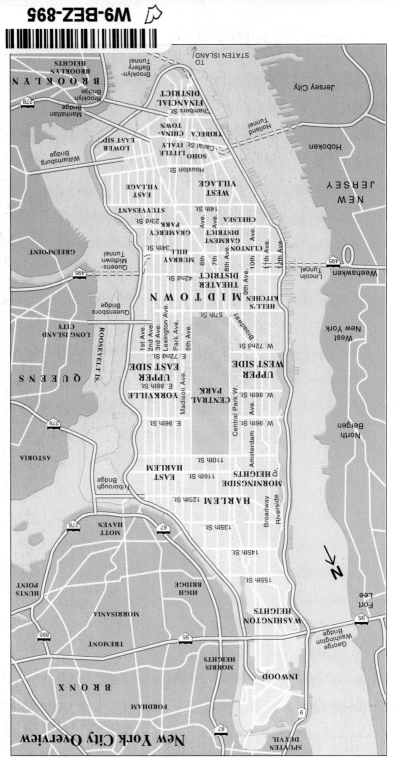

New York City Overview

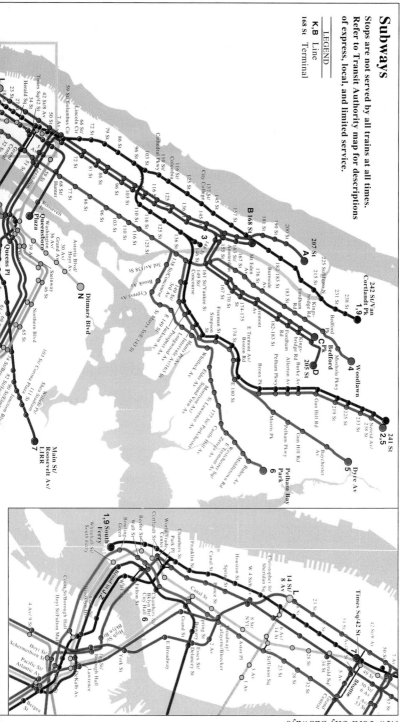

Subways

Stops are not served by all trains at all times.
Refer to Transit Authority map for descriptions
of express, local, and limited service.

LEGEND

K.B — Line

168 St — Terminal

New York City Subways

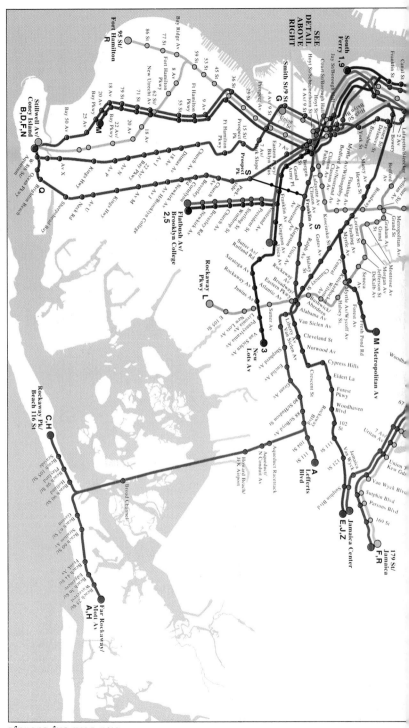

New York City Subways

Downtown Manhattan

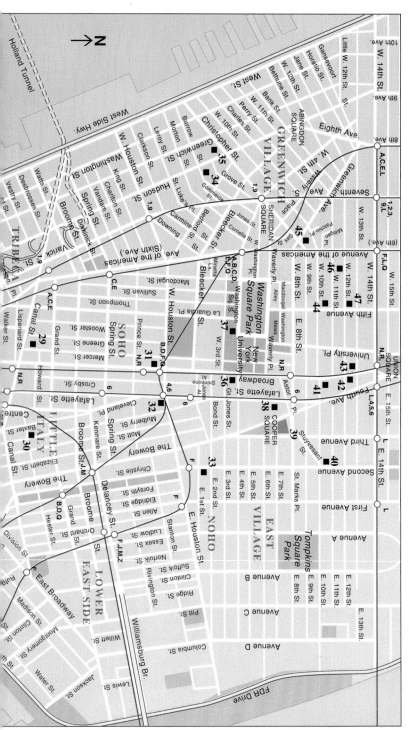

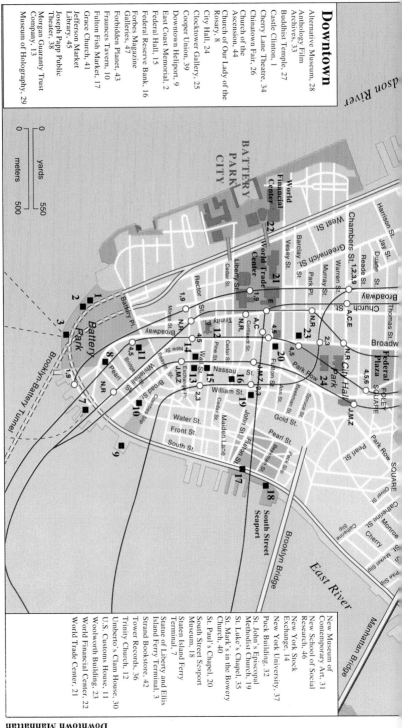

Downtown

Alternative Museum, 28
Anthology Film
Archives, 33
Buddhist Temple, 27
Castle Clinton, 1
Cherry Lane Theatre, 34
Chinatown Fair, 26
Church of the
Ascension, 44
Church of Our Lady of the
Rosary, 8
City Hall, 24
Clocktower Gallery, 25
Cooper Union, 39
Downtown Heliport, 9
East Coast Memorial, 2
Federal Hall, 15
Federal Reserve Bank, 16
Forbes Magazine
Galleries, 47
Forbidden Planet, 43
Fraunces Tavern, 10
Fulton Fish Market, 17
Grace Church, 41
Jefferson Market
Library, 45
Joseph Papp Public
Theater, 38
Morgan Guaranty Trust
Company, 13
Museum of Holography, 29

New Museum of
Contemporary Art, 31
New School of Social
Research, 46
New York Stock
Exchange, 14
New York University, 37
Puck Building, 32
St. John's Episcopal
Methodist Church, 19
St. Luke's Chapel, 35
St. Mark's in the Bowery
Church, 40
St. Paul's Chapel, 20
South Street Seaport
Museum, 18
Staten Island Ferry
Terminal, 7
Statue of Liberty and Ellis
Island Ferry Terminal, 3
Strand Bookstore, 42
Tower Records, 36
Trinity Church, 12
Umberto's Clam House, 30
U.S. Customs House, 11
Woolworth Building, 23
World Financial Center, 22
World Trade Center, 21

Downtown Manhattan

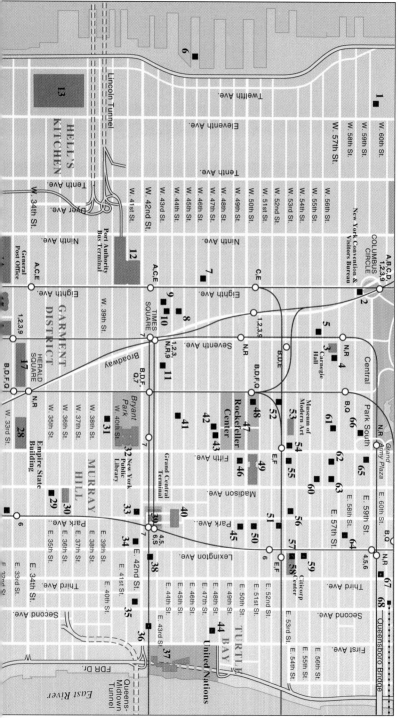

Midtown Manhattan

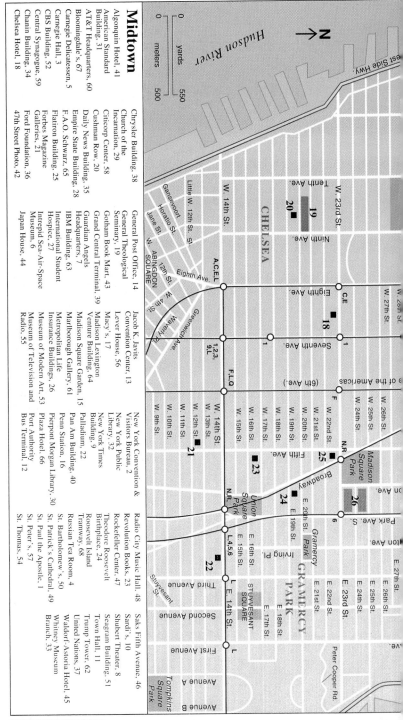

Midtown

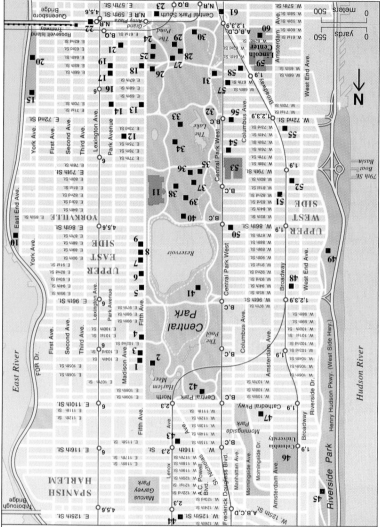

LET'S GO:
New York City

"Its yearly revision by a new crop of Harvard students makes it as valuable as ever." —*The New York Times*

"Value-packed, unbeatable, accurate, and comprehensive." —*The Los Angeles Times*

"A world-wise traveling companion—always ready with friendly advice and helpful hints, all sprinkled with a bit of wit." —*The Philadelphia Inquirer*

"Lighthearted and sophisticated, informative and fun to read. [Let's Go] helps the novice traveler navigate like a knowledgeable old hand." —*Atlanta Journal-Constitution*

"All the essential information you need, from making a phone call to exchanging money to contacting your embassy. [Let's Go] provides maps to help you find your way from every train station to a full range of youth hostels and hotels." —*Minneapolis Star Tribune*

"Unbeatable: good sight-seeing advice; up-to-date info on restaurants, hotels, and inns; a commitment to money-saving travel; and a wry style that brightens nearly every page." —*The Washington Post*

▪ Let's Go researchers have to make it on their own.

"The writers seem to have experienced every rooster-packed bus and lunar-surfaced mattress about which they write." —*The New York Times*

"Retains the spirit of the student-written publication it is: candid, opinionated, resourceful, amusing info for the traveler of limited means but broad curiosity." —*Mademoiselle*

▪ No other guidebook is as comprehensive.

"Whether you're touring the United States, Europe, Southeast Asia, or Central America, a Let's Go guide will clue you in to the cheapest, yet safe, hotels and hostels, food and transportation. Going beyond the call of duty, the guides reveal a country's latest news, cultural hints, and off-beat information that any tourist is likely to miss." —*Tulsa World*

▪ Let's Go is completely revised each year.

"Up-to-date travel tips for touring four continents on skimpy budgets." —*Time*

"Inimitable.... Let's Go's 24 guides are updated yearly (as opposed to the general guidebook standard of every two to three years), and in a marvelously spunky way." —*The New York Times*

Let's Go Publications

LET'S GO

The Budget Guide to
New York City

Kevin C. Murphy
Editor

St. Martin's Press ✹ New York

HELPING LET'S GO

If you want to share your discoveries, suggestions, or corrections, please drop us a line. We read every piece of correspondence, whether a postcard, a 10-page e-mail, or a coconut. All suggestions are passed along to our researcher-writers. Please note that mail received after May 1997 may be too late for the 1998 book, but will be retained for the following edition. **Address mail to:**

> **Let's Go: New York City**
> **67 Mt. Auburn Street**
> **Cambridge, MA 02138**
> **USA**

Visit Let's Go at **http://www.letsgo.com,** or send e-mail to:

> **Fanmail@letsgo.com**
> **Subject: "New York City"**

In addition to the invaluable travel advice our readers share with us, many are kind enough to offer their services as researchers or editors. Unfortunately, the charter of Let's Go, Inc. enables us to employ only currently enrolled Harvard-Radcliffe students.

Maps by David Lindroth copyright © 1997, 1996, 1995, 1994, 1993, 1992, 1991, 1990, 1989, 1988 by St. Martin's Press, Inc.

Map revisions pp. 57, 128-129, 202-203, 222-223 by Let's Go, Inc.

Distributed outside the USA and Canada by Macmillan.

ISBN: 0-312-14661-2

First edition
10 9 8 7 6 5 4 3 2 1

Let's Go: New York City is written by Let's Go Publications, 67 Mt. Auburn Street, Cambridge, MA 02138, USA.

About Let's Go

Back in 1960, a few students at Harvard University banded together to produce a 20-page pamphlet offering a collection of tips on budget travel in Europe. This modest, mimeographed packet, offered as an extra to passengers on student charter flights to Europe, met with instant popularity. The following year, students traveling to Europe researched the first, full-fledged edition of *Let's Go: Europe*, a pocket-sized book featuring honest, irreverent writing and a decidedly youthful outlook on the world. Throughout the 60s, our guides reflected the times; the 1969 guide to America led off by inviting travelers to "dig the scene" at San Francisco's Haight-Ashbury. During the 70s and 80s, we gradually added regional guides and expanded coverage into the Middle East and Central America. With the addition of our in-depth city guides, handy map guides, and extensive coverage of Asia, the 90s are also proving to be a time of explosive growth for Let's Go, and there's certainly no end in sight. The first editions of *Let's Go: India & Nepal* and *Let's Go: Ecuador & The Galapagos Islands* hit the shelves this year, and work toward next year's series has already begun.

We've seen a lot in 37 years. *Let's Go: Europe* is now the world's bestselling international guide, translated into seven languages. And our new guides bring Let's Go's total number of titles, with their spirit of adventure and their reputation for honesty, accuracy, and editorial integrity, to 30. But some things never change: our guides are still researched, written, and produced entirely by students who know first-hand how to see the world on the cheap.

HOW WE DO IT

Each guide is completely revised and thoroughly updated every year by a well-traveled set of 200 students. Every winter, we recruit over 120 researchers and 60 editors to write the books anew. After several months of training, Researcher-Writers hit the road for seven weeks of exploration, from Anchorage to Ankara, Estonia to El Salvador, Iceland to Indonesia. Hired for their rare combination of budget travel sense, writing ability, stamina, and courage, these adventurous travelers know that train strikes, stolen luggage, food poisoning, and marriage proposals are all part of a day's work. Back at our offices, editors work from spring to fall, massaging copy written on Himalayan bus rides into witty yet informative prose. A student staff of typesetters, cartographers, publicists, and managers keeps our lively team together. In September, the collected efforts of the summer are delivered to our printer, who turns them into books in record time, so that you have the most up-to-date information available for *your* vacation. And even as you read this, work on next year's editions is well underway.

WHY WE DO IT

At Let's Go, our goal is to give you a great vacation. We don't think of budget travel as the last recourse of the destitute; we believe that it's the only way to travel. Living cheaply and simply brings you closer to the people and places you've been saving up to visit. Our books will ease your anxieties and answer your questions about the basics—so you can get off the beaten track and explore. Once you learn the ropes, we encourage you to put Let's Go away now and then to strike out on your own. As any seasoned traveler will tell you, the best discoveries are often those you make yourself. When you find something worth sharing, drop us a line. We're Let's Go Publications, 67 Mt. Auburn St., Cambridge, MA 02138, USA (e-mail: fanmail@letsgo.com).

HAPPY TRAVELS!

Contents

Acknowledgements

This book is dedicated first and foremost to my sister Gillian, who chose this year to blaze her own trail through the capital of the world. Hopefully, these pages will keep her safe, well fed, intrigued, and having fun. Lisa Halliday and Allison Crapo had the unenviable task of massaging my prose into a coherent, readable guide—their advice and input were inestimable. Jace, Maika, and Vanessa incessantly traversed the beat, meticulously excavating the city's treasures with their trusty pens. The Domestic Room offered as healthy, stimulating, and enjoyable a work environment as one could ask for, A/C excepted. Intrepid NYU-ers Rob, Mike, and Katherine got me through the first time around. Special thanks to Dan H. for late-night Stratego sessions, Pogen M. for 42-foot thrills ($50) and 5.0 evasion strategies, DanO for Quake-a-thons, Alex T. for sloppy bike rides, Nick C., Liz A., and Jessica F. for their New York knowhow, AndyBruce for reviving office fun, Amanda/Mike/Tom for much-needed *Star Wars* viewings, Michelle S. for an unanticipated extra ball, Josh F. and Dave M. for multiple lunches, NASA for finding life on Mars, 71 Walker for the comfortable couch, Elissa G. for several on-the-spot philosophical discussions, and Liz Mayer for introducing me to the Let's Go Universe in the first place. A Tribe Called Quest kept it real and A Chinese Food Truck kept me alive. The antics at 18 Ilman Terrace distinguished the days—Shawn held Canada at bay, Lew spun the tunes, Danny was just happy to be here, and Jon kept the juice flowing. To the GSSM class of 1993 and the Harvard class of 1997, the journey is still the reward. New York, New York: Had I another 800 pages to fill, I still could never do justice to your splendor. Thad and Tessa: your tomes will follow. Mom and Dad, I owe everything that has or will come in this life to your love and wisdom, and I will always appreciate you and them both.
-KcM

Editor	Kevin C. Murphy
Managing Editor	Allison Crapo
Publishing Director	Michelle C. Sullivan
Production Manager	Daniel O. Williams
Associate Production Manager	Michael S. Campbell
Cartography Manager	Amanda K. Bean
Editorial Manager	John R. Brooks
Editorial Manager	Allison Crapo
Financial Manager	Stephen P. Janiak
Personnel Manager	Alexander H. Travelli
Publicity Manager	SoRelle B. Braun
Associate Publicity Manager	David Fagundes
Associate Publicity Manager	Elisabeth Mayer
Assistant Cartographer	Jonathan D. Kibera
Assistant Cartographer	Mark C. Staloff
Office Coordinator	Jennifer L. Schuberth
Director of Advertising and Sales	Amit Tiwari
Senior Sales Executives	Andrew T. Rourke
	Nicholas A. Valtz, Charles E. Varner
General Manager	Richard Olken
Assistant General Manager	Anne E. Chisholm

Maps

Color Maps

Researcher-Writers

Jace Clayton   *Manhattan, Brooklyn, Staten Island*
Evading another summer at the post office, Jace saw an opportunity to take on New York City and leapt for it. Scoffing the normal tourist tendencies, he set up shop in Brooklyn and promptly, diligently explored every nook of New York nightlife, finding time to sample jazz and jungle alike. By day, Jace exercised his trademark dry Claytonian wit upon Greenwich Village, Central Park, and Lower Manhattan while amassing enough vinyl along the way to warrant his own club night. Over the course of his expedition, Jace belied his mild-mannered New England exterior to become a full-fledged, gregarious, activity-hungry New Yorker—look for his return to Brooklyn's streets in the near future.

Vanessa Gil   *Manhattan, Queens, Long Island, Hoboken, Westchester*
Art historian extraordinaire and finder of gingham tablecloths, Vanessa brought an insider's sensibility to uptown and out-of-town. Undeterred by long commutes, she scoured the Upper East and Upper West for budget bargains, continually making new friends on her travels. Vanessa brought her trained eye to bear on the Met, the MoMA, and museums galore. When not sifting through Manhattan's many sights, Vanessa explored Hoboken, reinvented Queens, and learned much new about Long Island. Throughout it all, she never lost her cool and always managed to find cheap eats in the most unlikely of places. You go, Gil.

Maika Pollack   *Manhattan, the Bronx, Atlantic City*
Having sharpened her R-W teeth on the San Francisco Bay Area, Maika was more than ready to take a chomp out of the Big Apple. True to form, she braved itinerant junkies, would-be suitors, big birthday bashes, and fashion magazines to become an East Village expert and Queen of the SoHo gallery world. Moreover, Maika utilized her uncommon good luck (two, count 'em, two four-leaf clovers in one day) to break the bank in Atlantic City. When not carousing downtown, she found all manner of food, folks, and fun in Harlem and the Bronx. Having now taken on both the West and East coasts with efficiency and aplomb, Maika, as always, is well prepared for whatever challenge comes next.

How To Use This Book

It's rush hour, and, belongings in hand, you've just stepped out of a cab and into the biggest, baddest city in the world. As swarms of people hip and hurried scurry past to a million destinations, you look up to face an endless wall of stone and steel. Cars honk, music blares from a nearby radio, you are jostled by countless harassed-looking passers-by, and a fortyish man nearby keeps beckoning you to his briefcase of watches. At this point, you have two alternatives: panic and run screaming down the thoroughfare, or calmly reach into your knapsack and pull out your brand-spanking new *Let's Go: New York City 1997*. If you chose the former, then you've become another of the city's lost souls, and we can do nothing to help you. If, on the other hand, you grabbed your trusty neon-yellow traveling companion, then you, budget adventurer, have just taken your first step into a larger world.

In short, we're here to present the Big Apple in all its native glory. We want to help you to experience the city's scintillating history and leading-edge nightlife, get the most of world-class museums, or simply enjoy a good hot dog and view. We tell you what the local newspapers are and for what to use them. We help you budget your time and your money (for example, don't buy watches on the street), telling you where to go and what to expect when you get there.

New York City: An Introduction offers some background info on the city's history, politics, architecture, music, literature, and film. **Essentials** doles out sound practical advice. **Planning Your Trip** helps you get to the city safely and securely and tells you what to expect once there. We also attempt to aid travelers with special concerns, including senior citizens, disabled travelers, minority travelers, gays and lesbians, women, families, and travelers with special diets.

Getting Around explains the ins and outs of inter/intracity transportation and **Getting Acquainted** covers such necessities as health care, safety, banking, and the mail system. **Accommodations** lists budget beds, based on our R-W-tested scale of price, location, security, and comfort. **Food & Drink** presents extensive listings of cheap, tasty restaurants and watering holes from all corners of the city.

Once you've eaten, slept, and are ready to explore, flip to the crucial **Neighborhoods** section for in-depth summaries of the history, culture, and sights of New York's many impressive localities. For more specific interests, **Museums** and **Galleries** divvy up New York's thriving art world, **Sports** tells how to catch one of the city's star athletic teams along with how and where to break a sweat yourself, and **Entertainment & Nightlife** offers a golden pass to the New York City that never sleeps. **Shopping** tells you where to buy all manner of stuff, and **Daytripping** presents alternatives to the Big Apple when it all becomes too much. Last but not least, the **Appendices** yield more pertinent information, including a quick reference list of free activities and a calendar of over 100 annual events that take place in the area.

With the wind in your hair and *Let's Go* at your back, the Big Apple is your oyster. Read on, and happy hunting.

A NOTE TO OUR READERS

The information for this book is gathered by *Let's Go*'s researchers during the late spring and summer months. Each listing is derived from the assigned researcher's opinion based upon his or her visit at a particular time. The opinions are expressed in a candid and forthright manner. Other travelers might disagree. Those traveling at a different time may have different experiences since prices, dates, hours, and conditions are always subject to change. You are urged to check beforehand to avoid inconvenience and surprises. Travel always involves a certain degree of risk, especially in low-cost areas. When traveling, especially on a budget, always take particular care to ensure your safety.

BIG APPLE HOSTEL

The Place to Stay
for International
Travellers

Best Location
in Manhattan

Shared Rooms $ 19.00
Private Rooms $ 49.00

119 West 45th Street
New York, NY 10036

Tel. (212) 302-2603
Fax (212) 302-2605
E-Mail BigApple@concentric.net

New York City:
An Introduction

This rural America thing. It's a joke.

—Ed Koch

■ History

Since its earliest days, free-spirited New York has scoffed at the timid compromises of other American cities. In its immensity, diversity, and disdain for tradition, the city has become a remarkable metaphor for the American ideal, if not for all of modernity itself. It boasts the most immigrants, the tallest skyscrapers, and the trickiest con artists. Even the vast gray blocks of concrete have an indomitable charm. "There is more poetry in a block of New York than in 20 daisied lanes," rhapsodized resident talespinner O. Henry, returning from a dull vacation in rural Westchester. In the country, he said, "there was too much fresh scenery and fresh air. What I need is a steam-heated flat and no vacation or exercise."

New York's vaunted self-sufficiency began early. The colony was founded in 1624 by the Dutch West Indies Company as a trading post, but, as typical during the mercantilist age, England soon asserted rival claims to the land. While the mother countries squabbled, the colonists went about their burgeoning business: trading beaver skins, colorful wampum, and silver with the neighboring Native Americans. In 1626, New York's tradition of great bargains (and stiffing the unwary) began when Peter Minuit bought the island from natives for 60 guilders, or just under $24.

The land was rich and fertile, making European guidance hardly necessary. "Wild pigeons are as thick as the sparrows in Holland—children and pigs multiply here rapidly," gloated one colonist. When the Dutch West Indies Company did try to interfere, the settlers resented it. Calvinist Peter Stuyvesant, the governor appointed by Holland in the middle of the 17th century, enforced rigid rules on the happy-go-lucky settlement. He shot hogs, closed taverns, and whipped Quakers, sparking protest and anger among the citizenry. Inexplicably, the physically challenged Stuyvesant has since become a local folk hero. Several schools and businesses in New York are named for him and people refer to him fondly as "Peg-Leg" Peter.

As the early colonists were less than enthralled by Dutch rule, they put up only token resistance when the British finally invaded the settlement in 1664. The new British governors were less noxious, if only because they were less effective; an astounding number never even made it to the colony. Some got lost en route from England, a handful went down at sea, and others decided that New England was a more attractive spot and went there. Between 1664 and 1776, there were 22 hiatuses in governance.

Left to its own devices, the city continued to mature. In 1754, higher education came to New York in the form of King's College (later renamed Columbia University). By the late 1770s, the city had become a major port with a population of 20,000. The preoccupation with prosperity engendered by this early success meant that New Yorkers would be rather dull to the first whiffs of revolution. British rule was good for business—and, then as now, the dollar (or at least the gold coin) ruled in the soon-to-be capital of capitalism.

The new American army, understandably, made no great efforts to protect the ungrateful city, and New York was held by the British throughout the war. As a result, the American Revolution was a rough time for the Big Apple. The city had "a most melancholy appearance, being deserted and pillaged," wrote one observer. Fire destroyed a quarter of the city in 1776, and harbor ships had a tendency to spontaneously explode. When the defeated British finally left in 1783, most people were relieved—except for 6000 Tory loyalists, who followed the redcoats out of New York and went on to Nova Scotia.

With its buildings in heaps of rubble and one third of its population off roaming Canada, New York made a valiant effort to rebuild. Somewhat unexpectedly, it succeeded. "The progress of the city is, as usual, beyond all calculations," wrote one enraptured citizen. New York served a brief stint as the nation's capital; about the same time it acquired a bank and the first stock exchange, which met under a buttonwood tree on Wall Street. The Randel Plan simplified the organization of the city streets in 1811, establishing Manhattan's grid scheme. Merchants built mansions on the new streets, along with tenements for the increasing numbers of immigrants from Eastern and Northern Europe.

Administration and services continued to lag behind growth. Early in the 19th century, New York became the largest U.S. city, but pigs, dogs, and chickens continued to run freely. Fires and riots made streetlife precarious, while the foul water supply precipitated a cholera epidemic. The notorious corruption of Tammany Hall, a political machine set in motion in the 1850s and operative for nearly a century, aggravated the already desperate situation. "The New Yorker belongs to a community governed by lower and baser scum than any city in Western Christendom," complained perennial complainer George Templeton Strong.

Still, New Yorkers remained loyal to the city, often neglecting national concerns in favor of local interests. New York initially opposed the Civil War; its desire to protect trade with the South outweighed Abolitionist and constitutional principles. Abraham Lincoln, the *New York Times* wrote dismissively in 1860, was "a lawyer who has some local reputation in Illinois." The attack on South Carolina's Fort Sumter rallied New York to the Northern side, but a conscription act in July of 1863 led to the infamous New York City Draft Riots, which cost a thousand lives.

After the war, New York entered a half-century of prosperity, during which the elements of urban modernity began to coalesce. The Metropolitan Museum of Art was founded in 1870, and Bloomingdale's opened its venerable doors in 1872. Frederick Law Olmsted created Central Park on 82 rolling acres at the tail end of the century, and the Flatiron building, the first skyscraper, was erected in 1902. The city began to spread out, both horizontally and vertically. "It'll be a great place if they ever finish it," O. Henry quipped.

Booming construction and burgeoning industry helped to generate rosy urban bliss. Mayor Fiorello LaGuardia brought the city safely out of the Great Depression, and post-World War II prosperity brought still more immigrants and businesses to the city. But even as the country and the rest of the world celebrated New York as the capital of the 20th century, cracks in the city's foundations became apparent. By the 1960s, crises in public transportation, education, and housing exacerbated racial tensions and fostered the consolidation of a criminal underclass.

City officials raised taxes to provide more services, but higher taxes drove middle-class residents and corporations out of the city. As a series of recessions and budget crises swamped the government, critics deplored Mayor Robert Wagner's "dedicated inactivity." By 1975, the city was pleading with the federal government to rescue it from impending bankruptcy—and was rebuffed. The *Daily News* headline the next day read "Ford to New York: Drop Dead."

But New York, as it has been wont, bounced back. Budget wizard Felix Rohatyn trimmed the city's budget. The city's massive (if goofy) "I Love New York" campaign spread cheery hearts via bumper stickers. Large manufacturing, which had gone south and west of New York, was supplanted by fresh money from high finance and infotech, the big Reaganaut growth industries. In the 80s Wall Street was hip again, or at least grotesquely profitable, and the city seemed to recover some of its lost vitality.

As the rosy blush of the 80s faded to the gray recession of the early 90s, the city's problems seemed to reappear in full force. Bizarre outbreaks of violence received national attention; racial bigotry and threats of violent direct action littered the street-corners; and budget problems forced cuts in education and the police force.

And yet, nowadays, New York seems once again to be on the rebound. Community policing and the get-tough policies of mayor Rudy Giuliani have produced considerable drops in crime three years running, and formerly seamy areas like Times Square—not to mention the entire subway system—are now on the mend. It seems New York's history of comebacks is not yet over, at least in the hearts of its citizens. Former mayor Ed Koch's inaugural speech echoes the sentiments of generations. "New York is not a problem," he said, "New York is a stroke of genius."

■ Ethnic New York

> To Europe she was America, to America she was the gateway of the earth. But to tell the story of New York would be to write a social history of the world.
>
> —H.G. Wells

In 1643, Jesuit missionary Isaac Jogues wrote a description of a lively New Amsterdam fort. Among the 500 people living in this 17th-century melting-pot community were artisans, soldiers, trappers, sailors, and slaves—no fewer than 18 languages were spoken by this motley assemblage.

New Yorkers have always claimed a wide range of national origins. The first black settlement began in today's SoHo in 1644. Germans and Irish came over in droves between 1840 and 1860; in 1855, European-born immigrants constituted nearly half of New York's population.

After the Civil War, a massive wave of immigration began, cresting around the turn of the century. Europeans left famine, religious persecution, and political unrest in their native lands for the perils of seasickness and the promise of America. German and Irish immigrants were eventually joined, beginning in 1890, by Italians, Lithuanians, Russians, Poles, and Greeks.

Immigrants worked long hours in detestable and unsafe conditions for meager wages; only the Triangle Shirtwaist Fire of 1911, which killed 146 female factory workers, brought about enough public protest to force stricter regulations on working conditions. Meanwhile, Tammany Hall-based "ward bosses" stepped in to take care of the confused new arrivals, helping them find jobs and housing and even providing them with emergency funds in case of illness or accident, all in exchange for votes. Later, in the 1920s, the U.S. Congress restricted immigration, and the Great Depression of the 30s brought the influx to a virtual halt. The encroaching terrors in Europe in the late 30s, however, brought new waves of immigrants, particularly Jews seeking escape from Hitler's persecution.

Today the melting pot simmers with more than seven million people speaking 80 languages. New York has more Italians than Rome, more Irish than Dublin, and more Jews than Jerusalem. Immigrants from Asia and the Caribbean now make up most of the incoming population. The cultural diversity resulting from past and present immigration has recently made non-Hispanic whites a minority in the City for the first time in it's history. This vast melange of cultures has sadly by no means led to a smooth blend of harmonious racial unity. Ethnic divisions have been responsible for much of the city's strife, dating back to the 17th and 18th centuries. In the past few decades, ethnic conflict has led to, and been the result of, extreme segregation and distrust among neighboring communities. The 1960s saw rioting and looting in the South Bronx as angry African-Americans railed against perceived injustices by the government and the police. In the late 80s, racially related deaths in Bensonhurst, Howard Beach, and Crown Heights pointed out the lethal potential of ethnic tensions. Many enclaves throughout the city are similarly charged, as groups fight to gain political power and respect.

Still, New York continues to symbolize the promise of safe haven for thousands of immigrants, and while it takes years or lifetimes to assimilate into other cities, newcomers become New Yorkers almost instantly.

■ Politics

Despite its colonial flirtation with Toryism, New York has played a prominent role in American politics since the early days of the Republic. Much of our federal framework is indebted to the centralizing fiscal policies of the first Secretary of the Treasury, New Yorker and lousy shot Alexander Hamilton. Alas for the Big Apple, this strong central government was moved South of New York into a malarial swamp, eventually renamed Washington, D.C.

From then on, New York's political history is a murky one. Corruption, typified by "Boss" William Tweed and Tammany Hall, was long its hallmark, and honest politicians have had difficulty being effective. In the 1850s, Tweed took charge of Tammany and began promising money and jobs to people, often new immigrants, who agreed to vote for his candidates. With Tweed's men ruling city government, embezzlement and kickbacks were routine. Tweed managed to rob the city of somewhere between 20 and 300 million dollars. When citizens complained in 1871, Tweed said defiantly, "Well, what are you going to do about it?" And although a *New York Times* exposé led to Tweed's downfall in 1875, Tammany continued to try to influence elections without him.

Occasional reform movements bucked Tammany's power. In 1894, for example, Teddy Roosevelt was appointed to the police department. Dressed in a cape, he sallied forth at night like a judicial Masked Avenger, searching for policemen who were sleeping on the job or consorting with prostitutes. Even more successful as a reformer was Fiorello LaGuardia, New York's immensely popular mayor from 1933-1945. "Nobody wants me but the people," he said as he reorganized the government and revitalized the city.

John V. Lindsay ran in 1965 with the slogan "He is fresh and everyone else is tired," but even his freshness wilted under the barrage of crime, drought, racial problems, and labor unrest. After its mid-70s bankruptcy crisis, the city slowly began to rebound. Ed Koch became America's most visible mayor, appearing on *Saturday Night Live* and providing an endless stream of quotables, most notably, his catchphrase, "How'm I doing?" The economic boom of the late 80s made Wall Street—and, by extension, New York—once again glamorous and fashionable. In 1989, David Dinkins, the city's first black mayor, was elected on a platform of growth, harmony, and continued prosperity—even the most cynical New Yorkers seemed hopeful about the future.

During Dinkins's tenure, the Supreme Court abolished the Board of Estimate system of municipal government, under which each borough's president had one vote. (This system was blatantly unfair, since borough populations range from Brooklyn's 2.8 million to Staten Island's 350,000.) The old system was replaced with an expanded (35-member) City Council. Now, each borough can initiate zoning, propose legislation, and deal with contractors independently.

Dinkins ultimately failed to achieve his vision of racial harmony, though, and the continuing fiscal crises and persistent crime rate led to his defeat at the hands of Rudy Giuliani in the 1993 mayoral election. The campaign and the eventual election-night tallies were strongly divided along racial lines; many moderate whites who had supported Dinkins in 1989 defected to the side of the Republican Giuliani, who addressed a number of intertwining fears with a campaign that could be summed up in two words: Safety First.

Since his election, Giuliani has made a successful effort to increase police presence in the city. Imagine New Yorkers' surprise when they learned that in 1996 crime rates had gone down again for the third year in a row. Giuliani, for one, was pleased. The mayor also took a big risk for the city when he crossed party lines to support Governor Mario Cuomo in his bid for re-election. Cuomo subsequently lost to upstart George Pataki (the candidate favored by conservative upstate New York), who made a point of snubbing the mayor for several days after the election. Nonplussed, Giuliani deviated from the Republican camp again in 1996 to berate G.O.P Presidential candidate Bob Dole on his draconian immigration policies and refused to attend the party's August nominating convention. Priding himself on never taking a vacation and resting only five hours a night, tenacious Rudy Giuliani has slowly but surely won the hearts of many in the city that never sleeps, although his anti-crime Quality of Life Initiative has prompted concern among minority leaders.

■ Architecture

A hundred times have I thought New York is a catastrophe and fifty times:
It is a beautiful catastrophe.

—Le Corbusier, architect

THE EARLY YEARS AND EUROPEAN INFLUENCE

Capricious New York has always warmed to the latest trends in architecture, hastily demolishing old buildings to make way for their stylistic successors. In the 19th century the surging rhythm of endless destruction and renewal seemed to attest to the city's vigor and enthusiasm. Walt Whitman praised New York's "pull-down-and-build-over-again spirit," and *The Daily Mirror* was an isolated voice when, in 1831, it criticized the city's "irreverence for antiquity."

By the 20th century, many found that irreverence troubling. New York's history was quickly disappearing under the steamroller of modernization. Mounting public concern climaxed when developers destroyed gracious Penn Station in 1965, and the Landmarks Preservation Commission was created in response. Since then, the LPC has been vigorously designating buildings to protect. Developers, meanwhile, seek loopholes and air-rights to explode city buildings into the sky.

Despite the rear-guard efforts of the LPC, traces of Colonial New York are hard to find. The original Dutch settlement consisted mostly of traditional homes with gables and stoops. One example from 1699, the restored **Vechte-Cortelyou House,** stands near Fifth Avenue and 3rd St. in Brooklyn. The British, however, built over most of these with Federal-style buildings like **St. Paul's Church** on Madison Ave.

Even after the British had been forced out, their architectural tastes lingered, influencing the townhouses built by their prosperous colonists. Through the early 19th century, American architects continued to incorporate such Federal details as dormer windows, stoops, and doors with columns and fan lights. Federal houses still line Charlton St. and northern Vandam St., while the old **City Hall,** built by D.C. mastermind Pierre L'Enfant in 1802, employs Federal detailing on a public building.

The Greek Revival of the 1820s and 30s added porticoes and iron laurel wreaths to New York's streets. If you see a house with uneven bricks, it probably predates the 1830s, when bricks became machine-made. Greek Revival prevails on **Washington Square North,** Lafayette St., and W. 20th St. Gray granite **St. Peter's,** built in 1838, was the first Greek Revival Catholic Church in New York.

While cadging from the old country and the classical tradition, Americans did manage to introduce some architectural innovations. Beginning in the 1850s, thousands of brownstones (made from cheap stone quarried in New Jersey) sprang up all over New York. Next to skyscrapers, the **brownstone townhouse** may be New York's most characteristic structure. Although far beyond most people's means today, the houses were middle-class residences back then—the rich lived in block-long mansions on Fifth Avenue, and apartments were for the poor.

The social hierarchy of buildings was scandalized in 1883, when the luxurious **Dakota** apartment house (later John Lennon's home) went up. The building's name derives from its location on the far side of Central Park; it was so far removed from the social center of town, local wits joked, that it might as well be in Dakota Territory. But the relatively cheap, sumptuously appointed apartments offered an attractive alternative to the soaring real estate prices of Midtown. Soon, similar apartment buildings, like the **Ansonia,** were built in Harlem and on the Upper West Side.

In the 1890s, American architects studying abroad brought the Beaux Arts style back from France and captivated the nation. Beaux Arts, which blended Classical detail with lavish decoration, stamped itself on structures built through the 1930s. Especially fine examples are the **New York Customs House,** built by Cass Gilbert, and the **New York Public Library,** originally built to house James Lenox's overflowing book collection. Lenox, a wealthy recluse, accumulated so many books that keeping track of them in his apartment was nearly impossible; when he wanted to read one he already possessed, he often had to go out and buy another copy. He donated his collection to the city in 1895.

Architects lavished Beaux Arts detailing on the first specimens of New York's quintessential structure—the skyscraper. Made possible by the invention of the elevator in 1857, skyscrapers soon became the city's architectural trademark.

THE SKYSCRAPER: AN AMERICAN AESTHETIC

Permissive new building codes at the turn of the 20th century allowed the first skyscrapers to sprout. **The Flatiron Building,** erected in 1902, was triangular in shape and only 6 feet wide at its point; its wind currents blew women's skirts up, and people feared it would topple. But tall buildings proved a useful invention in a city forever short on space, and other monoliths soon joined the Flatiron.

In 1913, Cass Gilbert gilded the 55-story **Woolworth Building** with Gothic flourishes, piling terracotta salamanders onto antique "W"s. **The Empire State Building** and the **Chrysler Building,** fashioned from stone and steel and built like rockets, stand testimony to America's romance with science and space. Over the years, more dizzying buildings have joined the throng.

But not all of New York's towers look the same— the urban landscape does have some quirks and personality. Learn to read between the skylines and you'll be able to distinguish and date just about every building. New York's succession of zoning laws can be a better architectural guide than I.M. Pei.

Does the building have a ziggurat on top? Look like a wedding cake? Zoning restrictions of the late 1940s stipulated that tall buildings had to be set back at the summit. New York's first curtain of pure glass was the 1950 **United Nations Secretariat Building,** an air-conditioning nightmare. The building quickly inspired **Lever House,** a 24-story glass box. Then, in 1958, Ludwig Mies Van der Rohe and Philip Johnson created the **Seagram Building,** a glass tower set behind a plaza on Park Avenue. Crowds soon gathered to mingle, sunbathe, and picnic, much to the surprise of planners and builders. A delighted planning commission began offering financial incentives to every builder who offset a highrise with public open space. Over the next decade, many architects stuck empty plazas next to their towering office complexes. Some of them looked a little too empty to the picky planning commission, which changed the rules in 1975 to stipulate that every plaza should provide public seating. By the late 70s, plazas were moved indoors, and high-tech atriums with gurgling fountains and pricey cafés began to flourish.

The leaner skyscrapers you will see date from the early 80s, when shrewd developers realized they could get office space, bypass zoning regulations, *and* receive a bonus from the commission if they hoisted up "sliver" buildings. Composed largely of elevators and stairs, the disturbingly anorexic newcomers were generally disliked. Those tired of living in the shadow of shafts altered zoning policy in 1983 so that structural planning would encourage more room for air and sun.

Builders have finally recognized the overcrowding problem in East Midtown and expanded their horizons somewhat. New residential complexes have risen on the Upper East Side above 95th St.; in the near future, you can expect high-flying office complexes to stomp out the West Midtown culture of the 40s and 50s. Some developers, such as those who created 1989's **Citicorp Building,** have even ventured into the wilderness of Queens. And with the restructuring of the city government in 1989, citizens now have a greater say in development projects in their community.

The planning commission that oversees the beautiful catastrophe now takes overcrowding and environmental issues into account when it makes its decisions. As an added safeguard, the Landmarks Preservation Commission lurks ever-vigilant, ensuring that New York does not destroy its past as it steamrolls into the future.

■ New York in Music

Music in New York City dabbles in every genre and style. Classical music-related performances flourish uptown, especially at the series of halls composing **Lincoln Center** (Avery Fisher Hall is home to the **New York Philharmonic**). The 92nd Street Y is another showcase for serious music. Each summer the **Next Wave Festival** takes over the Brooklyn Academy of Music, offering spectacular, offbeat happenings, crackpot fusions of classical music, theater, and performance art. You can still even occasionally catch Hoboken's favorite son, **Frank Sinatra,** serenading the city that made him famous.

New York is assuredly the place to catch new music too. Nearly every performer who comes to the States plays here, and thousands of local bands compete to make a statement and win an audience. Venues range from stadiums to concert halls to back-alley sound-systems. Whatever your inclination, New York's expansive musical scene should be able to satisfy it. (See Entertainment & Nightlife: Music, p. 267.)

Jazz has been associated with the sound of the big city since the music's inception. The **Big Band** sound thrived here in the 20s and 30s, and **Duke Ellington** often played in clubs around the city. **Minton's Playhouse** in Harlem was home to **Thelonious Monk** and one of the birthplaces of **bebop,** a highly sophisticated jazz variant with a hard-edged sensibility. **Miles Davis, Charlie Parker, Dizzy Gillespie, Max Roach, Tommy Potter, Bud Powell,** and many others contributed to the New York sound of the late 40s and 50s, when beatniks, hepcats, and poor old souls filled 52nd St. clubs. **Free-jazz** pioneer **Cecil Taylor** and spaceman **Sun Ra** set up shop here during the 60s and 70s. Today, **wonko** experimentalists like **John Zorn** and **James Blood Ulmer** plot to destroy music at clubs like the **Knitting Factory;** meanwhile, in Brooklyn, a loose grouping of like-minded musicians called **M-Base** reconciles hot funk and cool jazz, to good effect.

True to the vicissitudes of city living, the New York rock sound has always had a harder edge than its West Coast or Southern counterparts. The **Velvet Underground,** Andy Warhol's favorite band and *the* seminal rock group of the 60s, combined deceptively jangling guitars with searing lyrics on sex, drugs, and violence that deeply influenced the next generation of bands. In 1976 ambitious avant-garde poets and sometime musicians took over the campy glam-rock scene in downtown barroom clubs like **CBGB's** and **Max's Kansas City:** bands and performers like the **Ramones, Patti Smith, Blondie,** and the **Talking Heads** brought venom, wit, and a calculated stupidity to the emerging **punk** scene. Ever since, New York has convulsed with musical shocks. In the 80s, angry kids imported **hardcore** from Washington, D.C.: a bevy of fast-rocking, non-drinking, non-smoking bands packed Sunday all-ages shows at CBGB's. In the 80s and early 90s the **"post-punk"** scene crystallized around bands such as **Sonic Youth** and **Pavement.** Obscure or out-of-print vinyl can be found in the city's many used record stores; prices are often absurd, but the selection far surpasses that of any other North American city (see Shopping: Record Stores, p. 290).

Rap and **hip-hop** also began here, on New York's streets, and the list of New York artists reads like the text of *The History of Urban Music,* including such heavyweight emcees as **KRS-1, Chuck D, LL Cool J, Run-DMC, EPMD,** and **Queen Latifah** (who leaped across the river from Jersey). **Grandmaster Flash** and Bronx DJ **Afrika Bambaataa** laid the foundations in the late 70s and early 80s with records rooted deeply in electronic processing, scratching, and sampling. In 1979, the **Sugarhill Gang** (see Sights: Harlem, p. 193, for more on Sugar Hill) released "Rapper's Delight," widely considered the first true rap record.

Predominant in the modern day East Coast hip-hop hierarchy are the **Native Tongues,** a loose collection of New York acts which includes **A Tribe Called Quest, De La Soul,** and **Black Sheep.** Another New York act gaining a lot of attention these days is the nefarious **Wu-tang Clan,** whose dense, brooding beats and clever use of kung-fu samples have made names for several of its coterie, including **Method Man** and the **GZA.** Pampered young funsters like the **Beastie Boys** and **Luscious Jackson** transcended racial lines to broaden the national appeal of the hip-hop genre, incorporating jazz loops, hardcore thrash, and funk samples into their stylistic repertoire. Other recent NY (and NY area) acts to climb the charts include **Nas, the Fugees,** and (the infamous) **Mobb Deep.** For a clearer glimpse of the hip-hop scene in New York (and across the country) pick up a copy of New York-based *The Source,* the genre's premier fanzine (now thicker and glossier than ever before).

Although the Big Apple can't hold a candle to many of its overseas rivals, New York City is currently ground zero for the east coast stage of the **rave** revolution that took hold of European and L.A. club culture. **Deelite** and **Moby** first got the city grooving where **disco** left off with their toe-tapping amalgamation of ambient and techno-funk, and now home-grown superstar D.J.'s like **Junior Vasquez, Frankie Bones,** and **James Christian** keep the home crowds dancing nightly to the newest **house, trance, jungle, breakbeat,** and **trip-hop**.

The newest aural concoction New York has to offer is **illbient**, a mix attitude that values sonic experiments over smooth dance mixes. At an illbient happening you might hear a hardcore rock single spliced with a minimalist piano piece, interrupted by a DJ cutup of two identical Sherlock Holmes spoken-word records which fades into Moroccan trance music. Illbient sessions often incorporate performance art, video installations, and dance in a commitment to "cultural alchemy." Illbient resonates with the density of cultures that only New York City can provide, and can be heard at SoundLab (726-1774), Cell (477-5005), and Analog (229-0786). Illbient performers to watch out for include **Loop, Olive, Spooky, Singe,** and **Bedouin.**

■ Literary New York

New York's reputation as the literary capital of the Americas has deep historical roots. English-born **William Bradford,** perhaps the city's first literary man of note, was appointed public printer—America's first—here in 1698. He went on to found the country's first newspaper, the *New York Gazette,* in 1725.

Even before it had become the publishing center of the country (supplanting Boston around the mid-19th century), New York was home to many pioneers of the national literature. Some of these writers—**Herman Melville,** for example—knew nothing of their own (or of New York's) impending literary fame. Melville, born in 1819 at 6 Pearl St. in lower Manhattan, was so disheartened by the critics' response to *Moby Dick* that he took a job at a New York customs house for four dollars a day and died unrecognized and unappreciated; to top it off, the *Times* called him Henry in his obituary. **Washington Irving** knew better how to work a room. Born at 131 William St., the author of *Knickerbocker's History of New York* made a name for himself penning satirical essays on New York society "from the beginning of the world to the end of the Dutch dynasty." In a moment of classic coinage, Irving gave New York its enduring pen-name, Gotham City. Other lower Manhattan writers of the times included **William Cullen Bryant, James Fenimore Cooper,** and **Walt Whitman,** who hung around for a while to work on the magazine *Aurora* and to rhapsodize in free verse on the Brooklyn Bridge and "Manahatta."

American writers have traditionally lived on the fringes of culture. Appropriately, most New York writers have lived on the *geographic* fringes of their city—either well above (in Harlem) or below (in the Village and on the Lower East Side) New York's social and commercial centers. Sometimes, as in **Edgar Allen Poe's** pitiful case, they were so brutally poor they had no choice in the matter. Poe, who rented a house all the way out in the rural Bronx, earned so little he used to send his aging mother-in-law to scour nearby fields for edible roots.

Literary deadbeats, hacks, and bohunks followed the wave of mostly Italian immigrants and Bohemians streaming into the Greenwich Village area in the early 20th century. Among the young-and-poor crowd were **Willa Cather, John Reed,** and **Theodore Dreiser,** parents of the modern American novel. For over fifty years the Village would be one of America's most important neighborhoods, hosting a full spectrum of poets, essayists, and novelists, including **Marianne Moore, Hart Crane, e.e. cummings, Edna St. Vincent Millay, John Dos Passos,** and **Thomas Wolfe.**

Although too expensive for most Village writers, spiffy Washington Square—immortalized by **Henry James's** book of that name and by **Edith Wharton's** *Age of Innocence*—was nevertheless the center of the literary scene. Radiating off the square to the north were the legendary **Salamagundi Club** (47 Fifth Ave. at 11th St.); the **Cedar Tavern**, one time gathering place for Beats **Allen Ginsberg** and **Jack Kerouac;** and the cobblestoned **Washington Mews**, home to **Sherwood Anderson** (No. 54), **"Jaundice" John Dos Passos** (in the studio between No. 14 and 15), and innumerable others. To the south of the Square once stood the boarding houses where **O. Henry** and **Eugene O'Neill** lived, and 133 MacDougal is the spot where O'Neill revved up his **Provincetown Players.** Down Bleecker and MacDougal you'll find some of the coffee houses the Beats made famous, along with former residences of James Fenimore Cooper (145 Bleecker), Theodore Dreiser, and **James Agee** (172 Bleecker). West of the square are the former pads of **Richard Wright, Edward Albee** (238 W. 4th St.), **Sinclair Lewis** (69 Charles St.), **Hart Crane** (79 Charles St.), and **Thomas Wolfe** (263 West 11th St.). **Dylan Thomas** was one of many writers who tanked up at the **White Horse Tavern** (567 Hudson St.). Few, however, were as unfortunate as Thomas, who, after pumping a purported 18 shots of scotch through his shredded gut, lapsed into a fatal coma.

The West Village, of course, did not have exclusive rights on New York's writerly set. On the other side of Broadway, the now-thriving, once-affordable East Village was headquarters to **Jack Kerouac, Allen Ginsberg, Amiri Baraka (Le Roi Jones),** and **W.H. Auden** (who spent a couple of decades at 77 St. Mark's Place, basement entrance). Many a writer whiled away his or her dying days in relative obscurity at the **Chelsea Hotel** (on 23rd St. between Seventh and Eighth Ave.). Among the surviving tenants are **Arthur Miller** and **Vladimir Nabokov.** In midtown lurks the legendary **Algonquin Hotel** (59 W. 44th St.). In 1919 the wits of the Round Table—writers like **Robert Benchley, Dorothy Parker, Alexander Woollcott,** and **Edna Ferber**—chose this hotel as the site of their famous weekly lunch meetings, making the Algonquin the site of inspiration for much of the *New Yorker* magazine.

The **Gotham Book Mart** (41 W. 47th St.), established in 1920, has long been one of New York's most important literary hangouts. The store is famous for its second-story readings, which has hosted some of the biggest writers of the century and once attracted all of literary New York. During the years when *Ulysses* was banned in the U.S., those in-the-know came to the Gotham to buy imported copies of Joyce's magnum opus under the counter. Check out the memorabilia and old photographs that document the bookstore's history. **Columbia University** has long been the intellectual magnet of the Upper West Side. The roving Beat crowd swarmed the area in the late 40s while Ginsberg was studying at the college. His friends were known to join him at the old **West End Café** (2911 Broadway), but unlike the White Horse, this delicatessen/bar doesn't play up its highfalutin' past.

While most of the Lost Generation mourned the lessons of World War I, New York witnessed one of the most vibrant and important moments in American literary history, the Harlem Renaissance. Novels like **George Schuyler's** *Black No More* and **Claude McKay's** *Home to Harlem* are energized accounts of the throbbing, grizzled underworld of speakeasies and nightclubs. **Zora Neale Hurston**, then an anthropology student at Columbia, helped plug the college intellectual scene into the hypercreative buzz up in Harlem, while **Langston Hughes** and his circle were busy founding radical journals. A downtown crowd of lefties, artists, and alternative lifestylists bypassed Midtown altogether in their relentless (often ignorantly condescending) explorations into black culture. For the next generation's impressions of this amazing neighborhood, look to the writings of **James Baldwin, Anne Petry,** and **Ralph Ellison**. Also see **Nathan Huggins's** *Harlem Renaissance*.

Some other must-reads involving the city of dreams:

Age of Innocence, House of Mirth, Edith Wharton: Two tales of turn-of-the-century romance and woe among the New York gentry.

A Tree Grows In Brooklyn, Betty Smith: An Irish woman's coming-of-age in early 20th-century Brooklyn. Also a 1945 film by Elia Kazan.

Bonfire of the Vanities, Tom Wolfe: A Wall Street financier takes a wrong turn off the TriBoro Bridge. Hijinks ensue. For your own sake, miss the movie.

Bright Lights, Big City, Jay MacInery: 80s New York. A columnist for the *New Yorker* divides his time between clubs and cocaine. Michael J. Fox starred in the film. Also see *Story of My Life*, another tale of Manhattan self-indulgence.

Call it Sleep, Henry Roth: The trials and tribulations of a Jewish immigrant family on the Depression-era lower east side. Also see *Mercy of a Rude Stream* for an autobiographical tale of youth in Harlem in the early 1900s.

Catcher in the Rye, J.D. Salinger: A now-classic fable of alienated youth. Prep-schooler Holden Caulfield visits the city and falls from innocence.

Eloise, Kay Thompson: A classic children's book. Young Eloise lives in the Plaza Hotel, wreaking havoc on every elegant floor and occasionally combing her hair with a fork.

The Great Gatsby, F. Scott Fitzgerald: An incisive commentary on the American dream, vis a vis the rise and fall of would-be New Yorker Jay Gatsby.

Invisible Man, Ralph Ellison: A definitive look at 1950s Harlem and one of the most telling portrayals of American racism ever written.

Mr. Sammler's Planet, Saul Bellow: Bellow takes no prisoners in this critical portrayal of 1970s New York youth culture, as seen through the single functioning eye of Holocaust survivor Sammler.

The New Negro, James Weldon Johnson: A collection of poems and essays capturing the optimism and spirit of the Harlem Renaissance.

New York Trilogy, Paul Auster: Three short stories that blur the boundaries between fiction and reality, set against the backdrop of Park Slope, Brooklyn.

Ragtime, E.L. Doctorow: Houdini, Henry Ford, and Emma Goldman populate this fictionalized account of New York life before World War I.

Six Degrees of Separation, John Guare: The award-winning play in which a young man claiming to be the son of Sidney Poitier has a profound effect on the lives of a wealthy Upper East Side couple.

Washington Square, Henry James: Typical Jamesian wit and scrutiny brought to bear on New York's 19th-century aristocracy. And he thought Daisy Miller had bad qualities.

▓ Lights, Camera, New York! (Film)

Since the earliest days of filmmaking, the Big Apple has been a popular setting for movies of all kinds, from big-budget musicals to independent art films. New York's role as a backdrop has not been limited to famous sights like the Statue of Liberty *(Remo Williams)* and the Empire State Building *(King Kong)*; filmmakers have gone down into the subways *(The Taking of Pelham 1-2-3)* and the corners of the outer boroughs *(Smoke)*. The following is a by-no-means comprehensive list of New York on celluloid:

After Hours: (1985) Griffin Dunne's absurdly nightmarish night out in the big city. Some consider this Scorsese's quietest masterpiece.

Annie Hall: (1977) Woody Allen and Diane Keaton play tennis, flirt, court, and part in this funny and romantic movie that captures Allen's love for the city and crystallizes his image as a neurotic Upper West Side intellectual.

Breakfast at Tiffany's: (1961) Audrey Hepburn as Holly Golightly frolics through Upper East Side high society.

City Hall: (1996) NYC Mayor Al Pacino wheels, deals and ultimately gets taken down by his protege, John Cusack.

Crossing Delancey: (1990) Amy Irving dates New York's premier pickle man.

Desperately Seeking Susan: (1985) A bored housewife finds excitement when she assumes the identity of that hippest of East Village hipsters, Madonna.

Die Hard With a Vengeance: (1995) Bruce Willis is forced to visit various NYC locales by evil mastermind Jeremy Irons. Watch the first half, then turn it off.

Do the Right Thing: (1989) Spike Lee's explosive look at one very hot day in the life of Bed-Stuy. Echoes the violence that erupted in New York at the same time.

Escape from New York: (1981) Kurt Russell must venture into the Manhattan of tomorrow, a rough-'n'-tough penal colony, to save the President.

Fort Apache, The Bronx: (1981) Cop Paul Newman learns why it's best to practice safety in and around the South Bronx.

Ghostbusters: (1984) Bill Murray and Dan Ackroyd try to rid the city (and Sigourney Weaver) of ghosts. Note the NYPL, among other landmarks.

The Godfather I, II, and III: (1972-1990) Coppola's searing study of one immigrant family and the price of the American dream. Next to *Star Wars,* the best film trilogy ever. Also a book by Mario Puzo.

Goodfellas: (1990) Scorsese's look at true-life gangster Henry Hill. Great location shots in the city, especially the Bamboo Lounge in Canarsie.

Hair: (1979) The love-child musical brought to the screen, complete with hippies tripping in Sheep Meadow in Central Park. Nell Carter sings a solo.

Independence Day: (1996) Aliens come to light up New York. Ouch.

Jacob's Ladder: (1991) Living in Brooklyn can be Hell. Just ask Tim Robbins.

James and the Giant Peach: (1996) Young James Henry Trotter travels to the Big Apple via a Big Peach. Note Richard Dreyfuss as a Brooklynite centipede.

Joe's Apartment: (1996) MTV's tale of a man, his NY apartment, and its multitude of roaches. Here's a fellow who could have used a *Let's Go* guide.

Kids: (1995) Larry Clark's study of some baaaaad NY kids. Not for the queasy.

Little Odessa: (1995) Tim Roth in a thriller about the emerging Russian-American mafia in Brooklyn's Brighton Beach. From the book by Joseph Koenig.

The Manchurian Candidate: (1962) Frank Sinatra is plagued by terrifying dreams in this cold-war thriller. Culminates in a terrifying scene at a Presidential convention in the old Madison Square Garden (MSG).

Manhattan: (1979) Woody Allen's hysterically funny love-note to New York, set to the tune of Gershwin's *Rhapsody in Blue.*

Marathon Man: (1976) Dustin Hoffman flees from Laurence Olivier's Nazi dentist, only to confront him in one of the pump-buildings at the Central Park reservoir.

Mean Streets: (1973) Harvey Keitel and Robert DeNiro cruise around Little Italy looking for trouble. Put Scorsese on the map.

Midnight Cowboy: (1969) "I ain't a for real cowboy, but I am one helluva stud." Jon Voight is a would-be hustler and Dustin Hoffman plays street rodent Ratso Rizzo in this devastating look at the seedy side of New York.

Moonstruck: (1987) Cher falls in love with baker Nicholas Cage in this romantic comedy set in Carroll Gardens. Watch for the scene in Lincoln Center.

The Muppets Take Manhattan: (1986) Kermit, Piggy, and the gang look to make it in the big city. Hey, in this town, even Gonzo fits right in.

New York Stories: (1989) Martin Scorsese, Francis Ford Coppola, and Woody Allen grind their cinematic axes on the Big Apple, to varying success.

On the Town: (1949) Start spreading the news—Gene Kelly and Frank Sinatra are sailors with time and money to burn in New York City.

On the Waterfront: (1954) Marlon Brando coulda been a contenda, had he ever gotten it in his head to get out of Hoboken.

Saturday Night Fever: (1977) John Travolta rules the dance floor. Forever.

Taxi Driver: (1976) Robert DeNiro is Travis Bickle, a taxi driver with issues. Don't look him in the eye and tip him well.

Wall Street: (1987) Oliver Stone's scathingly funny look at the craven life of Wall Street high-traders and why greed, for lack of a better word, is good.

The Warriors: (1975) Let's get down to it, boppers. A Coney Island gang must dodge their many rivals and cross the city at night to get back to their home turf.

West Side Story: (1961) Romeo and Juliet retold. Ironically, the area in which the film was shot is now some of the most prime real estate in the city.

When Harry Met Sally: (1989) Meg Ryan and Billy Crystal continually emote about their foibles against a New York backdrop. The ultimate date movie.

▓ Journalism and Publications

New York, the premiere society of information abundance, is a sounding board for the rest of the global village. ABC, CBS, NBC, two wire services, umpteen leading magazines, and more newspapers than anywhere else in the world have taken up residence here. Publicists, preachers, advertisers, sociologists, and community activists jockey for position, hoping to make enough noise to be heard above the information din. The stakes are immense, the opportunities unparalleled; the high concentration of media here amplifies every sound. Broadsheets, graffiti, posters, and billboards provide additional media outlets, public spaces for high-profile intervention. Meanwhile, a bizarre underground world awaits on public-access television, if you can find a friend with cable.

New York's romance with the media began almost three centuries ago. The city's first newspaper, the *Gazette,* appeared in 1725. Ten years later, John Peter Zenger, editor of the *New York Weekly Journal,* was charged with libel for satirizing public officials. His description of the city recorder as "a large spaniel...that has lately strayed from his kennel with his mouth full of fulsome panegyrics" was seen as especially offensive. The governor threw Zenger into jail and burned copies of his paper in public. Zenger's acquittal set a precedent for what would become a great U.S. tradition—the freedom of the press.

The city soon became the center of the nation's rapidly developing print network. Horace Greeley's *Tribune,* based in New York, became America's first nationally distributed paper. Despite his love for the city, Greeley's famous advice to young men around the country was to "Go West." As a result of the *Tribune* and its rivals, Nassau Street was dubbed "Newspaper Row" in the mid-19th century.

Today, New York supports well over 100 different newspapers, reflecting the diversity of its urban landscape. Weekly ethnic papers cater to the black, Hispanic, Irish, Japanese, Chinese, Indian, Korean, and Greek communities, among others. Candidates for local office frequently court voters in these communities by seeking endorsements from their papers. Other papers cater to the patrician, the pensive, and the prurient.

The *New York Post* and the *Daily News,* the city's two major tabloid dailies, are infamous for their less-than-demure sensibilities. The *News,* recently "rescued" by now-dead Robert Maxwell, has slightly better taste—it doesn't use red ink, and it reports fewer gruesome murders. *Post* headlines, often printed in unwieldy lettering three inches high, can have a nasty, toothsome ring. One of the *Post's* more brilliant offerings read "Headless Body Found in Topless Bar." Both papers have editorial policies more conservative than their headlines, as well as comics, advice pages, gossip columns, and horoscopes. The *Post* has a great sports section and both have good metropolitan coverage. *Newsday* also offers thorough local coverage. After more than 40 years as a successful Long Island paper—with a youngish staff, some entertaining columnists, and a special Sunday section just for the kids—*Newsday* had recently begun printing a New York City edition, only to shut down in 1995, a victim of a closed market and aggressive campaigns by its new rivals.

If you're a fan of headless body tales, the *New York Times* will not satisfy you. The distinguished elder statesperson of all city papers, the *Times,* New York's "Gray Lady," deals soberly and thoroughly with the news. Its editorial page provides a nationally respected forum for policy debates, and its political endorsements are prized by candidates across the country. Praise from its Book Review section can revitalize living authors and immortalize dead ones, and its Sunday crossword puzzles enliven brunches from Fresno to Tallahassee. The *Times* recently began "National Editions" geared toward audiences outside the city, but the paper remains staunchly centered on New York. Theater directors, nervous politicians, and other fervent readers often make late-night newsstand runs to buy the hefty Sunday *Times* around midnight on Saturday.

The Village Voice, the largest weekly leftist newspaper in the country, captures a spirit of the city each Wednesday that you won't find in the dailies. Printed on the same kind of paper as the conservative *Post* and *Daily News,* it has nothing else in common with them. Don't search here for syndicated advice columnists, baseball statistics, or the bikini-clad woman *du jour.* The *Voice* prefers to stage lively political debates and print quirky reflections on New York life. It also sponsors some excellent investigative city reporting—and the city's most intriguing set of personal ads. Aging rock-modernist Robert Christgau's music column grace the *Voice* every week, while the movie reviews are some of the most substantial (and sometimes most considered) in the nation. Best of all, it recently became free to Manhattanites and can be picked up at any street corner if you get up early enough. The *New York Press,* a free weekly, also has good club and nightlife listings in addition to entertaining articles on politics and culture.

The *Wall Street Journal* and the Upper East Side's *New York Observer* fill out the newspaper spectrum. The *Observer* prints articles and commentary on city politics on its dapper pink pages. The *Journal* gives a quick world-news summary on page one for breakfasting brokers more interested in the market pages. With its pen-and-ink drawings, conservative bent, market strategies, and continual obsession with the price of gold, the *Journal* offers to all a Wall Street insider's world perspective.

On the glossy side, New York is undoubtedly the magazine publishing capital of the country; most major publications have their headquarters somewhere in the city. Old venerables like *Time, Newsweek,* and *Rolling Stone* have been here for decades, while each week the newsstands seem to feature a new title dedicated to carrying the latest on food, film, or fashion. The newly spiced-up *New Yorker* publishes fiction and poetry by well known authors and the occasional fledgling discovery. The recent addition of former *Vanity Fair* editor Tina Brown as editor-in-chief has brought the magazine a new, updated style, photographs by Richard Avedon, occasional cartoons by Art Spiegelman, and more pieces on current events (no more six-parters on the history of wheat). The mag can still tend to be a little heady—even its ads contain measured prose. One world-famous cover by Saul Steinberg, showing the rest of the world dwarfed by New York, reflects the perspective of the typical *New Yorker* reader. *The New Yorker* also carries very thorough listings and reviews of films and events and the finest cartoons in the tri-state area. *New York* magazine also prints extensive listings but, unlike *The New Yorker,* focuses more on the city's (wealthy) lifestyle than its (pretentious) literati. Its final pages can prove very entertaining: they hold impossible British crossword puzzles, monthly word-game contests, and a slew of desperate personal ads. *Time Out: New York* magazine is the most recent weekly player in the local newsprint rivalry—its colorful nightlife-dense stories and extensive listings make it the *USA Today* of the Gen-X set, particularly for those alienated by the *Village Voice's* verbosity.

■ Etiquette

Like the French and the Visigoths, New Yorkers have a widespread reputation for rudeness. For most of them, lack of politeness is not a matter of principle; it's a strategy for survival. Nowhere is the anonymous rhythm of urban life more hammering than in New York City. Cramped into tiny spaces, millions of people find themselves confronting one another every day, rudderless in a vast sea of humanity. If the comfort of strangers seems overshadowed by the confusion, keep in mind that it's partly a question of scale. The city, by most fundamental human standards, is just too big and heterogeneous and jumbled. People react by developing thick skins and keeping to themselves, especially in public. If you feel that the city is intolerably unfriendly, remember the small humanitarian gestures that appear in the unlikeliest of places, and try on a frown yourself. Once you cultivate your own defensive New York attitude, you'll find the natives to be much more amiable.

Essentials

PLANNING YOUR TRIP

Start spreading the news; you're leaving today. Millions of penniless immigrants disembarked here and quickly learned to survive. Don't fret—you will, too.

An address book can be used as a supplementary travel guide; staying with friends, enemies, relatives, and acquaintances greatly alleviates the cost of living in New York. Visiting in the off-season helps, too: in May and September the weather improves, the waves of tourists recede, and prices plummet. Most facilities and sights stay open in the off-season—after all, New York is the city that never sleeps.

Travel offices, tourist information centers, and special-interest organizations will barrage you with an overwhelming amount of free information; it's best to write with specific requests (see Tourist Information, p. 66).

■ Useful Information

GOVERNMENT INFORMATION OFFICES

United States Tourist Offices, found in many countries, can provide you with armloads of free literature. If you can't find a U.S. Tourist Office in your area, write the **U.S. Travel and Tourism Administration,** Department of Commerce, 14th St. and Constitution Ave. NW, Rm. 1860, Washington, D.C. 20230 (202-482-4003). Or write or call N.Y. state and city tourist offices (see Tourist Information, p. 66)

TRAVEL ORGANIZATIONS

American Automobile Association (AAA) Travel Related Services, 1000 AAA Dr., Heathrow, FL 32746-5080 (407-444-8411). Provides free road maps and travel guides to members. Offers emergency road and travel services, and auto insurance (free for members, small fee otherwise). For emergency road services, call 800-222-4357; to become a member, call 800-926-4222 for the nearest office.

Council on International Educational Exchange (Council), 205 East 42nd St., New York, NY 10017-5706 (tel. (888) COUNCIL (268-6245); fax (212) 822-2699; e-mail info@ciee.org; http://www.ciee.org). A private, nonprofit organization, Council administers work, volunteer, and academic programs around the world. They also offer identity cards, including the ISIC and GO25, and a range of publications, including the magazine *Student Travels* (free). Call or write for more information.

Federation of International Youth Travel Organizations (FIYTO), Bredgade 25H, DK-1260 Copenhagen K, Denmark (tel. (45) 33 33 96 00; fax 33 93 96 76; e-mail mailbox@fiyto.org), is an international organization promoting educational, cultural, and social travel for young people. Member organizations include language schools, educational travel companies, national tourist boards, accommodation centers, and other suppliers of travel services to youth and students. FIYTO sponsors the GO25 Card.

International Student Travel Confederation, Herengracht 479, 10 17 BS Amsterdam, The Netherlands (tel. (31) 204 21 28 00; fax 20 421 28 10; http://www.istc.org; e-mail istcinfo@istc.org). The ISTC is a nonprofit confederation of student travel organizations whose focus is to develop, promote, and facilitate travel among young people and students. Member organizations include International Student Rail Association (ISRA), Student Air Travel Association (SATA), ISIS Travel Insurance, and the International Association for Educational and Work Exchange Programs (IAEWEP).

USEFUL PUBLICATIONS

In addition to this stylin' volume, Let's Go offers travelers the slim, sleek fold-out maps and textual highlights of Let's Go Map Guide: New York City. The following businesses and organizations also specialize in keeping travelers informed:

Adventurous Traveler Bookstore, P.O. Box 1468, Williston, VT 05495 (tel. 801-860-6776; fax 860-6607, or both at 800-282-3963; e-mail books@atbook.com; http://www.gorp.com/atbook.htm). Free 40-page catalogue upon request. Specializes in outdoor adventure travel books and maps for the U.S. and abroad. Their World Wide Web site offers extensive browsing opportunities.

Blue Guides, published in Britain by A&C Black Limited, 35 Bedford Row, London WC1R 4JH, in the U.S. by W.W. Norton & Co. Inc., 500 Fifth Ave., New York, NY 10110, and in Canada by Penguin Books Canada Ltd., 2801 John St., Markham, Ontario L3R 1B4. Blue Guides provide invaluable historical and cultural information as well as sightseeing routes, maps, tourist info, and listings of pricey hotels.

Bon Voyage!, 2069 W. Bullard Ave., Fresno, CA 93711-1200 (800-995-9716, from abroad 209-447-8441; e-mail 70754.3511@compuserve.com). Annual mail order catalog offers a range of products and publications for everyone from the luxury traveler to the diehard trekker. All merchandise may be returned for exchange or refund within 30 days of purchase, and prices are guaranteed (lower advertised prices will be matched and merchandise shipped free).

Hippocrene Books, Inc., 171 Madison Ave., New York, NY 10016 (212-685-4371; orders 718-454-2366; fax 454-1391). Free catalog. Publishes travel reference books, travel guides, foreign language dictionaries, and language learning guides which cover over 100 languages.

Michelin Travel Publications, Michelin Tire Corporation, P.O. Box 19001, Greenville, SC 29602-9001 (800-423-0485; fax 803-458-5665). Publishes three major lines of travel-related material: *Green Guides,* for sight-seeing, maps, and driving itineraries; *Red Guides,* which rate hotels and restaurants; and detailed, reliable road maps and atlases. All three are available at bookstores and distributors around the globe.

Rand McNally, 150 S. Wacker Dr., Chicago, IL 60606 (800-333-0136), publishes one of the most comprehensive road atlases of the U.S., Canada, and Mexico ($9), available in their stores and most other bookstores in the U.S. Phone orders accepted.

Travel Books & Language Center, Inc., 4931 Cordell Ave., Bethesda, MD 20814 (800-220-2665; fax 301-951-8546; e-mail travelbks@aol.com). Sells over 75,000 items, including books, cassettes, atlases, dictionaries, and a wide range of specialty travel maps, including wine and cheese maps of France, Michelin maps, and beer maps of the U.S. Free comprehensive catalogue upon request.

U.S. Customs Service, P.O. Box 7407, Washington, D.C., 20044 (202-927-5580). Publishes 35 books, booklets, leaflets, and flyers on various aspects of customs. *Know Before You Go* provides almost everything the international traveler needs to know about customs requirements; *Pockets Hints* summarizes the most important data from *Know Before You Go. Hints for Visitors* tells everything a foreign traveler visiting the U.S. for a year or less needs to know about customs requirements; *Customs Tips for Visitors* summarizes the most important information from *Hints for Visitors* (available in more than a dozen languages).

Wide World Books and Maps, 1911 N. 45th St., Seattle, WA 98103 (206-634-3453; fax 634-0558; e-mail travelbk@mail.nwlink.com; http://nwlink.com/travelbk). A good selection of travel guides, travel accessories, and hard-to-find maps.

LIBRARIES

New York Public Library, 11 W. 40th St. (661-7220, or 869-8089 for a recorded listing of exhibitions and events), entrance on Fifth Ave. at 42nd St. Non-lending central research library. Wide variety of exhibits on display. Open Tues.-Wed. 11am-6pm, Mon., Thurs.-Sat. 10am-6pm. Exhibitions open Mon., Thurs.-Sat. 10am-6pm, Tues.-Wed. 11am-6pm.

Midtown Manhattan, 455 Fifth Ave. (340-0833), at 40th St. Largest branch of the circulating libraries; specialized sections include Folklore and Women's Studies. Occasional exhibitions and presentations; pick up a free events calendar at any

NYPL location. Identification and proof of local address required to take out books. Open Mon.-Wed. 9am-9pm, Tues.-Thurs. 11am-7pm, Fri.-Sat. 10am-6pm.

Donnell Library Center, 20 W. 53rd St. (621-0618), between Fifth and Sixth Ave. Across the street from the Museum of Modern Art. Central Children's Room for "Curious George" fans. Largest circulation of foreign-language books. Open Mon., Wed., Fri.-Sat. 12:30-5:30pm, Tues., Thurs. 9:30am-8pm.

Performing Arts Research Center, at Lincoln Center, 111 Amsterdam Ave. (870-1630), entrance at 65th St. Specializes in theater, music, dance, film, and TV. Circulation section (for anybody with a NYC library card) includes CDs, CD-ROMs, tapes, and records. Tour (870-1608) Wed. at 2pm. Open Mon., Thurs. noon-8pm, Tues.-Wed., Fri.-Sat. noon-6pm.

Andrew Heiskell Library for the Blind and Physically Handicapped, 40 W. 20th St. (206-5400), near Sixth Ave. between Prince and Spring St. Braille and large type books. Open Mon.-Wed. 10am-5pm, Thurs. 1-7pm, Fri. 1-5pm. Librarians available by phone Mon.-Thurs. 10am-7pm, Fri. -Sat. 1-5pm.

Schomburg Center for Research in Black Culture, 515 Lenox Ave./Malcolm X Blvd. (491-2200), on the corner of 135th St. Largest collection of books by and about African-Americans anywhere in the world. Large, quiet reading rooms on the basement and second floor. Films and art exhibits shown regularly, call for schedule. Library open Mon.-Wed. noon-8pm, Thurs.-Sat. 10am-6pm; archives dept. open Mon.-Wed. noon-5pm, Fri.-Sat. 10am-5pm.

The other boroughs' head branches are: the **Bronx Reference Center,** 2556 Bainbridge Ave. (718-220-6565); the **St. George Library Center,** 5 Central Ave., Staten Island (718-442-8560); the **Queensborough Public Library,** 89-11 Merrick Blvd., Jamaica, Queens (718-990-0700); and the **Brooklyn Public Library,** Grand Army Plaza, Brooklyn (718-780-7700).

INTERNET RESOURCES

Along with everything else in the 90s, budget travel is moving rapidly into the information age. And with the growing user-friendliness of personal computers and internet technology, much of this information can be yours with the click of a mouse.

There are a number of ways to access the **Internet.** Most popular are commercial internet providers, such as **America On-Line** (800-827-6394) and **Compuserve** (800-433-0389). Many employers and schools also offer gateways to the Internet, often at no cost (unlike the corporate gateways above). The Internet itself has many uses, but the most benficial to net-surfing budget travelers are the World Wide Web and Usenet newsgroups.

The World Wide Web (WWW)

Increasingly the Internet forum of choice, the **World Wide Web** provides its users with graphics and sound, as well as textual information. This and the huge proliferation of "web pages" (individual sites within the World Wide Web) have made the Web the most active and exciting of the destinations on the Internet, though it has also made it the newest path from corporate advertisers to the minds of the masses; be sure to distinguish between what is good information and what is marketing. Another large difficulty with the Web is its lack of hierarchy (it is a web, after all). The introduction of **search engines** (services that search for web pages under specific subjects) has aided the search process some. **Lycos** (http://a2z.lycos.com) and **Infoseek** (http://guide.infoseek.com) are the two of the most popular. **Yahoo!** is a slightly more organized search engine; check out its travel links at http://www.yahoo.com/Recreation/Travel. However, it is often better to know a good site, and start "surfing" from there, through links from one web page to another. Here are some places to start surfing for budget travel information on the Web.

Dr. Memory's Favorite Travel Pages (http://www.access.digex.net/ldrmemory/cybertravel.html), is a great place to start surfing. Dr. Memory has links to hundreds of different web pages of interest to travelers of all kinds.

Rent-A-Wreck's Travel Links (http://www.rent-a-wreck.com/raw/travlist.html). Surprisingly, very good and very complete.

Big World Magazine (http://boss.cpcnet.com/personal/bigworld/bigworld.html), a budget travel 'zine, with a web page. Also has a great collection of links to travel pages.

City.Net (http://www.city.net) A very impressive collection of regional- and city-specific web pages. You just select a geographic area, and it provides you with links to web pages related to that area. **USA CityLink** (http://www.usacitylink.com/cityink) has a similar service for the U.S.

The CIA World Factbook (http://www.odci.gov/cia/publications/95fact) Tons of vital statistics on any city or country you want to visit. Check it out for an economic overview, an explanation of a nation's system of government, or a copy of the *Mission: Impossible* NOC list.

Shoestring Travel (http://www.stratpub.com) A budget travel e-zine, with feature articles, links, user exchange, and accommodations information.

The Student and Budget Travel Guide (http://asa.ugl.lib.umich.edu/chdocs/travel/travel-guide.html). Just what it sounds like.

The Interactive Travel Guide (http://www.developnet.com/travel). Began as the Cheap Travel Page and has expanded its scope some, but is still useful for the budget traveler.

If you're looking for New York specific web sites, you won't have to look too far; many organizations of interest to NYCers have their own web pages. Check for gopher and web sites maintained by ECHO ("East Coast HangOut"), New York's answer to California's WELL. ECHO is an internet service-provider based in Greenwich Village with a New York-centric world-view that attracts young professionals and perpetual Internet-surfers alike. They maintain listings for clubs, restaurant reviews, shopping tips, and other fun stuff. Some other interesting sites:

Internet Café (http://www.bigmagic.com).

totalny.com (http://www.totalny.com). Concerts, festivals, and other live events.

SonicNet (http://sonicnet.com). Alternative rock emphasis; chat with artists like Laurie Anderson.

Nightflight (http://www.echonyc.com/voice) Run in conjunction with the *Village Voice*. Guide to NY (and LA) nightlife.

Let's Go also lists relevant web sites throughout different sections of the Essentials chapter. One caveat: the Web can be as gossamer as its namesake; Web sites emerge and disappear very rapidly. Thus, as with normal travel, it is important for you to head out on your own in cyber-travel as well. Log on softly and carry a big virtual stick.

TELEPHONES

Most of the information you will need about telephones—including area codes for the U.S., foreign country codes, and rates—is in the front of the local **white pages** telephone directory. The **yellow pages,** published at the end of the white pages or in a separate book, is used to look up the phone numbers of businesses and other services. Federal, state, and local government listings are provided in the blue pages at the back of the directory. To obtain local phone numbers or area codes of other cities, call **directory assistance** at 411. Calling "0" will get you the **operator,** who can assist you in reaching a phone number and provide you with general information. For long-distance directory assistance, dial 1-(area code)-555-1212. The operator will help you with rates or other info and give assistance in an emergency. Calls to directory assistance or the operator are free from any pay phone.

Telephone numbers in the U.S. consist of a three-digit area code, a three-digit exchange, and a four-digit number, written as 123-456-7890. Only the last seven digits are used in a **local call. Non-local calls within the area code** from which you are dialing require a "1" before the last seven digits, while **long-distance calls outside the area code** from which you are dialing require a "1" and the area code. For example, to call the Film Forum in SoHo from outside Manhattan, you would dial 1-212-727-8110. Generally, discount rates apply after 5pm on weekdays and Sunday and economy rates every day between 11pm and 8am; on Saturday and on Sunday until 5pm, economy rates are also in effect. Numbers beginning with area code 800 are **toll-free calls** requiring no coin deposit. Numbers beginning with 900 are **toll calls** and charge you (often exorbitantly) for whatever "service" they provide.

Pay phones are plentiful, most often stationed on street corners and in public areas. Be wary of private, more expensive pay phones—the rate they charge per call should be printed on the phone. Put your coins (25¢ for a local call in NYC) into the slot and listen for a dial tone before dialing. If there is no answer or if you get a busy signal, you will get your money back after hanging up; connecting with answering machines will prevent this. To make a **long-distance direct call,** dial the number. An operator will tell you the cost for the first three minutes; deposit that amount in the coin slot. The operator or a recording will cut in when you must deposit more money. A rarer variety of pay phone found in some large train stations charges 25¢ for a one-minute call to any place in the continental U.S.

If you are at an ordinary telephone and don't have barrels of change, you may want to make a **collect call** (i.e., charge the call to the recipient). First dial "0" and then the area code and number you wish to reach. An operator will cut in and ask to help you. Tell him or her that you wish to place a collect call and give your name; anyone who answers may accept or refuse the call. If you tell the operator you are placing a **person-to-person collect call** (more expensive than a regular, **station-to-station collect call),** you must give both your name and the receiving person's name; the benefit is that a charge appears only if the person with whom you wish to speak is there (and accepts the charges, of course). The cheapest method of reversing the charges is MCI's new **1-800-COLLECT/265-5328** service: just dial 1-800-265-5328,

tell the operator what number you want to call (it can be anywhere in the world), and receive a 20% to 44% discount off normal rates. AT&T offers a similar program: dial **1-800-CALL-ATT/225-5288.** Finally, if you'd like to call someone who is as poor as you, simply **bill to a third party** by dialing "0," the area code, and then the number; the operator will call the third party for approval.

In addition to coin-operated pay phones, AT&T and its competitors operate a **coinless** version. Not only can collect and third-party calls be made on these ingenious gadgets, but you can also use a **telephone calling card;** begin dialing all these kinds of calls with "0." Generally, these phones are operated by passing the card through a slot before dialing, although you can always just punch in your calling-card number on the keypad (a desirable alternative if you happen to be traveling in an area where carrying around credit cards is unwise). Many of these phones—especially those located in airports, hotels, and truckstops—accept Visa, MasterCard, and American Express cards as well. The cheapest way to call long-distance from a pay phone is by using a calling card or credit card.

You can place **international calls** from any telephone. To call direct, dial the universal international access code (011) followed by the country code, the city/area code, and the local number. Country codes and city codes may sometimes be listed with a zero in front (e.g., 033), but when dialing 011 first, drop succeeding zeros (e.g., 011-33). In some areas you will have to give the operator the number and he or she will place the call. Rates are cheapest on calls to the United Kingdom and Ireland between 6pm and 7am (Eastern Time), to Australia between 3am and 2pm, and to New Zealand between 11pm and 10am.

The **country code** is 1 for the U.S. and Canada; 44 for the U.K.; 353 for the Republic of Ireland; 61 for Australia; 64 for New Zealand; and 27 for South Africa.

TELEGRAM

Sometimes **cabling** may be the only way to contact someone quickly (usually within 1-3 days). Within the U.S., the minimum cost for a same day, hand-delivered telegram is $30.90 for 15 words. A "Mailgram" is a telegram that arrives on the next mail-day and costs $18.95 for 50 words. For foreign telegrams, **Western Union** (800-325-6000) charges a base fee for the first seven words plus $9 delivery; after seven words, an additional per-word charge is assessed. To Canada, the rate is $12.85 plus 55¢ per additional word, to Great Britain and Ireland, $13.27/61¢, to Australia and New Zealand, $13.62/66¢, and $14.32/76¢ to Israel.

■ Documents & Formalities

Be sure to file all applications several weeks or months in advance of your planned departure date. Remember, you are relying on government agencies to complete these transactions. A backlog in processing can spoil your plans. U.S. citizens in particular should plan ahead; an unusually high number of U.S. passports are due to expire in 1996, creating even longer than normal delays in processing.

When you travel, always carry on your person two or more forms of identification, including at least one photo ID. A passport combined with a driver's license or birth certificate usually serves as adequate proof of your identity and citizenship. Many establishments, especially banks, require several IDs before cashing traveler's checks. Never carry all your forms of ID together, however; you risk being left entirely without ID or funds in case of theft or loss. Also, carry half a dozen extra passport-size photos that you can attach to the sundry IDs or railpasses you will eventually acquire. If you plan an extended stay, register your passport with the nearest embassy or consulate.

U.S. citizens seeking information about documents, formalities and travel abroad should request the booklet *Your Trip Abroad* ($1.25) from the **Superintendent of**

Documents, U.S. Government Printing Office, P.O. Box 371954, Pittsburgh, PA 15250-7954 (202-512-1800; fax 512-2250).

ENTRANCE REQUIREMENTS

Citizens of the U.S., Canada, the U.K., Ireland, Australia, New Zealand, and South Africa all need valid **passports** to enter most countries and to re-enter their own country. Some countries do not allow entrance if the holder's passport expires in under six months, and returning to the U.S. with an expired passport may result in a fine. Some countries also require a **visa;** an **invitation** from a sponsoring individual or organization is required by several Eastern European countries.

Upon entering a country, you must declare certain items from abroad and must pay a duty on the value of those articles that exceed the allowance established by that country's **customs** service. Holding onto receipts for purchases made abroad will help establish values when you return. It is wise to make a list, including serial numbers, of any valuables that you carry with you from home; if you register this list with customs before your departure and have a government official stamp it, you will avoid import duty charges and ensure an easy passage upon your return. Be especially careful to document items manufactured abroad.

When you enter a country, dress neatly and carry **proof of your financial independence,** such as a visa to the next country on your itinerary, an airplane ticket to depart, enough money to cover the cost of your living expenses, etc. Admission as a visitor does not include the right to work, which is authorized only by a work permit. Entering certain countries to study requires a special visa, and immigration officers may also want to see proof of acceptance from a school, proof that the course of study will take up most of your time in the country, and as always, proof that you can support yourself (see Visas, p. 22)

PASSPORTS

Before you leave, photocopy the page of your passport that contains your photograph and identifying information, especially your passport number. Carry this photocopy in a safe place apart from your passport, and leave another copy at home. These measures will help prove your citizenship and facilitate the issuing of a new passport if you lose the original document. Consulates also recommend you carry an expired passport or an official copy of your birth certificate in a part of your baggage separate from other documents. You can request a duplicate birth certificate from the Bureau of Vital Records and Statistics in your state or province of birth.

If you do lose your passport, it may take weeks to process a replacement, and your new one may be valid only for a limited time. In addition, any visas stamped in your old passport will be irretrievably lost. If this happens, immediately notify the local police and the nearest embassy or consulate of your home government. To expedite its replacement, you will need to know all information previously recorded and show identification and proof of citizenship. Some consulates can issue new passports within two days if you give them proof of citizenship. In an emergency, ask for immediate temporary traveling papers that will permit you to re-enter your home country.

Your passport is a public document belonging to your nation's government. You may have to surrender it to a foreign government official; but, if you don't get it back in a reasonable amount of time, inform the nearest mission of your home country.

United States Citizens may apply for a passport, valid for 10 years (five years if under 18), at any federal or state **courthouse** or **post office** authorized to accept passport applications, or at a **U.S. Passport Agency,** located in Boston, Chicago, Honolulu, Houston, Los Angeles, Miami, New Orleans, New York, Philadelphia, San Francisco, Seattle, Stamford, or Washington, D.C. Refer to the "U.S. Government, State Department" section of the telephone directory, or call your local post office for addresses. Parents must apply in person for children under age 13. You must apply in person if this is your first passport, if you're under age 18, or if your current passport is more than 12 years old or was issued before your 18th birthday. You must submit the following: (1) proof of U.S. citizenship (a certified birth certificate, certification of naturalization or of citizenship, or a previous passport); (2) identification bearing your signature and either your photograph or physical description (e.g. an unexpired driver's license or passport, student ID card, or government ID card); and (3) two identical, passport-size (2"x2") photographs with a white or off-white background taken within the last six months. It will cost $65 (under 18 $40). You can **renew** your passport by mail or in person for $55. Processing takes two to four weeks. Passport agencies offer **rush service** for a surcharge of $30 if you have proof that you're departing within ten working days (e.g., an airplane ticket or itinerary). Abroad, a U.S. embassy or consulate can usually issue a new passport, given proof of citizenship. If your passport is **lost or stolen in the U.S.**, report it in writing to Passport Services, U.S. Department of State, 111 19th St., NW, Washington, D.C., 20522-1705 or to the nearest passport agency. For more info, contact the U.S. Passport Information's **24-hour recorded message** (202-647-0518).

Canada Application forms in English and French are available at all **passport offices, post offices,** and most **travel agencies.** Citizens may apply in person at any one of 28 regional Passport Offices across Canada. Travel agents can direct the applicant to the nearest location. Canadian citizens residing abroad should contact the nearest Canadian embassy or consulate. Along with the application form, a citizen must provide: (1) citizenship documentation (an original Canadian birth certificate, or a certificate of Canadian citizenship); (2) two identical passport photos taken within the last year; (3) any previous Canadian passport; and (4) a CDN$60 fee (paid in cash, money order, or certified check) to Passport Office, Ottawa, Ont. K1A OG3. The application and one of the photographs must be signed by an eligible guarantor (someone who has known the applicant for two years and whose profession falls into one of the categories listed on the application). All above information is outlined in both English and French on the application form. Processing takes approximately five business days for in-person applications and three weeks for mailed ones. Children under 16 may be included on a parent's passport, though some countries require children to carry their own passports. A passport is valid for five years and is not renewable. If a passport is lost abroad, Canadians must be able to prove citizenship with another document. For additional info, call 800-567-6868 (24hr.; from Canada only) or call the Passport Office at 819-994-3500. In Metro Toronto, call 416-973-3251. Montréalers should dial 514-283-2152. Refer to the booklet *Bon Voyage, But...* for further help and a list of Canadian embassies and consulates abroad. It is available free of charge from any passport office.

Britain British citizens, British Dependent Territories citizens, British Nationals (overseas), and British Overseas citizens may apply for a **full passport.** For a full passport, valid for 10 years (five years if under 16), apply in person or by mail to a passport office, located in London, Liverpool, Newport, Peterborough, Glasgow, or Belfast. The fee is UK£18. Children under 16 may be included on a parent's passport. Processing by mail usually takes four to six weeks. The London office offers same-day, walk-in rush service; arrive early. The British Visitor's Passport, valid for one year in some western European countries and Bermuda only, is no longer available.

Ireland Citizens can apply for a passport by mail to either the Department of Foreign Affairs, Passport Office, Setanta Centre, Molesworth St., Dublin 2 (tel. (01) 671 16 33), or the Passport Office, 1A South Mall, Cork (tel. (021) 627 25 25). Obtain an application at a local Garda station or request one from a passport office. The new Passport Express Service offers a two-week turn-around and is available through post

ESSENTIALS

offices for an extra IR£3. Passports cost IR£45 and are valid for 10 years. Citizens under 18 or over 65 can request a three-year passport that costs IR£10.

Australia Citizens must apply for a passport in person at a post office, a passport office, or an Australian diplomatic mission overseas. An appointment may be necessary. Passport offices are located in Adelaide, Brisbane, Canberra City, Darwin, Hobart, Melbourne, Newcastle, Perth, and Sydney. A parent may file an application for a child who is under 18 and unmarried. Application fees are adjusted frequently. For more info, call toll-free (in Australia) 13 12 32.

New Zealand Application forms for passports are available in New Zealand from travel agents and Department of Internal Affairs Link Centres, and overseas from New Zealand embassies, high commissions, and consulates. Completed applications may be lodged at Link Centres and at overseas posts, or forwarded to the Passport Office, PO Box 10-526, Wellington, New Zealand. Processing time is 10 working days from receipt of a correctly completed application. An urgent passport service is also available. The application fee for an adult passport is NZ$80 in New Zealand and NZ$130 overseas for applications lodged under the standard service.

South Africa Citizens can apply for a passport at any Home Affairs Office. Two photos, either a birth certificate or an identity book, and a $12 fee must accompany a completed application. South African passports remain valid for 10 years. For further information, contact the nearest Department of Home Affairs Office.

VISAS

To acquire a visa for entrance to the U.S., you will need your passport and proof of intent to leave the U.S. Most visitors obtain a B-2 or "pleasure tourist" visa, valid for six months. Contact the nearest U.S. consulate in your home country to obtain yours. Upon arrival, the I-94 form (an arrival/departure certificate) will be attached to your

visa; if you lose this, replace it at the nearest **U.S. Immigration and Naturalization Service (INS)** office. (If you lose your passport in the U.S., you must replace it through your country's embassy.) The INS also grants extensions for visas (max. 6 months), which require form I-539 as well as a $70 fee.

Visitors from certain nations may enter the U.S. without visas through the **Visa Waiver Pilot Program.** Travelers qualify as long as they are traveling for business or pleasure, are staying for 90 days or less, have proof of intent to leave with a completed I-94W form, and enter aboard particular air or sea carriers. Participating countries are Andorra, Austria, Belgium, Brunei, Denmark, Finland, France, Germany, Iceland, Italy, Japan, Lichtenstein, Luxembourg, Monaco, the Netherlands, New Zealand, Norway, San Marino, Spain, Sweden, Switzerland, and the U.K. Contact the nearest U.S. consulate for more information.

Canadian citizens do not need a visa or passport, but must carry proof of citizenship (a passport, birth certificate, or voter registration card). Canadian citizens under 16 need notarized permission from both parents. Naturalized citizens should have their naturalization papers with them; occasionally officials will ask to see them. **Mexican citizens** may cross into the U.S. with an I-186 form.

Non-Tourist Visas For Work and Study

If you are not a citizen of the U.S. and hope to **work** in this country, there are numerous rules of which you must be aware. The place to start getting specific information on visa categories and requirements is your nearest U.S. Embassy or Consulate, or the Educational Advisory Service of the Fulbright Commission (a U.S. embassy-affiliated organization). You can also write to organizations such as Council, which have work-abroad programs. The alphabet soup of obtaining a worker's visa may seem complex, but it's critical that you go through the proper channels. Above all, do not try to give your consular officer any monkey-business. Working or studying in the U.S. with only a B-2 visa is grounds for deportation; if the U.S. consulate suspects that you may be trying to enter the country as a worker under the aegis of a pleasure trip, you will be denied a visa altogether.

Foreign students who wish to **study** in the United States must apply for either a J-1 visa (for exchange students) or an F-1 visa (for full-time students enrolled in an academic or language program). To obtain a J-1, you must fill out an IAP-66 eligibility form, issued by the program in which you will enroll. Both are valid for the duration of stay, which includes the length of your particular program and a brief grace period thereafter. In order to extend a student visa, submit an I-538 form 15 to 60 days before the original departure date.

If you are studying in the U.S., you can take any on-campus job to help pay the bills provided that (1) you have applied for a social security number, (2) you have completed an Employment Eligibility Form (I-9), and (3) you are not displacing a U.S. resident. On-campus employment is limited to 20 hours per week while school is in session, but you may work full-time during vacation if you plan to return to school. For further info, contact the international students office at the school you'll be attending.

TOEFL/TSE

Almost all institutions accept applications from foreign students directly. If English is not your native tongue, you will likely be required to take the **Test of English as a Foreign Language** and **Test of Spoken English (TOEFL/TSE),** which is administered in many countries. Requirements are set by each school. Contact the TOEFL/TSE Application Office, P.O. Box 6151, Princeton, NJ 08541-6151 (609-951-1100).

CUSTOMS: ENTERING THE U.S.

Customs restrictions should not impose an undue burden on budget travelers. You may bring the following into the U.S. duty free: 200 cigarettes, 50 cigars, or 2 kilograms of smoking tobacco; $100 in gifts; and personal belongings such as clothing and jewelry. Articles imported in excess of your exemption will be subject to varying duty rates, to be paid upon arrival. In general, customs officers ask how much money you have and your planned departure date in order to ensure that you'll be able to support yourself while here. In some cases they may ask about travel companions and political affiliation. Carry prescription drugs in labeled containers and have a written prescription or doctor's statement ready to show the customs officer. Women especially should be aware that certain prescription drugs, such as RU486, are illegal in the U.S. For more information, including the helpful pamphlet *U.S. Customs Hints for Visitors (Nonresidents)*, contact a U.S. embassy or write the U.S. Customs Service, P.O. Box 7407, Washington, D.C. 20004 (202-927-2095).

CUSTOMS: GOING HOME

Upon returning home, you must declare all articles you acquired abroad and must pay a duty on the value of those articles that exceed the allowance established by your country's customs service. Goods and gifts purchased at duty-free shops abroad are not exempt from duty or sales tax at your point of return; you must declare these items as well. "Duty-free" merely means that you need not pay a tax in the country of purchase.

Canada Citizens who remain abroad for at least one week may bring back up to CDN$500 worth of goods duty-free once per calendar year. Canadian citizens or residents who travel for a period between 48 hours and six days can bring back up to CDN$200 with the exception of tobacco and alcohol. You are permitted to ship goods except tobacco and alcohol home under this exemption as long as you declare them when you arrive. Citizens of legal age (which varies by province) may import in-person up to 200 cigarettes, 50 cigars, 400g loose tobacco, 400 tobacco sticks, 1.14L wine or alcohol, and 24 355mL cans/bottles of beer; the value of these products is included in the CDN$500. For more information, write to Canadian Customs, 2265 St. Laurent Blvd., Ottawa, Ontario K1G 4K3 (tel. (613) 993-0534).

Britain Citizens or visitors arriving in the U.K. from outside the EU must declare any goods in excess of the following allowances: 200 cigarettes, 100 cigarillos, 50 cigars, or 250g tobacco; still table wine (2L); strong liqueurs over 22% volume (1L), or fortified or sparkling wine, other liqueurs (2L); perfume (60 cc/mL); toilet water (250 cc/mL); and UK£136 worth of all other goods including gifts and souvenirs. You must be over 17 to import liquor or tobacco. These allowances also apply to duty-free purchases within the EU, except for the last category, other goods, which then has an allowance of UK£71. For more info about U.K. customs, contact Her Majesty's Customs and Excise, Custom House, Nettleton Road, Heathrow Airport, Hounslow, Middlesex TW6 2LA (tel. (0181) 910-3744; fax 910-3765).

Ireland Citizens must declare everything in excess of IR£34 (IR£17 per traveler under 15 years of age) obtained outside the EU or duty- and tax-free in the EU above the following allowances: 200 cigarettes, 100 cigarillos, 50 cigars, or 250g tobacco; 1L liquor or 2L wine; 2L still wine; 50g perfume; and 250mL toilet water. Goods obtained duty and tax paid in another EU country up to a value of IR£460 (IR£115 per traveler under 15) will not be subject to additional customs duties. Travelers under 17 are not entitled to any allowance for tobacco or alcoholic products. For more information, contact The Revenue Commissioners, Dublin Castle (tel. (01) 679 27 77; fax 671 20 21; e-mail taxes@ior.ie; WWW http:\\www.revenue.ie) or The Collector of Customs and Excise, The Custom House, Dublin 1.

Australia Citizens may import A$400 (under 18 A$200) of goods duty-free, in addition to the allowance of 1.125L alcohol and 250 cigarettes or 250g tobacco. You must be over 18 to import either of these. There is no limit to the amount of Australian and/or foreign cash that may be brought into or taken out of the country. However, amounts of A$5000 or more, or the equivalent in foreign currency, must be reported. All foodstuffs and animal products must be declared on arrival. For information, contact the Regional Director, Australian Customs Service, GPO Box 8, Sydney NSW 2001 (tel. (02) 213 20 00; fax 213 40 00).

New Zealand Citizens may bring home up to NZ$700 worth of goods duty-free if they are intended for personal use or are unsolicited gifts. The concession is 200 cigarettes (1 carton), 250g tobacco, 50 cigars, or a combination of all three not to exceed 250g. You may also bring in 4.5L of beer or wine and 1.125L of liquor. Only travelers over 17 may bring tobacco or alcoholic beverages into the country. For more information, consult the *New Zealand Customs Guide for Travelers,* available from customs offices, or contact New Zealand Customs, 50 Anzac Ave., Box 29, Auckland (tel. (09) 377 35 20; fax 309 29 78).

South Africa Citizens may import duty-free: 400 cigarettes, 50 cigars, 250g tobacco, 2L wine, 1L of spirits, 250mL toilet water, and 50mL perfume, and other items up to a value of SAR500. Amounts exceeding this limit but not SAR10,000 are dutiable at 20%. Certain items such as golf clubs and firearms require a duty higher than the standard 20%. Goods acquired abroad and sent to the Republic as unaccompanied baggage do not qualify for any allowances. You may not export or import South African bank notes in excess of SAR500. Persons who require specific information or advice concerning customs and excise duties can address their inquiries to the Commissioner for Customs and Excise, Private Bag X47, Pretoria 0001. This agency distributes the pamphlet *South African Customs Information,* for visitors and residents who travel abroad. South Africans residing in the U.S. should contact the Embassy of South Africa, 3051 Massachusetts Ave. NW, Washington D.C. 20008 (tel. (202) 232-4400; fax 244-9417) or the South African Home Annex, 3201 New Mexico Ave. #380, NW, Washington D.C. 20016 (tel. (202) 966-1650).

ESSENTIALS

YOUTH, STUDENT, & TEACHER IDENTIFICATION

The **International Student Identity Card (ISIC)** is the most widely accepted form of student identification. Flashing this card can procure you discounts for sights, theaters, museums, accommodations, train, ferry, airplane travel, and other services. Present the card wherever you go, and ask about discounts even when none are advertised. The card also provides accident insurance of up to $3000 with no daily limit. In addition, cardholders have access to a toll-free Traveler's Assistance hotline whose multilingual staff can provide help in medical, legal, and financial emergencies overseas.

Many student travel offices issue ISICs, including Council Travel, Let's Go Travel, and STA Travel in the U.S.; Travel CUTS in Canada; and any of the organizations under the auspices of the International Student Travel Confederation (ISTC) around the world (see Budget Travel Agencies, p. 43) When you apply for the card, request a copy of the *International Student Identity Card Handbook,* which lists by country some of the available discounts. You can also write to Council for a copy. The card is valid from September to December of the following year. The fee is $18. Applicants must be at least 12-years old and degree-seeking students of a secondary or post-secondary school. Because of the proliferation of phony ISICs, many airlines and some other services require other proof of student identity: a signed letter from the registrar attesting to your student status and stamped with the school seal and/or your school ID card. The $19 **International Teacher Identity Card (ITIC)** offers similar but limited discounts, as well as medical insurance coverage. For more info on these handy cards, consult ISTC's new web site (http:\\\\www.istc.org).

The Federation of International Youth Travel Organizations (FIYTO) issues a discount card to travelers who are under 26 but not students. Known as the **GO25 Card,** this one-year card offers many of the same benefits as the ISIC, and most organizations that sell the ISIC also sell the GO25 Card. A brochure that lists discounts is free when you purchase the card. To apply, you will need a passport, valid driver's license, or copy of a birth certificate; and a passport-sized photo with your name printed on the back. The fee is $16, CDN$15, or UK£5. For information, contact Council in the U.S. or FIYTO in Denmark.

INTERNATIONAL DRIVER'S LICENSE

If you plan to drive here, consider obtaining an International Driver's Permit (IDP) from your national automobile association before leaving (you can't get one here). Though not required by U.S. law, an IDP is a good idea for visitors from non-English-speaking countries, whose driver's licenses might be unfamiliar to American authorities. Make sure to have proper **insurance,** required by law in the U.S. You will need a green card or International Insurance Certificate to prove that you have liability insurance. Application forms are available at any AAA office or car rental agency.

Members of national automobile associations affiliated with the **American Automobile Association** (800-222-4357) can receive services from the AAA while they are in the U.S. Automobile Associations in 19 countries have full reciprocity agreements with the AAA. Check your country's association for details.

If your home country signed the Geneva Road Traffic Convention, you can legally drive in the U.S. for one year. However, unless you are from Canada or Mexico, your personal cars must exhibit the International Distinguishing Sign, which must be obtained in your home country. Consult the resident sages at your national automobile association before you leave. Remember that the usual **minimum age** for car rental and auto transport services is 21, occasionally 25.

■ Money

In Boston they ask, How much does he know? In New York, How much is he worth?

—Mark Twain

No matter how tight your budget, you won't be able to carry all your cash with you. Even if you can, don't: non-cash reserves are a necessary precaution in the big bad city. Unfortunately, out-of-state personal checks aren't readily accepted in NYC.

Before you arrive in New York, you might want to find out if your home bank is networked with any NYC banks; **Cirrus** (800-424-7787) and **Plus** (800-843-7587) are both popular **Automatic Teller Machine (ATM)** networks. If you're here for a while, open a savings account at one of the local banks and get an ATM card, which you can use at any time all over the city (see Financial Services in the city, p. 30)

New York **banks** are usually open Monday through Friday from 9am to 5pm. Some may also be open Saturdays from 9am to noon or 1pm. All banks, government agencies, and post offices are closed on legal holidays.

CURRENCY AND EXCHANGE

CDN$1 = $0.74	**$1 = CDN$1.37**
UK£1 = $1.55	**$1 = UK£0.64**
IR£1 = $1.58	**$1 = IR£0.62**
A$1 = $0.74	**$1= A$1.29**
NZ$1 = $0.66	**$1 = NZ$1.46**

U.S. currency uses a decimal system based on the **dollar ($).** Paper money ("bills") comes in six denominations, all the same size, shape, and dull green color. The bills now issued are $1, $5, $10, $20, $50, and $100. You may occasionally see funny denominations of $2 and $500, which are no longer printed but are still acceptable as currency. Some restaurants and stores may be squeamish about accepting bills larger than $50. The dollar is divided into 100 cents (¢). Pick your favorite notation for values of less than a dollar: 35 cents can be represented as 35¢ or $0.35. U.S. currency uses these coins: the penny (1¢), nickel (5¢), dime (10¢), and quarter (25¢). Half-dollar (50¢) and one-dollar coins are rarely seen (but are both legal tender).

Convert your currency infrequently and in large amounts to minimize exorbitant exchange fees. Try to buy traveler's checks in U.S. dollars so that you won't have to exchange them. Personal checks can be difficult to cash in the U.S. Most banks require that you have an account with them before they will cash a personal check, and opening an account can be a time-consuming affair.

If you stay in hostels and prepare your own food, expect to spend anywhere from $35-60 per person per day, depending on your eating habits and other needs. Transportation will increase these figures. Don't sacrifice your health or safety for a cheaper tab. No matter how low your budget, if you plan to travel for more than a couple of days, you will need to keep handy a larger amount of cash than usual. Carrying it around with you, even in a money belt, is risky; personal checks from home will probably not be acceptable no matter how many forms of identification you have (even some banks shy away from accepting checks).

It is more expensive to buy foreign currency than to buy domestic. In other words, Dutch guilders are less expensive in the Netherlands than in the U.S. However, converting some money before you go will allow you to zip through the airport while others languish in exchange lines. It will also prevent the problem of finding yourself stuck with no money after banking hours or on a holiday. It's a good idea to bring enough U.S. currency to last for the first 24 to 72 hours of a trip, depending on the day of the week you will be arriving. Also, observe commission rates closely and check newspapers to get the standard rate of exchange. Banks generally have the best rates, but this is by no means a hard and fast rule; sometimes tourist offices or exchange kiosks have the best rates. A good rule of thumb is to only go to places which have a 5% margin between their buy and sell prices. Anything more, and they are making too much profit. Be sure that both prices are listed.

TRAVELER'S CHECKS

Traveler's checks are one of the safest and least troublesome means of carrying funds. Several agencies and many banks sell them, usually for face value plus a 1% commission. (Members of the American Automobile Association can get American Express checks commission-free through AAA.) American Express and Visa are the most widely recognized, though other major checks are sold, exchanged, cashed, and refunded with almost equal ease. Keep in mind that in small towns, traveler's checks are less readily accepted than in cities with large tourist industries. Nonetheless, there will probably be at least one place in every town where you can exchange them for local currency. If you're ordering your checks, order them well in advance, especially if large sums are being requested.

Each agency provides refunds if your checks are lost or stolen, and many provide additional services. (Note that you may need a police report verifying the loss or theft.) Inquire about toll-free refund hotlines, emergency message relay services, and stolen credit card assistance when you purchase your checks.

You should expect a fair amount of red tape and delay in the event of theft or loss of traveler's checks. To expedite the refund process, keep your check receipts separate from your checks and store them in a safe place or with a traveling companion; record check numbers when you cash them and leave a list of check numbers with someone at home; and ask for a list of refund centers when you buy your checks. American Express and Bank of America have over 40,000 centers worldwide. Keep a separate supply of cash or traveler's checks for emergencies. Be sure never to countersign your checks until you're prepared to cash them. And always be sure to bring your passport with you when you plan to use the checks.

Buying traveler's checks in the currency of the country you're visiting can either be a wise measure or an exercise in futility. In some countries (the United States, for example) checks are accepted as readily as cash, whereas in others they are only beginning to gain acceptance. Depending on fluctuations in currency, you may gain or lose money by converting your currency beforehand. Use your best judgment.

American Express: Call 800-221-7282 in the U.S. and Canada; in the U.K. (0800) 52 13 13; in New Zealand (0800) 44 10 68; in Australia (008) 25 19 02. Elsewhere, call U.S. collect 801-964-6665. American Express traveler's checks are now available in 11 currencies: Australian, British, Canadian, Dutch, French, German, Japanese, Saudi Arabian, Spanish, Swiss, and U.S. They are the most widely recognized worldwide and the easiest to replace if lost or stolen. Checks can be purchased for a small fee at American Express Travel Service Offices, banks, and American Automobile Association offices (AAA members can buy the checks commission-free). Cardmembers can also purchase checks at American Express Dispensers, Travel Service Offices, airports, or by ordering them via phone (800-ORDER-TC/673-3782). American Express offices cash their checks commission-free (except where prohibited by national governments), although they often offer slightly worse rates than banks. You can also buy *Cheques for Two* which can be signed by either of two people traveling together. Request American Express' booklet "Traveler's Companion," which lists travel office addresses and stolen check hotlines. Traveler's checks are also available over America Online.

Citicorp: Call 800-645-6556 in the U.S. and Canada; in the U.K. (44) 18 12 97 47 81; from elsewhere call U.S. collect 813-623-1709. Sells both Citicorp and Citicorp Visa traveler's checks in U.S., Australian, and Canadian dollars, British pounds, German marks, Spanish pesetas, and Japanese yen. Commission is 1-2% on check purchases. Checkholders are automatically enrolled for 45 days in the Travel Assist Program (hotline 800-250-4377 or collect 202-296-8728) which provides travelers with English-speaking doctor, lawyer, and interpreter referrals as well as check refund assistance and general travel information. Citicorp's World Courier Service guarantees hand-delivery of traveler's checks when a refund location is not convenient. Call 24hr.

Thomas Cook MasterCard: Call 800-223-9920 in the U.S. and Canada; elsewhere call U.S. collect 609-987-7300; from the U.K. call 0800 622 101 free or 1733 502 995 collect or 44 1733 318 950 collect. Offers checks in U.S., Canadian, and Australian dollars, British and Cypriot pounds, French and Swiss francs, German marks, Japanese yen, Dutch guilders, Spanish pesetas, and ECUs. Commission 1-2% for purchases. Try buying the checks at a Thomas Cook office for potentially lower commissions. If you cash your checks at a Thomas Cook Office they will not charge you commission (whereas most banks will).

Visa: Call 800-227-6811 in the U.S.; in the U.K. (0800) 89 54 92; from anywhere else in the world call 017 33 31 89 49. It's a pay call, but can reverse the charges. Call any of the above numbers, and with your zip code, they can tell you the nearest place to get traveler's checks. Any kind of Visa traveler's checks can be reported lost at the Visa number.

CREDIT CARDS

In New York City, you are your credit rating. There are so many opportunities to purchase various one-of-a-kind consumer goods that you're going to want as much money at your disposal as possible. Few establishments in the city reject all of the major cards, but occasionally you'll come across a restaurant or bar who solely esteems cold hard cash. However, there are some nifty things that one can do with credit cards abroad that apply just about everywhere. Major credit cards—**MasterCard** and **Visa** are the most welcomed—instantly extract cash advances from associated banks and teller machines throughout the United States (and elsewhere, though it varies by country) in local currency. This can be a great way to make fast cash, but you will be charged massive interest rates if you don't pay off the bill quickly, so be careful when using this service. **American Express** cards also work in some ATMs, as well as at AmEx offices and major airports. All such machines require a **Personal Identification Number (PIN).** You must ask American Express, MasterCard, or Visa to assign you one; without this PIN, you will be unable to withdraw cash with your credit card. Keep in mind that MasterCard and Visa have different names elsewhere ("EuroCard" or "Access" for MasterCard and "Carte Bleue" or "Barclaycard" for Visa); some cashiers may not know this until they check their manuals.

Credit cards are also invaluable in an emergency—an unexpected hospital bill or ticket home or the loss of traveler's checks—which may leave you temporarily without other resources. Furthermore, credit cards offer an array of other services, from insurance to emergency assistance—these depend completely, however, on the issuer. Some even cover car rental collision insurance.

American Express (800-528-4800) has a hefty annual fee ($55) but offers a number of services. AmEx cardholders can cash personal checks at AmEx offices abroad. U.S. Assist, a 24-hour hotline offering medical and legal assistance in emergencies, is also available (800-554-2639 in U.S. and Canada; from abroad call U.S. collect 301-214-8228). Cardholders can also take advantage of the American Express Travel Service; benefits include assistance in changing airline, hotel, and car rental reservations, sending mailgrams and international cables, and holding your mail at one of the more than 1700 AmEx offices around the world.

MasterCard (800-999-0454) and **Visa** (800-336-8472) are issued in cooperation with individual banks and some other organizations.

CASH CARDS

Cash cards—popularly called ATM (Automated Teller Machine) cards—are widespread throughout New York and the United States. Depending on the system that your bank at home uses, you will probably be able to access your own personal bank account whenever you're in need of funds. Happily, the ATMs get the same wholesale exchange rate as credit cards. Despite these perks, do some research before relying too heavily on automation. There is often a limit on the amount of money you can withdraw per day, and computer network failures are not uncommon. If your PIN is longer than four digits, be sure to ask your bank whether the first four digits will work, or whether you need a new number. A great many ATMs are outdoors; don't let anyone distract you while at the machine and use discretion as you walk away from the machine.

The two international money networks you should know about are **Cirrus** (800-424-7787) and **PLUS** (800-843-7587). Both have ATMs all over New York City—access to your money shouldn't be a problem.

GETTING MONEY FROM HOME

One of the easiest ways to get money from home is to bring an **American Express** card. AmEx allows card holders to draw cash from their checking accounts at any of its major offices and many of its representatives' offices, up to $1000 every 21 days (no service charge, no interest). AmEx also offers Express Cash, with over 100,000 ATMs located in airports, hotels, banks, office complexes, and shopping areas around the world. Express Cash withdrawals are automatically debited from the Cardmember's specified bank account or line of credit. Card holders may withdraw up to $1000 in a seven day period. There is a 2% transaction fee for each cash withdrawal with a $2.50 minimum. To enroll in Express Cash, Cardmembers may call 800-CASH NOW/227-4669. Outside the U.S. call collect (904) 565-7875. Unless using the AmEx service, avoid cashing checks in foreign currencies; they usually take weeks and a $30 fee to clear.

Money can also be wired abroad through international money transfer services operated by **Western Union** (800-325-6000). In the U.S., call Western Union any time at (800-225-5227) to cable money with your Visa or MasterCard within the domestic United States. Credit card transfers do not work overseas, you must send cash. The rates for sending cash are generally $10 cheaper than with a credit card. The money is usually available in the country you're sending it to within an hour, although in some cases this may vary.

FINANCIAL SERVICES IN THE CITY

Travelers visiting New York will have no trouble finding a place to exchange foreign currencies and traveler's checks into U.S. dollars. Large banks—including **Citibank**

(627-3999, or 800-627-3999 from outside New York State), **Chase Manhattan** (800-282-4273), and **Chemical** (935-9935, or 800-935-9935 from outside NY, NJ, and CT)—blanket the city with subsidiary branches and ATMs, and fall over each other claiming to be the largest, nicest bank in town. Other companies specialize in providing foreign exchange services up to seven days a week, often quoting rates by phone.

American Express: Multi-task agency providing tourists with traveler's checks, gift checks, cashing services, you name it. Branches in Manhattan include: **American Express Tower,** 200 Vesey St. (640-2000), near the World Financial Center (open Mon.-Fri. 9:30am-5:30pm); **Macy's Herald Square,** 151 W. 34th St. (695-8075), at Seventh Ave. inside Macy's on the balcony level (open Mon.-Sat. 10am-6pm); **150 E. 42nd St.** (687-3700), between Lexington and Third Ave. (open Mon.-Fri. 9am-5pm); in **Bloomingdale's,** 59th St. and Lexington Ave. (705-3171; open Mon.-Sat. 10am-6pm); **822 Lexington Ave.** (758-6510), near 63rd St. (open Mon.-Fri. 9am-6pm, Sat. 10am-4pm).

Bank Leumi, 579 Fifth Ave. (343-5000), at 47th St. An account is not required to buy or sell foreign currencies and traveler's checks, issue foreign drafts, or make payments by wire, although Bank Leumi does charge for its services. Latest exchange rates are available by phone (343-5343). Open Mon.-Fri. 9am-5pm.

Cheque Point USA, 551 Madison Ave. (750-2255), between 55th and 56th St., with other branches throughout the city (call for locations). Wire funds to and from major foreign cities at rates cheaper than American Express's. Open Mon.-Fri. 8am-8pm, Sat. 9:45am-8pm, Sun. 10am-7pm.

TAXES AND TIPPING

The prices quoted throughout *Let's Go: New York City* are the amounts before sales tax has been added. Sales tax in New York is 8.25%. Hotel tax is 14.25%; there's also a $2 occupancy tax per single room per night and a $4 tax for suites.

Remember that service is never included on a New York tab. Tip cab drivers and waiters about 15%; especially good waiters—or those who work at especially good restaurants—are often tipped 20% of the tab. If you're in a large party at a restaurant (i.e. seven or more people) a gratuity of 15% may be automatically added to the bill. Tip hairdressers 10% and bellhops around $1 per bag. Bartenders usually expect between 50¢ and $1 per drink.

■ Safety and Security

> **Emergency:** Dial 911.
> **Police:** 374-5000. Use this for inquiries that are not urgent. 24hr.
> **TDD Police:** 374-5911.
> **Fire:** 999-2222.

Despite the recent dramatic decreases in crime levels throughout the city, personal safety should always be a consideration when visiting the Big Apple. With some precautions and awareness, you can emerge from your vacation unscathed, enriched, and more confident than ever about facing the vicissitudes of urban life.

ON FOOT

Acting like a tried-and-true New York City native (i.e. not making eye contact with strangers and not being overly friendly) may be your best protection. Petty criminals often attack tourists because they seem naive and hapless. As a city cop recently told reporters, "They go for the gawkers"—meaning that small-time crooks scam the unwary, the wide-eyed, and the slow-moving. The New Yorker walks briskly; the tourist wanders absently. Maintain at all times the fiction that you know where you are going. Be discreet with street maps and cameras and address questions about directions to police officers or store-owners. Consider covering your flagrantly yellow *Let's Go* guide with plain brown paper. Stay out of public bathrooms if you can; they

Aren't you going to rob me?

New Yorkers were amazed when recent statistics showed that city crime rates have substantially fallen three years in a row. According to recent figures, the murder rate is down 45%, robbery 31%, and assault 11%. For subway crimes, felonies are down 64%, and robberies are down an extraordinary 73%. (Alas, the staggering decrease in crime rates has been accompanied by a 50% increase in police brutality complaints.) Cops claim the decrease has to do with increased surveillance and arrests; Mayor Guliani claims (as did recently fired police Supt. William Bratton) that it's a tough attitude on crime; sociologists say its because of a lull in the high-crime 18-24 age bracket across the nation. Whatever the reasons, the results mean that living and traveling in the city have become safer, though you should still keep your guard up at all times.

tend to be filthy and unsafe. Instead, try department stores, hotels, or restaurants; even those with a sign on the door saying "Restrooms for Patrons Only" will usually allow you in if you look enough like a customer.

If, despite your confident swagger, you suspect you're being followed, duck into a nearby store or restaurant. Some East Side shops near school districts have yellow-and-black signs that say "safe haven" in their windows. The signs mean that shop managers have agreed to let people—especially students—who feel unsafe remain in their stores for long periods of time or call the police.

Rip-off artists seek the wealthy as well as the unwary, so hide your riches. Conceal watches, necklaces, and bracelets under your clothing if you're in a dangerous neighborhood. Turn that huge diamond ring around on your finger so jewelry-swipers can only see the band. Grip your handbag tightly and wear the strap diagonally. If you keep the bag and the strap on one side, it can easily be pulled off—or a clever thief with scissors may cut the strap so adeptly that you don't even notice. Statistically speaking, men are mugged more often than women, and while this fact shouldn't put either male or female travelers at ease, it should at least warn men that they are just as vulnerable.

Tourists are especially juicy prey because they tend to carry large quantities of cash. Transfer your money into traveler's checks and be careful with them. Don't count your money in public or use large bills. Tuck your wallet into a discreet pocket and keep an extra 10 bucks or so in a more obvious one. Many New Yorkers invest in a cheap extra wallet designated for "mugging money." Keep an extra bill for emergencies in an unlikely place, such as your shoe, sock, or any body cavity.

New York's streets are rife with con-artists. Their tricks are many. Beware of hustlers working in groups. And remember that no one ever wins at three-card monte. If someone spills ketchup on you, someone else may be picking your pocket. Be mistrustful of sob stories that require a donation from you. Chasten yourself for letting the city harden you if you must, but maintain your skepticism at all costs.

Pay attention to the neighborhood that surrounds you. A district can change character drastically in the course of a single block. The haughty Upper East Side, for example, segues into a dangerous bit of Harlem up in the triple digits. Simply being aware of the flow of people on the street can tell you a great deal about the relative safety of the area. Many notoriously dangerous districts have safe sections; look for children playing, women walking in the open, and other signs of an active community. If you feel uncomfortable, leave as quickly and directly as you can, but don't allow your fear of the new to close off whole worlds to you. Careful, persistent exploration will build confidence, strengthen your emerging New York attitude, and make your stay in the city that much more rewarding.

At night, of course, it's even more important to keep track of your environment. *Avoid poor or drug-ridden areas like the South Bronx, Washington Heights, Harlem, northeastern Brooklyn, and Alphabet City.* West Midtown and the lower part of East Midtown, both well populated commercial centers during the day, can be unpleasant at night. Follow the main thoroughfares; try to walk on avenues rather than streets. Residential areas with doormen are relatively safe even in the twilight. Fifth and Park are the least dangerous avenues in the evening on the East Side, Central Park West and Broadway the safest on the West.

Central Park, land of frisbees and Good Humor trucks by day, becomes dangerous and forbidding after sunset. If you find yourself penniless, tokenless, and on the wrong side of the park, walk around it by Central Park South rather than north of it or through it. If you're uptown, walk through the 85th St. Transverse near the police station. Avoid the woodsy deserted areas far from the main path. If you are visiting the gay bars near the West Side docks along the Hudson River, stay away from the abandoned waterfront area. Although the bars are trendy, the surrounding areas are considered unsafe. Bars and clubs in the Village may be a better bet. The areas around Times Square and Penn Station can also be dangerous. (For more info on safety, see Getting Around: Subways, Bicycles, and Walking, p. 59.)

IN VEHICLES

If you take a car into the city, try not to leave valuable possessions—such as radios or luggage—in it while you're off rambling. Radios are especially tempting. In fact, many thieves in New York actually make their living solely stealing radios. If your tape deck or radio is removable, hide it in the trunk or take it with you. If it isn't, at least conceal it under a lot of junk. Similarly, hide baggage in the trunk—although some savvy thieves can tell if a car is heavily loaded by the way it is settled on its tires. Park your vehicle in a garage or well traveled area. Sleeping in a car or van parked in the city is extremely dangerous—even the most dedicated budget traveler shouldn't consider it an option.

Late at night, take the bus rather than the subway, as buses are safer because the driver is in plain view. On weekends, taking the subway in the evening is less dangerous since most major lines are quite crowded then. If a station seems empty, stand near the token counter or look for a Guardian Angel, one of the self-appointed crimefighters clad in red berets. Alternatively, you can treat yourself to a taxi; although more expensive, they are probably the safest mode of travel at night.

In taxis, the dangers are more fiscal than physical. Don't let the driver, um, take you for a ride. Cab fares can be paid only at the end of the ride. New York taxis must drop off individuals and charge a bulk fare at the end; any driver who tries to charge you per person or by location has no business doing so. Take a yellow cab with a meter and a medallion on the hood rather than an illegal "gypsy" cab, which usually isn't yellow and doesn't have a meter (and may be driven by gypsies). The driver's name should be posted, and when you get out you can request a receipt with a phone number to call about complaints or lost articles. State your destination with authority and suggest the quickest route if you know it. If you hesitate or sound unsure, the driver will probably know—and possibly care—that you can be taken out of your way without noticing.

When disembarking from a plane or train, be wary of unlicensed taxi dispatchers. At Grand Central or Penn Station, a person may claim to be a porter, carry your bags, hail you a cab, and then ask for a commission or share of the fare. Don't fall for this baggage-carrying scam—give directions to the driver as fast as you can and drive off in style. Official dispatchers do not need to be paid.

ALCOHOL AND DRUGS

You must be 21 years old to purchase **alcoholic beverages** legally. Many bars and stores will want to see a photo ID (a driver's license or other valid government-issued document) before selling you alcohol. On the other hand, many won't—particularly in areas like Morningside Heights (Columbia University's neighborhood) and Greenwich Village (NYU's neighborhood), both of which meet the demands of large populations of underage college students. The more popular drinking spots, as well as more upscale liquor stores, are likely to card—and ruthlessly, at that.

Possession of marijuana, cocaine, heroin, MDMA ("ecstasy"), and most opiate deriv-atives (among many other chemicals) is punishable by stiff fines and imprisonment. But that doesn't stop New York's thriving **drug trade,** whose marketplaces are street corners, club bathrooms, and city parks throughout the city, most notably the Vil-lage's Washington Square Park and the Lower East Side. *Caveat emptor!*

If you carry **prescription drugs** while you travel, it is vital to have a copy of the prescriptions themselves readily accessible at U.S. Customs. In general, possession of illicit drugs during travel is a *very* bad idea. Check with the U.S. Customs Service before your trip (see Customs, p. 23) for more information on questionable drugs.

■ Health

Before you leave, check whether your insurance policy covers medical costs incurred while traveling (see Insurance, p. 36). Always have proof of insurance as well as pol-icy numbers with you. If you choose to risk traveling without insurance, you may have to rely on public health organizations and clinics that treat patients without demanding proof of solvency. Call the local hotline or crisis center listed in this book under Help Lines and Medical Care. Operators at these organizations have numbers for public-health organizations and clinics that treat patients without demanding proof of solvency. If you require **emergency treatment,** call **911** or go to the emer-gency room of the nearest hospital.

If you have a chronic medical condition that requires **medication** on a regular basis, be sure to consult your physician before you leave. Carry copies of your pre-scriptions and always distribute medication or syringes among all your carry-on and checked baggage in case any of your bags is lost. If you wear glasses or contact lenses, carry an extra prescription and perhaps a spare pair.

Any traveler with a medical condition that cannot be easily recognized (i.e., diabe-tes, epilepsy, heart conditions, allergies to antibiotics) may want to obtain a **Medic Alert Identification Tag.** The internationally recognized tag indicates the nature of the bearer's problem and provides the number for Medic Alert's 24-hour hotline. Attending medical personnel can call this number to obtain information about the member's medical history. Lifetime membership (tag, annually updated wallet card, and 24-hr. hotline access) begins at $35. Contact Medic Alert Foundation, P.O. Box 1009, Turlock, CA 95381-1009 (800-ID-ALERT/432-5378). The **American Diabetes Association,** 1660 Duke St., Alexandria, VA 22314 (800-232-3472), provides copies of the article "Travel and Diabetes" as well as diabetic ID cards, which show the car-rier's diabetic status. Contact your local ADA office for information.

All travelers should be concerned about **Acquired Immune Deficiency Syn-drome (AIDS),** which is transmitted through the bodily fluids of an infected (i.e., HIV-positive) individual. New York City has struggled with the epidemic for well over a decade now. Remember there is no assurance that someone is not infected; HIV tests show antibodies only after a six-month lapse, and there is no way to deter-mine through physical inspection whether or not a person carries the HIV virus. Do not have sex without using a condom, and don't ever share intravenous needles with anyone. (Latex condoms have smaller pores than sheepskin condoms and are thus more effective in preventing the spread of AIDS and other sexually transmitted dis-eases.) The Center for Disease Control's **AIDS Hotline** provides AIDS information in the U.S. (800-342-2437 24 hr.; TDD 800-243-7889, open daily 8am-2am). Council's brochure, *Travel Safe: AIDS and International Travel,* is available at all Council Travel offices (see p. 43).

Although reliable **contraception** is easily obtainable in New York City, women tak-ing birth control pills should bring enough to allow for extended stays. Condoms can be found in any pharmacy, usually right on the shelves; many of the city's pharma-cies, conveniently, stay open all the time.

If you are in the New York area and need an abortion, contact the **National Abor-tion Federation,** a professional association of abortion providers. Call its toll-free hot-line for information, counseling, and the names of qualified medical professionals in the area (800-772-9100; open Mon.-Fri. 9:30am-5:30pm). The NAF has informational publications for individuals and health-care clinics alike. Clinics they recommend must maintain certain safety and operational standards. In New York the NAF will refer you to the Planned Parenthood clinics. The number for the Manhattan clinic is 677-6474; in Brooklyn, 718-858-1819; in the Bronx, 718-292-8000.

MEDICAL CARE

Most hospitals will bill you later if you aren't covered by insurance, and most have multilingual (at least Spanish) services as well.

Bellevue Hospital Center, 462 First Ave. at 27th. St. (562-4141). Emergency Room 562-3015 (adult), 562-3025 (pediatric).

Beth Israel Medical Center, First Ave. and E. 16th St. (420-2000). Emergency Room 420-2840.

Columbia-Presbyterian Medical Center, Fort Washington Ave. and W. 168th St. (305-2500).

Mount Sinai Medical Center, Fifth Ave. and 100th St. Emergency Room (241-7171). Affiliated with CUNY Medical School.

New York Hospital-Cornell Medical Center, 520 E. 70th St., between York Ave. and FDR Dr. Emergency Room (726-5050).

New York Infirmary Beekman Downtown Hospital, 170 William St. (312-5000).

New York University Medical Center, 550 First Ave., between E. 32nd and E. 33rd St. Emergency Room (263-5550).

Walk-in Clinic, 55 E. 34th St. (252-6000), between Park and Madison Ave. Open Mon.-Fri. 8am-5pm, Sat. 10am-2pm. Affiliated with Beth Israel Hospital.

Kaufman's Pharmacy, 557 Lexington Ave. (755-2266), at 50th St. Free delivery within five blocks, otherwise customer pays two-way taxi fare. Open 24hr.

Eastern Women's Center, 44 E. 30th St. (686-6066), between Park and Madison Ave. Gynecological exams and surgical procedures for women, by appt. only.

Women's Health Line, New York City Department of Health (230-1111). Information and referrals concerning reproductive health. Open Mon.-Fri. 8am-6pm.

Planned Parenthood, Margaret Sanger Center at 380 Second Ave. (677-6474).

AIDS Information, (807-6655). Run by the Gay Men's Health Crisis. Mon.-Fri. 10am-9pm, Sat. noon-3pm.

AIDS Hotline, NYC Dept. of Health. (447-8200). Open daily 9am-9pm.

Venereal Disease Information, NYC Dept. of Health. (427-5120). Open Mon.-Fri. 8:30am-4:30pm.

■ Help Lines

Crime Victims' Hotline, 577-7777. 24-hr. counseling and referrals for victims of crime or domestic violence.

Sex Crimes Report Line, New York Police Department, 267-7273. 24-hr. information and referrals.

Poison Control Center, 764-7667.

Samaritans, 673-3000. 24-hr. suicide prevention. Confidential phone counseling.

Runaway Hotline, 619-6884. 24-hr. counseling and shelter referral.

Help Line, 532-2400. Crisis counseling and referrals. Open daily 9am-10pm.

Crisis Counseling, Intervention, and Referral Service, 516-679-1111. Focused primarily on youths, providing information and confidential counseling for all kinds of crises (AIDS, abortion, suicide, etc.). Includes the **Gay Peer Counseling Network.** Open 24hr.

New York Gay and Lesbian Anti-Violence Project, 807-0197. 24-hr. crisis intervention hotline, counseling, and referrals to support groups and legal services.

Gay and Lesbian Switchboard, 777-1800. Peer counseling and referral for the gay or lesbian traveler. Open daily 10am-midnight.

Lesbian Switchboard, 741-2610. Information on NYC-based activities and general support. Open Mon.-Fri. 6-10pm.

Alcohol and Substance Abuse Information Line, 800-274-2042. 24-hr. information and referrals on all drug-related problems.

Alcoholics Anonymous, 647-1680. Counseling and referrals to local AA meetings. Open daily 9am-10pm.

New York City Department for the Aging, 442-1000. Information and referrals. Open Mon.-Fri. 9am-5pm.

Consumer's Union, 914-378-2000. Consumer advice. Open Mon.-Fri. 9am-5pm.

Department of Consumer Affairs, 487-4444. Handles consumer complaints. Open Mon.-Fri. 9:30am-4:30pm.

■ Insurance

Beware of buying unnecessary travel coverage—your regular policies may well extend to many travel-related accidents. **Medical insurance** (especially university policies) often cover costs incurred abroad; check with your provider. **Medicare's** foreign travel coverage is valid only in Canada and Mexico. Canadians are protected by their home province's health insurance plan for up to 90 days after leaving the country; check with the provincial Ministry of Health or Health Plan Headquarters for details. Australia has Reciprocal Health Care Agreements (RHCAs) with several countries; when traveling in these nations Australians are entitled to many of the services that they would receive at home. The Commonwealth Department of Human Services and Health can provide more information. Your **homeowners' insurance** (or your family's coverage) often covers theft during travel. Homeowners are generally covered against loss of travel documents (passport, plane ticket, railpass, etc.) up to $500.

ISIC and **ITIC** provide $3000 worth of accident and illness insurance and $100 per day up to 60 days of hospitalization. They also offer up to $1000 for accidental death or dismemberment, up to $25,000 if injured due to an airline, and up to $25,000 for emergency evacuation due to an illness. The cards also give access to a toll-free Traveler's Assistance hotline (in the U.S. and Canada 800-626-2427; elsewhere call collect to the U.S. (713-267-2525) whose multilingual staff can provide help in emergencies overseas). To supplement ISIC's insurance, **Council** offers the inexpensive Trip-Safe plan with options covering medical treatment and hospitalization, accidents, baggage loss, and charter flights missed due to illness; they and **STA** also offer more comprehensive and expensive policies (p. 14). **American Express** cardholders receive automatic rental (required to decline collision insurance) and travel accident insurance on flight purchases made with the card. (Customer Service (800-528-4800)).

Remember that insurance companies usually require a copy of the police report for thefts, or evidence of having paid medical expenses (doctor's statements, receipts) before they will honor a claim and may have time limits on filing for reimbursement. Always carry policy numbers and proof of insurance. Check with each insurance carrier for specific restrictions and policies. Most of the carriers listed below have 24-hour hotlines.

Access America, 6600 West Broad St., P.O. Box 11188, Richmond, VA 23230 (800-284-8300; fax (804-673-1491). Covers trip cancellation/interruption, on-the-spot hospital admittance costs, emergency medical evacuation, sickness, and baggage loss. 24-hr. hotline.

The Berkley Group/Carefree Travel Insurance, 100 Garden City Plaza, P.O. Box 9366, Garden City, NY 11530-9366 (800-323-3149 or 516-294-0220; fax 516-294-1096). Offers two comprehensive packages including coverage for trip cancellation/interruption/delay, accident and sickness, medical needs, baggage loss, bag delay, accidental death and dismemberment, and travel supplier insolvency. Trip cancellation/interruption may be purchased separately at a rate of $5.50 per $100 of coverage. 24-hr. worldwide emergency assistance hotline.

Globalcare Travel Insurance, 220 Broadway Lynnfield, MA 01940 (800-821-2488; fax 617-592-7720; e-mail global@nebc.mv.com; nebc.mv.com/globalcare). Complete medical, legal, emergency, and travel-related services. On-the-spot payments and special student programs, including benefits for trip cancellation and interruption. GTI waives pre-existing medical conditions with their Globalcare Economy Plan for cruise and travel, and provides coverage for the bankruptcy or default of cruiselines, airlines, or tour operators.

Travel Assistance International, by Worldwide Assistance Services, Inc., 1133 15th St. NW, Suite 400, Washington, D.C. 20005-2710 (800-821-2828 or 202-828-5894; fax 202-828-5896; e-mail wassist@aol.com). TAI provides its members with a 24-hr. free hotline for travel emergencies and referrals. Their Per-Trip (starting at $52) and Frequent Traveler (starting at $226) plans include medical, travel, and financial insurance, translation, and lost document/item assistance.

Travel Guard International, 1145 Clark St., Stevens Point, WI 54481 (800 826-1300 or 715-345-0505; fax 715-345-0525). Comprehensive insurance programs starting at $44. Programs cover trip cancellation and interruption, bankruptcy and financial default, lost luggage, medical coverage abroad, emergency assistance, and accidental death. 24-hr. hotline.

■ Specific Concerns

WOMEN TRAVELERS

Women exploring on their own inevitably face additional safety concerns. Always trust your instincts: if you'd feel better somewhere else, move on. Always carry extra money for a phone call, bus, or taxi. Consider staying in hostels which offer single rooms that lock from the inside or in religious organizations that offer rooms for women only; avoid any hostel with "communal" showers. Stick to centrally located accommodations and avoid late-night treks or subway rides. Hitching is never safe for lone women, or even for two women traveling together. Choose subway compartments occupied by other women or couples.

When in New York City, the less you look like a tourist, the better off you'll be. Look as if you know where you're going (even when you don't) and consider approaching women or couples for directions if you're lost or feel uncomfortable. In general, dress conservatively, especially in less savory areas. If you spend time in New York, you may be harassed no matter how you're dressed. Your best answer to verbal harassment is no answer at all (a reaction is what the harasser wants). Wearing a conspicuous wedding band may help prevent such incidents. Don't hesitate to seek out a police officer or a passerby if you are being harassed. *Let's Go* lists emergency numbers (including rape crisis lines) in the Practical Information section. In crowds, you may be pinched or squeezed by over-sexed slimeballs; the look on the face is the key to avoiding unwanted attention. Feigned deafness, sitting motionless and staring at the ground will do more good than any reaction ever would achieve.

Don't hesitate to seek out a police officer or a passerby if you are being harassed. Think 911. Carry a whistle or an airhorn on your keychain, and don't hesitate to use it in an emergency. A **Model Mugging** course will not only prepare you for a potential mugging, but will also raise your level of awareness of your surroundings as well as your confidence (see Safety and Security, p. 31). Women also face additional health concerns when traveling (see Health, p. 33). All of these warnings and suggestions, however, should not discourage women from traveling alone. Don't take unnecessary risks, but don't lose your spirit of adventure either.

For general information, contact the **National Organization for Women (NOW),** which boasts branches across the country that can refer women travelers to rape crisis centers and counseling services, and provide lists of feminist events. Main offices include 22 W. 21st St., 7th Fl., **New York,** NY 10010 (212-260-4422); 1000 16th St. NW, 7th Fl., **Washington, D.C.** 20004 (202-331-0066); and 3543 18th St., **San Francisco,** CA 94110 (415-861-8960).

Handbook For Women Travelers by Maggie and Gemma Moss (UK£9). Encyclopedic and well written. From Piaktus Books, 5 Windmill St., London W1P 1HF (tel. (0171) 631 07 10).

Directory of Women's Media available from the National Council for Research on Women, 530 Broadway, 10th Floor, New York, NY 10012 (274-0730; fax 274-0821). The publication lists women's publishers, bookstores, theaters, and news organizations (mail orders, $30).

A Journey of One's Own, by Thalia Zepatos, Eighth Mountain Press $17. The latest thing on the market, interesting and full of good advice, plus a specific and manageable bibliography of books and resources.

Places of Interest to Women, Ferrari Publications, P.O. Box 37887, Phoenix, AZ 85069 (602-863-2408), an annual guide for women (especially lesbians) traveling in the U.S., Canada, the Caribbean, and Mexico ($14, plus shipping).

Women Going Places, a women's travel and resource guide emphasizing women-owned enterprises. Geared towards lesbians, but offers advice appropriate for all women. $14 from Inland Book Company, 1436 W. Randolph St. Chicago, IL 60607 (800-243-0138) or order from a local bookstore.

OLDER TRAVELERS

Senior citizens are eligible for a wide range of discounts on transportation, museums, movies, theaters, concerts, restaurants, and accommodations throughout New York City. Heck, Frank Sinatra is 80 and he still croons about how much he loves the place. If you don't see a senior citizen price listed, ask and you may be surprised.

AARP (American Association of Retired Persons), 601 E St. NW, Washington, D.C. 20049 (202-434-2277). Members 50 and over receive benefits and services including the AARP Motoring Plan from AMOCO (800-334-3300), and discounts on lodging, car rental, and sight-seeing. Annual fee $8 per couple; lifetime membership $75.

Elderhostel, 75 Federal St., 3rd Fl., Boston, MA 02110-1941 (617-426-7788; fax 426-8351; www at http://www.elderhostel.org). For those 55 or over (spouse of any age). Programs at colleges, universities, and other learning centers in over 50 countries on varied subjects lasting one to four weeks.

National Council of Senior Citizens, 1331 F St. NW, Washington, D.C. 20004 (202-347-8800). Memberships are $12 a year, $30 for three years, or $150 for a lifetime. Individuals or couples can receive hotel and auto rental discounts, a senior citizen newspaper, use of a discount travel agency, supplemental Medicare insurance (if you're over 65), and a mail-order prescription drug service.

Unbelievably Good Deals and Great Adventures That You Absolutely Can't Get Unless You're Over 50, by Joan Rattner Heilman. After you finish reading the title page, check inside for some great tips on senior discounts and the like. Contemporary Books, $10

BISEXUAL, GAY, AND LESBIAN TRAVELERS

New York City has a large, active, and supportive gay and lesbian population. Gay and lesbian visitors will have no trouble finding bars, clubs, bookstores, and special events in the city. The NYC Gay Pride Parade, in late June of each year, is one of the biggest in the world. *Let's Go* lists many information lines, community centers, entertainment, and special services for gays and lesbians. Consult New York's many gay papers, most of which are available at corner newsstands (especially in Greenwich Village), for the most current information. *NY Native* is one of the most useful. *Homo-Xtra,* which bills itself as the "politically incorrect" weekly, directs its readers to all kinds of sexy services. The nationally distributed *Advocate* magazine has a New York section; also check the *Village Voice,* which details events, services, and occasional feature articles of interest to gays and lesbians. The quarterly *Metrosource* covers bars, bookstores, and various gay resources, and is available at most gay bookstores.

Damron Travel Guides, P.O. Box 422458, San Francisco, CA 94142 (415-255-0404 or 800-462-6654). Publishers of the *Damron Address Book* ($15), which lists bars, restaurants, guest houses, and services in the United States, Canada, and Mexico catering to gay men. The *Damron Road Atlas* ($15) contains color maps of 56 major U.S. and Canadian cities and gay and lesbian resorts and listings of bars and accommodations. *The Women's Traveller* ($12) includes maps of 50 major U.S. cities and lists bars, restaurants, accommodations, bookstores, and services catering to lesbians. Forthcoming in 1997 is *Damron's Accommodations*, listing lesbigay hotels around the world ($19). For mail order, add $5 shipping.

Ferrari Guides, P.O. Box 37887, Phoenix, AZ 85069 (602-863-2408; fax 439-3952; e-mail ferrari@q-net.com). Gay and lesbian travel guides: *Ferrari Guides' Gay Travel A to Z* ($16), *Ferrari Guides' Men's Travel in Your Pocket* ($14), *Ferrari Guides' Women's Travel in Your Pocket* ($14), *Ferrari Guides' Inn Places* ($16). Available in bookstores or by mail order (postage/handling $4.50 for the first item, $1 for each additional item mailed within the US.

Gayellow Pages, P.O. Box 533, Village Station, New York, NY 10014 (212-674-0120; fax 420-1126). An annually updated listing of accommodations, resorts, hotlines, and other items of interest to the gay traveler. USA/Canada edition $16. You can also order the spin-off *NY Gayellow,* which focuses exclusively on establishments in New York City.

Giovanni's Room, 345 S. 12th St., Philadelphia, PA 19107 (215-923-2960; fax 923-0813; e-mail gilphilp@netaxs.com). An international feminist and lesbigay bookstore with mail-order service. Carries many of the publications listed in *Let's Go*.

International Gay Travel Association, Box 4974, Key West, FL 33041 (800-448-8550; fax 305-296-6633; e-mail IGTA@aol.com; http://www.rainbow-mall.com/igta.) An organization of over 1100 companies serving gay and lesbian travelers worldwide. Call for lists of travel agents, accommodations, and events.

International Lesbian and Gay Association (ILGA), 81 rue Marché-au-Charbon, B-1000 Bruxelles, Belgium (tel./fax 32 25 02 24 71; e-mail ilga@ilga.org). Not a travel service. Provides political information, such as homosexuality laws of individual countries.

Spartacus International Gay Guides, published by Bruno Gmunder, Postfach 110729, D-10837 Berlin, Germany (tel. (30) 615 00 30; fax (30) 615-9134). Lists bars, restaurants, hotels, and bookstores around the world catering to gays. Also lists hotlines for gays in various countries and homosexuality laws for each country. Available in bookstores and in the U.S. by mail from Giovanni's Room (listed above), $33.

The number for the **Gay and Lesbian Switchboard** in New York is 777-1800 (phone staffed daily 10am-midnight; interactive recording gives info on bars and nightlife, including lists of which places are popular which nights of the week); the number for the **Lesbian Switchboard** is 741-2610. When you first arrive in the city, stop by the

Rainbow Pride

New York has been a major center for American gay life since the 19th century, when an open and accepting bohemian lifestyle flourished in Greenwich Village and eventually in Harlem as well. As a result of this open and vocal community, the city has been the site of several firsts in American homosexuality:

1966: The first gay student organization was created at Columbia University; it was soon followed in 1967 by one at NYU.

1969: The Stonewall Rebellion signalled the beginning of the gay pride movement and established the legitimacy of gays in New York. The riots are now commemorated yearly.

1980s: In the face of the AIDS epidemic, gay leaders developed the Gay Men's Health Crisis, the first medical organization dedicated to serving those with AIDS (1981). A few years later, gays angry at the lack of funding and attention paid to AIDS formed ACT-Up, the first gay militant activist group (1987).

1994: The 1994 Gay Pride parade—with the aid of the hugely successful Gay Games athletic competition and a rally marking the 25th anniversary of the Stonewall riots—transformed New York into the undisputed cynosure of the gay and lesbian community. Estimates of attendance at the final rally on the Great Lawn in Central Park ranged from 100,000 to 500,000.

Lesbian and Gay Community Services Center (620-7310; phones staffed daily 9am-11pm), located at 208 W. 13th St., between Seventh and Eighth Avenue. Over 400 meeting groups hold their gatherings in this three-story converted schoolhouse. The center houses a medical walk-in clinic, holds dances, and will refer you to various support groups. The **Gay and Lesbian Visitors Center** (463-9030), at 135 W. 20th St., between Sixth and Seventh Avenue, publishes the bi-monthly magazine *The List* ($3), which carries advertisements for gay-friendly hotels, restaurants, and cultural events. Membership in the center costs $35 per year; members receive a year-long subscription to *The List,* mailed notices of interest to the gay and lesbian community, and a number of useful discounts.

DISABLED TRAVELERS

Particularly since President George Bush signed the Americans with Disabilities act in 1992, New York City has slowly but surely removed many of the impediments to disabled travel. Those with disabilities should inform airlines and hotels of their disabilities when making arrangements for travel; some time may be needed to prepare special accommodations. Hotels and hostels have become more and more accessible to disabled persons, and many attractions are even trying to make exploring the outdoors more feasible. Call restaurants, hotels, parks, and other facilities to find out about the existence of ramps, the widths of doors, the dimensions of elevators, etc.

Arrange transportation well in advance to ensure a smooth trip. Hertz, Avis, and National **car rental agencies** have hand-controlled vehicles at some locations. In the U.S., both **Amtrak** (800-872-7245, in PA 800-322-9537) and the airlines will accommodate disabled passengers if notified at least 72 hours in advance. Hearing-impaired travelers may contact Amtrak in advance using teletype printers. **Greyhound** buses will also provide free travel for a companion; if you are without a fellow traveler, call Greyhound (800-752-4841) at least 48 hours, but no more than one week before you plan to leave and it will make arrangements to assist you. For information on transportation availability in individual U.S. cities, contact the local chapter of the Easter Seals Society.

If you are planning to visit a national park or attraction in the United States run by the National Park Service, you should obtain a free **Golden Access Passport,** which is available at all park entrances and from federal offices whose functions relate to land, forests, or wildlife. The Golden Access Passport entitles disabled travelers and their families to enter parks for free and provides a 50% reduction on all campsite and parking fees.

You can also explore a number of more general books helpful to travelers with disabilities. The following organizations provide info or publications that might be of assistance:

American Foundation for the Blind, 11 Penn Plaza, New York, NY 10011 (212 - 502-7600). Provides information and services for the visually impaired. For a catalogue of products, contact Lighthouse Y, 10011 (800-829-0500).Open Mon.-Fri. 8:30am-4:30pm.

Facts on File, 11 Penn Plaza, 15th Floor, New York, NY 10001 (212-967-8800). Publishers of *Disability Resource,* a reference guide for travelers with disabilities ($45, plus shipping). Retail bookstores or by mail order.

Graphic Language Press, P.O. Box 270, Cardiff by the Sea, CA 92007 (619-944-9594). Publishers of *Wheelchair Through Europe* ($13). Comprehensive advice for the wheelchair-bound traveler. Specifics on wheelchair-related resources and accessible sites in various cities throughout Europe.

Moss Rehab Hospital Travel Information Service (215-456-9600, TDD 215- 456-9602). A telephone information resource center on international travel accessibility and other travel-related concerns for those with disabilities.

Society for the Advancement of Travel for the Handicapped (SATH), 347 Fifth Ave., #610, New York, NY 10016 (212-447-7284; fax 212-725-8253). Publishes quarterly travel newsletter *SATH News* and information booklets (free for members, $13 each for nonmembers) with advice on trip planning for people with disabilities. Annual membership $45, students and seniors $25.

Twin Peaks Press, P.O. Box 129, Vancouver, WA 98666-0129 Publishers of *Travel for the Disabled,* which provides travel tips, lists of accessible tourist attractions, and advice on other resources for disabled travelers ($20). Also publishes *Directory for Travel Agencies of the Disabled* ($20), *Wheelchair Vagabond* ($15), and *Directory of Accessible Van Rentals* ($10). Postage $3 for first book, $1.50 for each additional book. (360-694-2462, orders only MC and Visa (800-637-2256; fax 360-696-3210)

The following organizations arrange tours or trips for disabled travelers:

Directions Unlimited, 720 N. Bedford Rd., Bedford Hills, NY 10507 (800-533-5343; in NY 914-241-1700; fax 241-0243). Specializes in arranging individual and group vacations, tours, and cruises for the physically disabled.

Flying Wheels Travel Service, 143 W. Bridge St., Owatonne, MN 55060 (800-535-6790; fax 451-1685). Arranges trips in the U.S. and abroad for groups and individuals in wheelchairs or with other sorts of limited mobility.

The Guided Tour Inc., Elkins Park House, Suite 114B, 7900 Old York Road, Elkins Park, PA 19027-2339 (800-783-5841 or 215-782-1370; fax 635-2637). Organizes travel programs for persons with developmental and physical challenges and those requiring renal dialysis. Call, fax, or write for a free brochure.

TRAVELERS WITH CHILDREN

Family vacations to New York City are recipes for disaster (remember *Home Alone 2?*)—unless you slow your pace and plan ahead a bit. When deciding where to stay, remember the special needs of young children; if you pick a B&B, call and make sure it's child-friendly. If you rent a car, make sure the rental company provides a car seat for younger children. Consider using a papoose-style device to carry your baby on walking trips.

Restaurants often have children's menus and discounts. Virtually all museums and tourist attractions also have a children's rate. Be sure that your child carries some sort of ID in case of an emergency or he or she gets lost. And arrange a reunion spot in case of separation when sight-seeing (e.g., next to Perseus at the Met).

Children under two generally fly for 10% of the adult airfare on international flights (this does not necessarily include a seat). International fares are usually discounted 25% for children from two to 11.

Some of the following publications offer tips for adults traveling with children or distractions for the kids themselves. You can also contact the publishers to see if they have other related publications that you might find useful.

Backpacking with Babies and Small Children ($10). Published by Wilderness Press, 2440 Bancroft Way, Berkeley, CA 94704 (800-443-7227 or 510-843-8080; fax 548-1355).

Kidding Around ($10-13, postage under $5). A series of illustrated books for children about Spain, Paris, London, Boston, New York, L.A., Chicago, and Hawaii. Educational (and distracting) books that could prove invaluable for keeping little ones happy on long trips. Published by John Muir Publications, P.O. Box 613, Santa Fe, NM 87504 (800-285-4078; fax 505-988-1680).

Travel with Children by Maureen Wheeler ($11.95, postage $1.50). Published by Lonely Planet Publications, Embarcadero West, 155 Filbert St., #251, Oakland, CA 94607 (800-275-8555 or 510-893-8555; fax 893-8563; e-mail info@lonelyplanet.com; http://www.lonelyplanet.com). Also P.O. Box 617, Hawthorn, Victoria 3122, Australia.

VEGETARIAN, KOSHER, AND HALAL TRAVELERS

Vegetarians won't have any problem eating cheap and well in New York. Try Barbara Holmes's *Vegetarian Dining in New York City* ($9). Write to P.O. Box 845, Midwood Station, Brooklyn, NY 11230 (718-434-3180).

ESSENTIALS

Travelers who keep **kosher** should contact New York synagogues for information about kosher restaurants; your own synagogue or college Hillel office should have lists of Jewish institutions in New York. The *Jewish Travel Guide* ($13, $2.50 postage) is available in the U.S. from Sepher-Hermon Press, 1265 46th St., Brooklyn, NY 11219 (718-972-9010), and lists Jewish institutions, synagogues, and kosher restaurants. The guide is also available in the U.K. from Ballantine-Mitchell Publishers, Newbury House 890-900, Eastern Ave., Newbury Park, Illford, Essex IG2 7HH, (tel. (0181) 599 88 66; fax (0181) 599 09 84). Muslim travelers seeking **halal** foods should check the local Yellow Pages listings under "halal."

MINORITY TRAVELERS

New York City is a dialectic of diversity. On one hand, America's melting pot features a thriving network of interconnected ethnic communities, with more Irish than Dublin, more Italians than Rome, more Jews than Jerusalem, and what's considered by many to be the African-American capital of the world. On the other hand, ugly episodes of ethnic strife have plagued many areas of the city, such as Bensonhurst and Crown Heights. Your best bet is to keep your eyes open and exercise discretion when traveling—run-down neighborhoods at night aren't safe for members of any ethnicity. **Hippocrene Books** offers several widely-available travel guides for minorities, including *Black New York* ($15) (see Useful Information, p. 14).

GETTING TO NEW YORK CITY

▇ Budget Travel Agencies

Students and people under 26 ("youth") with proper ID qualify for enticing reduced airfares. These are rarely available from airlines or travel agents, but instead from student travel agencies like **Let's Go Travel, STA, Travel CUTS, USTN** and **Council Travel** (see Useful Information, p. 14). These agencies negotiate special reduced-rate bulk purchases with the airlines, then resell them to the youth market; in 1996, peak season roundtrip rates from even the offbeat corners of Europe to New York City rarely topped $800 and off-season fares or fares from common destinations like London were considerably lower. Roundtrip fares from Australia or New Zealand through STA cost around $1400. Return-date change fees also tend to be low (around $50 per segment through Council or Let's Go Travel). Most flights are on major airlines, though in peak season some agencies may sell seats on less reliable chartered aircraft. Student travel agencies can also help non-students and people over 26, but they probably won't be able to get the same low fares.

Campus Travel, 52 Grosvenor Gardens, London SW1W 0AG (http://www.campus-travel.co.uk.) 41 branches in the U.K. Student and youth fares on plane, train, boat, and bus travel. Flexible airline tickets. Discount and ID cards for youths, travel insurance for students and those under 35, and maps and guides. Puts out travel suggestion booklets. Telephone booking service: in Europe call (0171) 730 34 02; in North America call (0171) 730 21 01; worldwide call (0171) 730 81 11; in Manchester call (0161) 273 17 21; in Scotland (0131) 668 33 03.

Council Travel (http://www.ciee.org/cts/ctshome.htm), the travel division of Council, is a full-service travel agency specializing in youth and budget travel. They offer railpasses, discount airfares, hosteling cards, guidebooks, budget tours, travel gear, and student (ISIC), youth (GO25), and teacher (ITIC) identity cards. U.S. offices include: Emory Village, 1561 N. Decatur Rd., **Atlanta,** GA 30307 (tel. (404) 377-9997); 2000 Guadalupe, **Austin,** TX 78705 (tel. (512) 472-4931); 273 Newbury St., **Boston,** MA 02116 (tel. (617) 266-1926); 1138 13th St., **Boulder,** CO 80302 (tel. (303) 447-8101); 1153 N. Dearborn, **Chicago,** IL 60610 (tel. (312) 951-0585); 10904 Lindbrook Dr., **Los Angeles,** CA 90024 (tel. (310) 208-3551); 1501

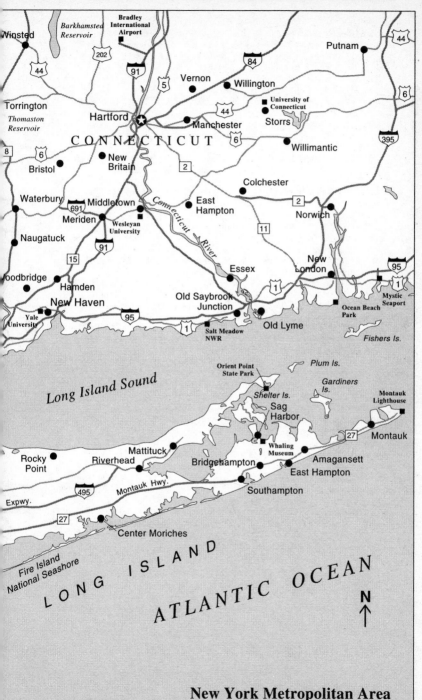

New York Metropolitan Area

University Ave. SE, **Minneapolis,** MN 55414 (tel. (612) 379-2323); 205 E. 42nd St., **New York,** NY 10017 (tel. (212) 822-2700); 953 Garnet Ave., **San Diego,** CA 92109 (tel. (619) 270-6401); 530 Bush St., **San Francisco,** CA 94108 (tel. (415) 421-3473); 4311½ University Way, **Seattle,** WA 98105 (tel. (206) 632-2448); 3300 M St. NW, **Washington, D.C.** 20007 (tel. (202) 337-6464). **For U.S. cities not listed,** call 800-2-COUNCIL (226-8624). Also 28A Poland St. (Oxford Circus), **London,** W1V 3DB (tel. (0171) 437 7767).

Council Charter: 205 E. 42nd St., New York, NY 10017 (212-661-0311; fax 212-972-0194). Offers a combination of inexpensive charter and scheduled airfares from a variety of U.S. gateways to most major European destinations. One-way fares and open jaws (fly into one city and out of another) are available.

CTS Travel, 220 Kensington High St., W8 (tel. (0171) 937 3388 for travel world-wide). Specializes in student/youth travel and discount flights. Kensington. Open Mon.-Fri. 9:30am-6pm, Sat. 10am-5pm. Also at 44 Goodge St., W1.

Let's Go Travel, Harvard Student Agencies, 67 Mt. Auburn St., Cambridge, MA 02138 (800-5-LETS GO/553-8746 or 617-495-9649). Railpasses, HI-AYH member-ships, ISICs, ITICs, FIYTO cards, guidebooks (including all of the Let's Go guides and Map Guides), maps, bargain flights, and a complete line of budget travel gear. All items available by mail; call or write for a catalog.

STA Travel, 6560 Scottsdale Rd. #F100, Scottsdale, AZ 85253 (800-777-0112 nation-wide; fax (602-922-0793). A student and youth travel organization with over 100 offices worldwide offering discount airfares for young travelers, railpasses, accom-modations, tours, insurance, and ISICs. 16 offices in the U.S. including: 297 New-bury St., **Boston,** MA 02115 (617-266-6014); 429 S. Dearborn St., **Chicago** IL 60605 (312-786-9050; 7202 Melrose Ave., **Los Angeles**, CA 90046 (213-934-8722); 10 Downing St., Ste. G, **New York,** NY 10003 (212-627-3111); 4341 University Way NE, **Seattle,** WA 98105 (206-633-5000); 2401 Pennsylvania Ave., **Washing-ton, D.C.** 20037 (202-887-0912); 51 Grant Ave., **San Francisco,** CA 94108 (415-391-8407), **Miami,** FL 33133 (305-461-3444). In the U.K., 6 Wrights Ln., **London** W8 6TA (tel. (0171) 938 47 11 for North American travel). In New Zealand, 10 High St., **Auckland** (tel. (09) 309 97 23). In Australia, 222 Faraday St., **Melbourne** VIC 3050 (tel. (03) 349 69 11).

Travel CUTS (Canadian Universities Travel Services Limited): 187 College St., Toronto, Ont. M5T 1P7 (416-979-2406; fax 979-8167; e-mail mail@travelcuts). Can-ada's national student travel bureau and equivalent of Council, with 40 offices across Canada. Also in the U.K., 295-A Regent St., **London** W1R 7YA (tel. (0171) 637 31 61). Discounted domestic and international airfares open to all; special stu-dent fares to all destinations with valid ISIC. Issues ISIC, FIYTO, GO25, and HI hos-tel cards, as well as railpasses. Offers free *Student Traveller* magazine, as well as information on the Student Work Abroad Program (SWAP).

Travel Management International (TMI), 3617 Dupont Avenue South, Minneap-olis, MN 55409 (617-661-8187 or 800-245-3672). Usually a diligent, prompt, and very helpful travel service offering student fares and discounts.

USIT Youth and Student Travel: 19-21 Aston Quay, O'Connell Bridge, Dublin 2 (tel. (01) 602 12 00; fax 671 24 08). In the U.S.A.: **New York** Student Center, 895 Amsterdam Ave., New York, NY, 10025 (212-663-5435). Additional offices in Cork, Galway, Limerick, Waterford, Maynooth, Coleraine, Derry, Athlone, Jordanstown, Belfast, and Greece. Specializes in youth and student travel—hence the name! Offers low cost tickets and flexible travel arrangements all over the world. Supplies ISIC and GO25 cards.

■ By Plane

If you're planning to fly into New York, you will have to choose not only a carrier but an airport as well. Three airports serve the New York metropolitan region. The larg-est, **John F. Kennedy Airport,** or JFK (718-244-4444), is 12 miles from midtown Manhattan in southern Queens and handles most international flights. **LaGuardia Airport** (718-533-3400), 6 miles from midtown in northwestern Queens, is the small-est, offering domestic flights and hourly shuttles to and from Boston and Washington, D.C. **Newark International Airport** (201-762-5100 or 201-961-6000), 12 miles from

Midtown in Newark, NJ, offers both domestic and international flights at budget fares often not available at the other airports (though getting to and from Newark can be expensive). Bi-monthly *Airport Guides* by the Port Authority have comprehensive information on all flights arriving and departing New York's airports. The guides' most useful aspect is that they let you know all the airlines—budget and charter as well as the biggies—flying any particular route into or out of the city. Armed with this info, you can then call all these airlines in search of the best deal. The guides do not carry any information on ticket prices themselves. Write to Airport Customer Services, One World Trade Center 65N, New York, NY 10048, or call 435-4877 8am-5pm on weekdays. The guides cost $7 for a year's subscription through the mail but are free if picked up in person. (If you only want one, they'll usually send it to you free.)

FROM WITHIN THE U.S.

When dealing with any commercial airline, buying in advance is always the best bet. To obtain the cheapest fare, buy a roundtrip ticket and stay over at least one Saturday; traveling on **off-peak** days (Mon.-Thurs. morning) is usually $30 to $40 cheaper than traveling on the weekends. You will need to pay for the ticket within 24 hours of booking the flight, and tickets are entirely non-refundable. Any change in plans incurs a fee of between $25 and $150, even if only to change the date of departure or return. Since travel peaks between June and August and around holidays, you may want to reserve a seat several months in advance for these times. When inquiring about fares, be sure to get advance purchase and length of stay requirements, or else you may not be able to buy your ticket in time or be forced to return home sooner than expected.

The commercial carriers' lowest regular offer is the **APEX** (Advanced Purchase Excursion Fare); specials advertised in newspapers may be cheaper, but have correspondingly more restrictions and fewer available seats. APEX fares provide you with confirmed reservations and often allow **"open-jaw" tickets** (landing in and returning from different cities). APEX tickets usually must be purchased two to three weeks ahead of the departure date. Be sure to inquire about any restrictions on length of stay (the minimum is most often 7 days, the maximum 2 months; shorter or longer stays usually mean more money).

Most airlines allow children under two to fly for free on the lap of an adult (see Travelers with Children, p. 41). Students and seniors get good deals on the **Delta** and **USAir** Boston-New York and New York-Washington **shuttles.** Travel from 10am to 2pm and after 7pm on weekdays and all day on weekends costs $75 each way for both sets of travelers. Youths (16-25) can also purchase a four-pack of shuttle passes at the discount rate of $58 per ticket. The discount applies during peak hours, but you must fly standby. No advance purchase is required. The standard fare for adults is generally $150 each way. Last-minute travelers should also ask about **"red-eye"** (i.e., all-night) flights, which are common on popular business routes.

Consider **discount travel agencies** such as **Travel Avenue,** 10 S. Riverside Plaza, Chicago, IL, 60606 (800-333-3335), which rebates 4-7% on the price of all airline tickets (domestic and international) minus a $15 ticketing fee. Also try **Last Minute Travel** (800-527-8646). Student-oriented agencies such as **Council, Travel CUTS,** and **STA Travel** sometimes have special deals that regular travel agents can't offer (see Budget Travel Agencies, p. 43).

FLIGHTS FROM ABROAD

Many major U.S. airlines offer special **"Visit USA" air passes** and fares to international travelers. You must purchase these passes outside the U.S., paying one price for a certain number of "flight coupons." Each coupon is good for one flight segment on an airline's domestic system within a certain time period; typically, all travel must be completed within 30 to 60 days. Some cross-country trips may require two segments. The point of departure and the destination must be specified for each coupon at the time of purchase, and once in the States, any change in route will incur a fee of between $50 and $75. Dates of travel may be changed once travel has begun at no extra charge. **USAir** offers vouchers good for travel on the east coast for $589-649, or in all 48 states for $649-679. **United, Continental, Delta,** and **TWA** also offer programs. Remember that there is **no smoking** on any flight with a duration less than six hours within the U.S.

From Europe

Travelers from Europe will experience the least competition for inexpensive seats during the off-season; "off-season" need not mean the dead of winter. Peak season rates generally take effect on either May 15 or June 1 and run until about September 15. You can take advantage of cheap off-season flights within Europe to reach an advantageous point of departure for North America. London is a major connecting point for budget flights to the U.S.; New York City is often the destination. Discount travel agencies offer reasonable rates even during the peak season.

If you decide to fly with a commercial airline rather than through a charter agency or ticket consolidator, you'll be purchasing greater reliability, security, and flexibility. Many major airlines offer reduced-fare options, such as three-day advance-purchase fares; these tickets can be purchased only within 72 hours of the time of the departure, and are restricted to youths under a certain age (often 24). Check with a travel agent for availability. The lowest major airline fares for a roundtrip ticket from Europe in July 1996: **British Airways** (London to NYC $673; 800-247-9297), **Continental** (London to Newark, NJ $810; 800-525-0280), **Northwest** (London to NYC $714; 800-225-2525), **TWA** (London to NYC $710; 800-221-2000), **United** (London to NYC $673; 800-538-2929). Smaller, budget airlines often undercut major carriers by offering bargain fares on regularly scheduled flights. Competition for seats on these smaller carriers can be fierce—book early. Discount trans-Atlantic airlines include **Virgin Atlantic Airways** (London to NYC $714; 800-862-8621) and **IcelandAir** (London to NYC $708; 800-223-5500).

From Australia and New Zealand

A good place to start searching for tickets is the local branch of one of the budget-travel agencies listed above. STA Travel is the largest international agency, with offices in Sydney, Melbourne, and Auckland. (see Budget Travel Agencies, p. 43). **Qantas, Air New Zealand, United,** and **Northwest** fly between Australia or New Zealand and the United States. Prices are roughly equivalent among the four (American carriers tend to be a bit less), but the cities they serve differ. Advance purchase fares from Australia have extremely tough restrictions. If you are uncertain about your plans, pay extra for an advance purchase ticket that has only a 50% penalty for cancellation. Many travelers from Australia and New Zealand reportedly take **Singapore Air** or other Far East-based carriers during the initial leg of their trips; check with STA or another budget agency for more comprehensive information.

TO AND FROM THE AIRPORTS

Travel between each of the airports and New York City without a car of your own becomes simpler as cost increases; you pay in time or money. Though **public transportation** is generally the cheapest option, this mode can be time-consuming and usually involves changing mid-route from a bus to a subway or train (especially tricky if you're loaded with baggage). **Private bus companies** will charge slightly more, but will take you directly from the airport to any one of many Manhattan destinations: Grand Central Station (42nd St. and Park Avenue), the Port Authority Bus Terminal (41st St. and Eighth Avenue), or the World Trade Center (1 West St.), along with several prominent hotels. Private companies run frequently and according to a set schedule (see individual listings below). Some services peter out or vanish entirely between midnight and 6am. If you want to set your own destination and schedule, and if you're willing to pay, you can take one of New York's infamous **yellow cabs.** Heavy traffic makes the trip more expensive: traveling during rush hour (7:30-10am and 4-7:30pm) can devastate a wallet. You are responsible for paying **bridge and**

tunnel tolls. For the most up-to-date guide to reaching the airports, call **AirRide,** the Port Authority's airport travel hotline, at 800-247-7433. It's an automated interactive system offering very detailed information on how to reach any of the three airports by car, public transportation, or private bus line. Also try the **MTA/New York City Transit Center** at 718-330-1234 for similar information. Finally, if you make lodging reservations ahead of time, be sure to ask about limousine services—some hostels offer transportation from the airports for reasonable fares.

From JFK Airport

The cheapest route into the city is on the **subway.** Catch a free brown-and-white JFK long-term parking lot bus from any airport terminal (every 10-15min.) to the **Howard Beach-JFK Airport subway station.** You can take the **A train** from there to the city (1hr.); the A stops several times in lower Manhattan, as well as at Washington Sq., 34th St.-Penn Station, 42nd St.-Port Authority, and 59th St.-Columbus Circle ($1.50). Heading from Manhattan to JFK, take the Far Rockaway A train. Or you can take one of the local buses (Q10 or Q3; fare $1.50, exact change required) from the airport into Queens. The Q10 bus heads to Lefferts Blvd., where it connects with the A train, and to Kew Gardens, where it connects with the E and F trains. You can then take the subway into Manhattan ($1.50). The Q3 connects JFK with the F train at 179th St.-Jamaica and 159th St. Ask the driver where to get off, and be sure you know which subway line you want. Although these routes are safer during the day, nighttime travelers should check with the information desk to find the safest way into the city.

Those willing to pay a little more can take the **Carey Airport Express** (718-632-0500 or 0509), a private line that runs between JFK (also LaGuardia, see below) and Grand Central Station and the Port Authority Terminal. Buses leave every 30 minutes from JFK to Manhattan from 5am to 1am daily (45-75min., $13). If you want to save a few dollars, Carey will take you to Jamaica station in Queens ($5), from where you can catch the E, J, or Z subway trains into the city ($1.50). If you are heading to JFK from Manhattan, get on the Carey bus at one of six locations, including 125 Park Avenue at Grand Central Station (every 30min., 6am-midnight, 1hr.) or at the Port Authority Terminal (1½hr.). **Students** get half-price tickets, which can be purchased only at the company office in Manhattan at 125 Park Avenue at Grand Central Station; buy two in Manhattan if you plan to take the express back into the city. The **Gray Line Air Shuttle** (800-451-0455) will drop you off (not pick you up) at any hotel in Manhattan between 23rd and 63rd St. ($16). Inquire at a Ground Transportation Center in JFK. A **taxi** from JFK to midtown costs about $35.

From LaGuardia Airport

The journey to LaGuardia takes about half as long as the trek out to JFK. If you have extra time and light luggage when leaving the airport, take the MTA Q33 **bus** ($1.25) to the 74th St.-Broadway-Roosevelt Ave.-Jackson Hts. subway stop in Queens. From there, take the #7, E, F, G, or R train into Manhattan ($1.50). You can catch the Q33 bus from the lower level of the terminal. Allow at least 1½ hours travel time. Be especially careful traveling these routes at night. The **Carey Airport Express** also runs to and from LaGuardia every 30 minutes, stopping at a number of locations in Manhattan, including Grand Central Station and Port Authority (30min.-1hr., $9). If you can't afford a cab but you still crave door-to-door service, the **Gray Line Air Shuttle** (800-451-0455) will take you to any hotel between 23rd and 63rd for $13 (6am-7pm). Be prepared for a long ride: the bus runs the circuit of large midtown hotels before stopping at smaller hotels. A **taxi** to Manhattan costs around $25, a sum not all that unreasonable if split between two or more people; at LaGuardia, it is relatively easy to find someone to share a cab.

From Newark Airport

The trip from New Jersey's Newark Airport takes about as long as from JFK. **New Jersey Transit Authority (NJTA)** (201-762-5100 or 212-629-8767) runs a fast, efficient **bus** (NJTA #300) between the airport and Port Authority every 15-30 minutes during the day, less frequently at night (24hr., $7; travel time 30-45min.). For the same fare, the **Olympia Trails Coach** (212-964-6233) travels between the airport and Grand Central, Penn Station, or the World Trade Center (daily 5am-11pm, every 20-30min.; 25min.-1hr. travel time; $7; tickets may be purchased on the bus). **NJTA Bus #107** will take you to midtown for $3.25 (exact change required), but don't try it unless you have little luggage and lots of time. The NJTA also runs an **Air Link bus #302** ($4) between the airport and Newark's Penn Station (*not* Manhattan's); and from there **PATH** trains ($1) run into Manhattan, stopping at the World Trade Center, Christopher St., Sixth Avenue, 9th St., 14th St., 23rd St. and 33rd St. Expect to travel 15-30 min. For PATH information call 1-800-234-7284. A taxi should run you about $45, but be sure to negotiate the price with the driver before departing.

■ By Bus

Getting in and out of New York can be less expensive and more scenic by bus or train than by plane. **Greyhound** (800-231-2222) operates the largest number of lines, departing to New York from Boston (4½hrs.; $27 one way, $51 roundtrip), Philadelphia (2hrs.; Mon.-Thurs. $14 one way, $26 roundtrip), Washington, D.C. (4½hrs.; $27 one way, $51 roundtrip), and Montreal (8 hrs.; $65 one way, $79 roundtrip). The fares listed here require no advance purchase; significant discounts off these fares can be had by purchasing tickets 3, 7, or 14 days in advance. Some buses to these cities take longer (up to 2 hours more) due to additional stops or time of travel.

A number of **discounts** are available on Greyhound's standard-fare tickets: senior citizens ride for 10% off, children under 11 ride for half-fare, and children under 2 ride for free in the lap of an adult. A traveler with a physical disability may bring along a companion for free, and active and retired U.S. military personnel and National Guard Reserves (and their spouses and dependents) may take a roundtrip between any two points in the U.S. for $169.

Greyhound allows passengers to carry two pieces of luggage (up to 45 lbs. total) and to check two pieces of luggage (up to 100 lbs.). Whatever you stow in compartments underneath the bus should be clearly marked; be sure to get a claim check for it, and watch to make sure your luggage is on the same bus as you. As always, keep your essential documents and valuables on you. Take a jacket, too; surprisingly efficient air-conditioning brings the temperature down to arctic levels.

If you plan to tour a great deal by bus within the U.S., you may save money with the **Ameripass,** which entitles you to unlimited travel for 7 days ($179), 15 days ($289), or 30 days ($399); extensions for the 7- and 15-day passes cost $15 per day. The pass takes effect the first day used, so make sure you have a pretty good idea of your itinerary before you start. Before purchasing an Ameripass, total up the separate bus fares between towns to make sure that the pass is indeed more economical, or at least worth the unlimited flexibility it provides. Greyhound offers an **International Ameripass** for visitors from outside North America. A 7-day adult pass sells for $159, a 15-day pass for $219, a 30-day pass for $299, and a 60-day pass for $499. (There are no special rates for children.)

Always check bus schedules and routes personally, and don't rely on old printed schedules since listings change seasonally. Greyhound schedule information can be obtained from any Greyhound terminal or from the reservation center at 800-231-2222. Greyhound has implemented a reservation system much like that of the airlines, which will allow you to call and reserve a seat or purchase a ticket by mail. If you call seven or more days in advance and want to purchase your ticket with a credit card, reservations can be made and the ticket mailed to you. Otherwise, you may make reservations up to 24 hours in advance.

If you are boarding at a remote "flag stop," be sure you know exactly where the bus stops. Call the nearest agency and let them know you'll be waiting at the flag stop for the bus at a certain time. Catch the driver's attention by standing on the side of the road and flailing your arms wildly—better to be embarrassed than stranded.

The hub of the Northeast bus network, New York's **Port Authority Terminal,** 41st St. and Eighth Avenue (435-7000; Subway: A, C, or E to 42nd St.-Port Authority), is a tremendous modern facility with labyrinthine bus terminals. The Port Authority has good information and security services, but the surrounding neighborhood is somewhat deserted at night, when it pays to be wary of pickpockets and to call a cab. Avoid the terminal's bathrooms at all times and costs.

A recent addition to bus travel is **East Coast Explorer,** a bus service connecting the cities of Boston, New York, and Washington, D.C. For $3-7 more than Greyhound, travel all day with 13 other people on back roads, stopping at sites of historic interest—a good bargain for those trying to tour the East Coast for cheap. Trips from Washington to New York leave Friday mornings, stopping at Newcastle, DE, and Philadelphia. Trips from New York to Washington leave Thursday mornings and visit the Amish countryside of Lancaster, Pennsylvania. From Boston, the bus departs for New York on Tuesday mornings and passes through Massachusetts and Dinosaur State Park. Trips head back to Boston from New York on Monday mornings, with stops at the seaside towns of Mystic, Connecticut and Newport, Rhode Island. The air-conditioned bus makes pick-ups and drop-offs at most hostels and budget hotels; call between one month and one day in advance for reservations (718-694-9667 or 800-610-2680, between 8am and 11pm). Trips between New York and Washington cost $32; $29 between New York and Boston. Costs for all trips include tolls and tour guide (Larry Lustig, the company's founder and operator). Each passenger is limited to two bags.

■ By Train

The train is still one of the cheapest and most comfortable ways to travel in the U.S. You can stretch your legs, buy overpriced victuals, and shut out the sun to sleep in a reclining chair (avoid paying unnecessarily for a roomette or bedroom). If *Silver Streak* is any indication, you may have an adventure along the way to boot. Travel light; not all stations will check baggage and not all trains carry large amounts.

Amtrak, 60 Massachusetts Ave. NE, Washington, D.C. 20002 (800-872-7245), offers a discount **All-Aboard America** fare that divides the continental U.S. into three regions—Eastern, Central, and Western. Amtrak permits three stopovers and a maximum trip duration of 45 days. During the summer, rates are $198 if you travel in one region, $278 to travel in two regions, and $338 for all three (from late Aug. to mid- Dec. and early Jan. to mid-June, rates are $178, $238, and $278). (See below for regular fare information.) Your itinerary, including cities and dates, must be set at the time the passes are purchased; the route may not be changed once travel has begun, although times and dates may be changed at no cost. All-Aboard fares are subject to availability; reserve two to three months in advance for summer travel.

Another discount option, available only to those who aren't citizens of North America, is the **USA Rail Pass,** which allows unlimited travel and unlimited stops over a period of either 15 or 30 days. As with the All-Aboard America program, the cost of the pass depends on the number of regions in which you wish to travel. The pass, allowing 30 days of travel nationwide, sells for $425 during the peak season and for $339 off-season; the 15-day nationwide pass sells for $340 during the peak season and for $229 off-season. Another discount option on Amtrak is the **Air-Rail Travel Plan,** offered in conjunction with United Airlines, which allows you to travel in one direction by train and then fly home, or vice-versa. The transcontinental plan, which allows coast-to-coast travel originating in either coast, sells for $605 peak-season and $516 off-season. The East Coast plan, which allows travel roughly as far west as Atlanta, is $417 during peak season, $373 off-peak.

Full fares on Amtrak vary according to time, date, and destination. Amtrak seldom places advance-purchase requirements on its fares, although the number of seats sold at discount prices is always limited. These discount tickets are naturally the first to sell, so it's best to plan in advance and reserve early. In fact, you'll want to call and reserve as soon as your travel dates are set—if you reserve well ahead of your date of

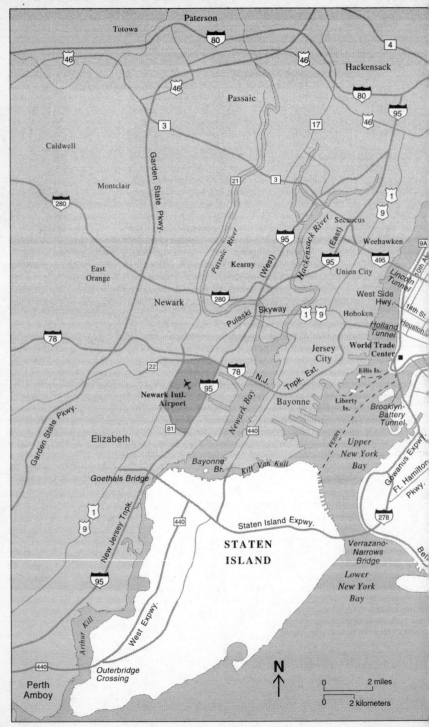

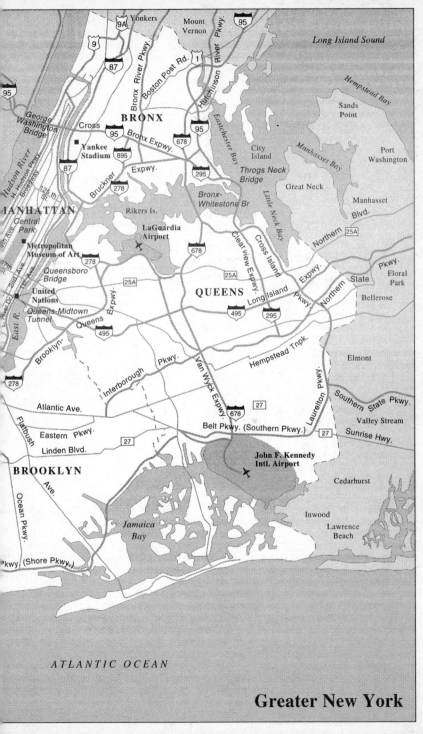

Greater New York

departure, Amtrak will often give you a grace period of several weeks or months before requiring you to actually pay for your tickets (e.g., reserve in August for a trip the following June and you'll often be given until November to pay). Amtrak accepts reservations up to 11 months in advance. One way fares don't vary with the season, but roundtrip tickets can be significantly cheaper between late August and late May, with the exception of Christmastime. The *Maple Leaf* connects Toronto with New York for $62 one-way and as little as $86 roundtrip; the *Crescent* connects New Orleans with New York for $160 one way and between $168 and $258 roundtrip. From Washington, tickets to New York cost $51 one way and $92 roundtrip. Tickets from Chicago to New York are $128 one way and between $128 and $256 roundtrip.

Amtrak offers several **discounts** off its full fares for certain travelers: children ages two to 15 accompanied by a parent (½-fare); children under age two (free on the lap of an adult); senior citizens (15% off Mon.-Thurs.); travelers with disabilities (25% off); and current members of the U.S. Armed Forces and active-duty veterans (20% off), as well as their dependents (12½% off). Circle trips and special holiday packages can save you money as well. Keep in mind that discounted air travel, particularly for longer distances, may be cheaper than train travel. For up-to-date information and reservations, contact your local Amtrak office or call **800-USA-RAIL/872-7245** from a touch-tone phone.

TRAIN STATIONS

Grand Central Station, 42nd St. and Park Avenue (subway: #4, 5, 6, 7 or S to 42nd St.-Grand Central), handles more than 550 trains a day. It handles the three **Metro-North** (800-METRO-INFO/532-4900) commuter lines to Connecticut and the New York suburbs (the Hudson, Harlem, and New Haven lines). Longer train routes run out of the smaller **Penn Station,** 33rd St. and Eighth Avenue (subway: #1, 2, 3, 9, or A, C, E to 34th St.-Penn Station); the major line is **Amtrak** (800-872-7245 or 212-582-6875), which serves upstate New York and most major cities in the U.S. and Canada, especially those in the Northeast (to Washington, D.C., 3¾hrs., $51 one way, $92 roundtrip; Boston 4-5hrs., $52 one way, $72-86 roundtrip depending on time of travel). Penn Station also handles the **Long Island Railroad (LIRR)** (718-822-5477; fares range from $3-14 and service is fairly extensive, extending to the eastern tip of the island; see Daytripping: Long Island, p. 303), and **NJ Transit** service to New Jersey (201-762-5100).

■ By Car

The **speed limit** in New York State, as in most other states, is 55 miles per hour; a number of states, or sections of states, have limits of 65 miles per hour. There are several major approaches to driving into New York. From New Jersey there are three choices. The **Holland Tunnel** connects to lower Manhattan, exiting into the SoHo area. From the NJ Turnpike you'll probably end up at the **Lincoln Tunnel,** which exits in midtown in the West 40s. The third and arguably easiest option is the **George Washington Bridge,** which crosses the Hudson River into northern Manhattan, offering access to either Harlem River Drive or the West Side Highway. Coming from New England or Connecticut on I-95, follow signs for the **TriBoro Bridge.** From there get onto FDR Drive, which runs along the east side of Manhattan and exits onto city streets every 10 blocks or so. Or look for the Willis Avenue Bridge exit on I-95 to avoid the toll, and enter Manhattan farther north on FDR Drive.

For information on renting a car, see Getting Around, below.

HITCHHIKING

Hitchhiking is illegal in New York State and the laws tend to be strictly enforced within New York City. Offenders will usually be asked to move on. It's best to take the train or bus out of the metropolitan area; hitching in and around New York City is dangerous. If someone you don't know offers you a free ride, don't take it. *Let's Go* cannot recommend hitchhiking as a safe means of transport. We cannot emphasize this enough. *Do not hitchhike.*

GETTING AROUND

> I have two faults to find with New York. In the first place, there is nothing to see; and in the second place, there is no mode of getting about to see anything.
>
> —Anthony Trollope, North America, 1862

To be equipped for the New York City navigation experience, you will need more than an understanding of the logic underlying its streets. You will need to know how to use the **public transportation system.** Get a free subway or bus map from station token booths or the visitors bureau, which also has a free street map (see Tourist Information, p. 66). For a more detailed program of travel, find a Manhattan Yellow Pages, which has detailed subway, PATH, and bus maps. Since bus routes vary for each of the boroughs, you may want to get other bus maps; send a self-addressed, stamped envelope to **NYC Transit,** 370 Jay St., Brooklyn, NY 11201. Then wait about a month. The **NYC Transit Information Bureau** (718-330-1234) dispenses subway and bus info.

■ Orientation

New York City is composed of five boroughs: Brooklyn, the Bronx, Queens, Staten Island, and Manhattan. Nevertheless, plenty of tourists and Manhattanites alike have been known to confuse Manhattan with New York. This Manhattancentric perspective has deep historical roots. The island's original inhabitants, the Algonquin, called it "Man-a-hat-ta" or "Heavenly Land." The British were the first to call the island "New York," after James, Duke of York, the brother of Charles II. It was only in 1898 that the other four boroughs joined the city's government. No matter how often you hear Manhattan referred to as "The City," each of the other boroughs really does have a right to share the name. Flanked on the east by the East River (actually a strait) and on the west by the Hudson River, Manhattan is a sliver of an island. It measures only 13 miles long and 2½ miles wide. Fatter Queens and Brooklyn look onto their svelte neighbor from the other side of the East River, and pudgy, self-reliant Staten Island averts its eyes in the south. **Queens,** the city's largest and most ethnically diverse borough, is dotted with light industry, airports, and stadiums. **Brooklyn,** the city's most populous borough (with 2.24 million residents), is even older than Manhattan. Founded by the Dutch in 1600, the borough today cradles several diverse residential neighborhoods along with pockets of dangerous slums. **Staten Island** has remained a staunchly residential borough, similar to the suburban bedroom communities of eastern Long Island. North of Manhattan sits the **Bronx,** the only borough connected by land to the rest of the U.S. Supposedly, the whole borough was once a Dutch estate owned by Jonas Bronck; an excursion to his family's farm was referred to as a visit to "the Broncks'." Today's Bronx encompasses both the genteel suburb of Riverdale and New York's most devastated area, the South Bronx.

DISTRICTS OF MANHATTAN

Despite the unending urban chaos within its borders, New York can be broken down into manageable neighborhoods, each with a history and personality of its own. As a result of city zoning ordinances, quirks of history, and random forces of urban evolution, boundaries between these neighborhoods can often be abrupt.

The city began at the southern tip of Manhattan, in the area around **Battery Park** where the first Dutch settlers made their homes. The nearby harbor, now jazzed up with the touristy **South Street Seaport,** provided the growing city with the commercial opportunities that helped it succeed. Historic Manhattan, however, lies in the shadows of the imposing financial buildings around **Wall Street** and the civic offices around **City Hall.** A bit farther north, neighborhoods rich in the ethnic culture brought by late 19th-century immigrants rub elbows below Houston Street—**Little Italy, Chinatown,** and the southern blocks of the **Lower East Side.** Formerly home to Russian Jews, Delancey and Elizabeth Streets now offer pasta and silks. To the west lies the fashionable **TriBeCa** ("Triangle Below Canal St."). **SoHo** ("South of Houston"), a former warehouse district west of Little Italy, has transformed into a pocket of gleaming art studios and galleries. Above SoHo huddles **Greenwich Village,** whose lower buildings and jumbled streets have for decades been home to intense political and artistic activity. To its east the **East Village** and **Alphabet City** are bohemian and anarcho-punk hangouts, with crowded streets and an active (though sometimes seedy) nightlife.

A few blocks north of Greenwich Village, stretching across the west teens and twenties, lies **Chelsea,** the late artist Andy Warhol's favorite hangout and former home of Dylan Thomas and Arthur Miller. East of Chelsea, presiding over the East River, is **Gramercy Park,** a pastoral collection of elegant brownstones. **Midtown Manhattan** towers from 34th to 59th St., where traditional and controversial new skyscrapers stand side by side, supporting over a million elevated offices. Here department stores outfit New York; the nearby **Theater District** attempts to entertain the world, or at least people who like musicals, and **Times Square** continues to pulse in neon as the city's energy center.

North of Midtown, **Central Park** slices Manhattan into East and West. On the **Upper West Side,** the gracious museums and residences of Central Park West neighbor the chic boutiques and sidewalk cafés of Columbus Avenue and the hubbub of Broadway. On the **Upper East Side,** the galleries and museums scattered among the elegant apartments of Fifth and Park Avenue create an even more elegant, old-money atmosphere.

Above 97th St., the Upper East Side's opulence ends with a whimper where commuter trains emerge from the tunnel and the *barrio* begins. Above 110th St. on the Upper West Side sits majestic **Columbia University** (founded as King's College in 1754), an urban member of the Ivy League. The communities of **Harlem, East Harlem,** and **Morningside Heights** produced the Harlem Renaissance of black artists and writers in the 1920s and the revolutionary Black Power movement of the 1960s. Although torn by crime, **Washington Heights,** just north of St. Nicholas Park, is nevertheless somewhat safer and more attractive than much of Harlem and is home to Fort Tryon Park, the Met's Medieval Cloisters museum, and a quiet community of Old and New World immigrants. Manhattan ends in a rural patch of wooded land with caves inhabited at various times by the Algonquin and homeless New Yorkers.

MANHATTAN'S STREET PLAN

The city of right angles and tough, damaged people.

—Pete Hamill

Most of Manhattan's street plan was the result of an organized expansion scheme adopted in 1811—from then on, the major part of the city grew in straight lines and at right angles. Above 14th St., the streets form a grid that a novice can quickly master. In the older areas of lower Manhattan, though, the streets are named rather than numbered. Here, the orderly grid of the northern section dissolves into a charming but confusing tangle of old, narrow streets. Bring a map; even long-time neighborhood residents may have trouble directing you to an address.

Above Washington Square, avenues run north-south and streets run east-west. Avenue numbers increase from east to west, and street numbers increase from moving north. Traffic flows east on most even-numbered streets and west on most odd-numbered ones. Two-way traffic flows on the wider streets—Canal, Houston, 14th, 23rd, 34th, 42nd, 57th, 72nd, 79th, 86th, 96th, 110th, 116th, 125th, 145th, and 155th. Four **transverses** cross Central Park: 65/66th St., 79th/81st St., 85/86th and 96/97th St.

ESSENTIALS

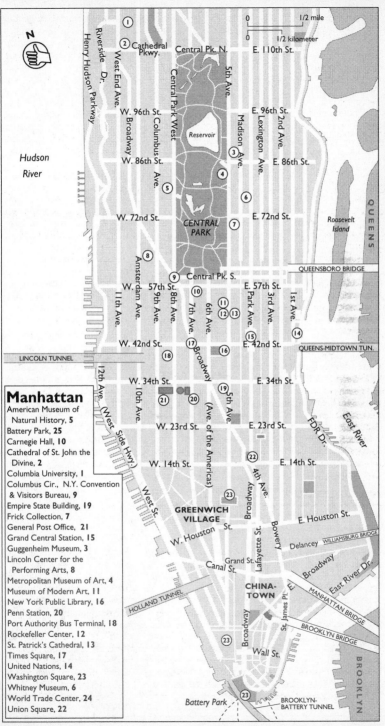

Manhattan

American Museum of
  Natural History, **5**
Battery Park, **25**
Carnegie Hall, **10**
Cathedral of St. John the
  Divine, **2**
Columbia University, **1**
Columbus Cir., N.Y. Convention
  & Visitors Bureau, **9**
Empire State Building, **19**
Frick Collection, **7**
General Post Office, **21**
Grand Central Station, **15**
Guggenheim Museum, **3**
Lincoln Center for the
  Performing Arts, **8**
Metropolitan Museum of Art, **4**
Museum of Modern Art, **11**
New York Public Library, **16**
Penn Station, **20**
Port Authority Bus Terminal, **18**
Rockefeller Center, **12**
St. Patrick's Cathedral, **13**
Times Square, **17**
United Nations, **14**
Washington Square, **23**
Whitney Museum, **6**
World Trade Center, **24**
Union Square, **22**

Most avenues are **one-way.** Tenth, Amsterdam, Hudson, Eighth, Sixth, Madison, Fourth, Third, and First Ave. are northbound. Ninth, Columbus, Broadway below 59th Street, Seventh, Fifth, Lexington, and Second Avenues are southbound. Some avenues allow **two-way traffic:** York, Park, Central Park West, Broadway above 59th St., Third below 24th St., West End, and Riverside Dr.

New York's east/west division refers to an address's location in relation to the two borders of Central Park—**Fifth Avenue** along the east side and **Central Park West** along the west. Below 59th St. (where the park ends), the West Side begins at Fifth Ave. Looking for adjectives to describe where you are relative to something else? Uptown is anywhere north of you, downtown is south, and crosstown means to the east or the west. Want to use nouns? Uptown (above 59th St.) is the area north of Midtown. Downtown (below 34th St.) is the area south of Midtown.

Now for the discrepancies in the system. You may hear **Sixth Avenue** referred to by its new name, **Avenue of the Americas,** though using this moniker is a surefire way to be identified as an out-of-towner. Lexington, Park, and Madison Ave. lie *between* Third and Fifth Ave., where there is no Fourth Ave. On the Lower East Side, there are several avenues east of First Avenue that are lettered rather than numbered: **Avenues A, B, C,** and **D.** Finally, above 59th St. on the West Side, Eighth Avenue becomes Central Park West, Ninth Avenue becomes Columbus Avenue, Tenth Avenue becomes Amsterdam Avenue, and Eleventh Avenue becomes West End Avenue. **Broadway,** which follows an old Algonquin trail, cavalierly defies the rectangular pattern and cuts diagonally across the island, veering west of Fifth Ave. above 23rd St. and east of Fifth Ave. below 23rd St.

Tracking down an address in Manhattan is easy. When given the street number of an address (e.g. #250 E. 52nd St.), find the avenue closest to the address by thinking of Fifth Ave. as point zero on the given street. Address numbers increase as you move east or west of Fifth Ave., in stages of 100. On the East Side, address numbers are 1 at Fifth Ave., 100 at Park Ave., 200 at Third Ave., 300 at Second Ave., 400 at First Ave., 500 at York Ave. (uptown) or Avenue A (in the Village). On the West Side, address

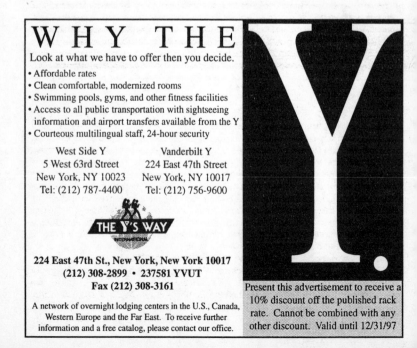

numbers are 1 at Fifth Ave., 100 at Avenue of the Americas (Sixth Ave.), 200 at Seventh Ave., 300 at Eighth Ave., 400 at Ninth Ave., 500 at Tenth Ave., and 600 at Eleventh Ave. In general, numbers increase from south to north along the avenues, but you should always ask for a cross street when you are getting an avenue address.

■ Subways

Operated by **New York City Transit** (718-330-1234, open daily 6am-9pm), the 230-mile New York subway system operates 24 hours a day, 365 days a year. It moves 3.5 million people daily, and has 469 stations with 25 free transfer points. The fare for Metropolitan Transit Authority (MTA) subways is a hefty $1.50 (and there are never discounts for bulk purchases), so groups of four may find a cab ride to be cheaper and more expedient for short distances. Long distances are best traveled by subway, since once inside a passenger may transfer onto any of the other trains without restrictions.

Although by far the quickest means of transportation in Manhattan, the subways are much more useful for traveling north-south than east-west, as there are only two crosstown shuttle trains (42nd and 14th St.). In upper Manhattan and in Queens, Brooklyn, and the Bronx, some lines become "El" trains (for "elevated") and ride above street level to the city's nether regions.

"Express" trains run at all hours and stop only at certain major stations; "locals" stop everywhere. Be sure to check the letter or number and the destination of each train, since trains with different destinations often use the same track. When in doubt, ask a friendly passenger or the conductor, who usually sits near the middle of the train. Once you're on the train, pay attention to the often garbled announcements—trains occasionally change mid-route from local to express or vice-versa, especially when entering or leaving Manhattan.

Efforts at aesthetic sterility in the trains have by no means erased the perils of subway crime, though the numbers are rapidly shrinking. In crowded stations (most notably those around 42nd St.), pickpockets find work; violent crimes, although infrequent, tend to occur in stations that are deserted. Always watch yourself and your belongings, and try to stay in well lit areas near a transit cop or token clerk. Some stations have clearly marked "off-hours" waiting areas that are under observation and significantly safer. Don't stand too close to the platform edge (some people have been pushed, though others have fallen in of their own accord) and keep to well lit areas when waiting for a train. When boarding the train, pick a car with a number of other passengers in it, or sit near the middle of the train, in the conductor's car.

For safety reasons, try to avoid riding the subways between 11pm and 7am, especially above E. 96th St. and W. 120th St. and outside Manhattan. Try also to avoid rush-hour crowds, where you'll be fortunate to find air, let alone seating—on an average morning, more commuters take the E and the F than use the entire rapid-transit system of Chicago (which has the nation's second-largest system). If you must travel at rush hour (7:30-9:30am and 5-6:30pm on every train in every direction), the local train is usually less crowded than the express. Buy a bunch of tokens at once at the booth or, preferably, at the new and more efficient token-vending machines now at many stations; you'll not only avoid a long line, but you'll be able to use all the entrances to a station (some token booths close late at night). You'll see glass globes outside of most subway entrances. If the globe is green it means that the entrance is staffed 24 hours a day. A red globe indicates that the entrance is closed or restricted in some way; read the sign posted above the stairs.

The subway network integrates the **IRT, IND,** and **BMT** lines, now operated by NYC Transit. The names of these lines are still used, although they are no longer of functional significance. The IRT (#1, -#9) and the IND (A, C, D, E, F, Z) are two groups of lines that run through Manhattan; the BMT (B, J, L, M, N, Q, R) runs mostly from lower Manhattan to Queens and Brooklyn. Certain routes also have common, unofficial names based on where they travel, such as the "7th Ave. Line" or the

"Broadway Line" for the #1, 2, 3, or 9; the "8th Ave. Line" for the A and C; the "Lexington Line" for the #4, 5, or 6; and the "Flushing Line" for the #7.

■ Buses

Because buses are often mired in traffic, they can take twice as long as subways, but they are almost always safer, cleaner, and quieter. They'll also get you closer to your destination, since they stop every two blocks or so and run crosstown (east-west), as well as uptown and downtown (north-south). For long-distance travel (over 40 north-south blocks) buses can be a nightmare (except at night and on weekends, when traffic is manageable), but for shorter and especially crosstown trips, buses are often as quick as, and more convenient than, trains. The MTA transfer system provides north-south travelers with a slip valid for a free ride east-west, or vice-versa, but you must ask the driver for a transfer when you board and pay your fare. Make sure you ring when you want to get off. Bus stops are indicated by a yellow-painted curb, but you're better off looking for the blue sign post announcing the bus number or for a glass-walled shelter displaying a map of the bus's route and a schedule of arrival times. A flat fare of $1.50 is charged during peak hours (10am-6pm) when you board; either exact change or a subway token is required (dollar bills are not accepted). Off-peak rides cost $1.

Queens is served in addition by five bus lines: **MTA/Long Island Bus** (516-766-6722; covers mainly Nassau Cty., Long Island) and four private companies: **Green Bus Lines** (718-995-4700; covers mainly Jamaica and central Queens), **Jamaica Buses, Inc.** (718-526-0800; covers mainly Jamaica and Rockaway in Queens), **Queens Surface Corp.** (718-445-3100), and **TriBoro Coach Corp.** (718-335-1000; covers Forest Hills, Ridgewood, and Jackson Hts.), while the Bronx has two: **Liberty Lines Express** (718-652-8400) and **New York Bus Service** (718-994-5500). All of these companies charge $1.50 and accept MTA tokens, though trips back and forth from Manhattan and other boroughs can cost as much as $4. Most of these bus routes do not appear on MTA schedules.

■ Taxis

With drivers cruising at warp speed along near-deserted avenues or dodging through bumper-to-bumper traffic, cab rides can give you painful ulcers. And even if your stomach survives the ride, your budget may not. Still, it's likely that you'll have to take a taxi once in a while, in the interest of convenience or safety. Rides are expensive: the meter starts at $2 and clicks 30¢ for each additional one-fifth of a mile; 30¢ is tacked on for every 75 seconds spent in slow or stopped traffic, a 50¢ surcharge is levied from 8pm to 6am, and passengers pay for all tolls. Don't forget to tip 15%; cabbies need and expect the dough. Before you leave the cab, ask for a receipt, which will have the taxi's identification number (which can be either its meter number or its medallion). This number is necessary to trace lost articles or to make a complaint to the **Taxi Commission** (221-TAXI/8294; 221 W. 41st St., between Times Sq. and the Port Authority Bus Terminal; open Mon.-Fri. 9am-5pm). Since some drivers may illegally try to show the naive visitor the "scenic route," quickly glance at a street map before embarking so you'll have some clue if you're being taken to your destination, or just being taken for a ride. Use only yellow cabs—they're licensed by the state of New York. Cabs of other colors are unlicensed and illegal in NYC. If you can't find anything on the street, commandeer a radio-dispatched cab (see the Yellow Pages under "Taxicabs"). Use common sense to make rides cheaper—catch a cab going your direction and get off at a nearby street corner. When shared with friends a cab can be cheaper, safer, and more convenient than the subway, especially late at night. But you can't cram more than four people into the cab.

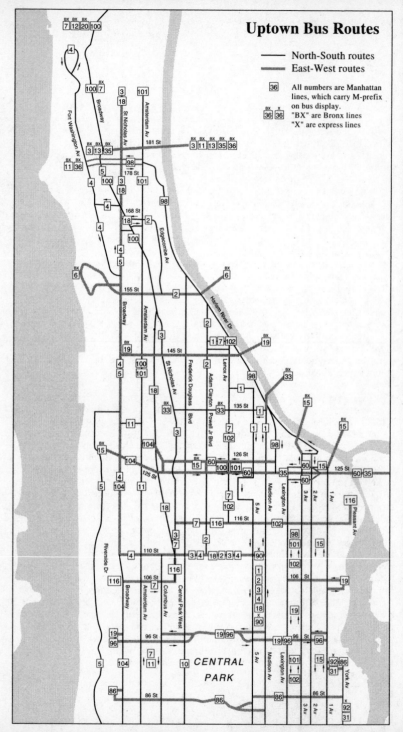

Uptown Bus Routes

—— North-South routes

══ East-West routes

36 All numbers are Manhattan lines, which carry M-prefix on bus display. "BX" are Bronx lines "X" are express lines

Downtown Bus Routes

— North-South routes

— East-West routes

15 All numbers are Manhattan lines, which carry M-prefix on bus display.

15 15 15 "Q" are Queens lines; "B" are Brooklyn lines "X" are express lines

■ Driving

Driving in New York is not something to look forward to. Most New Yorkers only learn to drive in order to escape from the city, and some Manhattanites never learn to drive at all, terrified by the prospect of learning to make wide right turns in midtown traffic. When behind the wheel in New York, you are locked in combat with aggressive taxis, careless pedestrians, and crazed bicycle messengers. Stopped in traffic, you may have to fight off over-eager windshield washers who expect to be paid either to wash the windshield or not to wash the windshield.

Once in Manhattan, traffic continues to be a problem, especially between 57th and 34th St. The even greater hassle of parking joins in to plague the weary. Would-be parallel parkers can rise to this challenge in one of three ways. **Parking lots** are the easiest but the most expensive. In Midtown, where lots are the only option, expect to pay at least $25 per day and up to $15 for two hours. The cheapest parking lots are downtown—try the far west end of Houston St.—but make sure you feel comfortable with the area. Is it populated? Is the lot guarded? Is it well lit?

The second alternative is short-term parking. On the streets, **parking meters** cost 25¢ per 15 minutes, with a limit of one or two hours. Competition is ferocious for the third option, **free parking** at spots on the crosstown streets in residential areas. Read the signs carefully; a space is usually legal only on certain days of the week. The city has never been squeamish about towing, and recovering your car once it's towed will cost $100 or more. Break-ins and car theft are definite possibilities, particularly if you have a radio. Note the preponderance of "No radio in car" signs stuck in car windows. The wailing of a car alarm, a noise as familiar to city residents as the crowing of a rooster is to rural Americans, attracts little if any attention.

Accommodations

If you know someone who knows someone who lives in New York, get that person's phone number. The cost of living in New York can rip the seams out of your wallet. Don't expect to fall into a hotel; if you do, odds are it will be a pit. At true full-service establishments, a night will cost around $125. Hotel tax is 14.25%, with an additional $2 occupancy tax per night on a single room and $4 for suites. Many reasonable choices are available for under $60 a night, but it depends on your priorities. People traveling alone may want to spend more to stay in a safer neighborhood. The young and the outgoing may prefer a budget-style place crowded with students. Honeymooning couples may not.

Hostels offer fewer amenities than more commercial establishments yet manage to preserve a greater feeling of homeyness and camaraderie. Cheap YMCAs and YWCAs offer another budget option, but young backpackers may miss the intimacy and social life a hostel can offer. All of these places advise you to reserve in advance—even once you get to New York, you should call to make sure there are rooms available prior to making the trek there with your bags. Cheap hotels lasso hapless innocents and ingenues around the Penn Station and Times Square areas of Midtown, but you should avoid these honky-tonk spots; the hotel rooms often rent by the hour. Another high concentration of budget hotels can be found in the lower part of East Midtown, south of the Empire State Building. These spots, around Park Avenue South in the 20s, can vary widely in quality.

Crime-free neighborhoods in the city exist only in dreams; never leave anything of value in your room. Most places have safes or lockers available, some for an extra fee. Don't sleep in your car, and never, ever sleep outdoors, anywhere in New York. The city has a hard enough time protecting its vast homeless population—tourists simply would not stand a chance.

■ Hostels

Hostels offer unbeatable deals on indoor lodging and are great places to meet budget travelers from all over the world. Hostels are generally dorm-style accommodations where the sexes usually sleep apart, often in large rooms with bunk beds. Because most hostelers don't place a huge premium on luxury or privacy, hostel beds can cost as little as $15 per night. Expenses and frills are kept to a minimum as a tradeoff. Guests often must rent or bring their own sheets or "sleep sacks" (two sheets sewn together); sleeping bags are usually not allowed. Many hostels make kitchens and utensils available for their guests, and some provide storage areas and laundry facilities. Some hostels are in former hotels, while others like to call themselves hotels; hybrids may offer private singles and doubles in addition to the communal dorms. In most other hostels, you can get a room with fewer occupants and more conveniences for a little more money. Most hostel guests are students or of student age, often from outside the U.S., but the clientele can be surprisingly mixed. This diversity of backgrounds and experiences leads to many late-night conversations in the common room.

If you're going to be traveling extensively in the rest of the U.S. or Canada, you should consider joining **Hostelling International-American Youth Hostels (HI-AYH)** the leading organization of U.S. hostels. There are over 300 HI-AYH-affiliated hostels throughout North America; these are usually kept up to a higher standard than most private hostels, though they tend to be more strict and institutional. HI-AYH runs an excellent hostel in New York, with much space and many amenities (see below). Yearly **HI-AYH membership** is $25 for adults, $15 for those over 54, $10 for those under 18, $35 for families. **Non-members** who wish to stay at an HI-AYH hostel usually pay $3 extra, which can be applied toward membership. For more information, contact HI-AYH, 733 15th St. NW, Ste. 840, Washington, D.C. 20005 (202-783-6161; fax 202-783-6171), or inquire at any HI-affiliated hostel.

Though you may not be as enthusiastic as the Village People, don't overlook the **Young Men's Christian Association (YMCA)** or the **Young Women's Christian Association (YWCA).** The YMCA's and YWCA's rates are often better those of city hotels, and Christianity is neither a requirement nor much of a presence. Singles average $25-42 per night, around $110 per week; rooms include use of a library, pool, and other facilities. You may have to share a room and use a communal bath or shower, however. Some YMCAs in New York (listed below) accept women and families as well as men. Reserve two months in advance, and expect to pay a refundable key deposit of about $5. For information and reservations, write or call **The Y's Way,** 224 E. 47th St., New York, NY 10017 (212-308-2899).

Let's Go lists New York's best hostels and YMCA/YWCAs, ranked according to price, safety, and location.

New York International HI-AYH Hostel, 891 Amsterdam Ave. (932-2300; fax 932-2574), at 103rd St. Subway: #1, 9, B, or C to 102nd St. Located in a block-long, landmark building, this is the mother of all youth hostels—the largest in the U.S., with 90 dorm-style rooms and 530 beds. Shares its site with the **CIEE Student Center** (666-3619), an information depot for travelers, as well as a Council Travel office and supply store where you can buy everything from a money pouch to your next *Let's Go* guide. Spiffy new soft carpets, blonde-wood bunks, and spotless bathrooms. Members' kitchens and dining rooms, coin-operated laundry machines ($1), communal TV lounges, and a large outdoor garden. Walking tours and outings. Key-card entry to individual rooms. Secure storage area and individual lockers. 29-night max. stay, 7-night in summer. Open 24hr. Check-in any time, check-out 11am (late check-out fee $5). No curfew. Members $22 per night; non-members pay $3 more. Family room $66. Groups of 4-12 may get private rooms; groups of 10 or more definitely will. Linen rental $3 per night. Towel $2. Excellent wheelchair access.

International Student Center, 38 W. 88th St. (787-7706; fax 580-9283), between Central Park West and Columbus Ave. Subway: B or C to 86th St. Open only to foreigners (but not Canadians) aged 20-30; you must show a foreign passport or valid visa to be admitted. A once-gracious, welcoming brownstone on a cheerful, tree-lined street noted for frequent celebrity sightings. Single-sex, no-frills bunk rooms. Large basement TV lounge with affable, satisfied guests. Five-day max. stay when full in the summer, 7-day max. the rest of the year. Open daily 8am-11pm. No curfew. A bargain at $12 a night. Key deposit $10. No reservations, and generally full in summer, but call by 10pm for a bed, and they'll hold it for you for two hours. Call before your arrival. No wheelchair access; lots of stairs.

Sugar Hill International House, 722 Saint Nicholas Ave. (926-7030; fax 283-0108), at 146th St. Subway A, B, C, or D to 145th St. Located on Sugar Hill in Harlem, across from the subway station. Reassuring, lively neighborhood. Converted brownstone with huge, well lit, comfortable rooms. Two to ten people fit in rooms that feature sturdy bunkbeds, hand-built by the owners. Staff is usually stunningly friendly and helpful, with a vast knowledge of NYC and the Harlem area. Facilities include kitchens, TV, stereo, and paperback library. Beautiful garden in back. All-female room available. Check-in 9am-10pm. No lockout. Incredible deal at $14 per person. Call in advance. The owners of Sugar Hill also run the new 4-floor hostel next door at 730 Saint Nicholas Ave., the **Blue Rabbit Hostel** (491-3892, 800-610-2030). Similar to the Sugar Hill, but with more doubles and hence more of a sense of privacy. Friendly kittycats, common room, and kitchen. Amazingly spacious rooms. Check-in 9am-10pm. Also $14 per person, $16 for a bed in a double. No lockout. Call in advance. Two week limit.

Banana Bungalow, 250 W. 77th St. (800-6-HOSTEL/467835 or 769-2441; fax 877-5733), between Broadway and 11th Ave. Subway: #1 or 9 to 79th St. Walk two blocks south and turn right. A vast, continually expanding and renovating hostel, with a sun deck on the top floor, a tropical-themed lounge/kitchen, and dorm-style rooms sleeping 4-7 people; the more expensive ones have their own bathrooms, the less expensive share a bathroom among three rooms. Beds $18, less in the off season. Reservations required a few days in advance. Wheelchair access.

De Hirsch Residence, 1395 Lexington Ave. (415-5650 or 800-858-4692; fax 415-5578), at 92nd St. Subway: #6 to 96th St. Affiliated with the 92nd St. YMHA/YWHA, de Hirsch has some of the larger, cleaner, and more convenient hostel housing in the city. Huge hall bathrooms, kitchens, and laundry machines on every other floor give this hostel a collegiate feel. Single-sex floors, strictly enforced. A/C available for $3 per day or $45 per month. Access to the many facilities of the 92nd St. Y, including free Nautilus and reduced rates for concerts. Organized activities such as video nights in the many common rooms and walking tours of New York. The rates are quite reasonable: singles $294 per week ($42 per night); beds in doubles $210 per week ($30 per night). 3-day min. stay. Long-term stays from 2 months to 1 yr. available for $625 per month for singles, $420-500 per month for beds in doubles. Application required at least a month in advance; must be a student or working in the city, and must supply references.

International Student Hospice, 154 E. 33rd St. (228-7470), between Lexington and Third Ave. Subway: #6 to 33rd St. Up a flight of stairs in an inconspicuous converted brownstone with a brass plaque saying "I.S.H." Hostel with helpful and knowledgeable owner; populated by a predominantly European crowd of backpackers and dotted with postcards from former residents. Good location in Murray Hill. Twenty very small rooms with bunk beds bursting with antiques, Old World memorabilia, cracked porcelain tea cups, and clunky oak night tables. The ceilings are crumbling and the stairs slant precariously, but the house is slowly being restored by willing residents. Rooms for 2-4 people and hall bathroom. Large common room, lounge, and enough dusty books to last a summer. $25 per night, with some weekly discounts.

Big Apple Hostel, 119th W. 45th St. (302-2603; fax 302-2605) between Sixth and Seventh Ave. Subway: #1, 2, 3, 9, N, or R to 42nd St.; or B, D, or E to Seventh Ave. Centrally located, this hostel offers clean, comfortable, carpeted rooms, a full kitchen with refrigerator, a big back deck, a luggage room, a grill for barbecuing, a few common rooms, and laundry facilities. Passport nominally required; Americans accepted with out-of-state photo ID or some other convincing means of proving themselves tourists. Open 24hr. Bunk in dorm-style room with shared bath $22. Singles $58. Lockers in some rooms, but bring your own lock. Free coffee and tea in the kitchen. There's even a playful house cat, Caesar. No reservations accepted Aug.-Sept., but they'll hold a bed if you call after 11am on the day you want to arrive. Reservations accepted Oct.-July; make them a few weeks in advance for June and July.

Chelsea International Hostel, 251 W. 20th St. (647-0010), between Seventh and Eighth Ave. Subway: #1, 9, C, or E to 23rd St. As Chelsea continues to gentrify, this 47-bed hostel becomes an increasingly better deal. The congenial staff offers their guests free beer and pizza on Wed. nights, and free beer (bring your own pizza) on Sun. All rooms have windows, and all guests have access to a backyard garden. Located in south Chelsea on a block with a police precinct, this hostel is fairly safe. Cramped but adequate 4-person dorm rooms $20 per bed; private rooms $45. Reservations recommended; call ahead.

Gershwin Hotel, 7 E. 27th St. (545-8000; fax 684-5546), between Fifth and Madison Ave. Subway: N or R to 28th St. With a large, cool building full of pop art and twenty-somethings, the Gershwin seems more like a living MTV show idea than a place to stay. The hotel hosts a next-door gallery, an amateur band night (Sat.), and a hip bar, all of which throw frequent parties, including a recent Andy Warhol seance. There is a "Love Boat" feel here—summer days in the rooftop garden often become unabashed scamming sessions. Passport or ID proving out-of-state or foreign residence required. 21-day max. stay. 24-hr. reception. Check-out 11am. No curfew. 4-bed dorms $20 per bed. Private rooms are also available. Doubles and triples $75-105. Continental breakfast $2.50.

Mid-City Hostel, 608 Eighth Ave. (704-0562), between 39th and 40th St. on the 3rd and 4th floors. Subway: #1, 2, 3, 9, N, or R to 42nd St.-Seventh Ave.; or A, C, or E to 42nd St.-Ninth Ave. On the east side of Eighth Ave. No sign: just look for a yellow building with the street number on the small door (and the sign advertising the fortune teller who works inside at the base of the stairs). Don't be intimidated by the lively neighborhood and busy streets that surround this comfortable, homey hostel. Brick walls, skylights, and old wooden beams across the ceiling make it feel like a friend's apartment. Caters mainly to an international backpacking crowd—a passport or valid student ID is required. Small breakfast included. 7-day max. stay in summer. Lock out noon-6pm. Curfew Sun.-Thurs. midnight, Fri.-Sat. 1am. Bunk in mixed dorm-style room with shared bath $20 (Oct. to late June, $18). Reservations are required and should be made weeks in advance for summer. Absolutely no smoking allowed in the hostel.

Chelsea Center Hostel, 313 W. 29th St. (643-0214), between Eighth and Ninth Ave. Subway: #1, 2, 3, 9, A, C, E to 34th St. Gregarious, knowledgeable staff will help you out with New York tips in multiple languages. Room for 28 guests—16 of these must stay in the same windowless basement room. The lovely backyard garden helps to alleviate the cramped feeling, and the hostel is one of the friendlier and more accommodating around. 2 showers. Check in anytime, but lockout 11am-5pm. Dorm beds in summer $20, in winter $18. Light breakfast included. Blankets and sheets provided. Be sure to call ahead; it's usually full in summer.

Uptown Hostel, 239 Lenox/Malcolm X Ave. (666-0559), at 122nd St. Subway: #2 or 3 to 125th St. Currently run by the knowledgeable and helpful Gisèle out of the New York Bed and Breakfast (p. 78). Bunk beds, sparkling clean, comfy rooms, and spacious hall bathrooms. Wonderful new common room and recently sanded floors. $12 per night. Call 1-2 weeks in advance during the summer and at least 2 days in advance any other time.

YMCA—Vanderbilt, 224 E. 47th St. (756-9600; fax 752-0210), between Second and Third Ave. Subway: #6 to 51st St. or E, F to Lexington-Third Ave. Five blocks from Grand Central Station. Convenient and well run, with reasonable prices and vigilant security. Clean, brightly lit lobby bustles with jabbering internationals touting internal-frame backpacks. Rooms are quite small, and bathroom-to-people ratio is pretty low, but aah, the perks! Lodgers get free run of the copious athletic facilities (StairMasters, aerobics classes, Nautilus machines, pool, and sauna), safe-deposit boxes, and guided tours of the city. 25-day max. stay; no NYC residents. Check-in 1-6pm; after 6pm must have major credit card to check in. Check-out at noon, but luggage storage until departure ($1 per bag). Five shuttles daily to the airports. Singles $51. Doubles $63. Key deposit $10 (refundable). Make reservations 1-2 weeks in advance and guarantee with a deposit. Wheelchair access.

YMCA—West Side, 5 W. 63rd St. (787-4400, fax 580-0441). Subway: #1, 9, A, B, C, or D to 59th St.-Columbus Circle. Small, well maintained rooms but dilapidated halls in a big, popular Y with an impressive, Islamic-inspired façade. Free access to 2 pools, indoor track, racquet courts, and Nautilus equipment. Showers on every floor and spotless bathrooms. A/C and cable TV in every room. Check-out at noon; no curfew. Singles $51, with bath $75. Doubles $53, with bath $85. Reservations recommended. A few stairs at entrance; otherwise wheelchair-friendly.

YMCA—McBurney, 206 W. 24th St. (741-9226; fax 741-0012), between Seventh and Eighth Ave. Subway: #1, 9, C, or E to 23rd St. A working YMCA with a lot of activity on the ground floor. The no-frills rooms upstairs are livable, but no A/C. Mix of elderly locals, students, and other travelers. Good security. The familiar scent of chlorine pervades throughout. Singles $38, with TV $43. Doubles $52. Triples $68. Quads $86. Rooms with TVs available. Free access to gym. 25-day limit on stays. $122-per-week student rate. Usually has vacancies, but reservations are advisable. Wheelchair access.

YMCA—Flushing, 138-46 Northern Blvd., Flushing, Queens (718-961-6880; fax 718-461-4691), between Union and Bowne St. Subway: #7 to Main St.; the "Y" is about a 10-min. walk. Walk north on Main St. (the Ave. numbers should get smaller as you walk), and turn right onto Northern Blvd. **Men only.** The area between the Y and Flushing's nearby shopping district is lively and well populated, but the neighborhood quickly deteriorates north of Northern Blvd. Standard Y rooms—clean but worn, with hall bathroom. Daily maid service provided. Gym, Nautilus, squash, and swimming facilities included. $28-37 per night, $130-180 per week. 28-day maximum stay. Key deposit $10. Passport or driver's license required. Make reservations at least a week in advance.

YMCA—Central Queens, 89-25 Parsons Blvd., Jamaica, Queens (718-739-6600, fax 718-658-7233), at 90th Ave. Subway: E or J to Jamaica Center. Parsons Blvd. joins Archer Ave. right at the subway station; walk north along it across Jamaica Ave. and one block farther to 90th Ave. **Men only.** In a bustling, noisy downtown district. Concrete prevails in the small but neat private rooms. Gym, Nautilus, racquetball, and swimming facilities included. $36 per night; $138.50 per week. Key deposit $10. Passport or driver's license required. No reservations.

■ Dormitories

Miss that two-by-four dorm ambience? Now you can experience it while traveling, too. Some colleges and universities open their residence halls to conferences and travelers, especially during the summer. You may have to share a bath, but rates are often low and facilities are usually clean and well maintained. If you hope to stay at a school, contact its housing office before you leave.

Columbia University, 1230 Amsterdam Ave. (678-3235; fax 678-3222), at 120th St. Subway: #1 or 9 to 116th St. Whittier Hall sets aside some rooms for visitors year-round. Rooms are small but clean. 24-hr. tight security. Not the safest neighborhood, but well populated until fairly late at night. Singles $35. Doubles with A/C and bath (some with kitchen) $65. Reserve in advance.

New York University, 14a Washington Pl. (998-4621). NYU's Summer Housing Office rents rooms on a weekly basis (3-week min., 12-week max.) from mid-May to mid-August. Rooms available with or without A/C, bath, or kitchenette; boarders without kitchens must join the meal plan for $70 per person per week. Anyone is eligible. Singles without A/C or meal plan $105 per week, doubles $70 per person per week. Doubles with kitchen and A/C $130 per person per week. Rooms are located in various dorms of NYU's campus in Greenwich Village and vary in size but are all eminently livable. Call after Jan. 1 for more information and reservations; reserve by May 1.

Fashion Institute of Technology, 210 W. 27th St. (760-7885), between Seventh and Eighth Ave. Subway: #1 or 9 to 28th St. Decent neighborhood, but adjacent to the sleazy Penn Station area; exercise caution at night. Most residents are F.I.T. summer students, but others can rent rooms by the week or month, space permitting. Application required; call or pick one up, but allow a couple of days for processing. Office open Mon.-Fri. 8am-7pm. Spartan dorm-style doubles with communal baths in a gray, boxy building. $157 per person per week (1-week min. stay). Double-occupancy suites with kitchen and bath, $790 per person per month (1-month min. stay). Reservations necessary; full payment in advance. Housing offered from first week of June until July 31. Some rooms wheelchair-accessible. $5 charge per guest signed in from 2am-9am.

■ Hotels

No chocolate dainties for you, O budget traveler; consider yourself lucky if you've found a reasonably priced room. A single in a cheap hotel should cost $35-60. Most hotel rooms can (and should) be reserved in advance. Ask the hotel owner if you can see a room before you pay for it. You should be told in advance whether the bathroom is communal or private. Most hotels require a key deposit when you register. Check-in usually takes place between 11am and 6pm, check-out before 11am. You may be able to store your gear for the day even after vacating your room and returning the key, but most proprietors will not take responsibility for the safety of your belongings. Some hotels require a *non-refundable* deposit for reservations. However, the hotel may allow you to use your deposit on a future stay at the hotel.

If you have a particular fondness for Hiltons and Marriotts beyond your means, consider joining **Discount Travel International,** 114 Forrest Ave. #203, Narberth, PA 19072 (215-668-7184; fax 215-668-9182). For an annual membership fee of $45, you and your household will have access to a wealth of discounts on unsold hotel rooms, airline tickets, cruises, car rentals, etc., which can save you as much as 50%.

Let's Go has found the best budget hotels and ranked them in order of value, based on price, facilities, safety, and location.

Carlton Arms Hotel, 160 E. 25th St. (684-8337, for reservations 679-0680), between Lexington and Third Ave. Subway: #6 to 23rd St. Stay inside a submarine and peer through windows at the lost city of Atlantis, travel to Renaissance Venice, or stow your clothes in a dresser suspended on an Astroturf wall. Each room has been designed in a different motif by a different avant-garde artist. "I sought to create a resounding rhythm that echoed wall-to-wall, layer upon layer, to fuse our separate impressions into one existence," writes the artist of room 5B. Hmm. Aggressive adornment doesn't completely obscure the age of these budget rooms, but it goes a long way toward providing distractions. You won't pay that much, either. Singles $49, with bath $57. Doubles $62, with bath $69. Triples $74, with bath $84. Pay for seven or more nights up front and get a 10% discount. Make reservations for summer at least two months in advance. Confirm reservations at least 10 days in advance. Discounts for students and foreign travelers: Single $44, with bath $53. Double $57, with bath $65. Triple $68, with bath $78.

Roger Williams Hotel, 28 E. 31st St. (684-7500, reservations 800-637-9773; fax 576-4343), at Madison Ave. in pleasant Murray Hill neighborhood. Subway: #6 to 33rd St. You can't fit all of your friends into the elevator, but this hotel under renovation, with its spacious, clean rooms, should suit your every need. Small refrigerators will hold leftovers from the many take-out restaurants lining Madison Ave. All rooms with toilet, bath, phone, stove, and kitchenette. 24-hr. security. Singles $79. Doubles or twins $89. Triples $99. Quads $109.

Portland Square Hotel, 132 W. 47th St. (382-0600 or 800-388-8988; fax 382-0684), between Sixth and Seventh Ave. Subway: B, D, F, Q to 50th St.-Sixth Ave. Rooms are carpeted, clean, comfortable, and A/C-equipped. Perks include cable TV, sink, and safe in every room, but the hotel's main asset is its great location. Attracts mostly foreigners. Singles with shared bath $50, with private bath $70. Doubles $94. Triples $99. Quads $104.

Herald Square Hotel, 19 W. 31st St. (279-4017 or 800-727-1888; fax 643-9208), at Fifth Ave. Subway: B, D, F, N, or R to 34th St. In the original Beaux Arts home of Life magazine (built in 1893). Above the entrance note the reading cherub entitled "Winged Life," carved by Philip Martiny. The sculpture was a frequent presence on the pages of early Life magazines. Work by some of America's most noted illustrators adorns the lobby, halls, and rooms. Tiny, clean, newly renovated rooms with color TV, small refrigerators, phones, and A/C. Singles with shared bath $45, with private bath $60. Doubles $65, with 2 beds $99. International students get a 10% discount. Reservations recommended for the cheaper rooms; without them you may have to take something more expensive.

Pioneer Hotel, 341 Broome St. (226-1482), between Elizabeth St. and the Bowery. Located between Little Italy and the Lower East Side in a century-old (but recently renovated) building, the Pioneer is a great place to stay if you want to be close to the hip nightlife of SoHo and the East Village. NYU film students like to shoot their film projects in this hotel's classic rooms. All rooms have TVs and sinks; there are public telephones in the lobby and messages can be left at the desk. Singles $34, with A/C $40. Doubles $48, with A/C $56, with bath $60. Singles also rent for $210 per week

Pickwick Arms Hotel, 230 E. 51st St. (355-0300 or 800-PICKWIK/742-5945; fax 755-5029), between Second and Third Ave. Subway: #6 to 51st St. or E, F to Lexington-Third Ave. Business types congregate in this well located and well priced mid-sized hotel. Chandeliered marble lobby filled with the silken strains of Top-40 Muzak contrasts with tiny rooms and microscopic hall bathrooms. Roof garden and airport service available. Check-in 2pm; check-out 1pm. Singles $50, with shared bath $60. Doubles with bath $99. Studios (two double beds) $148. Additional person in room $12. Gets very busy, so make reservations.

Hotel Wolcott, 4 W. 31st St. (268-2900; fax 563-0096), between Fifth and Sixth Ave. Subway: B, D, F, N, or R to 34th St. An ornately mirrored and marbled entrance hall leads into this newly renovated hotel. New furniture and carpeting, cable TV, and efficient A/C. Singles $80. Doubles $85. Triples $95. ISIC will get you a 10% discount. Self-service laundry in building. Reservations recommended a month or more in advance for summer.

Washington Square Hotel, 103 Waverly Pl. (777-9515 or 800-222-0418; fax 979-8373), at MacDougal St. Subway: A, B, C, D, E, F, or Q to W. 4th St. Fantastic location. Glitzy marble and brass lobby, with a peachy medieval gate in front. A/C, TV, and key-card entry to individual rooms. Recent improvements include the addition of a restaurant/bar, lounge, meeting room, and exercise room. Clean and comfortable; friendly and multilingual staff. Singles $85. Doubles $110. Two twin beds $117. Quads $138. Rollaway bed $12. ISIC holders get a 10% discount. Reservation required 2-3 weeks in advance.

Hotel Iroquois, 49 W. 44th St. (840-3080 or 800-332-7220; fax 398-1754), near Fifth Ave. Subway: B, D, or F to 47th St.-Rockefeller Ctr. Pink and blue, slightly worn but spacious rooms in an old pre-war building. This hotel once hosted James Dean and is now the stop of choice for Greenpeace and other environmental activists when in town. Check-out noon. Singles and doubles $75-100. Suites (5-person max.) $125-150. Student discounts available, and all prices negotiable during winter. Reservations advisable a few weeks in advance in summer.

Hotel Grand Union, 34 E. 32nd St. (683-5890; fax 689-7397), between Madison and Park Ave. Subway: #6 to 33rd St. Centrally located and recently renovated rooms equipped with cable TV, phone, A/C, a mini-fridge, and full bathroom. 24-hr. security. Singles and doubles $79-95. Triples $90-104. Quads $105+. Two-room suite from $105.

Hotel Stanford, 43 W. 32nd St. (563-1480; fax 629-0043), between Fifth Ave. and Broadway in NY's Korean district. Subway: B, D, F, N, or R to 34th St. A glitzy Korean confection of a hotel, the lobby glitters with sparkling ceiling lights and a well polished marble floor. Moreover, the Stanford adjoins the extremely authentic **Gam Mee OK** restaurant, which serves up such delicacies as ox-bone soup ($7), pork bellies, and cows' feet ($15). There's also a coffee shop in the lobby. Rooms are well cooled and impeccably clean, with firm mattresses and plush carpeting. TV, A/C, and small refrigerators in every room. Check-out at noon. Reservations strongly recommended. Singles $85. Doubles $100. Triples $130.

Senton Hotel, 39-41 W. 27th St. (684-5800), at Broadway. Subway: R to 28th St. Comfortable beds in spacious quarters, amid a bevy of large-print floral wallpapers. TV, including cable (HBO and dirty movies). Basic accommodations—Spartan, but most rooms are newly renovated, with a shockingly incongruous bright-blue paint job. Home to many locals. The hotel has 24-hr. security and guests are not allowed. Singles with hall bath $40. Doubles $50. Suites (2 double beds) $65.

Arlington Hotel, 18-20 W. 25th St. (645-3990 or 800-488-0920; fax 633-8952), between Broadway and Sixth Ave. Subway: F or R to 23rd St. Prides itself on hospitality and courteous service. Caters to foreign travelers, especially those from Asia: signs are translated into Chinese, Korean, and Japanese. Clean-smelling refurbished rooms, all with TV and A/C. Single or double (1 bed) $85, Twin (2 beds) $98. 10% ISIC discount. Credit card reservations guaranteed.

Malibu Studios Hotel, 2688 Broadway (222-2954; fax 678-6842), at 103rd St. Subway: #1 or 9 to 103rd St. Tropical motif. Located on a fun and funky block. Brightly lit blue rooms with refrigerator and hot plate. Variable rates. Single with shared bath $35, with private bath $60. Doubles $50, with private bath $70. Triples $60, with private bath $80. Quads $80, with private bath $90. Triples and quads consist of two double beds. The friendly staff often doles out VIP passes to popular clubs, including the Tunnel and Webster Hall. Ask about student, off-season, and weekly/monthly discounts. No wheelchair access.

Madison Hotel, 21 E. 27th St. (532-7373 or 595-9100; fax 686-0092), at Madison Ave. Subway: #6, N, or R to 28th St. Dark, tight hallways with precipitous stairs, but big rooms with color TV, refrigerators, and newly renovated private baths. 14-day max. stay. $5 cable deposit. Singles $60-70. Doubles $75.

Hotel Remington, 129 W. 46th St. (221-2600; fax 764-7481), between Broadway and Sixth Ave. Subway: B, D, or F to 47th St.-Rockefeller Ctr.; or #1, 2, 3, 9, N, or R to 42nd St.-Times Sq. Centrally located and close to theaters and Fifth Avenue shopping attractions. Plush carpeting, bedspread, and curtains in matching orange hang in reasonably large rooms. All rooms with color TV, cable, self-dialing telephones, and A/C. Barber shop downstairs just in case you need a quick trim before dinner and a show. Prices range from approx. $90 for a single to $120 for a quad with two double beds.

Riverview Hotel, 113 Jane St. (929-0060; fax 675-8581), near West St. on the Hudson in Greenwich Village, and between W. 12th and W. 14th St. Subway: #1 or 9 to Christopher St. Moderately safe area. Clean and relatively friendly, but no frills. Singles are cramp-inducingly small but doubles are decent. No deadbolts on room doors. Shared co-ed bathrooms on the hall. Singles with TV $34 or $155 per week., plus a $5 key deposit. Doubles $54 or $275 per week., plus $5 deposit.

■ Bed and Breakfasts

Bed and Breakfasts (private homes that rent out one or more spare rooms to travelers) are a great alternative to impersonal hotel and motel rooms. They're hardly your stereotypical B&Bs—no sleepy New England village squares or big front porches—but Manhattan does have a wide selection. Many don't have phones, TVs, or showers with their rooms. Reservations should be made a few weeks in advance, usually with a deposit. Most apartments listed have two-night minimums. Listings are divided into "hosted"—meaning traditional B&B arrangements—and "unhosted," meaning that the people renting you the apartment will not be there. Most agencies offer a wide range of prices, depending on the accommodation's size and quality and the neighborhood's safety. Apartments in the West Village and the Upper East Side cost the most. Most agencies also list accommodations in boroughs other than Manhattan; these can be an excellent budget alternative.

New York Bed and Breakfast, 134 W. 119th St. (666-0559), between Lenox and Adam Clayton Powell Ave. in Harlem. Subway: #2 or 3 to 116th St. or 125th St. Run by the incredibly warm and friendly Gisèle, this B&B features a double and single bed in every well kept room, croissants, and the aloof black cat Alain. (Alain is restricted to certain rooms, so folks with allergies need not fret.) Gisèle runs tours of Harlem, trips to jazz clubs and gospel choirs, speaks French, rents bicycles, and will help you find an apartment. Two-day min. stay. Gisèle lives in the brownstone; no lockout time. $35 per person per night or $20 per person per room for a double. Call 1-2 weeks in advance during the summer.

Bed and Breakfast of New York (645-8134). 300 listings throughout the city. 25% deposit required when you make your reservations, refundable up to 10 days before your visit, minus $20 booking fee. Deposits payable by personal check, but only cash, certified checks, or traveler's checks accepted for the bill. Hosted accommodations: singles $60-80 per night, doubles $90-100 per night. Unhosted one-bedroom apartments from $90-200. Weekly and monthly rates available.

New World Bed and Breakfast (675-5600 or toll-free from the U.S. and Canada, 800-443-3800; fax 675-6366). About 150 listings, in all parts of Manhattan. When you make your reservation, you must pay with a credit card 25% of the total bill as a deposit; refundable up to ten days before your visit, with $25 cancellation fee. Hosted accommodations. Singles start at $65, doubles at $80. Studio (1 bedroom) apartments begin at $100.

Urban Ventures (594-5650; fax 947-9320). The oldest and most established agency in the city. A whopping 700 listings covering most neighborhoods in Manhattan, plus additional listings for Brooklyn and Queens. 2-night min. in bed and breakfasts, 3-night min. in unhosted accommodations. Hosted accommodations: singles $55-80, doubles $65-90, triples from $120. Unhosted accommodations: studio apartments $75-110, one-bedroom $110-140, two-bedroom $165-230.

Food & Drink

This city takes its food seriously. For those whose culinary experience has been limited to the classic American strip-mall fast-food joint, New York will dazzle you with its stupendously diverse culinary bounty. Ranging from mom-and-pop diners to elegant five-star eateries, the food offered here will suit all appetites and pocketbooks.

New York's restaurants do more than the United Nations to promote international goodwill and cross-cultural exchanges. City dining spans the globe, with restaurants ranging from relatively tame sushi bars to wild combinations like Afghani/Italian and Mexican/Lebanese. In a city where the melting pot is sometimes less than tranquil, one can still peacefully sample Chinese pizza or a Cajun knish. Just remember to be open-minded: you won't get very far in New York if you eat only what you can pronounce.

Chinese restaurants spice up every neighborhood and even fill up a town of their own. For a taste of bell'Italia, cruise to Mulberry Street in Little Italy. For the most realistic of post-post-revolutionary Russian cuisine, make a trip to Brooklyn's Brighton Beach, where Soviet emigrés have built their community. Many Eastern European dishes have become New York staples. The plump traditional dumplings (*knishes*) make a great lunch; eat potato knishes with mustard or meat knishes with *yoich* (gravy). Fill up on *pirogi,* Polish (or Ukrainian or Russian) dough creations stuffed with fruit, potato, or cheese and garnished with fried onions and sour cream; sample some spicy Polish *kielbasa* (sausage), or pig out on *blintzes,* thin pancakes rolled around sweet cheese, blueberries, and other divine fillings. Grab a *bialy,* a flat, soft, onion-flavored bagel cognate, from a local bakery.

And of course there are always two old favorites: pizza and bagels. New Yorkers like their pizza thin and hot, with no small amount of grease. Warfare between pizzerias has been going on for years; the major issue is not the taste but the name. There are now a full 22 institutions fighting over the right to call themselves the Original Ray's. Who is Ray? Who cares? No-name pizzerias can offer fare as fine as titled competitors. The humble bagel is mighty Brooklyn's major contribution to Western civilization. Bagels come in a rainbow of flavors—the most common being plain, egg, poppyseed, and onion—but only one shape, well suited for a thick layer of cream cheese. Exiles from the city often find bagel deprivation to be one of the biggest indignities of life outside of New York.

Those low on cash can take advantage of the inexpensive lunch specials offered by otherwise unapproachable restaurants—a large Hungarian lunch can be yours for $5. Almost any local coffeeshop will serve you a full American breakfast with eggs, bacon, toast, and coffee for $2-3. Don't expect to find any gargantuan supermarkets in this town; the many bakeries, corner markets, and greengrocers make New York's streets more fruitful than air-conditioned aisles. Atriums and public parks throughout the city provide idyllic urban settings for picnics, and many of the larger museums offer picturesque, artwork-filled cafés to facilitate your digestion. For those who like to eat on the street, pushcart vendors abound. Sidewalk gourmands can stick with the old roving standbys on wheels (hot dogs, pretzels, roasted chestnuts), or try something more adventurous (shish kebabs, falafel, knishes).

New Yorkers dine later than most Americans. In New York you can find a restaurant open and serving dinner almost anytime between afternoon and midnight. Make reservations or arrive before 7pm to beat the crowds to the best tables in the house. Remember to read the daily specials on the wall, and don't judge a restaurant by its façade; good things often come in a dingy package.

ORGANIZATION

We have prefaced the restaurant listings, which are organized by neighborhood, with a list of the same restaurants, categorized by type of food and by features (delivery, open late, outdoor dining, etc.). Restaurants in the "*Let's Go* Pick" category feature extraordinary combinations of low prices and quality and are denoted in the *By Type of Food*, *By Feature*, and *By Neighborhood* listings with a star (★). Every restaurant listed in the *By Type of Food* and *By Feature* sections is followed by an abbreviated neighborhood label, which directs you to the section within the *By Neighborhood* list where you'll find the restaurant's complete write-up. The abbreviations used are as follows:

EM	East Midtown	EV	East Village, Lower East Side, and Alphabet City
WM	West Midtown	CHT	Chinatown
UG	Union Square,Gramercy Park	LI	Little Italy
CH	Chelsea	LM	Lower Manhattan
UES	Upper East Side	B	Brooklyn
UWS	Upper West Side	Q	Queens
H	Harlem	BX	Bronx
GV	Greenwich Village	SI	Staten Island
ST	SoHo and TriBeCa	HO	Hoboken, NJ
★	*Let's Go* pick		

BY TYPE OF FOOD

New American
★Barking Dog Luncheonette *UES*
 Blue Collar Café *MH*
 Bubby's *ST*
 Chat n' Chew *UG*
 Eighteenth and Eighth *CH*
 Elephant and Castle *GV*
 Hourglass Tavern *WM*
 Prince St. Bar and Restaurant *ST*
 Quantum Leap *GV*
 Short Ribs *B*
★Yaffa's Tea Room *ST*

Standard American
 Diane's Uptown *UWS*
 EJ's Luncheonette *UES*
 Empire Kosher Chicken
  Restaurant *Q*
 First Edition *Q*
 Hamburger Harry's *FD*
 Happy Burger *UWS*
 Jackson Hole Wyoming *UES*
 Jimmy's Famous Heros *B*
 Junior's *B*
 Mama's Food Shop *EV*
 Moon Dance Diner *ST*
 Ottomanelli's Café *UES*
 Oysters Bar and Restaurant *EM*
 Space Untitled *ST*
 Utopia-W-Restaurant *CH*
 Viand *UES*
 Washington Square Restaurant *GV*

Bakery
 Bel Gusto Bagel Smashery and
  Café *HO*
 Damascus Bakery *B*
 D.G. Bakery *IT*
 Egidio's Pastry Shop *BX*
 Galaxy Pastry Shop *Q*
★H&H Bagels *UWS*
 Hammond's Finger Lickin' Bakery *B*
 Hot Bagels and Tasty Bakery *UWS*
★The Hungarian Pastry Shop *MH*
 New Lung Fong Bakery *CHT*
★Poseidon Bakery *WM*
 Sarabeth's Kitchen *UES*
 Sea Lane Bakery *B*
 Soutine *UWS*
 Yonah Schimmel Knishery *EV*

Barbecue and Ribs
★Brother Jimmy's BBQ *UES*
 Brother's BBQ *ST*
 Dallas BBQ *UWS*
 Short Ribs *B*

British and Irish
 Siné *EV*
 Tea and Sympathy *UWS*

Café
 Bagel Point Café *B*
★Bell Caffe *ST*
 Biblio's *ST*
 Big Cup *CH*
 B.M.W. Gallery and Coffee Magic *CH*

Café Classico *EM*
Café Gitane *LI*
Café La Fortuna *UWS*
Café Lalo *UWS*
Café Mozart *UWS*
Caffè Borgia *GV*
Caffè Dante *GV*
Caffè Egidio *BX*
Caffè Mona Lisa *GV*
Caffè Reggio *GV*
Caffè Roma *LI*
De Lillo Pastry Shop *BX*
Ferrara *LI*
First Street Café *EV*
Kokobar *B*
L Café *B*
La Bella Ferrara *LI*
Le Gamin Café *ST*
Lo Spuntino *LI*
Lucky's Juice Joint *ST*
Maria Caffè *EM*
Ottomanelli's Café *UES*
Pink Pony Café *EV*
Sarabeth's Kitchen *UES*

Candy

Eddie's Sweet Shop *Q*
★Philip's Confections *B*

Central and Eastern European

Kiev *EV*
K.K. Restaurant *EV*
Knish Knosh *Q*
★Primorski Restaurant *B*
Ratner's Restaurant *EV*
Rush'n Express *UES*
Stylowa Restaurant *B*
★Teresa's *B*
Uncle Vanya Café *WM*
Veselka *EV*
Yonah Schimmel Knishery *EV*

Chinese

Empire Szechuan Balcony *UG*
Empire Szechuan Gourmet *UWS*
Excellent Dumpling House *CHT*
Fortune Garden *EM*
Hong Fat *CHT*
House of Vegetarian *CHT*
HSF *CHT*
★La Caridad *UWS*
La Favorita *CH*
Mee Noodle Shop and Grill *EV*
New Lung Fong Bakery *CHT*
New Oriental Pearl Restaurant *CHT*
Ollie's *UWS*
Oriental Palace *B*

Peking Duck House *CHT*
Sam Chinita *CH*
Szechuan Cottage *Q*
Taipei Noodle House *EM*
Tibetan Shambala *UWS*
20 Mott St. Restaurant *CHT*
Tang Tang Noodles and More *UES*
Yeun Yeun Restaurant *CHT*
★Zen Palate *UG*

Creole, Cajun, and Caribbean

Ray's Jerk Chicken *B*
Hammond's Finger Lickin' Bakery *B*
Negril *CH*

Deli

Carnegie Delicatessen *WM*
Jimmy's Famous Heros *B*
Katz's Delicatessen *EV*
★Pastrami King *Q*
Second Ave. Delicatessen *EV*

Diner

Bendix Diner *CH*
The Den *UES*
★EJ's Luncheonette *UES*
Frank's Papaya *FD*
Jackson Hole, Wyoming *UES*
Johnny Rocket's *HO*
Moon Dance Diner *ST*
Moonstruck *EM*
Sunburnt Espresso Bar *UG*
★Tom's Restaurant *B*
★Tom's Restaurant *MH*
Washington Square Restaurant *GV*

Ethiopian

Abyssinia *ST*
★Massawa *MH*

Fast Food

Frank's Papaya *FD*
McDonald's *FD*
Nathan's *B*
Rush'n Express *UES*

French

★Florent *GV*

Greek and Middle Eastern

Amir's Falafel *MH*
Andalousia *GV*
★Cleopatra's Needle *UWS*
★Damask Falafel *EV*
Fountain Café *B*
Happy Burger *UWS*
Khyber Pass Restaurant *EV*
★Moroccan Star *B*

FOOD AND DRINK

Olive Tree Café *GV*
Oznaut's Dish *B*
★Poseidon Bakery *WM*
Time-Out Kosher Pizza and
Israeli Food *H*
★Uncle George's *Q*
Yaffa Café *EV*

Indian, Pakistani, and Afghan

Anand Bhavan *Q*
★Ariana Afghan Kebab *WM*
Indian Café *UWS*
Khyber Pass Restaurant *EV*
Madras Mahat *UG*
Minar *WM*
Rose of India *EV*

Italian

Ann & Tony's *BX*
Ballato *LI*
Benito One *LI*
Carmine's *UWS*
Cucina di Pesce *EV*
★Cucina Stagionale *GV*
D.G. Bakery *IT*
Dominick's *BX*
ecco'la *UES*
Il Fornaio *LI*
La Mela *LI*
Mappamondo *GV*
Maria Caffè *EM*
Mario's *BX*
Paninoteca *LI*
Pasquale's Rigoletto *BX*
Pietro and Vanessa *LI*
Puglia Restaurant *LI*
Ramdazzo's Clam Bar *B*
Red Rose Restaurant *B*
Ristorante Taormina *LI*
Rocky's Italian Restaurant *LI*
Taormina Ristorante *BX*
Tutta Pasta *GV*
Vincent's Clam Bar *LI*
Zigolini's *FD*

Japanese and Korean

Daikichi Sushi *UWS*
★Dosanko *EM*
Mill Korean Restaurant *MH*
Obento Delight *UWS*
★Sapporo *WM*
Woo Chon Restaurant *Q*

Kosher

Empire K.'s Roasters *Q*
Gertel's Bake Shop *EV*
Knish Knosh *Q*
Ratner's Restaurant *EV*

Time-Out Kosher Pizza and
Israeli Food *H*

Latin American and Spanish

El Chivito D'Oro *Q*
El Gran Castillo de Jagua *B*
El Pollo *UES*
Emporium Brasil *WM*
Meson Sevilla *WM*
★La Caridad *UWS*
★La Casita Restaurant *H*
La Isla *HO*
La Rosita *MH*
Las Tres Palmas *B*
National Café *EV*
Piu Bello *Q*
Rice and Beans *WM*
Sam Chinita *CH*
Spain *GV*

Mexican/Tex-Mex

Arriba! Arriba! *UES*
★Benny's Burritos *EV*
Bright Food Shop *CH*
Buddy's Burrito and Taco Bar *B*
Burritoville *UES*
Dallas BBQ *UWS*
El Teddy's *ST*
Fresco Tortilla Grill *UG*
★Kitchen *CH*
Lupe's East L.A. Kitchen *ST*
Manganaros *WM*
Mary Ann's *CH*

Pickles

Essex St. (Gus's) Pickle Corp. *EV*

Pizza

Original Ray's Pizza and
Restaurant *UWS*
Ray's Pizza *GV*
Time Out Kosher Pizza *H*
Tony's Pizza *BX*

Roughage

Bennie's Café *UWS*

Seafood

Cucina di Pesce *EV*
Coldwaters *EM*
Mary Ann's *CH*
Oyster's Bar and Restaurant *EM*
Ramdazzo's Clam Bar *B*
Vincent's Clam Bar *LI*
Waterfront Crabhouse *Q*

FOOD AND DRINK

Soul Food and Southern Cookin'

★Copeland's *H*
Dallas BBQ *UWS*
Jack 'n' Jill's *Q*
Monck's Corner *WM*
The Pink Teacup *GV*
Ray's Soul Kitchen *HO*
Sylvia's *H*

Southeast Asian

Bali Nusa Indah *WM*
Bendix Diner *CH*
Café Ceylon *WM*
Gia Lam *B*
★Jai-ya *LEM*
The Lemongrass Grill *UWS*
★Mingala West *UWS*

Mueng Thai Restaurant *CHT*
Nam *B*
PlanEat Thailand *B*
Pongrisi Thai Restaurant *CHT*
Prince St. Bar and Restaurant *ST*
Rain *UWS*
Road to Mandalay *CHT*
Thai House Café *ST*

Tibetan

Tibetan Kitchen *UG*
Tibetan Shambala *UW*

Vegetarian

★Dojo Restaurant *EV*
Eva's *GV*
House of Vegetarian *CHT*
Quantum Leap *GV*
★Zen Palate *UG*

BY FEATURES

Delivery

★Ariana Afghan Kebab *WM*
Bali Nusa Indah *WM*
Brother's BBQ *ST*
Bubby's *ST*
Daikichi Sushi *UWS*
Fortune Garden *EM*
Hamburger Harry's *FD*
Maria Caffe *EM*
Minar *WM*
Obento Delight *UWS*
Tibetan Kitchen *LEM*
★Zen Palate *UG*

Open Late

Café Lalo *UWS*
Café Mozart *UWS*
Caffè Borgia *GV*
Caffè Reggio *GV*
Carnegie Delicatessen *WM*
Diane's Uptown *UWS*
Empire Szechuan Gourmet *UWS*
First Edition *Q*
Fulton Seaport Deli *FD*
★H&H Bagels *UWS*
Hong Fat *CHT*
Hot Bagels and Tasty Bakery *UWS*
HSF *CHT*
★The Hungarian Pastry Shop *MH*
Kiev *EV*
Moon Dance Diner *ST*
Nathan's *B*
Olive Tree Café *GV*
★Philip's Confections *B*
Pink Pony Café *EV*

★Tom's Restaurant *H*
★Uncle George's *Q*
Veselka *EV*
Washington Square Restaurant *GV*
Woo Chon Restaurant *Q*
Yaffa Café *EV*

Outdoor Dining

Bubby's *ST*
The Cloister Café *EV*
Il Fornaio *LI*
Indian Café *UWS*
La Bella Ferrara *LI*
La Mela *LI*
Pietro and Vanessa *LI*

Let's Go Picks

★Ariana Afghan Kebab *WM*
★Barking Dog Luncheonette *UES*
★Benny's Burritos *EV*
★Bell Caffè *ST*
★Big Cup *CH*
★Brother Jimmy's BBQ *UES*
★Cleopatra's Needle *UWS*
★Coldwaters *EM*
★Copeland's *H*
★Cucina Stagionale *GV*
★Damask Falafel *EV*
★Dojo Restaurant *EV*
★Dosanko *EM*
★EJ's Luncheonette *UES*
★Florent *GV*
★H&H Bagels *UWS*
★Hungarian Pastry Shop *MH*
★Jai-ya *LEM*
★Lucky's Juice Joint *ST*

FOOD AND DRINK

★Kitchen *CH*
★La Caridad *UWS*
★Massawa *MH*
★Moroccan Star *B*
★Oznaut's Dish *B*
★Pastrami King *Q*
★Phillip's Confections *Q*
★PlanEat Thailand *B*
★Poseidon Bakery

★Primorski Restaurant *B*
★Soutine *UWS*
★Teresa's *B*
★Tom's Restaurant *B*
★Tom's Restaurant *H*
★Uncle George's *Q*
★Veselka *EV*
★Yaffa's Tea Room *ST*
★Zen Palate *UG*

Not Quite a Free Lunch

Most budget travelers spend their sojourn in NYC without ever stepping foot in one of the city's swankier restaurants: New York's most famous chefs don't come cheap. But there are ways to splurge and treat yourself to an *extremely* fine meal without completely busting your wallet. Every summer, city restaurants across the boroughs can participate in **NY Restaurant Week,** during which the price of lunch corresponds to the current year. Thus, for 1997, the price will be $19.97. While this might seem like a lot, at ritzy places like Lutece, Gramercy Tavern, Union Square Café, Peter Luger, and Le Cirque it's quite a bargain. The program has begun expanding to include the entire summer, and reservations tend to go quickly. For a complete list of participating restaurants, send a stamped self-addressed envelope to:

NYC Restaurants
New York Convention and Visitors Bureau
2 Columbus Circle
New York, NY 10019

BY NEIGHBORHOOD

The restaurants listed under each neighborhood have been ranked by Let's Go according to our somewhat subjective appraisals of prices, quality, and atmosphere. Restaurants at the bottom of the listings are not necessarily crummy, as we don't list places that we wouldn't recommend. And if you're in the mood for Italian food, don't feel like you have to eat at the great Indian place at the top of our listings. The only restaurants we'll be mad at you for missing are denoted with our "Let's Go Pick" stars (★); these places are a true cut above the rest.

■ East Midtown

In this area, where tycoons run their corporate empires by wining and dining their clients well, prices can run up pretty quickly. Don't despair yet—the tycoons' underpaid underlings all eat cheap lunches in this same area. From around noon to 2pm, the many delis and cafés become swamped with harried junior executives trying to eat quickly and get back to work. The 50s on Second Ave. and the area immediately surrounding Grand Central Station are filled with good, cheap fare. You might also check out grocery stores, such as the **Food Emporium,** 969 Second Ave. (593-2224) between 51st and 52nd; **D'Agostino,** Third Ave. (684-3133), between 35th and 36th; or **Associated Group Grocers,** 1396 Second Ave., between E. 48th and E. 49th St. These upscale supermarket chains, with branches scattered throughout Manhattan, feature reliable, well stocked delis, fresh fruit and salad bars, ice cold drinks, gourmet ice cream, tons of munchies, and lots more—all at reasonable prices. This part of town also has many public plazas, lobbies, and parks in which to picnic with your new purchases; try **Greenacre Park,** 51st St. between Second and Third Ave.; **Paley Park,** 53rd St. between Fifth and Madison; or the **United Nations Plaza,** 48th St. at First Ave.

★**Dosanko,** 423 Madison Ave. (688-8575), at E. 47th St. Japanese fast food—very cheap, very fast, and very good. All is tranquil at this aromatic pit-stop; the food is so tasty it seems criminal to waste time talking. The scrumptious *gyoza* ($4.50) is a favorite, as are the many varieties of ramen ($5.30-7). Another Dosanko with more seating sits a few blocks away at 217 E. 59th St. (752-3936) between Second and Third Ave. Open Mon.-Fri. 11:30am-10pm, Sat.-Sun. noon-8pm.

★**Coldwaters,** 988 Second Ave. (888-2122), between E. 52nd and E. 53rd St. Seafood ($6-11) is served under nautical paraphernalia and stained-glass lamps. Lunch is a bargain: two drinks (alcoholic or non-), choice of entree, salad, and fries for $8 (daily 11:30am-4pm). Dinner is also a good deal: soup, salad, entree, and dessert for $12 (Mon.-Thurs. 4-7pm). Try the Idaho Rainbow Trout ($9), Cajun Catfish ($9), or Boston Cod ($9). Open daily 11am-3am.

Moonstruck, 449 Third Ave. (213-1100), at 31st St. This restaurant/diner offers four floors of culinary pleasure, with huge bay windows bathing the first floor in moon- (and streetlamp) light. Offers a staggering array of sandwich options including the Sliced Young Maryland Turkey ($8), as well as diner fare such as Silver Dollar Griddlecakes ($4.15). Most entrees hover between $9-12, but pasta dishes are a tad cheaper ($8). Open daily 6am-1am.

Taipei Noodle House, 986 Second Ave. (759-7070/7553/7554), at E. 53rd St. The sheer assortment of vegetable and meat dishes is sure to satisfy dieters, vegetarians, and proud carnivores alike. Most entrees run $6.50-9. The real deal is the weekday lunch special (Mon.-Fri. 11am-4pm), with entree, soup, rice, and egg roll for $4.75-6. Friendly service. Open Mon.-Sat. 11am-midnight.

Maria Caffè, 973 Second Ave. (832-9053; fax 750-7125), between E. 51st and E. 52nd St. Pastries and pizzas made on the premises and an incredible combo deal—$5.50 for pasta, salad, roll, and drink (daily 11am-3pm). Pita pizza $1.50, mozzarella and dried tomato sandwich $5. Portions are small but very filling. Open daily 8am-9pm.

Fortune Garden, 845 Second Ave. (687-7471; fax 687-3838), between E. 45th and E. 46th St. As indicated by the "corporate accounts welcome" sign, the prices in this restaurant are sky-high ($15-20). If you get take-out, though, it's much cheaper. Weekday lunch special is two appetizers and an entree (beef and broccoli, General Tso's chicken, or 16 other choices) for $6. Dinner entrees $7-11, Chef's specialities (such as Crystal Prawns or Sea Dragon) $9-16. Open Mon.-Fri. 11:30am-11pm, Sat.-Sun. 12:30-11pm.

Oysters Bar and Restaurant (490-6650) in Grand Central Station. Excellent (if exorbitant) seafood for the weary traveler. Opened soon after Grand Central itself, the restaurant has hosted many celebrities, including Lillian Russell and famous eater Diamond Jim Brady. The prices are high, but the chowder is a great deal—$3.25 for a huge bowl. The sandwich menu is also worth a peek, as are, of course, the oysters ($1.50-2 per piece). Open Mon.-Fri. 11:30am-9:30pm.

Café Classico, 35 West 57th St. (355-5411), between 5th and 6th Ave. This little restaurant upstairs specializes in Kosher, healthy, and gourmet delights. Sandwiches ($5-9) and eight varieties of healthy shakes ($2.50) are offered here. Open daily 11:30am-10pm.

■ West Midtown

Home to ritzy theaters and dilapidated tenements, West Midtown embraces a full range of culinary flavors. Your best bets are generally along Eighth Ave. between 34th and 59th St., in the area known as **Hell's Kitchen.** Once much more deserving of its name, this area has within the past few years given birth to a fantastically diverse array of restaurants. These eateries cater to a wide mix of people, many of whom arrive from swankier parts of the city and leave secure in the knowledge that, not only have they been to Hell and back, but they've been well fed and left a tip. Those whose resources reach deeper should try a meal on posh **Restaurant Row** on 46th St. between Eighth and Ninth Ave. The block consistently offers elegant dining to a pre-theater crowd. (Arriving after 8pm will make getting a table easier.)

FOOD AND DRINK

The area's cheapest meals can be had along the **fast food** version of Restaurant Row on the east side of Seventh Ave. between 33rd and 34th St. Besides the requisite McDonald's, you'll find Italian food and pizza, good buffet Chinese food sold by the pound (only $3.69 at **Chinatown Express**), gyros, and Philly cheesesteaks. Yet, even the fast food value meals tend to be only one or two dollars less than the price of a hearty spread at one of Hell's Kitchen's small, genuine, ethnic restaurants.

The neighborhood's several swanky restaurants are just as much sights as they are eating establishments. West Midtown is home to the slick, nationally franchised restaurants **Planet Hollywood, Hard Rock Café, All-Sports Diner,** and the **Harley-Davidson Café.** While you might want to get their t-shirts, these are not distinctively New York restaurants and aren't really worth the hour-long wait to get a table.

Celebrities occasionally drift over to **Sardi's,** 234 W. 44th St., and take a seat on the plush red leather, surrounded by caricatures of themselves and their best friends. Traditionally, on the opening night of a major Broadway play, the main star makes an exalted entrance following the show—to hearty cheers for a superb performance or polite applause for a bomb. If the literati grow bored, they may head to appealing but expensive Restaurant Row. Farther uptown, near Carnegie Hall, sits the **Russian Tea Room,** 150 W. 57th St., a New York institution currently under renovation until 1997, where dancers, musicians, and businesspeople meet to down caviar and vodka.

★**Ariana Afghan Kebab,** 787 Ninth Ave. (262-2323), between 52nd and 53rd St. With the approximate dimensions of a shoebox, this family-run restaurant serves up excellent Afghani food at reasonable prices. The beef *tikka kebab,* chunks of beef marinated and cooked over wood charcoal, is excellent served with rice, bread, and salad ($7), as is the *aushak,* leek-filled dumplings topped with yogurt and a spicy meat sauce. Vegetarian entrees range from $5.50-7.25. Open Mon.-Sat. noon-10:30pm, Sun. 3-10pm.

★**Poseidon Bakery,** 629 Ninth Ave. (757-6173), near 44th St. This fifty-year old bakery serves up authentic Greek pastries and delicacies. They even make their own filo dough for their sweet, sweet *baklava,* their *kreatopita* (meat pie), *tiropita* (cheese pie), and *spanakopita* (spinach pie)—all delicious and sold for around $2. Open July-Aug. Tues.-Sat. 9am-7pm. Also open Sept.-June Sun. 10am-4pm.

Hourglass Tavern, 373 W. 46th St. (265-2060), between Eighth and Ninth Ave. A dark, tiny, theater-crowd-crowded triangular joint with a limited menu that changes weekly. Servers flip an hourglass at your table when you sit down—the 59-min. time limit is strictly enforced when people are waiting. The menu describes this policy as "part of the game we play!" Dramatized in John Grisham's *The Firm* as the covert meeting place for two cloak-and-dagger types. Prix fixe entrees ($12.75) include soup or salad. Lunch entrees, offered a la carte, are less expensive ($7.25-9.50). Open Wed.-Fri. noon-2:00pm, Mon.-Sat. 5-11:15pm, Sun. 5-10:30pm. Cash only.

Monck's Corner, 644 Ninth Ave. (397-1117; fax 262-6517), at 45th St. The home of truly delectable Southern homestyle cooking. Those new to Southern cooking should opt for the mainstays: Southern fried chicken $7 or spare ribs $8, both served with collard greens and potato salad. Veterans looking for a little adventure might want to sample the oxtail stew ($7) or the vegetarian entree ($7), which includes yams, mac and cheese, okra, mixed vegetables, and string beans. The sweet potato pie is a great finish. Takeout only. Open Mon.-Sat. 1-9pm.

Sapporo, 152 W. 49th St. (869-8972), near Seventh Ave. A Japanese translation of the American diner, with the grill in full view. A favorite snack spot for Broadway cast members and corporate types alike, as well as many who can converse with the waiters in their native tongue. Menu items are listed on the wall in Japanese (but don't worry—the menu explains in English). Filling portions and astounding flavors. The Sapporo ramen special is a big bowl of noodles with assorted meats and vegetables, all floating around in a miso soup base ($6-6.75). Open Mon.-Sat. 11am-1am, Sun. 11am-11pm.

Bali Nusa Indah, 651 Ninth Ave. (765-6500), between 45th and 46th St. Sheer white walls, batiked tablecloths, and soothing Burmese pipe music all contribute to the subdued atmosphere of this restaurant. Great food served in plentiful portions. The fried rice noodles with shrimp and chicken ($7) are a favorite and the lunch specials, served with salad topped with a warm, spicy peanut dressing ($5, served daily 11:30am-4pm) are a great bargain. Try the mango ice cream for dessert ($2.50). Open daily 11:30am-10:30pm.

Manganaros, 488 Ninth Ave. (563-5331 or 800-4SALAMI/472-5264), between 37th and 38th St. This effortlessly classy Italian grocery and restaurant retains all the sights, sounds, smells, and flavors of pre-Gentrification Hell's Kitchen. The staff will construct the sandwich of your dreams, or you can select from their vast menu ($3-8). Eggplant parmigiana ($5.25) is a local favorite, as are the pastas of the day ($7.50). Open Sept.-June Mon.-Fri. 8am-7pm, Sat. 8am-9pm; July-Aug. Mon.-Fri. 8am-4pm.

Minar, 9 W. 31st St. (684-2199), between Fifth Ave. and Broadway. Long, narrow and colored like a subway platform, this Indian restaurant still manages to pack in many of the neighborhood's South Asians for lunch and dinner. Tasty, spicy vegetable curries ($4-4.25) and "non-vegetable" curries ($4-5) are served with a small salad and choice of bread (the *naan*, an unleavened flour variety, is delicious). Open daily 10:30am-10pm.

Uncle Vanya Café, 315 W. 54th St. (262-0542; fax 262-0554), between Eighth and Ninth Ave. Marionettes hang from the ceiling and the samovar reigns in this cheerful café. Delicacies of czarist Russia range from *borscht* (a hot or cold soup of beets, cabbage, and tomatoes served with sour cream and dill, $3) to *teftley* (Russian meatballs in sour cream sauce, $5.50) to caviar (market price—a concession to capitalism). Don't forget to ask about their dessert of the day. Undiscovered, homey, and very good. Open Mon.-Sat. noon-11pm, Sun. 2-10pm.

Rice & Beans, 744 Ninth Ave. (265-4444), between 50th and 51st St. This small Brazilian restaurant offers healthy, hearty food to a *salsa* beat. Lunch specials are served from 11am-4pm and, for $6.50, you can get an entree with white or yellow rice and fried plantains on the side. The tropical fruit shake ($2.75) is the dessert of choice here. Open Mon.-Thurs. 11am-10pm, Fri.-Sat. 11am-11pm, Sun. 1-9pm.

Emporium Brasil, 15 W. 46th St. (764-4646), between Broadway and Sixth Ave. A part of "Little Brazil" which runs along central 46th St., this small café serves excellent pastries and sandwiches. Coffee drinks served in single ($1-2.25) and double sizes ($1.25-3.50). They also sell a number of Brazilian newspapers and grocery products. Sit back, sip a double cappuccino, and watch the Brazilian news on their big screen TV. Open Mon.-Fri. 9am-7pm; Sat. 9am-5pm.

Carnegie Delicatessen, 854 Seventh Ave. (757-2245), at 55th St. One of New York's great delis. Ceiling fans whir gently overhead as photos of famous (and, after eating here, well fed) people stare out from the walls; you'll find everyone from Willis Reed to Oliver North. Eat elbow-to-elbow at long tables and chomp on the free dill pickles. The "Woody Allen," an incredible pastrami and corned beef sandwich, could easily stuff two people ($13), but sharing incurs a $3 penalty. First-timers shouldn't leave without trying the sinfully rich (and gargantuan) cheesecake topped with strawberries, blueberries, or cherries ($6). Open daily 6:30am-4am. Cash only.

■ Union Square and Gramercy Park

Straddling the extremes, the lower Midtown dining scene is neither fast-food commercial nor *haute cuisine* trendy. Instead, this slightly gentrified, ethnically diverse neighborhood features many places where honest meals are wed to reasonable prices. On Lexington in the upper 20s, Pakistani and Indian restaurants battle for customers, some catering to a tablecloth crowd, others serving take-out. Liberally sprinkled throughout are Korean corner shops that are equal parts grocery and buffet bars. You can often fill up on prepared pastas, salads, and hot entrees, paying for them by the pound. The area around Union Square offers an equally diverse dining experience, with funky diners and a hip crowd. On 18th Street and Irving Place, among rows of 19th-century red-brick houses, you'll run into **Pete's Tavern,** a legendary

New York watering hole since 1864. Legend has it that O. Henry, who lived nearby, wrote "The Gift of the Magi" in one of the booths.

★**Jaiya,** 396 Third Ave. (889-1330), between 28th and 29th St. Critics rave over Thai and other Asian food, with three degrees of spiciness, from mild to "help-me-I'm-on-fire." *Pad thai* $7.25—a definite steal. Lunch specials Mon.-Fri. 11:30am-3pm. Most dishes $5-6. Open Mon.-Fri. 11:30am-midnight, Sat. noon-midnight, Sun. 5pm-midnight. Another location at 81-11 Broadway in Elmhurst, Queens.

★**Zen Palate,** 34 E. Union Sq. (614-9345), across from the park. Fantastic Asian-inspired vegetarian cuisine, including soothing, healthy, and fabulously fresh treats like "shredded heaven" (assorted veggies and spring rolls with brown rice) for $8, stir fried rice fettuccini with mushrooms $7, or other concoctions on the brown rice/seaweed/kale and soy tip. Fresh-squeezed juices or soy milkshakes $1.50. Crazy desserts like tofu-honey pie. A very stylish decor for the Union Square area. Open Mon.-Sat. 11am-11pm, Sun. noon-10:30pm. Other locations at 663 9th Ave. (582-1669) at 46th St. and 2170 Broadway (501-7768) at 76th St.

Chat 'n' Chew, 10 E. 16th St. (243-1616), between Union Square and Fifth Ave. Self-described "trailer park food"—heaping plates of tasty macaroni and cheese (with a crunchy top) $7.25, a classic grilled cheese with tomato $6, and huge rice krispie treats with mini-marshmallows $2. Quintessentially and unabashedly American cuisine. Open Mon.-Thurs. 11:30am-11:30pm, Fri. 11:30am-midnight, Sat. 10am-midnight, Sun. 10am-11pm.

Fresco Tortilla Grill, 36 Lexington Ave. (475-7380), at 24th St. Unlike most of NYC's thousands of anonymous holes-in-the-wall, this one has good, very cheap Mexican food. Tacos $1, big and delicious burritos $4-5. No tables; just a few stools—most customers get take-out. The best bargain for a large group is 12 flour tortillas, grilled pepper and onions, beans and salsa, and 1lb. of chicken for only $13. Open Mon.-Fri. 11am-10pm, Sat.-Sun. noon-7pm.

Tibetan Kitchen, 444 Third Ave. (679-6286), between 30th and 31st St. This tiny place serves excellent food—meatier than Chinese, with a dollop of Indian thrown in. *Momo,* beef dumplings, "Tibet's most popular dish," $7.25 and *bocha,* Tibetan buttered and salted tea, are both worth a taste. Veggie dishes $6.75-7.25. An authentic cultural experience—note the Dalai Lama smiling serenely from the wall. Open Mon.-Fri. noon-3pm and 5:30-11pm, Sat. 5:30-11pm.

Empire Szechuan Balcony, 381 Third Ave. (685-6215, 685-6961, 685-6962, or 685-6670), between 27th and 28th St. Mirrored walls and leafy plants rim this purple-trimmed, multi-tiered Chinese food emporium. Well-cooked, tasty Chinese fare, refreshingly free of goo, oil, and MSG, with such exquisite names as "A galaxy of prawns" ($10.45) and "chow fun" ($6). Entrees $6-10. Open Mon.-Fri. 10:30am-midnight, Sat.-Sun. 11:30am-midnight.

Madras Mahat, 104 Lexington Ave. (684-4010), between 27th and 28th St. In a paean to multicultural correctness, this vegetarian Indian restaurant is owned by a Catholic and has been approved as strictly kosher. All-you-can-eat veggie chow-down $7 (Mon.-Fri. 11:30am-3pm), crepes $5.50-8, curries $9. For $7, the restaurant also features several exotically named lunch specials, such as the Madras lunch or Bombay lunch. Open Mon.-Fri. 11:30am-3pm and 5-10:30pm, Sat.-Sun. noon-10:30pm.

Sunburnt Espresso Bar, 206 3rd Ave. (674-1702), at 18th St. Cheerful red coffee place with an impressive selection of tasty snacks: corn and red pepper salad $3, and prosciuto with sun-dried tomato, basil, and brie $5. Dreamy shakes, smoothies, and frappes ($3.25-4.50),and fat-free muffins ($1.75) round out the dessert menu. Cute waiters, too. Open Mon.-Fri. 7am-11pm, Sat.-Sun. 8am-11pm.

■ Chelsea

Nestled between the oh-so-chic West Village and the rapidly upscaling West Midtown, Chelsea is dotted with fake-retro diners that offer unexceptional $6 hamburgers and $7 omelettes. But, crammed amid these soulless joints are plenty of quality diners and restaurants serving up food from all over the Americas. The best offerings are the products of the large Mexican and Central American community in the southern section of the neighborhood. From 14th Street to 22nd Street, restaurants offer combinations of Central American and Chinese cuisine as well as varieties of Cajun and Creole specialties. Eighth Ave. provides the best restaurant browsing. Pool sharks willing to pay a little more for their meal for the chance to play a game of eight-ball should check out the echoing, cavernous **Billiard Club,** 220 W. 19th St. (206-7665), where you can get lunch for two and an hour on a table for $17 (pool table alone $5 per hr.).

★**Kitchen,** 218 Eighth Ave. (243-4433), near 21st St. A real kitchen specializing in Mexican food, with hot red peppers dangling from the ceiling. All food to go; there's no dining room. Burrito stuffed with pinto beans, rice, and green salsa ($5.70). Dried fruit, nuts, and shrimp by the pound ($1-5), as well as other grocery items are available in Kitchen's authentic Mexican grocery. Very serious about chilis and chips. Open daily 11:30am-10:30pm.

★**Big Cup,** 228 8th Ave. (206-0059), between 21st and 22nd St. Lots of colorful and comfy velvet couches and overstuffed chairs make this a great place to curl up with a cup of joe ($1), plug in a powerbook, or cruise for cute guys. Predominantly gay clientele. Crazy coffee flavors like toffee-coffee and sandwiches like cactus, red pepper, and chipotle ($5) for daring tongues. Tarot readings in house on Tues. nights at 8pm. Open Sun.-Thurs. 7am-2am, Fri.-Sat. 8am-3am.

Negril, 362 West 23rd St. (807-6411), between 8th and 9th Ave. The Jamaican fare served here is light yet incredibly spicy. *Bon Appetit* magazine once printed the recipe for their ginger lime chicken ($8.50). Beans or jerk chicken ($7.50) comes with rice or grilled banana and steamed vegetables. Sandwiches $6.50-7.50, "light meals" (salads, etc.) $3.50-8.50, and entrees $6.50-8.50; dinner $8-15. Spicy ginger beer $2. Festive Sunday brunch with live band 11am-4pm. Wheelchair accessible. Open Mon.-Sat. noon-11pm, Sun. 11am-4pm and 5-10pm.

Utopia-W-Restaurant, 338 Eighth Ave. (807-8052), at 27th St. Located in the boxy shadow of the Fashion Institute of Technology, this is the school's chic diner, populated by the equally chic student body. Heavy-duty meaty burgers on toasted buns (cheeseburger with fries, coleslaw, and pickle $5)—this is not model fare. Dinner often comes with a complimentary glass of wine. Open daily 6am-9:30pm.

Sam Chinita Restaurant, 176 Eighth Ave., at 19th St. A 50s diner complete with red curtains serves up Spanish-and-Chinese cuisine (perhaps a little more Chinese than Spanish). Dozens of deals under $6. Favorites include yellow rice with chicken Latin-style ($6) and lobster Cantonese with fried rice and eggroll ($9). Daily lunch specials $3-6 (noon-4pm). Open daily 11:45am-11pm.

Bright Food Shop, 216 Eighth Ave. (243-4433), at 21st St. This red-and-white-checkered diner, "where the Southwest meets the Far East," serves a delicious mix of Mexican and Asian cuisine. The corner green salad, topped with sunflower seeds and sherry cumin vinaigrette ($5), is excellent, as is the quesadilla with shrimp, watercress, and goat cheese ($12). Beverages include such exotic offerings as honey limeade ($1-1.75) and amé herbal soda ($2.25). You can't miss their neon sign—when they say "bright," they mean it. Open Mon.-Sat. 10:45am-3:30pm and 6-10:30pm, Sat.-Sun. brunch 11am-4pm.

Eighteenth and Eighth, Eighth Ave. (242-5000), at 18th St. (duh). Between the artsy-looking regular customers and the art display, this slightly cramped room has the feel of a downtown gallery. The masterpiece is a healthy and subtly flavored menu, which does wonderful things to chicken, fish, vegetables, and tropical fruit. Curry-mango chicken $10; other entrees $7-15. Desserts $3-5. Open Mon.-Fri. 8am-midnight, Sat.-Sun. 9am-12:30am.

Eureka Joe, 168 Fifth Ave. (741-7500), at 22nd St. Mainly a coffee joint; this is one of the few in the area with true style. Though they have sandwiches ($5-7) and plates ($8), you'll probably want to skip straight to their mouth-watering desserts ($1-4). Where else in the city can you get a fruit-glazed organic doughnut? Coffee is only 50¢ on weekday mornings from 7-10am. Open Mon.-Fri. 7am-10pm, Sat. 9am-10pm, Sun. 10am-6pm.

Mary Ann's, 116 Eighth Ave. (633-0877), at 16th St. Benevolent waiters serve up huge portions in this white-walled, wood-finished restaurant hung with *piñatas* and slung with lights. Inventive and unusual Mexican cuisine, often in surprising marriages with seafood. The enchilada stuffed with shrimp and snowcrab served in *tomatillo* sauce ($9.25) and the roasted eggplant quesadilla with salad and avocado ($8) keep the locals happy. Most entrees $9-11. Margaritas $4.50. Popular and crowded. Open Mon.-Tues. 11:30am-10:30pm, Wed.-Thurs. 11:30am-10:45pm, Sat. 11:30am-11:15pm, Sun. noon-10pm.

Bendix Diner, 219 Eighth Ave. (366-0560), at 21st St. A new hybrid—the Thai greasy spoon. Try the stir-fried noodles with vegetables ($7) or play it safe with a burger ($3.75). Pies and sandwiches, too. Veggie stir fries $6. Grilled ½ chicken with potatoes and veggies $6.45. Open Mon.-Sat. 7am-1am, Sun. 7am-11pm.

B.M.W. Gallery and Coffee Magic Espresso Bar, 199 7th Ave. (229-1807), between 21st and 22nd St. Drapes, sofas, and hanging art make this coffee shop and wine bar a step above the rest. Good selection of wines, microbrews, and gay-friendly magazines. Inexpensive treats: vegetable sandwiches ($3), large iced Mochaccino ($2.60), and coffee (80¢). Open Mon.-Wed. 7am-10:30pm, Thurs.-Fri. 7am-1am, Sat. 10am-1am, Sun. 10am-9pm.

■ Upper East Side

Meals on the Upper East Side descend in price as you move east from Fifth Ave.'s glitzy, overpriced museum cafés towards Lexington, Third, and Second Ave. Visitors aiming to experience the classic New York bagel should try **H&H East** (734-7441), at 1551 Second Ave. between 80th and 81st St. Open 24 hours, H&H still uses a century-old formula to deliver its promise: to send you to bagel heaven. But don't feel confined to restaurant dining; grocery stores, delis, and bakeries speckle every block. If nothing strikes your fancy, you may buy provisions here and picnic in Central Park.

★**Barking Dog Luncheonette,** 1678 Third Ave. (831-1800), at 94th St. As the staff's shirts command, "SIT–STAY!" and satisfy your hunger pangs with helpings fit for the biggest dog on the block. The breakfast special ($4.50), with two eggs, hash browns, and your choice of bacon or sausage biscuit, tastes delicious, while late risers may prefer the burger platter ($6.50). With huge bay windows overlooking Third Ave., this charming corner restaurant features delightful dog decor and a peaceful atmosphere not unlike canine heaven. Open daily 8am-11pm.

★**Brother Jimmy's BBQ,** 1461 First Ave. (545-7427), at 76th St. The sign proclaims "BBQ and booze, the stuff that makes America strong," and this greasy-chops Carolina kitchen serves up plenty of both, along with a healthy dose of southern hospitality, in the form of free food for kids under 12, 25% off entrees for southerners on Wednesday nights, and free margaritas with dinner on Monday nights. Ribs $13, with 2 side dishes and corn bread. Sandwiches, for the less strong, $6-7. Kitchen open Sun.-Thurs. 5pm-midnight, Fri.-Sat. 11am-1am. Bar open "until you finish your last drink" or until around 4am.

★**EJ's Luncheonette,** 1271 Third Ave. (472-0600), at 73rd St. The understated American elegance and huge portions of good food in this hip 50s style diner has fostered a legion of devoted Upper East Siders—the scrumptious fare (buttermilk pancakes $5, hamburgers $5.75) is rumored to have attracted such neighborhood luminaries as JFK, Jr. Open Mon.-Thurs. 8am-11pm, Fri.-Sat. 8am-midnight, Sun. 8am-10:30pm.

Tang Tang Noodles and More, 1328 Third Ave. (249-2102/3/4), at 76th St. Cheap, hot, tasty Chinese noodles and dumplings. Not one noodle dish over $5.75—most around $5. Dense crowds but lightning-quick service, and very authentic food. Open Sun.-Thurs. 11am-11pm, Fri.-Sat. 11:30am-11:15pm.

Burritoville, 1489 First Ave. (472-8800), between 77th and 78th St. Also at 1606 Third Ave. (410-2255), between 90th and 91st St. Venture past the narrow door into the mystical town of Burritoville, "where the shadows are of ancient animal shapes and the sky is a harmony of clay flutes and whistles." Tasty Tex-Mex with 15 different varieties of burrito, including the Rte. 66 Burrito (vegetarian, $4.95) and Davy Crockett's Last Burrito (grilled lamb, $7.25). Six locations around NYC. Open daily noon-11pm.

Viand, 673 Madison Ave. (751-6622), between 61st and 62nd St. An excellent post-shopping pit stop. The food is all pricey except for the exceptional burgers.

Cheeseburger $4.10; with fries, cole slaw, and toppings $6. Great atmosphere and friendly staff. Open daily 6am-10pm.

El Pollo, 1746 First Ave. (996-7810), between 90th and 91st. This under-hyped Peruvian dive's grilled chicken dishes, served with complimentary wine in a cramped bowling alley of a restaurant, have locals raving. Plump chickens are marinated, spit-roasted, and topped with a variety of sauces. In addition to poultry, exotic Peruvian delicacies make the menu an affordable epicurean adventure. Half chicken $5. BYOB. Another location at 482 Broome St (431-5666) in Soho. Open daily 11:30am-11pm.

Sarabeth's Kitchen, 1295 Madison Ave. (410-7335), at 92nd St. Well dressed parents and children sup in grand style in this erstwhile local bakery, now a bustling glossy duplex. Dinner prices are steep, but brunch addicts should join the masses, put their names down an hour early, stroll around the neighborhood, then return to sink their teeth into Dr. Seussian "green and white" eggs scrambled with cream cheese and scallions ($7.50). Dessert lovers can sample the amazingly delectable assortment of pastries, custards, and muffins while sipping cappuccino in the small café. Also at 423 Amsterdam Ave. (496-6280), at 81st St. Open Mon.-Fri. 8am-3:30pm and 6-10:30pm, Sat. 9am-4pm and 6-10:30pm, Sun. 9am-4pm and 6-9:30pm.

Ottomanelli's Café, 1626 York Ave. (772-7722), between 85th and 86th St. An outpost of the vast and powerful Ottomanelli Empire that has supplied New York with meat and baked goods since 1900. Venture down the steps into this charming, darkly-lit café for a pastry respite from your East Side travels. The small café's menu offers grilled breast of chicken, pizza, and their unique steakburgers, ground fresh daily. Many other locations on the Upper East Side, including 439 E. 82nd St. at York Ave. (737-1888), 1518 First Ave. at 79th St. (734-5544), 1370 York Ave. at 73rd St. (794-9696), and 1199 First Ave. at 65th St. (249-7878). Open daily noon-10pm.

The Den, 1500 Third Ave. (628-7165), between 84th and 85th St. Despite the dark and gloomy connotations associated with its name, the Den is large, bright, and altogether cheerful, with pink walls and painted windows opening onto an idyllic nature scene. Entrees are on the pricey side ($8-14), but the large burgers are well within budget range ($3-6). Look for your waitperson's caricature on the menu. Smoking lounge available. Open daily 8:30am-10:30pm.

Arriba! Arriba!, 1463 Third Ave. (249-1423), between 82nd and 83rd St. Cattle skulls, a black-lit bar, and a deer head sporting an eyepatch all lend this Mexican restaurant a vaguely surreal ambience. Most entrees $7-10, though some of the fajita dishes are a bit pricier (beef $11.45, shrimp $14). Open Mon.-Fri. noon-midnight, Sat.-Sun. noon-1am.

Jackson Hole Wyoming, 1270 Madison Ave. (427-2820), at 91st St. Huge windows on both Madison and 91st St. allow you to people-watch while feasting on these super-human burgers. 30 different kinds of 7-oz. burgers ($4-8, $6.50-10 for a platter). Also at 64th St. between Second and Third Ave., and on Columbus between 83rd and 84th St. Open daily 7am-11pm.

ecco-la, 1660 Third Ave. (860-5609), corner of 93rd st. After practicing your art criticism at the Met or the Whitney, come debate the aesthetics of ecco-la's hand-painted tables and clock-adorned walls while feasting on fresh pasta pockets filled with lobster, mushrooms, scallions, and parsley in an avocado cream sauce ($10). Less adventurous souls can stick with pizza ($9) or pasta ($10). Open Sun.-Thurs. noon-midnight, Fri.-Sat. noon-12:30am.

Rush'n Express, 306 E. 86th St. (517-4949), between First and Second Ave. Russian delights featured at low prices make a tasty meal alternative to fast food chains. Walls decorated with scenes from Russian folklore and Russian pop music will get you in the mood while scrumptious *piroshki* ($1.35) transports you to the old country. Open daily 11am-10pm.

Papaya King, 179 E. 86th St. (369-0648), at Third Ave. New Yorkers tolerate the outrageously long lines at this establishment all for a taste of the "tastier than filet mignon" hot dogs (2 for $3.79). Any of the fresh fruit shakes ($1.69) should put a spring in your step. Open Sun.-Thurs. 8am-1am, Fri.-Sat. 9am-3am.

■ Upper West Side

Unlike many other New York neighborhoods, the Upper West Side lacks a definitive restaurant typology. Cheap pizza joints often neighbor chic eateries; street vendors hawk sausages in the shadow of pricey specialty stores. If browsing in Betsey Johnson or Charivari makes you grumpy, haggle at the Columbus Ave. Street Fair; if it makes you hungry, wander down the tempting aisles of **Zabar's,** 2245 Broadway (787-2002), the deli *cum* grocery that never ends. The vast array of restaurants in the area offers meals for the solitary as well as the social.

★**Cleopatra's Needle,** 2485 Broadway (769-6969), between 92nd and 93rd St. Jazz and authentic Middle Eastern fare served up nightly to faithful locals. Take-out lunch counter also available to those who can't stop at dinner (*baba ghanoush*) or Egyptian burrito for less than $4. Patrons have fun pronouncing exotic dishes like *Kibbehsinaya* ($8) and *Imam Bayildi* ($9), or else stick to familiar friends like roast cornish hen ($8.25). Takeout/deli open daily 8am-11pm, dinner Sun.-Thurs. 5-11pm, Fri.-Sat. 5pm-midnight.

★**La Caridad,** 2199 Broadway (874-2780), at 78th St. One of New York's most successful Chinese-Spanish hybrids. You could eat here 160 times and never have the same dish twice. The ebullient waiters charm in three languages. The decor isn't elaborate, but the delicious homestyle cooking should remind you of your *abuelita*. Prices stay decidedly south of the $10 border. Open Mon.-Sat. 11:30am-1am, Sun. 11:30am-10:30pm.

★**Soutine,** 104 W.70th St. (496-1450), at Amsterdam Ave. This thimble of a bakery has packed a punch since 1983—its lovingly baked treats even gained the approval of food critic Ed Levine. Try their sacristans (puff pastries) or fruit tarts for under $2. Sandwiches $3.50. Open Mon.-Fri. 8am-7pm, Sat. 9am-5pm.

★**H&H Bagels,** 2239 Broadway (595-8000), at 80th St. With bagels that are cheap (70¢) and baked fresh daily, H&H has been nourishing the huddled masses of the Upper West Side for years. Open 24hr.

Ollie's, 2315 Broadway (362-3111 or 362-3712), at 84th St. The requisite whole chickens hang inside the window, but the real mark of quality here is the sound of content slurping that provides background music to any meal eaten at Ollie's. Noodle soups and fried rice dishes are the best budget deals (most around $5.25). Varnished wooden tabletops lend a sophisticated air to this crowded little restaurant. Open Mon.-Sat. 11am-midnight, Sun. 11am-11:30pm. Other locations (same hours and menus): 2957 Broadway at 116th St., and 190 W. 44th St., between Sixth and Seventh Ave.

Carmine's, 2450 Broadway (362-2200), between 90th and 91st St. This lively, noisy, family-style Italian restaurant serves huge portions; one plate can easily feed three people. Although prices are not quite in the budget range for dinner, the delicious hero combos ($8) sold at the lunch/take-out section next door are a gourmet deal. Decent free wine with your meal. Open Mon.-Thurs. 5-11pm, Fri. and Sat. 5pm to midnight, Sun. 3-11pm; Mon.-Sat. bar opens at 4:30pm.

Café Lalo, 201 83rd St. (496-6031), at Amsterdam Ave. This super-chic locale with floor-to-ceiling windows is the place to come after a movie if you want to be seen racking up the fat grams. Sinfully rich desserts and European posters make one feel as if one were transported to a more refined, elegant era (or tax bracket). More than 60 different pastry and cake desserts, each $3-6. Open Sun.-Thurs. 9am-2am, Fri.-Sat. 9am-4am.

Tibet Shambala, 488 Amsterdam Ave. (721-1270), between 83rd and 84th St. Tasty Tibetan food, including many vegetarian and "no-moo" dishes. Lunch specials Mon.-Fri. noon-4pm $5.50, dinner entrees $7.25-9. Reincarnation not included. Open Mon.-Fri. 1-4pm and 6-11pm, Sat.-Sun. noon-11pm.

Daikichi Sushi, 2345 Broadway (362-4283), between 85th and 86th St. This no-frills sushi boutique offers 30 low-priced sushi combinations ($4-8). Fast service illustrates how seriously these folks take their *nigiri*. Carry-out only; perfect for your picnic in Central Park. Open daily 11am-10pm.

Rain, 100 W. 82nd St. (501-0776), at Columbus Ave. This building-lobby-turned-restaurant is a hip world unto itself. Trendy music pumps over the sound system as the stylish crowd slurps up Thai noodles. Not a budget bargain (lunch entrees $9-11, dinners $11-22), but good for a sumptuous treat and to see how the other half lives. Open Mon.-Fri. noon-3pm and 6-11pm; Fri.-Sun. noon-4pm and Fri. 6pm-midnight, Sat. 5pm-midnight, Sun. 5-10pm.

Obento Delight, 210 W. 94th St. (222-2010), between Amsterdam Ave. and Broadway. Fresh Japanese food at low prices. Don't be put off by the off-the-avenue location—Obento is a classy operation: cute little tables in beige-colored wood, with a well mannered, conscientious waitstaff. Vegetable tempura $6.75, shrimp shumai (10 pieces) $5.50. Free delivery ($7 min.). Open daily 11:30am-11pm.

Hot Bagels & Tasty Bakery, 2079 Broadway (699-5611), between 71st and 72nd St. New Yorkers wouldn't survive without little bakeries like this one with a full assortment of breads, pastries, and sandwiches (most under $5) to satisfy hunger pangs at any hour of the day or night. Open 24hr.

Café Mozart, 154 70th St. (595-9797), between Broadway and Columbus Ave. A pleasantly unpretentious café, off hurried Broadway. A perfect place for gourmet coffee, reading a free paper, and gazing at passers-by. Lunch special (Mon.-Fri. 11am-2pm) includes sandwich, quiches, or omelette with soda or coffee and dessert ($6). Salads ($4-9) generously proportioned. Live classical music Mon.-Sat. 9pm-midnight, Sun. 3-6pm and 7-10pm. Open Mon.-Thurs. 11am-2am, Fri. 11am-3am, Sat. 10am-3am, Sun. 10am-2am.

Dallas BBQ, 27 W. 72nd St. (873-2004), between Columbus and Central Park West. Although the bright awning is a bit out of place on this mostly residential block, inside you'll see private booths and kitschy Tex-Mex decor (including the *de rigeur* skulls and rugs) that lend a familiar air to your dining, pardner. The bar at the left is better for more raucous pursuits. Sorry, no electric bronco. Open Sun.-Thurs. noon-midnight, Fri.-Sat. noon-1am.

Mingala West, 325 Amsterdam Ave. (873-0787), at 75th St. Burmese cooking uses rice noodles, peanut sauces, coconuts, and curries, yet tastes nothing like Thai or Indonesian food. With its lavender walls, ebony elephants, and photo of 1991 Burmese Nobel laureate Aung San Soo Kyi (who was recently released from house arrest), the place makes for a friendly introduction to a new cuisine. Generous $5 lunch specials (soup or salad, plus your choice of among 20 tantalizing entrees with rice or noodles) offered Mon.-Fri. noon-4pm; $6-9 "light meal" samplers 4:30-6:30pm. Glass noodles and beef dishes on the main menu ($7-13). Open Sun.-Thurs. noon-11:30pm, Fri.-Sat. noon-midnight.

Café La Fortuna, 69 W. 71st St. (724-5846), at Columbus Ave. Delicious Italian pastries, coffees, and sandwiches served in a dark grotto of a café. A definite local favorite; high school swingers sit in clumps and wish they could smoke, scholars stretch out with books and papers at corner tables, and families bring their children out on the back patio. Try the delicious iced cappuccino served with chocolate Italian ice ($3.50). Open Sun.-Thurs. noon-midnight, Fri.-Sat. noon-1:30am.

Diane's Uptown, 251 Columbus Ave. (799-6750), near 71st St. Hip young students bop to the music as they chomp on hearty burgers in this brass-railed café. Little old ladies from the neighborhood can be seen taking their lunches here as well. 7-oz. burgers ($4.50) can be enjoyed with chili, chutney, or your choice of seven cheeses (85¢ per topping). Frequently, burgers and omelettes are $1 off. Open Sun.-Thurs. 11am-midnight, Fri.-Sat. 11am-1am.

Indian Café, 2791 Broadway (749-9200), at 108th St. and West End Ave. Authentic Indian food served here—the airy, glass-walled patio and the shady bar are both tranquil eating spots. Elephant posters and Indian music inspire visions of the mother country. Clay-oven-baked dishes ($8) are the house special, but many cheaper dishes hover around the $6 mark. Open daily 11:30am-midnight.

The Lemongrass Grill, 2534 Broadway (666-0888), at 95th St. Another adventurous, delicious culinary tradition of the Upper West. Thai noodles and vegetables ($5-7) sate locals among the bamboo shoots. Open Sun.-Thurs. noon-11:30pm. Fri.-Sat. noon-12:30am. Also in Park Slope at 61 Seventh Ave. (718-399-7100).

The Happy Burger, 2489 Broadway (799-7719), between 92nd and 93rd St. This charming little dive serves up sixteen varieties of 8-oz. burgers, all under $5. Greek specialties (such as baked *mousaka*) can be also be had for less than $7. Weightwatchers and broadly-defined vegetarians can stick to the turkey burger ($3.65) or salads ($5.25). Open daily 7am-10pm.

Empire Szechuan Gourmet, 2574 Broadway (663-6004/5/6), at 97th St. A favorite of Upper West Siders (hence the 3 telephone numbers). Modern decor and efficient waitstaff have this spacious establishment running like clockwork. Fifteen diet entrees for the calorie-challenged. Beef and lamb dishes ($8.25) offered alongside the usual poultry and pork fare. Hors d'oeuvres (mostly $1) and dim sum ($1-6, Mon.-Fri. 10:30am-3:30pm and Sat.-Sun. 10am-3:30pm), as well as Japanese dishes and a sushi bar. Generous lunch specials $5 Mon.-Fri. 11:30am-3pm. Dinner coupons on take-out menus handed out in front of the restaurant. Free delivery. Open daily 10:30am-2am.

■ Morningside Heights

The cafés and restaurants in Morningside Heights cater mostly to Columbia students, faculty, and their families. This usually means that hours run very late and the price range fits that of a starving student. Old-fashioned coffeeshops abound, and there are plenty of places to grab a fine meal after touring the area's grand churches, although the cuisine alone isn't worth the journey.

★**Massawa,** 1239 Amsterdam Ave. (663-0505), at 121st St. You'll want to make sure your hands are spotless before heading here, a restaurant that specializes in cheap well prepared Ethiopian and Eritrean cuisine—traditionally eaten by hand. The various vegetarian dishes range from $5-6, and are served with spongy *ingera* bread or rice. Between 11:30am and 3pm, they offer kicking lunch specials like lamb stew and collard-green/potato platters ($4-5.75). Open daily noon-midnight.

★**Tom's Restaurant,** 2880 Broadway (864-6137), at 112th St. "Doo-doo-doo-doo..." Suzanne Vega wrote that darn catchy tune about this diner, and Tom's is featured in most episodes of *Seinfeld*, but this eatery is mainly known for its luxurious milkshakes ($2.45). Greasy burgers for $3-5, dinner under $6.50. Open Mon.-Wed. 6am-1:30am and open continuously from Thurs. 6am to Sun. 1:30am. "Doo-doo-doo-doo..."

★**The Hungarian Pastry Shop,** 1030 Amsterdam Ave. (866-4230), at 111th St. For those of you who don't know the difference between Fila and *phyllo,* lace up the former and head over to the West Side's worst-kept secret to find out about the latter. Plain, friendly, Boho pastry shop. Eclairs, cake slices, and other goodies all around $2. Fine coffee, too ($1.30). The outdoor garden is great for reading, writing, or watching passers-by on Amsterdam Ave. Open Mon.-Sat. 8am-11:15pm, Sun. 8am-10pm.

Mill Korean Restaurant, 2895 Broadway (666-7653), at 112th St. Traditional, freshly prepared Korean food. Lunch specials Mon.-Fri. 11am-3pm ($5-7). Complete dinners with side dishes ($7-10). Try the fiery stir-fried squid ($8 at dinner, $5.50 at lunch). Open daily 11am-10pm.

La Rosita Restaurant, 2809 Broadway (663-7804), between 108th and 109th St. The restaurant may lack the romantic atmosphere that seems fitting for its name, but the genuine Spanish cuisine more than makes up for it. The daily specials range from $5.25-6.25; among them is roast pork with brown rice and casaba. The menu is in both Spanish and English, just in case you're brushing up on either. Excellent café con leché (espresso with milk $1). Open daily 9am-10pm.

Amir's Falafel, 2911A Broadway (749-7500), between 113th and 114th St. Low-priced Middle Eastern fare for vegetarians and meat-lovers alike. Sandwiches ($3) and salads ($2) made with care. Mirrors and paintings of belly dancers await your contemplation. Open daily 11am-11pm.

■ Harlem and Washington Heights

Cheap food abounds in Harlem and Washington Heights. Whether you stop at one of the many fast food restaurants (chains or independent) or pick up a snack from one of the many street vendors, you most likely won't pay as much in Harlem as you would in the rest of the city. A plethora of fast food joints can be found on 181st and 125th St. Along **Nagle Ave.,** in a predominantly Dominican section of Washington Heights, many street vendors sell fresh fruit shakes which they'll blend up for you on command for a few dollars—the perfect solution to summer heat.

Ethnic food is everywhere, with Jewish food in Washington Heights, various Latino and Cuban foods in the Hispanic communities and, of course, all kinds of African-American cuisine—East and West African, Caribbean and Creole, and some of the best soul food north of the Mason-Dixon Line. Try Lenox Ave., 125th St., or 116th St. in Harlem, the Columbia area, or the Yeshiva/Fort Washington area. Harlem isn't the most traveler-friendly area in the city; try to follow the directions to the restaurants given below—these will keep you on the most populated streets and take you to the most convenient subway stops.

★**Copeland's,** 547 W. 145th St. (234-2357), between Broadway and Amsterdam Ave. Subway: #1 or 9 to 145th St. Sylvia's without the tourists; excellent soul food without the slick presentation. Smothered chicken $6.50; fried pork chop $7.20. Smorgasbord next door—cafeteria-style but just as good. The Southern-style breakfasts and Sunday brunch are simply amazing. Open Tues.-Thurs. 4:30-11pm, Fri. 4:30pm-midnight, Sat. 4:30pm-midnight, Sun. 11am-9:30pm.

Sylvia's, 328 Lenox/Malcolm X Ave. (996-0660), at 126th St. Subway: #2 or 3 to 125th St. This sleek touristed restaurant has magnetized New York for over 20 years with enticing soul-food dishes. Sylvia highlights her "World-Famous talked-about BBQ ribs special" with "sweet spicy sauce" (served with collard greens and macaroni and cheese, $10.50). Lunch special is a pork chop, collard greens, and candied yams for $6. Gospel Brunch Sun. 1-7pm with live music and soul food. Live music (Wed.-Fri. 7-9pm; no cover) features jazz and R&B. Open Mon.-Sat. 7:30am-10:30pm, Sun. 1-7pm.

Time-Out Kosher Pizza and Israeli Food, 1186 Amsterdam Ave. (923-1180), between 186th and 187th St. on the campus of Yeshiva University. Subway: #1 or 9 to 181st St. Walk a few blocks east on 181st St. to Amsterdam Ave. and then walk five blocks north through Yeshiva's area. The name says it all. Slice of kosher pizza $1.50. Kosher falafel plate $4.75. Bagel with lox $2.25. Seven kinds of knishes and three kinds of *burekas,* each only $1.50. Open Sun.-Fri. 7am-6pm.

La Casita Restaurant, 2755 Broadway (663-2811), at 106th St. Colorful Spanish restaurant with some of the best prices in town—eggs with rice and beans ($3), chicken cracklings ($6.25), mixed salad with avocado ($3.50), and tropical fruit shakes ($2.50) are just some of the good eats to be had here. Desserts include flan ($1.10) and sweet milk ($1.25). Open daily 6:30am-12:30am.

■ Greenwich Village

All the free-floating artistic angst of the West Village spawns many creative (and inexpensive) food venues. The aggressive and entertaining street life makes stumbling around and deciding where to go almost as much fun as eating.

Try the major avenues for cheap, decent food. The European-style bistros of Bleecker and MacDougal Streets, south of Washington Square Park, have perfected the homey "antique" look. **Bleecker St.** between Sixth and Seventh Ave. offers a great variety of eateries—classy and kitschy. If you're in a picnic mood, a good bet is the **Murray Cheese Shop,** 257 Bleecker St. (243-3289), at Cornelia St. This aromatic establishment contains over 400 kinds of cheese, with dietary information available for the dairy-paranoid. Try the camembert in rosemary and sage ($4; open Mon.-Sat. 8am-8pm, Sun. 9am-6pm).

Late night in the Village is a unique New York treat: as the sky darkens, the streets become increasingly crowded and crazy. A ringside seat at one of the many outdoor cafés or restaurants is a perfect venue to watch the creatures of the night take over. Exploration of the many twisting side streets and alleyways yields many fruits—you can drop into a jazz club or join Off-Broadway theater-goers as they settle down over a burger and a beer to write their own reviews. Alternatively, you can ditch the high life completely and slump down 8th St. to Sixth Ave. to join the freak scene and find some of the most respectable pizzerias in the city.

★**Cucina Stagionale,** 275 Bleecker St. (924-2707), at Jones St. Unpretentious Italian dining in a pretty environment. Packed on weekends—the lines reach the street at times. A sample of the soft *calimari* in spicy red sauce ($6) or the spinach and cheese ravioli ($7) will tell you why. Pasta dishes $6-8; veal, chicken, and fish dishes $8-10. Once you've been seated, might as well get a dessert too; the bill still won't be over $15. Open Sun.-Thurs. noon-midnight, Fri.-Sat. noon-1am.

★**Florent,** 69 Gansevoort St. (489-5779), between Washington and Greenwich Ave. In the terminally hip bowels of this meat-packing district is a 24-hr French diner that's not to be missed. Clientele ranges from drag queens to rastafarians, the food is fab, and the place is full even at 4am. Goat cheese and apple or portobello mushroom salads $6. Entrees range from burgers to gourmet, $9-20. Good wine list. It may not be very budget, but it's the best place to celebrate Bastille Day this side of Paris. Open 24hr.

Ray's Pizza, 465 Sixth Ave. (243-2253), at 11th St. Half of the uptown pizza joints claim to be the "Original Ray's," but this one is the real McCoy. People have been known to fly here from Europe just to bring back a few pies—it's the best pizza in town. Well worth braving the lines and paying upwards of $1.75 for a cheese-heavy slice. Scant seating; this is pizza on the go. Open Sun.-Thurs. 11am-2am, Fri.-Sat. 11am-3am.

Quantum Leap, 88 W. 3rd St. (677-8050), between Thompson and Sullivan St. Brown rice galore at this aggressively veggie restaurant. Exotic ways to save the planet, including BBQ Teriyaki Tofu ($8.50), soyburger delight ($5), spicy Szechuan beancurd ($8.95), and the lunch special—salad, spaghetti, and wheat ball ($5). For dessert, try the Cocoa-Peanut Tofu Pie ($3) or perhaps a glass of carrot juice ($2). Don't worry, carnivores—it's all very tasty. Open Mon.-Thurs. 11:30am-11pm, Fri. 11:30am-midnight, Sat. 11am-midnight, Sun. 11am-10pm.

Olive Tree Café, 117 MacDougal St. (254-3480), north of Bleecker St. Standard Middle Eastern food offset by seemingly endless stimulation. If you get bored by the old movies on the wide screen, you can rent chess, backgammon, and Scrabble sets ($1), doodle with colored chalk on the slate tables, or sit on the patio and survey the Village nightlife. Falafel $2.75, chicken kebab platter with salad, rice pilaf, and vegetable, $7.50. Delicious egg creams only $1.75. Open Sun.-Thurs. 11am-3am, Fri.-Sat. 11am-5am.

Mappamondo, 11 Abingdon St. (675-3100), at W. 8th St. Small, cozy, and filled with globes, this place serves pasta with a range of creative toppings, as well as antipasti and meat dishes. Pasta plates $7-8, pizzas $7-7.50. Kitty-corner across Abingdon Sq. is **Mappamondo Due,** 581 Hudson St. (675-7474), a more bustling version with the same menu and slightly more food. Open Mon.-Fri. noon-midnight, Sat.-Sun. 11am-1am.

The Pink Teacup, 42 Grove St. (807-6755), between Bleecker and Bedford St. Soul food in a small, pink, and friendly environment. As multiple Martin Luther King Jrs. gaze at you from the walls, you can sit at the table of brotherhood and swoon over the tasty fried chicken. Dinner prices are steep, but the $6.25 lunch special includes choice of fried chicken or stew, soup or salad, two vegetables, and dessert (served 11am-2pm). Coffee, eggs, and fritters can feed two well for under $10. Dinner prices are steep. BYOB. Open Sun.-Thurs. 8am-midnight, Fri.-Sat. 8am-1am.

Tutta Pasta, 26 Carmine St. (463-9653), south of Bleecker. A modern establishment with glass doors that slide open in summer. The treats here are the fresh home-made pastas, including tortellini, manicotti, and linguine ($8-15). Offers a 10% discount for students and seniors. Open daily noon-midnight. Another location at 504 La Guardia Pl. (420-0652), between Bleecker and Houston St.

Andalousia, 28 Cornelia St. (979-3693), between Bleecker and 4th St. Festooned with beautiful Moroccan rugs and maps of Africa, this restaurant offers large portions of authentic Moroccan cuisine. Be sure to try a *breewat* (flaky pastry, $2.50) or two before digging into some couscous or *tajine* stew ($10-15). Open Sun.-Thurs. noon-3pm and 5pm-midnight, Fri.-Sat. 5pm-1am.

Washington Square Restaurant, 150 W. 4th St. (533-9306), at Sixth Ave. All-American diner-style fare to satisfy your cravings. Power ballads on the radio and large booths, ideal for eavesdropping on Villagers eating pancakes ($3-5) or omelettes ($2.50-6) at 8pm. Sandwiches and burgers $5-6. Open 24hr.

Spain, 113 W. 13th St. (929-9580), between Sixth and Seventh Ave. This restaurant offers enormous tureens of traditional Spanish food for $11-16. The entrees can easily satisfy 2 or even 3 people (sharing incurs an extra $2 charge). Try the *paellas* or anything with garlic. You even get a tantalizing selection of free appetizers such as *chorizo*. Open daily noon-1am.

Elephant and Castle, 68 Greenwich Ave. (243-1400), near Seventh Ave. Their motto is *"j'adore les omelettes,"* and boy, are those omelettes adorable ($5.50-7.50). The apple, cheddar, and walnut creation, the spinach-cheddar combo, and all the rest of the strange omelette mixtures are a tad unnerving, but well worth the culinary experience. The non-omelette options are also delectable; main entrees involve intriguing toppings on chicken or pasta for $9-10.50. Open Mon.-Thurs. 8:30am-midnight, Fri. 8:30am-1am, Sat. 10am-1am, Sun. 10am-midnight.

Tea and Sympathy, 108 Greenwich Ave. (807-8329), between Jane and W. 13th St. An English tea house—high tea, cream tea, and good old-fashioned British cuisine. Filled with kitschy teacups and salt shakers, fading photos of obviously English families, and beautiful chipped china. The waitresses all speak the Queen's English. Afternoon tea (the whole shebang—sandwiches, tea, scones, rarebit) $13, cream tea (tea, scones, and jam) $6, shepherd pie $6.75. Open Mon.-Fri. 11:30am-10pm, Sat.10am-10pm, Sun. 10am-9pm.

Eva's, 11 W. 8th St. (677-3496), between MacDougal St. and Fifth Ave. Refreshing fast-service health food with a seating parlor. Massive meatless combo plate with falafel, grape leaves, and eggplant $5.35. The menus outside often contain coupons. Open daily 11am-11pm.

CAFÉS

Caffè Reggio, 119 MacDougal St. (475-9557), south of W. 3rd St. Celebs, wannabes, and students crowd the oldest café in the Village. Open since 1927, this place showcases busts and madonnas in every corner, and pours a mean cup of cappuccino ($2.25). Choose from a wide selection of pastries ($2.50-3.50). You'll bounce off the walls. Open Sun.-Thurs. 10am-2am, Fri.-Sat 10am-4am.

Caffè Borgia, 185 Bleecker St. (673-2290), at MacDougal St. Moody, dark café has the look and feel of mother Italy. Cult figures who frequent the place include Pacino and De Niro. Virtually endless coffee list ($1.50-2.75) and many sweet desserts. Open Sun.-Thurs. 10am-2am, Fri. 10am-4am, Sat. 10am-5am.

Caffè Dante, 79 MacDougal St. (982-5275), south of Bleecker St. A Village staple, decorated with black and white photos of the Old World. *Frutta di bosco,* $4.50. Coffee-based liquids $2-6. Nice *gelati* and Italian ices ($4.50). A great place to take Beatrice. Open Sun.-Thurs. 10am-2am, Fri.-Sat. 10am-3pm.

Caffè Mona Lisa, 282 Bleecker St. (929-1262), near Jones St. The presence of *La Gioconda* imagery is strong but not overpowering, much like the coffee. In addition to the well brewed beverages ($1.50-2.75) and the usual café fare, Mona Lisa entices with oversized mirrors hanging above stuffed chairs and other personality-filled furniture pieces. Open daily 11am-2am.

■ SoHo

As with everything else in SoHo, the food is all about image. Down with the diner; food here comes in a variety of exquisite and pricey forms, none of it fried or served over a counter. Most of the restaurants in SoHo demonstrate a strong preoccupation with decor, and most aim to serve a stylishly healthful cuisine which, like *Life* cereal, is both good and good for you. With the image lifestyle, of course, comes money, so don't be surprised if you find it hard to get a cheap meal. Often the best deal in SoHo is brunch, when the neighborhood shows its most cozy and good-natured front (and puts the calorie-counter away for a while). Omelettes, pancakes, and coffee are served piping hot in any number of café/bar establishments.

FOOD AND DRINK

Even more than its restaurants, SoHo's grocery stores tend to champion the organic side of gourmet dining. At **Dean and Deluca,** 560 Broadway (431-1691), at Prince St., gallery quality art surrounds a huge selection of gourmet coffees, pastas, produce, and seafood (open Mon.-Sat. 10am-8pm, Sun. 10am-7pm). Much less chic and more budget-friendly, the **Gourmet Garage,** 453 Broome St. (941-5850), at Mercer St., is organic-intensive in its stock of pastas, produce, fresh salads, and teas (open daily 8am-8:30pm).

★**Bell Caffè,** 310 Spring St. (334-BELL/2355), between Hudson and Greenwich. This low-key restaurant in an old bell factory may be off the beaten path, but there are good reasons to walk the extra blocks. Bell sports a global-village-meets-garage-sale aesthetic with a delicious multicultural menu to match, offering Indian, African, Mexican, Jewish, and Japanese "ethno-healthy" cuisine, including "Spring Street Rolls" made with shrimp, ginger, port vinaigrette, and couscous. Always laid back, always healthy, and everything on the menu is under $10. Free live music nightly 9:30pm-midnight and monthly receptions for the new art that goes up on the restaurant's walls. Catch a cool breeze off the Hudson while enjoying the backyard patio seating. Open Sun.-Thurs. noon-2am, Fri.-Sat. noon-4am.

★**Lucky's Juice Joint,** 75 W. Houston St. (388-0300), near W. Broadway. *Three's Company* meets SoHo at this small restaurant specializing in fresh juice combinations. Smoothies ($3.50) are made with a whole banana and a choice of everything from soy milk to peaches; a variety of other additions—from ginseng to bee pollen—can be put into your smoothie for under a dollar more. Lucky's is not just a vegetarian's dream; it also serves up fresh and tasty food to the weary gallery-goer. Veggie sandwiches $4-5, chilled 10-oz "shots" of wheat grass, $1.50. Open Mon-Sat. 9am-8pm; Sun. 10am-8pm.

Lupe's East L.A. Kitchen, 110 Sixth Ave. (966-1326), at Watts St. Lupe's is small, down-scale, and diner-esque; not elegant but one of the cheaper and tastier spots around. Burritos and enchiladas ($7-8), and beer are standard. Super Vegetarian Burrito ($7.25) and the Taquito Platter ($7.25) are super-tasty, as are the *huevos cubanos*—eggs any style with black beans and sweet plantain ($5); four types of hot-pepper sauce are provided on every table for those who need a little more fire. Brunch ($3.75-7.25) served Sat.-Sun. 11:30am-4pm. Better atmosphere than East L.A. Open Sun.-Tues. 11:30am-11pm, Wed.-Sat. 11:30am-midnight.

Abyssinia, 35 Grand St. (226-5959), at Thompson St. Terrific Ethiopian restaurant with low-to-the-ground, hand-carved stools at tables made of woven fibers akin to wicker. Combine the decor with the experience of eating most dishes with your hands, scooping up the food with pieces of dense and spongy *injera* bread, and you get a very comfortable, communal atmosphere. Vegetarian entrees $6-8, meat dishes $8.50-12. The *azefa wotólentils*—red onions, garlic ginger, and hot green peppers, served cold—is great in the summer (as is a St. George, the Ethiopian-style beer served here). Open Mon. 6-10pm, Tues.-Thurs. 6-11pm, Fri. 6pm-midnight, Sat. 1pm-midnight, Sun. 1-11pm.

Moon Dance Diner, 80 Sixth Ave. (226-1191), at Grand St. The real thing—an authentic old diner-car replete with curved ceilings and counter service. Excellent short-order breakfasts are served all day, but breakfast specials, served in the morning, are particularly rewarding. The cheese omelette with toast and home- fries ($3.50) is mighty tasty. Wed. nights offer all-you-can-eat pasta (with a big selection of pastas and sauces) for $8. Dollar draft beers all day every day. Sandwiches $6.50-9. Open Mon.-Fri. 8:30-11am for breakfast. Also open Sun.-Wed. 8am-midnight; Thurs.-Sat. 24hr.

Space Untitled, 133 Greene Street (260-6677), near Houston St. Joint exhibition space and café with a strangely cafeteria-like atmosphere for chic SoHo. Still, the $1 cups of coffee may be nicer than the school lunch swill you may remember. Sandwiches and salads $4-7, desserts $1.50-3.50. Wine and beer $4.50-5.50. Open Sun.-Mon. 7am-10pm, Tues.-Thurs. 7am-11pm, Fri.-Sat. 7am-midnight.

Brother's BBQ, 225 W. Houston St. (727-2775), at Varick St. An authentic barbecue shack may seem out of place in artsy SoHo, but Brother's down-to-earth atmosphere is a welcome respite in this land of high style. Friendly service, delicious ribs, and mashed potatoes—what a combo! Bring a bib. Most entrees roll in at $8.

Sandwiches $4.75-6.50. Mon. nights all-you-can-eat BBQ $11. During lunch (Mon.-Fri. 11:30am-4pm) all prices about $2 less. ½-chicken buttermilk-fried, $7. Open Mon.-Thurs. 11:30am-11pm, Fri. 11:30am-2am, Sat. 11am-2am, Sun. 11am-11pm; kitchen closes at midnight Fri.-Sat.

Prince St. Bar and Restaurant, 125 Prince St. (228-8130), at Wooster St. High ceilings, spare decor, and a wall of large windows exemplify the SoHo style; hardwood floors and a couple of cacti complete the effect. But hey, Prince St. has been here since 1975, so at least it can say it got here first. An excellent selection of Indonesian specialties ($6-11)—the stir-fry noodles with steamed vegetables and choice of sauce (peanut, garlic, or ginger) are great for dinner, as is the challah French toast for breakfast. The burgers are grand, too ($6-8.50). Full bar with a selection of microbrews (pints $3-4). Open Sun.-Mon. 11:30am-11pm, Tues.-Wed. 11:30am-midnight, Fri.-Sat. 11:30am-1am.

Le Gamin Café, 50 MacDougal St. (254-4678), near Houston St. Always packed with locals, this very European café offers simple and tasty breakfast, lunch, and dinner over one of the best magazine selections in town. Café au lait ($3) in hand, you can read to your heart's content. People-watching is fun too—Le Gamin is notorious for its cute waitstaff. Open daily 8am-midnight.

■ TriBeCa

Dining in TriBeCa is generally a much funkier (and blessedly cheaper) experience than in chic SoHo. It's not that restaurants here don't put a lot of thought into style, but that the style of choice has a dressed-down, folksy, flea market flavor. TriBeCa is much more industrial than SoHo, and restaurants often hide like little oases among the hulking warehouses and decaying buildings.

★Yaffa's Tea Room, 19 Harrison St. (274-9403), near Greenwich St. Situated in a pleasingly uncommercial and hidden corner of TriBeCa, Yaffa's is one of the few places in Manhattan that serves high tea—and definitely the coolest. The decor is straight out of yard sales and used furniture stores—not ratty, just "unusual." Wide selection of healthful sandwiches ($7.50) and entrees ($7-15). Brunch served daily 8:30am-5pm (omelettes and main selections $4.50-6.50, pastries $4-6). High tea ($15, reservations required) served Mon.-Fri. 2-6pm, and includes a "savory course,"—cucumber, salmon, or watercress finger sandwiches—fresh baked scones, dessert sampler, and a pot of tea. There's also "Couscous Night" every Thursday from 6:30 to midnight. The attached bar/restaurant, at the corner of Greenwich St., is a little less subdued, with a different menu (including tapas ($2-3) like marinated mushrooms and mozzarella with sundried tomatoes) to complement small tables covered with green, corrugated aluminum. Bar open daily 8:30am-4am, restaurant open 8:30am-midnight.

Biblio's, 317 Church St. (334-6990), between Walker and Lipsenard. Stop by this café/bookstore to find out what's happening in TriBeCa from the people who live there. Pictures of the owners and founders adorn the walls, and the staff is quite conversational and friendly. The bookstore half specializes in small press, eastern philosophy, film books, and unusual periodicals. Most pasta salads and sandwiches under $5, good coffee drinks and desserts as well. Poetry and free live jazz on many nights; call ahead for the schedule. A bulletin board just inside the door lists events at other establishments and parks in the area. Open 7:30am-8pm daily.

Bubby's, 120 Hudson St. (219-0666), at N. Moore St. This café's rough brick walls with white woodwork, unupholstered wooden window benches, and two walls of windows all add to its stylish simplicity. Great scones, muffins, and pies keep this place, originally a pie company, packed with locals, but lunch and dinner are excellent as well; the spinach and black bean quesadilla ($7) and the half-spicy jerk chicken with homemade mashed potatoes and greens ($10)—each served with yummy sweet corn muffins—are both favorites. Soups $2.75-3.75, salads $4-10, and sandwiches $6.75-7.75. Full breakfast menu as well. Expect a wait on weekend mornings. Open daily 7am-11pm.

El Teddy's, 219 West Broadway (941-7070), between Franklin and White St. You'll definitely have no trouble finding it—the huge, colorful awning made in stained glass window fashion from many colors of paper is *nada* if not obvious. First-rate, creative Mexican cuisine (yes, cuisine) conceived with a strong dose of California health food. The baby-artichoke-and-sundried-tomato quesadilla ($7) and the shrimp tostada with jalapeños, avocados, and refried beans ($9) are both excellent. TriBeCa residents also rave about El Teddy's margaritas ($7.50 for a shaker). Open Mon.-Fri. noon-3pm and 6-11:30pm, Sat. 6-11:30pm, Sun.6-11pm.

■ East Village and Lower East Side

Culinary cultures clash on the lower end of the East Side, where pasty-faced punks and starving artists dine alongside an older generation conversing in Polish, Hungarian, and Yiddish. The neighborhood took in the huddled masses, and, in return, got lots of cool places to eat; immigrant culture after immigrant culture has left its culinary residue in the form of cheap restaurants. As Chinatown gradually dissipates along East Broadway, you can still find the city's finest kosher Jewish eateries. Farther north, the Ukrainians made their mark in the form of cheap places serving borscht, *pirogi*, and other inexpensive yet hearty foods. Twenty-six Indian restaurants line 6th St. between First and Second Ave. This area is crammed full of $3-4 afternoon lunch specials.

Lately, the most noticeable immigrant culture in the East Village has been that of its artsy youth; they, too, brought their restaurants and cafés, and because the East Village has yet to experience the gentrification of its western counterpart, there are still many undiscovered and quiet establishments. **First** and **Second Ave.** are the best for restaurant-exploring, St. Mark's Place hosts a slew of inexpensive and popular village institutions, and at night, Ave. A bustles with bars and sidewalk cafés.

★**Dojo Restaurant,** 24 St. Mark's Pl. (674-9821), between Second and Third Ave. Dojo is one of the most popular restaurants and hangouts in the East Village, and rightly so; it offers an incredible variety of vegetarian and Japanese food that manages to be simultaneously healthy, delicious, and inexplicably inexpensive. Tasty soyburgers with brown rice and salad $3. Spinach and pita sandwich with assorted veggies $3. Outdoor tables allow for interaction with slick passers-by, though the loud chaos of St. Mark's might give you a headache. New location (same menu) on Washington Square South at 14 W. 4th St. (505-8934). Open Sun.-Thurs. 11am-1am, Fri.-Sat. 11am-2am.

★**Benny's Burritos,** 93 Ave. A (254-2054), at 6th St. This colorful, shiny Cal-Mex hot spot is dirt-cheap and always hoppin'. Trendy, tasteful decor, lots of windows for excellent people-watching, and great food—plump, tasty burritos with black or pinto beans $5-6. Fab frozen margaritas $5. Locals swear by it. Open Sun.-Thurs. 11am-midnight, Fri.-Sat. 11am-1am. No credit cards accepted, traveler's checks only with ID.

★**Damask Falafel,** 85 Ave. A. (673-5016) between 5th and 6th St. This closet-sized stand serves the cheapest and best falafel in the area—$1.75 for a sandwich, $3.50 for a falafel platter with tabouli, chick peas, salad, and pita bread. $1.25 for two succulent stuffed grape leaves. Banana milk shakes $1.25. Open Mon.-Fri. 11am-2am, Sat.-Sun. 11am-4am.

★**Veselka,** 144 Second Ave. (228-9682), at 9th St. Down-to-earth, soup-and-bread, Polish-Ukrainian joint. Traditional food served in a friendly, untraditional setting. Big, beautiful murals cover everything, including the dumpster around the corner. Enormous menu includes about 10 varieties of soups, as well as salads, blintzes, meats, and other Eastern European fare. Blintzes $3.50, soup $1.95 a cup (the chicken noodle is sumptuous). Combination special gets you soup, salad, stuffed cabbage, and four melt-in-your-mouth *pirogi* ($7.95). Great breakfast specials: challah french toast, OJ, and coffee for $3.75. Open 24hr.

Mama's Food Shop, 200 E. 3rd St. (777-4425), between Ave. A and B. A wall of framed pictures of Mama-looking women greet you as you enter this tiny shop which, as you might guess, specializes in Home cooking with a capital H. See trendy villagers and up-towners settling in to heaping plates of fried chicken ($5) or salmon ($7), with sides ranging from honey-glazed sweet potatoes to broccoli to couscous for only $1 each. Scrape your leftovers and turn in your plate at the end of the meal, just like at good ole Mom's. Bread pudding and cobbler by the ½ pint ($3) are available for dessert if you have room. Open Mon.-Sat. 11am-11pm.

Siné, 122 St. Mark's Pl. (475-3991, 982-0370 for band info), between First Ave. and Ave. A. Subway: #6 to Astor Pl. Name means "That's it" in Gaelic. Down-to-earth, folksy crowd comes here after a long day at the farm. Three or four bands per night starting at 8pm and ranging from folk to blues to rock. Food also served—the ginger veggie stew with brown rice, bread, and salad is a great deal at $5. Traditional Irish breakfasts 10am-4pm. Breads and desserts baked daily. Never a cover. Open daily 10am-1am.

First Street Café, 72 E. 1st St. (420-0701), by First Ave. Perfect for people-watching, this small, hip café serves up free jazz nightly at 9pm, as well as the best morning breakfast deal in the area: bagels, eggs, and coffee for $2.50. Bowls of cappuccino big enough to drown in $3. Open Sun.-Thurs. 8am-midnight, Fri.-Sat. 8am-2 or 3am.

National Café, 210 First Ave. (473-9354), at 13th St. It would be hard to find a better Cuban lunch special in the city; from 10:30am-3pm, the National serves an entree of the day, a choice of rice and beans or salad plus plantain, a cup of soup, and bread for $4. Even without the specials, everything on the menu is well under $10. Open Mon.-Sat. 10:30am-10pm.

Second Ave. Delicatessen, 156 Second Ave. (677-0606), at 10th St. The definitive New York deli, established in 1954. People come into the city just to be snubbed by the waiters here. Strictly kosher, and proudly so. Try a free sample of chopped chicken liver on rye—even if you don't like liver, you'll love theirs. Have pastrami (reputed to be the best in the city) or tongue on rye bread for $7.50, a fabulous burger deluxe for $7, or matzah ball soup for $3. Meals served with an array of pickles (kosher dill, cucumber, and sour tomato). Note the Hollywood-style star plaques embedded in the sidewalk outside; this was once the heart of the Yiddish theater district. Open Sun.-Thurs. 8am-midnight, Fri.-Sat. 8am-2am.

Yaffa Café, 97 St. Mark's Place (647-9302), between First Ave. and Ave. A. The highest decor-to-price ratio in the Village. Diners peruse a 5-page menu offering all sorts of salads ($5-6), sandwiches ($3.50-6), and beer ($3.50) in an interior right out of I-Dream-of-Jeannie's bottle. The outdoor garden in the back is open all summer, complete with abandoned bathtubs, a working fountain, and random Duchamps-inspired sentence fragments spray-painted on the walls. Open 24hr.

K.K. Restaurant, 194 First Ave. (777-4430), between 11th and 12th St. This light-wood panelled restaurant has a down-home feel and serves well-prepared Polish cuisine. The $5.75 lunch special comes with a choice of soup or salad, an entree, a choice of vegetable, and coffee or soda. Try the *kielbasa* or the Polish beer. The patio makes for great outdoor dining. Free delivery, too. Open daily 7am-11pm.

Rose of India, 308 E. 6th St. (533-5011, 473-9758), between First and Second Ave. Decorated like a Christmas tree turned inside out and spread across a subway car, the Rose of India stands out even on a street of 26 Indian restaurants as the liveliest and tastiest. Curries with rice, dal, and chutney $5-7. Nine different breads $1.75-$3. Samosas for $2. On your birthday, they'll throw a mini "party" for you, replete with cakes and lights. BYOB, and make reservations on weekends to beat the long lines. Open daily 11am-1am.

Mee Noodle Shop and Grill, 219 First Ave. (995-0333), at 13th St. Fresh ingredients make for very good, simple Chinese food. The noodle soups are grand ($2.75-5), as are the *dan-dan* noodles ($4.25). Other entrees $4-8.50. Open daily 11am-11pm. Other locations at 795 Ninth Ave. and 53rd St. (995-0396), and 922 Second Ave. at 49th St. (995-0563).

Pink Pony Café, 176 Ludlow St., between E. Houston and Stanton St. Self-consciously trendy café/ice cream parlor/bookshop catering to the Lower East Side artistic set, located in a neighborhood that stays quiet even at night. A great place to study, read, or write over an espresso ($1.50). Or, try their iced lemon and ginger drink ($1.50). Perhaps a smoothie? At $3.50, they're the best in the city. Several shelves of second-hand books for sale or perusal, tending toward the trashy spy-thriller genre. Comfy chairs and couches. Open Sun.-Thurs. 10:30am-midnight, Fri.-Sat. 10:30am-4am.

The Kiev, 117 Second Ave. (674-4040), at 7th St. A funky Eastern European breakfast extravaganza. A great place to end up at 4am when you have the munchies. A stack of heaven-sent fresh buttermilk peach pancakes $3 (also come in fresh banana, blueberry, cheese, and cherry). A cup of homemade soup ($1.75) comes with an inch-thick slab of challah bread. Lengthy menu features sandwiches of all sorts, along with many other breakfast specialties. Open 24hr.

Khyber Pass Restaurant, 34 St. Mark's Pl. (473-0989), between Second and Third Ave. Retreat from St. Mark's and relax on cushy pillows and afghan rugs. A dainty place on the central artery of the East Village serving Afghani food. The unusual cuisine served here recalls more familiar Middle Eastern foods but with surprising twists and turns. There are plenty of unusual vegetarian selections, such as pumpkin dumplings ($3 for 4). One can sit on pillows at a traditional, low-to-the-ground table and enjoy *bouranee baunjaun,* eggplant with mint yogurt and fresh coriander ($7.50), or *phirnee,* a delicate rice pudding with pistachios and rosewater ($2.25). Free delivery. Open daily noon-midnight.

Cucina di Pesce, 87 E. 4th St. (260-6800), between Second and Third Ave. A classic little Italian place, complete with checkered table cloths, cute waiters, and sidewalk (and backyard) seating. You can sit in the backyard and pretend you're in Firenze. Dishes are inexpensive if not excellent, and the large portions will fill you up. Spinach penne (spinach pasta with asparagus, sundried tomatoes, and fontina cheese) $7. Salmon with sauteed mushrooms and a side of pasta $10. Weekday special 4:30-6:30pm; weekends 4-6pm. Full dinner with bread, soup, entree, and wine $10. Open Sun.-Thurs. 4pm-midnight, Fri.-Sat. 4pm-1am.

For Jewish food, hold on to your yarmulke and head on down to the Lower East Side around and south of East Houston St. **Kossar's Hot Bialys,** 367 Grand St. (473-4810) at Essex St., makes bialys that recall the heyday of the Lower East Side (open 24 hr.). Here are some more of the more famed establishments:

Katz's Delicatessen, 205 E. Houston St. (254-2246), near Orchard St. Established in 1888, Katz's is an archetypal New York deli. It gets lots of mileage from being the site of Meg Ryan's fake orgasm in *When Harry Met Sally.* You better know what you want; the staff here means business. The food is good and the portions ample, but you pay extra for the atmosphere. Heroes cost $5.10, sandwiches around $8. They also provide a salami-shipping service, dating from the days when our boys overseas asked for nothing better than to receive cold cuts in the mail. Open Sun.-Tues. 8am-10pm, Wed.-Thurs. 8am-11pm, Fri.-Sat. 8am-midnight.

Ratner's Restaurant, 138 Delancey St. (677-5588), just west of the Manhattan Bridge. The most famous of the kosher restaurants, partly because of its frozen-food line. In odd contrast to its run-down surroundings, this place is large, shiny, and popular. Jewish dietary laws are strictly followed and only dairy food is served—but oy vey! Such matzah brei ($8.95)! Also feast on fruit blintzes and sour cream ($9) or simmering vegetarian soups ($4). Open Sun.-Thurs. 6am-midnight, Fri. 6am-3pm, Sat. sundown-2am.

Yonah Schimmel Knishery, 137 E. Houston St. (477-2858). Rabbi Schimmel's establishment, around since the heyday of the Jewish Lower East Side (around 1910), has honed the knish to an art. A dozen varieties available for $1.50. Try yogurt from the 87-year-old strain for $1.25. Open daily 8:30am-5:30pm.

Gertel's Bake Shoppe & Luncheonette, 53 Hester St. (982-3250), near Essex St. Gertel's is a hole-in-the-wall kosher sandwich and baked goods shop with great food (sandwiches $3-4) and no sit-down service. Open Sun.-Thurs. 6:30am-5pm, Fri. 6:30am-3pm.

Essex St. (Gus's) Pickle Corp., 35 Essex St. (254-4477). Pickles galore, as seen in *Crossing Delancey.* A vast variety of gherkins, from super sour to sweet, sold individually ($.50 to $2.00) and by the pound. Also offers coleslaw, pickled tomatoes and carrots, and the like. Open Sun.-Thurs. 9am-6pm, Fri. 9am-4pm.

■ Little Italy

Immortalized by Billy Joel, who used to have dinner in the local *ristoranti*, **Mulberry Street** is the main drag and the appetite avenue of Little Italy. Here, among the strings of tiny Italian flags that fly above the street, *trattorie* and *caffè* crowd the sidewalks with their outdoor tables. Daylight during the work-week finds Little Italy quieter than most districts of New York; at night and on weekends, however, tourists and natives released from their jobs come here to stroll, feast, and finally relax in the sidewalk *caffè*. After 7pm, the street comes to life, but you'll have to arrive a little earlier to get one of the better tables. For the sake of variety and thrift, dine at a *ristorante* and then move to a *caffè* to get your just desserts. The *caffè* atmosphere is more conducive to lingering and contemplation (and the coffee's usually better to boot). Beginning with the second Thursday in September, Mulberry Street goes wild as Little Italy toasts the Saint of Naples during the raucous 10-day **Feast of San Gennaro.** To get to Little Italy, take the #4, 5, or 6, the N or R, or the J, M, or Z to Canal St.; or take the B, D, F, or Q to Broadway-Lafayette.

Ballato, 55 E. Houston St. (274-8881), at Mott St. Gracefully stemmed wine glasses and glistening chocolate-covered cherries greet you. Although clearly cross-bred with SoHo style, Ballato serves impeccable southern Italian cooking to a small crowd of couples, tourists, and students. Pasta $7.50-11.50, trout in olive oil $12.50. *Antipasti* $5.50-8. Two-course lunch (Mon.-Fri. noon-4pm; $7.50) includes choice from a wide selection of entrees and either an appetizer or dessert. *Prix fixe* dinner (Sun.-Fri. 4-6:30pm, Sat. 5-6:30pm; $14.50) includes all 3 courses. Open Mon.-Fri. noon-11pm, Sat. 4pm-midnight, Sun. 4pm-11pm.

Puglia Restaurant, 189 Hester St. (966-6006), at Mulberry St. Long tables yield fun and rowdiness. Venture into four separate dining rooms, ranging from diner-like to batcave-like (lined with stones and mildly cavernous). A favorite of New Yorkers and bold tourists. Pastas $7-10, entrees $8.75-10.75. Monstrous plate of mussels $9.25. Try the "famous" *rigatoni alla vodka* ($9.75). Live Italian folk music nightly beginning at 5pm. Occasional "interactive comedy/mystery theater" involves the whole dinner crowd in a mob show—call for info and reservations. Open Sun.-Thurs. 11:30am-midnight, Fri.-Sat. 11:30am-1am.

Vincent's Clam Bar, 119 Mott St. (226-8133), at Hester St. A New York institution. Archaic photos line the walls of the *ristorante* that Giuseppe and Carmela Siano established in 1904 and named after their son. Ravioli with Vincent's famous hot clam sauce $8, pasta from $6.50. Entrees are mainly seafood ($6.50-17). Vincent's Shrimp Balls $8.50. Open Sun.-Thurs. 11:30am-1:30am, Fri.-Sat. 11:30am-3:30am.

Pietro & Vanessa, 23 Cleveland Pl. (941-0286), between Spring and Lafayette St. Removed from the main fray of crowded and hectic outdoor tables along Mulberry St.; the large, relaxing patio out back is a welcome change. *Trattoria* with a very good standard menu. Baked clam *antipasto* $5.25, pasta such as *fusilli primavera* (with fresh vegetables) $8-9, chicken entrees $9-11, fish and veal $10. Open Mon.-Fri. noon-11pm, Sat. 4-11pm, Sun. 4-10pm.

La Mela, 167 Mulberry St. (431-9493), between Broome and Grand St. Kitschy photos and postcards dot the walls; tables and chairs endlessly shift and merge to accommodate large groups and families, and super-friendly waitstaff merrily chortle as you chew. Equally rambunctious outdoor seating in their backyard, complete with a guitar-touting bard. A wide assortment of pasta and *gnocchi* ($6.50-10), along with a large number of entrees ($12-15). Always specials; the waiters love to shout you through your order. Open daily noon-11pm.

Benito One, 174 Mulberry St. (226-9171). Another location at 163 Mulberry St. (226-9012), between Grand and Broome St. A small, very friendly *trattoria* featuring a menu of excellent Italian fare. A favorite is *pollo scarpariello,* chicken on the bone with garlic, olive oil, and basil ($11). Pasta $7-11, veal $13, poultry $11-13, seafood $12.50-20. Open Sun.-Thurs. noon-11pm, Fri.-Sat. noon-midnight.

Paninoteca, 250 Mulberry St. (219-1351), at Prince St. Unlike most Little Italy *trattorie*, Paninoteca isn't afraid of sunlight. Two walls of windows and lots of blonde-wood; the lighter, simpler decor complements a lighter, simpler, healthier menu.

Salads $4-7, pastas $6-8, entrees $11-13. The *carbonara alla panna* ($9), cheese-filled tortellini with bacon, ham, peas, and onions, will leave you smiling. Brunch served daily until 4pm. Open Mon.-Thurs. 11am-midnight, Fri 11am-1am, Sat. 9am-1am, Sun. 9am-midnight.

Rocky's Italian Restaurant, 45 Spring St. (274-9756), at Mulberry St. This Italian stallion punches out *primi* dishes a few blocks away from the heart of the action. Billy Crystal and his uncle are regulars in this family eatery that's been cooking up consistently good Italian fare for over 20 years. For lunch try a pizza hero ($4) or sandwiches ($4-7), served until 5pm. Pastas $6.50-11, entrees $11-17. Or come up with your own idea—special orders don't upset them. The house specialty, chicken in wine sauce with mushrooms ($11), is a definite treat. Open daily 11am-11pm. Closed Sun. July-Aug.

The D.G. Bakery, 45 Spring St. (226-6688), at Mulberry St. This neighborhood mainstay has baked heavenly thick-crusted Italian-style loaves, arguably the best bread in the city, since 1963. The bread is available throughout New York, but it's best when bought here. The selection diffuses quickly after 11am on weekends. Open daily 8am-2pm or until supplies last.

Il Fornaio, 132A Mulberry St. (226-8306), between Broome and Grand St. A clean and simple white-tiled interior, with perfectly symmetrical jars and tins of olive oil. Sreetside features a plethora of green tables and wooden chairs in the midst of side-walk traffic. Upbeat, reasonable menu; the excellent thin-crust pizzas ($4-10) are a specialty. Hot sandwiches start at $4.50, pasta dinners at $6. *Antipasti* $5-6. Open Sun.-Thurs. 11:30am-11:30pm, Fri.-Sat. 11:30am-midnight.

Ristorante Taormina, 147 Mulberry St. (219-1007/8/9), between Grand and Hester St. Upscale and right in the heart of Mulberry Street's restaurant row, with large windows, graceful green plants, exposed brick walls, and blondewood fittings. Dressy but comfortable clientele enjoys gourmet food and bottles of wine. The tux-edoed maitre'd completes the picture of Italian elegance. *Penne arrabiate* $13, *saltinbocca alla romana* (veal with prosciutto, white wine, and sage) $13. Pastas $10-16, entrees $12-18. Open Mon.-Thurs. noon-11:30pm, Fri. noon-12:30am, Sat. noon-1am, Sun. noon-10:30pm.

Caffè

Caffè Roma, 385 Broome St. (226-8413), at Mulberry St. A good *caffè* gets better with time. A full-fledged saloon in the 1890s, Roma has kept its original furnishings intact: dark green walls with polished brass ornaments, sinuous wire chairs, marble tables, chandeliers, and darkwood cabinets where liquor bottles used to roost. The pastries and coffee, Roma's *raison d'être*, prove as refined as the setting. Try the neapolitan *cannoli* or the *baba au rhum* ($1.50 to take out, $2.25 to eat in). Potent espresso $1.75, obligatory cappuccino, with a tiara of foamed milk, $2.50. Open Sun.-Thurs. 8am-midnight, Fri.-Sat. 9am-1am.

La Bella Ferrara, 110 Mulberry St. (966-7867). Named after the city that brought you turbo power, La Bella Ferrara maintains the dual imperatives of power and grace in its dynamic production of *dolci*. Sleek glass and checkered tile in two rooms designed for conversational intimacy and wolfing down desserts. Pastries $1.50-2, desserts $3-4.50, cappuccino $2.50, biscuits $4.75 per lb. Breakfast special (served Mon.-Fri. 9am-noon; $2.75) includes cappuccino or espresso, juice, and croissant, bagel, or muffin. Lunch special (soup and sandwich; until 5pm) $5.50. Worth a visit on a nice evening—it's one of the few places on Mulberry St. that gives you outdoor seating removed from pedestrian flow. Open Sun.-Thurs. 9am-1am, Fri.-Sat. 9am-2am.

Ferrara, 195-201 Grand St. (226-6150). Less a café than an institution, Ferrara rolls out the red carpet for your sweet tooth. America's first espresso bar (since 1892) has become one of the city's most popular places for caffeination. In good weather the bar extends up two floors and onto the sidewalk, where a counter dispenses authentic Italian *gelati* ($4.75). *Cannoli* $2.85, *tiramisu* $4.50, strawberry short-cake $4.25, other pastries $2, mini-pastries 75¢. Excellent sandwiches like the *focaccia imbottita,* with broccoli, artichoke, provolone, roasted peppers, and pesto ($4.50). Open Sun.-Fri. 7:30am-midnight, Sat. 7:30am-1am.

Café Gitane, 242 Mott St. (334-9552), at Prince St. More SoHo than Mulberry, this trendy but relaxed café caters to the young, beautiful, and bohemian. Inside it's small, retro, and diner-esque, with bold-colored chairs upholstered in vinyl, tables topped with linoleum, and full counter service. Hang out with a book or over conversation; a magazine rack invites you to linger. Creative, healthful salads $4.25-6.75. Sandwiches $6-7.50. Espresso $1.75, café au lait $2.75, cheesecake $3.75, chocolate torte $4. Selection of teas $1.75-2. Open Sun.-Thurs. 9am-11:30pm, Fri.-Sat. 9am-midnight.

Lo Spuntino, 117 Mulberry St. (226-9280), between Hester and Canal St. Small and simple, but gorgeous desserts compensate for lackluster decor. Lengthy list of mousses includes pumpkin mousse (in season). Pear mousse with raspberry puree $5, chocolate mousse $4.50, espresso $2. Iced cappuccino with ice cream $5. *Cannoli* $2.25. Open Mon.-Fri. 5pm-1am, Sat.-Sun. 11:30am-1am.

■ Chinatown

If you're looking for cheap, authentic, and tasty Asian fare, join the crowds that push through the narrow, chaotic streets of one of the oldest Chinatowns in the nation. A trip to this rapidly expanding district is sure to result in at least some degree of culture shock; the streets here are trafficked almost exclusively by Chinese and other Asians, and the businesses which line them are guided by (and cater to) a sensibility that shows little influence of mainstream America. In the numerous small stores that operate here, you can find rare items like Chinese housewares, hermetically sealed whole fish, roots, and all sorts of spices. If you decide you're up to doing some cooking of your own, head to **Kam Kuo Food Corp.,** 7 Mott St. (349-3097), just north of Chatham Sq., or **Hong Kong Supermarket** at the junction of East Broadway and Pike St. Multitudinous wonders occupy these local supermarkets. In the frozen meats section, London broil is supplanted by pork toes, chicken feet, and duck wings. The produce section features Chinese versions of broccoli and eggplant. Look out for the sweetened, dried cuttlefish (80¢-$2). Upstairs, chinaware and cooking utensils can supplement your food purchases (open daily 9am-8:30pm).

The neighborhood's 200-plus restaurants cook up some of the best Chinese, Thai, and Vietnamese cooking in the city and, better yet, compared to prices in nearby French and Italian eateries, these restaurants are remarkably inexpensive. This is mostly due to the fierce culinary competition. The great Vietnamese place you ate in last year may now be serving Malaysian cuisine under a different name. Such competition has been a boon for palates; once-predominantly Cantonese cooking has now burgeoned into several different cuisines from the various regions of China: hot and spicy Hunan or Szechuan food, the sweet and mildly spiced seafood of Soochow, or the hearty and filling fare of Beijing. This competition has not diminished the popularity of Cantonese *dim sum,* however. In this Sunday afternoon tradition, waiters roll carts filled with assorted dishes of bite-sized goodies up and down the aisles. To partake, you simply point at what you want (beware of "Chinese Bubblegum," a euphemism for tripe). At the end of the meal, the number of empty dishes on your table is tallied up.

For dessert (especially in summer), check out the **Chinatown Ice Cream Factory,** 65 Bayard St. (608-4170), at Mott St. Many of the flavors here are Baskin-Robbins standards, but others, such as lychee, mango, ginger, red bean, and green tea are authentic, homemade, and truly unique. (One scoop $1.90, two $3.40, three $4.50. Open Mon.-Thurs. 11:30am-11pm, Fri. and Sun. 11:30am-11:30pm, Sat. 11:30am-midnight.) The **May May Gourmet Bakery,** 35 Pell St. (267-0733), between Mott and Bowery, offers countless interesting pastries (all under 75¢). Make the commonplace seem strangely exotic with a black bean paste, lotus seed pastry (each 50¢), or coconut tart (60¢; open daily 9am-8:30pm). To reach Chinatown, take the # 6, J, M, N, R, or Z to Canal St., walk east on Canal to Mott St., go right on Mott, and follow the curved street toward the Bowery, Confucius Plaza, and E. Broadway.

FOOD AND DRINK

Excellent Dumpling House, 111 Lafayette St. (219-0212 or 219-0213), just south of Canal. True to its name, this restaurant offers absolutely terrific vegetarian and meat dumplings fried, steamed, or boiled ($4 for 8 sizeable pieces). Also great pan-fried noodles ($5-6.50) and huge bowls of noodle soups (mostly $3.50-4). Lunch specials (served Mon.-Fri. 11am-3pm) include entree such as shredded pork with garlic sauce or chicken with black bean sauce, choice of soup, and fried rice and a wonton (all specials $5.50). Small, unassuming, and populated with tourists. Nevertheless, splendid food and fast service. Open daily 11am-9pm.

House of Vegetarian, 68 Mott St. (226-6572), between Canal and Bayard St. Faux chicken, faux beef, faux lamb, and faux fish comprise the huge menu of this small and appropriately green eatery; all the animals are ersatz here, made from soy and wheat by-products. Great *lo mein* (with three kinds of mushrooms $6.75) and gluten with black bean sauce ($7). Most entrees $6-10. An ice-cold lotus-seed or lychee drink ($2) hits the spot on summer days. Open daily 11am-11pm.

HSF (Hee Sheung Fung), 46 Bowery (374-1319), just south of Canal St. Tasteful, large, crowded, and festooned with Chinese neon placards and rotating poultry in the window. Well known for its fantastic *dim sum* (served daily 7:30am-5pm) and for its "Hot Pot" buffet. The Hot Pot is the Asian equivalent to fondue, in which a huge pot of boiling broth is placed in the center of your table with a platter of more than 50 raw ingredients spread around it for dipping. Ingredients are unlimited ($18 per person) and range from fresh scallops, squid, shrimp, clams, mussels, and periwinkles to spinach, watercress, and Chinese cabbage. Range of other entrees ($7.50-17) as well, including delicacies like prawns in Yushan garlic sauce ($13). Open daily 7:30am-5am.

Peking Duck House, 22 Mott St. (227-1810), at Park St. This place won seven stars from the *Daily News* and former mayor Ed Koch called it "the best Chinese restaurant in the world." While you shouldn't believe all the hype, the Duck House does offer a well priced, enjoyable meal. If someone else is paying, order the Peking Duck Extravaganza ($29). If not, you'll probably want to stick with one of the entrees ($5.50-13), like the fried carp with scallions, carrots, ginger and sweet and sour sauce ($12.25). *Dim sum* ($2.40-7 per dish) served Sat.-Sun. 11:30am-3pm. Open Sun.-Thurs. 11:30am-10:30pm, Fri.-Sat. 11:30am-11:30pm.

Road to Mandalay, 380 Broome St. (226-4218), at Mulberry St. A rare Burmese pearl washed up on the Italian shores of Mulberry St. Refined Burmese cuisine (a marriage of Indian and Thai food) served in a cozy setting enhanced by overflowing fruit baskets. Start with the coconut noodle soup ($3.25) and the 1000-layered pancake, a delicate Burmese bread ($2.50). Entrees range from $8 (Burmese curry) to $10.50 (mixed seafood). Lighter fare features street-market noodles fried with duck and garlic $5.50-7. Open Mon.-Fri. 4-11pm, Sat.-Sun. noon-11pm.

Pongrisi Thai Restaurant, 106 Bayard St. (349-3132 or 766-0939) A soothing, exotic, air-conditioned haven in the clatter of Chinatown. Pad Thai to die for $5.50. Glass noodles with beef, squid, and veggies in soup with black bean sauce $6. Roasted duck in curry with coconut milk, bamboo shoots, onions, and bell peppers $9.50. Known for homemade Thai desserts like sweet rice with egg custard and coconut milk ($1.50). Open daily 11:30am-11:30pm.

Hong Fat, 63 Mott St. (349-4735 or 349-4860), near Bayard St. No-frills meals in a small formica heaven done up in reds and yellows, with a small, hot Szechuan menu. The Szechuan-style *kung po* beef ($7.50) and the fat noodles, a.k.a. *chow fon* ($5.50), keep 'em coming. Other noodle dishes $3-5. Entrees $6-11.25, house specialties $7-11.25. With massive air-conditioned support, Hong Fat stays chilly all night long. Very friendly staff. Open daily 10am-5am.

Mueng Thai Restaurant, 23 Pell St. (406-4259), between Mott St. and Broadway. The curry comes in 4 different colors—props to those who choose hot green. Try the Matsuman curry ($9) or the chicken in coconut milk soup ($3). Noodle dishes $8. Extensive selection of meat and seafood entrees (most $8-11). Lunch special (Tues.-Fri. 11:30am-3pm): rice and your choice of curry for $5. Open Sun., Tues.-Thurs. 11:30am-10pm, Fri.-Sat. 11:30am-11pm.

New Lung Fong Bakery, 41 Mott St. (233-7447), at Bayard St. Unlike many other bakeries around here, a clean, spacious, airy place. The "New" refers to the eating area installed toward the back. A classic Chinese coffeeshop, where locals sit and sip coffee cooled with sweetened condensed milk 60¢. Amazingly cheap selection of pastries (40-75¢ each). Almond cookies 50¢, pineapple sponge cake 50¢, chicken rolls 60¢, ham and cheese or sausage buns 50¢. Open daily 7am-9pm.

New Oriental Pearl Restaurant, 103-105 Mott St. (219-8388), between Hester and Canal St. Huge, garishly red, and family-filled, this place dazzles its clientele with huge dragons and glitzy gold Chinese lettering on shiny walls. You can choose your meal from the aquariums in the front, where fish, eels, and manta rays attempt to look more inconspicuous than their delectable neighbors. Try the orange beef Hunan-style ($9) or the shrimp fried rice ($6). Most entrees $9-12, fried rice and noodle dishes $5-9. Open daily noon-11pm.

20 Mott St. Restaurant, 20 Mott St. (964-0380), near Pell St. This two-story restaurant's entrees are so good you may want to skip the daily *dim sum*. The jasmine tea is excellent, too. Entrees $7-13, except for the abalone dishes ($40), the bird's nest soup ($65), and the shark's fin ($65.25). Open Sun.-Thurs. 8am-midnight, Fri.-Sat. 8am-2am.

Yeun Yeun Restaurant, 61A Bayard St. (406-2100). Chinese food in an American diner atmosphere—shoebox-shaped, full of booths, and downscale. Small menu seems straight out of the 50s. If you can break the language barrier, order the chicken chop suey ($6.50) or shrimp chow mein ($4.25). Entrees $3.50-7. For dessert try a lychee ice—a milkshake with syrup and fresh lychees at the bottom ($1.50). Open 4-11pm daily.

▓ Lower Manhattan

Lower Manhattan eateries cater to sharply clad Wall St. brokers and bankers on lunch break; they offer cheap food prepared lightning-fast at ultra-low prices, always available as take-out and sometimes with free delivery. Bargain-basement cafeterias are low on atmosphere but can fill you up with everything from gazpacho to Italian sausages. Fast-food joints pepper Broadway near Dey and John St. just a few feet from the overpriced offerings of the Main Concourse of the World Trade Center. In the summer, food pushcarts form a solid wall along Broadway between Cedar and Liberty St. In addition to the usual fare, vendors sell falafel and eggplant plates ($2.75), burritos ($4.50), and chilled gazpacho with an onion roll ($3.75). You can sup in Liberty Park, across the street.

At the pedestrian plaza at Coenties Slip, between Pearl and South William St., you can choose among the small budget restaurants. Select from a bounteous buffet at the **Golden Chopsticks** (825-0314) for $4 per pound; venture into the adjacent Indian or fish and chips restaurants, or trek over to nearby Chinatown for hearty cuisine. North of City Hall, food kiosks fill **St. Andrew's Plaza,** a no-frills alternative for the local crowd of office workers doing lunch.

For those who miss the queasy charm of shopping-mall cuisine, a food court near South Street Seaport also takes a stab at providing every imaginable type of ethnic cuisine in a single, convenient location. **The Promenade,** on the third floor of Pier 17 at South Street Seaport (732-7678), juxtaposes the **Wok-n'-Roll** (sweet-n'-sour pork, egg roll, and fried rice $5.99), with the **Athenian Express** (gyro or souvlaki $4.70), **The Salad Bowl** (pita sandwich with tuna, chicken, or hummus $4.50), with the **Raj'n Cajun,** where crawfish are $5.49 (promenade open Sun.-Thurs. 10am-10pm, Fri.-Sat. 10am-1am; some bars/restaurants open later).

Zigolini's, 66 Pearl St. (425-7171), at Coenties Alley. One of the few places in the area where indoor air-conditioned seating abounds, this authentically Italian restaurant serves huge and filling sandwiches ($5-7), as well as some great pasta dishes. Try the tomato spirals with sundried tomatoes, artichokes, roasted peppers, and parsley ($6.50). Come up with an appealing combo of your own and they might add it to the menu—it's happened before. Open Mon.-Fri. 7am-7pm.

Frank's Papaya, 192 Broadway (693-2763), at John St. Excellent value, quick service. Very close to the World Trade Center. Jumbo turkey burger $1.60, all-beef hot dog 50¢. Breakfast (egg, ham, cheese, coffee) $1.50. Stand and eat at one of the counters inside. Open Mon.-Sat. 5:30am-10pm, Sun. 5:30am-5:30pm.

Hamburger Harry's, 157 Chambers St. (267-4446), between West and Greenwich St. Gourmet burgers for the connoisseur: 7-oz. beef patty or chicken broiled over applewood with exotic toppings like avocado, alfalfa sprouts, chili, salsa, and béarnaise sauce ($6, with red slaw and fries or potato salad $8). Regular burger $4, nacho cheese fries $3. Open Mon.-Sat. 11:30am-10pm, Sun. 11:30am-9pm.

McDonald's, 160 Broadway (385-2063), at Liberty St. Step inside and witness one of New York's finest examples of postmodern kitsch. A $3 million double decker McPalace that seats 320 at marble tabletops. A doorperson in a tux and the strains of a baby grand piano greet you for a Wall St. McPower lunch during peak hours, and you can even keep track of stock prices as they whiz by on a computer ticker-tape. Check out the McBoutique for cheesy merchandise. Down a fruit tart ($2.50) and espresso ($2) in addition to the typical McDonald's cuisine. Fruit nectar ($1.50) and herbal tea ($1) to quench that Big McThirst. Prices run about 25% higher than the usual McDonald's fare. Open Mon.-Fri. 6am-11pm, Sat.-Sun. 7:30am-9pm.

■ Brooklyn

Brooklyn's restaurants, delis, and cafés offer all the flavors and varieties of cuisine that can be found in Manhattan, and often at lower prices. Brooklyn Heights and Park Slope offer nouvelle cuisine but specialize in pita bread and *baba ghanoush*. Williamsburg has cheap eats in a funky, low-fi atmosphere, Greenpoint is a borscht-lover's paradise, and Flatbush serves up Jamaican and other West Indian cuisine. For those who didn't get their international fill in Manhattan, Brooklyn has its own China-town in Sunset Park and its own Little Italy in Carroll Gardens.

DOWNTOWN

★**Moroccan Star,** 205 Atlantic Ave. (718-643-0800), in Brooklyn Heights. Subway: #2, 3, 4, 5, M, N, or R to Borough Hall, then 4 blocks on Court St. Ensconced in the local Arab community, this restaurant serves delicious and reasonably cheap food. Try the *pastello*, a delicate semi-sweet chicken pie with almonds ($8.75, lunch $6). Open Sun. noon-10pm, Tues.-Thurs. 10am-11pm, Fri.-Sat. 11am-11pm.

★**Teresa's,** 80 Montague St. (718-797-3996), in Brooklyn Heights. Subway: #2, 3, 4, 5, M, or R to Borough Hall; Montague St. is right there, and Teresa's is at the Prome-nade end. Good, cheap Polish food in a pleasant wood and off-white interior. Stuffed pepper ($6.75). *A pierogi* ($3.50) stuffed with cheese, potatoes, meat, or sauerkraut and mushrooms makes a filling meal. Weekday lunch specials (Mon.-Fri. 11am-4pm): entree, soup, and beverage for $6. Open daily 9am-11pm.

Red Rose Restaurant, 315 Smith St. (718-625-0963), in Carroll Gardens. Subway: F or G to Bergen St. Classy Italian dining that's heavy on the garlic and light on the wallet. The well stocked menu offers pastas from $5.25-8, and there's an additional list of 27 house specials (around $8) from which to choose from. Powerful garlic bread ($2). Open daily 11am-11pm.

Damascus Bakery, 195 Atlantic Ave. (718-855-1456), in Brooklyn Heights. Subway: #2, 3, 4, 5, M, or R to Borough Hall, then down 4 blocks on Court St. Friendly bak-ery serving up all kinds of baked goods, Middle Eastern and otherwise. Package of fresh pita bread 55¢. Superior *baklava* $1.50, spinach and feta pies $1.20, others $1-2. Open daily 7:30am-7pm.

Las Tres Palmas, 124 Court St. (718-596-2740, 624-9565), near Atlantic Ave. Sub-way: #2, 3, 4, 5, M, or R to Borough Hall, then 3½ blocks on Court St. What this small, clean restaurant lacks in polish it makes up for with excellent, affordable food. Locals come to the self-proclaimed "best Spanish restaurant in downtown Brooklyn" to enjoy hefty bowls of soup ($2.35-3) and meat dishes like chicken fric-assee ($6.40) or Palomilla steak with onions ($7.60). Entrees served with rice and beans or plantains and salad. Open daily 10am-11pm.

Buddy's Burritos and Taco Bar, 260 Court St. (718-488-8695), between Kane and Douglass St. in Carroll Gardens. Subway: F or G to Bergen St., west one block to Court St., then left 4 blocks. Italian food is the specialty in this neighborhood, but if you want a well stuffed burrito made with fresh ingredients ($3.25-6), this is the place. Open Mon.-Sat. 11:30am-11pm, Sun. 11:30am-10pm.

Junior's, 986 Flatbush Ave. Extension (718-852-5257), across the Manhattan Bridge at De Kalb St. Subway: #2, 3, 4, 5, B, D, M, N, Q, or R to Atlantic Ave. Cream, sugar, cholesterol, and the suburbanites who trek for hours to consume it. Lit up like a jukebox, Junior's feeds classic roast beef and brisket to hordes of loyals. 10-oz. steakburgers start at $5.50, full entree lunch specials around $8. This place is famous for its killer cheesecake (plain slice $3.75). Open Sun.-Thurs. 6:30am-12:30am, Fri.-Sat. 6:30am-2am.

Bagel Point Café, 231 Court St. (718-522-2220), in Carroll Gardens. Subway: F or G to Bergen St., then walk one block east to Court St. The chic and stylish set of Carroll Gardens come here to indulge in the café's delicate European pastries and desserts ($1-4). Top-notch bagels only 50¢. You can sit in their garden and enjoy a fresh mozzarella and sun-dried tomato sandwich ($3.75). Open Mon.-Thurs. 7am-1pm, Fri.-Sat. 8am-1am, Sun. 8am-midnight.

Fountain Café, 183 Atlantic Ave. (718-624-6764), in Brooklyn Heights. Subway: #2, 3, 4, 5, M, or R to Borough Hall, then four blocks on Court St. This place, named for the rumbly little fountain standing in its center, serves up inexpensive and filling Middle Eastern food to a predominantly Middle Eastern clientele. *Shwarma* $4, shish kebab $4, falafel sandwich $2.85, Syrian spinach pie $1.50. Open Sun.-Thurs. 10:30am-10:30pm, Fri.-Sat. 10:30am-11:30pm.

Kokobar, 59 Lafayette St. (718-243-9040). Subway: G to Fulton. Right around the corner from Spike's Joint, this cybercafé/bookstore was co-founded by Alice Walker's daughter. This café exemplifies the Fort Greene mentality—intellectual multiculturalism and social activism in an environment comfortable to wealthy minority artists and publishers. Excellent *orzata* ($1.75) to be had while browsing through the selection of urban contemporary writings, black classics, and Zen literature. The house brew, like the minimalist interior design, is a fusion of African and Asian flavors (90¢). Kokobar hosts frequent readings by up-and-coming minority writers, and is a good place to get flyers about Brooklyn's black gay nightlife. Oh yes, you can get sandwiches ($4-7) and check your e-mail, too. Open Mon.-Fri. 7am-11pm, Sat. 10am-midnight, Sun. 10am-10pm.

NORTH BROOKLYN

★**Oznaut's Dish,** 79 Berry St. (718-599-6596). Subway: L to Bedford Ave. From the subway, walk west to Berry St. and head north. Beautiful, beautiful, beautiful, with good food to boot. Scene: Antoni Gaudi meets ex-Manhattanite artists in laid-back Williamsburg and they build a restaurant in *kif*-dream Morocco. Lamb burger on peasant bread $6.50. Granola, yogurt, and fruit $4. Forty teas (and lots of wine) to choose from, like Iron Goddess of Mercy and Lapsang Crocodile. North African/American-eclectic fare, with plenty of cross-pollinated goodies like coconut Indian curry ($8). Open Tues.-Sun. 6am-midnight.

★**PlanEat Thailand,** 184 Bedford Ave. (718-599-5758). Subway: L to Bedford Ave. A restaurant that could only exist in Brooklyn: the city's best inexpensive Thai food served in a small restaurant decorated with high-quality graffiti on the walls. All beef dishes under $6, all chicken dishes under $7, and a killer pad thai for only $5.25. If you ask for spicy, they'll give you medium—it'll be enough to clear your sinuses (unlike most eateries, hot means *hot!* and is reserved for those who know what they're getting into). Open Mon.-Sat. 11:30am-11:30pm, Sun. 1pm-11pm.

Stylowa Restaurant, 694 Manhattan Ave. (718-383-8993), between Norman and Nassau Ave. in Greenpoint. Subway: G to Nassau Ave. Polish cuisine at its best and cheapest. Sit among Polish-speakers and sample *kielbasa* (Polish sausage) with fried onions, sauerkraut, and bread ($4), or roast beef in homemade gravy with potatoes ($4). Excellent potato pancakes $3. All other entrees ($2.75-7.25) served with a glass of compote (pink, apple-flavored fruit drink). Open Mon.-Thurs. noon-9pm, Fri. noon-10pm, Sat. 11am-10pm, Sun. 11am-9pm.

L Café, 189 Bedford Ave. (718-388-6792). Subway: L to Bedford Ave. Rotating local art adorns the walls of this chill Williamsburg café. The few food offerings are creative—the Leonard Cohen ($3.75) is a mixture of brie, scallions, and balsamic vinegar on bread. Fine cups of coffee help visitors absorb this emerging artist enclave. Open Mon.-Fri. 8:15am-midnight, Sat.-Sun. 10am-midnight.

CENTRAL BROOKLYN

In central Brooklyn, good ethnic fare abounds. Because of its recent yuppification and growing chic, the Park Slope area has become a home to artsy coffee shops and gourmet-minded restaurants. While other areas of Central Brooklyn remain a haven for international specialties. Eighth Ave. in Sunset Park is the heart of Brooklyn's Chinatown, and Church Ave. in Flatbush is the place for Jamaican and other West Indian cuisine.

★**Tom's Restaurant,** 782 Washington Ave. (718-636-9738), at Sterling Pl. Subway: #2 or 3 to Brooklyn Museum. Head to Washington St. on the left side of the museum and follow it northward across the multi-lane intersection. A quintessential Brooklyn breakfast place—an old-time luncheonette complete with a soda fountain and 50s-style hyper-friendly service. Two eggs with fries or grits, toast, and coffee or tea $2. Famous golden *challah* french toast $3. Breakfast served all day. Open Mon.-Sat. 6:30am-4pm.

Ray's Jerk Chicken, 3125 Church Ave. (718-826-0987), between 31st and 32nd St. in Flatbush. Subway: #2 or 5 to Church Ave. and 2 blocks east. Jerked chicken is a delicious Jamaican specialty—crispy chicken roasted with a sweet and very peppery marinade and served either hot or cold. You can also sample one of the many other enticing entrees ($6-7). Open Mon.-Thurs. 9am-3am, Fri.-Sun. 24hr.

Oriental Palace, 5609 Eighth Ave. (718-633-6688), near 56th St. in Sunset. Subway: N to Eighth Ave. Authentic and inexpensive. *Dim sum* $1-1.50 per order, including chicken feet and bird's nest (daily 7:30am-4pm). Lunch around $5, roast pork bun 50¢. Juicy roasted meats on rice $6.75-8.75. Open Sun.-Thurs. 7:30am-midnight, Fri.-Sat. 7:30am-1am.

El Gran Castillo de Jagua, 345 Flatbush Ave. (718-622-8700), at Carlton St. across from the subway. Subway: D or Q to Seventh Ave. A terrific place for cheap, authentic Latino food. Meat dinners with rice and beans or plantains and salad $5-12. The *mofungo* (crushed green plantains with roast pork and gravy, $3.50) is absolutely grand. Open daily 7am-midnight.

Short Ribs, 9101 Third Ave. (718-745-0614), in Bay Ridge. Subway: R to 86th St. Walk one block west and south a few blocks. The best barbecue around—especially if someone else foots the somewhat hefty bill. French onion soup is served in a round loaf of semolina bread ($4.50). A solid meal with onion rings costs $15. Incredibly popular; this two-story joint fills at mealtimes. Open Mon.-Thurs. noon-11pm, Fri.-Sat. noon-1am, Sun. noon-10pm.

Nam, 222 Seventh Ave. (718-788-5036), in Park Slope. Subway: D or Q to Seventh Ave. Walk several blocks along Seventh Ave. Thriving on the patronage of health-minded Park Slopers, Nam serves up delicate Vietnamese cuisine at prices even the starving yuppie can afford. Rice noodle dish bun ($7) is a satisfying standard choice, but more adventurous entrees await. Plenty of vegetarian options available, such as *ca tim nuong xao dam ot,* stir-fried charred eggplant in spicy sweet and sour sauce ($6.50). Open Mon.-Fri. 10am-10:30pm, Sat.-Sun. 11am-11:30pm.

Hammond's Finger Lickin' Bakery, 5014 Church Ave. (718-342-5770), at Utica Ave. in Flatbush. Subway: #3 or 4 to Utica Ave., then 2 blocks east. Jamaican and other West Indian pastries all $1-2, including sweet, sweet fruit turnovers ($1.60). Open daily 8:30am-7pm.

Gia Lam, 5402 Eighth Ave. (718-854-8818), at 54th St. in Sunset Park. Subway: N to Eighth Ave. This popular Vietnamese restaurant serves large portions at low prices. The squid with lemongrass on rice ($3.50) is an excellent lunch choice. Lunches $3-5, dinner entrees $6-9. Open Mon.-Thurs. 11am-10:15pm, Fri. 11am-10:30pm, Sat.-Sun. 10:30am-10:30pm.

Sundaes & Cones, 5622 Eighth Ave. (718-439-9398), between 56th and 57th St., in Sunset Park. Subway: N to Eighth Ave. 36 flavors of ice cream, including green tea, red bean, mango, and lychee. Cones start at $1.40 and go up if you want them dipped or topped. Frozen yogurt and ice cream drinks also available. Take a turn riding the coin-operated horses in front of the store. Open daily 10am-midnight.

SOUTH BROOKLYN

The shores of Brooklyn present a welcome culinary quandary: the choices are endless. Try authentic Russian knishes (heated, flaky dough with a choice of filling) on **Brighton Beach Ave.**, Italian *calamari* (fried squid) in spicy marinara sauce along Emmons Ave. in Sheepshead Bay, or tri-colored candy on Coney Island. Eat until you feel ill—it still won't make a dent in your wallet.

★**Primorski Restaurant,** 282 Brighton Beach Ave. (718-891-3111), between Brighton Beach 2nd St. and Brighton Beach 3rd St. Subway: D or Q to Brighton Beach, then four blocks east on Brighton Beach Ave. Populated by Russian-speaking Brooklynites, this vaguely nautically themed restaurant serves some of the Western Hemisphere's best Ukrainian borscht ($2.25) in an atmosphere of gritty Slavic decadence. Many of the waiters struggle with English, but whatever you end up with will be tasty. Eminently affordable lunch special (Mon.-Fri. 11am-5pm, Sat.-Sun. 11am-4pm; $4) is the best lunch deal in NYC—your choice of among three soups and about 15 entrees, bread, salad, and coffee or tea. At night, prices rise as the disco ball begins to spin. Nightly entertainment, including live disco music. Open daily 11am-2am.

★**Philip's Confections,** 1237 Surf Ave. (718-372-8783), at the entrance to the B, D, F, or N train in Coney Island. Sate your inner child. Famous salt-water taffy (95¢ for a ¼lb.). Candy or caramel apple $1. Cotton candy $1. Lime rickeys (60¢) are one of the cheaper and better Coney Island refreshment sources on hot summer days. Open Sun.-Thurs. 11am-3am, Fri.-Sat. 11am-4am.

Nathan's, Surf and Stillwell Ave. (718-946-2206), in Coney Island. Subway: B, D, F, or N to Coney Island; across from the subway stop. 74 years ago, Nathan Handwerker became famous for underselling his competitors on the boardwalk: his hot dogs cost a nickel; theirs were a dime. His crunchy dogs have since become nationally famous, sold in franchises of the restaurant and in supermarkets. A classic frank at this crowded place—the original Nathan's—sells for $1.85. Open Sun.-Thurs. 8am-4am, Fri.-Sat. 8am-5am.

Jimmy's Famous Heros, 1786 Sheepshead Bay Rd. (718-648-8001), near Emmons Ave. Subway: D or Q to Sheepshead Bay, then southeast on Sheepshead Bay Rd. Heros—New Yorkese for subs or grinders (from the Greek gyros)—cost about $4.50 and can be shared by two. Always ask for "the works" on whatever you order; you'll thank us later. Primarily take-out; you can eat out by the Bay. Open Mon.-Sat. 9am-6pm, Sun. 9am-5pm.

Ramdazzo's Clam Bar, 2017 Emmons Ave. (718-615-0010), in Sheepshead Bay. Subway: D or Q to Sheepshead Bay, then south on Sheepshead Bay Rd. to Emmons Ave. A beautiful waterfront location and a seafood menu account for the large crowd and the slightly higher prices. Many dishes, though, are still within budget range: linguine with red or white clam sauce $8, fried scallop sandwich $5.50. Open Sun.-Thurs. 11:30am-12:30am, Fri-Sat. 11:30am-2:30am.

Sea Lane Bakery, 615 Brighton Beach Ave. (718-934-8877). Subway: D or Q to Brighton Beach. The best Jewish bakery in Brighton. It may be best to try a little of everything (9 kinds of pastry cost 90¢ each). Then again, you can't go wrong with a loaf of honey cake with almonds and cherries ($4). Open daily 6am-9pm.

Taste of Russia, 219 Brighton Beach Ave. (718-934-6167), in Brighton Beach. Subway: D or Q to Brighton Beach. This well kept Russian deli stocks everything from fresh-baked delicacies to mango-flavored soft drinks. Favorites include the chicken Kiev ($4 per lb.) stuffed cabbage ($3.50 per lb.), or blintzes ($3.50 per lb.) Open daily 8am-10pm.

■ Queens

With nearly every ethnic group represented in Queens, this often overlooked borough offers visitors authentic and reasonably priced international cuisine away from

Manhattan's urban neighborhoods. **Astoria** specializes in discount shopping and cheap eats. Take the G or R train to Steinway St. and Broadway and start browsing—the pickings are good in every direction. The number of Greek and Italian restaurants increases right around the elevated station at Broadway and 31st St., where you can catch the N train north to Ditmars Blvd. for still more Astorian cuisine. In **Flushing,** excellent Chinese, Japanese, and Korean restaurants flourish. Restaurants here often make use of authentic and somewhat exotic ingredients, such as skatefish, squid, and tripe, from which more Americanized Asian restaurants tend to shy away. Always check the prices; an identical dish may cost half as much only a few doors away. **Bell Boulevard** in Bayside, out east near the Nassau border, is the center of Queens nightlife for the young and semi-affluent; on most weekends you can find crowds of locals bar-hopping here.

In **Jamaica** and the other African-American and West Indian neighborhoods to the southeast, you can try fast food like Jamaican beef patties or West Indian *rito* (flour tortillas filled with potatoes, meat, and spices). Jamaica Ave. in downtown Jamaica and Linden Blvd. in neighboring St. Albans are lined with restaurants specializing in this type of cuisine. Jamaica also holds a **farmer's market** at 159-15 Jamaica Ave. (718-291-0282; open Mon.-Sat. 7am-7pm), where a few farmers offer their bounty indoors, next to a food court that offers Caribbean and Carolina-Southern restaurants, among others. To get to Jamaica, take the E or J train to Jamaica Center; from there the Q4 bus goes to Linden Blvd. in St. Albans. Traversing this area safely requires extra care and attentiveness.

★**Pastrami King,** 124-24 Queens Blvd. (718-263-1717), near 82nd Ave., in Kew Gardens. Subway: E or F to Union Tpke./Kew Gardens. Exit station following sign that says "Courthouse" and "Q10 bus," then go left past the sign to the north side of Queens Blvd. It's 2 blocks ahead and across the street. Everything here, from the meats to the slaw to the pickles, is made on the premises. Meat-lovers will be full for days on the open grilled-salami sandwich ($7.25), while the fat-averse can stick to salads ($5.75-9) and omelettes ($4-9). Open Tues.-Sun. 9:30am-11pm.

★**Uncle George's,** 33-19 Broadway, Astoria (718-626-0593), at 33rd St. Subway: N to Broadway, then 2 blocks east; or G or R to Steinway St., then 4 blocks west. This popular Greek restaurant, known as "Barba Yiogis O Ksenihtis" to the locals, serves inexpensive and hearty Greek delicacies around the clock. Almost all entrees are under $10: Die-hard fans feed on roast leg of lamb with potatoes ($8), or octopus sauteed with vinegar ($7). Goat soup ($6) and chick pea soup ($3) are part of the lighter fare. Excellent Greek salad with feta cheese ($6). Open 24hr.

Anand Bhavan, 35-66 73rd St., Jackson Heights (718-507-1600). Subway: F, G, H, R, or 7 to 74th St./Broadway, then walk two blocks down 73rd St. Tasty vegetarian South Indian restaurant—you'll wonder if you're in Queens or Bombay. Picant lunch specials ($6-8; served noon-4pm) are an incredible bargain, as is the Madras special, a filling 4-course meal that includes *sambar* (spicy lentil soup) and a choice of *iddly* (rice crepe with peppers and onions) or *vada* (stuffed lentil dough). When they say spicy, they mean spicy. Open daily 11am-9:30pm.

First Edition, Bell Blvd. at 41st Ave., Bayside (718-428-8522). Subway: #7 to Main St.-Flushing, then the Q12 bus (catch it in front of Stern's Department Store, next to the station) along Northern Ave. to Bell Blvd., then walk north 3 blocks. This bar/restaurant tries to lure you in with cheap, filling food specials and then stick it to you with costly drinks. If you can control your thirst, you'll eat for cheap. Mon. 25¢ wings; Tues. half-price pizzas and pastas; Wed. half-price chili nachos; Thurs. half-price fajitas and quesadillas; Sun. half-price chicken fingers. Specials run all day. Crowded, lively, and meat-marketish at night. Open daily 11am-4am.

Galaxy Pastry Shop, 37-11 30th Ave., Astoria (718-545-3181). Subway: N to 30th Ave. (Grand Ave.). Make a right on 30th Ave. and walk east to 37th St. A favored spot for young locals on the make, the Galaxy offers great pastries with which to break your diet. It's not just the baklava ($1)—almost everything offered here is worth eating. Open daily 6:30am-3am.

Woo Chon Restaurant, 41-19 Kissena Blvd., Flushing (718-463-0803). Subway: #7 to Main St., then walk south 2 blocks to where Kissena Blvd. forks off to your left;

it's just ahead on the left. Behind the waterfall lies some of the finest Korean food in Flushing. Korean barbeque prices climb a bit above budget boundaries, but the Pan-Asian noodle offerings are nearly all shy of $9. This little restaurant's ability to satiate its mainly Asian clientele lets you know you're in good hands. Open 24hr.

Empire K.'s Roasters, 100-19 Queens Blvd. (718-997-7315), in Forest Hills. Subway: G or R to 67th Ave.; when leaving the station, head right following the sign that says "67th Ave.-North Side Queens Blvd." Cheap chicken is prepared according to Jewish law by one of the major kosher meat manufacturers. Although the zillion variations of chicken are tempting, the fish offerings (tuna, salmon, whitefish, herring, and gefilte) all bite below $10. Open Sun.-Thurs. 11am-9:30pm, Fri. 11am-2:30pm.

Waterfront Crabhouse, 2-03 Borden Ave., Long Island City (718-729-4862). Subway: #7 to Vernon Blvd./Jackson Ave., then south on Vernon; turn right on Borden Ave. and walk all the way to the river. Perhaps better named the "Across-the-Street-from-the-Waterfront" Crabhouse, this is the former home of the turn-of-the-century Miller's Hotel, through which the rich and famous passed as they escaped to Long Island by ferry. Theodore Roosevelt and Grover Cleveland once dined in this building, which lost its third floor in a fire in 1975. Today the Crabhouse's wooden booths are decorated with the requisite antiques and touches of stained glass. You can kindle a romance with the "Loveboat," a stuffed lobster floating in an ocean of shrimp scampi ($19). Beef steaks $8-15. Daily entertainment. Reservations recommended. Open Mon., Tues. noon-10pm, Wed.-Thurs. noon-11pm, Fri. noon-midnight, Sat. noon-midnight, Sun. 1-10pm.

Più Bello, 70-09 Austin St., Forest Hills (718-268-4400). Subway: E or F to 71st-Continental Ave. Walk west on Queens Blvd. past 70th Rd. to 70th Ave., then take a left and walk one block to the corner of Austin St. A slick, family-owned restaurant where the neighborhood's cool kids hang out. The Argentinian expatriate owners make their smooth *gelato* and many of the delicious cakes on the premises. A kitschy waterfall adds to the ambience. Mozzarella and tomato or prosciutto sandwiches $5-7. More than 20 *gelato* desserts to choose from, including *coppa lamponi* (raspberry *gelato*) and *coppa fragola* (strawberry *gelato*), $5. Open Mon.-Thurs. 10am-midnight, Fri.-Sun. 10am-1am, Sat. 10am-2am.

Knish Knosh, 101-02 Queens Blvd., Rego Park (718-897-5554). Subway: G or R to 67th Ave. This storefront knishery may not offer much seating, but the fruits of their ovens will fill you with the urge to walk off calories. Succulent knishes ($1.50) stuffed to plumpness with potato, Kasha, broccoli or onion. Lunch special ($2.50) includes large knish or kosher frank in a blanket and soda or coffee. Open Mon. 9am-7pm, Tues.-Fri. 9am-7:30pm, Sat.-Sun. 9am-6pm.

Szechuan Cottage, 102-09 Queens Blvd., Rego Park (718-997-6227), at 67th Dr. Subway: G or R to 67th Ave. This unbeatable eatery has proven its mettle with picky local palettes for many years. Chef's specialties include such familiars as General Tso's Chicken ($8.50), while the kitchen puts a unique spin on the diet cycle with asparagus dishes and basil specials. Open daily 11:30am-11pm.

Eddie's Sweet Shop, 105-29 Metropolitan Ave., Forest Hills (718-520-8514), at 72nd Rd. Subway: E or F to 71st Continental Ave., then take the Q23 to Metropolitan Ave. Turn left on the Ave. and walk two blocks to the corner of 72nd Rd. This sweet shop has been serving homemade ice cream and savory cappuccino to diehards for thirty years. Scoops $1. Old-fashioned marble floors and wooden stools evoke the parlors of the 50s. Open Tues.-Fri. 1-11:30pm, Sat.-Sun. noon-11:30pm.

El Chivito D'Oro, 40-08 Junction Blvd. (718-335-4827). Subway: #7 to Junction Blvd. Discriminating Uruguayan and Argentinian locals come to this sleekly renovated establishment to enjoy dishes from the homeland. The meat dishes are the main specialty, such as the *parrillada*, a grilled meat smorgasbord including sweetbread (cow glands), tripe (intestines), sausage, skirt steak, and other fruits of the *gaucho's* toil ($21). Open daily noon-2am.

■ The Bronx

When Italian immigrants settled the Bronx, they brought with them their recipes and a tradition of hearty communal dining. While much of the Bronx is a culinary disaster zone, the New York *cognoscenti* have discovered the few oases along Arthur Ave. and in Westchester where the fare is as robust and the patrons as rambunctious as their counterparts in Naples. The neighborhood of **Belmont,** which centers around the intersection of Arthur Ave. and 187th St., brims with pastry shops, streetside *caffè,* pizzerias, restaurants, and mom-and-pop emporiums vending Madonna 45s and battalions of imported espresso machines, all without the touristy flair of Little Italy. If you're in for a tasty, cheap, and exotic treat, you may want to try a dixie cup full of **Italian ice** (50¢) from one of the local street vendors—flavors include coconut, lime, and mango. To get to Arthur Ave., take the #2 train to Pelham Pkwy., then Bronx bus #Bx12 two stops west; alternatively, take the C or D train to Fordham Rd. and walk five blocks east.

Mario's, 2342 Arthur Ave. (718-584-1188), near 186th St. Five generations of the Migliucci *famiglia* have worked the kitchen of this celebrated southern Italian *trattoria.* The original clan left Naples in the early 1900s and opened the first Italian restaurant in Egypt, then came to the U.S. and cooked themselves into local lore; unsurprisingly, Mario's appears in Puzo's *The Godfather.* Celebrities often pass through, among them the starting lineups for the Yankees and the Giants. A room-length couch embraces patrons with familial arms amid an out-of-this-world pink decor. Proudly serves such delicacies as escargot ($5.50) or *spiedini alla romana,* a deep-fried sandwich made with anchovy sauce and mozzarella ($8). Traditional pasta $9.50-11.50, eggplant stuffed with ricotta $6.25. Open Tues.-Thurs. noon-11pm, Fri.-Sat. noon-midnight, Sun. noon-10pm.

Tony's Pizza, 34 E. Bedford Park Blvd. (718-367-2854). Subway: #4 to Bedford Park Blvd. Classic (and good-natured) pizza joint with slabs so good that students from the nearby Bronx High School of Science will skip class to grab a slice. Crisp crust slathered with generous amounts of cheese. Slice $1.50, extra topping 75¢. Open Mon.-Fri. 11am-8pm.

Ann & Tony's, 2407 Arthur Ave. (718-933-1469), at 187th St. Typical of Arthur Ave., this bistro established in 1927 may specialize in comfortable, no-frills decor but, unlike most restaurants in the area, Ann & Tony's has specials for dinner that run as low as $6, salad included. For lunch, sandwiches begin at $5. Open Mon.-Thurs. 11am-10pm, Fri. 11am-11pm, Sat. 1pm-midnight, Sun. 1-9pm.

Taormina Ristorante, 1805 Edison Ave. (718-823-1646). Subway: #6 to Buhre Ave. Hearty Italian fare in the shadow of the subway tracks. Combine any pasta with any sauce to suit your fancy. Pasta $9.50-10, sandwiches $5-8. Chicken dishes from $10, veal from $12. Open Mon.-Fri. 11am-10pm, Sat. noon-11pm, Sun. noon-10pm.

De Lillo Pastry Shop, 606 E. 187 St. (718-367-8198), near Arthur Ave. Although this small shop is often crowded, it's worth your while to sit here and sample the excellent baked goods ($1-2) along with a cappuccino ($1.75) or espresso ($1.25). Open Mon.-Fri. 8am-7pm, Sat.-Sun. 8am-8pm.

Egidio Pastry Shop, 622 E. 187th St. (718-295-6077). Since 1912, Egidio has been baking up mountains of Italian pastries and cakes—the colorful cases display over 100 different fresh-baked goodies! The ever-popular *cannolis* ($1.20) and the linzer torte ($1.20) are house favorites, and go perfect with a steaming cappuccino ($2) and bag of mini-cookies (sold by the pound). Most desserts $1.20-2. A neighborhood tradition. Open daily 7am-8pm.

Pasquale's Rigoletto, 2311 Arthur Ave. (718-365-6644). A relative newcomer to the Arthur Ave. pasta scene, Pasquale's cooks with the best of them. As the name suggests, Pasquale's will soothe you with potent arias; if you have a favorite in mind, asked to have it played. Favorite customer Joe Pesci's pictures adorn the front door. You can either bring your own wine for a $5 corking fee, or drink from their well stocked bar. Pasta $12.50, meat dishes $15, poultry $14.50, seafood $16. Open Sun.-Thurs. noon-10pm, Fri.-Sat. noon-10:30pm.

Dominick's, 2335 Arthur Ave. (718-733-2807), near 186th St. Small authentic Italian eatery. Waiters will seat you and your sweetie at a long table of gruff-but-friendly Italians eager to discuss the menu and the neighborhood, but they won't offer you a menu or a check—they'll recite the specials of the day and bark out what you owe at the end of the meal. The linguine with mussels and marinara ($7), the marinated artichoke ($6), and the special veal *francese* ($12) are all time-honored house specials. Arrive before 6pm or after 9pm, or expect at least a 20-min. wait. Open Mon., Wed.-Sat. noon-10pm, Fri. noon-11pm, Sun. 1-9pm.

■ Hoboken, NJ

To tell the truth, there are few restaurants in Hoboken to get really excited about. Then again, one comes to Hoboken not to eat, but to drink (p. 121). Many of the hottest bars have restaurants attached—snag your munchies there instead. To get to Hoboken, take the B, D, F, N, Q, or R train to 34th St., then the PATH train ($1) to the first Hoboken stop. (The PATH train also leaves from the 23rd and 14th St. stations of the F train, as well as from its own stations at 9th St./Sixth Ave. and Christopher St./ Greenwich St.) To get to the main drag of Washington St. from the PATH station, walk along Hudson Pl. to Hudson St., up one block to Newark St., left two blocks to Washington St., and right onto Washington St.

Johnny Rocket's, 134 Washington St. (659-2620), at 2nd St. Before Quentin Tarantino made retro hip with Jack Rabbit Slims, Johnny Rocket's was taking its customers on a sentimental journey back to the 50s via its old-school diner feel and juicy cheap hamburgers ($3.45). Most of the red booths come equipped with a 5¢ jukebox that plays Patsy Cline, Nat King Cole, and other oldies per your request. Even better, the soda fountain has Dr. Pepper and flavored Cokes. A spanking-clean floor and gracious waitstaff complete the time trip. Open Sun.-Thurs. 10am-11pm, Fri.-Sat. 10pm-3am.

Imposto's Restaurant and Deli, 102 Washington St. (963-9077). A humble, friendly pizza stop. After a long night of drinking hard at Hoboken's many alehouses, you can stop here for a quick slice ($1.50) before catching the PATH train back to Manhattan. All-American pizza parlor like those found on practically every college campus. The lunch special is a deal—2 slices and a drink for $3, or get a "Hoboken's favorite," sauteed chicken and broccoli ($2.50). Open Mon.-Wed. 11am-11pm, Thurs. 11am-3am, Fri.-Sat. 11am-4am, Sun. noon-midnight.

Bel Gusto Bagel Smashery and Café, 718 Washington St. (201-217-9119), between 7th and 8th St. They claim to attack your food with hammers here. "Potato smash" with cheese $2.75, "Pizza bagel smash" $3.50. Bel Gusto also offers such purportedly delectable combinations as grilled chocolate and peanut butter bagel ($2.70) or grilled eggplant and cheese bagel ($4). Open Mon.-Fri. 7:15am-6:15pm, Sat.-Sun. 8am-3pm.

La Isla, 104 Washington St. (201-659-8197). If you're homesick for the homeland, or if you just love Cuban food, this charming diner-turned-family-restaurant is for you. Specials change daily; servings are large and no plate is over $7. Adventurous vegetarians might try the *yuca*, a tasty Caribbean potato-like vegetable (and, according to the menu, an acronym for Young Upscale Cuban American). Open daily 6am-10pm.

Ray's Soul Kitchen, 1039 Washington St. (201-798-4064), at 11th St. in Maxwell's. Southern-style soul food meant for enjoyment during Maxwell's shows (p. 275). Unless you're tuned in for a particular act, it's probably cheaper to go elsewhere. Platter o' food $11. Maxwell's is in the process of adding a microbrewery to its entertainment repertoire. Open Fri.-Sun. 4pm-1am.

■ Miscellaneous Food Stores

Balducci's, 424 Sixth Ave. (673-2600), between 9th and 10th St. Subway: #1, 9 to Christopher St.-Sheridan Sq. Expect to fight long lines at any given hour in this shrine to the art of fine dining. A huge selection of prepared foods, cheese, breads, and desserts. Open daily 7am-8:30pm.

East Village Cheese, 40 Third Ave. (477-2601), between 9th and 10th St. Subway: #6 to Astor Pl. The name says it all. Actually, it doesn't, because this store also sells many varieties of crackers and snack foods in addition to the many different varieties of *fromage*. Check out the bargain bin and the appetizer section. Open Mon.-Fri. 8:30am-6:30pm, Sat.-Sun. 8:30am-6pm.

Ecce Panis, 1120 Third Ave. (535-2099), between 65th and 66th St. Subway: #6 to 68th St.-Hunter College. The name means "behold the bread" in Latin, and that's the only thing to be done in this baked-goods mecca. Try one of the sun-dried tomato or onion loaves, a *focaccia,* or one of the four varieties of sweet *biscotti.* Discreetly nibble on the free chunks on the counter while selecting. Open Mon.-Fri. 8am-8pm, Sat.-Sun. 8am-6pm.

Economy Candy, 108 Rivington St. (254-1531), on the Lower East Side. Subway: F, J, M, or Z to Delancey St.-Essex St. Imaginatively named store purveys sugar in all its most attractive forms. Imported chocolates, jams, oils, and spices, plus countless bins of confections, all at rock-bottom prices. Treat yourself to a huge bag of gummi bears ($1) or a pound of chocolate-covered espresso beans ($5). Open Sun.-Fri. 8:30am-5:30pm, Sat. 10am-5pm.

The Erotic Baker, 582 Amsterdam Ave. (721-3217), between 88th and 89th St. Subway: #1 or 9 to 86th St. Decadent baked goods, shaped to approximate nature's designs. Some PG-13 baking, too. Place custom orders (usually around $20) 24hr. in advance (phone orders only). Open Tues.-Fri. 10am-6pm.

La Piccola Cucina, 2770 Broadway (222-2381), between 106th and 107th St. This tiny gourmet shop is a great place to stock up that picnic basket before heading to the park. Get a curried chicken salad ($2) or a sandwich with fresh mozzarella, arugula, and tomatoes ($5.50). Make the difficult choice between Sicilian-style and Tuscan-style *biscotti,* or go with the delicious *cannolis* ($1.25). Open Mon.-Fri. 10am-9pm; Sat. 10am-10pm, and Sun. 11am-8pm.

Sahadi Importing Company, 187 Atlantic Ave. (718-624-4550), between Court and Clinton St. in Brooklyn. Subway: #2, 3, 4, or 5 to Borough Hall. This Middle Eastern emporium draws clientele from all over the city, stocking spices and seasonings, dried fruits, twenty kinds of olives, and an array of spreads and dips like hummus and *baba ghanoush.* Locals love the *lebany,* made with yogurt and spices. Open Mon.-Fri. 9am-7pm, Sat. 8:30am-7pm.

Teuscher Chocolatier, 620 Fifth Ave. (246-4416), at Rockefeller Center. Subway #6 to 51st St. or E to Fifth Ave. and 53rd St. On the promenade at Rockefeller Center, duck into this fragrant little sweet shop. From *marron glace* to Dom Perignon filled truffles, Teuscher is the ultimate in fresh chocolate (flown in from Zurich weekly). Ultra-expensive, but you can try a piece at about $2 a pop. Open Mon.-Sat. 10am-6pm.

Zabar's, 2245 Broadway (787-2000), between 80th and 81st St. Subway; #1 or 9 to 79th St. A New York institution. Loaves of bread and lines of shoppers stretching as far as the eye can see, with wings devoted to prepared foods, coffee and teas, cookware, ad infinitum. The adjoining café serves pastries and great coffee. Open Mon.-Fri. 8am-7:30pm, Sat. 8am-midnight, Sun. 8:30am-7pm.

BARS

New York soaks in bars. Every major street has a couple of dark holes where the locals burrow on weeknights. Most keep prices tied down and music pumped up. To capture the essence of a particular New York subset, venture into the wild Venn diagram of the city's bar life. Many music and dance clubs (see Entertainment and Nightlife p. 255) are also festive places to quaff; the following listings are for places where the focus is on conversing and imbibing.

■ Greenwich Village

Polly Esther's, 21 E. 8th St. (979-1970), near University Pl. Subway: 4, 5, 6, L, N, or R to Union Square. There's a story of a pub named Polly that was trying to recreate the 70s. They had pics of Jaws, Charlie's Angels, and the folks from Three's Company. Then one day Village hip cats heard the disco, and they knew it was much more than a hunch. They swarmed the place, got down and boogied, and then they all got drunk on Brady punch ($4.75). Beer $3. Two-for-one happy hour 1-9pm on weekdays and 1-7pm on weekends. Open Mon.-Fri. 11am-2am, Sat.-Sun. 11am-4am. Another location at 249 W. 26th St. (929-4782).

The Slaughtered Lamb Pub, 182 W. 4th St. (800-627-5262), at Jones St. Subway: A, B, C, D, E, F, or Q to W. 4th St. A rather sinister-looking English pub dedicated to the werewolf, from lore to Lon Chaney, Jr., Jack's *Wolf* to Jackson's *Thriller*. More than 150 types of beer ($5-20 per bottle), yards of ale, and darts and billiards downstairs in the "dungeon." Check out the skeleton at the front door and plan around the full moon. Open Sun.-Wed. noon-3am, Thurs.-Sat. noon-4am.

Barrow Street Ale House, 15 Barrow St. (206-7302), near Seventh Ave. and W. 4th St. Subway: A, B, C, D, E, F, or Q to W. 4th St. Ignore the unsightly murals and enjoy this roomy neighborhood bar. Don't miss the tremendous deals: $1 drafts all day Sun. and Mon. and between 5:30-9:30pm on Tues. and Wed. You'll be laughing and stumbling all the way to the bank. Pool and pinball downstairs. The black and tans are revolutionary. Open Mon.-Wed. 4pm-3am, Thurs. 4pm-4am, Fri.-Sat. 3pm-4am, Sun. 3pm-3am.

Automatic Slims, 733 Washington St. (645-8660), at Bank St. Subway: A, C, or E to 14th St. Simple bar in the West Village with an excellent selection of blues and soul, in an old-time bar environment decorated with pictures of the Velvet Underground. Twenty-somethings sit at tables with classic 45s under the glass top. Packed on weekends with a more diverse crowd. American cooking served 6pm-midnight. Entrees $7-15. Open Sun.-Mon. 5:30pm-2:30am, Tues.-Sat. 5:30pm-4am.

The Whitehorse Tavern, 567 Hudson St. (243-9260), at W. 11th St. Subway: #1 or 9 to Christopher St. Dylan Thomas drank himself to death here, pouring 19 straight whiskies through an already tattered liver. Boisterous students (and waiters) pay a strange and twisted homage to the poet. Beer $3-5. Outdoor patio for those hot summer nights. Open Sun.-Thurs. 11am-2am, Fri.-Sat. 11am-4am.

Julius, 159 W. 10th St. (929-9672), at Waverly Pl., between Sixth and Seventh Ave. Subway: A, C, or E to 14th St. This bar has been a hot spot for gay men since 1966, when a protest was staged against the laws denying service to homosexuals. Today commemorative plaques explain the event as older, more conservative men drink legally amid the rainbow flags. Happy hour Mon.-Sat. 4pm-9pm, drinks half price.

Peculier Pub, 145 Bleecker St. (353-1327). Subway: #6 to Bleecker St. Over 400 kinds of beer from 43 countries. When people from New Jersey ask you where Bleecker Street is, this is where they're headed. A neighborhood crowd during the week but packed with tourists and the "bridge-and-tunnel" crowd on weekends. Beer can get a little pricey: domestic beers $3-4, imports $5-6. Open Mon.-Thurs. 5pm-2am, Fri. 4pm-4am, Sat. 2pm-4am, Sun. 4pm-1am.

▓ East Village and Lower East Side

Beauty Bar, 231 E. 14 St. (539-1389), between Second and Third Ave. Remember Frenchie's dream sequence in *Grease,* where Frankie Avalon sang "Beauty School Dropout" in a haze of 1950s salon paraphernalia? That dream can now be your reality in this former hair parlor and current hot spot. People leave the primping for bathroom mirrors and settle here to quaff $3.50-4.50 beers and take in the funky decor. Crowded with East Village natives any night of the week. Open daily 5pm-4am.

The International Bar, 120½ First Ave. (777-9244), between 7th St. and St. Mark's Pl. Grimy and authentic East Village. This long and skinny bar has only two tables in the back, but the large, friendly counter seats many. Christmas lights and yellow sponge-painted walls give this bar a fiery glow. With domestic beers priced at $2.50, it's the "most reasonably priced bar on the Ave.," and a good scene at night. Clientele includes immigrants, lost youths, and college kids. A long history of regulars. Open Mon.-Fri. 11am-4am, Sat.-Sun. noon-4am.

Nation, 50 Ave. A, between 4th and 3rd St. A sleek dark glass box that's a stylish cross between a club and a café, with the best of both. A good place for a drink on the ever-popular Ave. A—live DJs every night spin everything from jungle to house, trip-hop to old school, but it's usually mellow enough for conversation over a drink (if you're not a dancer). No cover. Coffee shop open daily 8am-6pm. Bar open 8:30pm-4:30am daily.

Tenth Street Lounge, 212 E. 10th St. (473-5252), between First and Second Ave. A Soho bar east of 5th Ave. Mahogany panelling and fresh squeezed juices almost merit the $4-5 cost of beer at this chic-as-hell village hangout. A very expensive club, colored in discreet red lighting, with a clientele to match. Gorgeous place for an early-evening drink—the front bar is open to the street until 9pm. Occasional $10 cover Thurs.-Sat. evenings. Open Mon.-Sat. 5pm-3am, Sun. 4pm-2am.

Sophie's, 507 E. 5th St. (228-5680), between Ave. A and B. Subway: F to Second Ave. or #6 to Astor Pl. Packed with leather jackets and baseball caps on weekends. Cheap cheap cheap. Draft beer $1 for a large mug (imported draft $2). Mixed drinks start at $2.50. Pool table and soulful jukebox. Open daily noon-4am.

Max Fish, 178 Ludlow St. (529-3959), at Houston St. in the Lower East Side. Subway: F to Delancey St. or Second Ave., or J, M, or Z to Essex St. This aggressively hip bar draws big crowds of cool people on Thurs., Fri., and Sat., and small crowds of cool people on other days. The decor is decidedly *avant:* found objects, original cartoons, and the like. The jukebox is easily the best in town, with everyone from the Fugees to the Stooges to Folk Implosion. Beer $2.50. Open daily 5:30pm-4am.

McSorley's Old Ale House, 15 E. 7th St. (473-9148), at Third Ave. Subway: #6 to Astor Pl. Their motto is "We were here before you were born," and unless you're 130 years old, they're right. One of the oldest bars in New York City, McSorley's has played host to such luminaries as Abe Lincoln, the male Roosevelts, and John Kennedy since it opened in 1854 (women were not allowed in until 1970). Nowadays the crowd is somewhat scruffier, especially on Fri. and Sat., but the sense of history pervades. Only 2 beers: light and dark. Two-fisters take note: mugs come 2 at a time ($3 for 2). Open Mon.-Sat. 11am-1am, Sun. 1pm-1am.

d.b.a., 41 First Ave. (475-5097), between 2nd and 3rd St. It could mean "drink better ale" or "don't bother asking," depending on who you consult. With 19 premium beers on tap, 100 bottled imports and microbrews, and 24 different tequilas, this extremely friendly, out of the way bar lives up to its motto—"where every drink is a meal." New beers debut here, and tastings are held every month; call for info. Open daily 1pm-4am.

Joe's Bar, 520 E. 6th St. (473-9093 payphone), between Ave. A and B. Young and eclectic neighborhood crowd makes up most of the regulars. Very laid-back and unpretentious. Great jukebox. Pilsner, Bass, and Foster's on tap. Beers $2-3 a mug. Serious pool on Mon. nights. Open daily noon-4am.

■ SoHo and TriBeCa

The Ear Inn, 326 Spring St. (226-9060), near the Hudson. Established in 1817 and once a big bohemian/activist hangout, this bar now tends to the TriBeCa mellow crowd—dark wood, an uneven ceiling that's done some settling, and dusty old bottles behind the bar. Mellow jazz and blues are played at low volume so as not to stem the flow of conversation. Very comfortable; tables are covered with paper and stocked with crayons. Good American food served from noon-4:30pm everyday and Mon.-Thurs. 6pm-2am, Fri.and Sat. 6pm-3am, Sun. 6pm-1am. Appetizers and salads $2-6, dinner $6-8, specials and entrees $5-9. Pint of domestic beer $3.50. Bar open until 4am.

Spy, 101 Greene St. (343-9000), near Spring St. If you want to glimpse (or spy on) the legendary SoHo fashion/music/film crowd, a couch at this ultra glam bar may be your best bet. A cross between an 18th-century salon and an MTV video, Spy's chandeliers and gilt everything decor competes with the menu in ostentation: cold asparagus $8, beluga caviar $50, cigars $10-15. Before you throw the budget guide in disgust, the beers are reasonably priced ($4-5), and the view of SoHo society from here is incomparable. Get here early and wait for the fun to start. Lounge-y music, DJs Mon. and Wed.-Sat. nights. Open daily 5pm-4am.

Naked Lunch Bar and Lounge, 17 Thompson St. (343-0828). Adorned with the roach and typewriter motif found in the novel and movie of the same name, Naked Lunch serves as a memorable drinking atmosphere. Play with the Royal typewriter displayed on the back bar if you get bored. Good selection of microbrews and 25 kinds of specialty martinis to sip. According to the bartenders, "anything served in a martini glass is a martini." Take that, James Bond. All beers $5. DJ Wed.-Sat., no cover. Open Sun.-Mon. 5pm-2am, Tues.-Sat. 5pm-4am.

Lucky Strike, 59 Grand St. (941-0479), at W. Broadway. Favorite hunting ground of the SoHo ultra-magna-beautiful, but $3.50 Budweisers with similar prices in the restaurant in back make this more a sight than a watering hole. Both are almost always crowded. Expect to be stared at as you walk in the door; if you're prepared to stare right back, then you'll have a good time. Open daily noon-4am.

Buddha Bar, 150 Varick St. (929-4254), at Vandam. With hundreds of gold Buddhas over the bar and huge red vinyl booths decorated with gold dragons, this joint looks like a Chinese restaurant on steroids. Roomy enough for privacy, yet established and popular enough to be a scene. Cover $5-7 some nights. Open Mon.-Thurs. 10:30pm-3am, Fri.-Sat. 10:30pm-4am, and Sun. 9:30pm-3:30am.

Fanelli's, 94 Prince St. (226-9412), at Mercer St. Established in 1872 in a beautiful building of black cast iron. A mellow neighborhood hangout, where it always feels like it's late at night. Standard bar fare and cheap brew ($3 for domestic drafts, $3.50 for imports and microbrews), and the location—right in the midst of SoHo's busiest streets—means you won't have to look hard to find the place. Open Mon.-Thurs. 10am-2am, Fri.-Sat. 10am-3am.

■ Upper West Side and Morningside Heights

★**The Westend Gate,** 2911 Broadway (662-8830), between 113th and 114th St. Subway: #1 or 9 to 116th St. Once frequented by Kerouac, the Gate is now playpen to the young, highly educated Columbia crowd. The Gate sprawls over nearly a block, allowing for huge sitting areas, both inside and out. Live music and comedy events held here seasonally, so call ahead. A great selection of cheap pitchers. Food served until 11pm. Open daily 11am-2am.

The Bear Bar, 2156 Broadway (362-2145), at 76th St. A bit removed from the Amsterdam Ave. yupbar scene—thus cheaper and less boring. Keeps in touch with its sensitive side via bears, cuddly stuffed and carved wooden ones alike. Terrific beer selection with over 75 microbrews. Lots of cheap drink promotions, like a "drink early" scheme, whereby beer starts at 50¢ at 5pm and goes up 25¢ every hour, and "Ladies Drink Lite" nights (Mon.-Wed. 8pm-close), when women drink all the Lite beer they can for free. Open Mon.-Fri. 5pm-4am, Sat. 4pm-4am, Sun. 1pm-4am.

Hi-Life Bar and Grill, 477 Amsterdam Ave. (787-7199), at 83rd St. Step back into the 50s at this sleek retro hangout. A bit cramped, but friendly waitstaff and a late-night menu are a big draw. Live music Wed., DJ Thurs.-Sat. Open Mon.-Fri. 4pm-late night, Sat.-Sun. 10:30am-4pm for lunch and 4:30pm-late night.

Tap-A-Keg Bar, 2731 Broadway (749-1734), between 104th and 105th St. This small, unpretentious bar has hand-painted tables, a friendly bartender, pinball machines, and jazz on the stereo. Open daily 2pm-4am.

Amsterdam Café, 1207 Amsterdam Ave. (662-6330), between 119th and 120th St. This café serves up a full menu of sandwiches, salads, and pasta dishes for under $10 during the day to an older, more professional Morningside Heights crowd. At night, though, the dark, wood-paneled space fills up with a younger set, who come to enjoy the summer draft specials at $4.50 per pitcher and other thirst-quenching quaffs. Open daily 6:30am-1am.

Abbey Pub, 237 W. 105th St. (222-8713), at Amsterdam Ave. One of the more down-to-earth bars in the area, the Abbey is a great place to stop in for a few beers after a hectic day of sightseeing in Morningside Heights' grand churches. Open daily 4pm-4am (Kitchen opens at 5pm).

Night Café, 938 Amsterdam Ave. (864-8889), at 106th St. With weekly pool tournaments, a great juke box, and a huge TV cable-ready with SportsChannel, this little bar pulls in locals and a young college-kid set. Pool tournaments on Tues. nights. Happy hour from 4-7pm offers $1 off every drink. Open daily noon-4am.

The Shark Bar, 307 Amsterdam Ave. (874-8500), between 74th and 75th. High-class, enjoyable bar and soul-food restaurant; possibly the only truly interracial establishment on the Upper West Side below 110th St. Well dressed after-work crowd nurses stiff drinks. Live jazz on Tues. with a $5 cover; "gospel brunch" Sat. 12:30pm and 2pm (no cover). Reasonable drink prices (bottled beer from $3). Entrees from $11. Open Mon.-Tues. 5:30-11:30pm, Wed. 5:30pm-midnight, Thurs. 5:30pm-12:30am, Fri.-Sat. 5:30pm-1am, Sun. 5:30-11pm.

■ Upper East Side

★**Crossroads,** 300 E. 77th St. (988-9737), on Second Ave. This bar arguably has the friendliest clientele and best live music on the Upper East Side. Cartoon images of Jimi, Jerry, and others in the rock-god pantheon beam down upon you as you savor $5 pitchers (Sun. and Mon. nights) or $2 pints (Tues.). Open 6pm-2am weekdays, 6pm-4am Fri. and Sat.

★**The Deadline,** 1649 Third Ave. (289-9982), between 92nd and 93rd St. With 3 satellites, 5 TVs, and a huge movie screen, this pub should satisfy the needs of any Big 4 sports fan. Sunday night pool tournaments (7pm) and a 25¢ basketball shooting game occupy aspiring athletes, while the more philosophically inclined can ponder the homey plastic gingham tablecloths or the sled, trumpet, fire truck, and other assorted objects hanging from the ceiling. Look for the all you can drink specials on weekends from 1-6pm. Open daily 11am-4am.

Manny's Car Wash, 1558 Third Ave. (369-2583), between 87th and 88th Ave. Done up like a drive-thru car wash on Muddy Waters Drive, this place hosts some smokin' blues. Come between 4 and 9pm and drink all you want for $6. Women drink free Mon. night. Happy hour Wed.-Sat. 5-8pm. Open daily 5pm-3:30am.

Kinsale Tavern, 1672 Third Ave. (348-4370), between 94th and 95th St. A traditional Irish bar, complete with green walls, a massive wooden bar, and 101 beers for your drinking pleasure. 20-oz. of Guinness $4; those audacious enough to ingest American suds can get Bud for $3. A special on a beer-of-the-day most nights after 6pm. Sit back and soak up some Irish hospitality. Open Mon.-Sat. 8am-4am, Sun. noon-4am.

Australia, 1733 First Ave. (876-0203), at 90th St. The land down under transported to the Upper East Side pub scene. National pride is apparent, from the boomerangs on the walls to the Aussie natives behind the bar. Very friendly staff, typical after-work crowd. Women drink free on Wed. and Thurs. Draft beers $3. Open Mon.-Fri. 5pm-4am, Sat.-Sun. noon-4pm.

American Trash, 1471 First Ave. (988-9008), between 76th and 77th St. Cavernous barroom hung with "trash" from NASCAR go-carts to Molly Hatchet posters. Baby busters have a wild-'n'-crazy time celebrating lowbrow culture. Drink specials change every night; call for details. Happy hour daily 4-7pm. Pints $2. Women drink at happy hour prices Tues. 4pm-midnight. Open daily noon-4am.

■ Midtown and Chelsea

Coffee Shop Bar, 29 Union Sq. West (243-7969), facing Union Sq. Park. Subway: #4, 5, 6, L, N, or R to Union Sq. A chic diner for fashion victims, owned by three models. Sure, it's a bar, but more importantly, it's a spectacle. Good for a very late dinner, or to watch others have dinner. Beers $3.75-4.50. Open daily 6am-5am.

Old Town Bar and Grill, 45 E. 18th St. (473-8874), between Park Ave. and Broadway. Subway: #4, 5, 6, L, N, or R to Union Sq. A quiet 104-year-old hideaway with wood, brass, and an aging clientele to match, as seen on the old "Late Night" opening montage. Beer on tap $4, Heineken $3.75, domestics $3. Open Mon.-Sat. 11:30am-1am, Sun. 3pm-midnight.

Live Bait, 14 E. 23rd St. (353-2492), between Madison and Broadway. Subway: 6, N, or R to 23rd St. Run by the same folks who brought you the Coffee Shop Bar, Live Bait offers an equally pretty, though more raucous crowd, full of business people by day and tourists by night. Relatively good Cajun menu, including beer-steamed shrimp ($8) and cajun-fried calamari with marinara ($7), also available for dinner and late-night snacks. Open Mon.-Thurs. 11:30am-1:30am, Fri. 11:30am-2:30am, Sat. 11:30am-3am, Sun. noon-midnight.

O'Flaherty's, 334 W. 46th St. (246-8928), between Eighth and Ninth Ave. Subway: A, C, or E to 50th St. Although located on ritzy Restaurant Row, this small bar manages to keep the feel of a true neighborhood pub. Great selection of beers on tap, including Murphy's ($4 per pint). Live music Tues.-Sat. at 10:00pm ranges from rock-and-roll to blues unplugged to bluegrass. Call for schedule.

Peter McManus, 152 Seventh Ave. (929-9691 ot 463-7620), at 19th St. Made famous by a *New York Times* article on the timeless appeal of ordinary bars, of which this is the epitome. Ordinary drinks, ordinary clientele, ordinary prices, and ordinary bathrooms. The carved mahogany bar and leaded glass windows add to the charm. $2 drafts. Open daily 11am-4am.

■ The Outer Boroughs

Adobe Blues, 63 Lafayette Ave. (718-720-2583), at Fillmore St. in Staten Island. Take the Staten Island Ferry, then the S40 bus to Lafayette Ave. A lively mix of beer and chili-lovers fill this bar, which is styled after the saloons of the Old West. Features the second-largest selection of beers in all of NYC—more than 230. Bottles arrive from the Czech Republic, Korea, Columbia, and France, as well as much of the rest of our Global Village. And the prices aren't bad either: a 20-oz. glass of Newcastle Brown runs $4 (but selection of drafts changes frequently). Also sample 1 (or 2 or 3) of their 35 brands of tequila. Ask the bartender to give you a look at Jake the one-eyed king snake—he lost his eye in an unfortunate shedding accident. Lunch entrees $5-7, dinner entrees $8-13. Live jazz Wed., Fri., and Sat. nights with no cover. Lunch served Mon.-Sat. 11:30am-5pm; dinner nightly 5-11pm; late-night menu available. Bar open Sun.-Thurs. 11:30am-midnight, Fri.-Sat. 11:30am-2am.

Teddy's, N. 8th St. and Berry St. (718-384-9787), in Greenpoint, Brooklyn. Subway: L to Bedford Ave. and 1 block west. The new artiste crowd starts drinking here, and only you can find out where they end up. Cheap drinks ($1-3). Occasional kitsch-ful 70s lounge nite. Jazz on Thurs. from Nov.-March. Open daily 11am-1am.

Mugs Ale House, 125 Bedford Ave. (no phone), in Greenpoint, Brooklyn. Subway: L to Bedford Ave. This quiet neighborhood pub serves reasonably priced beers, dark ales, and lagers ($2-5) to local artists and the young, working-class residents of the area. Open daily 3pm-3am.

Montague Street Saloon, 122 Montague St. (718-522-6770), near Court St. Subway: 2 or 3 to Clark St.; take Henry St. to Montague. Young wanna-be yuppies congregate to eat, drink, and be merry on this fashionable street in Brooklyn Heights. Open daily 11:30am-4am.

Johnny Macks, 1114 Eighth Ave. (718-832-7961), in Park Slope, Brooklyn. Subway: F to Seventh Ave.-Park Slope; walk east 1 block to Eighth Ave., then south 3 blocks. Recent college grads frequent this dark-wood-panelled bar, which prides itself on its selection of microbrews ($3 on tap). Look for drink specials during the summer. Open Mon.-Fri. 4pm-4am, Sat.-Sun. noon-4am.

■ Hoboken, NJ

Hoboken swims in alcohol. Bars come in countless guises—as faux-Caribbean dives, soul music speakeasies, or Wild West saloons. Your best bets are the mile of Washington St. (1st to 14th St.), the area from Newark St. to 4th St. in the south of town, and the region surrounding the PATH station. PATH runs 24 hours., so even Manhattanites can come and drink 'til they drop. Bring proof of age.

In June 1994 the City Council—worried about rampant drunkenness, particularly potential World Cup fervor—ruled that all bars in Hoboken must close at 1am. They then decreed that bars could stay open until 3am, but with a "one-way" policy of no admittance or re-admittance after 1am. These days the law is still on the books, but the situation is still working itself out.

To get to Hoboken, take the B, D, F, N, Q, or R train to 34th St., then the PATH train ($1) to the 1st stop in Hoboken. (The PATH train also leaves from the 23rd and 14th

St. stations of the F train, as well as from its own stations at 9th St./Sixth Ave. and Christopher St./Greenwich St.)

Scotland Yard, 72 Hudson St. (201-222-9273). From the PATH station, walk along Hudson Pl. to Hudson St. and up two blocks. A spacious wood-paneled bar is the centerpiece of this English pub. British memorabilia covers the walls—a perfect place for Anglophiles and expatriates. Beers $2.50-3. Open daily 11:30am-1am.

Miss Kitty's Saloon and Dance Hall Floozies, 94-98 Bloomfield St. (201-792-0041), at First St. From the PATH station, walk along Hudson Pl. to Hudson St., up three blocks to First St., then left four blocks to Bloomfield St. This spacious Wild West-style saloon features a large dining area and lots of yuppies. Beers $3-3.50. Open Mon.-Wed. 4:30pm-2am, Thurs. noon-2am, Fri. noon-3am, Sat. 11:30am-3am, Sun. 11:30am-2am.

Cryan's Exchange, 110 First St. (201-798-6700), at Bloomfield St. From the PATH station, walk along Hudson Pl. to Hudson St., up three blocks to First St., left four blocks to Bloomfield St. This brightly colored, lively bar features authentic Irish bartenders and a New York Stock Exchange ticker for those who just can't leave it at the office. Happy hour (Mon.-Wed.) and Super Happy Hour (Thurs.-Fri) 4-7pm. Open daily 11am-2am.

Bahama Mama's, 215 Washington St. (201-217-1642). From the PATH station, walk along Hudson Pl. to Hudson St., up one block to Newark St., left two blocks to Washington St., and right a few blocks. Frat-boy heaven. Palm trees and a big surfer mural indicate that this is *the* Caribbean dance club in Hoboken. $2.50 shots, $3 drafts, $4 drinks, and $5 multi-layered drinks. Saturdays are classic rock, Fridays are "clubby," and Thursdays are retro-80s. Open daily 8pm-3am.

Traps Back Door, 333 Washington St. (795-1665). Hot nightspot with $1 shots, $3 drafts, $3.50 bottles, and $4 drinks. Monday night football parties are a particular draw for the local crowd. Also features a back room with a DJ. No cover. Open daily 11am-2am.

Neighborhoods

Far below and around lay the city like a ragged purple dream, the wonderful, cruel, enchanting, bewildering, fatal, great city.

—O. Henry

The classic sightseeing quandary experienced by New York tourists is finding the Empire State Building. They've seen it in dozens of pictures and drawings, captured in sharp silhouettes or against a steamy pink sky as a monument of dreams. They've seen it towering over the grey landscape as their plane descends onto the runway, or in perspective down long avenues or from a river tour. But they can't see it when they're standing right next to it.

This optical illusion may explain why many New Yorkers have never visited some of the major sights in their hometown. When you're smack in the middle of them, the tallest skyscrapers seem like a casual part of the scenery. In this densely-packed city, even the most mind-boggling sights are awash in the endless combination of environments that serve as backdrops for everyday life. Not all sights are as glaringly obvious as the Statue of Liberty. Sometimes you'll enter a modest doorway to find treasures inside, and sometimes you'll need to take a long elevator ride to see what everybody's raving about. If it's your first time in the big city, you'll notice even more subtle attractions—the neighborhoods and personalities jumbled together on shared turf, the frenzy of throngs at rush hour, the metropolitan murmur at dusk. And if it's your hundredth time in the city, there will still be parts of town you don't know too well, architectural quirks you've never noticed, and streetscapes you've never appreciated. Seeing New York takes a lifetime.

▓ Sightseeing Tours

The best way to discover New York City is on foot. Stare at a map, learn the layout of the city, and hit the streets. **Walking tours** offer the inside scoop on neighborhoods and sights you might overlook—knowledgeable New Yorkers share their love for the city with you. Many of these tours are thematic or highly specialized. Call around to get a sense of what's being offered on the days you plan to be in the city (and see Walking Tours, below).

Standard **bus tours** whisk you around Manhattan in cushy splendor, often stopping at a pre-printed list of sights and directing you to a slew of souvenir stands. These tours are good for an overview of the city but offer little to those willing to use the subway and do some legwork. More specialized bus tours are usually more rewarding, though there are probably better walking tours of the same areas. **Boat tours** offer breathtaking views of the cityscape, but don't expect to see much more.

A number of New York landmarks offer tours of their inner workings. Imperial **Lincoln Center** sponsors guided tours of its theaters: The Metropolitan Opera House, New York State Theater, and Avery Fisher Hall. There are four to eight tours every day, depending on rehearsal schedules, from 10am to 5pm, and they last about an hour (admission $7.75, students and seniors $6.75, children $4.50). For information or to make a reservation, call 875-5351. Reservations are recommended but not required. In addition, a free tour every Wednesday at 2pm instructs the curious in the art of locating items in the library's mammoth collection of musical soundtracks and movie scores. The tour passes through the center's three art galleries. No reservations necessary; meet at the information desk at the plaza entrance. For information, call 870-1670.

Historic **Carnegie Hall,** at Seventh Ave. and 57th St., opens its doors to tourists Mondays, Tuesdays, Thursdays, and Fridays at 11:30am, 2pm, and 3pm. The tour grants entrance to the main hall itself, discusses the history and architecture of the building, visits other performance spaces, and lasts about an hour. Tours cost $6, seniors and students $5, children under 10 $3. For information, call 903-9790.

A true shrine to an era long past, **Radio City Music Hall,** 1260 Sixth Ave. (632-4041), between 50th and 51st St., gives behind-the-scenes tours every day between 10am and 5pm, leaving every 30 to 45 minutes. Billed as "the one-hour tour that will last you a lifetime," the tour grants access to the Great Stage, the 6000-seat auditorium, and the mighty Wurlitzer; lets you talk with a current member of the Rockettes; and fills you in on the full history of the place. Admission is $9 for adults and $4.50 for children under 7.

Check out "Late Night" arrival Conan O'Brien on the **NBC Studio Tour,** where you'll also see **Saturday Night Live's** famous Studio 8H. (Tours given daily 9:30am-4:30pm, leaving every 15 minutes. Extended hours for summer months and holidays. Each tour is limited to 17 people, and tickets go on a first-come, first-serve basis. No one under 6 admitted. Admission $8.25.)

Madison Square Garden (465-5800), on Seventh Ave. between 31st and 33rd St., also offers a tour of its inner workings. Tours include a trip into the 20,000 seat arena and the Paramount (the Garden's concert stage), visits into the locker rooms of the 1994 Stanley Cup-winning Rangers and the 1994 and 1995 almost-NBA-title-winning Knicks, and a step up into the luxury suites. (Tours offered on the hour Mon.-Fri. 10am-3pm, Sat. 10am-2pm, and Sun. and designated holidays 11am-2pm. Admission $7.50.)

A visit to the world's financial capital wouldn't be complete without a trip to the **New York Stock Exchange,** on 20 Broad St. (656-5168). A self-guided tour of the building—including the zoo-like main trading floor— is free, but tickets are required (open Mon.-Fri. 9:15am-4pm; you will not be admitted after 2pm; tickets are first-come, first-serve).

Housing a quarter of the world's gold reserves in a vault sinking five stories below street level, the immense **Federal Reserve Bank of New York,** 33 Liberty St. (720-6130), conducts 40min. free tours of the premises from Monday to Friday at 10:30am, 11:30am, 1:30pm, and 2:30pm. A minimum of seven working days' prior notification is required; minimum age 16; maximum group of 30 people. Behind-the-scenes tours of the **Fulton Fish Market** are given on the first and third Thursdays each month beginning at 6am and lasting 1[hrs., June through September (admission $10; reservations required at least a week in advance; call 669-9416 or, for group tours, 748-8590).

WALKING TOURS

92nd Street Y, 1395 Lexington Ave. (996-1100). The Y leads an astounding variety of walking tours covering all boroughs and many aspects of New York life, from Beaux Arts Fifth Ave., the Botanical Gardens, and the Brooklyn Navy Yards to literary tours, museum visits, even a murder mystery. Tours are given on Sun., last about 3 hrs., and cost $15-25. Call for the latest tours.

City Walks (989-2456). Run by the friendly and knowledgable John Wilson, a Yalie and a New Yorker for over 35 years. Walking tours of Manhattan cost $12 and usually last 2 hrs., although he'll arrange for private trips. Covering all parts of the city, from Battery Park City to Greenwich Village to the Upper West Side, Mr. Wilson's excursions focus on history and architecture. Call to confirm schedule and make reservations; meeting places vary according to the area on which the tour is focusing.

Adventure on a Shoestring, 300 W. 53rd St. (265-2663). Walking tours of all parts of Manhattan, all the boroughs, and even the more interesting parts of northern New Jersey (e.g. Hoboken). 75-minute tours incorporate chats with members of the various communities. In Manhattan, the tour of Gramercy Park and the tour of Greenwich Village are especially entertaining. Tours cost $5; the price has never increased during the organizations's 31 years of existence. Some excursions—like touring backstage at the Met, or chatting with those who claim to have had out-of-body experiences—are open only to members ($3 per event; membership $40 per year).

Sidewalks of New York (517-0201 for a recorded schedule; 662-5300 to reach the office). Anecdotal, amusing, and offbeat walking tours with titles like "Hundred-and-One-Year-Old Broadway Baby" and "All in the Family," a survey of popular Mafia hangouts in Little Italy. All tours cost $10 and last 2 hrs. No reservations required. Call to find out about the next few forays.

Museum of the City of New York, Fifth Ave. and 103rd St. (534-1672). In spring and early fall the museum sponsors popular walking tours ($15) every other Sun., starting at 1pm and lasting for a leisurely 1-2 hrs. Areas covered include Chelsea, the Lower East Side, and Greenwich Village, with a focus on the history and architecture of the particular district. Call to sign up a few days beforehand.

Joyce Gold's Tours, 141 W. 17th St. (242-5762). The devoted Ms. Gold has read over 900 books on Manhattan, the subject she teaches at NYU and at the New School. 40 Sundays per year she and a company of intrepid adventurers set out on tours focusing on architecture, history, and the movements of ethnic groups within the city. Tours last approx. 3hrs., depending on the subject, and cost $15.

Radical Walking Tours (718-492-0069). Bruce Kayton leads tours that cover the alternative and underground history of New York City. For example, tours of Greenwich Village feature radicals and revolutionaries like John Reed and Emma Goldman, as well art and theatrical movements. Other tours include trips to Chelsea, Wall Street, and the Lower East Side. All tours are $6 and last 2-3 hrs. No reservations required. Call for schedule and departure sites.

Lower East Side Tenement Museum Walking Tours, 90 Orchard St. (431-0233). On Saturdays from June to Sept. at 1:30pm and 2:30pm, you can embark upon the hour-long "The Streets Where We Lived: A Multi-Ethnic Heritage Tour" tour ($12, students and seniors $10, price includes admission to the Tenement Museum, tour only $7, students and seniors $6).

Municipal Art Society, at the Urban Center, 457 Madison Ave. (935-3960) near 50th St., leads guided walking tours ($10 during the week from 12:30-2pm, $15-30 on weekends); destinations change with the seasons but include most major districts of Manhattan, such as SoHo, Greenwich Village, and Times Square. Their free tour of Grand Central Station meets every Wed. at 12:30pm, in front of the Chemical Commuter Bank. Call in advance with an idea of where you'd like to go, or ask for a schedule of their tentatively-planned future tours.

Times Square Exposé, Seventh Ave. at 42nd St. (768-1560), in the Times Square Visitors Center. This free, 2-hr. walking tour unfolds the theatrical history of Times Square, along with its celebrated scandals and electronic "miracles." Tours given every Fri. at noon.

Heritage Trails New York, starting at Federal Hall, between Wall and Broad St. In an attempt to capture some of the spirit of similar tours in Boston, Philadelphia, and Washington, D.C., Mayor Giuliani recently helped to organize 4 walking paths exploring the history and culture of Lower Manhattan. Detailed maps and info for the trails (red, blue, green, and orange) can be found in the *Heritage Trails Guidebook* ($5), available at Federal Hall and selected bookstores.

BOAT TOURS

The Petrel (825-1976), a 70-ft. pecan mahogany yacht, leaves from Battery Park and will take 40 passengers around New York Harbor, visiting Governor's Island, Ellis Island, the Brooklyn Bridge, or the Verrazano-Narrows Bridge—depending on Mother Nature's whims. On weekdays, the Petrel makes 45-min. trips at noon, 1pm, and 5:30pm (45 min., $9), and 1½-hr. trips at 5:30pm ($20). On weekends, the Petrel sails for 2 hrs. at 3pm and 5:30pm ($28). On Sundays, there are 1 ½ hr. sails at 1pm ($17, $12 children and seniors), 3pm (90 min.), and 7:30pm (2 hrs.); weekends at 3, 5:30, and 8pm (all 2 hrs.). Make reservations in advance.

Circle Line Tours, Pier 83, W. 42nd St. (563-3200), at the Hudson River and Twelfth Ave. Boats circumnavigate Manhattan island on a 3-hr. tour. Cruises run daily every hour on the ½-hr. from 9:30am to 3:30pm from mid-June to early Sept.; call for specific times and to hear the reduced off-season schedule. Admission $18, seniors $16, children under 12 $9. Also conducts romantic, 2-hr. "harbor lights" tours around Manhattan in the lovely light of sunset. You'll hear the sirens singing if you're not careful. Daily at 7pm early May-early Oct.; weekends only throughout the off-season. Same rates as daytime tour. Light snacks and cocktails served. All boats operate late March-Dec. 24. No reservations necessary; get there ½hr-45min. early.

Pioneer, Pier 16, South Street Seaport Museum (669-9417). This 109-yr.-old sailing schooner was originally built to carry cargo but will now carry you around the harbor south of Manhattan—you can help hoist the mainsail or take a turn at the wheel. Fantastic views of the skyline and Statue of Liberty. Two-hr. cruises daily at 3:30 and 7pm, Fri.-Sat. also at 9:30pm ($16, seniors and students $13, children under 13 $6). 1½ hour lunchtime cruises sail Mon.-Fri. at 12:30pm ($12). Reservations recommended, especially for weekend cruises; you can make them up to three weeks in advance.

Staten Island Ferry, South St. (718-390-5253), near Battery Park. Offers one of the best deals in Manhattan, and round the clock to boot: it operates every half hour, 24 hrs. a day, 7 days a week. Amazing views of the lower Manhattan skyline, Ellis Island, the Statue of Liberty, and Governor's Island. Don't miss the trip at night, but exercise caution around the Staten Island terminal. Fare 50¢ round-trip (!!!). No reservations required.

BUS TOURS

Lou Singer Tours (718-875-9084), offers tours of the "Twin cities of Brooklyn and Manhattan." The tours, now in their 24th year, are still led by the colorful Mr. Singer, who regales his audience with zesty little nuggets while driving from place to place. The 5-hr. Manhattan Noshing Tour ($25 plus $18 food charge) is a multi-ethnic food-sampling extravaganza, with 12 food stops peppered with Lou's intriguing commentary on the history and architecture of the Lower East Side. Also offered is a tour of Brooklyn Brownstones ($25 plus $2 admission charges), which includes a jaunt through an historic house and a visit to a church with Tiffany windows. Advance reservations are required; reserve 2 wks. in advance during the summer. Bus departs from 325 E. 41st St., between First and Second Ave.

Rock and Roll Tour NY (941-9464). Created by Danny Fields, currently manager of the Ramones and Iggy Pop and long-time music industry insider, this 2-hr. bus tour takes you to over 50 places where rock history was made in New York from the mid-50s to the present. The tour covers everything from where Dylan and Zappa lived to where John Lennon was murdered and where Sid and Nancy wrote the script of their demise. Call for a current schedule and the location of tour departures. Tickets $25; student discount available. Reservations required.

Gray Line Sight-Seeing, 900 Eighth Ave. (397-2600), between 53rd and 54th St., or 166 W. 46th St. (397-2620), near Seventh Ave. Huge bus-tour company offering more than 20 different trips, including jaunts through Manhattan and gambling junkets to Atlantic City, conducted in English, French, German, Haitian, and Portuguese. The tour of lower Manhattan ($29) runs about 3½ hrs. and includes a guided walk through the Financial District. Other good bets include a 4½-hr. trip through Harlem ($29), and the grand, 6-hr. NYC-immersion tour ($40). The launder-your-money unescorted voyage to Atlantic City costs $26. They also offer daylong trips to Washington, DC., Philadelphia, and Niagara Falls. Reservations aren't required for the in-city tours, but arrive at the terminal ½ hr. in advance.

Harlem Spirituals, 1697 Broadway (757-0425), at 53rd St. Offered are tours of upper Manhattan (in English, French, German, Spanish, Portuguese, and Italian) including the "Spirituals and Gospel" tour, which includes trips to historic homes and participation in a Baptist service ($32 for 4 hrs., leaves Sun. at 8:45am). The "Soul Food and Jazz" tour ($69, offered Thurs.-Sat. 7pm-midnight) features a short tour of Harlem, a filling meal at a Harlem restaurant (usually Sylvia's), and an evening at a jazz club. Tickets should be purchased in advance; call for info.

Harlem Renaissance Tours (722-9534). The 4-hr. "Sunday Gospel Tour" features the history of Harlem and includes 1 hr. at a gospel-church service and lunch or brunch at a local restaurant ($35). Call ahead for a schedule and to make reservations, as tours are only offered to groups and will not accept individuals.

■ Lower Manhattan

Its zillion dollar facade glistening on a thousand postcards, the southern tip of Manhattan is a motley assortment of antiquated cobblestones and sleek financial powerhouses. The Wall Street area is the densest in all of New York, though the Street itself measures less than one-half-mile long. Home of the frenzied New York Stock Exchange, Wall Street is regarded as the cornerstone of the Financial District—an area that sees one trillion dollars of capital and commerce exchange hands every day. High above only a handful of streets, corporate masterminds negotiate the global economy from one of the highest concentrations of skyscrapers in the world. Yet this density has a rich history: lower Manhattan was the first part of the island to be settled by Europeans, and many of the city's historically significant sights lie buried amid the chasms of glass and steel. The neighborhood's crooked streets serve as a reminder of New York City's chaotic youth, before it grew up and straightened out into an orderly grid. Omnipresent **Heritage Trail** markers indicate the most significant spots and provide historical information and anecdotes about many sights. For a detailed walking tour of lower Manhattan, call Heritage Trails at 767-0637.

Touring lower Manhattan shouldn't cost much. Parks, churches, and cathedrals of commerce, such as the New York Stock Exchange, charge no admission. For a slice of life, visit during the work week, when suspendered and high-heeled natives brandishing *Wall Street Journals* and cellular phones rush around between deals. After hours, these titans of trade loosen their ties, slip on their Reeboks, and suck in the ocean breeze (and a few drinks) at **South Street Seaport.**

■ The Financial District

Battery Park, named for a British gun battery stored there from 1683 to 1687, is now a monument-heavy chunk of green forming the southernmost tip of Manhattan Island. The #1 and 9 trains to South Ferry terminate at the southeastern tip of the park; the #4 and 5 stop at Bowling Green. With its plethora of memorials, the grounds are a great place to enjoy a morning cup of java. One can spend the waking hours admiring Tony Smith's abstract metal sculpture, perusing historical plaques, or just inhaling some sea air near the Hope Garden. But beware: on weekends the park is often mobbed with people on their way to the Liberty/Ellis Island ferries, which depart from here.

As you enter the park from the north, walk past the **Netherlands Memorial Flagpole** toward Castle Clinton and the water. On the way is **Hope Garden,** an AIDS memorial dedicated in 1992 where 100,000 roses bloom and fade each year. This park also contains an eclectic collection of war monuments and memorials to various immigrants, many who risked all to come to the States. A stroll through this affecting assortment indicates the massive number of commemorated individuals in this park.

Castle Clinton, the main structure in the park, contains an information center and a circular pavilion where you can purchase tickets for the Liberty/Ellis Island ferry (see Sights: Liberty Island and Ellis Island, p. 138). More than a glorified ticket booth, this structure was completed just before the War of 1812, as tensions between Britain and the newly independent United States were coming to a boil. It then stood in 35 ft. of water, connected by a drawbridge to the shore 200 ft. away. Not a single shot was ever fired from the fort, and by 1824 the city felt safe enough from British invasion to lease the area for public entertainment, including firework displays and balloon ascents. Later, in the 1840s, the castle was roofed over and turned into a concert hall. By 1855, enough landfill from nearby construction had accumulated to connect Castle Clinton to the mainland, and it became New York's immigrant landing-depot. Between 1855 and 1889, more than eight million immigrants passed through these walls. In later years, when Ellis Island had assumed this function, Castle Clinton turned into the site of the beloved New York Aquarium; the aquarium eventually moved to Coney Island, however, and the building was left vacant. When the city declared the fort a National Historic Site in 1950, wreckers had already removed the

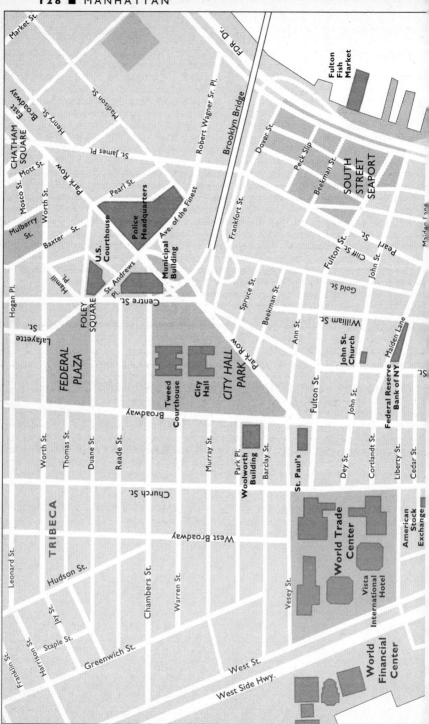

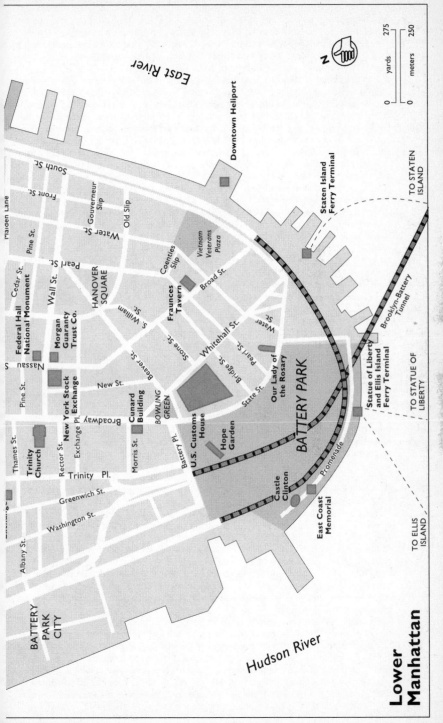

Lower
Manhattan

East River

Hudson River

BATTERY PARK CITY

Downtown Heliport

Staten Island Ferry Terminal

TO STATEN ISLAND

Brooklyn-Battery Tunnel

Statue of Liberty and Ellis Island Ferry Terminal

TO STATUE OF LIBERTY

TO ELLIS ISLAND

East Coast Memorial

Castle Clinton

Promenade

BATTERY PARK

Our Lady of the Rosary

Hope Garden

U.S. Customs House

Vietnam Veterans Plaza

Coenties Slip

Fraunces Tavern

HANOVER SQUARE

BOWLING GREEN

Cunard Building

Morgan Guaranty Trust Co.

New York Stock Exchange

Federal Hall National Monument

Trinity Church

Maiden Lane
South St.
Front St.
Pine St.
Cedar St.
Wall St.
Pearl St.
Water St.
Gouverneur Slip
Old Slip
Broad St.
S. William St.
S. William St.
Stone St.
Beaver St.
Whitehall St.
Water St.
Pearl St.
Bridge St.
State St.
Battery Pl.
Morris St.
Exchange Pl.
New St.
Broadway
Rector St.
Pine St.
Nassau
Thames St.
Trinity Pl.
Greenwich St.
Washington St.
Albany St.

N

yards   275
meters   250

second story, the roof, and other expansions, leaving the building at its present dimensions, the same as those of 1811. The fort is now under the care of the National Park Service and is attended by Park Rangers. The Rangers lead 15-20 minute walking tours of Castle Clinton (every hour from 10:05am-4:05pm daily). Tours are free and leave from the castle (Castle Clinton open daily 8:30am-5pm).

The vista from Castle Clinton offers a clear view of lush New Jersey (on the right), Ellis Island (dominated by a large brick building), Liberty Island (she's waving at you), Staten Island (where the big orange ferries are heading), and Governor's Island, a command center for the U.S. Coast Guard (on the left). Near the castle stands a particularly striking group of structures, the **East Coast Memorial,** a monument to those who died in coastal waters in World War II. A large sculpture of a swooping eagle stands in front of two rows of granite monoliths engraved with the names of the dead. If the weather's good, catch a view from the other direction on a 90-minute cruise around lower Manhattan and the islands, offered by **NY Waterways** ($14; mid-March to Nov. Mon.-Fri. 10:15am, 12:15pm, 2:15pm; call 800-533-3779 for departure locations and info on foreign language tours).

Just north lies State St., which forms the northeast border of the park. Before this area was filled with land, State St. was the shorefront, and by the 1790s it had become the most fashionable residential street in Manhattan. State St.'s domestic glamor has vanished today, but you can still sense its former elegance in the two brick and wooden ghosts of a bygone era, the **Church of Our Lady of the Rosary** and the adjoining **Shrine of St. Elizabeth Ann Seton,** at 7-8 State St. (269-6865). Originally built as the James Watson House from 1792 to 1805 in the Federal style, the shrine still retains its original façade, with columns supposedly cut from ship masts. St. Elizabeth Ann Seton, canonized in 1975 as the first U.S.-born saint, lived here with her family from 1801 to 1803. The adjoining church, to the left as you face it, dates from 1883, when it served as a shelter for Irish immigrant women.

North on State St., at the rear of the courtyard adjacent to the church, stands the quirky museum **New York Unearthed** (748-8628), which, under the sponsorship of the South St. Seaport Museum, features artifacts from ancient Manhattan. Excavators discovered most of the items here during preparations for new construction in the downtown area. The small collection runs from clay pipes dated AD 1250 to small displays depicting "Meetings at the Tavern, ca. 1700" and "Lunch at the Counter, ca. 1950." In the basement you can observe archaeologists working in a glass-walled laboratory or hop inside the "Systems Elevator" for a pre-virtual simulation of a journey to a "dig" (museum open Mon.-Sat. noon-6pm; closed Sat. Dec.-March; free). Right next to the museum stands the sheer, elegant, and largely empty wedge of **17 State St.** Built in 1989, this great white whale of a building stands on the site of the house where Herman Melville was born in 1819. Melville soon left to pen his masterpiece *Moby Dick* as well as "Bartleby the Scrivener," a mid-19th century vision of the soulless financial district.

A walk along the edge of Battery Park leads to the **U.S. Custom House,** off the northeastern corner of the park. This stunning palace of trade was completed in 1907, when the majority of U.S. revenues came from customs duties and the majority of customs duties came from New York. Fort Amsterdam stood here in 1626, facing out at the harbor and defending the Dutch colony. In 1790, a Georgian mansion was built here as the presidential residence, but George Washington never moved in because the U.S. capital moved to Philadelphia the very same year (Washington, D.C. didn't become the nation's capital until 1803). The building now houses the **National Museum of the American Indian** (see Museums, p. 245).

The Beaux Arts masterpiece that stands here today combines Baroque and Renaissance inspiration with aggressive decoration. All of the sculpture and artwork on the building relates directly to its function over the years. The 12 statues on top of the façade represent the 12 great trading centers of the world. On the ground level, four large sculptures of enthroned women typify a sadly dated white supremacist worldview: Africa sleeps with her arms atop a crumbling sphinx and a lion, dozing Asia rests on a throne of skulls, and self-satisfied Europe sits stately and dignified. America seems ready to leap forward out of her chair, carrying the torch of Liberty—although a Native American peeps timidly over her shoulder, in sharp contrast to the building's current function. The four women were seated there by Daniel Chester French, the same sculptor who placed Lincoln in his memorial in Washington, D.C., and John Harvard in his high chair in Cambridge, MA. On the façade, the window arches are adorned with the heads of the six "races" of the world.

The Custom House faces egg-shaped **Bowling Green,** the city's first park. It was rented out as a bowling green in 1733 for the price of one peppercorn a year—hence the oddball name. Here occurred the city's first shady business transaction, when Dutch settler Peter Minuit bought Manhattan Island from Native Americans for $24. Colonists later rioted here in the 1760s against the taxes imposed by George III's Stamp Act. When George repealed the act in 1770, New Yorkers forgave him by commissioning an equestrian statue of the king. After the Declaration of Independence was read in front of City Hall on July 9, 1776, however, the joyous (if fickle) populace raced to Bowling Green and tore down the statue, bits of which were later used as bullets during the Revolutionary War.

Poised to run from the tip of Bowling Green right up Broadway is the **Bull,** whose massive head is lowered as he paws the ground. As the symbol of a good market, the bull was the gift of Italian artist Arturo DiModica, who mischievously planted the 7000 lb. bronze sculpture in front of the New York Stock Exchange in the dead of night a few winters back. Looking the gift bull in the mouth, unamused brokers had it promptly removed; as a compromise, it now grazes here, at a distance.

At 24 Broadway, next to the bull, is the **Museum of Financial History** (908-4110), located in the former Standard Oil building. The exhibits and displays here provide a good means of contextualizing the neighborhood (open Mon.-Fri. 11:30am-2:30pm; free).

At Whitehall and Pearl St., on the east side of Bowling Green, stands the **Broad Financial Center,** with one of the most whimsical lobbies in New York. Tapering pylons with revolving metal globes on top balance on surreal spheres of marble, and a wall-sized clockface stares over a sloping pool of water. Exit onto Pearl St.; walking northeast one block leads to Broad St., where Dutch colonists trying to recreate their homeland dug a canal that ran through their settlement. Unfortunately, the water soon became putrid. The disappointed Dutch filled in the filthy canal to create the present street.

At 54 Pearl St. lies the pseudo-historic **Fraunces Tavern** block, an island of traditional buildings in a sea of architectural aggrandizement. The block contains structures built between 1719 and 1883, with many 20th-century additions and reconstructions. The Fraunces Tavern museum (425-1778) is a reconstruction of one of George Washington's favorite New York hangouts. It was on the second floor of this tavern that the general said his final farewell to the officers of his victorious revolution (see Museums, p. 247).

Following Broad St. north leads to the junction of Stone and South William St. This anonymous little block was the site of the great fire of 1835, which destroyed all of Manhattan's original Dutch city, though a nostalgic merchant refitted two of his South William storefronts with Dutch-style façades. Continue up South William St. to Hanover Square, a paved-over intersection that provides benches for the weary. Note the statue of the Dutch goldsmith Abraham De Peyster, moved to this spot in the 1970s from Bowling Green. Once the northern border of the New Amsterdam settlement, **Wall Street** takes its name from the wall built here in 1653 to shield the Dutch colony from a British invasion from the north. By the early 19th century, it had already become the financial capital of the U.S., and many a populist reformer used its name to refer to the entire financial district and its baleful menace to the nation. Its mystique endures today—Wall Street means big business, big money, and occasionally, big losses.

Although it is currently behind locked gates, take note of historic **55 Wall St.** This building once housed the Second Merchants' Exchange (1836-1854), the predecessor of the modern stock exchange. Its 16 Ionic columns, each weighing 41 tons and cut from a single slab of stone, were dragged here by teams of oxen. Across the street at No. 60 hovers the unmistakable headquarters of the **Morgan Bank,** 52 stories of bizarre but eye-catching 1980s neoclassicism. Feel free to wander through the vast public atrium of white and gray marble and gaze at the mirrored, white-latticed ceiling (open daily 7am-10pm).

Just a bit farther down Wall St., at its intersection with Broad St. (which turns into Nassau St. to the north), cluster a mass of sights. **Federal Hall** (825-6888), with its larger-than-life statue of a tightly pantalooned George Washington on its steps (several historians have commented on the heft of Washington's rump), stands at 26 Wall Street. After 1703, this classical building housed the original City Hall, where the trial of John Peter Zenger helped to establish freedom of the press in 1735. Perhaps most notably, Washington was first sworn in here (roughly on the spot where his big-boned likeness stands today). The building served as the first seat of the constitutional government—here James Madison submitted the Bill of Rights to Congress. The building also served as the original meeting place of the House of Representatives and the Senate. Unfortunately, the original building was demolished in 1812. In 1955 its replacement became a national memorial, and its exhibits now include the illustrated Bible used by Washington at his inauguration, a 10-minute animated program called "Journey to Federal Hall," and models of the building's predecessor. Tours and an animated film are offered upon request (open Mon.-Fri. 9am-5pm; disabled entrance at 15 Pine St.).

South on Broad St., between Wall St. and Exchange Pl. stands the current home of the **New York Stock Exchange** (656-5168). The main building, constructed in 1903, has a relief sculpture on its pediment entitled *Integrity Protecting the Works of Man*, made by J.Q.A. Ward, creator of the Washington statue outside Federal Hall. The Stock Exchange was first created as a marketplace for handling the $80 million in U.S. bonds that were issued in 1789 and 1790 to pay Revolutionary War debts. Over the course of the 19th century, the exchange became increasingly formalized. The 1867 invention of the stock ticker revolutionized the market. The ticker recorded every sale of stock and made transaction information instantly available to the public (and, of course, provided the necessary material for New York's famous "ticker tape" parades). The stock market cooked throughout the 1920s, only to collapse suddenly on Black Monday, October 7, 1929. The early 1980s saw another impressively "bullish" market, but its nosedive on October 19, 1987, gave broken traders an unpleasant history lesson. Recent heavy speculation in emerging infotainment technologies has brought the market once again to unprecedented heights, causing no small share of angst to Wall Street's plethora of predictive pundits.

To get to the Stock Exchange's visitors' entrance, walk to the left, down Broad St., to the main doors at No. 20, where a stock exchange staff member distributes free admission tickets, each labeled with a session time. A limited number of tickets are available for each session, and the later in the day you arrive the more likely it is that only tickets for sessions several hours away will be left. Tickets sometimes run out entirely by 1pm, and it's preferable to arrive around 9am to ensure a convenient admission time. On crowded days, you'll be forced to wait in a long line for the elevator once you are admitted to the building (open to public Mon.-Fri. 9am-4pm, with last session beginning at 2:45pm).

Upstairs, you can see exhibits detailing the workings and history of the stock market, along with a wide-screen "experience theater," which shows an 11-minute video on the history of the exchange (narrated in logical fashion by Leonard Nimoy). But the real draw is the observation gallery that overlooks the zoo-like main trading floor of the exchange. From the glass-enclosed gallery, you can observe the frenzy that fills all 37,000 sq. ft. of the room (which claims 50-ft. high ceilings). Recorded introductions to the floor activity are available in any of a number of languages. The visitors' gallery has been enclosed ever since the 60s, when leftist hooligans invented creative ways to disrupt trading activity, such as throwing dollar bills at the traders.

Observe the chaos of murmuring and milling in this paper-strewn pen, as anxious people huddle around honeycombed banks of green video screens. The all-important

TV monitors, grouped in clusters called "trading posts," nearly outnumber the people. More than 2000 companies deal on the New York Stock Exchange, the world's largest with 79 billion shares of stock valued at $3 trillion. Note the color-coded jackets sported by the folks on the trading floor; brokers are clad in yellow, reporters in navy, and pages in light blue. To your left, at the rostrum, the bell rings for opening at 9:30am and closing at 4pm.

Around the corner, at the end of Wall St., the seemingly ancient **Trinity Church** has the last laugh over its towering billionaire neighbors. Its Gothic spire was the tallest structure in the city when it was first erected in 1846, and the Episcopal congregation here dates from 1696. The hourly bells will remind you that Wall Street existed before it was consumed by skyscrapers —the church has kept time for this community for 150 years. Trinity Church owns much of the land upon which the nearby architectural giants reside, ensuring that sizable mounds of moolah support the church. Behind the altar is a small **museum** (602-0872; open Mon.-Fri. 9-11:45am and 1-3:45pm, Sat. 10am-3:45pm, Sun. 1-3:45pm; daily tours given at 2pm). The church's 2½-acre yard, dating from 1681, houses the graves of Alexander Hamilton and other historical notables. De-stressing corporate execs often come here for a shady respite from the material world.

From September through June, Trinity Church and St. Paul's Chapel present the **Noonday concert** series (see Entertainment & Nightlife: Classical Music, p. 270). The church also hosts changing exhibitions of contemporary sculpture in both its north and south courtyards. Trinity Church commissions these works in an attempt to combine contemporary art with venerable architecture (courtyards open Mon.-Fri. 7am-4pm, Sat. 8am-3pm, Sun. 7am-3pm).

■ World Trade Center and Battery Park City

Walk up Broadway to Liberty Park, and in the distance you'll see the twin towers of the **World Trade Center.** The main plaza, on Church and Dey St., contains two sculptures, a large fountain, ample seating space, daily lunchtime entertainment, and front-row views of the 1377-ft.-tall towers. Bosom companions at 110 stories each, the sleekly striped shafts (constructed in 1973) dwarf every other building in the city. They provide 10 million sq. ft. of office space for their creator, the Port Authority of New York and New Jersey. The bombing of the complex in 1993 has left no visible scars other than the ubiquitous "All visitors must carry ID" signs.

Two World Trade Center has the **observation deck** (323-2340). When you enter the lobby from Liberty St., take an escalator to the ticket booth on the mezzanine (open daily June-Sept. 9:30am-11:30pm; Oct.-May 9:30am-9:30pm; admission $8, seniors and children 6-12 $3). A branch of the Visitor Information Center is also located on the mezzanine, dispensing all the maps, brochures, and schedules that make it worthy of its name (open Mon.-Fri. 9am-5pm; also Sat. in summer). You'll also find on the mezzanine a **TKTS booth** which sells discounted same-day tickets to Broadway and off-Broadway shows Tuesday through Friday (See Entertainment and Nightlife: Theater p. 257).

Once you've stood in line for observation deck tickets and had your bag searched, ride the elevator up to the 107th floor, where everyone ignores exhibits on trade history and economics to enjoy the best view in New York. Unfortunately, looking out the window can be a little bit frustrating, since the stainless steel stripes on the building walls preclude any panoramic picture-window views. The architects opted to place much of the skeleton of the building on the outside, in order to leave large, unbroken spaces inside the building. You may want to use the coin-operated telescopes or the diagrams of landmarks distributed throughout the observatory. Nevertheless, the view is spectacular; get your bearings and pick out your favorite sights from one of the most famous skylines in the world.

In good weather, the **rooftop observatory** opens. Unless you suffer from vertigo, take the escalator up for an extraordinary viewing experience. The top of the neighboring twin seems only a few feet away (though it's actually farther away at the top than at the bottom due to the curve of the earth). You can't get much higher than this without hopping a jet or climbing the Himalayas—it's the world's tallest outdoor platform. They also have quarter-operated telescopes with which to survey the city below.

To the west glimmers the golden-hued World Financial Center. Across the river, a flat New Jersey stretches into the distance on a glorious plane of radon. To the south, you can see (from right to left) Ellis Island, Liberty Island, and Governor's Island, with Staten Island in the distance behind them. You can also see the entrance to the Brooklyn-Battery Tunnel; look for the red paved area just north of Battery Park, where cars seem to disappear and re-appear from inside a boxy structure. To the east, the far-away Manhattan and Brooklyn bridges steal the show. It's hard to believe that the arches of the Brooklyn Bridge once overshadowed the rest of the New York skyline.

Weekdays throughout July and August, the World Trade Center hosts a series of free lunchtime concerts called **Centerstage**. The concerts are held on the mezzanine-level plaza at One World Trade Center (call 435-4170 or see Entertainment and Nightlife: Music, p. 270).

One level below ground at the Trade Center lurks an underground shopping mall—the largest (and arguably the most mundane) in New York. If subterranean shopping fazes you, skip out of consumer Hades and follow the signs directing you to the **World Financial Center** and **Battery Park City.** Whatever the city dug up to build the World Trade Center, it dumped west of West St. The 100 new acres were recently developed to form Battery Park City. Reached via the pedestrian overpass, the development lies less than a mile from Wall Street.

Next door, Cesar Pelli's **World Financial Center** rises in a pleasingly geometric fashion. Each of its 40-story towers is more spacious than the 102-story Empire State Building, as the buildings were constructed for computers requiring huge window-less rooms—not people who need a view to survive. The Center's main public space is the vaulted and glass-enclosed **Winter Garden,** an expanse of sixteen 40-ft.-tall palm trees and numerous expensive cafés and shops. The space regularly hosts free concerts, dance programs, poetry readings, and other art and cultural events, from dancing to diverse world music groups, ethnic art exhibitions, and family programs (call 945-0505 for information or see Entertainment and Nightlife: Music, p. 270). The garden looks out on the esplanade, which takes you right out to the water. A **ferry** makes an eight-minute crossing from here to Hoboken and back on weekdays (fare $2; call 908-463-3379 for more information).

Head onto the Battery Park City **promenade** and stroll through this patch of post-modern residences. Sculptures by Fischer, Artschwager, Ned Smyth, Scott Burton, and Mary Miss line the esplanade. The loyal and insightful sentiments of two New York poets, Frank O'Hara and Walt Whitman, have also been inscribed on the terrace here.

The best way to get back to the street is to return the way you came, back through the Winter Garden to the walkway and the plaza.

■ City Hall and the Civic Center

The aura of 19th-century New York, bulldozed out of existence elsewhere in the city, still dominates this area. A number of magnificent municipal buildings stand in the neighborhood surrounding City Hall; nearly all house some branch of city, state, or federal government, and most of them are set back atop a huge flight of stone steps. Munching a hot dog as you sit high on these flights of steps is sure to put some happiness in your heart.

At 111 Centre St., between Leonard and White St., sits the **Civil Court Building.** Across the street at 100 Centre St. sits the imposing **Criminal Courts Building,** with the hopeful words of Thomas Jefferson inscribed on the façade: "Equal justice for all men of whatever state or persuasion." Decide for yourself by sitting in on a proceeding. Visit the clerk's office in room 150 or call ahead (374-6261) to see what's on the docket.

As you proceed south down Centre to its intersection with Lafayette St., you can observe a group of sizeable office buildings housing anonymous parts of the city bureaucracy. While unremarkable at street level, the pillared **United States Courthouse,** at 40 Centre St., bears a gold roof that crowns the skyline. Next door, to the left on St. Andrew's Place and past a group of inexpensive food kiosks, the **Church of St. Andrew** (962-3972) is tucked away in the shadow of the Municipal Building. The serene space of the church, built in 1938, houses a lovely dark wood crucifix set against a crimson background and framed by dark pillars (open daily 7am-5:30pm).

At the corner of Duane and Elk St., archaeologists recently discovered the remains from thousands of burials, thought to be part of a 17th- and 18th-century **African-American burial ground.** One of New York's major colonial sights, the area has been made a national landmark by an act of Congress, following protests that the sight should not be ignored in favor of a new Federal Court building.

Its towering neighbor, One Centre St., also known as the **Municipal Building,** was completed in 1914. A striking free-standing colonnade distinguishes its enormous façade, and its mammoth base actually straddles Chambers St. Across Centre St., on the north side of Chambers St., you'll find the former Hall of Records, which now houses the **Surrogate's Court.** Two sculpture groups—*New York in Its Infancy* and *New York in Revolutionary Times*—grace the turn-of-the-century Beaux Arts exterior. Twenty-four statues of notable New Yorkers also enliven the building. Come into the subdued marble entrance hall and step up to the balcony to get closer to the unique curved ceiling. In the strangely pagan lobby, the ceiling is covered with Egyptian tile mosaics and the 12 signs of the Zodiac.

Across the street in City Hall Park stands the infamous **Tweed Courthouse,** a historic municipal financial disaster. Builders laid the foundations of the courthouse on a $150,000 budget in 1862 and finished it a decade and $14 million later. Pop mythology has it that $10 million of this money was actually embezzled into the corrupt Tweed political machine, leading to a public outcry that marked the beginning of the end of the Tweed party's rule. Politics aside, today you can admire the building's Victorian reinterpretation of the classical column.

Exit from the other side of the Tweed Courthouse and you'll find yourself in City Hall Park, facing the rear of **City Hall** itself. The hall still serves as the focus of the city's administration. The Colonial chateau-style structure, completed in 1811, is a lovely antidote to the mammoth skyscrapers and stocky municipal buildings that surround it. During its restoration in 1956, a durable limestone façade replaced the original marble, and the northern side was refinished and improved (which was originally left rough in the belief that the city would never expand north of this point anyway). In 1865, thousands of mourners filed past the body of Abraham Lincoln, paying final respect to the assassinated president in the vaulting rotunda of City Hall. The winding stairs lead to the **Governor's Room,** which was originally intended for the use of its namesake during his trips to the city. The room is now used to display a number of important early portraits, including ones of Jefferson, Monroe, Jackson, Hamilton, Jay, and Washington. On one side of the Governor's Room sits the **City Council Chamber;** on the other side, down the short hallway to the right, are the **Mayor's Offices,** which are closed to the public. The building is officially open to tourists on weekdays from 10am to 4pm, but public meetings here often run later (sometimes through the night) and can be interesting.

The surrounding **City Hall Park** has been a public space since 1686—home to an almshouse, a jail, a public-execution ground, and a barracks for British soldiers. On July 9, 1776, George Washington and his troops encamped here to hear the Declaration of Independence. Today it is pleasantly landscaped with colorful gardens and a fountain. This welcoming spot of green amid the stone and steel hosts a small but welcome **Farmer's Market** every Tues. and Fri. 8am-6pm (Fri. only Jan.-March).

Towering at 233 Broadway, off the southern tip of the park, is the Gothic **Woolworth Building,** one of the most sublime and ornate commercial buildings in the world. Erected in 1913 by F.W. Woolworth to house the offices of his corner-store empire, it was known as the "Cathedral of Commerce," until the Chrysler Building opened in 1930 and replaced it as the world's tallest structure. The lobby of this five-and-dime Notre Dame is littered with Gothic arches and flourishes, its glittering mosaic ceilings complemented by carved caricatures high up in the four corners of the lobby; note the one of Woolworth himself counting change and the one of architect Cass Gilbert holding a model of the building.

A block and a half farther south on Broadway, near Fulton St., **St. Paul's Chapel** was inspired by London's St. Martin-in-the-Fields. Constructed in 1766, with a spire and clocktower added in 1794, St. Paul's is Manhattan's oldest public building in continuous use. Gaze at the green churchyard and the surprising shades of the interior—baby blue, soft pink, and cream, with gold highlights. You can see George Washington's pew, where the first President worshipped on Inauguration Day, April 30, 1789. Above the pew hangs an oil painting of the nation's Great Seal—the first such rendition of the Seal that was officially adopted in 1782. Below the east window outside the church is a memorial to Major General Richard Montgomery, killed in the famous 1775 attack on Quebec. The chapel presents classical music concerts from September through June (see Entertainment & Nightlife: Classical Music, p. 270). For information on the chapel, call the office of the Trinity Museum (602-0773; chapel open Mon.-Fri. 9am-3pm, Sun. 7am-3pm).

Head across Broadway again, then east on Ann St., to the **Nassau Street pedestrian mall,** a little-known and slightly run-down shopping district characterized by fabulous 19th-century architecture and cheesy ground-level clothing stores. Packed with shoppers during the day, the area has acquired a nice gritty feel (in spite of the one large restored building painted pastel pink and green). Like too many places in New York, it's worth avoiding at night.

South on Nassau St. and across Maiden Lane, the **Federal Reserve Bank of New York** (720-6130) occupies an entire block. Built in 1924, this neo-Renaissance building was modeled after the Palazzo Strozzi of a 15th-century Florentine banking family. More than 200 tons of iron went into the decorative treatment. Be vewwy vewwy qwiet, but this building stores more gold than Fort Knox—many nations store their gold reserves here in a vault sinking five levels below the street. The interior of the vault is a cell-block of 121 triple-locked compartments, each a separate storehouse, most containing the gold of a single nation. When the balance of trade shifts between nations, the gold is physically moved from one country's compartment to another's. Free one-hour tours of the building and vault are offered by the Fed, but reservations are required at least seven working days in advance (tours Mon.-Fri.10:30am, 11:30am, 1:30pm, and 2:30pm; free).

A one block jaunt back up Nassau St. and right onto John St. will bring you to **John Street United Methodist Church** (269-0014). Established in 1766, the church houses the oldest Methodist society in the country, along with a museum specializing in Colonial and 19th-century memorabilia (sanctuary and museum both open Mon., Wed., and Fri. noon-4pm).

■ South Street Seaport

Walking east on Fulton St. toward the East River leads you past a large strip of moderately priced restaurants and ultimately to **South Street Seaport.** New York's shipping industry thrived here for most of the 19th century, when New York was the nation's prime port and shipping was one of its leading commercial activities. Like many other waterfront areas of lower Manhattan, its size has increased considerably through the use of landfill. At the beginning of the 18th century, Water Street marked the end of Manhattan. Soon landfills had stretched the island to Front Street, and by the early 19th century they stretched it to its present dimensions, with South Street bordering the water.

Despite its history, the area is not exactly as authentic as it makes itself out to be. Zoning and development decisions of the early 80s rescued the neighborhood from its seedy state of decay, steering it in the alternative direction of homogenized commercialization and architectural restoration. If you get a feeling of déjà vu as you tread the cobbled streets or wander among the overpriced novelty shops, that may be because the Rouse Corporation, which designed the rejuvenated area, sponsored similar gentrification at Boston's Quincy Market and Baltimore's Harborplace.

The process succeeded and the historic district, in all its fishy and foul-smelling glory, became a ritzy Reagan-era playground. The fresh-fish market became a yuppie meat market. Now the South Street Seaport complex has 18th-century shops, graceful galleries, and seafaring schooners in addition to the fish. After 5pm, masses of crisply attired professionals—sneakers lurking under skirts and ties trailing over shoulders—flee their offices and converge here for much-anticipated cocktails. Tourists and natives alike mingle among the expensive shops and greasy food.

The seaport begins at the intersection of Fulton, Pearl, and Water St., as car traffic gives way to street performers. Nearby stands the ironically miniature **Titanic Memorial Lighthouse.** To the left, on Water St., a number of 19th-century buildings have been restored and now house some shops. Lovers of the printing process can get their fix at **Bowne & Co.,** 211 Water St., a restored 19th-century printing shop where employees give demonstrations on a working letterpress (748-8660; open Mon.-Sat. 10am-5pm). Next door is the **Whitman Gallery,** which displays antique ship models and historic maritime prints (open in summer Mon.-Wed., Fri.-Sun. 10am-6pm, Thurs. 10am-8pm; after Labor Day Mon., Wed., Fri.-Sun. 10am-5pm, Thurs. 10am-8pm). On the Fulton St. side of this block, you can escape to enjoy a quiet lunch in **Cannon's Walk,** a sparkling-clean alley behind these shops.

Back in the main square, the right side of Fulton St. is home to famous **Schermerhorn Row,** the oldest block of buildings in Manhattan, constructed mostly between 1811 and 1812. When Peter Schermerhorn purchased this tract in the 1790s as an investment, it was a "water lot," and the city sold him the right to fill it in with solid surface. Schermerhorn's just-add-landfill purchase proved to be profitable, as this spot rapidly became the focus of much of New York's sea-related commerce. At the **Seaport Museum Visitors' Center** (748-8659), you can buy tickets to many of the attractions at the Seaport (open April-Sept. Mon.-Wed., Fri.-Sun. 10am-6pm, Thurs. 10am-8pm; Oct.-March Mon.,Wed.-Sun. 10am-6pm, Tues. 10am-5pm). Tickets are also available at the museum's gift shop or at Pier 16 (see below).

Across Fulton St. from Schermerhorn Row stands one of the focuses of the seaport, the **Fulton Market Building.** Currently undergoing renovations, the ground floor still offers a restaurant and some shops, but the action has moved to Pier 17. At the end of Fulton St., the river rises suddenly into view—and so does the smell, as the spirits of dead fish assault your nostrils. The stench comes from the **Fulton Fish Market,** the largest fresh-fish market in the country, hidden to the left on South St. under the overpass. The city has tried to dislodge the market, but it has held fast for over 160 years and still opens at 4am, despite all efforts at displacement. New York's store and restaurant owners have bought their fresh fish here by the East River since the Dutch colonial period. A recent fire caused thousands of dollars in damage and renewed Mayor Giuliani's desire to weed out the mob influences that allegedly control the market's activities. Between midnight and 8am you can see buyers making their pick from the gasping catch, just trucked here in refrigerated vehicles. Those who can stomach wriggling scaly things might be interested in the behind-the-scenes tour of the market given some Thursday mornings from June to October (see Sightseeing Tours, p. 123). Take care not to offend the local mafia hoods—you just may end up sleeping with the fishes.

Farther on toward the river on Fulton St., you'll find the **Pier 17 Pavilion** to your left, the **Pier 16 Ticketbooth** straight ahead, and a number of sailing ships docked to your right. At Pier 17 you can play on a three-story, glass-enclosed "recreation pier" filled with small, upscale specialty shops, restaurants, and food stands. The top-floor eating complex here engages in fast-food multiculturalism with its quick-service eateries. Outside you can feast your eyes on striking views of the Brooklyn Bridge from lounge chairs in the shade (marketplace information 732-7678).

The Pier 16 kiosk, the main ticket booth for the seaport, stays open from 10am to 7pm (open one hour later on summer weekends). You can buy tickets here for sev-

NEIGHBORHOODS

eral cruises, each carrying predictably overstarched company aboard. The **Seaport Line** offers one-hour day cruises and two-hour evening cruises with live music ranging from $12-22 (see Sightseeing Tours, p. 123).

An admission ticket, sold at both the Pier 16 booth and the Museum Visitors' Center, serves as a full-day pass to many small galleries, ships, and tours. The ticket includes entrance to the **Melville Gallery** (213 Water St.), which features changing exhibits, the **Whitman Gallery** (209 Water St.), home of ocean liner memorabilia; the **Children's Center** (165 John St.), which hosts craft workshops for kids; the **Norway Galleries** (171 John St.), which has exhibitions on the history of New York's seamen; and the ships *Ambrose, Wavertree,* and *Peking* (see below). Take a "Hard Tack and Hard Times Ship Tour" which explores both the *Ambrose* and the *Peking* (daily 2pm) or board a "Ships Restoration Tour" (daily 1pm). For recorded information about the museums, call 748-8600. (Admission $6, students $4, seniors $5, children 4-12 $3.) Finally, combination rates are available if you want to take a cruise and visit the museums.

Harbored at Pier 16, next to the ticket kiosk, bobs the **Peking,** the second-largest sailing ship ever built. The *Peking,* built in 1911 by a Hamburg-based company, spent most of its career on the "nitrate run" to Chile, a route that passes around Cape Horn, one of the most dangerous stretches of water in the world. Powered purely by shifting winds and brute force, ships like the *Peking* represent the culmination of 2000 years of sailing history. For an intriguing sample of this rich history, don't miss the 15-minute 1929 film of the ship during an actual passage around Cape Horn (shown daily 10am-6pm). Also on board, you can see reconstructed living quarters and a photo exhibit about sailing life. If you're in the mood for manual labor, you can help the current crew raise one of the ship's 32 sails (Wed.-Sun. 3:30pm) after half-hour tours beginning at 2pm. Be sure to pick up a schedule at the visitors' center. You can get in with a museum ticket or by paying a suggested donation of $3 from 10am-6pm.

Several other ships have been docked in the seaport for good. Smaller ones include the *Wavertree,* an iron-hulled, three-masted ship built in 1885. In addition, you can see the *Ambrose,* a floating lighthouse built in 1907 to mark an entrance to the New York harbor. The *Pioneer* sailing ship gives two- and three-hour cruises on which you can assist with sailing duties (see Sightseeing Tours, p. 123).

The Seaport also hosts a number of concerts and performances outdoors on the Ambrose Stage throughout the summer. The "Twilight Dance Series" brings such notable companies as Paul Taylor II and the Dance Theatre of Harlem School Ensemble. Past events have also included "NHL Street Hockey at the Seaport," a crafts fair, and a Gospel Night (for information, call 732-7678).

▨ Liberty Island: The Statue of Liberty

Give me your tired, your poor,
Your huddled masses yearning to breath free,
The wretched refuse of your teeming shore.
Send these, the homeless, tempest-tossed to me.
I lift my lamp beside the golden door!

—Emma Lazarus

The Statue of Liberty, deeply embedded in the heart of American identity and consciousness, is to the United States as Versailles and the Eiffel Tower are to France, the Leaning Tower is to Italy, and Buckingham Palace and the Tower of London are to England. The colossal sculpture, rivaled only by the Empire State Building (and, more recently, the Twin Towers) as *the* symbol of New York City, has represented the most attractive element of the American Dream for over a century and has become recognized throughout the world as a universal image of freedom, as evidenced by Chinese youngsters' invocation of Lady Liberty just prior to the Tiananmen Square massacres in 1989. The statue has also made appearances in countless novels, television shows and films, including *Escape from New York, Working Girl, Splash,*

Planet of the Apes, and *Remo Williams*, and was recently blown to smithereens in the alien epic *Independence Day*. For all these reasons, the Statue of Liberty has become a world-renowned tourist draw—an up-close view of this striking modern-day colossus offers a chance to experience and reflect upon one of the cornerstones of the American myth.

Like most things American, the statue has roots in the Old World. The sculpture originated as Frenchman Frederic-Auguste Bartholdi's idea for a lighthouse at the Suez Canal, a plan he shelved when the prospect of a monument to Franco-American friendship was first entertained. The new statue was to commemorate the victory of the Union in the Civil War and the constitutional extension of liberty to black slaves; more pragmatically, the gift would improve the chances that America would oppose the decidedly libertyless government of Napoleon III in France. The reference to liberation was reduced over time as the project was stalled, and now remains only as a set of broken manacles (invisible from the ground) at the statue's feet. In 1871, as the Paris Commune made things increasingly inhospitable for Bartholdi in France, the sculptor finally came to America to line up support for his vision. While his countrymen were plotting against the establishment of the workers' paradise in Paris, Bartholdi, with President Grant and others, plotted production on the biggest statue the world had ever seen, *Liberty Enlightening the World*.

Bartholdi was convinced that, in America, size mattered. He wrote to his mother that everything was bigger here, "even the peas." Along with classical and philosophical notions of the "colossus," Bartholdi also wished to incorporate the feminine embodiment of Liberty that had sustained the early years of the French Revolution, as in Delacroix's *Liberty Leading the People*. The resulting work of art was a 151-ft.-tall (300 with pedestal) woman in a toga holding a lamp aloft (her face was modeled after Bartholdi's mother).

Even before its inauguration on October 28, 1886, this monument to Franco-American relations (something few Americans, then or now, tend to get choked up about) had begun to acquire symbolic significance: immigrants, and not just French ones, had made a claim to the statue. Publishing magnate Joseph Pulitzer, a millionaire Hungarian immigrant who had realized the American Dream in his publishing empire, raised the money for the required pedestal by guilt-tripping ordinary New Yorkers into giving whatever they could. Locals of all ages responded to his efforts with words (and hard-earned pennies) of generosity—"A lonely and very aged woman with limited means wishes to add her mite"; "Enclosed please find five cents as a poor office boy's mite to the pedestal fund"; and the Tiny Tim-esque "We send you $1.00, the money we saved to go to the circus with." After the pedestal was completed, the finishing touch to *Liberty Enlightening the World* was penned by poet Emma Lazarus in 1883, when she imbued the New Colossus with its now-famous words of welcome. America's destiny as the home of the homeless, a nation of settlers, was sealed.

The Statue of Liberty officially opened in 1886. Women were barred from the opening ceremonies in 1886, but a group of determined suffragettes chartered a boat and sailed themselves over to the statue, interrupting speakers by pointing out the irony of a female embodiment of Liberty in a country where women could not vote. 1965 saw a more extreme protest on Liberty Island as four terrorists tried to sever the Lady's head and torch-arm with explosives.

Even the most famous American icon requires an occasional facelift, and Lady Liberty's came amidst a great deal of hoopla that some might characterize as an excess of liberty, including corruption, grandstanding, and media saturation. The mid-Eighties restoration led by Chrysler chairman Lee Iacocca vastly improved the statue's internal design and removed the wire mesh around the staircase so visitors could view Liberty's innards as they climb. The only visible exterior change is the gold-plated copper flame—Bartholdi's original conception—replacing the ancient glass and copper one. Shrouded in scaffolding for two years, Lady Liberty was unveiled in a huge centennial party on July 4th, 1986, replete with Elvis impersonators, 25,000 boats in the harbor, 40,000 fireworks, and an estimated 1.52 million people crowding downtown for a glimpse of the 100-year-old birthday girl.

NEIGHBORHOODS

Lady Liberty's copper sheeting (2.5 mm thick) has acquired its green patina over the last 100 years as a form of self-protection against the elements and the not-quite-pristine city air. Bartholdi chose the symbols of the statue to represent the ideals of rational republicanism. The seven points of the crown stand for the seven seas and seven continents. The toga recalls the ancient republic of Rome. The tablet in her left hand is the keystone of liberty and bears the inscription "July 4, 1776." More obscurely, each window in the visor represents one of the "natural minerals" of the earth. Finally, the torch burns as a symbol of the Masonic ideal—Enlightenment.

The statue draws colossal crowds, particularly in the summer, when you may find yourself standing in line for up to three hours. Winter is a better time to visit; spring and fall, on the other hand, are often dominated by howling packs of schoolchildren who each year refine the art of spitting on the heads of those below them climbing the statue. If you do attempt a visit in the summer, try to get there on the first or second ferry, or bring someone you feel like standing next to for a few hours. The nicer the day, the longer the line (and the greater the number of heat-exhaustion cases). Eat before you go; the climb, with its endless stairs, can be strenuous, and food on the island is priced according to international-monopoly rules: in other words, whatever foreign tourists can bear.

An ideal summer trip will have you on the boat for Liberty at 9am, off the island in a few hours, and over to the air-conditioned comfort of Ellis Island by noon. Ferries run in a Battery Park-Liberty-Ellis loop; listen for your stop (you're unlikely to miss it). The ticket costs the same no matter how long you stay and regardless of whether you want to see only the statue or the immigration station, so you might as well do both.

The ferry ride is one long photo-op, with jaw-dropping views of the lower Manhattan skyline, the Brooklyn Bridge, and, of course, Ms. Liberty. Being a ferry for tourists and tourists alone, the boat will lean dramatically toward the island so that the camera-ready can snap away by the rail.

Once you're on the island, it's in your best interest to head quickly for the entrance at the back of the statue. (Don't incite a riot, but keep in mind that every person you can maneuver in front of means less time in line.) Enter through Fort Wood, part of the system of New York Harbor defenses during the War of 1812. The line on the left is the only way to get to the crown. It's all stairs: 22 stories' worth, or 300-plus of them, many narrow and spiraling, the last leg a narrow spiral staircase that claustrophobes and vertigo sufferers may want to avoid. There are really only two reasons to go to the crown: (1) like Mt. Everest, because it's there, or (2) to glimpse Gustave Eiffel's (yes, that Eiffel) internal support-system. The only way to see the intricate, web-like structure is to clamber to the crown. Be warned—the view is highly anticlimactic: the tiny windows, resembling those on an airplane, look out not on Manhattan but on the Brooklyn dockyards. Senior citizens, young children with a propensity to whine or spit, and anyone with a heart, respiratory, or leg ailment should probably avoid the climb. For those who are inclined to back down midway, there are plenty of chances to stop climbing and return to the bottom. Make sure you use *Dial;* you're going to wish everybody did.

Back on terra firma, the usually faster line on the right is for the elevator, which goes to the observation decks atop Richard Morris Hunt's pedestal. There, you can admire the enchanting views of New York, Ellis, and the towering statue above you. Don't bother being sneaky; you can't take the elevator halfway up and climb to the top. An exhibit on Lady Liberty's history, from creation to restoration, is located over the entrance doors on the second level. Some of the artifacts on display include a actual-size mold of Ms. Liberty's face, various artists' renderings of the sculpture, and a history of the statue's cultural influence, including the cover of Supertramp's *Breakfast in America* LP. On the third floor rests a small immigration exhibit which should whet your appetite for the much more fascinating Ellis Island.

Rangers are a friendly and knowledgeable lot and are willing to answer any question you have, just as long as you're not attempting a smokescreen to jump ahead in line. If they do occasionally appear testy, rattled, or preoccupied with medical cases, it's only because they're ridiculously outnumbered: 15 of them to 10,000 tourists on a busy day. Outdoor ranger-conducted tours are held at 45 minutes past the hour, from 10:45am-3:45pm daily.

If you have some time before the next ferry departs, the well manicured grounds are nice for a quick walk-around. Of particular interest are the small, cartoonish sculptures of important folk in Liberty's history. Or you may want to take in the gift shop and cafeteria. In the shop you can buy useful things like $2 foam Liberty crowns, $70 Liberty hologram watches, and 50¢ Statue of Liberty erasers. In the cafeteria, food names struggle to sound tantalizing while jumbled in a variety of languages (fried fish and french fries $4).

Buy tickets for the ferry at Castle Clinton in the southwest corner of Battery Park, the "toe" of Manhattan Island, right outside the Bowling Green subway station (subway: #4, 5) or across the park from the South Ferry terminal (subway: #1, 9; see Sights: Lower Manhattan, p. 127). Ferries leave for Liberty Island from the piers at Battery Park every half hour from 9am to 3:30pm weekdays, 9am-4:30pm weekends. The last return ferry normally runs at 5:15 pm, in July and August at 7pm. (Ferry information 269-5755. Tickets $7, seniors $5, children 3-17 $3, under 2 free.)

▓ Ellis Island

While the Statue of Liberty may be the embodiment of the American Dream, nearby Ellis Island chronicles the often harsh realities of starting over in the New World. The island re-opened to huddled masses of tourists in 1990 after an infusion of hundreds of millions of dollars. During its three functional decades (1890-1920), approximately 15 million immigrants were processed here, many winding up with new names in addition to a new homeland.

World War II saw Ellis Island used as a detaining center for war criminals. Fueled by the allegations of Senator Joseph McCarthy, Ellis served as a center for screening the political beliefs of non-Americans trying to visit the U.S. throughout the early 50s. In 1970, five years after Ellis Island became a national monument, Native American activists attempted to occupy Ellis in a protest reminding the public that European immigrants destroyed America's often forgotten original inhabitants.

The exhibits on the island are divided between Ellis's history proper and the history of the peopling of America in general. Most of the first floor, used as a baggage storage area in Ellis's heyday, now displays a colorful statistical survey of America's remarkable diversity—rivaled only by the diversity of tourists milling about. For those who can trace an ancestor back to Ellis, the first floor also features a computer to help track immigration records.

The second floor is the focal point of the installation, where exhibits on the history of Ellis Island speak volumes about the arrival of the modern bureaucratic state's border control. "Through America's Gate" describes step by step the batteries of physical and mental tests, fitness exams, financial and criminal checks, and occasional hearings and detentions undergone by the newly arrived. Each step is illustrated by a documentary-style photographs and an oral history program featuring recorded memories of those who came through here. Also on the second floor is the overwhelming Registry Room, also known as the "great hall," where most of the processing took place. The great windows flood the room with light, making it an ideal place to rest up on a hard day of touring, if echoes of shuffling lines of exhausted, fearful immigrants don't disquiet you.

On the other end of the second floor, across the great hall, "Peak Immigration Years" tells the story behind the story, including depictions of ethnic neighborhoods in the U.S. after waves of immigration and the poverty, racism, community, and kinship that characterized them. The exhibit includes a wall of American political cartoons on immigration (most more than a little politically incorrect), and a computer that tests your citizenship knowledge (it's harder than you might think).

The third floor plays host to numerous intriguing exhibits, including "Treasures from Home," a collection of artifacts and clothing, and "Becoming American Women," a discussion of the cultural adjustments immigrant women had to make to become Americans in practice as well as in name. Various sculptures and large black and white photographs of grim-faced arrivals festoon the restored halls. Offices and the extensive immigration library of ship records and the like, open to researchers with prior permission, round out the third floor.

Those who don't feel like reading each exhibit in detail or deciphering the reminiscences on the headphones at each stop will want to check out the film *Island of Hope, Island of Tears,* presented twice an hour in one of the two theaters (one theater starts shows at 10:35am and continues every 45 minutes until 3:50pm, the other is prefaced by a 15 minute ranger talk and starts at 11:10am, continuing every hour until 4:10pm) on the island. The film is free, but tickets must be picked up at the information desk near the entrance in advance of the showing. This should be done early on if you want to see the film. Alternatively, you can listen to the (slightly rushed) audio taped guided tour narrated by Tom Brokaw ($3.50, seniors and students $3, children under 17 $2.50). Reading the signs yourself is probably a better bet. The restaurant has better food than the one over on Liberty Island, but the prices are equally exorbitant (fish and fries $4).

Two ferries bring you to and from Liberty and Ellis islands. One runs Battery Park-Liberty-Ellis, and the other Liberty State Park-Jersey City, NJ-Ellis-Liberty. Both run daily every half hour from 9:15am until 3:30pm, or 4:30pm on weekends and holidays. (Ferry information 269-5755. Tickets $7, seniors $5, children 2-17 $3, children under 2 free.) Guided tours of the island at 11am and 2pm daily.

■ Lower East Side

NEIGHBORHOODS

Down below Houston lurks the trendily seedy Lower East Side, where old-timers, who remember the days when the Second Ave. El ran from the power station at Allen and Pike St., rub shoulders with heroin dealers and hip twenty-somethings. A huge influx of Jews swelled the population of the Lower East Side in the century between 1850 and 1950; two million arrived in the 20 years before World War I, fleeing the Czar's bloody pogroms. The Lower East Side is still a neighborhood of immigrants, though now they are mostly Asian and Hispanic. Chinatown has expanded across the Bowery and along the stretch of East Broadway, one of the district's main thoroughfares. A lot of East Village-type artists and musicians have recently moved in as well, especially near Houston St., but despite the influx of artists, a seedy element remains—in an age of heroin *chic*, the Lower East Side has the dubious distinction of being the heroin capital of New York City.

Despite the population shift, remnants persist of the Jewish ghetto that inspired Jacob Riis's compelling work, *How the Other Half Lives*. New Yorks oldest synagogue building is the red-painted **Congregation Anshe Chesed** at 172-176 Norfolk St. (529-7194), just off Stanton St. This Gothic Revival structure, built in 1849 to seat 1500, now houses a small art gallery. Further down Norfolk, at #60 between Grand and Broome St., sits the **Beth Hamedrash Hagadol Synagogue** (674-3330), the best-preserved of the Lower East Side houses of worship. This synagogue was purchased in 1885 by the Orthodox congregation which is still housed there; it is the oldest Orthodox congregation in New York to be continually housed in one location. From Grand St., follow Essex St. three blocks south to **East Broadway.** This street epitomizes the Lower East Side's flux of cultures. You will find Buddhist prayer centers next to (mostly boarded up) Jewish religious supply stores, and the offices of several Jewish civic organizations. Across from Seward Park, the **Forward Building** stands watch at 175 East Broadway, on the block once known as "Publishers Row." Now occupied by a Chinese church, this tower once housed the offices of the Yiddish daily newspaper that bore its name (in Yiddish: *Foreverts*) and, at the beginning of this century, was the bastion of Yiddish intellectual culture. The *Forward* still publishes weekly from its midtown offices. Near East Broadway, at 15 Pike St., sits the dilapidated **Congregation Sons of Israel Kalvarie,** the former Pike St. *shul*. Graffiti covers this once-grand temple, whose congregation exists in name only. At 12 Eldridge St. near Canal St., another synagogue, the **Eldridge St. Synagogue** (219-0903), is in the midst of a multi-million dollar renovation that will yield a synagogue and museum. Tours are available with advance notice (open Sun., Tues.-Thurs. noon-4pm; Admission $4, children, students, and seniors $2).

The area around Orchard and Delancey Streets is one of Manhattan's bargain shopping centers. On Sundays, Orchard Street fills up with salesmen hawking their discount goods to multitudes of potential customers. Stop in at **Schapiro's House of Kosher Wines,** 126 Rivington St. (674-4404), for a tour of the only operational winery left in NYC, famous for once giving a bottle of "the wine you can cut with a knife" to every immigrant family. (Tours Sun. 11am-4pm; you can stop in and taste the wine anytime.) At 97 Orchard St., between Broome and Delancey St., you can visit the **Lower East Side Tenement Museum** (431-0233), a preserved tenement house of the type that proliferated in this neighborhood in the early part of the century. Buy tickets for a slide show, video, and guided tour at 90 Orchard St., at the corner of Broome St. ($7, seniors and students $6. Tours conducted Tues.-Fri. at 1, 2, and 3pm, and Sat.-Sun. every 45min. between 11am-4:15pm. The museum gallery at 90 Orchard St. (open Tues.-Sun. 11am-5pm) offers free exhibits and photographs documenting Jewish life on the Lower East Side. Guided historical walking tours depart from the corner at 90 Orchard St. at 1:30pm on Sat. and Sun. (Tickets $7, seniors and students $6. Combo tickets for tour and museum $12, seniors and students $10.)

■ Little Italy and Chinatown

Substituting the shores of Canal Street for the canals of Venice, touristed **Little Italy** brings a tasty slice of the Old World to the Big Apple. Raging Bull Robert DeNiro stalked the *Mean Streets* here in 1973 and then returned a year later to run the place in *The Godfather II* (you can still see the remnants of the set). Unfortunately, in recent years emphasis has moved away from the "Italy" and toward the "Little," as the neighborhood's borders have begun to collapse and recede in the face of an aggressively expanding Chinatown. Walk a few blocks in any direction from Mulberry Street—the main, Italian flag-flying drag—and you're almost certain to encounter a number of Chinese shops and signs. These days, many young Italians are moving out; meanwhile, more authentic (and thus less tourist-conscious) Italian neighborhoods flourish in Bensonhurst, Brooklyn, and in Belmont, in the Bronx. Nevertheless, between Broome and Canal St. on Mulberry St., the flavor of the old Little Italy lives on.

In truth, the Little Italy experience is less about sights and more about tastes. Most area restaurants are reasonable, but some can be horrendously overpriced—a full meal can run to $60-70, particularly when a bottle of wine is brought into the equation. Save money by dining on sizable appetizers (usually referred to as *antipasti* on the more authentic menus) or grabbing a snack at one of the many shops and groceries. (See Eating & Drinking: Little Italy, p. 103.)

Although its name fails to evoke images of Italy, **Mulberry Street** remains the heart of the neighborhood. At **Umberto's Clam House,** 129 Mulberry St., at Hester St., "Crazy Joey" Gallo was slain in 1972 while celebrating his birthday; he had allegedly offended a rival "family." No Italian neighborhood could be considered complete without an appropriately imposing Catholic house of worship— **St. Patrick's Old Cathedral,** completed in 1815, rests at 264 Mulberry St., near Prince St. The area, known to some as East SoHo, is developing its own galleries, cafés, and hipster hangouts. One of America's earliest Gothic Revival churches, the façade was damaged in an 1866 fire. The Cathedral still administers marriages and baptisms (by appt. only; call 226-8075).

If antiquated fire stations ring your bell, the well kept (and newly renovated) **Engine Co. 55** stands at 363 Broome St., between Mott and Elizabeth St., dating from 1898. You can continue your tour of historic buildings devoted to civil protection by walking west on Broome St. a few blocks to Centre St. At this corner looms the massive and elegant **former police headquarters** of the city. Alas for tourists, this domed

Neoclassical giant has been a private residence since 1909. Still, it's worth a peek inside the lobby nevertheless.

On the northern fringe of Little Italy, at the corner of Lafayette St. and E. Houston St., stands the **Puck Building,** appropriately enough the former home of the monthly humor magazine *Spy*. This beautiful 1899 red-brick building originally housed *Spy's* humor-magazine predecessor *Puck*; to honor its namesake, a cute golden Puck stands over the Lafayette St. door, awaiting mischief.

Meanwhile, on Little Italy's southern front, commercial **Canal Street** divides Little Italy from its nearest neighbor, Chinatown. Stepping south across Canal St., Italian *caffè* and *gelaterie* give way to pagoda-topped phone booths, steaming tea shops, and multiple varieties of Asian food. New York's **Chinatown** maintains seven Chinese newspapers, over 300 garment factories, innumerable food shops, and the largest Asian community in the U.S. outside San Francisco (over 300,000 estimated residents). Vaguely bounded by Worth St. to the south and Canal St. to the north, Broadway to the west and the Bowery to the east, Chinatown spills out farther into the surrounding streets every year, especially towards Little Italy.

Mott and Pell Streets, the unofficial center of Chinatown, are a hubbub of commercial activity, paved with brightly colored businesses and restaurants vying for tourist attention, with everything from shelves of dried ginseng to bucketfuls of baby turtles glistening like jade. Don't be snookered by the low prices on merchandise—creative labeling abounds in several stores. Just because those Walkmans say Sony doesn't mean they're made in Japan. Gift shops also line the streets, peddling miniature Buddhas, exotic swords, spherical stress relievers, and dragon-shaped clogs. During the Chinese New Year (in late Jan. or Feb.), the area's frenetic pace accelerates to a fever pitch. Also be careful down here around the Fourth of July. Fireworks of all stripes are sold here, but most are illegal and dealing with the crafty sales techniques of illicit fire-hawkers can be intimidating. Moreover, Mayor Giuliani's "Quality of Life" crackdown has made many fireworks even *more* illegal.

One of New York's stranger melting pot amalgamations, the **Ling Liang Church,** rests at 173-175 East Broadway. Here lies a postmodern Christ surrounded by biblical blessings on a bed of red Chinese characters. Southwest along East Broadway, left (south) on Market St. and one block down, on the corner at 61 Henry St., stands the mysteriously spireless **First Chinese Presbyterian Church,** a large dark stone building built in 1817. Back to East Broadway and one block further southwest is Chatham Square and its **Kimlau War Memorial.** The Memorial, a large Chinese-style stone arch, was erected in memory of those Chinese-Americans killed in pursuit of, as the statue reads, "freedom and democracy." Just north on the Bowery, a huge stone **Confucius** stands with clasped hands on his namesake plaza at the corner of Division St., spreading the Chapter of Harmony to any person or pigeon who happens along. On the south side of Chatham Square, on St. James Pl. between James and Oliver St., is the **First Shearith Israel Graveyard.** This site served as the cemetery for New York City's first Jewish congregation, the Spanish-Portuguese Shearith Israel Synagogue; some of the gravestones here date from as early as 1683.

Head northwest back across Chatham Square to reach Chinatown proper, west of the Bowery. Scholars should ascend to the **Oriental Enterprises Company,** 13 Elizabeth St. (2nd floor), a bookstore specializing in Chinese literature. Its extensive collection includes books, tapes, CDs, and newspapers, as well as some interesting calligraphy equipment (open daily 10am-7pm). For a less academic and more theological treat, note the reds and golds of the **Buddhist Temple,** 16 Pell St., off Mott St. Here, the devout are invited to kneel and give offerings in front of a porcelain statue,

---

Fowl Play?

When we say that the Chinatown fair chicken is tough to beat, we're not kidding. One disgruntled sore loser, upon falling to the mighty bird, was overheard to remark: "I'm not normally so terrible at tic-tac-toe—the chicken confused me." Hmmm. Better watch that cockiness—you might just run afoul.

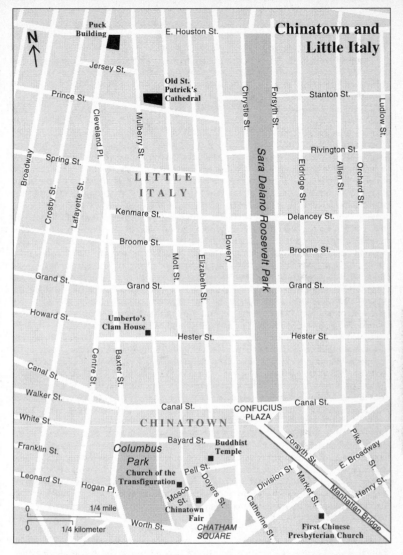

Chinatown and Little Italy

Puck Building

E. Houston St.

Jersey St.

Old St. Patrick's Cathedral

Prince St.

Chrystie St.

Forsyth St.

Stanton St.

Ludlow St.

Cleveland Pl.

Mulberry St.

Broadway

Spring St.

Rivington St.

Eldridge St.

Allen St.

Orchard St.

LITTLE ITALY

Kenmare St.

Broome St.

Bowery

Mott St.

Elizabeth St.

Sara Delano Roosevelt Park

Delancey St.

Broome St.

Grand St.

Grand St.

Howard St.

Crosby St.

Lafayette St.

Grand St.

Umberto's Clam House

Hester St.

Hester St.

Centre St.

Baxter St.

Canal St.

Walker St.

White St.

Franklin St.

Leonard St.

Canal St.

CONFUCIUS PLAZA

Canal St.

CHINATOWN

Columbus Park

Bayard St.

Buddhist Temple

Church of the Transfiguration

Pell St.

Dovers St.

Mosco St.

Chinatown Fair

Hogan Pl.

Worth St.

CHATHAM SQUARE

Forsyth St.

Division St.

Market St.

Catherine St.

Manhattan Bridge

Pike St.

E. Broadway

Henry St.

First Chinese Presbyterian Church

0 —— 1/4 mile
0 —— 1/4 kilometer

NEIGHBORHOODS

while the less devout can browse through the gift shop in the rear of the same room. If your pleasures run a more earthly course, try some of the truly unique flavors at the **Chinatown Ice Cream Factory,** including ginger, lychee, and papaya ice creams (see Eating and Drinking: Chinatown, p. 105).

The **Chinatown Fair,** 8 Mott St., features old-school video games and one clever chicken. If all the arcade rats keep killing you in Kombat games and Galaga and Mrs. Pacman just don't carry the same thrill they once did, you can take on the fair's resident chicken genius. For 50¢, the resident fowl will engage you in an arduous battle of tic-tac-toe. Don't write off the bird just yet—remember, this is its livelihood.

Speaking of birds, early-rising ornithologists (or curiosity-seekers) will want to take an early morning stroll to Sara Delano Roosevelt Park, west of the Bowery, at the corner of Chrystie and Delancey St. There, between about 7 and 9am, a number of older Chinese men gather each morning from spring through fall to give sun to the songbirds—an old tradition intended as a distraction from vice. The men arrive with caged birds in hand, the cages still covered in cloth so that their occupants don't wake too early. After positioning their cages in a small, grassy area at the park's northern edge, the men gingerly remove the cages' coverings, and bid their songbirds good morning. The men do some stretching exercises and socialize as they wait for their birds to warm to the sun and begin singing. Once sufficiently bathed in the sun's warmth and light, the birds awaken to the day—their songs are amazingly loud and melodic, easily heard over the roar of the heavy morning traffic.

■ SoHo

Artist Barbara Kruger's statement "You are where you are shown" is a sentiment widely shared in SoHo, the district **So**uth of **Ho**uston St. (pronounced "HOW-ston"), north of Canal St., west of Broadway, and east of Sullivan St. Over the years, SoHo has become as much a style of life as a place to live—the artists and artistic types who inhabit the area thrive on the energy of its image-intensive bars, galleries, boutiques, and restaurants. This is a great place for star-gazing, too, so bring your autograph book and a bright flash for your camera. Celebrities like that.

The architecture here is American Industrial (1860-1890), notable for its cast-iron façades. The architects used iron to imitate stone, often painting it to look like limestone, and they laced the columns and pediments with ornate detail (you can still see an 1861 building made by James Bogardus, the inventor of iron buildings, at 85 Leonard St.). The iron frames made heavy walls unnecessary and allowed for the eventual installation of vast windows. The sweatshops and factories that filled the structures were outlawed in time, and decades of decay led to the City Club's declaration in 1962 that the area was "the wasteland of New York." Developer Robert Moses saw the dilapidated blocks as the prime location for his Lower Manhattan Expressway, but residents fought the construction and instead embarked on a program of redevelopment and rehabilitation. In 1973 the city declared the neighborhood an historic district.

The huge open spaces of these building proved strongly attractive to New York's artistic community, and the past three decades have seen SoHo transformed into the city's high-priced gallery mecca. Here, art is nothing if not for sale. Every block has its own set of galleries (dozens line the streets between Broadway and West Broadway). Don't be put off by snooty gallery-owners unless you're interrupting a private showing to a visiting head of state. Galleries are best viewed with a grain of salt and a pinch of attitude. Most hold some interesting work behind the scenes—with the right line, you may be able to talk someone into showing you the reserve artwork. Many galleries also host fun (and pretentious) parties for openings and closings of shows—you may be able to finagle an invitation from the staff. Most close Sundays and Mondays from September to June and often close altogether through the heat of July and August (see Galleries, p. 252).

A few museums make their home amid the SoHo galleries. **The Alternative Museum** (966-4444) claims a space on the fourth floor of 594 Broadway, a building which also houses nine commercial galleries. Across the street is **The Museum for African Art,** 593 Broadway (966-1313), which exhibits a stunning variety of African and African-American art. At 583 Broadway, just north of Prince St., you'll find **The New Museum of Contemporary Art** showing the newest and latest on the art scene. At 575 Broadway, the Guggenheim's new downtown branch, the **Guggenheim Museum SoHo** (423-3500), fills two spacious floors of an historic 19th-century building with selections from the museum's permanent collection of modern and contemporary works (See Museums, p. 245).

When you're in the mood to buy (and believe us, you won't be buying the art), browse through SoHo's extensive selection of clothing boutiques, handmade stationers, and home furnishing stores. SoHo is home to a large number of designer boutiques (which explains why most of the passersby on the streets of SoHo look as if they've just stepped off the runway). But be forewarned: these aren't bargain

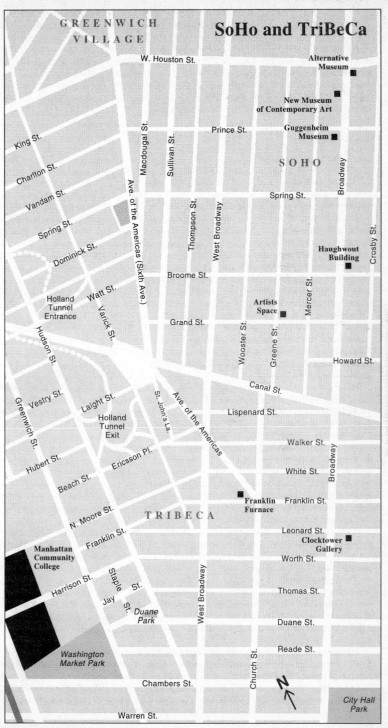

GREENWICH
VILLAGE

SoHo and TriBeCa

W. Houston St.

Alternative
Museum

New Museum
of Contemporary Art

Prince St.

Guggenheim
Museum

King St.

S O H O

Charlton St.

Broadway

Vandam St.

Spring St.

Macdougal St.

Sullivan St.

Spring St.

Dominick St.

Ave. of the Americas (Sixth Ave.)

Thompson St.

West Broadway

Broome St.

Haughwout
Building

Holland
Tunnel
Entrance

Watt St.

Varick St.

Grand St.

Artists
Space

Wooster St.

Greene St.

Mercer St.

Crosby St.

Howard St.

Hudson St.

Canal St.

Vestry St.

Laight St.

St. John's La.

Ave. of the Americas

Lispenard St.

Greenwich St.

Holland
Tunnel
Exit

Walker St.

Hubert St.

Ericsson Pl.

White St.

Broadway

Beach St.

N. Moore St.

Franklin
Furnace

Franklin St.

T R I B E C A

Franklin St.

Leonard St.

Clocktower
Gallery

Manhattan
Community
College

Worth St.

Harrison St.

Staple St.

Jay St.

West Broadway

Thomas St.

Duane
Park

Duane St.

Church St.

Reade St.

Washington
Market Park

Chambers St.

N

City Hall
Park

Warren St.

designer boutiques. The fact that there aren't price tags on the clothes mean that if you have to ask, you probably can't afford it. However, there are a surprising number of good buys to be found in the district's vintage clothing stores and streetside stands. Be sure to check out the daily "fair" which sets up shop on a lot on Wooster at Spring St. The bargain hunt continues on Broadway with a wide selection of used clothing stores. Flea market devotees should check out the outdoor **Antiques Fair and Collectibles Market** (682-2000), held year-round, hosting some 50-100 vendors (depending on the season), from 9am to 5pm on Saturdays and Sundays on the corner of Broadway and Grand St.

■ TriBeCa

If you're looking for genuine starving artists, you may find a few in TriBeCa ("**TRI**angle **BE**low **CA**nal St."), an area bounded by Chambers St., Broadway, Canal St., and the West Side Highway. Lacking the Rodeo Drive-ish feel of SoHo, TriBeCa seems much more akin to the rest of the city—a visit won't leave you wondering whether the graffiti you see really is graffiti or just an artist's subtle attempt to create something that resembles graffiti but which will really confront you with your secret prejudices and thus open your eyes.

The avant-garde art world has migrated south from SoHo; new galleries offer exhibitions by less-established artists. Art lovers should look to the **Franklin Furnace,** 112 Franklin St. (925-4671), which battles fire regulations in its continuing quest to display the most alternative of alternative art. The Institute for Contemporary Art's **Clocktower Gallery** (233-1096) stands at 108 Leonard St., between Broadway and Lafayette, as TriBeCa recedes into Chinatown. The avant-garde gallery and studio space resides in the former home of the New York Life Insurance Company, on the 13th floor. Although the gallery and exhibition space will be closed to the public until 1996 (the gallery will be exclusively an artists' studio space until then while its sister gallery, P.S. 1 in Long Island City, Queens, undergoes renovations), on Thursday afternoons (after 2pm) you can still climb inside the clocktower to observe its eye-boggling mechanism and a fine view of lower Manhattan. And while the upstairs lofts here are still flanked by butter and egg warehouses, they have undergone art gentrification similar to those in SoHo. The seemingly decaying building that you see most likely harbors a number of beautifully restored lofts and studios.

While TriBeCa may not seem as pretty or vibrant as SoHo, residents of the area are very proud of their neighborhood—streets and community facilities are under constant renewal and improvement. West along White St., at 2 White St. and West Broadway, stands an anachronistic 1809 Federal house, a small brick structure whose paint is aged and peeling but whose interior has been completely refurbished and now houses a stylish and comfortable (although nameless) bar. Southwest of here, on Harrison St. between Greenwich and West St., stands a row of beautifully restored 18th-century townhouses. Just to the south, in an open triangular space bounded by Greenwich, Chambers, and West St., is **Washington Market Park,** which holds a surprisingly big and green spread of grass, as well as a killer playground/sandbox which attracts kids of all ages. The park hosts Thursday evening concerts each week from late June to early August; performances include every type of music, from jazz to R&B to country (call the Parks Dept. at 408-0100 for info, or just visit the bulletin board by the main gate to the park, where a schedule is always posted). Between Chambers and N. Moore St. stands **Manhattan Community College,** part of the City University system. TriBeCa also has its own local newspaper, called the "TriBeCa Trib," which can be picked up for free in many of the area's eating establishments and is a good guide to many of the community's festivals and events.

Southeast TriBeCa, along Broadway and Chambers St., has a more commercial feel than the rest of the area. Discount stores and cheap restaurants of all types line these streets, and with City Hall and the Financial District nearby, this area tends to be rather busy during the day. But along some of TriBeCa's quieter streets, like Hudson and W. Broadway, you'll find quite a few second-hand stores selling everything from

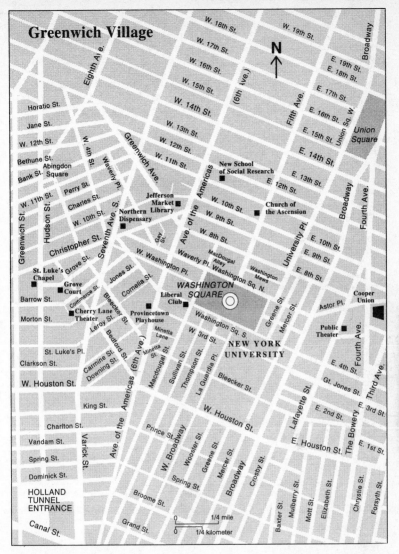

Greenwich Village

W. 18th St.
W. 17th St.
W. 16th St.
W. 15th St.
W. 14th St.
W. 13th St.
W. 12th St.
W. 11th St.

W. 19th St.
E. 19th St.
E. 18th St.
E. 17th St.
E. 16th St.
E. 15th St.
E. 14th St.
E. 13th St.
E. 12th St.

Broadway
(6th Ave.)
Fifth Ave.
Union Sq. W.
Union Square

Eighth Ave.

Horatio St.
Jane St.
W. 12th St.
Bethune St.
Bank St.
Abingdon Square

W. 4th St.
Waverly Pl.
Greenwich Ave.

New School
of Social Research

Fourth Ave.

W. 11th St.
Perry St.
Charles St.
W. 10th St.

Jefferson
Market
Library
Northern
Dispensary

W. 10th St.
W. 9th St.
W. 8th St.

Church of
the Ascension

E. 10th St.
E. 9th St.
E. 8th St.

Broadway

Greenwich St.
Hudson St.
Christopher St.
Seventh Ave. S.

Gay St.
MacDougal
Alley
Waverly Pl. Washington Sq. N.
Washington
Mews

University Pl.

St. Luke's
Chapel
Grove
Court

W. Washington Pl.
Jones St.
Cornelia St.
Liberal
Club

WASHINGTON
SQUARE

Greene St.
Mercer St.

Astor Pl.
Cooper
Union

Barrow St.
Morton St.

Cherry Lane
Theater
Commerce St.
Bedford St.

Provincetown
Playhouse

Washington Sq. S.
W. 3rd St.

Public
Theater

E. 4th St.
Fourth Ave.

St. Luke's Pl.
Clarkson St.

Leroy St.
Minetta
Lane
Minetta St.

NEW YORK
UNIVERSITY

Bleecker St.

Gt. Jones St.
Third Ave.

W. Houston St.

Carmine St.
Downing St.
Ave. of the Americas (6th Ave.)
MacDougal St.
Sullivan St.
Thompson St.
La Guardia Pl.

Lafayette St.
E. 2nd St.
E. 3rd St.

King St.

Charlton St.
Vandam St.
Spring St.
Dominick St.

HOLLAND
TUNNEL
ENTRANCE

Canal St.

Varick St.

Prince St.
W. Broadway
Wooster St.
Greene St.
Mercer St.
Broadway
Crosby St.

Spring St.
Broome St.

Grand St.

W. Houston St.
E. Houston St.
The Bowery
E. 1st St.

Baxter St.
Mulberry St.
Mott St.
Elizabeth St.
Chrystie St.
Forsyth St.

0   1/4 mile
0   1/4 kilometer

NEIGHBORHOODS

furniture to vintage clothing. The thing to remember about TriBeCa is that although a street may look barren, one of the best restaurants in the city (and probably one of the cheapest as well) is likely to be hidden somewhere on the block. TriBeCa may not be as polished as SoHo, but its odd mix of *couture* and squatter can be at once less pretentious and more exciting.

■ Greenwich Village

Located between Chelsea and SoHo on the lower West Side of Manhattan, Greenwich Village (or, more simply put, "the Village") and its residents have defied convention for almost a century to become the nexus of New York bohemia and the counter-cultural capital of the East Coast. In contrast to the orderly, skyscraper-encrusted streets of Midtown, the Village's narrow thoroughfares meander haphazardly without regard to any underlying grid or sense of numerical order. Tall buildings yield to brownstones of varying ages and architectural styles. Although high rents have reduced the diversity of its residents, the Village has long been a haven for artists, activists, musicians, writers, and amusement-seekers eager to embrace the alternative. Nowadays, when bohemians do so, they must withstand the gawking stares of tourists, and after the embrace is over, many return home to the East Village, Brooklyn's Williamsburg, and other areas where struggling artists can afford the cost of living.

The Village's prominence began with Tom Paine, who in 1808 had the derring-do to live on Bleecker St. Herman Melville and James Fenimore Cooper wrote American masterworks here, and Mark Twain and Willa Cather explored the U.S. heartland from their homes near Washington Square. Henry James was born on the square during the Village's High Society days, and Edith Wharton lived nearby. John Reed, John Dos Passos, and e.e. cummings all made the move to the Village straight from Harvard, followed by James Agee. Rents here were lower then, and many writers came to begin their careers in poverty and obscurity. Eugene O'Neill created the Provincetown Playhouse in the West Village; it became the site of his first theatrical successes. Theodore Dreiser wrote here, as did Edna St. Vincent Millay and Thomas Wolfe. Tennessee Williams, James Baldwin, and William Styron all found their way to small apartments in the area, and Richard Wright lived in the same building as Willa Cather, 35 years later.

"Greenwich Village" used to refer to the entire strip of Manhattan between Houston and 14th Streets but now refers primarily to the western part of the Village (from Broadway west to the Hudson River), while the area east of Broadway is now called the "East Village." If you hear anyone refer to "the Village," they probably mean this western area, although bohemians to the east would argue that true "Village" life has shifted to the east.

Today there are fewer and fewer aspiring artists in the Village as young professionals take over block by block. Nevertheless, the neighborhood remains one of the liveliest in Manhattan, with crowds of locals and tourists in varying states of substance-induced delirium wandering the streets well into the night. A particular treat is the wild **Village Halloween Parade.** If you ever wanted to see people dressed as toilets or carrots or giant condoms, this is your chance; if you're lucky, you may even receive a personal benediction from Rollerina, the city's cross-dressing fairy godmother on wheels.

In the Village, no matter what the hour, there's always a good time going on somewhere. If nothing else, there are few areas in the city so prime for people-watching. Residents with various pierced body parts share the street with NYU business students, an amazing panoply of dogs and the owners who love them, and wealthy urbanites eager to be confused with struggling artists. Sit at one of the sidewalk cafés and watch the world pass by.

■ Washington Square Park Area

Washington Square Park has been the universally acknowledged heart of the Village since the district's days as a little-known suburb. Native Americans once inhabited the marshland here, and by the mid-17th century it became home for black slaves freed by the Dutch. The latter half of the 18th century saw the area converted into a potter's field for the burial of the poor and unknown (around 15,000 bodies lie buried here) and then as a hanging-grounds during the Revolutionary War (people swung from trees that still stand today). In the 1820s the area was converted into a park and parade ground, and high-toned residences soon made the area the center of New York's social scene.

High society has long since gone north, and **New York University** has moved in. The country's largest private university and one of the city's biggest landowners (along with the municipal government, the Catholic Church, and Columbia University), NYU is most notable for its hip students, its top-of-the-line communications and film departments, its takeover of historic buildings, and some of the least appealing architecture in the Village. Many of the most unattractive buildings around the Square proudly display the purple NYU flag.

At the north end of Washington Square Park and the south end of Fifth Ave. stands the majestic **Washington Memorial Arch**, built in 1889 to commemorate the centennial of Washington's inauguration. The two statues on either side depict America's versatile founding father in poses of war and peace. The arch is actually hollow—every year the NYU band opens the door at the base and trudges up the 110 stairs to kick off the NYU commencement with *Pomp and Circumstance.*

In the late 1970s and early 80s Washington Square Park became a base for low-level drug dealers, and a rough resident scene sprang up. The mid-80s saw a noisy clean-up campaign that has made the park fairly safe and allowed a more diverse cast of characters to return, though the burgeoning drug industry was not completely displaced. Today musicians play, misunderstood teenagers congregate, dealers mutter cryptic code words, homeless people try to sleep, pigeons strut on the lawn, and children romp in the playground. In the southwest corner of the park, a dozen perpetual games of chess wend their ways toward inevitable checkmate while circles of youths engage in hours of hacky-sacking. The fountain in the center of the park provides an amphitheater for comics and musicians of widely varying degrees of talent. Judge for yourself how well Beethoven's *Moonlight Sonata* translates to the steel drum. Sadly, like many of the city's public areas, the park is markedly less safe after sunset, when the drug merchants set up shop in and around the area.

The north side of the park, called the **Row,** showcases some of the most elegant architecture in the city. Built largely in the 1830s, this stretch of stately Federal-style brick residences soon became an urban center roamed by 19th-century professionals, dandies, and novelists. No. 18, now demolished, was the home of Henry James's grandmother and the setting for his novel *Washington Square,* while farther west at 29 Washington Square West stands the home of Eleanor Roosevelt in the years after her husband's death. Nowadays the Row is mostly NYU administration buildings. The NYU Admissions Office at #22 (998-4500) offers tours of the campus (Mon.-Fri. 11am and 2:30pm; 2 and 3:30pm tours are often available too; call ahead).

A few steps north up Fifth Ave. on the east side is **Washington Mews,** a quirky, cobblestoned alleyway directly behind the Row. The boxy little brick houses, originally constructed as stables for the houses facing the park, are now NYU faculty housing.

Nearby **Eighth Street,** lined with offbeat shops and stores like **Wild Generation** and **Psychedelic Solutions,** is an anti-mall for the alternakids: strips of punky, funky, and commercial shops await perusal. Famous residents have included Jimi Hendrix, whose Electric Lady studio was located at **52 W. 8th Street.** Eighth St.'s stores offer, among other things, anti-establishment t-shirts and Cobain memorial apparel for disaffected anarchic types, leather restraints and assorted bondage gear for the adventurous, and plenty of creative smoking apparati for the "tobacco" enthusiast.

Back on Fifth Ave., at the corner of 10th St., rises the **Church of the Ascension,** an 1841 Gothic church with a lovely altar and stained-glass windows. President John Tyler consummated a secret elopement with his second wife here in 1844 (open daily noon-2pm and 5-7pm). **The Pen and Brush Club,** at 16 E. 10th St., was founded to promote female intelligentsia networking; among its members were such notables as Pearl Buck, Eleanor Roosevelt, Marianne Moore, and Ida Tarbell.

11th Street. features several stunning examples of turn-of-the-century architecture. That is, except for 18 W. 11th St., where an anomalous new building was built to replace the house destroyed in 1970 by a bomb-making mishap perpetrated by the Weathermen, a radical group residing in the basement. At Fifth Ave. and 11th St. is the **Salmagundi Club,** New York's oldest club for artists. Founded in 1870, the club's building is the only mansion left from the area's heyday as the pinnacle of New York society (open daily 1-5pm; call 255-7740 for details on exhibitions).

The corner of Fifth Ave. and 12th St. is dominated by the eccentric **Forbes Magazine Galleries** (206-5548), Malcolm Forbes's vast collection of random objects (see

Museums, p. 247). Up one more block, off Fifth Ave. at 2 W. 13th St., lies the **Parsons School of Design,** with its own exhibition galleries and cigarette-wielding, black-garbed *artistes.*

One avenue to the east is **University Place.** At 12th St. and University Pl. is the **New School for Social Research,** an institution dedicated to continuing adult education; former faculty include John Dewey and W. E. B. DuBois. During World War II, the New School made itself famous when it offered positions to European intellectuals fleeing the Nazis.

At 12th St. and Broadway lies the **Forbidden Planet,** purported to be the world's largest science fiction store. You can browse through vintage film memorabilia, a wide selection of comics, hundreds of science-fiction paperbacks, and a sizable collection of role-playing paraphernalia. Across the street is one of the world's most famous bookstores, the **Strand,** which bills itself as the "largest used bookstore in the world." You'll want plenty of time to search through the collection of over two million books on eight miles of shelves. (See Shopping: Bookstores, p. 296.)

Grace Church, constructed in 1845, asserts its powerful Gothic presence at 800 Broadway between 10th and 11th. The church, despite its dark medieval interior and vaguely creepy exterior, used to be *the* place for weddings (open Mon.-Thurs. 10am-5pm, Fri. 10am-4pm, Sat. noon-4pm, Sun. open for services only).

Broadway to the south reveals a strange conglomeration of cheap futon stores, "antique" and "vintage" (read: used yet expensive) clothing outlets, bars, and health food markets which line the street between electronic stores and fast-food joints. Here the styles are usually a few steps behind the truly avant-garde and a few dollars above the truly bohemian. At Broadway and 4th St., you'll find another of the Village's spiritual landmarks, **Tower Records,** a store with three floors and hundreds of racks full of music (but no actual records—only CDs and cassettes; see Shopping: Record Stores, p. 290.) If a star is going to do a PR stint in the Village, it'll be here.

At 721 Broadway and Washington Pl., NYU's **Tisch School of the Arts,** named for CBS president/NYU benefactor Larry Tisch, has produced such ground-breaking filmmakers as Spike Lee and Martin Scorcese.

At Greene Street and Waverly Place, one block up from Washington Pl., lies NYU's **Brown Building,** the former site of the Triangle Shirtwaist Company where a 1911 fire killed most of the primarily female staff (the doors had been chained shut to prevent the workers from taking too many breaks). The resulting uproar led to new workplace regulations and a rejuvenated worker safety movement (although the owners escaped charges of manslaughter and were instead awarded $6445 of insurance money for each victim).

One block west, Washington Sq. East is lined with NYU classrooms and administrative offices; the **Main Building** is located at Waverly Pl. After a recent year-long renovation, the **Grey Art Gallery** (998-6780) reopened at 100 Washington Sq. East. The gallery features community and student artists as well as works on the Village. (Open Sept.-May Mon.-Fri. 11am-6pm; June-Aug. Tues. and Thurs.-Fri. 11am-6:30pm, Wed. 11am-8:30pm, Sat. 11-5pm; closed Aug.) Further down Washington Sq. East, at the southeast corner of the park, is **NYU Information** at 70 Washington Sq. South. Come here for free maps and answers to your NYU-relevant questions.

One block east at Greene St. and W. 4th St. is a red-sandstone monolith—NYU's **Tisch Hall** (Larry again), home to the Stern Business School. The vast space before it and the brown cinderblock **Courant Institute of Mathematical Sciences** is known as **Gould Plaza.** A shiny aluminum Dadaist sculpture by Jean Arp, which bears an uncanny resemblance to a bunny rabbit or a deformed maple leaf, sits in the plaza inviting disparaging artistic commentary. Two blocks west at Washington Sq. South and LaGuardia Pl. looms another rust-colored bulk, the **Elmer Holmes Bobst Library.** Designed by architects Phillip Johnson and Richard Foster with the intention of unifying the campus through red-sandstone facades, only the Library, Tisch Hall, and Meyer Physics building were completed before money ran low. Rethinking its strategies, NYU opted for cheap purple flags instead. Across the street is the **Loeb**

Student Center, festooned with pieces of scrap metal that are purported to represent birds in flight.

Farther west, at 55 Washington Sq. South and Thompson St., stands the **Judson Memorial Baptist Church,** built in 1892 in a grand style, complete with stained glass, ornate trim, and an impressive tower. Known for its liberal stance on religion, Judson hosted a good deal of avant-garde art activity in the 50s and 60s and now prides itself on being a positive force for tolerance in the Village. Farther west along Washington Sq. South, across the street from the park, stands NYU's brick-arched **Vanderbilt Law School.** Inside the arch lies a surprisingly pleasant atrium, where anxious-looking law students cram amid the green of the garden.

The area directly south of Washington Square Park, from W. 4th St. to Houston St., is probably the most heavily touristed area of the Village, since it contains many of the more famous clubs, cafés, and bars. On MacDougal St., Sullivan St., Thompson St., and Bleecker St., one could spend days or weeks sipping cappuccinos, flipping through records, going to small clubs, and generally emulating bohemia. Just south of Washington Sq. Park, at 133 MacDougal St., is the landmark **Provincetown Playhouse.** Originally based on Cape Cod, the Provincetown Players were joined by the young Eugene O'Neill in 1916 and brought here that same year to perform his successful play *Bound East for Cardiff.* The playhouse went on to premiere many of O'Neill's works, as well as the work of other Village writers such as Edna St. Vincent Millay. Farther south on **MacDougal Street** are the Village's finest (and most tourist-trampled) coffeehouses. At the intersection of MacDougal and **Bleecker Street** in particular, café powerhouses **MacDougal, Le Figaro,** and **Café Borgia** vie for coffee lovers' patronage. Authors Jack Kerouac and Allen Ginsberg once graced Le Figaro and Café Borgia with their Beat presences, howling out poetry with free jazz accompaniment. These sidewalk cafés still provide some of the best coffee and people watching in the city (see Eating & Drinking, p. 97).

Parallel to MacDougal St. runs **Sullivan Street,** home to the **Sullivan St. Theater** and its *Fantastiks*, the longest running show in American theater history (see Entertainment and Nightlife: Theater, p. 263). **Bleecker Street,** made famous by Simon and Garfunkel, features a number of jazz clubs and bars. On the corner of Bleecker St. and LaGuardia Pl. stands a Picasso sculpture, proclaimed by the *New York Times* to be the ugliest piece of public art in the city. (It *is* relatively unattractive.) Farther down LaGuardia Pl., a statue of sprightly former mayor and street namesake **Fiorello LaGuardia** waves to passers-by with his mouth gaping open. Finally, at the corner of LaGuardia and E. Houston St., stands the **Time Landscape,** an "environmental sculpture" purported to depict the way Greenwich Village looked some 30,000 years ago. The effect, however, is severely curtailed by the fence surrounding it and the cars zipping along the street.

■ West of Sixth Ave.

The less-touristy bulk of Greenwich Village lies west of Sixth Ave. Despite rising property prices, the West Village still boasts an eclectic summer street life and excellent nightlife. The streets are equally eclectic; West 4th even crosses W. 10th and W. 11th St., while other roads will appear to cross themselves.

When walking up Sixth Ave., beware the speeding cars desperately trying to negotiate the non-rectilinear driving patterns created when the uptown avenues plowed through pre-existing Village streets. This also made for very large intersections; exercise caution or follow the crowds when crossing the streets.

At the northeast corner of the intersection of Sixth Ave. and W. 8th St. lies **Balducci's,** the legendary Italian grocery at 422 Sixth Ave., which has grown over the years from a sidewalk stand to a gourmand's paradise (see p. 115). Balducci's offers an orgy of aromatic cheese barrels, bread loaves, and fresh chilled vegetables—in case the food doesn't pique your interest, you can get into a staring contest with the live, bug-eyed lobsters (they'll win, but you can eat them in retaliation).

Across the street at 425 Sixth Ave. stands the landmark **Jefferson Market Library** (243-4334), a Gothic structure complete with detailed brickwork, stained-glass windows, and a turreted clock tower. Built as a courthouse in 1874, it occupies the triangle formed by the intersection of W. 10th St., Sixth Ave., and Greenwich Ave. Once voted one of the 10 most beautiful buildings in the country, the remarkable structure faced and beat a demolition plot in the early 60s. Carefully restored in 1967, the building reopened as a public library. Inside, the original pre-Raphaelite stained glass graces the spiral staircase. A pamphlet detailing the history of the site and the restoration can be obtained at the front desk (open Mon. and Thurs. noon-6pm, Tues. 10am-6pm, Wed. noon-8pm, Sat. 10am-5pm).

Left out of the library onto 10th St. and across the street rests an iron gate and a street sign that says **Patchin Place.** Behind the gate lies a tiny courtyard, little more than a paved alley. These 145-year-old buildings housed writers e.e. cummings, Theodore Dreiser, and Djuna Barnes during their Village sojourns.

Seventh Ave. is another crossroads of sorts. The next huge snarl of roads leads to **Sheridan Square,** the intersection of Seventh Ave., Christopher St., W. 4th St., and Grove St. Rioters against the Civil War draft thronged here in 1863 during some of the darkest days in New York City's history; some protesters brutally attacked freed slaves. Since then, the area has become much more tolerant, as evidenced by **Christopher Street's** large and very visible gay community. This is the territory of the Guppie (Gay Urban Professional), though gay males and lesbians from all socio-economic and cultural groups shop, eat, and live here. Here and throughout the Village, same-sex couples can and do walk together openly (see also Entertainment and Nightlife: Gay and Lesbian Clubs, p. 278). The area of Christopher St. near Sheridan Sq. has been renamed Stonewall Place, alluding to the **Stonewall Inn,** site of the 1969 police raid that sparked the gay rights movement. A plaque marks the former site of the club at 53 Christopher St.; the bar that resides there now is not the same one of 27 years ago. Within Sheridan Square two sculptures of same-sex couples stand locked in embraces, a tribute to the vibrant gay community. Scrutinizing the whole scene, a rather forlornly single General Sheridan stands nearby.

Christopher St. runs into **Bedford Street,** a remarkably narrow old-fashioned strip mapped prior to 1799 and named after a similar street in London. **Chumley's** bar and restaurant, at Number 86 between Grove and Barrow St., became a speakeasy in Prohibition days, serving to literary Johns (Dos Passos and Steinbeck), Ernest Hemingway, and Thornton Wilder, among others. As if out of respect for its surreptitious past, no sign of any kind indicates that the neglected structure might be a commercial establishment. Near the corner of Commerce St. stands No. 75½ Bedford St. Constructed in a former alley, this is the narrowest building in the Village; it measures a mere 9½ feet across. Edna St. Vincent Millay lived here until 1950. In 1924, Millay founded the **Cherry Lane Theater** at 38 Commerce St. (989-2020), which has showcased Off-Broadway theater (such as Beckett's *Waiting for Godot)* ever since.

Across the way at 39-41 Commerce St. and Bedford St. stand a pair of identical houses separated by a garden, known as the **Twin Sisters.** Completely unsubstantiated legend has it that they were built by a sea-captain for his spinster daughters, who were not on speaking terms. One block up Bedford St. is more twin action—102 Bedford St. at Grove St. is known as **Twin Peaks.** No need to worry about dancing dwarves here; just check out the two-roofed structure.

At the western end of Grove St. is the **Church of St. Luke's in the Fields,** 179-485 Hudson St. The third-oldest church in Manhattan, it was named for the once-remote location at which it was built in 1821. Walking up Hudson St. will lead you to the **meat-packing district,** around W. 12th and Gansevoort St. Here you can watch **slabs of meat** get loaded onto **large trucks,** if that's your idea of **a good time.**

From Hudson St., it's just a few blocks over to the docks along West St., which used to handle a great deal of New York's freight traffic as well as the occasional ocean liner. Recently, gay teenagers have been hanging out on the piers, and Mayor Giuliani, always ready to shut down a good time, has begun to enforce "quality of life" laws against these young ruffians. So if you're here late at night, don't drink outside,

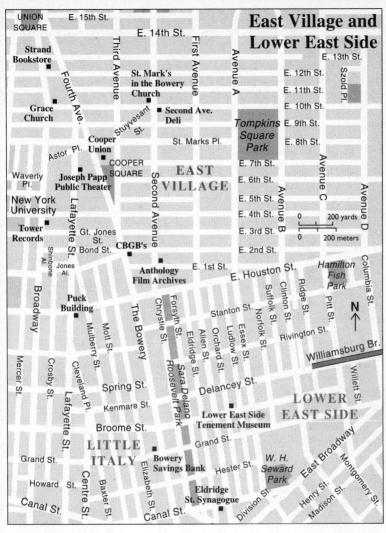

East Village and Lower East Side

and try not to urinate on the street. From here, you can peer across the water at Hoboken or down the island at the World Trade Center.

East Village

The old Lower East Side, once home to many Eastern European immigrants, extended from East Broadway to 14th St. Now this area has developed a three-way split personality, encompassing the part south of Houston and east of the Bowery (now considered to be the whole of the Lower East Side), the section east of Broadway and north of Houston (known as the "East Village"), and the part of the East Village east of First Ave. (known as "Alphabet City").

The East Village, a comparatively new creation, was carved out of the Bowery and the Lower East Side as rents in the West Village soared and its residents sought accommodations elsewhere. Allen Ginsberg, Jack Kerouac, and William Burroughs all eschewed the Village establishment to develop their junked-up "beat" sensibility east of Washington Square Park. Billie Holiday sang here; more recently, the East Village provided Buster Poindexter, Sonic Youth, and the Talking Heads with their early audiences. The eastward movement has recaptured much of the gritty feel of the old Village, and the population here is less homogeneous than in the West, with older Eastern European immigrants living alongside newer Hispanic and Asian arrivals. East Village residents embody the alternative spectrum, with punks, hippies, ravers, rastas, guppies, goths, beatniks, and virtually every other imaginable group coexisting amidst a myriad of cafés, bars, clubs, shops, and theaters. This multicultural compromise has not come easily; many poorer denizens of the East Village feel they have been pushed out by the newcomers. These tensions have most assuredly not been eased by glimmers of gentrification and rising rents in the East. Yet, despite these difficulties, the East Village will likely stay both ethnically and socio-economically diverse for quite some time to come.

A crowded, busy stretch of Broadway marks the western boundary of the East Village and the eastern edge of the Greenwich Village/NYU area. Everyone and their grandmother seems to know about this browser's paradise (see Greenwich Village, p. 149. for more on Broadway). Lafayette St. lies to the east of Broadway and runs parallel to it. At Lafayette and 4th St. stands **Colonnade Row,** with the Public Theater across the street. Colonnade Row consists of four magnificently columned houses, built in 1833. These were the homes of New York's most famous 19th-century millionaires: John Jacob Astor and Cornelius "Commodore" Vanderbilt, as well as the Delano family (as in Franklin Delano Roosevelt). There used to be nine of these houses; the ones that remain, at 428-434 Lafayette St., reflect the wear and tear of the ages.

The **Joseph Papp Public Theatre,** a grand brownstone structure across the street at 425 Lafayette St. (598-7150) was constructed by John Jacob Astor in 1853 to serve as the city's first free library. After its collection moved uptown, the building became the headquarters of the Hebrew Immigrant Aid Society, an organization dedicated to assisting thousands of poor Jewish immigrants in the early years of this century. In 1967, Joseph Papp's **New York Shakespeare Festival** converted the building to its current use as a theatrical center. Look for long lines of people waiting for free tickets to Shakespeare in the Park. These queues form in the early morning every day throughout June and July and wrap around the block in what has become an annual city tradition (see Entertainment & Nightlife: Theater, p. 256).

Up Lafayette St., **Astor Place,** both a small road and a large intersection, simmers with street life. The street signs were recently covered with stickers bearing the words "Peltier Place," in honor of Leonard Peltier, a Native American currently in prison for allegedly killing two FBI agents in 1985, and in protest against John Jacob Astor, whose fur trading is seen by some as exploitation of the Native American population. Check out the ever-popular **Beaver Murals** at the Astor Subway Stop— they pay homage to Astor's prolific fur trade.

At 2 Astor Pl. and Broadway, you can complement your new Village wardrobe with a distinctive trim at the largest haircutting establishment in the world, **Astor Place Hair Stylists** (475-9854), famous for its low-priced production-line approach to style. As one observer noted, "It's like Club MTV with clippers." Scissors are trés passé here—everything here is done with mechanical clippers. Matt Dillon, JFK, Jr., and Susan Sarandon are just some of the celeb clients who frequent this establishment. Stay away if you're finicky—Astor is suited to those who enjoy living dangerously. A total of 110 people (including a DJ) are employed in this three-story complex (open Mon.-Sat. 8am-8pm, Sun. 9am-6pm; short hair cuts $10, long hair cuts $12; Sun. and holidays $2 extra).

Astor Place, the intersection (at the juncture of Lafayette, Fourth Ave., Astor Pl., and E. 8th St.), is distinguished by a sculpture of a large black **cube** balanced on its corner. If you and your friends push hard enough the cube will rotate, but somebody sitting or sleeping underneath may complicate the process. "The Cube" is a frequent

---

Not to be Outdone

Industrialist Peter Cooper contributed much to the Big Apple when he founded his school in 1859. Yet, perhaps the most lasting contribution to society was made by his wife. Not to be outdone by the philanthropy of her husband, Mrs. Cooper exercised her prodigious culinary skills to create one of the world's favorite dishes—Jell-O, everyone's favorite quivering, translucent jelly dessert.

---

meeting point for rallies, marches, demonstrations, and site-specific performance art pieces, as well as for hordes of 12-year-old skaters who converge here most nights. Note the subway kiosk, a cast-iron Beaux Arts beauty that was built—believe it or not—in 1985 as part of a reconstruction of the station (the #6 train stops here).

The **Cooper Union Foundation Building**, 7 E. 7th St. (353-4199), at Cooper Square, stands as a proud and prominent feature of Astor Place. It was built in 1859 to house the Cooper Union for the Advancement of Science and Art, a tuition-free technical and design school founded by the self-educated industrialist Peter Cooper. While other American universities emulated the British university system in their ideals and design, Cooper Union was one of the first uniquely American places of education— the first college intended for the underprivileged, the first co-educational college, the first racially open college, and the first college to offer free adult-education classes. The school's free lecture series has hosted practically every notable American since the mid-19th century. Both the American Red Cross and the NAACP were founded here. It's also the oldest standing building in the U.S. incorporating steel beams; in fact, the building is made of old railroad rails. Appropriately enough, its namesake founder was among the industrial pioneers who laid down the steel rails that accelerated railroad construction. On the second floor, the **Houghton Gallery** hosts changing exhibits on design and American history, as well as displays of student-produced work, but usually not during the summer (open Mon.-Fri. noon-7pm, Sat. noon-5pm).

Stuyvesant Street angles off to the northeast from Astor Place, cutting north over 9th St. and terminating at Second Ave. and 10th St., right in front of the pretty **St. Mark's in the Bowery Church,** 131 E. 10th St. (674-6377). The church was built in 1799, on the site of a chapel that was on the estate of Peter Stuyvesant, the much-reviled last Dutch governor of the colony of New Amsterdam. He lies buried in the small cobblestone graveyard here. Restored in the mid-70s, the church building burned to a near-crisp in a 1978 fire, and re-restoration was not completed until a few years ago.

The building plays host to several community dramatic companies, including the much-lauded **Ontological Theater** (533-4650), with some of the better small off-Broadway plays, the **Danspace Project** (674-8194), and the **Poetry Project** (674-0910). Call for info on upcoming events; you'll need to make reservations for theater tickets and arrive 15 minutes early for the show—otherwise your seats may go to those on the waiting list.

Across from the church at 156 Second Ave. stands a famous Jewish landmark, the **Second Ave. Deli** (677-0606). This is all that remains of the "Yiddish Rialto," the stretch of Second Ave. between Houston and 14th St. that comprised the Yiddish theater district in the early part of this century. The Stars of David embedded in the sidewalk out front contain the names of some of the great actors and actresses who spent their lives entertaining the poor Jewish immigrants of the city. One can order sublime chicken soup or splash out on a pastrami sandwich while watching a Broadway schedule on an electronic stock ticker.

St. Mark's Place, running from Third Ave. to Ave. A where E. 8th St. would be, is the geographical and spiritual center of the East Village. In the 1960s, the street was the Haight-Ashbury of the East Coast, full of pot-smoking flower children waiting for the next concert at the Electric Circus. In the late 1970s it became the Kings Road of New York, as mohawked youths hassled passers-by from the brownstone steps off Astor Place. Nowadays, St. Mark's is the East Village's answer to a small town's Main Street. People know one another here—sometimes, they even talk to one another.

NEIGHBORHOODS

Dark little restaurants and cafés elbow for space with leather boutiques and trinket vendors. Though many grumpy "Village types" now shun the commercialized and crowded areas of the street, St. Mark's is still central to life in this part of town and a good place to start a tour of the neighborhood.

Farther east, First and Second Ave. are filled mostly with restaurants, cafés, and bars, but a few remnants of old New York remain. The **New York Marble Cemeteries,** on Second Ave. between 2nd and 3rd St., and on 2nd St. just east of Second Ave., were the city's first two non-sectarian graveyards. One can gaze through the fences at the dilapidated tombstones, or just sit by the fence in the shade of the cemetery trees. Many prominent New Yorkers have been buried here, including (at the 2nd St. yard) the improbably named Preserved Fish, a prominent local merchant.

■ Alphabet City

East of First Ave., south of 14th St., and north of Houston, the avenues run out of numbers and take on letters. For better or for worse, this part of the East Village has so far escaped the escalating yuppification campaign that has claimed much of St. Mark's Place. In the area's heyday in the 60s, Jimi Hendrix and the Fugs would play open-air shows to bright-eyed love children. Rent is still relatively reasonable; here you'll find the stately residences of the East Village's deadbeatniks and hard-core anarchists, as well as artists, students, and some occasional regular people. The low rent also attracts the city's most interesting poetry slams and hipster hangouts, not to mention the plethora of loud bands who have claimed Alphabet City's side streets as their rehearsal space. Not designed for tourists and potentially unsafe for a solitary late-night prowl, Alphabet City is full of East Villagers doing their thing.

The neighborhood may have been brought to you by the letters A, B, C, and D, but Alphabet City is no Sesame Street. There has been a great deal of drug-related crime in the recent past; however, the community has done an admirable job of making the area livable again. Alphabet City is generally safe during the day, and the addictive nightlife on Ave. A ensures some protection there, but try to avoid straying east of Ave. B at night. During the summer of 1995, this part of the East Village saw violent clashes between New York's finest and squatters in abandoned buildings claimed by the city. The NYPD have been actively attempting to return law and order to the East Village, at the expense of many of the area's less law-abiding residents.

Alphabet City's extremist Boho activism (and the sometimes brutish behavior of the NYPD) has made the neighborhood chronically ungovernable in the last several years. A few years ago, police officers precipitated a riot when they attempted to forcibly evict a band of the homeless and their supporters in **Tompkins Square Park,** bordered by E. 10th St., E. 7th St., Ave. A, and Ave. B. An aspiring video artist recorded scenes of police depravity, setting off a public outcry and a further round of police-inspired violence. Today, the park is no longer a glum testament to the progress of gentrification—it has recently reopened after a two-year hiatus, and officials have high hopes for the area. The park still serves as a psycho-geographical epicenter for many a churlish misfit; one of the many riots that erupted in New York City following the Rodney King verdict in 1992 was led by the "East Side Anarchists," who hoofed down to Tompkins Square after tearing through St. Mark's Place. There are basketball courts and a playground in the northwest section of the park (quite popular with the younger, less politically concerned East Village set), and the park hosts free outdoor concerts during the summer.

East of the park, countless memorial murals attest to the scars left by drugs and the drug war. A mural on an old burned-out crack house on Ave. C between 8th and 9th St. pleads for action against drugs at home rather than on the streets, and a mural on the northwest corner of 8th St. and Ave. C hangs "in memory of Cesar." Many other murals in the area offer colorful celebrations of the neighborhood (most of them done by a somewhat mythical artist named Chico). Other less solemn projects include the community gardens that bloom next to some of these murals and blasted buildings, including one on 9th St. between Ave. B and Ave. C. At the corner of Ave.

Steal This Radio

Activated on Thanksgiving 1995, *Steal This Radio* (voice mail: 539-3884) is a micro-power pirate radio station that can be heard from the western edge of Williamsburg to the Bowery, with a similar North-South range centered on the Lower East Side. Born from Loisaida's "squatters, low-income tenants, activists, and non-activists," STR is committed to serving as a "giant community drum," pounding out anarchist/grassroots music, news, politics, and radio drama, along with substantial Spanish-language broadcasting. Shows ranging from homemade music to Native American-focused attest to the Loisaida's cultural diversity and commitment to the community. The signal is difficult to receive and the station itself is elusive—but, as with New York's anarchist paper *The Shadow*, you're likely to hear a unique take on current events. The truth is out there...

B and 2nd St., the "Space 2B" is surrounded by a fence made of pipes and car parts and serves as an outdoor gallery and performance space. For information on current issues and events, check for free local papers at St. Mark's Bookshop and other stores in the area. The often extravagant street art and neighborhood posters can also give you an update on some of the current issues. Or you can sit at one of the sidewalk cafés that line Ave. A between 6th and 10th St. and watch for yourself.

■ Lower Midtown: Madison Square, Union Square, and Gramercy Park

Neither coldly commercial nor hotly trendy, lower Midtown, like the third little bear's bowl of porridge, seems just right. Neoclassical architecture and generous avenues create an aura of refinement. At the 23rd St.-Madison Square intersection, for example, four of the earliest skyscrapers form a sub-skyline, one of the city's hidden visual treasures. This end of Midtown is also home to a burgeoning population of young professionals; new cafés, restaurants, and clubs have sprung up in the past ten years as this formerly exclusively residential neighborhood has developed into a center for graphic design and publishing.

To escape the roar of the midtown crowds, walk downtown from the Empire State Building area. On 29th St., between Fifth and Madison Ave., is the **Church of the Transfiguration,** better known as "The Little Church Around the Corner." This has been the home parish of New York's theater world ever since a liberal pastor agreed to bury Shakespearean actor George Holland here in 1870, when no other church would. The diminutive Victorian brick structure features peculiar green roofs, cherub-like gargoyles, and a tangled garden out front. Check out the stained-glass windows: they may look like a scene from the Bible, but look again—the vignette is from *Hamlet* (open daily 8am-6pm).

Madison Ave. ends, appropriately enough, at **Madison Square Park.** The park, opened in 1847, originally served as a public cemetery. Check out the statues of your favorite Civil War generals. Since developers have only just started to sink their cranes into this area, a number of the landmark buildings from years past remain, forming a miniature skyline. The area near the park sparkles with funky architectural gems.

The first of the old-but-tall buildings in this collection is the **New York Life Insurance Building,** located northeast of the park, occupying the northeast corner of 26th St. and Madison Ave. Built by Cass Gilbert (of Woolworth Building fame) in 1928, it wears its distinctive golden pyramid hat with aplomb. The building is located on the former site of P.T. Barnum's "Hippodrome," which was rebuilt by Stanford White and renamed Madison Square Garden in 1879. It soon became the premier spot for New York's trademark entertainment spectacles, as well as the spectacle of the 1906 rooftop shooting death of Stanford White by his reputed mistress's husband (the story was later fictionalized in E.L. Doctorow's *Ragtime*). The Garden's present-day descendant now sits on top of Penn Station.

One block south, at the corner of Madison Ave. and 25th St., sits the **Appellate Division of the Supreme Court.** Check out the allegorical statuary which decorates the outside, including the mild men Wisdom and Force. Civil and criminal defendants from the upstate counties plead their cases inside and the courthouse also hosts a small exhibition pertaining to court-related notables. It's free, but the bailiff and the intimidating "Be Prepared to be Frisked at Any Time" sign may discourage excessive lingering. Next door are the clock faces of the 700-foot-high **Metropolitan Life Insurance Tower,** which survey Madison Square Park from the corner of Madison Ave. and 23rd St. The tower, a 1909 addition to an 1893 building, also belongs to New York's I-used-to-be-the-tallest-building-in-the-world club. The annex on 24th St., connected by a walkway, features an eye-catchingly neo-Gothic façade.

Just west, off the southwest corner of the park, is yet another distinguished club member—the eminently photogenic **Flatiron Building,** often considered the world's first (and finest) skyscraper. It was originally named the Fuller Building, but its dramatic wedge shape, imposed by the intersection of Broadway, Fifth Ave., and 23rd St., quickly earned it its current *nom de plume.*

Until he was 15, Teddy Roosevelt lived in the 1840s brownstone at 28 E. 20th St., between Broadway and Park Ave. South. The **Theodore Roosevelt Birthplace** (260-1616) consists of five elegant period rooms from Teddy's childhood. Though not the original rooms, they have been reconstructed along the same lines (open Wed.-Sun. 9am-5pm, guided tours 9am-4pm; admission $2).

Farther east along 20th St. lies the gorgeous and gated **Gramercy Park,** the largest private park in Manhattan, located at the foot of Lexington Ave. between 20th and 21st St. The park was built in 1831 by Samuel B. Ruggles, a developer fond of greenery. He drained an old marsh and then laid out 66 building lots around the periphery of the central space. Buyers of his lots received keys to enter the private park; for many years, the keys were made of solid gold. Residents of the buildings now pay annual maintenance fees for the upkeep of the park and can obtain keys to the park's heavy iron gate from their buildings' doorpeople.

Ruggles believed that the park would not only improve the quality of life of residents, but also increase property values and city tax revenues over the years. Over 150 years later, little has changed, as the park, with its wide gravel paths, remains the only private park in New York, immaculately kept by its owners. The surrounding real estate is some of the choicest in the city. The tree-lined sidewalks with conveniently placed stoops offer a breather from the traffic and noise dominating the neighborhoods east and west of the park. With its full-fledged foliage, nearby 19th St. is known as "Block Beautiful" to locals and boasts most of the one-family homes in the neighborhood.

The **Brotherhood Synagogue** faces the park at No. 28 Gramercy Park South. It was formerly a Friends Meeting House, commissioned in 1859 by the Quakers. They asked the firm of King and Kellum to design "an entirely plain, neat, and chaste structure of good taste, but avoiding all useless ornamentation." This tan building—constructed in the Anglo-Italianate style with simple cornices, pediments, and arched windows—fits the bill.

Just east, between Second and Third Ave., lies the **Police Academy Museum,** 235 E. 20th St. (477-9753), located on the second floor of the NYC Police Academy (see Museums, p. 251). Up Lexington Ave. at 26th St. is the **69th Regiment Armory,** notable for having hosted the infamous art exhibition in 1913 that brought Picasso, Matisse, and Duchamp to the shores of America; Teddy Roosevelt called these artists "a bunch of lunatics."

It's just a few increasingly offbeat blocks to **Union Square,** between Broadway and Park Ave. South, and 17th and 14th St. So named because it was a "union" of two main roads, Union Square and its surrounding area sizzled with High Society intrigue before the Civil War. Early in this century, the name gained dual significance when the neighborhood became a focal point of New York's large Socialist movement, which held its popular May Day celebrations in **Union Square Park.** Later, the workers united with everyone else in abandoning the park to drug dealers and derelicts,

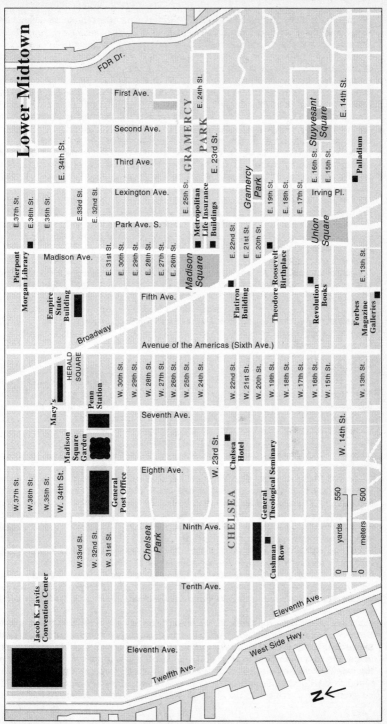

Lower Midtown

FDR Dr.

First Ave.

Second Ave.

Third Ave.

Lexington Ave.

Park Ave. S.

Madison Ave.

Fifth Ave.

Broadway

Avenue of the Americas (Sixth Ave.)

Seventh Ave.

Eighth Ave.

Ninth Ave.

Tenth Ave.

Eleventh Ave.

Twelfth Ave.

Eleventh Ave.

West Side Hwy.

GRAMERCY PARK

Gramercy Park

Union Square

Stuyvesant Square

Palladium

E. 14th St.

E. 15th St.
E. 16th St.
E. 17th St.
E. 18th St.
E. 19th St.

E. 20th St.
E. 21st St.
E. 22nd St.

E. 23rd St.
E. 24th St.
E. 25th St.

Irving Pl.

Metropolitan
Life Insurance
Buildings

Madison
Square

Flatiron
Building

Theodore Roosevelt
Birthplace

Revolution
Books

Forbes
Magazine
Galleries

E. 13th St.

E. 34th St.

E. 37th St.
E. 36th St.
E. 35th St.

E. 33rd St.
E. 32nd St.

E. 31st St.
E. 30th St.
E. 29th St.
E. 28th St.
E. 27th St.
E. 26th St.

Pierpont
Morgan Library

Empire
State
Building

Macy's

HERALD
SQUARE

Penn
Station

Madison
Square
Garden

General
Post Office

Chelsea
Park

CHELSEA

W. 23rd St.

W. 14th St.

Chelsea
Hotel

General
Theological Seminary

Cushman
Row

W. 30th St.
W. 29th St.
W. 28th St.
W. 27th St.
W. 26th St.
W. 25th St.
W. 24th St.

W. 22nd St.
W. 21st St.
W. 20th St.
W. 19th St.
W. 18th St.
W. 17th St.
W. 16th St.
W. 15th St.

W. 13th St.

W. 37th St.
W. 36th St.
W. 35th St.
W. 34th St.

W. 33rd St.
W. 32nd St.
W. 31st St.

Jacob K. Javits
Convention Center

yards   550
meters   500

0   0

N

but in 1989 the city attempted to reclaim it. The park is now pleasant and generally safe, though not pristine; as in much of Manhattan, denizens run the gamut from homeless people to sunbathers to pigeons. Check out the sculpture of George Washington, which is said to be the finest equestrian statue in the country. The scent of herbs and fresh bread wafts through the park, courtesy of the **Union Square Greenmarket,** which makes its home here every Wednesday, Friday, and Saturday. Farmers and bakers from all over the state and the region come to hawk their fresh produce, jellies, and baked goods.

On the east side of the park stands the old Neoclassical **American Savings Bank;** although designed by Henry Bacon, architect of the Lincoln Memorial in Washington, D.C., the building was never declared an historical landmark. The bank was sent into receivership by New York regulators in 1992 and was purchased in August 1993 (for a whopping $2 million) to become the newest **House of Blues** restaurant and blues bar. The building will be renovated to hold a 300-seat dining room and a hall for live music and will open sometime in the future.

Overlooking the ruckus, a number of modern apartment buildings wear levitating party hats that glow at night. The **Zeckendorf Towers,** built in 1987, are at One Irving Pl., between W. 14th and 15th St. The triangular caps and four-sided clock faces seem to gently parody Cass Gilbert's pyramid-topped buildings, including the nearby New York Life building.

Make a left onto 14th St. to reach the **Palladium,** at 126 E. 14th St. between Third Ave. and Irving Pl. This former movie palace, converted into a disco in 1985 by Japanese designer Arata Isozaki, contains a mural by Keith Haring and a staircase with 2400 round lights. Once, Madonna and her friends used to party inside while fans waited for hours to get in; since then, the Material Girl has brought her show elsewhere and New Jersey's bridge-and-tunnel crowd has taken over. Still, the nightclub hosts huge parties and special events and boasts the world's largest dance floor. (See Entertainment & Nightlife: Dance Clubs, p. 277.)

■ Chelsea

Clement Clark Moore (of "'Twas the Night Before Christmas" fame) was more than just a long-winded poet with visions of sugarplums. He also owned and developed most of Chelsea during the mid-1800s. This relatively uniform development resulted in an architecturally consistent residential neighborhood in the Greek Revival and Italianate styles, instead of the architectural stew that characterizes other neighborhoods. Strangely named after the Chelsea Hospital in London, the original Chelsea estate stretched from Eighth Ave. west to the Hudson River, and from 14th to 23rd St. Present-day Chelsea extends a few blocks farther to the north and east. Home to some of the most fashionable clubs and bars in the city, Chelsea has lately witnessed something of a rebirth. A large and visible lesbigay community and an increasing artsy-yuppie population have given Chelsea the flavor of a lower-rent West Village. Many stores, bars, and restaurants in the area prominently display gay pride flags and support gay pride days, marches, and other activities. Chelsea feels like a neighborhood, and unlike other parts of New York, you'll often see its denizens sunbathing, talking, or reading out on their stoops—they might even say hi as you walk by.

Chelsea's 20th-century gay pride is set against a background of 19th century architecture. At 356 W. 20th St., between Eighth and Ninth Ave., **St. Peter's Church** towers imposingly. This is the oldest Gothic revival church in the U.S. An example of Clement Moore's architectural work lives on at **Cushman Row,** 406-418 W. 20th St., a terrace of Greek Revival brownstones, complete with wrought-iron railings. These posh homes face the brick cathedral and the grounds of the **General Theological Seminary,** a grassy oasis that blooms with roses in the summer (243-5150; entrance at 125 Ninth Ave. between 20th and 21st). If you're lucky, you may catch some aspiring monks playing tennis. (Grounds open Mon.-Fri. noon-3pm, Sat. 11am-3pm.) Take in the wonder of the fancy co-op housing of the **London Terrace Apartments,** spanning an entire block since 1929, and a similarly elegant Greek revival-style mansion at 414-16 W. 22nd St., also between Ninth and Tenth Avenue.

Present-day Chelsea bears marks of past industrialism. To the west, along Tenth and Eleventh Ave., Chelsea transforms from a residential neighborhood into an industrial district. Like most of Manhattan's warehouse-y areas, West Chelsea is gentrifying as islands of trendiness move into its large, low-rent spaces. The wide, largely non-residential streets and the huge scale of the buildings, windows, and driveways lend comic inflation to the district, culminating in the mammoth **Chelsea Piers,** once a trans-Atlantic travel port and now a mammoth sports and entertainment complex. In this premier yuppie watering hole, the locals play indoor golf and drink microbrews by the gallon nightly. The central stores of the **Terminal Warehouse Company** tower along Eleventh and Twelfth Ave. between 27th and 28th St., and the once-grand and still-fetching **Starett-Lehigh Building** sits at Eleventh Ave. and 26th St. Exercise caution in this somewhat deserted area at night.

Few buildings in the world have housed as many important cultural figures as the historic **Hotel Chelsea,** 222 W. 23rd St. (243-3700), between Seventh and Eighth Ave. In this cavernous 400 room complex some 150 books have been penned, including works by Arthur C. Clarke, Arthur Miller, William Burroughs, Mark Twain, Eugene O'Neill, Vladimir Nabokov, and Dylan Thomas. Joni Mitchell, John Lennon, and Jasper Johns all called this hotel home at some point in their careers. Yet, despite the hype surrounding the place where Sid killed Nancy, *9½ Weeks* was filmed, and Robert Mappelthorpe and Patti Smith rented rooms, the hotel is admirably discreet. Ethan Hawke is now rumored to live here, but the doorpeople certainly aren't telling secrets. Every room is unique—singles start at $110, doubles at $135.

Chelsea's **flower district,** on 28th St. between Sixth and Seventh Ave., blooms most colorfully during the wee hours of the morning. Later in the day, if you wander around 27th St. and Broadway, you can witness the wholesale trading of cheap imports ranging from porn videos to imitation Barbie dolls to wigs made from 100% human hair. On the weekends (when weather permits), Chelsea's parking lots are home to numerous outdoor antique shows and flea markets, particularly along 25th, 26th, and 27th St. near Sixth Ave. Some are quite pricey, while others provide the perfect opportunity to find cheap stuff you've never seen before but suddenly need to ensure your continued happiness.

▓ West Midtown

Decidedly more grungy than its eastern counterpart, West Midtown offers a break from the ritzy boutiques, corporate wonderworlds, and neck-craning tourists that clutter East Midtown. This area, west of Sixth Ave. between 31st and 59th St., shines in a more neon, less gold-foiled way, with Broadway theaters, inexpensive eateries, countless hotels, and peep shows—all beckoning through the grime. If you want to see the city of *Midnight Cowboy,* where the Broadway lights splash on the dingy canvas of old warehouses and steamy streets, shuffle through the west side.

■ Herald Square area and the Garment District

Pennsylvania Station, at the corner of 33rd St. and Seventh Ave., is one of the less engrossing architectural examples in West Midtown but, as a major subway stop and train terminal, it can at least claim to be highly functional. The original Penn Station, a classical marble building modeled on the Roman Baths of Caracalla, was gratuitously demolished in the 60s. The railway tracks leading in and out of the station were covered with **Madison Square Garden (MSG),** New York's premier entertainment complex. The venue hosts a fine array of top acts, including both the Knicks and the 1994 Stanley Cup champion Rangers. Behind-the-scenes tours of the complex, including glimpses of the locker rooms and luxury boxes, are offered daily (see Sightseeing Tours, p. 123). Facing the Garden at 421 Eighth Ave., New York's immense main post office, the **James A. Farley Building,** sits complacently in its primary 10001 ZIP code.

Upper Midtown

Lincoln Center

W. 62nd St.

W. 61st St.

CENTRAL PARK

W. 60th St.

St. Paul the Apostle

W. 59th St.

Maine Monument

Central Park South

W. 58th St.

COLUMBUS CIRCLE

W. 57th St.

New York Convention & Visitors Bureau

Russian Tea Room

W. 56th St.

Carnegie Hall

W. 55th St.

Eleventh Ave.

Tenth Ave.

W. 54th St.

Ninth Ave.

W. 53rd St.

Eighth Ave.

W. 52nd St.

Seventh Ave.

W. 51st St.

W. 50th St.

W. 49th St.

W. 48th St.

W. 47th St.

Guardian Angels Headquarters

THEATER DISTRICT

W. 46th St.

W. 45th St.

Shubert Theater

W. 44th St.

DUFFY SQUARE

W. 43rd St.

Sardi's

W. 42nd St.

Central Synagogue

TIMES SQUARE

W. 41st St.

Port Authority Bus Terminal

W. 40th St.

Broadway

Lincoln Tunnel

Dyer Ave.

W. 39th St.

W. 38th St.

Eighth Ave.

W. 37th St.

Seventh Ave.

Jacob K. Javits Convention Center

W. 36th St.

W. 35th St.

Macy's

W. 34th St.

Eleventh Ave.

Tenth Ave.

W. 33rd St.

Ninth Ave.

General Post Office

Madison Square Garden

W. 32nd St.

Penn Station

W. 31st St.

W. 30th St.

GARMENT DISTRICT

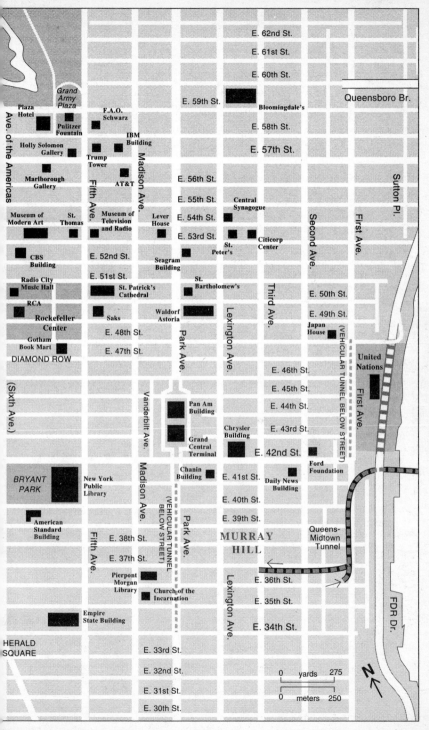

Completed in 1913, it mirrors the neoclassical magnificence of the former Penn Station. The broad portico bears the often-quoted motto of the U.S. Postal Service: "Neither snow nor rain nor heat nor gloom of night stays these couriers from the swift completion of their appointed rounds." During business hours, one can see the small poster of mugshots and fingerprints of the real-life "America's Most Wanted," or look around its one-room **Post Office Museum** that proudly displays such things as postal clerk ties, scales, and hats of decades past.

East on 34th St., between Seventh Ave. and Broadway, stands monolithic **Macy's.** (see Shopping: Department Stores, p. 287). This giant, which occupies a full city block, was recently forced to relinquish its title as the "World's Largest Department Store" and change its billing to the "World's Finest Department Store" when a new store in Germany was built one square foot larger. With nine floors (plus a lower level) and some two million square feet of merchandise, Macy's has come a long way from its beginnings in 1857, when it grossed $11.06 on its first day of business. Recently, however, it was forced to revisit its humble roots when it filed for bankruptcy and its fate still remains uncertain. The store sponsors the **Macy's Thanksgiving Day Parade,** a New York tradition buoyed by helium-filled 10-story Snoopies, Barneys, and other such cultural-icon inflatable blobs, marching bands, floats, and general hoopla. Santa Claus always glides by last in the parade, heralding the arrival of the Christmas shopping season and joy to kids (and merchants) everywhere. If you're in town in August, watch for the store's "Tapamania," when hundreds of tap-dancers cut loose on the sidewalks of 34th St.

Farther east along 34th St. are hundreds of discount stores offering everything from manufacturer's irregulars to downright cheap stuff. You can browse to your heart's content, but be advised that most of these stores are inevitably crowded and plagued by long lines at the cash register.

To the north is the **Garment District,** which extends along Seventh Ave. (also known as Fashion Ave. in this area) from 34th St to 42nd St. As Kathie Lee Gifford could tell you, the Garment District gained its name by once housing the bulk of the city's often inhumane clothing manufacturers. Today a small statue named "The Garment Worker," depicting an aged man huddled over a sewing machine, sits near the corner of 39th St. to commemorate (or romanticize) the formative era. Throughout this area there are still plenty of inexpensive wholesale and retail fabric, jewelry, clothing, and leather stores.

Down 34th St., at the convergence of Broadway and Sixth Ave., lies hectic **Herald Square.** Here a bronze statue of Minerva presiding over bellringers sits at the center of a small triangle of asphalt and park benches, heralding you to take a respite from your travels.

■ Times Square and the Theater District

Just north of the Garment District rests **Times Square,** which is centered around the intersection of 42nd St., Seventh Ave., and Broadway. Although probably still considered the dark and seedy core of the Big Apple (by most New Yorkers), the Square has worked hard in the past few years to straighten its laces and improve its image. The prime mover in this effort at urban renewal has been the Times Square Business Improvement District (BID), which began operations in 1992, funded by area residents and businesses. The BID began by putting 45 cherry-red jumpsuited sanitation workers on the streets daily, along with 40 public safety officers. According to the Mayor's Sanitation Scorecard, the rating of sidewalks alone jumped from 54% to 94.4% clean in just over a year. Robberies are down by 40%, pick-pocketing and purse-snatching by 43%, and the number of area porn shops has plummeted by more than 100 from its late-70s climax of 140. The flip side of this gentrification is that the crime and seediness is only being displaced westward— these statistics are only for the Times Square region. Along with BID, Disney is playing an important role in restructuring the area with its planned entertainment complex and 47-story hotel replacing the closed-down porn shops along 42nd St. between 7th and 8th Ave. Disney's restoration of the aging New Amsterdam Theater, where the Ziegfeld Follies performed their original chorus line routine for more than 20 years, is nearing completion. Across the street, Madame Tussaud's and AMC will rebuild the Liberty, Empire, and Harris theaters into a wax museum and 29-screen movie megaplex. The historic Victory Theater, where Abbot met Costello and Houdini made an elephant disappear, is also undergoing renovation and will be the site of a new children's theater.

Still, Times Square is Times Square. In fact, a recent city ordinance required new offices to cover their facades with electronic and neon glitz—explaining the enormous stock ticker atop the Morgan Stanley building. Teens continue to roam about in search of fake IDs and hustlers are still as eager as ever to scam suckers. One-and-a-half million people pass through Times Square every day. The streets are crowded with theatergoers, tourists, and wanderers well into the night. The carnival-like excitement here—endless bustle and chaos—is unique and, perhaps, endangered. Be sure to stop by the **Visitors' Center,** 229 West 42nd St., at the northwest corner of 42nd St. and Seventh Ave. for a variety of information and suggestions (open daily 9am-6pm). The center offers a free, two-hour walking tour of the area every Friday at noon.

Just west of Times Square, at 229 W. 43rd St., are the offices of the **New York Times** (556-1600), founded in 1851, for which the square was named in 1904 (although the *Times* was then housed at One Times Square—the big, triangular building at the head of the square). A short trip south down Eighth Ave. to 41st St. brings you in front of the multi-storied **Port Authority Bus Terminal,** the departure point for a volley of buses. Despite high-profile police presence, this area and the terminal itself are a little seedier than the area north of 42nd St. and can be dangerous, especially at night; stay on the major streets and try not to look like a tourist.

Further west, on 42nd St. between Ninth and Tenth Ave., lies **Theater Row,** a block of renovated Broadway theaters. The nearby **Theater District** stretches from 41st to 57th St. along Broadway, Eighth Ave., and the streets which connect them. Some of the theaters have been converted into movie houses or simply left to rot as the cost of live productions has skyrocketed. Approximately 37 theaters remain active, most of them grouped around 45th St. and 22 of them have been declared landmarks in testament to their historical importance (see Entertainment: Theater, p. 255). Between 44th and 45th St., a half-block west of Broadway just in front of the Shubert Theater, lies **Shubert Alley,** a private street for pedestrians originally built as a fire exit between the Booth and Shubert Theaters. After shows, fans often hover at stage doors to get their playbills signed.

Behind the scenes of every show are the playwrights, composers, and lyricists; protecting their interests is the **Dramatists Guild,** 234 W. 44th St. (398-9366), located in the former penthouse suite of J.J. Schubert, the Broadway mogul who popularized theater in the 1920s and 30s. Members of the guild include luminaries Stephen Sondheim, Peter Stone, and Mary Rodgers. According to their charter, "producers, directors, agents, students, academicians, and patrons of the arts" can all become members for $50 per year. Hard-core autograph hunters prey outside.

A few blocks uptown and to the west is the **Meat-Packing District.** A mix of warehouses, piers, loft apartments, and theater overflow, this area of Manhattan is fighting its reputation as a crime-infested neighborhood and undergoing some gentrification in the process. A good example of the mix is 46th Street—at the helm of **Restaurant Row** (a strip of posh eateries catering to the free-spending pre-theater crowd), the **Guardian Angels** (397-7822) work out of a small space off the corner of Eighth Ave. and W. 46th St. Wearing red berets rather than halos, these angels are self-declared vigilantes and martial artists who have taken city crime into their own hands. They carry no weapons, yet rarely hesitate to make a citizen's arrest. Angels are renowned for their stamina; controversial founder Curtis Sliwa managed to strike fear into his attackers even after being shot twice and thrown out of a taxi. The Angels have launched a pre-emptive graffiti strike against the corrugated metal front door of their headquarters, spray-painting a beautiful scene there in order to keep anyone else from doing so in a less appealing fashion.

Up several blocks at 130 W. 55th St. between Sixth and Seventh Ave., a former Muslim mosque was converted into the **City Center Theater** in 1943. Sickles and crescents still adorn each doorway, four tiny windows face Mecca from the limestone upper stories, and a Moorish dome caps the roof. Venture inside the lobby to see the elaborate tile mosaics surrounding the elevators.

How do you get to **Carnegie Hall?** Practice, practice, practice. This institution at 57th St. and Seventh Ave. was established in 1891 and remains New York's foremost soundstage. Over the years, Carnegie Hall has become synonymous with musical success. During its illustrious existence, the likes of Tchaikovsky, Caruso, Toscanini, and Bernstein have played Carnegie; Dizzy Gillespie, Ella Fitzgerald, and Charlie Parker all took the stage in 1957; and the Beatles and the Rolling Stones performed here within five months of each other in 1964. Other notable events from Carnegie's playlist include the world premiere of Dvořák's Symphony No. 9 *(From the New World)* on December 16, 1893, Winston Churchill's landmark lecture *The Boer War as I Saw It* in 1901, an energetic lecture by Albert Einstein in 1934, and Martin Luther King, Jr.'s last public speech on February 28, 1968.

Apparently suffering from the same "Great Music Hall Syndrome" as Radio City, Carnegie Hall was in danger of being demolished in the 1950s and being replaced by a large office building. Luckily, outraged citizens managed to stop the impending destruction through special state legislation in 1960. In 1985, in commemoration of the 25th anniversary of the rescue, a $50 million restoration and renovation program gave the worn façade a face-lift, enlarged the street-level lobby, and modernized the backstage. During renovations, the stage ceiling, which had been damaged during the filming of *Carnegie Hall* in 1946 (and subsequently covered with only some canvas and a curtain), was finally repaired. Legend has it that it was actually this hole that gave Carnegie Hall its better-than-perfect acoustics. (Tours are given Mon., Tues., Thurs., and Fri. at 11:30am, 2, and 3pm; Admission $6, $5 students and seniors, children under 9 $3; call 903-9790 for more information). Carnegie Hall's **museum** displays artifacts and memorabilia from its illustrious century of existence (open Thurs.-Tues. 11am-4:30pm; free; see Entertainment and Nightlife: Classical Music, p. 268).

■ Columbus Circle and Hell's Kitchen

Columbus Circle, at Eighth Ave. and Central Park South, marks the northern end of West Midtown, the southwest corner of Central Park, and the beginning of the Upper West Side. Christopher Columbus poses atop his pedestal, unmindful of the hubbub that surrounds him. The **Maine Monument,** on the northeast side of Columbus Circle, pays tribute to the seamen who died on the *U.S.S. Maine* in 1898, the sinking of which sparked the Spanish-American War. The **New York Convention and Visitors Bureau,** Two Columbus Circle, assists tourists with all manner of brochures, discount coupons, and suggestions (397-8222; open Mon.-Fri. 9am-6pm, Sat.-Sun. 10am-3pm).

Nearby, on the west side of the circle, is the **New York Coliseum,** built in 1954 by the TriBoro Bridge and Tunnel Authority to serve as the city's convention center. Nowadays, the **Jacob K. Javits Convention Center,** which sits along Twelfth Ave. between 34th and 38th St., has stolen the spotlight, leaving the Coliseum somewhat empty and its future uncertain, especially now that Mort Zuckerman has dropped his multimillion-dollar bid to develop the site into a huge office complex. Its front has become an unofficial shelter for the homeless, protecting them from the winds whipping across the circle. The city periodically evicts these homeless people in order to clean up the area in preparation for special events, like the 1992 Democratic National Convention.

Hell's Kitchen, west of Ninth Ave. between 34th and 59th St., was formerly a violent area inhabited by impoverished immigrants. Until the turn of the century, gangs, with names such as the misleading "Battle Row Annie's Ladies' Social and Athletic Club" and pigs roamed its swarming streets. Hell's Kitchen, home to Marvel's comic crimefighter Daredevil, was once regarded as one of the most dangerous areas in North America, where policemen would only patrol in groups of four or more. Now, the district's overcrowded tenements have been replaced with an artsier crowd, who are trying to give this area the less ominous (though still loaded) name **Clinton.** Ninth and Tenth Ave. are loaded with restaurants, delis, and pubs—the neighborhood is one of New York's best sampling of various inexpensive ethnic cuisines. The low-slung Gothic brownstone **Church of St. Paul the Apostle** (entrance on Ninth Ave.) sits placidly amid the action at 415 W. 59th St., between Ninth and Tenth Ave. A high-relief above a sky-blue mosaic rests above an impressive front door of carved wood, and dioramas of Christ's Passion flank the interior. Be sure to heed the sign warning you not to throw coins into the Baptismal Font which sits just inside the entrance—it does resemble a wishing well and the temptation will be there. Services are given in both English and Spanish.

Student protests over tuition hikes culminated in a two-week takeover of CUNY's **John Jay College of Criminal Justice,** 899 Tenth Ave. at 58th St., in May 1990. The turmoil ended in a violent reinstatement of power by administration officials. Renovations have given the 1903 neo-Victorian building, formerly the DeWitt Clinton High School (attended by Calvin Klein), a postmodern atrium and extension. Statues in niches, somber gargoyles, fretful nuthatches, and grape leaves adorn the building's white façade, while the American eagle stares blankly overhead.

■ East Midtown

East of Sixth Ave., from about 34th St. to 59th St., lies the bulk of East Midtown. This is the New York most tourists probably envision when reflecting on the Big Apple. Here, star-struck, camera-happy visitors, hurried businesswomen in Ann Taylor suits and white Keds, and shifty-eyed salesmen with briefcases full of watches crowd the sidewalks amid honking taxis and towering skyscrapers. In East Midtown, buildings are judged by their proximity to the heavens, hotels by the size of their chandeliers, and people by the size of their wallets and/or credit ratings. Don't let the enormity or hustle-bustle of East Midtown frighten you—keep an eye on your finances and let yourself be swept up in the urban frenzy.

■ The Empire State Building

New York impressed me tremendously because, more than any other city in the world, it is the fullest expression of our modern age.

—Leo Trotsky

Ever since King Kong first climbed the Empire State Building (or, as it is often slurred by natives, "Empire Staybuilding") with his main squeeze in 1933, the world-renowned landmark has attracted scores of other view-seeking tourists eager for a respite from the furor at street level, lovers hoping to wax romantic with their objects of desire, and the occasional tragic Kong-emulating suicide. Just recently, even alien tourists chose the landmark as the epicenter of their destructive visit in the movie blockbuster *Independence Day*. Completed in 1929, the building has become a revered element of the skyline, as integral to conceptions of New York as yellow cabs, bagels, and the Statue of Liberty. Although no longer the tallest building in the world (the Chicago Sears Tower holds the title) or even the tallest in New York (the Twin Towers beat it by several floors), the towering spire still dominates postcards, movies, and the hearts of city residents.

Built on the site of the original Waldorf and Astoria hotels, the limestone, granite, and stainless steel-sheathed structure is a pioneer in Art Deco design. Stretching 1454 feet into the sky and containing two miles of shafts for its 73 elevators, the Empire State was among the first of the truly spectacular skyscrapers. It stands in relative solitude in midtown, proudly distinguishing itself from the forest of monoliths that has grown around Wall St. To add to its distinctiveness, the upper 30 floors of the building are illuminated nightly until midnight in appropriate color schemes for holidays or special events, such as red, white, and blue for Independence Day or the Rangers' victory in the 1994 Stanley Cup hockey finals.

The Empire State's lobby stands as a gleaming shrine to Art Deco interior decorating, right down to the mail drops and the elevator doors. The Empire State is optimistically featured in "textured light" along with the Seven Wonders of the Ancient World. The arrows on the wall lead to the escalator accessing the concourse level, where you can purchase tickets to the observatory. Of primary importance is the sign indicating the visibility level—a day with perfect visibility offers views for 80 miles in any direction but, even on a day with a visibility of only five miles, one can still spot the Statue of Liberty. (Observatory open daily 9:30am-midnight, tickets sold until 11:30pm. Admission $4.50, children under 12 and seniors $2.25. Call 736-3100 for observatory information.)

Once atop the main observatory, 1050 feet above the nearest cab or honking horn, venture onto the windswept outdoor walkways or opt to stay in the temperature-controlled interior. Either way, the view, particularly at night, is absolutely breathtaking—enough to warm the heart of the most jaded of individuals. From this height one can understand why the Empire State Building has been featured in so many romantic films, from *Sleepless in Seattle* to *An Affair to Remember* to, of course, *King Kong*. Equally impressive from this lofty perspective is the thought of just how many people are crammed onto this relatively small piece of land. Overwhelming sentiments aside, the Empire State lays out a huge diagram of the city from the center of Manhattan's grid—the gorgeous view to the north gives a feel for the monumental scale of Central Park, while the view to the south provides the opportunity to make faces at the tourists atop the World Trade Center.

If the view doesn't inspire enough awe, the Empire State also features the **New York Skyride,** a seat-convulsing simulation of spaceship journey through the city, narrated by *Star Trek's* Scotty and peppered with lousy jokes by Yakov Smirnoff. (Skyride open 10am-10pm; admission $8, seniors and children under 12 $6, combination pass with observatory $10; call 564-2224 for more info.)

Also catering to the uneasily stupefied is the **Guinness World's Record Exhibit Hall** (947-2335) on the Concourse level. Here, wax and plastic conglomerations commemorate such "wonders" as the world's tallest man, heaviest man, and most tattooed lady in gaudy P.T. Barnum style. They don't come much more kitschy than this. (Exhibit wall open 9am-10pm, admission $7, children $3.50, combination pass with observatory $10 adults, children $5.)

■ Murray Hill

Back on the ground lies the **Murray Hill** area, east of Fifth Ave. between 34th and 42nd St., the home of the late 19th-century "robber barons." In this neighborhood, warm brownstones and condos lie in the shadow of the glass-and-steel business citadels farther uptown. At 205 Madison Ave. and 35th St. stands the impressive **Church of the Incarnation.** Built in 1864, the church features stained glass by Tiffany, sculptures by Augustus Saint Gaudens, and memorials by Daniel Chester French. A handy pink pamphlet near the entrance details the church's art (open Mon.-Fri. from about 11:30am-2pm, but the times are variable—try your luck at the church door).

The highlight of Murray Hill is the **Pierpont Morgan Library,** 29 E. 36th St. (685-0610), at Madison Ave., where the J. Pierpont Morgan clan developed the concept of the book as fetish object. With regular exhibitions and lots and lots of books inside, this Low Renaissance-style *palazzo* is worth a visit (see Museums, p. 244).

■ 42nd Street

On Fifth Ave., north past the upscale shopping of **Lord and Taylor** (See Shopping: Department Stores, p. 287), the hubbub of 42nd Street bustles all day and long into the evening. The **New York Public Library** reposes placidly on the west side of Fifth Ave. between 40th and 42nd St. On sunny afternoons, throngs of people recline on its marble steps, watching the world go by or watching others watch them from behind a book. Dutifully guarding these steps from intruders are two mighty lions, aptly named Patience and Fortitude. In addition to the kings of the jungle, Grecian urns, sculptural groups, and fountains (the one on the right representing Truth, the other Beauty) all reflect the importance attached to this storehouse of culture. The free brochure offered inside ("A Building to Celebrate") details all the nuances of the library's interior and exterior architecture.

The building's temple-like interior is equally majestic. The grandeur of the rotating exhibits (recent ones have included a retrospective on "Books of the Century" and a study on the future of on-line libraries) coupled with the immensity of the architecture and the ornamentation (such as a huge mural depicting the presentation of the "the book" from Moses to modernity) should remind any visitor that these folks take reading seriously. Unfortunately, this particular branch is solely for research purposes—you're better off across the street at the Mid-Manhattan branch for reading material (see Essentials: Libraries, p. 15). Free tours of the library take place Tuesday through Saturday at 12:30pm and 2:30pm, leaving from the Friends Desk in Astor Hall (call 930-0502 for info). For a recorded announcement of exhibitions and events, call 869-8089 (library open Mon. and Thurs.-Sat. 10am-6pm, Tues.-Wed. 11am-7:30pm).

Spreading out against the back of the library along 42nd St. to Sixth Ave. is soothing **Bryant Park.** Site of the World's Fair in 1853, the park's recent renovations make it an even nicer respite from the asphalt and steel in every direction. In the afternoon, people of all descriptions crowd into the large, grassy, tree-rimmed expanse to talk, relax, and sunbathe. The stage that sits at the head of the park's open field plays host to a variety of free cultural events throughout the summer, including screenings of classic films, jazz concerts, and live comedy. Call the New York Convention and Visitors Bureau (397-8222) for an up-to-date schedule of events. The park is open 7am-9pm.

To the east along 42nd St., **Grand Central Terminal** sits between Madison and Lexington Ave., where Park Ave. would be if it continued. Once *the* transportation hub where visitors received their introduction to the Big Apple, Grand Central has been partially supplanted by Penn Station, the Port Authority, and various area airports, but it maintains its dignity nonetheless. As if to remind travelers and commuters that they're running late, wing-footed **Mercury** leaps atop the famed 13-foot-high clock in front. Inside rests the **Main Concourse,** a huge lobby area which becomes zebra-striped by the sun falling through the slatted windows. This recently renovated landmark, where countless commuters cross paths daily, breathes elegance in its marble simplicity and majestic grandeur. Occasionally, jazz and classical amateur musicians will set up here and entertain the harried passers-by.

Jutting out from the Main Concourse, store-filled arcades snake their way underground to many of the surrounding buildings. Buy some newspapers, roses, or New York memorabilia here and people-watch as specimens of all descriptions hobble, stride, meander, and dash across the marble floor, but keep your eyes peeled for the bag-snatchers and pickpockets who also roam the halls. Free tours are given at 12:30pm on Wednesdays from the Chemical Bank in the Main Concourse and on Fridays from the Phillip Morris building across the street.

Growing out of the back of Grand Central, the **Pan Am Building** looms over most of 44th and 45th St. This 59-story blue monolith slices Park Ave. in half, much to the chagrin of many a New Yorker. Although the once-familiar Pan Am logo atop the building has been replaced by that of Met Life, the skyscraper retains its old name and vaguely aerodynamic shape. The largest commercial office space ever built, the Pan Am building contains 2.4 million sq. ft. of corporate cubicles, swankier stores than Grand Central, pink rather than white marble, and a nice but unfortunately benchless atrium. Deep inside the lobby, right above the escalators, hangs an immense red-and-white Josef Albers mural. In the building's other lobby, at E. 44th and Vanderbilt, an intriguing wire-and-light sculpture encloses what appears to be an energized atom. Right across E. 45th St. sits the **Helmsley Building,** which also truncates Park Ave. but which is redeemed in the eyes of city denizens by its regal appearance from further up the road.

Another familiar notch in the Midtown skyline is the Empire State Building's smaller, flashier Art Deco cousin, the **Chrysler Building,** at 42nd St. and Lexington Ave., which appears to Charleston madly even as the latest postmodern constructions go up nearby. The Chrysler is topped by a spire modeled on a radiator grille, one of many details meant to evoke the romance of the automobile in the Golden Age of the Chrysler Automobile Company. Other monuments to motoring include a frieze of idealized cars in white and gray brick on the 26th floor, flared gargoyles at the fourth setback styled after 1929 hood ornaments and hubcaps, and stylized lightning-bolt designs symbolizing the energy of the new machine. In a display of capitalist ingenuity, the Chrysler building was once engaged in a race with the Bank of Manhattan building for the title of the world's tallest structure. Work on the bank was stopped when it seemed as if it had already won. The devious Chrysler machinists then brought out and strapped on the spire that had been secretly assembled inside. And so, when completed in 1929, this elegantly seductive building stood as the world's tallest—that is, until the Empire State topped it a year later.

East on 42nd St. between Park and Second Ave., the **Daily News Building,** home to the country's first successful tabloid, delivers itself with pomp and self-importance. The paper and building are considered to be the inspiration for the *Daily Planet* of Superman fame. Though the *Daily News* caters to an exclusively New York readership, the lobby is dominated by a gigantic rotating globe, a clock for every time zone in the world, and an inexplicable tribute to our solar system. Perhaps consistent with tabloid journalism's penchant for accuracy, the huge globe still features East Germany, Yugoslavia, and the U.S.S.R.

Nearby shady **Tudor Park,** between 42nd and 43rd St. on Tudor Pl. (which is itself between First and Second Ave.), offers an ideal spot to take a break from checking out architecture. The park's gravel paths, metal benches, ornate fence, and outsized oaks—congregating in a refreshingly uncluttered silence—lend a European charm to this grassy nook (open daily 7am-midnight). Down a flight of curved stairs from Tudor Park lies **Ralph J. Bunche Park,** right in front of the United Nations. A tall sculpture, ivy-covered walls, and carved faces grace this small area, as does an inspirational quote from Isaiah.

If you feel an urgent need to get out of the city for a while, head for the **United Nations Building** (963-4475), which may seem as if it's located along New York's First Ave. between 42nd and 48th St. However, this area is international territory and thus not subject to the laws and jurisdiction of the U.S., as evidenced by the 184 flags flying outside at equal height, in flagrant violation of American custom. An understated skyscraper and kicky little lobby make up the bulk of the place. Outside, a multicultural rose garden and a statuary park provide a lovely view of the East River (and a rather un-lovely one of Queens). Note the statue depicting a muscle-bound man beating a sword into a plowshare. The buff Socialist was a 1959 gift of the former U.S.S.R. Also of interest is a striking (and surprisingly Christian-oriented for a world council) statue of St. George exterminating a dragon-serpent that oddly resembles fuselage.

Informative tours of the very 60s-styled **General Assembly** meet at the back of the U.N. lobby. The tours last about 45 minutes, leaving every 15 minutes from 9:15am to 4:45pm daily and are available in 20 languages if there is sufficient demand. Make sure to buy the special U.N. postage stamps, which can only be mailed from the U.N., but which will ship that postcard to Dubuque all the same. (Tours $6.50, seniors over 60 and students $4.50, children under 16 $3.50, children under 5 not admitted on tour. Visitors' Entrance at First Ave. and 46th St.) You must take the tour to get past the lobby. Sometimes free tickets to G.A. sessions can be obtained during the diplomat work year (Oct.-May); call 963-1234 for more info.

Just up the street at First Ave. and E. 44th St. is the **UNICEF House,** devoted to advocacy for children in the international arena. The **Danny Kaye Visitors Center** opened in July 1994, with exhibits and explanations of UNICEF's mission. A gift shop also sells cards and other paraphernalia, with all profits going to the UNICEF Children's Fund.

Located a few blocks north of the U.N. at 333 E. 47th St. and First. Ave., the deceptively modernist **Japan House** (832-1155) stands as the first example of contemporary Japanese design in New York City. The designer, Junzo Yoshimura, sought to integrate Western with Asian style and the result is a half-Japanese, half-American amalgamation—Western on the outside but completely Asian on the inside. In the spirit of a traditional Japanese home, there is an interior pool garden on the first floor, complete with stones and bamboo trees, while a gallery on the second floor exhibits traditional and contemporary Japanese art. The mission of the **Japan Society,** headquartered within, is similar. An association dedicated to bringing the people of Japan and America closer together, the Society sponsors Japanese language courses, conferences, lectures, meetings with notable leaders, a film series, and various performances (Society open Mon.-Fri. 9:30am-5:30pm; gallery open Sept.-May Mon.-Fri. 11am-5pm; suggested donation $3).

■ Lexington, Park, and Madison

The area between First and Third Ave. consists mainly of high-rise residences interspersed with various embassies. Further west, skyscrapers and ritzy hotels reclaim the territory. At 570 Lexington Ave. and 51st St., the **General Electric Building** was originally the headquarters of the Radio Corporation of America (RCA) when it was completed in 1931. The famous orange-and-buff eight-sided brick tower is alive with bolts and flashes that crackle off the surface, an allegorical reference to the power of radio. G.E. keeps tight security, but the elegantly designed Art Deco lobby and elevators are worth a quick peek.

The *crème-de-la-crème* of the Park Ave. hotels is undoubtedly the **Waldorf-Astoria Hotel** at 301 Park Ave. between 49th and 50th. Cole Porter's piano sits in the front lounge, while a huge chandelier and an actual red carpet greet you as you slink humbly down the hallways. The Duchess of Windsor, King Faisal of Saudi Arabia, and the Emperors Hirohito and Akihito of Japan all have stayed here (as have about a million business travelers) and every U.S. President since Hoover has spent a night or two away from the White House at the hotel. The beautiful Westminster clock in the drawing room deserves note. Toast of the 1893 World's Fair, the octagonal timepiece features reliefs of founding fathers Washington, Jackson, and Lincoln, among others. With its neoclassical murals and huge chandeliers, this hotel is hardly budget accommodations, but the lobby is certainly worth a peek if you have the nerve to venture in.

To see the more garish end of the hotel spectrum, walk one block west to 451-455 Madison Ave. and 50th St. The **New York Palace Hotel** has incorporated the six powerful, graceful brownstones that comprise the former **Villard Houses,** which date from 1884. At press time the Palace was still undergoing renovations—whether the outcome will equal its predecessor (the Helmsley Palace) in overdone ostentation remains to be seen.

Up Park Ave., between 50th and 51st St., stands the Byzantine **St. Bartholomew's Church** (751-1616), which draws heavily upon medieval European religious architecture for its inspiration. Completed in 1919, the temple features a large mosaic of the Resurrection glittering with golden halos, while less subtle paper flames dangle from the quilt-like dome. The life-size marble angel in the devotional area left of the altar has been a favorite of visitors and worshippers for many years.

On the flip side of ecclesiastical architecture, at 619 Lexington Ave. and 53rd St., **Saint Peter's Church** (935-2200) foregoes the classical religious styles to create a more contemporary and urban space of worship that resembles a futuristic oxygen tent. Replete with sofa pews, this funky church sponsors services, jazz vespers, musical concerts, social groups, and off-Broadway theater. (See Entertainment and Nightlife: Jazz, p. 271.) Built as a modern-day equivalent of the medieval-church-as-social-center, St. Peter's was developed in conjunction with the Citicorp Building behind it in an attempt to fuse the corporate with the celestial.

NEIGHBORHOODS

St. Peter's neighbor, the shiny, slanted **Citicorp Center** stands on four 10-story stilts at Lexington and 53rd St. so as not to crush the temple at its base. The entire structure, sheathed in reflective grayish aluminum, is known to radiate warmly at sunrise and sunset. The distinctive 45-degree-angled roof was originally intended for use as a solar collector, but this plan never saw the light of day. Instead the roof supports an intriguing gadget, the so-called TMD, or Tuned Mass Damper, which senses and records the tremors of the earth and warns of earthquakes (an important feature for a building on stilts).

Central Synagogue at 652 Lexington Ave. and 55th St, the oldest continuously operating synagogue in the city, is currently undergoing renovations, but its beautiful architectural details are still visible. Built in 1870 by Henry Fernbach, its Moorish-revival architecture combines a lavish façade of onion domes and intricate trim with an exquisite display of stained glass within.

Although just barely seven years old, the stylish **Madison Lexington Venture Building,** up a few blocks at 135 E. 57th St., has already garnered quite a few awards. The front of the main building curves inward, creating an arc around four pairs of green Italian marble columns arranged in a Stonehenge circle and highlighted by a fountain, perfect for weary tourists and druids to congregate around.

Philip Johnson's postmodern AT&T Building stands farther west on Madison Ave. between 55th and 56th St. Sony recently leased out the building and renamed it **Sony Plaza.** It now features two massive Sony superstores featuring hands-on interaction with state-of-the-art products and free movie screenings of releases by Sony-owned Columbia. Sony has also answered its charge to provide free education for the children of New York with its new **Sony Wonder** museum, an interactive introduction to communications technology which should not be missed. It's free! (open Tues.-Sat. 10am-6pm, Sun. noon-6pm).

Two more blocks up on Madison Ave., between 57th and 58th St., sits the **Fuller Building,** a big, black, shiny Art Deco building that looks like it just came off the set of *The Shadow.* Completed in 1929, it was one of the first office buildings to be situated this far north in Manhattan and served as the headquarters of America's leading construction firm during the Great Depression. Inside, the Fuller contains 12 floors of art galleries (see Galleries, p. 254).

■ Rockefeller Center

Between 48th and 51st St. and Fifth and Sixth Ave. stretches **Rockefeller Center,** a monument to the conjunction of business and aesthetics. In the American tradition of "bigger is better," Rockefeller Center is the world's largest privately owned business and entertainment complex, occupying 22 acres of midtown Manhattan.

On Fifth Ave. between 49th and 50th St., the famous gold-leaf statue of Prometheus ("My hand's on fire!") sprawls out on a ledge of the sunken **Tower Plaza,** surrounded by pulsing jet streams of water that taunt his burning appendage. The Plaza serves as an overpriced open-air café in the spring and summer and as a world-famous ice-skating rink and tree stand in the winter. Over 100 flags from the member nations of the U.N. flap around the Plaza in simultaneous obedience to the winds. The 70-story **RCA Building** (now owned by General Electric), seated at Sixth Ave., remains the most accomplished artistic creation in this complex. Every chair in the building sits less than 28 feet from natural light. In the lobby, hulking workers (and, oddly enough, Lincoln) heave and strain on a heroic mural, a mute and ironic testament to the idealized glory of manual labor. The RCA building also acts as headquarters to G.E. subsidiary **NBC.** The network offers an hour-long tour which traces the history of NBC, from their first radio broadcast in 1926 through the heyday of TV programming in the 50s and 60s. The tour visits the studios of *Conan O'Brien* and the once infamous 8H studio, home of *Saturday Night Live.* (Tours run Mon.-Sat. every 15min. from 9:30am-4:30pm; $8.25.) For information on audience tickets to an NBC show, see Entertainment & Nightlife: Television, p. 265.)

Escaping demolition in 1979 to receive a complete interior restoration (due to public outcry), **Radio City Music Hall** still thrives as a multi-program entertainment venue. First opened in 1932 at the corner of Sixth Ave. and 51st St., the 5874-seat theater remains the largest in the world. The 144-foot-wide stage is equipped with a revolving turntable comprised of three separate sections, each of which can be elevated or dropped 40 feet. The hydraulic stage elevator system was so sophisticated that the U.S. Navy borrowed the design for World War II aircraft carriers.

The brainchild of Roxy Rothafel, the hall was originally intended as a variety showcase, yet functioned primarily as a movie theater. Over 650 feature films debuted here from 1933 to 1979, including *King Kong, Breakfast at Tiffany's, To Kill a Mockingbird,* and *Doctor Zhivago.* Nowadays, the hall is probably more famous for its Rockettes, Radio City's world-renowned chorus line. The current dancers range in height from 65½ to 68½ inches, but seem to be of equal height onstage thanks to the marvels of perspective. Their complicated routines and eye-high kicks still enthrall audiences. Tours of the great hall are given daily 10am-5pm. (Tickets $12, children $6, for more info call 632-4041. See Entertainment and Nightlife: Music, p. 273 for information on concerts and performances in the hall.)

■ Fifth Ave.

The section of Fifth Ave. between 42nd and 59th St., once the most desired residence of New York's elite, has been taken over by the stores and institutions that originated to serve them. The grand scale of the establishments here and the centrality of Fifth Ave. itself combine to make this stretch of street arguably the most famous avenue in the U.S. Protestors and celebrators of all types choose this thoroughfare for their parade routes, while parading consumers and tourists revel in the unsurpassed opportunities for window-shopping. Fascinating stores and boutiques, most catering to the six-digit crowd, line the streets here—don't be afraid to go in and poke around. Just don't break anything.

Just off Fifth Ave. on 44th St. between Fifth and Sixth Ave., is the **Algonquin Hotel,** which in the 1920s hosted Alexander Woollcott's "Round Table," a regular gathering of the brightest luminaries of the theatrical and literary world, recently immortalized in *Mrs. Parker and the Vicious Circle.* The hotel's major attraction was its proximity to the offices of *The New Yorker;* thus Robert Benchley, Dorothy Parker, and Edna Ferber, among others, came here frequently for dinner, drinks, and witty quips. The Oak Room still serves tea every afternoon, but now exclusively to Algonquin guests (and their friends). On the southeast corner of Fifth Ave. and 51st St. stands **St. Patrick's Cathedral** (753-2261), New York's most famous church and the largest Catholic cathedral in America. Completed in 1879 after 21 years of labor, the structure captures the essence of great European cathedrals while retaining its own unique spirit. The calming aroma of incense and the relative quietude of the cathedral offers a great contrast to the midday rush outside. The twin spires on the Fifth Ave. façade, captured in countless photos and postcards, streak 330 feet into the air. Artisans in Chartres and Nantes created most of St. Patrick's stained-glass windows, under which the controversial Cardinal O'Connor communes with God.

Up one block and just west of Fifth Ave. at 25 W. 52nd St. is the newly relocated **Museum of Television and Radio** (621-6800), formerly the Museum of Broadcasting. The museum spent $50 million on its recent move and expansion and the new building is quadruple the size of its predecessor. It has only one small gallery of exhibits, though; it works almost entirely as a "viewing museum," allowing visitors to attend scheduled screenings in one of its theaters, or to choose and enjoy privately a TV or radio show from its library of 60,000 (see Museums, p. 250). Down the block at 51 W. 52nd St., the **CBS Building** (975-4321), a dour spectacle reminiscent of *2001's* monolith (no stars in this one, though—"Black Rock" only has corporate offices), maintains a cold but fervid watch over arch-enemy NBC. For the greatest dramatic effect, view the smoke-colored granite tower from Sixth Ave. (For info on tickets to CBS shows, see Entertainment: Television, p. 265.)

St. Thomas's Church (757-7013), with its famously heavy, lopsided left tower, has anchored down the northwest corner of Fifth Ave. and 53rd St. since 1911. From above the door, numerous saints, apostles, and missionaries gaze down at Fifth Ave.'s materialistic idolatry with expressions ranging from dispassionate to aghast. Guided tours are offered Sundays following the 11am service. If you continue down W. 53rd St. towards Sixth Ave., you can take in a handful of masterpieces in the windows of the **American Craft Museum** and the **Museum of Modern Art** (see Museums, p. 238). If you have some time (and the money for admission), rest your tired feet in MoMA's sculpture garden, which features works by Rodin, Renoir, Miró, Lipschitz, and Picasso. And if you have a few hours, you can explore the museum's considerable collection of modern masterpieces.

The imposing **University Club** on the northwest corner of Fifth Ave. and 54th St., is a turn-of-the-century granite palace meant to accommodate aging, affluent Caucasian males. As indicated by its name, this organization was one of the first men's clubs that required its members to hold college degrees. 20 prestigious university crests adorn its façade. In June of 1987, the previously all-male club voted to admit women in accordance with a city ordinance. Welcome to the 20th century.

The impressive **Fifth Ave. Presbyterian Church,** built in 1875 at the northwest corner of Fifth Ave. and 55th St., is the largest Presbyterian sanctuary in Manhattan, seating 1800. The old clock, visible on three sides of the steeple, still runs on its own gravitational weight—a huge box of rocks. Inside, the stern pews and pulpit make for a much-needed aesthetic relief from the glass and gilt of Midtown. For a view of an even more elaborate top, check out the **Crown Building,** 730 Fifth Ave. at 57th St. Originally designed by Warren and Wetmore in 1924, the upper tier has now been overlaid with over 85 pounds of 23-carat gold leaf. At sunset, the reflected light creates a crown of fire.

Just across Fifth Ave. lie the king and queen of shiny baubles, Trump and Tiffany. The **Trump Tower** at 56th St., unsurprisingly shines like a beacon to excess. Inside, a ludicrous five-story waterfall-on-a-wall washes down an atrium composed of orange, pink, and brown marble. The result is tacky with a capital Trump. There are enough fashion boutiques here to satisfy even the most depraved world leader.

Speaking of tacky, Marla Maples and Donald Trump named their daughter Tiffany after their glittery neighbor at 727 Fifth Ave., between 56th and 57th St. At **Tiffany & Co.** (755-8000), everything is beautiful. Nervous (and rich) couples pick out rings and jewelry on the first floor and register for housewares on the second. It's best to ignore the "you can't afford that" sneers if you want to ooh and aah at the massive diamonds. Alternatively, you can go up to the third floor and see which famous people have registered for what. New York-related exhibitions show regularly and the window displays can be art in themselves, especially around Christmas (open Mon.-Wed., Fri.-Sat. 10am-6pm, Thurs. 10am-7pm).

Two blocks north, you can reclaim that inner child at **F.A.O. Schwarz,** 767 Fifth Ave. (644-9400) at 58th St. Toys, toys, toys; automated toys greet visitors and talk (endlessly). Home to complex Lego constructions, the latest action figures, adorable huggy bears, and a separate annex exclusively for Barbie dolls, this is where Tom Hanks soothed the savage Robert Loggia with a toe-tappin' rendition of "Heart and Soul" in *Big.* Come Christmas, the store is jam-packed with frenzied shoppers celebrating the holiday season in a ritual that resembles the running of the bulls in Pamplona (open Mon.-Wed. 10am-6pm, Thurs.-Sat. 10am-7pm, Sun. 11am-6pm).

On Fifth Ave. and 59th St. at the southeast corner of Central Park sits the legendary **Plaza Hotel,** built in 1907 by Henry J. Hardenberg. Built at the then-astronomical cost of $12.5 million, its 18-story, 800-room French Renaissance interior is opulence incarnate, flaunting five marble staircases, countless ludicrously named suites, and a two-story Grand Ballroom. Past guests and residents have included Frank Lloyd Wright, the Beatles, F. Scott Fitzgerald, and, of course, the eminent Eloise. When Donald Trump bought this national landmark in 1988, locals shuddered; so far, his Midas touch hasn't altered the place. Flash the doorman a charming smile as he opens the door for you and head in to have a look. The wealth inside is amazing—marble, glass, brass, and gold—but more to the point, it's extremely well cooled and will always provide a great break from summer heat and humidity. *Let's Go* recommends the $15,000-per-night suite.

Double-billing as a forecourt to the Plaza Hotel and as an entrance to Central Park, the **Grand Army Plaza** absorbs the Pulitzer Memorial Fountain. Along with Karl Bitter's Statue of Abundance sits Saint-Gaudens' gaudy, gilt equestrian statue of Union General William Tecumseh Sherman, proving that war may be hell, but it definitely pays to win.

■ Upper East Side

Until the end of the Civil War, 19th-century jet-setters chose this part of town for their summer retreats, building elaborate mansions in garden settings. By the late 1860s, however, simply summering uptown would not suffice. Landowners converted their warm-weather residences into year-round settlements. The building of elevated railroads during the Gilded Age brought an influx of the urban proletariat, swelling the local population. In 1896, Caroline Schermerhorn Astor built a mansion on Fifth Ave. at 65th St., and the rest of high society soon followed. The posh East Side lifestyle flourished until the outbreak of World War I. During this Golden Age, the old-money crowd took advantage of improvements in technology to produce sumptuous mansions outfitted with everything from elevators to intercoms. Scores of the wealthy moved into the area and refused to budge, even during the Great Depression when armies of the unemployed pitched their tents across the way in Central Park.

So it was that hotels, mansions, and churches first colonized the former wilderness of the Upper East Side. The lawns of Central Park covered the land where squatters had dwelt; **Fifth Ave.**, now occupied by millionaires, parades, and unbearably slow buses, rolled over a stretch once grazed by pigs. Today, Fifth Ave. is home to **Museum Mile**, which includes the Metropolitan, the Guggenheim, the International Center of Photography, the Cooper-Hewitt, the Museum of the City of New York, and the Jewish Museum, among others. Nearby on **Madison Ave.** artists, market psychologists, and salespeople conspire to manipulate the present through the advertising industry. These jingle factories are well concealed from the unsuspecting consumer above the unbroken façade of expensive boutiques and superb galleries. The high-art and high-fashion windows of Madison Ave. offer endless hours of aesthetic bliss and materialistic glee.

Flanked by uniform gray and brown apartment buildings and interrupted only by the occasional Gothic church, **Park Ave.** sidesteps the glitz of other parts of town in favor of an austere demeanor. The landscaped green islands that divide the avenue down the middle complete the picture of a Park Ave. destined to remain the same for decades to come. Gaze at the view down the avenue to the hazy indigo outline of midtown's starscraping silhouettes. Grittier **Lexington Ave.** injects a little reality into the East Side. Here and on **Third, Second,** and **First Ave.,** you'll find vibrant crowds and a happening singles scene. Farther north, highrise projects and grimmer urban settings replace the street party atmosphere of the 70s and 80s.

A walk through the Upper East Side, land of conspicuous consumption, might as well be kicked off at 59th St. and Third Ave., where, flag-festooned **Bloomingdale's** sits in regal splendor (see Shopping: Department Stores, p. 287). Try on designer clothes, spray on a little perfume—get ready for the Upper East Side.

Reeking of the latest Calvin Klein scent, waft over to 60th St. and Madison Ave. to see where the "old boys" cavort and establish their networks of power. The **Metropolitan Club,** at 1 E. 60th St., was built by the dynamic trio of McKim, Mead and White on a commission from J.P. Morgan for his friends who had not been accepted at the **Union Club** (101 E. 69th St.). The **Knickerbocker Club,** at 2 E. 62nd St., was founded by disgruntled Union Club men who were growing unhappy with the club's "liberal" admissions policy.

Down the block from the Metropolitan Club, at 47 E. 60th St. between Madison and Park Ave., stands the less snooty (but no less exclusive) **Grolier Club.** Built in

1917 in honor of 16th-century bibliophile Jean Grolier, this Georgian structure houses a collection of fine bookbindings, a public exhibition room, and a specialized research library (open by appointment; call 838-6690 for details). Though built and decorated in the 1930s, nearby **Christ Church,** 520 Park Ave. at 60th St., manages to appear quite ancient. Ralph Adams Cram decorated the exterior of this Byzantine-Romanesque hybrid with Venetian mosaics and marble columns. Note the iconic panels (taken from an old Russian church) inside, above the altar. (Open daily 9am-5pm for meditation, prayer, and respectful viewing. Occasional concerts featuring classical church music; call 838-3036 for information.) Just around the corner, at 22 E. 60th St., the **French Institute** (355-6100), the cultural mission of the French Embassy, offers a variety of Gallic lectures and films (open Mon.-Thurs. 10am-8pm, Fri. 10am-6pm).

Nearby preens the latest location of New York's fashion ground zero, **Barneys New York** at 660 Madison Ave. between 60th and 61st St. Designers such as Vera Wang, Jean-Paul Gaultier, Armani, and many more all sell here at extraordinary prices. Celeb-spotting is a sport here—look for JFK, Jr.; he's reputed to show up a lot (see Shopping: Department Stores, p. 287). Barney has recently been joined on this block by high-fashion pals **Calvin Klein** and **Ann Taylor.**

Between Lexington and Park Ave., at 128 E. 63rd St., stands the **Society of American Illustrators** (838-2560) and its **Museum of American Illustration** (see Museums, p. 249). At 1190 Second Ave. and 63rd St., check out the **Elizabeth Street Garden Galleries.** A gallery devoted to garden statuary, this outdoor exhibition features a large fountain and several marble giants.

West on Fifth Ave., check out the building at 63rd St. Past residents of **810 Fifth Ave.** include publisher William Randolph Hearst and a pre-presidential Richard Nixon. Tricky Dick could go upstairs to borrow butter, eggs, and wire-taps from Nelson Rockefeller, a former shoeshine boy and anxious owner of New York's only fully equipped bomb shelter. At the corner of Fifth Ave. and 65th St. stands **Temple Emanu-El** ("God is with us"), the largest synagogue in the U.S. Outside, Eastern details speckle the otherwise Romanesque structure, creating an interesting hybrid. Inside, the nave bears Byzantine-style ornaments and seats 2500 worshippers—more than St. Patrick's Cathedral (744-1400; open daily 10:30am-4:30pm).

Next door stands the Richard Hunt-designed **Lotos Club,** on E. 66th St. between Madison and Fifth, an organization of actors, musicians, and journalists. The building is distinguished by its odd, layered look and gaudy trimwork. East 67th and 68th Streets between Fifth and Madison Ave. furnish several examples of turn-of-the-century mansion architecture with a distinct French accent.

History buffs may want to stop and view **The Sarah Delano Roosevelt Memorial House,** actually a pair of identical buildings designed by Charles Platt in 1908, at 45-47 E. 65th St. between Madison and Park Ave. The Roosevelt matriarch commissioned the construction on the occasion of her son Franklin's wedding. In these buildings, FDR recovered from polio in the early 20s and launched his political career. The building is now home to the Institute for Rational-Emotive Therapy (don't ask—we don't know).

Occupying virtually an entire block, the **Seventh Regiment Armory** makes its stand between 66th and 67th St. on Park Ave. The Seventh Regiment fought in every major U.S. campaign from 1812 on, including a valiant outing for the Union during the Civil War. Much of the armory's original 19th-century decoration and furnishing remain in place today. Particularly remarkable are the Veterans' Room and the adjoining former library, now a display room for the Regiment's silver. The front hallway boasts a gargantuan staircase sheathed in venerable red plush, as well as a whole host of decomposing flags. The eerily impenetrable gloom makes it virtually impossible to see the portraits, but they can see you. The Armory still serves as an active military facility; call ahead for a tour (744-8180).

The swarms of purple insignia sweatshirts harken the presence of **Hunter College,** part of the City University of New York. The main building presents its unsightly modernist façade to Park Ave. and its even less attractive posterior to Lex-

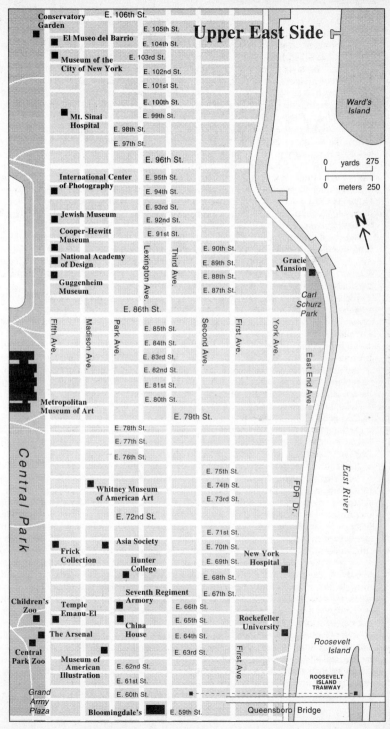

Upper East Side

Conservatory Garden

El Museo del Barrio

Museum of the City of New York

E. 106th St.
E. 105th St.
E. 104th St.
E. 103rd St.
E. 102nd St.
E. 101st St.
E. 100th St.
E. 99th St.

Mt. Sinai Hospital

E. 98th St.
E. 97th St.

Ward's Island

E. 96th St.

International Center of Photography

E. 95th St.
E. 94th St.
E. 93rd St.
E. 92nd St.
E. 91st St.

Jewish Museum

Cooper-Hewitt Museum

National Academy of Design

Guggenheim Museum

0 yards 275
0 meters 250

N

Lexington Ave.
Third Ave.

E. 90th St.
E. 89th St.
E. 88th St.
E. 87th St.

Gracie Mansion

Carl Schurz Park

E. 86th St.

Fifth Ave.
Madison Ave.
Park Ave.
Second Ave.
First Ave.
York Ave.
East End Ave.

E. 85th St.
E. 84th St.
E. 83rd St.
E. 82nd St.
E. 81st St.
E. 80th St.

Metropolitan Museum of Art

E. 79th St.

E. 78th St.
E. 77th St.
E. 76th St.

Central Park

E. 75th St.
E. 74th St.
E. 73rd St.

East River

Whitney Museum of American Art

E. 72nd St.

E. 71st St.
E. 70th St.
E. 69th St.
E. 68th St.

FDR Dr.

Asia Society

Frick Collection

Hunter College

New York Hospital

Children's Zoo

Temple Emanu-El

Seventh Regiment Armory

E. 67th St.
E. 66th St.
E. 65th St.
E. 64th St.
E. 63rd St.

China House

Rockefeller University

The Arsenal

Central Park Zoo

Museum of American Illustration

First Ave.

Roosevelt Island

E. 62nd St.
E. 61st St.
E. 60th St.

ROOSEVELT ISLAND TRAMWAY

Grand Army Plaza

Bloomingdale's

E. 59th St.

Queensboro Bridge

ington Ave., between 67th and 69th St. Note the innovative walkways stretching across 68th St. and Lexington Ave. that connect the various buildings.

Three foreign art galleries stand on Park Ave. at 69th St.: the **Americas Society** at 680 Park Ave., the **Spanish Institute** at 684 Park Ave., and the **Italian Institute** at 688 Park Ave. The **Asia Society,** 725 Park Ave. at 70th St., celebrates Asian cultural awareness with lectures, films, and an impressive art collection assembled by John D. Rockefeller III (see Museums, p. 245). Wealthy philanthropic industrialist Henry Clay Frick's marvelous mansion, home of the **Frick Collection,** sits at 1 E. 70th St. at Fifth Ave., kicking off Museum Mile in grand style (see Museums, p. 243).

The **Polo–Ralph Lauren** boutique (606-2100) wallows in its pretentious splendor at 867 Madison Ave., between 71st and 72nd St. Look wealthy or Ralph's cronies may ignore you...until you touch something (open Mon.-Sat. 10am-6pm, Thurs. 10am-8pm). The building was originally a private home; the store's interior reflects that eternal old-money style.

Resembling an upside-down ziggurat or a hard-to-place Tetris piece, the **Whitney Museum of American Art** and all of its treasures await your aesthetic scrutiny at the corner of Madison Ave. and 75th St. Bring an inquisitive friend and an open mind (see Museums, p. 242).

Slightly removed from the mayhem of Madison where it once stood, **Sotheby's** (606-7000) conducts its affairs and auctions at 1334 York Ave. at 72nd St. Viewings are open to the public, although admission to a few of the biggest auctions requires tickets (open Mon.-Fri. 9am-5pm; gallery open Mon.-Sat. 10am-5pm, Sun. 1-5pm). On the corner of Lexington Ave. and 76th St. sits the multi-domed **Church of St. Jean Baptiste.** Recently renovated after a bout of divine vandalism (God smote the cross off the top in a thunderstorm), St. Jean still displays Italianate style and swagger. Inside, examine the sculpture in the shrine to St. Anne, as well as the Vatican-esque altar pieces.

The front door of **900 Park Ave.,** at 79th St., may look familiar: the once-wholesome cast of *Diff'rent Strokes* drove up in a limousine to Mr. Drummond's residence at the beginning of every episode. No, the naked female statue on the pedestal up front is not Kimberly.

Even after passing on to the great Big Apple in the sky, celebrity New Yorkers manage to uphold their status and maintain their coteries. The grave roll call of the **Frank E. Campbell Chapel,** a prestigious funeral chapel (1076 Madison Ave. at 81st St.), reads like Mortuaries of the Rich and Famous: Robert Kennedy, John Lennon, Elizabeth Arden, James Cagney, Jack Dempsey, Tommy Dorsey, Judy Garland, Howard Johnson, Mae West, and Arturo Toscanini all rest their bones here while spiritually engaged elsewhere.

New York's cultural flagship, The **Metropolitan Museum of Art,** holds court at 1000 Fifth Ave., near 82nd St.; fountains and sore-footed museum-goers flank its majestic presence. The largest in the Western hemisphere, the Met's art collection encompasses some 33 million works (see Museums, p. 234). Across the street at 1014 Fifth Ave., **Goethe House** (439-8700) offers a Germanic cultural respite from the *Sturm und Drang* of New York through films and lectures (library open Tues. and Thurs. noon-7pm, Wed. and Fri.-Sat. noon-5pm; see Movies, p. 264).

For more Germanic culture, head east of Lexington Ave. between 77th and 96th St.—this is the **Yorkville** area. Originally settled by Germans, Yorkville welcomed immigrants from the Rhine Valley throughout the first half of this century. Although the heavy German flavor that once marked local restaurant menus, beer gardens, pastry shops, and deli counters has been diluted in the wake of newer chain stores and pizza parlors, establishments such as **Schaller and Weber** at 1654 Second Ave. (879-3047) testify to a continued German presence.

Starting on 82nd St. and East End Ave. is the **John Finley Walk,** a sidewalk overlooking the East River and speeding cars on FDR Drive. Stroll down the path and come to the **Carl Schurz Park,** between 84th and 90th St. along East End Ave., named for the many-hatted German immigrant who served as a Civil War general, a Missouri senator, President Rutherford B. Hayes's Secretary of the Interior, and finally as editor of the *New York Evening Post* and *Harper's Weekly*. The park is a haven of greenery with many nooks for asphalt-weary metropolites, courts for urban athletes, and playgrounds for their offspring. The park sponsors free jazz concerts on Wednesdays from 7pm to 9pm. **Gracie Mansion,** at the northern end of the park, has been the residence of every New York mayor since Fiorello LaGuardia moved in during World War II. Rudy Giuliani presently occupies this hottest of hot seats. To reserve a tour of the colonial mansion, call 570-4751 (tours Wed. only; suggested admission $3, seniors $2).

Henderson Place lines East End Ave. near 86th St.; although this series of Queen Anne-style houses were created in 1882 for "persons of moderate means," they nevertheless flaunt multiple turrets, parapets, and ivy-colored walls. Ghostbusters beware: rumor has it that some of these houses are haunted. Nearby, the fanciful **Church of the Holy Trinity** offers folk, choral, and Spanish eucharists every Sunday at 316 E. 88th St. between First and Second Ave. Note the amazing Claymation-style doorwork.

Back over on Museum mile, at Fifth Ave. and 88th St., the oddly-shaped **Guggenheim Museum,** designed by Frank Lloyd Wright, spirals away (see Museums, p. 241). Down the street, the **National Academy Museum,** 1083 Fifth Ave. at 89th St., serves as both a school and a museum for the academy, founded in 1825. Works by 11 of the 30 founding members reside over at the Metropolitan Museum.

When Andrew Carnegie requested that architects Babb, Cook, and Willard construct "the most modest, plainest, and most roomy house in New York" on 91st St. at Fifth Ave., he received a large Renaissance-Georgian combination of red brick and limestone, situated in a luxurious garden. Within, dark oak paneling, textured wallpaper, and demure atriums create the perfect setting for a society ball. When Carnegie moved up and out, the Smithsonian moved in, relocating their National Museum of Design here in the **Cooper-Hewitt Museum** (see Museums, p. 243).

Take a break from museum-going at the **Church of the Heavenly Rest,** located at the corner of Fifth Ave. and 90th St. Sit down, rest your bones, and note the breathtaking stained glass window above the altar.

Next up on the Mile are The **Jewish Museum,** at 92nd St. and Fifth Ave., a French Renaissance structure containing the country's largest collection of Judaica, and the **International Center of Photography,** 130 Fifth Ave. at 94th St., which maintains a huge collection of photographs while operating workshops, photolabs, and a screening room (see Museums, p. 248).

Wandering back on to Park Ave., note the Lippincott Sculpture at 92nd St. This modernist piece, vaguely resembling a pawn and knight under a wave, offers a unique respite from the usual manicured medians. Continuing north stands the **Synod of Bishops of the Russian Orthodox Church Outside Russia,** which inhabits the 1917 Georgian mansion at Park Ave. and 93rd St. The bishops scattered a few icons about but left the interior decoration virtually unchanged, except for a former ballroom converted into a cathedral.

New York's most prominent mosque, the **Islamic Cultural Center,** at Third Ave. and 96th St., was precisely oriented by computer to face the holy city of Mecca. Meanwhile the Russians continued their conquest of the Upper East Side with the **Russian Orthodox Cathedral of St. Nicholas** at 15 E. 97th St. The cathedral's onion domes lend a dose of Russian authenticity to the Upper East Side.

Hunter College High School, located at Park Ave. and 94th St., is housed in a former armory; its sheer, windowless walls have inspired the nickname "the brick prison" among the school's students. The courtyard façade looks impressive from Madison Ave.—it has been used in a number of films, most recently *The Fisher King*—but is actually a free-standing wall, a stage-set backdrop for the cement courtyard. Hunter is one of a kind: a public school which is also supported by the City University of New York. Founded at the turn of the century as an all-female teacher-training school, H.C.H.S. went co-ed in the 70s when a few parents sued the city for the right to give their sons a Hunter education. Famous alums include Young MC and Adam "SANE" Smith, the late graffiti artist.

NEIGHBORHOODS

Museum Mile finally ends up in East Harlem with the **Museum of the City of New York,** on Fifth Ave. and 103rd St., and **El Museo del Barrio,** on Fifth Ave. and 104th St., the only museum in the U.S. specializing in Latin American and Puerto Rican art (see Museums, p. 249).

▓ Roosevelt Island

"New York's Island Paradise," as the ad for the luxury apartments here croons, has a long and complicated history. This minute strip of land floating in the East River between Manhattan and Queens was originally occupied by the Canarsie Indians and known as Minnahannock (loosely translated "It's nice to be on the island"). After the Canarsie sold the land to the Dutch in 1637, it changed hands many more times, from Dutch hog farmers to an English farmer named Robert Blackwell to the City of New York in 1828. The city then used the island as a dumping ground for unwanted people—establishing jails, hospitals, and a lunatic asylum here. Roosevelt Island has also functioned as the city's St Helena: Boss Tweed of the politically murky Tammany Hall was incarcerated here, as was the hardened criminal Mae West (for her role, prefiguring Madonna, in a play called "Sex"). Finally, in 1969, architects Phillip Johnson and John Burgee redesigned the island as a state-sponsored utopia of mixed-income housing, safety, and handicapped-accessibility. In 1986 the island's name was changed from Welfare Island to Roosevelt Island, in honor of Franklin Delano.

Most of Roosevelt Island's action, such as it is, is on the north end. Here, people seem to live one of the most idyllic suburban existences, not even 300 yards away from the hustle and bustle of East Midtown. Aided by state funding and extensive planning, the past 25 years have seen the construction of residential complexes for a variety of income groups, with a concerted effort at racial diversity. The community runs a communal garden (open May-Sept. Sat.-Sun. 8am-6pm), and, as the great number of running tracks, tennis courts, soccer fields, and softball diamonds attests, they have the choice of keeping in shape as well. Other than these options, though, there is little in the way of entertainment: no movie theater, record store, or bowling alley. Apartments in this model community are nevertheless hard to come by, except for the luxury apartments ($2400 per month). Another, and probably final, housing complex is in the development stages, even though it was originally slated for completion in 1995. The Roosevelt Island community has its own public services, stores, restaurants, and public school, as well as cheerfully colored buses and garbage trucks—Battlestar Galactica comes to Manhattan.

To add to the general unreality of the place, a bright orange tram shuttles residents and tourists across the East River. Featured in the action movie *Nighthawks* (starring Sylvester Stallone), the tram ride allows a grand view of the East Side. As you hover almost 250 feet above the river, you can see the United Nations complex and the distinctive hats of the Chrysler Building and the Empire State Building to your right. One of the only publicly operated commuter cable cars in the world, it operates at an annual deficit of $1 million, and its future is especially uncertain now that the subway line has been extended to the island.

You can pick up the tram at 59th St. and Second Ave. Look for the big red cable rotors next to the Queensboro Bridge. Round-trip fare costs $2.80 and the ride takes about 6 minutes each way. (Cars run every 15min., Sun.-Thurs. 6am-2am, Fri.-Sat. 6am-3:30am; twice as frequently during rush hour.) Those with a fear of heights can take the Q and B subway line, which was finally extended here in 1989. The Q102 bus also makes the trip.

Once on the island, take the mini-bus (10¢) up Main St. and roam around a bit. A walking/rollerblading path encircles the island, and gardens and playgrounds are abundant on the northern half. You can also check out the ruins of the insane asylum and hospital. (Projects are now underway to restore the ruins and turn them into an arts complex.) Lighthouse Park, at the northernmost tip of the island, is a pleasant pastoral retreat with great views of the swirling waters of the East River.

■ Central Park

Beloved Central Park has certainly had its moments in the sun: from Simon and Garfunkel's historic 1981 concert, to Dustin Hoffman's refuge here in *Marathon Man,* to the annual meeting of stars in the summertime Shakespeare-in-the-Park festival. From Pavarotti to *Pocahontas,* New York's 843-acre metropolitan oasis has set the verdant stage for many events, from ardent suitors proposing marriage on horse-drawn carriages to huge Stonewall gay-and-lesbian rallies. Enormous Central Park offers a pastoral refuge from the fast-paced urban jungle of New York City.

Despite its bucolic appearance, Central Park was never an original wilderness; the landscaped gardens were carved out of the city's grid, between 59th and 110th St. for several blocks west of Fifth Ave. The campaign for a public park in New York began in the mid-1840s with William Cullen Bryant, the vociferous editor of the *New York Evening Post,* and the project received support from the acclaimed architect Andrew Jackson Downing in his magazine *The Horticulturist.* The creation of the park became a unifying issue in the mayoral campaign of 1851—both the Democrat and Whig candidates were strongly in favor of the project. In 1853, the state authorized the purchase of land from 59th to 106th St. (The 106th-110th St. addendum was purchased in 1863.) Alas, Downing drowned and was unable to design his dream project. The city held a competition to determine the new designer.

The winning design, selected in 1858 from 33 competing entries, came out of a collaboration between Frederick Law Olmsted and Calvert Vaux. Because Olmsted had a day job heading the construction crews that cleared the debris and edifices from the proto-park, most of the plans for Central Park were drawn at night. Olmsted and Vaux transformed 843 acres of bogs, cliffs, glacial leftovers, bone-boiling works, and pig farms into a living masterwork they called Greensward. The whole landscape took 15 years to build and 40 years to grow.

The Park may be roughly divided between north and south at the main reservoir; the southern section of the Park affords more intimate settings, serene lakes, and graceful promenades, while the northern end has a few ragged edges. Nearly 1400 species of trees, shrubs, and flowers grow here, the work of distinguished horticulturist Ignaz Anton Pilat. Lose yourself in the flora without fear of getting lost: look to the nearest aluminum lamppost for guidance, and check the small metal four-digit plaque bolted to it. The first two digits tell you what street you're nearest (89, for example), and the second two whether you're on the east or west side of the Park (an even number means east, an odd west). In an emergency, call the **24-hour Park Line** (570-4820; call boxes located throughout the Park).

Along 59th St. (also known as Central Park South), horses chomp on oats as children and couples clamor for **carriage tours** of the Park ($34 for a 20min. ride; 246-0520 for information). Debate has surrounded this practice for many years. Even if you disapprove of the animals being used for such labor, try to be better-behaved than the radical activists, who recently punched out a driver. These self-same activists would probably prefer the new (and much more environmentally correct) **Bite of the Apple bicycle tour** ($25 for 2hr ride, children $20; tours leave daily at 10am, 1 and 4pm from 2 Columbus Circle; call 541-8759 for more information).

Start off your own walking tour of Central Park at the **Central Park Zoo** (recently renamed the **Central Park Wildlife Center)** at E. 64th St. and Fifth Ave. (861-6030). Built in 1934, it has attracted flocks of visitors ever since. Roving herds of sugar-hyped children make even the drowsy reptiles of the Tropical Rainforest pavilion tremble in fear, and solitary tourists find a safe haven from sweat in the deliciously chilly Penguin room. A sign of the times: a couple of years ago an obsessively backstroking polar bear was treated for depression. (Open April-Oct. Mon.-Fri. 10am-5pm, Sat.-Sun. 10:30am-5:30pm; Nov.-March daily 10am-4:30pm. Last entry ½-hr. before closing. Admission $2.50, seniors $1.25, children 3-12 50¢.) Above the archway, north of the main zoo, hangs the **Delacorte Musical Clock,** made in 1965 by Andrea Spaldini. Every half-hour from 8am to 6pm, bears, monkeys, and other bronze creatures perform a hop-and-skip routine. North of the 65th St. transverse lies the Children's Zoo, currently undergoing renovation.

In front of the Zoo at Fifth Ave. and E. 64th St. sits the dumpy, ivy-covered **Arsenal,** which holds the Park's administrative offices. The third-floor **Arsenal Gallery** (360-8236) hosts free Park-related exhibitions (open Mon.-Fri. 9:30am-4:30pm).

Walking west from the Arsenal (to the left, if you're facing the clock), you'll reach the Children's District. The area south of 65th St. was specifically designated by Vaux and Olmsted as a place for the young (and the young at heart) to play, ride rides, and get good, clean food. In those days, the food was distributed at the **Dairy,** built by Vaux in 1870 so that purity-tested milk could be distributed to poor families susceptible to food poisoning. The building now houses the **Central Park Reception Center** (794-6564). Brochures and calendars are available here, as are exhibitions on Park history. Pick up the **free map** of Central Park and the seasonal list of events. (Open Tues.-Thurs., Sat.-Sun. 11am-5pm, Fri. 1-5pm; Nov.-Feb. Tues.-Thurs., Sat.-Sun. 11am-4pm, Fri. 1-4pm.)

Next to the Dairy is what Olmsted and Vaux called the *Kinderberg* (children's mountain). Although the **Chess and Checkers House** has closed, with a $20 deposit you can rent equipment at the Dairy and square off at any of the 24 outdoor boards. Follow the blaring beat to the **Wollman Skating Rink** (396-1010), which features children defying death and adults clinging cautiously to the railing. When it gets cold enough at this outdoor rink, wheels turn to blades for ice-skating. (Whole complex open Mon.-Thurs. 10am-6pm, Fri. 10am-10pm, Sat. 11am-11pm, Sun. 11am-7pm. Ice- or roller-skating $4, children under 12 and seniors over 55 $3, plus $6.50 skate or rollerblade rental.) A nice addition to the roller rink is the railed ledge overlooking it, from which an unparalleled view of midtown can be had free of charge. Wollman also rents skates and rollerblades for use throughout the park ($15 for 2 hr., $25 all day; includes helmet and pads; deposit required).

If you enjoy going in circles while listening to calliope renditions of easy-listening hits, visit the hand-carved horses of the **Friedsam Memorial Carousel** (879-0244), located at 65th St. west of Center Dr. The 58-horsepower carousel was brought from Coney Island and fully restored in 1983. (Open daily 10am-6:30pm, weather permitting. Thanksgiving to mid-March Sat.-Sun. 10:30am-4:30pm. Admission 90¢.)

Directly north of the Carousel lies **Sheep Meadow,** from about 66th to 69th St. on the western side of the Park. This is the largest chunk of Greensward, exemplifying the pastoral ideals of the Park's designers and today's teenage crowds. Sheep did graze here until 1934, but after that the Park could afford lawn mowers and so terminated the flock. A popular spot for love-ins and be-ins of the 60s and 70s, "The Meadow" remains a countercultural enclave where teenagers gather to get high and hangout alongside frisbee-tossers and picnicking families. This is where TV star Jerry Seinfeld met his young paramour, Shoshonna Lonstein. Directly north of the meadow, the crowd instantly ages about 50 years. Complexions turn noticeably less bronzed under the broad straw hats and white clothes of the lawn bowlers and croquet players who gather in shady hedge-rimmed patches from May through November. (Call 688-5495 during summer months for info on a free croquet clinic offered Tues. nights at 6pm. White sports clothes and flat-soled shoes required.)

West of Sheep Meadow, between 66th and 67th St.,**Tavern on the Green** (873-3200), said to be the city's most profitable eatery, specializes in pricey meals with a view of brilliantly illuminated greenery (lunch $11-26, dinner $13-29; open Mon.-Fri. noon-3:30pm and 5:30-11:30pm, Sat.-Sun. 10am-3:30pm and 5pm-11:30pm).

Along West Drive, at 67th St., stands the **Seventh Regiment Civil War Monument,** sculpted by John Quincy Adams Ward in 1870. Although bureaucrats deemed the Park "too chipper" for "sepulchral monuments," someone somewhere pushed the statue design through. In subsequent years it became a prototype for Civil War monuments throughout the country.

To the east of Sheep Meadow lies the cool dark path of the **Mall.** Bronze statues of literary lions, including Shakespeare and Robert Burns, decorate this tree-lined thor-

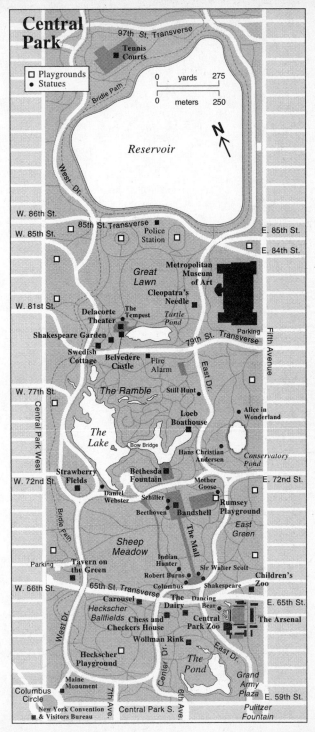

Central Park

97th St. Transverse

Tennis Courts

□ Playgrounds
• Statues

0 yards 275
0 meters 250

Bridle Path

West Dr.

Reservoir

N

W. 86th St.

85th St. Transverse
Police Station

E. 85th St.

W. 85th St.

E. 84th St.

Great Lawn

Metropolitan Museum of Art

Cleopatra's Needle

W. 81st St.

Delacorte Theater
The Tempest
Turtle Pond

Parking

Fifth Avenue

Shakespeare Garden

79th St. Transverse

Swedish Cottage
Belvedere Castle
Fire Alarm

East Dr.

The Ramble
Still Hunt

W. 77th St.

Alice in Wonderland

Loeb Boathouse

Central Park West

The Lake
Bow Bridge
Hans Christian Andersen

Conservatory Pond

Strawberry Fields
Bethesda Fountain

W. 72nd St.
Daniel Webster
Schiller
Mother Goose

E. 72nd St.

Beethoven
Bandshell
Rumsey Playground

East Green

Sheep Meadow

Bridle Path

Indian Hunter
Sir Walter Scott

Parking
Tavern on the Green
Robert Burns

Columbus
Shakespeare
Children's Zoo

W. 66th St.
65th St. Transverse
Carousel
The Dairy
Dancing Bear

E. 65th St.

Heckscher Ballfields
Chess and Checkers House
Central Park Zoo
The Arsenal

West Dr.
Wollman Rink

Heckscher Playground

Center Dr.

East Dr.

The Pond

Grand Army Plaza

Maine Monument

Columbus Circle

7th Ave.

Central Park S.

6th Ave.

E. 59th St.

New York Convention & Visitors Bureau

Pulitzer Fountain

oughfare. Off the southwestern end of the Mall is the first American statue placed in the Park—**The Indian Hunter** (1869), also by J.Q.A. Ward.

At the north end of the Mall is the Rumsey Playfield and a bandshell. The Dairy can give you calendars for the '97 **Central Park Summerstage** program, which is held here. In years past Summerstage has sponsored free concerts by big names in genres from opera to punk rock. Past performers include Stereolab, The Master Musicians of Jajouka, and A Tribe Called Quest, among others. The Summerstage is not limited to music: writers such as Suzan-Lori Parks and Paul Auster have been known to read from their latest works here as well. (For recorded Summerstage info, call 360-2777.)

North of the 72nd St. Transverse is the **Terrace,** linking the Mall with the Lake and boasting elaborate carvings of plants, birds, and park animals. The bas-relief along the grand central staircase depict the four seasons. The centerpiece of the Terrace and the Park as a whole is **Bethesda Fountain,** containing the 1865 statue of the **Angel of the Waters,** sculpted in Rome by Emma Stebins. Benches in the sun and the pleasant sound of running water against the ubiquitous drone of New York crowds make this an ideal picnic spot—bring your sandwich or buy your (overpriced) hot dog here.

On the northern edge of the Terrace and spreading out to the west from underneath the Bow Bridge is the **Lake,** green with algae but still a very dramatic sight in the heart of the City. The 1954 **Loeb Boathouse** (517-2233), a late but indispensable addition to the Park, supplies rowboats. (Open daily April-Sept.10:30am-5pm, weather permitting. Rowboats $10 per hr., refundable $30 deposit.)

Aquaphobes can rent a bike from the boathouse instead and make their own journeys on *terra firma.* (Bike rental April-Sept. Mon.-Fri. 10am-6pm, Sat.-Sun. 9am-6pm, in clement weather. $8 per hr. for 3-speeds, $10 per hr. for 10-speeds, $14 per hr. for tandems; credit card, ID, or $100 deposit required for all bikes; 10-speeds require additional $20 deposit. Call the Boathouse.)

To the east of the Terrace and the Lake, model boats set sail daily on the pacific swells of **Conservatory Water.** This formal basin, site of the yacht race in E.B. White's *Stuart Little,* vibrates in summertime with the sounds of carefree children. Competitive model-yachters gather to race (they observe Olympic yachting regulations) Saturdays at 10am from late March to mid-November. A statue of **Hans Christian Andersen,** a gift from Copenhagen in 1956, stands near dreamchild **Alice in Wonderland** and several of her friends—another gift of the Danes in 1959. Children perpetually scramble over both statues, sitting in Andersen's lap or clinging precariously to the Mad Hatter's oversized *chapeau.* The Andersen statue has become a prime storytelling spot in the summer; tales are spun Saturdays at 11am and in July on Wednesdays as well (sponsored by the New York Public Library; call 340-0849 for information). More stories for the 3- to 8-year-old set are told on the playgrounds in July and August; check the schedules posted in the playgrounds.

Strawberry Fields, sculpted as Yoko Ono's memorial to her late husband, is located to the west of the Lake at 72nd St. and West Dr., directly across from the **Dakota Apartments** where John Lennon was assassinated and where Ono still lives with their son. Ono battled for this space against city-council members who had planned a Bing Crosby memorial on the same spot. Picnickers and 161 varieties of plants now inhabit the rolling hills around the star-shaped "Imagine" mosaic on sunny spring days. And on John Lennon's birthday in October, in one of the largest unofficial Park events, thousands gather here to remember—or, as time passes, to "imagine"—what the legend was really like.

North of the Lake, the **Ramble** features winding footpaths that cover dense forestry and intimate clearings. Frequented by birdwatchers seeking a glimpse of the variety of migratory species that reside here, after nightfall the Ramble transforms into an infamous site for anonymous male sex. The possibility of anti-gay violence makes this activity ill-advised; club-hopping is much safer (see Gay and Lesbian Clubs, p. 268). The high point of the Park, literally, is **Belvedere Castle,** a whimsical fancy designed by the restless Vaux in 1869. The castle, which looks like something out of a fairy tale, rises just off the 79th St. Transverse from the **Vista Rock,** commanding a view of the Ramble to the south and the Great Lawn to the north. For many years a weather station, Belvedere Castle has been reincarnated as an education and information center and serves as the stronghold of the green knights—the **Urban Park Rangers** (772-0210) who provide visitor and emergency services for the Park (castle open Wed.-Fri. 11am-4pm, Sat.-Sun. 11am-5pm; free).

The **Swedish Cottage Marionette Theater,** at the base of Vista Rock, puts on regular puppet shows, such as 1996's *Cinderella.* (Shows Mon.-Fri. at 10:30am and noon; season runs from early June through mid-August. Admission $5, children $4. Call 988-9093 for information and reservations; reservations are required.) **The Shakespeare Garden,** containing plants, flowers, and herbs mentioned in the Bard's works, sits near the Cottage.

Up the hill from the Cottage Theater lies the round wooden space of the **Delacorte Theater,** hosting the wildly popular **Shakespeare in the Park** series each midsummer. Performances often feature renowned actors and are always free, though getting tickets takes initiative and long periods of time waiting in line. One of the 1995 shows, *The Tempest,* featured Patrick Stewart. Come early: the theater seats only 1936 lucky souls (see Entertainment & Nightlife: Theater, p. 256).

Immediately north of the castle lies a dried up **Turtle Pond** and a fenced-in **Great Lawn**—this grassy expanse is closed for restoration until fall 1997. Here Paul Simon and Disney's Pocahontas crooned, the Stonewall 25 marchers rallied, and the New York Philharmonic Metropolitan Opera held its performances—they have now moved to the North Meadow (see Opera, p. 266).

Encircled by joggers (the track around it is 1.58 miles), the shiny, placid **Reservoir**—recently renamed to honor frequent jogger Jacqueline Kennedy Onassis—may be the most tranquil sight in Manhattan. North of the Reservoir at the 97th St. Transverse are the basketball courts of the **North Meadow Recreation Center** (348-4867), which also sponsors board games, pool, wall climbing, baseball, tennis, and kite-flying. Most of these are free, but some that require equipment have a small fee.

Above the reach of the Park's tourist crowds, at 105th St. and 5th Ave., is the attractive **Conservatory Garden** (860-1382; gates open spring-fall daily 8am-dusk). Free tours of the Garden are offered every Saturday through the summer at 11am. Up at the northeast corner of the Park lies the recently reopened **Harlem Meer,** an 11-acre lake. The **Harlem Meer Performance Festival** enlivens the shores with free jazz, reggae, and Latin music performances, as well as multicultural dance and theater (shows late May to Oct., Sat. at 2pm; call 860-1370). **The Charles A. Dana Discovery Center** here at 110th St. and Fifth Ave. features exhibitions and activities presenting Central Park as an environmental (as opposed to historical or cultural) space (860-1370; open Tues.-Sun. 11am-5pm). Check out the relatively new (as of the summer of '95) exhibit of carved birds entitled "Wood on the Wing." The Center also leads tours and loans out fishing rods for use in the Meer (you do have to throw the fish back, though).

Central Park is fairly safe during the day, but less so at night. Don't be afraid to go see the shows or Shakespeare in the Park at night, but stay on the path and try to go with someone else. Do not go wandering on the darker paths at night. Women especially should use caution after dark.

For general Central Park information, call 360-3444; for general parks and recreation info, call 360-8111 Mon.-Fri. 9am-5pm.

The Haunted Pond of Central Park

If you go out to the Pond tonight, you're in for a big surprise. According to the "Secrets of Central Park" walking tour in *Time Out* magazine, the ghostly Van der Voort sisters, dead of old age since 1880, can still be seen "skating" about the large pond in the southeastern corner of the park. Such intimate friends in life that they endlessly rejected their mother's marriage arrangements, they have been witnessed by many a disquieted Plaza Hotel guest since World War I, glissading about in their matching red and purple skating outfits.

▓ Upper West Side

The **Upper West Side** is one of the friendliest areas of Manhattan. Lacking the uptight pretention of the East Side, the Upper West Side manages to be tastefully elegant while incorporating some ethnic areas and some happening nightlife. Central Park West luxuriously borders the area—don't be surprised to see a familiar face from the big screen strolling leisurely about.

The population of the Upper West Side tends to reflect the presence of its cultural and academic institutions; **Lincoln Center** and nearby **Columbia University** provide residents of the Upper West with the best in culture and learning. As a result, the Upper West Side is the enclave of a lively and spirited intelligentsia, peacefully co-existing with—even embracing—the flavors brought in by assiduous Caribbean immigrant groups.

While Central Park West and West End Ave. flank the Upper West with residential quietude, **Columbus Ave.** and **Broadway** are exciting thoroughfares for dining, shopping, and people-watching both day and night. Although originally conceived as a residential thoroughfare, Broadway is the principal and most colorful street on the West Side. Today the street is crammed with delis, theaters, and boutiques; on the sidewalk hawkers peddle everything from bun dumplings to worn copies of *Juggs* magazine to the kitchenware of yesteryear. Because of this continuous activity, Broadway is bustling enough to feel safe even late at night, though the same can't be said of the side streets that intersect the avenue.

■ Lincoln Center

Broadway intersects Columbus Ave. at **Lincoln Center,** the cultural hub of upper-crust New York. The seven facilities that constitute Lincoln Center—Avery Fisher Hall, the New York State Theater, the Metropolitan Opera House, the Library and Museum of Performing Arts, the Vivian Beaumont Theater, the Walter Reade Theater, and the Juilliard School of Music—accommodate over 13,000 spectators at a time and take up the space between 62nd and 66th St. and Amsterdam and Columbus Ave. Power broker Robert Moses masterminded this project in 1955 when Carnegie Hall seemed fated for destruction. The complex was designed as a modern version of the public plazas of Rome and Venice, and despite the criticisms of its architecture that met its opening (the *Times* called it a hulking disgrace), it has become one of New York's most frequented and popular locales.

The **plaza** is especially lively on weekend afternoons, when young hopeful dancers glide by and other student performing artists mill about with their instrument cases. The plaza's impressive fountain is a favored lovers' rendezvous, where Cher and Nicholas Cage were *Moonstruck* and the cast of *Fame* danced at the beginning of each show. This open area is also a favorite spot for fashion photographers; models sweat under faux fur coats in August. The uniform white monumentality of the eight-block complex is worth marveling at. On your left, with your back to Columbus Ave., is an automated information booth.

When your back is to Columbus Ave., **Avery Fisher Hall** stands on your right. The hall was designed in 1966 by Max Abramovitz and houses the New York Philharmonic under the direction of Kurt Masur, to whom the baton was recently passed by conductor Zubin Mehta. Previous Philharmonic directors include Leonard Bernstein, Arturo Toscanini, and Leopold Stokowski (see Entertainment & Nightlife: Classical Music, p. 267). To your left, if your back is to Columbus Ave., beams the monolithic **New York State Theater,** which plays host to the New York City Ballet and the New York City Opera. December is *Nutcracker* month, a yearly ritual for many New Yorkers.

Straight ahead and beyond the fountain is the centerpiece of Lincoln Center, the **Metropolitan Opera House.** This 1966 work by Wallace K. Harrison echoes behind a Mondrian-inspired glass façade. Beautiful Chagall murals span the lobby, and a grand, many-tiered staircase curves down to the humble opera buff. The gift shop

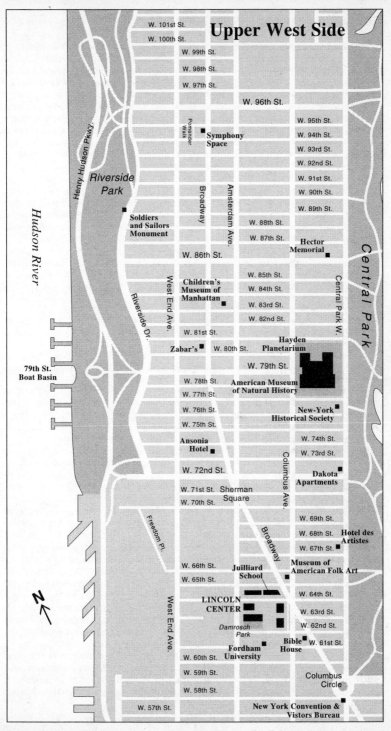

Upper West Side

W. 101st St.
W. 100th St.
W. 99th St.
W. 98th St.
W. 97th St.
W. 96th St.
W. 95th St.
W. 94th St.
W. 93rd St.
W. 92nd St.
W. 91st St.
W. 90th St.
W. 89th St.
W. 88th St.
W. 87th St.
W. 86th St.
W. 85th St.
W. 84th St.
W. 83rd St.
W. 82nd St.
W. 81st St.
W. 80th St.
W. 79th St.
W. 78th St.
W. 77th St.
W. 76th St.
W. 75th St.
W. 74th St.
W. 73rd St.
W. 72nd St.
W. 71st St.
W. 70th St.
W. 69th St.
W. 68th St.
W. 67th St.
W. 66th St.
W. 65th St.
W. 64th St.
W. 63rd St.
W. 62nd St.
W. 61st St.
W. 60th St.
W. 59th St.
W. 58th St.
W. 57th St.

Henry Hudson Pkwy.

Hudson River

Riverside Park

Soldiers and Sailors Monument

Pomander Walk

Symphony Space

Broadway

Amsterdam Ave.

Hector Memorial

West End Ave.

Children's Museum of Manhattan

Riverside Dr.

Central Park W.

Central Park

Zabar's

Hayden Planetarium

American Museum of Natural History

79th St. Boat Basin

New-York Historical Society

Ansonia Hotel

Columbus Ave.

Dakota Apartments

Sherman Square

Hotel des Artistes

Museum of American Folk Art

Freedom Pl.

Broadway

Juilliard School

LINCOLN CENTER

Damrosch Park

Fordham University

Bible House

West End Ave.

Columbus Circle

New York Convention & Vistors Bureau

N

here broadcasts performances live on house monitors; sneaky budgeteers can get a quick opera-fix just browsing in the shop at performance time. (Shop open Mon.-Sat. 10am-5:30pm or until 2nd intermission of performance, Sun. noon-6pm.)

To your left as you face the opera house, in the southwest corner of Lincoln Center, is **Damrosch Park,** which hosts frequent outdoor concerts at its Guggenheim Bandshell, as well as the perennially popular **Big Apple Circus.** On the north side of the opera house, Henri Moore's 1965 *Lincoln Center Reclining Figure* reclines in the reflecting pool. Across the pool squats the **Vivian Beaumont Theater,** a tidy glass box under a heavy cement helmet, built by Eero Saarinen in 1965. Recent theatrical premieres here have included *Six Degrees of Separation* and *Arcadia.* **The New York Public Library for the Performing Arts** (870-1630) joins the opera house and the theater and holds over eight million items, from videotapes to manuscripts, all available for loan to anyone with a NYC library card. (Library open Mon., Thurs. noon-8pm, Tues.-Wed., Fri.-Sat. noon-6pm. See Essentials: Libraries, p. 15.)

The combined terrace and bridge leads across 66th St. to the halls of the prestigious **Juilliard School of Music,** Pietro Belluschi's Brutalist-inspired building. Here Itzhak Perlman and Pinchas Zukerman fine-tuned their skills, Robin Williams tried out his first comedy routines, and Val Kilmer learned to pout dramatically. For information on student concerts, call the Juilliard box office at 769-7406 (open Mon.-Thurs. 10am-5pm). There are no student performances during the summer. Within the Juilliard building complex is the intimate **Alice Tully Hall,** where the Chamber Music Society of Lincoln Center resides (see Entertainment and Nightlife: Classical Music, p. 267). To your left and about 200 feet away as you face Juilliard, a beige office building conceals Lincoln Center's newest offering, the **Walter E. Reade Theater.** Scan the schedule in the front window; the theater often features foreign films and special festivals (see Entertainment and Nightlife: Movies, p. 264).

Guided tours of Lincoln Center's theaters and galleries are offered daily (see Sightseeing Tours, p. 123).

■ The Rest of the Upper West

Columbus Circle, on Broadway at 59th St., is a bustling nexus of pedestrian and automobile traffic, marking the end of Midtown and the symbolic entrance to the Upper West Side (see Sights: West Midtown, p. 163). At 1865 Broadway near 61st St., the **Bible House** (408-1200), run by the American Bible Society, distributes the Good Book in nearly every tongue. Its exhibition gallery showcases rare and unorthodox Bibles, plus a smattering of Gutenberg pages and an on-line Good News Bible. (Gallery open Mon.-Fri. 9:30am-4:30pm; free. Library open Mon.-Fri. 9am-4:30pm. Bookstore open Mon.-Fri. 9am-5pm.)

Directly across from Lincoln Center, on a triangular plot just south of the intersection of Broadway and Columbus Ave., is **Dante Park,** designed in 1921 to commemorate the 600th anniversary of the poet's death. Presiding over the minuscule park is an imposing bronze of the man himself. Juilliard students often play jazz or chamber music here on Tuesdays at 6:30pm during the summer. Throughout the year, tired strollers or elderly people can be seen here sitting or feeding the pigeons.

The undistinguished modern façade of the **Museum of American Folk Art,** across from Lincoln Center, on Columbus Ave. between 65th and 66th St., gives way to a cool interior, where you can rest on a bench when you've had your fill of 18th-century quilts (see Museums, p. 249).

Edging Central Park, at 5 W. 63rd St., is the mammoth, Moorish-inspired **West Side Y** (787-4400, 787-1301), the nestling place of many a struggling young artist. A block up Central Park West at 2 W. 64th, the **New York Society for Ethical Culture** (874-5210) gives sporadic lectures, readings, and classical recitals for the intelligentsia. This venerable organization helped found many others, including the American Civil Liberties Union. The school is favored by many resident yuppies for the education of their young. One of New York City's **armories** holds down the fort at 56 W. 66th St., between Central Park West and Broadway; the turrets and battlements of the First

Battery of the New York National Guard now defend the ABC television studios hidden behind the Fisher-Price castle.

At 1 W. 67th St., poised between Central Park West and Columbus Ave., stands the stately **Hotel des Artistes,** a mass of luxury co-ops originally designed to house bohemians who had moved beyond their romantic garret stage. Built by George Mort Pollard in 1913, the building has quartered Isadora Duncan, Alexander Wollcott, Norman Rockwell, and Noel Coward. The opulence is mostly on the inside, but note the ivy-shaped exterior stonework. Here you will also find the chic **Café des Artistes.** The menu may be a little on the *cher* side, but the pastoral murals of reclining nudes, painted in 1934 by Howard Chandler Christy, are worth a peek.

The stone-hewn glory of Imperial Egypt meets the principles of streamlined design at **135 W. 70th St.,** between Columbus and Amsterdam Ave. This apartment house, the original home of the Knights of Pythias club, flaunts sapphire-blue columns with bearded men as capitals, as well as hawks whose lengthy wingspans are immediately recognizable to any Grateful Dead fan.

Constructed in 1970, the curvaceous, sunken **Lincoln Square Synagogue** (known in Jewish circles as "Wink and Stare" synagogue), at 69th St. and Amsterdam, is a granite cousin of Lincoln Center. The bow-tie-shaped **Sherman Square** knots at 72nd St. and Broadway. Unsurprisingly, a statue of Giuseppe Verdi presides over **Verdi Square,** on the northern half.

At 2109 Broadway between 73rd and 74th St., the famed **Ansonia Hotel,** *grande dame* of *belle* apartments, bristles with heavy ornaments, curved Veronese balconies, and towers. Its soundproof walls and thick floors enticed illustrious tenants like Enrico Caruso, Arturo Toscanini, and Igor Stravinsky. Theodore Dreiser did his own composing here, and Babe Ruth stayed just a few doors away.

A few blocks east are the stately apartment buildings that line Central Park West and contrast with the lively businesses of Broadway and Columbus Ave. As Manhattan's urbanization peaked in the late 19th century, wealthy residents sought tranquility in the elegant **Dakota Apartments,** 1 W. 72nd St. at Central Park West. When the apartment house was built in 1884, someone thought it was so remote from the heart of the city that "it might as well be in the Dakota Territory." The idea caught on and inspired the building's official name. Henry J. Hardenburg designed the luxury complex, which featured the first passenger elevators in the city and an ingenious design that made each apartment unique. John Lennon's streetside murder here in 1981 brought modern notoriety to the mammoth building.

Secure in their block-long neoclassical building, the staff of the **New York Historical Society,** at 77th St. and Central Park West (873-3400), will help you uncover obscure facts about the past or provide pop trivia about the present. The galleries reopened in the summer of 1995 after an economically necessitated hiatus. The library is open for scholarly pursuits Wednesday through Friday from noon to 5pm.

The **American Museum of Natural History,** at Central Park between 78th and 81st St., New York's celebration of evolution, is another of the Upper West Side's prized cultural treasures. J. C. Cady and Co. built the museum in 1899, though the original structure has since become surrounded by additions and new wings—its most recent renovation was concluded in 1995. Holden Caulfield used to hang out in the museum's Hayden Planetarium. The museum's patron saint Teddy Roosevelt is honored at the main entrance on Central Park West by a Beaux Arts triumphal arch and an embarrassingly unsavory sculpture of non-European peoples. The pre-modern meets the post-modern in the museum's excellent new dinosaur exhibit, which is currently reveling in the distinction of being one of the museum's most popular exhibits ever. (See Museums, p. 240 and *Catcher in the Rye*.)

Over on West End Ave., between 76th and 77th St., is a block of Victorian townhouses designed by master masons Lamb and Rich in 1891. It is rumored that graft king and former mayor Jimmy "Gentleman Jim" Walker's mistress once occupied an apartment at 76th and Broadway above the townhouses, and that the doting mayor had the block zoned off to stop construction on high-rises that might obscure the lovely view.

NEIGHBORHOODS

In 1637, Dutch settlers constructed the **West End Collegiate Church and School,** 370 West End Ave. at 77th St., as a reproduction of a market building in Holland. Robert Gibson overhauled it in 1893, using characteristically Dutch stepped gables and elongated bricks. Collegiate now preps the sons of New York's elite for the Ivy League lifestyle. Another prestigious prep school, the **Trinity School** at 139 West 91st St., dates from 1709 and boasts a similar heritage. Its marble-floored lobby is worth a quick visit.

With ornate iron gates and a spacious interior courtyard, the **Apthorp Apartments,** 2207 Broadway at 79th St., have starred in a number of New York-based films: *Heartburn, Network, Eyewitness, The Cotton Club, The Changeling, Rosemary's Baby,* and *The Money Pit.* Its simple marble facade features bas-relief vestal virgins, ensuring the good fortune of the affluent residents within. The apartments were built by Clinton and Russell in 1908 on a commission from William Waldorf Astor, who named them after the man who owned the site in 1763. Ask the guard to let you check out the courtyard. The lopsided spires across 79th St. belong to the First Baptist Church.

A few blocks up Broadway lie two icons of the Upper West Side lifestyle— **Zabar's,** 2245 Broadway, at 80th St. (787-2000), is the huge gourmet grocery of choice. Stop in to buy a bagel and walk out with enough gourmet treats to last you a week. **Shakespeare and Co.,** 2259 Broadway at 81st St. (580-7800), which at presstime was struggling to maintain its lease, has for many years garnered a fiercely loyal clientele. Its windows had a brief cameo in the romantic classic *When Harry met Sally* (See Shopping: Food Stores and Bookstores, "Shopping" on page 287).

The **West Park Presbyterian Church** has been a fixture at Amsterdam Ave. and 86th St. since 1890. It exhibits fine Romanesque styling, with a rough-hewn red sandstone surface that makes it look as if it just popped out of a clay oven. Strangely, Byzantine doorways and capitals top it off. On 86th St. at West End Ave. you'll also find the **Church of St. Paul and St. Andrew,** which dates from 1897. Check out the octagonal tower and the angels in the spandrels.

Central Park creator Frederick Law Olmsted's other green contribution to Manhattan, **Riverside Park,** stretches from 72nd to 145th St. along the Hudson River. As in the case of Central Park, Olmsted had a little help from Calvert Vaux. Directly across the intersection of Riverside Drive and 89th St., the **Soldiers and Sailors Monument,** more tomb than memorial, mourns the Union lives lost in the Civil War. **The Carrère Memorial,** a small terrace and plaque at 99th St., honors one of the city's great architects, John Merven Carrère, who died in an automobile accident. His partner Thomas Hastings designed the monument. Back east at 87th St., between Columbus Ave. and Central Park West, is another memorial: a brightly colored mural entitled "In Memory of Hector" (by "Chico").

Next to a vacant lot, at 175 W. 89th St. and Amsterdam Ave., stands the only surviving stable in Manhattan: the multi-story **Claremont Stables,** which serve as equine condos for high-pedigree horses and also offer riding lessons (see Horseback Riding, p. 286). Claremont riders can often be seen trotting alongside the cars on Central Park West, but the urbane Westsiders seem to take it in stride. The appropriately named **El Dorado Apartments,** on Central Park West between 90th and 91St, showcase flashy Art Deco detailing in a full array of golds. A national landmark, the lobby at the El Dorado is worth a stop, if you can convince the numerous security guards that you won't sneak a visit to the various stars who reside there.

Originally a skating rink, **Symphony Space,** 2537 Broadway at 95th St. has distinguished itself with brilliant if wacky programming. Their "Wall to Wall Bach" took a walk on the wild side, as did their gala birthday salute to the late avant-garde composer John Cage. Every Bloomsday (June 16) Symphony Space celebrates James Joyce's *Ulysses* with readings, lectures, and parties. The space also hosts a giant foreign-film fest each summer to complement its classical music, world-beat, and literary programs during the year; stop in for a monthly program (or ask to be added to their mailing list). (box office 864-5400/5414; open Thurs.-Sat. noon-7pm; tickets by phone Thurs.-Sat. noon-6pm) (see Classical Music, p. 267).

From the masters Carrère and Hastings comes the English Renaissance-style **First Church of Christ, Scientist,** on location at the corner of 96th St. and Central Park West. The exterior of the **Cliff Dwellers' Apartments** at Riverside and 96th St. features a marriage of Art Deco and Native American styles.

Throughout the Upper West Side, if not all over the city, apartment-dwellers have conspired to break the city's colorless monotony by planting and maintaining cozy, informal public gardens. Especially verdant, varied, and flowerful is the **Lotus Garden** (580-4897), up a flight of stairs on 97th St. between Broadway and West End Ave. You can sit on benches and admire the fat tulips on Sundays from 1-4pm.

If the old buildings of the Upper West Side make you nostalgic for things past, check out the **Broadway Barber Shop** at 2713 Broadway, between 103rd and 104th St. The gilt lettering on the windows has faded, but 1907 trappings, like the antique barber chairs and the storefront swizzle stick, remain.

■ Harlem

Half a million people are packed into the three square miles that make up greater Harlem. On the East Side above 96th St. lies **Spanish Harlem,** known as El Barrio (the neighborhood), and on the West Side lies Harlem proper, stretching from 110th to 155th St. West of Morningside Ave., and south of 125th St. is the Columbia University area, known more commonly as **Morningside Heights** than as a part of Harlem. On the West Side from 125th to 160th St. lies **Central Harlem,** where much of the cultural and social life of the area takes place, and to the far north, from 160th St. to 220th St., stand **Washington Heights** and **Inwood,** areas populated by thriving Dominican and Jewish communities. All these neighborhoods heat up with street activity, not always of the wholesome variety; visit Harlem during the day or with someone who knows the area. If you lack the street wisdom or can't find your own guide, opt for a commercial tour (see Sightseeing Tours, p. 123).

Yet it is a colossal (and frequent) misconception to let Harlem's problems overshadow its positive aspects. Although poorer than most neighborhoods, it is culturally rich; and, contrary to popular opinion, some of it is as safe as the rest of New York. Known as the "city within the City," Harlem is considered by many to be the black capital of the Western world. Over the years Harlem has entered the popular consciousness as the archetype of America's frayed cities, but you won't believe that hype after you've visited the place.

Harlem's rich history contributes to its prominence and attraction today. During most of the 19th century, West Harlem held the large country estates of affluent Manhattanites. When subway construction began in the 1890s, speculators built expensive housing in Harlem, anticipating an influx of middle-class residents. They never came. The owners rented the empty buildings to people who for the first time could obtain respectable New York housing. Over the next 30 years blacks flocked to Harlem by the thousands, more than doubling its population of 80,000 between 1920 and 1930 alone. As the population increased, culture flourished. The 1920s were Harlem's Renaissance: a thriving scene of musicians, writers, and scholars lived fast and loose, producing artistic masterworks in the process. The Cotton Club and the Apollo Theater, along with numerous other jazz clubs, were a part of the musical vanguard. Authors like Langston Hughes and Zora Neale Hurston wrote novels and poems that changed the face of literature. Harlem also supported a flourishing gay and lesbian underground in the 20s and 30s; they flocked to the clubs here, which were more tolerant than those downtown.

After the Depression and World War II, Harlem continued to thrive culturally, if not economically. Music fans of the 1950s could easily find themselves overwhelmed by the diversity of offerings. In one bar Charles Mingus would be strumming on his dancing bass; next door Charlie Parker would be blowing solos over the newest bebop tune from a hocked horn, while across the street Billie Holiday would be mellifluously reducing her audience to pools of tears. Many small jazz clubs still exist and are worth seeking out, despite the necessary extra legwork.

NEIGHBORHOODS

In the 1960s, riding the charged tidal wave of the Civil Rights movement that began in the South but quickly spread northward, the radical Black Power movement flourished here. The Revolutionary Theater of LeRoi Jones performed consciousness-raising one-act plays in the streets and Malcolm X, Stokely Carmichael, and H. Rap Brown spoke eloquently against racism and injustice. Recognizing the need for economic revitalization as a route to empowerment, members of the community began an attempt at redevelopment in the 1970s. This attempt continues today as the City pumps money into the area and communities bond together to beautify their neighborhood and actively resist crime. There is a definite strand of separatism in the current Harlem philosophy, as Malcolm X's teachings of self-empowerment gain increasing popularity, but it would be an exaggeration to say whites are wholly unwelcome here. You may feel somewhat like an outsider, especially in areas that don't see a lot of tourists, but many storeowners and residents are proud to have visitors and will go out of their way to make you feel welcome.

In fact, today's Harlem is home to a population that is increasingly diverse, both ethnically and socio-economically. In recent years, an influx of Dominicans has changed the culture of much of the western part of Harlem. **Hamilton Heights,** concentrated around St. Nicholas and Convent Ave. in the 140s, is home to professionals of all types. The stereotypical Harlem which attracts all the negative publicity is largely represented south of 125th St. in the Manhattan Valley, particularly along Frederick Douglass Ave. and Adam Clayton Powell Blvd.; you will want to avoid these avenues after dark. For more information on Harlem, call the Uptown Chamber of Commerce at 996-2288.

■ Morningside Heights and Columbia University

Morningside Heights, south of 125th St. and west of Morningside Park, is a good place to start a tour of the Harlem area (Subway: #1 or 9 to 110th St. or 116th St.). The neighborhood is filled with cheap, unassuming restaurants, but the area is also rich with marble memorials, monuments, and sights. Majestic and unfinished, the **Cathedral of St. John the Divine,** between 110th and 113th St. along Amsterdam Ave., is already the world's largest cathedral; when finished, it will break its own record. Construction, begun in 1892, still continues and is not expected to be completed for another century or two. You'll probably see sculptors working on the cathedral's gargoyles and fixtures as you walk by. At a stoneyard nearby, artisans carve blocks much as they would have in the age of the great medieval cathedrals. The original design called for a Byzantine church with some Romanesque ornamentation. Twenty years and several bishops later, Ralph Adams Cram drew up new designs that betrayed his admiration for the French Gothic. The façade resembles the cathedral of Notre Dame, with its centerpiece rose window, symmetrical twin towers, and heavy arched portals. The bronze door of the central portal was cast in Paris by M. Barbedienne, who also cast the Statue of Liberty (which would fit underneath the central dome of this church).

A "living cathedral," St. John's features naves dedicated not only to the sufferings of Christ, but to the beauty of abstract geometry and the experience of immigrants. Stained glass windows portray TV sets and George Washington as well as the usual religious scenes. Amble down the overwhelming central nave to see the altar dedicated to AIDS victims, a 100 million-year-old nautilus fossil, a modern sculpture for 12 firefighters who died in 1966, and a 2000-lb. natural quartz crystal. The cathedral also has a "Poet's Corner" dedicated to American literature and featuring the names of, and quotations from, writers such as Wharton, Faulkner, and Hawthorne. The church currently maintains an extensive secular schedule, hosting concerts, art exhibitions, lectures, theater, and dance events (for information call 316-7540). The complex also has a homeless shelter, a school, and countless other community services. Vertical tours of the church are given on the first and third Saturday of the month at noon and 2pm ($10; make reservations); regular horizontal tours Tues.-Sat. at 11am and Sunday

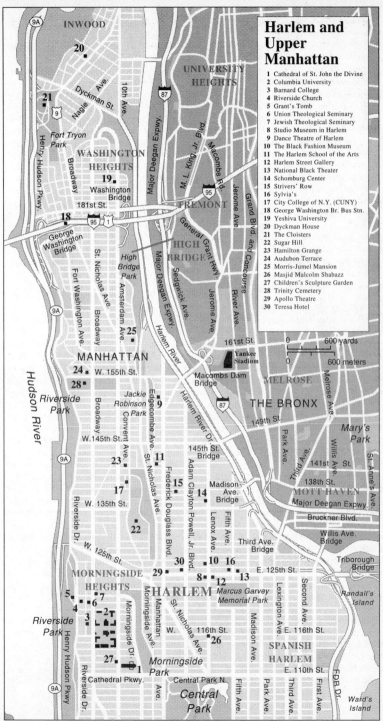

Harlem and Upper Manhattan

1 Cathedral of St. John the Divine
2 Columbia University
3 Barnard College
4 Riverside Church
5 Grant's Tomb
6 Union Theological Seminary
7 Jewish Theological Seminary
8 Studio Museum in Harlem
9 Dance Theatre of Harlem
10 The Black Fashion Museum
11 The Harlem School of the Arts
12 Harlem Street Gallery
13 National Black Theater
14 Schomburg Center
15 Strivers' Row
16 Sylvia's
17 City College of N.Y. (CUNY)
18 George Washington Br. Bus Stn.
19 Yeshiva University
20 Dyckman House
21 The Cloisters
22 Sugar Hill
23 Hamilton Grange
24 Audubon Terrace
25 Morris-Jumel Mansion
26 Masjid Malcolm Shabazz
27 Children's Sculpture Garden
28 Trinity Cemetery
29 Apollo Theatre
30 Teresa Hotel

at 1pm (church open daily 7am-5pm; tours $3; call 932-7347; admission $1, students and seniors 50¢).

Next to the cathedral, the **Children's Sculpture Garden,** at 111th St. and Amsterdam Ave., is crowned by a huge, grotesque fountain of a winged warrior on a smiling disc that explodes with spiraling jets of water. The Ring of Freedom surrounds the fountain, topped with small bronze sculptures created annually by schoolchildren. The little bronze plaques which surround the garden include historical footnotes written by children about fable-teller Aesop's escape from slavery, the Spaniard Goya's commitment to social action through art, and similar tales of pancultural help (open 24 hr., but safest during the daytime).

To the east of St. John's, down the cliffs from Morningside Dr., lies **Morningside Park,** a bit of greenery stretching from 110th to 123rd St. Featured in *When Harry Met Sally,* this sloping park offers a recreational space and rambling paths where you too can discuss your sexual fantasies. The wooded park is not very safe, however, especially at night.

New York City's member of the Ivy League, **Columbia University,** chartered in 1754, is tucked between Morningside Dr. and Broadway, stretching from 114th to 120th St. Now co-ed, Columbia also has cross-registration with all-female **Barnard College,** across Broadway. The centerpiece of this elevated, urban campus is the magisterial Low Library, named after former Columbia president Seth Low. Daniel Chester French's statue of Alma Mater, stationed on the front steps of the building, became a rallying point during the riots of 1968. The small, green quad in front of the library is a good place to find a game of ultimate frisbee or pick-up soccer on just about any sunny, weekend day. Group tours are given to prospective students from late fall through spring, but there are no regularly scheduled tours for the public during the year (you must call ahead to make an appointment). Call 854-2842 for information or to schedule a tour.

Near Columbia, at 120th St. and Riverside Dr., is the **Riverside Church.** This steel-framed Gothic structure sprang up in only two years thanks to the powerful pockets of John D. Rockefeller, Jr. Its well known pastor, William Sloane Coffin, uses his pulpit to champion the struggle for civil rights and the fight against AIDS (he was once a leading crusader against the war in Vietnam). The observation deck in the tower commands an amazing view of the bells within and the expanse of the Hudson River and Riverside Park below. Or you can hear concerts on the world's largest carillon (74 bells, Sunday afternoons at 2:30pm), another gift of Mr. Rockefeller, Jr. (Open Tues.-Sat. 11am-4pm; admission to observation deck Mon.-Sat. $1, Sun. $2; Sun. service 10:45am; free church tours given Sun. 12:30pm.)

Diagonally across Riverside Dr. lies **Grant's Tomb** (666-1640). The massive granite mausoleum, once covered with graffiti but now under renovation, rests in peace atop a hill overlooking the river. Inside, the black marble sarcophagus of ("who's buried in Grant's tomb?") Ulysses S. Grant and his wife Julia are surrounded by bronze casts of the general's cronies. Informal and individualized ranger-guided tours are available upon request and can last anywhere from 5 to 90 minutes, depending on how many questions you ask. (Open daily 9am-5pm; free.) Take a rest on the whimsically tacky mosaic tile benches around the monument, added in the mid-70s.

A walk down Broadway affords a wide assortment of college-catering bookstores, grocery stores, and restaurants, including the famous **Tom's Restaurant** (864-6137) at 2880 Broadway, which has been featured in an inescapable remix by Suzanne Vega and many, many episodes of *Seinfeld* (see Food & Drink, p. 79).

■ Central Harlem

125th Street, also known as Martin Luther King Jr. Boulevard, spans the heart of traditional Harlem (Subway: #2, 3, A, B, C, or D to 125th St.). Fast-food joints, jazz bars, and the **Apollo Theatre,** at 253 W. 125th St. (222-0992, box office 749-5838), keep the street humming day and night. 125th has recently resurged as a center of urban life; street vendors, small shops, and families with children have combined to make this part of Harlem a lively community center and cultural hub.

Most of the streets around here have been renamed. Sixth Ave. is now Lenox Ave. but is also known as Malcolm X Blvd. Seventh Ave. is Adam Clayton Powell, Jr. Blvd., and Eighth Ave. is Frederick Douglass Blvd.

The recently built **Adam Clayton Powell, Jr., State Office Building,** at 163 W. 125th St. between Lenox Ave. and Powell Blvd., has brought bureaucratic life to 125th St. The building also sponsors speakers and films of relevance to the community. The **Studio Museum in Harlem** rests at 144 W. 125th St. (see Museums, p. 251). The former **Teresa Hotel,** at the northwest corner of 125th St. and Powell Ave., has housed Malcolm X and Fidel Castro, who once preached solidarity and brotherhood to the people of Harlem from these balconies. An unconventional tourist, Castro felt safer in Harlem than in other parts of New York; still, charmingly paranoid, he transported live Cuban chickens for his meals. Off 125th St., at 328 Lenox Ave., **Sylvia's** (966-0660) has been the "Queen of Soul Food" for over 20 years (see Eating and Drinking, p. 95). The silver dome of the **Masjid Malcolm Shabazz,** where Malcolm X was once a minister, glitters on 116th St. at Lenox Ave. (visit Fri. at 1pm and Sun. at 10am for services and information, or call 662-2200).

A walk up Lenox Ave. often yields an intriguing slice of Harlem life. Teenagers, families, and older professionals all mingle on the wide sidewalks. Older residents sit on stoops and watch the world whiz by. There's an incredibly large number of people on the streets at all times of day. The **Liberation Bookstore,** 421 Lenox Ave. at 131st St., has a great selection of African and African-American history, art, poetry, and fiction (open Mon.-Fri. 11am-7pm, Sat. 11:30am-6:30pm). Nearby at 132nd and Lenox Ave. is the **Lenox Terrace Apartment complex** where many black politicians live, including Percy Sutton. On 135th St. and Lenox Ave., the **Schomburg Center,** a branch of the public library, houses the city's African archives and presents exhibits of local artists' work (see Museums, p. 251 and Essentials: Libraries, p. 15). The #2 and 3 subway lines run up Lenox Ave. from 125th to 135th St.

Just north, at 132 W. 138th St. between Lenox Ave. and Powell Blvd., is New York's oldest African-American church, the **Abyssinian Baptist Church.** It was at one time presided over by the ubiquitous congressman Adam Clayton Powell, Jr. The church has 14,000 members and the pastor, Calvin Butts, is a well known local political leader. A notable upper-class Harlem neighborhood is one block west, on 138th St. between Powell and Douglass Blvd. **Striver's Row,** consisting mainly of brownstones, was built by David King in 1891. Three different architects designed these buildings, now part of the St. Nicholas Historic District. Spike Lee filmed *Jungle Fever* here and Bob Dylan owns a house on this street.

Farther west, across St. Nicholas Park, is the **City College,** at 138th St. and Convent Ave. (650-5310). The northernmost outpost of the City University of New York, it sports an odd mix of Gothic and 70s-esque architecture. The college had an open admissions policy since its 1849 founding and was populated primarily by Jewish students until after World War II. Today the school, which has no dorms, educates mostly commuter students from the city. The less appealing south campus lies between 130th and 135th St. The college can be reached by walking up Morningside/Convent Ave. from 125th St. or by taking the #1 or 9 subway to 137th St. and walking two blocks east.

Just north of the college, along Convent Ave. between 140th and 145th St., is **Hamilton Heights,** home to many upper-middle-class black families living in some of the city's most intricately designed brownstones. Walk down Hamilton Terrace, which is between Convent and St. Nicholas Ave., for a good example of these homes. Alexander Hamilton built his two-story Colonial-style country home, **Hamilton Grange,** at what is now 287 Convent Ave. (283-5154), at 141st St. (open Wed.-Sun. 9am-4pm; free). The National Park Service wants to restore the house to its original state and make it a bona fide national landmark; if funding comes through, the house will be moved to nearby St. Nicholas Park. Up a couple of blocks, **Sugar Hill,** which stretches from 143rd to 155th St. between St. Nicholas and Edgecombe Ave., was at

NEIGHBORHOODS

one time home to some of the city's wealthiest and most important gangsters and was recently the setting for the film *Sugar Hill.* Today the neighborhood is better known for the Sugarhill Gang, the rap act that emerged from its streets in 1979 to release the first rap crossover success, "Rapper's Delight." These areas can be reached by the A, B, C, or D subway to 145th St. West of Amsterdam Ave., the neighborhood becomes predominantly Dominican. Spanish is the language of choice here and a business here even runs a $60 express bus to Miami.

Farther north at Broadway and 155th St. are the four buildings in **Audubon Terrace,** the Beaux Arts complex that houses the **Numismatic Society Museum,** the **Hispanic Society of America,** the **American Academy of Arts and Letters** (see Museums, p. 246), and **Boricua College,** a private Hispanic liberal arts college. The Italian Renaissance courtyard has huge reliefs and sculptures. Diagonally across Broadway, you can wander around the **Trinity Cemetery,** between 153rd and 155th St., and Amsterdam Ave. and Riverside Dr. (take the #1 subway to 157th St. or the A or B subway to 155th St.). John James Audubon's grave is near the Church of the Intercession. John Jacob Astor and ex-mayor Fernando Wood are also rumored to be buried here. Exercise caution visiting the cemetery, especially if alone.

Farther west and across the West Side Hwy. is the newly-opened **Riverbank State Park.** In 1993 the state decided to put a sewage plant here, an act which many members of the African-American community considered racist, so Governor Cuomo decided that a state-run park would be built over the new plant. The park, with year-round ice-skating, an indoor pool, tennis, tracks, roller-skating rinks, baseball diamonds, and picnic fields, is extremely popular. The funny odor you detect is tidewater—honest. Call 694-3643 or 694-3610 for times and rates of the various activities. The M11 bus runs directly into the park, as does the Bx11, which also runs to the Bronx Zoo. The #9 subway to 145th St. and the #1 or 9 subway to 157th St. will also take you near the park.

■ Spanish Harlem

East Harlem, better known as **Spanish Harlem** or El Barrio ("The Neighborhood"), hugs the northeast corner of Central Park and extends to the 140s, where it is bounded by the Harlem River. At the main artery on 116th St., the streets bustle with people selling fruit, shirts, and diverse sorts of chow. The famous "ice man" cometh and flavors ground-up ice with mango, papaya, coconut, or banana syrup to save you from the summer heat (50¢-$1). Anti-crack murals and memorials to the drug's victims adorn the walls. Spanish Harlem north of 110th St. is only safe on certain streets; areas below 110th are usually safe during the day. The northern tip of Fifth Ave.'s Museum Mile stretches up to the **Museum of the City of New York** at 103rd St. and **El Museo del Barrio** at 105th St. (see p. 249).

■ Washington Heights

Once upon a time the area north of 155th St., known as Washington Heights, was an all-Irish enclave, but the sounds of rhumba and calypso soon drowned out those of the fife and drum as Puerto Ricans and Latin Americans began to claim the neighborhood for their own. Blacks, Greeks, Armenians, and a large Jewish community subsequently moved in. Unfortunately, the newest noise is the police siren: crack, cocaine, and other drugs have begun to litter the Heights' urban landscape. Nevertheless, the residents of Washington Heights continue to take pride in their neighborhood; the first **Washington Heights & Innwood Week** was held in October of 1996. The festival included oral history workshops, folk dance, food festivals, and photo exhibitions honoring this multi-ethnic community.

During the day, Washington Heights affords a taste of urban life with a thick ethnic flavor. On the same block, you can eat a Greek dinner, buy Armenian pastries and vegetables from a South African, and discuss the Talmud with a student at nearby Yeshiva University. These communities are very tight and, in some ways, exclusive;

most tourists don't venture up this far. Throughout much of the area, you'll see signs in Spanish or in Hebrew, without English translations; many of the residents here have never spoken—or even found it necessary to speak—English. You may feel like an outsider, but that shouldn't stop you from exploring this neighborhood and all that it has to offer.

Bargain-shop along trinket-filled St. Nicholas Ave. or Broadway. Street vendors sell swimwear, Italian shoes, and household items for half the original price. You can find discount electronics stores here too. Prices fall as the street numbers rise.

The Georgian **Morris-Jumel Mansion,** at 65 Jumel Terrace, between 160th and 162nd St. (923-8008), was built in 1765 and is Manhattan's oldest existing house. Washington lived here while planning his successful (but little-known) Battle of Harlem Heights in the autumn of 1776. In 1810, Stephen and Eliza Jumel bought the house; Eliza seems to have spent most of her time primping, as seen by the vast numbers of parlors and dressing rooms in the house. Stephen died in 1832 and in 1833 Eliza up and married Aaron Burr in the front room. Don't be afraid to knock if the house seems closed (open Wed.-Sun. 10am-4pm; $3, seniors and students $1, children under 12 free; tours Tues.-Fri.; take the A or B subway to 163rd St.). The gardens are exceptional as well, with a great view of the Harlem River. Nearby, at St. Nicholas Ave. and 161st St. (take the A or B subway to 163rd St.), more brownstones with architecturally varied façades vie for attention on **Sylvan Terrace,** at 161st St.

Columbia University recently ignited a controversy when it decided to buy the abandoned **Audubon Ballroom** on 165th St. between St. Nicholas Ave. and Broadway. The ballroom was the site of Malcolm X's assassination; protesters have covered the doorway with plaques calling for a memorial to the Black Power advocate. Nonetheless, all that remains now is the front façade.

You can either walk to Broadway and up to 178th St. or take the A train to 181st St. to view the **George Washington Bridge Bus Station** on 178th St. between Broadway and Fort Washington Ave. It resembles a huge Christmas tree cookie-cutter. The **George Washington Bridge** heads west and across the Hudson from the station. Constructed in 1931 by Othmar Amman, this 14-lane, 3500-foot suspension bridge was once pronounced "the most beautiful bridge in the world" by Le Corbusier. Just beneath the bridge, accessible by steps from the intersection of 181st St. and Pinehurst, lies **Fort Washington Park,** home to the **Little Red Lighthouse** and the remnants of the original fort. Originally constructed to steer barges away from Jeffrey's Hook, the lighthouse became the thinly disguised subject of Hildegarde Hoyt Swift's obscure children's book *The Little Red Lighthouse and the Great Grey Bridge.*

Back on Amsterdam Ave., from 182nd to 186th St., stands **Yeshiva University,** surrounded by kosher bakeries and butcher shops. This is the oldest Jewish-studies center in the U.S., dating from 1886. The **Yeshiva University Museum** (960-5390) on 185th St. features exhibits concerning the Jewish community (open Tues.-Thurs. 10:30am-5pm, Sun. noon-6pm, or call for appointment. Admission $3, seniors and children under 17 $1.50). **Tannenbaum Hall** is the centerpiece of the campus at 186th St., featuring Romanesque windows and colorful minarets. Take the #1 or 9 train to 181st or 190th St.

Five blocks west along 181st St. leads to the gently (and not-so-gently) sloping hill that is Fort Washington Ave. The journey north along Fort Washington Ave. takes you past a succession of mid-rise apartment buildings (c. 1920), home to Jewish and Hispanic families. At 190th St. and Ft. Washington Ave., the **St. Francis Xavier Cabrini Chapel** shelters the remains of Mother Cabrini, the patron saint of immigrants. Her fleshy body lies in a crystal casket under the altar, but her smiling face is made of wax—Rome has her head. Ack. Legend has it that shortly after her death, a lock of her hair restored the eyesight of an infant who has since grown up to be a Texan priest (open Tues.-Sun. 9am-4:30pm). One more block down is Margaret Corbin Circle and the official (and safest) entrance to **Fort Tryon Park,** lovingly landscaped by Central Park's Frederick Law Olmsted. John D. Rockefeller donated this land to the city in exchange for permission to construct Rockefeller University. You can still see the crusty remains of Fort Tryon, a Revolutionary War bulwark. The park also contains a magnificent expanse of gardens and **The Cloisters,** the Met's sanctuary for medieval art (see Museums, p. 247). This is one of the most peaceful sights in Manhattan and is worth the trip even if you don't have a taste for medieval art. To get to the Cabrini Chapel or Ft. Tryon Park by subway, take the A train to 190th St., then take the elevator up from the station; otherwise, you'll end up at the base of a less lovingly landscaped mountain.

At Broadway and 204th St. stands a modest but charming 18th-century Dutch dwelling. Donated to the city as a museum in 1915, **Dyckman Farmhouse Museum** (304-9422), which is the only remaining 18th-century farmhouse in Manhattan, has been restored and filled with period Dutch and English family furnishings (open Tues.-Sun. 11am-4pm; free. Subway: A to Dyckman or 207th St.).

Washington Heights and neighboring Inwood can be safe on one block and plagued by crack dealers on the next. It's best to reach the neighborhood by the A train, which will bring you closer to the intriguing sights than will the #1 or 9 trains.

■ Brooklyn

If the borough of Brooklyn left New York City, it would become America's fourth largest city. As the two and a quarter million residents would tell you, Brooklyn can and does exist as an independent entity—one well worth the visit. Brooklyn's collection of ethnically diverse neighborhoods fascinates the imagination and is often mythologized and commemorated in literature, song, and film. If you need an escape from tourist-infested Manhattan, it may be time to explore the streets of the borough called Brooklyn. Always a gregarious town, Brooklyn is perfect for an adventurous stroll—what goes on here tends to go on outdoors, be it neighborhood banter, baseball games in the park, ethnic festivals, or gang violence.

When some romantics ponder Brooklyn, they conjure up images of the rough stickball players who grew up to be the one and only Dodgers, or think of Woody Allen's boyhood home, presided over by his raucous mother and stubby aunt under the roller coaster in *Annie Hall.* The communities that gave rise to these now-nostalgic images remain (and someone still lives in the house under Coney Island's now-defunct Thunderbolt Rollercoaster), but Brooklyn has many more faces, and a visit to each one yields a rich and rewarding look into urban life, from the ultra-orthodox Hasidim of Crown Heights to the wealthy black bohemia of Fort Greene (home of filmmaker Spike Lee). Recently, Eighth Ave. in Sunset Park has become Brooklyn's Chinatown, and reasonable loft rents in Williamsburg has brought in ambitious droves of struggling artists.

Brooklyn's pride in its distinct culture has deep historical roots. The Dutch originally settled the borough in the 17th century. Although Brits shared the land, Dutch culture flourished well into the early 19th century. When asked to join New York in 1833, Brooklyn refused, saying that the two cities shared no interests except common waterways. Not until 1898 did Brooklyn decide, in a close vote, to become a borough of New York City.

ORIENTATION

Brooklyn's main avenues dissect the borough. The Brooklyn-Queens Expressway pours into the Belt Parkway and circumscribes Brooklyn. Ocean Parkway, Ocean Ave., Coney Island Ave., and diagonal Flatbush Ave. run from the beaches of southern Brooklyn to Prospect Park in the heart of the borough. Flatbush Ave. eventually leads to the Manhattan Bridge. The streets of western Brooklyn (including those in Sunset Park, Bensonhurst, Borough Park, and Park Slope) are aligned with the western shore and thus collide at a 45-degree angle with central Brooklyn's main arteries. In northern Brooklyn, several avenues—Atlantic Ave., Eastern Parkway, and Flushing Ave.—travel from downtown far east into Queens.

Brooklyn is also spliced by subway lines. Most lines serving the borough pass through the Atlantic Ave. Station downtown. The D and Q lines continue southeast through Prospect Park and Flatbush to Brighton Beach. The #2 and 5 trains head east to Brooklyn College in Flatbush. The B and N trains travel south through Bensonhurst, terminating in Coney Island. The J, M, and Z trains serve Williamsburg and Bushwick and continue east and north into Queens. The Brooklyn-Queens crosstown G train shuttles from southern Brooklyn through Greenpoint into Queens. For maps and other material on Brooklyn, visit the **Fund for the Borough of Brooklyn,** 16 Court St. (subway #2, 3, 4, 5, M, or R to Borough Hall; 718-855-7882), near Montague St. The MTA also provides maps of the entire city transit system (including Brooklyn) which are available in every city station.

■ Brooklyn Bridge

Walking a mile across the **Brooklyn Bridge** at sunrise or sunset is one of the most exhilarating strolls New York City has to offer. The bridge that gracefully spans the gap between Lower Manhattan's dense skyscraper cluster and Brooklyn's less intimidating shore is considered by many to be the world's most beautiful. Georgia O'Keeffe and Joseph Stella have memorialized this triumph of technology and aesthetics on canvas, and Walt Whitman expressed his admiration through verse. (Subway 4, 5, or 6 to Brooklyn Bridge/City Hall.) A ramp across from City Hall begins the journey from Manhattan.

The setting sun weaving through shifting grids of suspension cables combines with the majestic Gothic arches for a powerful architectural experience, heightened by the rush of cars below and the cyclists and rollerbladers whizzing by in the right lane. Iron rungs lead to the top of the bridge, but neither the law nor extreme danger deters a fearless few from occasionally climbing to the top.

The arched towers of New York's suspended cathedral, the greatest engineering achievement of an age, loomed far above the rest of the city when completed in 1883, the product of engineering wizardry and 15 years of steady work. After chief architect John Augustus Roebling crushed his foot in a surveying accident and died of gangrene, Roebling's son Washington (and subsequently Washington's wife Emily Warren, after he succumbed to the bends) took over the management of the job. In the end, the trio achieved a combination of delicacy and power that made other New York bridges look cumbersome or flimsy. Plaques at either end of the walkway commemorate the Roeblings and 20 workers who died during construction. You'll notice the piers and warehouses of Brooklyn's waterfront stretching ahead; behind spreads the cityscape that puts all others to shame.

Like all great bridges, this one has had its share of post-construction deaths as well. A few days after its opening, a frantic mob feared the bridge was collapsing and trampled 12 pedestrians to death in their struggle to escape. A Mr. Brody leaped off the bridge in 1920, marking the first suicide. Locals say if only he had tucked and rolled, dived and not belly flopped, he might have lived.

■ Downtown Brooklyn

Start a tour of downtown Brooklyn at the Atlantic Ave. subway station (#2, 3, 4, 5, D, and Q) or the Pacific Street station (B, M, N, and R). The **Williamsburg Savings Bank,** at the corner of Flatbush Ave. and Hanson Place, is Brooklyn's tallest building at 512 feet. The building was completed in 1929 and has a splendid Romanesque interior with arches, pillars, patterned marble floors, and a gold and green tiled ceiling. A huge painting of the sun shines down on Brooklyn while a blackened Manhattan lurks in the shadows (open Mon. and Thurs.-Fri. 8:30am-9pm, Tues.-Wed. 9am-3pm). Walk up Flatbush Ave. a few blocks to Fulton St. and take a left. The stretch of Fulton St. to Borough Hall is now called **Fulton Mall.** The eight blocks were renamed in the 70s in an effort to spark investment in the disintegrating street that had been Brooklyn's main commercial thoroughfare in the 30s and 40s. Instead of the department stores of yesteryear, Fulton Street is now known for smaller, cheaper stores with bargains galore on clothes, shoes, and electronics. The mall gets as crowded as any Manhattan street; you can mingle and enjoy the bustle.

NEIGHBORHOODS

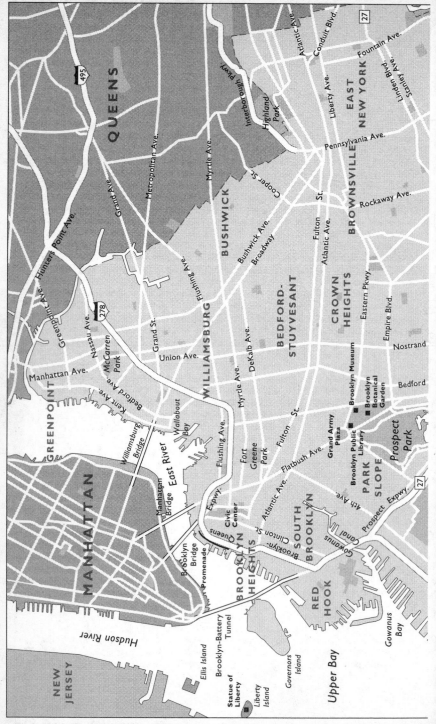

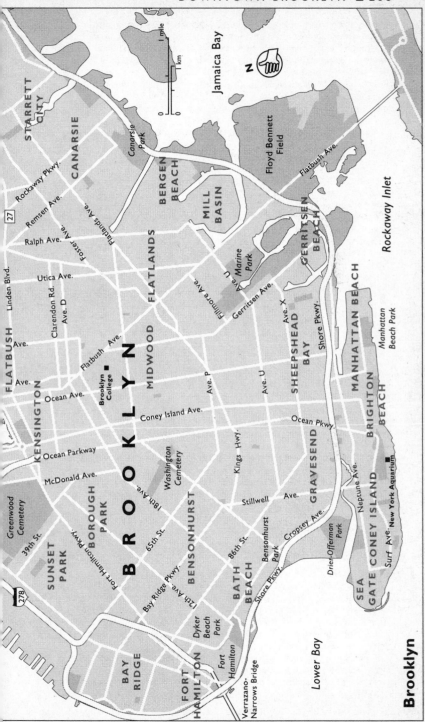

Brooklyn

Over to the north, along DeKalb Ave., lies **Fort Greene.** A vibrant and financially secure group of blacks and other minorities compose the upscale multicultural neighborhood of Fort Greene. The community is bounded by the Navy yard and Atlantic Ave. on the north and south, and Flatbush Ave. Extension and Clinton Ave. on the east and west. A stroll down DeKalb will take you past Afro-centric stores, pleasant **Fort Greene Park** (designed by the Central Park duo of Olmstead and Vaux), and right to **Spike's Joint,** filmmaker Spike Lee's boutique (see p. 294). Lee makes his home here, as do many powerful art and entertainment figures contributing to Fort Greene's pan-ethnic renaissance.

Back at the end of Fulton Mall, Fulton St. turns into Joralemon St. **Borough Hall** sits to your right at 209 Joralemon St. This eclectic Victorian/Greek Revival hulk, built in 1851, once housed the city hall of an independent Brooklyn and is now the oldest building in Brooklyn (tours Tues. at 1pm). If you walk to the opposite side of the building, into **Columbus Park,** you can see that the figure Justice, standing firmly with scales and sword on top of the hall, isn't wearing a blindfold. Cynics may find this peculiarity significant.

Just north of Borough Hall, past the statue of Columbus and a bust of Robert Kennedy, is the **New York State Supreme Court.** The building lies at the southern end of **Cadman Plaza Park,** a long stretch of greenery extending from Columbus Park to the Brooklyn Bridge. The Romanesque Revival lives on at the granite **Brooklyn General Post Office,** 271 Cadman Plaza East, between Tillary and Johnson St. At the northern end of the park is the **Brooklyn War Memorial.**

As Cadman Plaza Park ends at the entrance to the Brooklyn Bridge, Cadman Plaza West becomes Old Fulton St. and runs down to the waterfront, where you can catch a throat-parching view of Manhattan. The **Eagle Warehouse and Storage Co.,** 28 Old Fulton St. at Front St., once housed Walt Whitman's *Brooklyn Eagle* and has been converted into apartments.

This neighborhood, known as **DUMBO** (Down Under the Manhattan Bridge Overpass), consists largely of industrial warehouse spaces with "For Lease or Sale" signs on their doors. Some of these spaces have been taken over by Brooklyn's volunteer artist militias, who have converted them into galleries. For example, the building at 135 Plymouth St. and Anchorage St. houses several makeshift galleries, including the **Ammo Exhibitions Space.** Another gallery, the **Brooklyn Anchorage,** is housed within the bridge suspension cable storage chambers at Front St. 1996 saw large-scale multimedia installations making good use of the 80-foot-high vaulted ceilings (open mid-May to mid-Oct. Thurs.-Sun. noon-6pm). Recently, landlords of buildings in DUMBO have tried to squeeze artists out in favor of more upscale renters. As the fear of gentrification grows, locals have banded together in an attempt to maintain the low-rent atmosphere. At the northern end of Main St., between the Manhattan and Brooklyn Bridges, reposes the **Empire-Fulton-Ferry State Park,** a pleasant, grassy, waterfront area. The DUMBO neighborhood is largely deserted, even during the day, except for a steady stream of slow, lumbering trucks; after dark, there is no reason to visit.

■ Brooklyn Heights

In 1814, when the invention of the steamboat made development in Brooklyn Heights possible, rows of now-posh Greek Revival and Italianate houses sprang up. The shady lanes of New York's first suburb were later targeted for preservation, and in 1965 Brooklyn Heights became New York's—and the nation's—first Historic District. Brooklyn Heights is just west of Cadman Plaza Park and south of Old Fulton St. Today the brownstones of the 19th century house the young, upwardly mobile set and a diverse collection of families.

Beneath the plain brick facade of **111 Court Street,** near the Court St. subway stop, lies an historic apartment building, home to various dancers, writers, and filmmakers through the years. The enclave now acts as headquarters of such artistic up-and-comers as the *Spider Arts Alliance* and the 'zine *Indignant Gingham.*

Atlantic Ave. is the place to sample Middle Eastern food. Aside from the many restaurants, **Sahadi Importing Company,** 187 Atlantic Ave., stocks an immense and delicious array of Middle Eastern groceries and prepared foods and is open Monday through Saturday from 9am to 7pm (see Miscellaneous Food Stores, p. 115). From Atlantic Ave., take a right onto Hicks St. for a stroll through the heart of historic Brooklyn. A few blocks down, **Grace Church,** 254 Hicks St. at Grace Ct., is bedecked with Tiffany windows depicting the life of Christ. Across from the church, **Grace Court Alley,** a cul-de-sac intended for the motorless transport of the well-to-do, is flanked by elegant apartments that recall a time when the pleasures of the bourgeoisie were simpler.

A left on Henry St., followed by a right on Montague St., will take you to **St. Ann and the Holy Trinity Episcopal Church** (718-834-8794), on the corner of Clinton St. The church is currently undergoing extensive restoration; call about the availability of tours. This is the first church in America to have painted and stained-glass windows; at present, it contains over 4000 square feet of glass. An alternative high school is run out of the church, which is also quite a cultural center; **Arts at St. Ann's** (718-858-2424) is based here and brings performers like Lou Reed and Marianne Faithfull to the acoustically superb space.

Take a left on Clinton St. to get to Pierrepont St., which is parallel to Montague St. and Remsen St. At 128 Pierrepont St. stands the **Brooklyn Historical Society** (718-624-0890), housed in a striking building lined with spooky gargoyle-busts of Shakespeare, Beethoven, and others. There is a museum and a research library here for those interested in the esoterica of the borough (718-624-0890; museum open Tues.-Sat. noon-5pm; admission $2, seniors and children under 12 $1; Wed. free).

Pierrepont St. leads directly to the **Promenade** (also known as the Esplanade). This waterfront walkway, which spans from Remsen St. to Orange St., also serves as the roof of the toxic Brooklyn-Queens expressway. The view of lower Manhattan exceeds the descriptive and evocative powers of all puny adjectives. To the left, the Statue of Liberty can be seen peeping out from behind Staten Island. In fair weather, Ellis Island appears in full view, to the right of Liberty Island. The large green protrusion at the southernmost tip of Manhattan is the Staten Island Ferry terminal. The bright-orange ferry can be seen crossing back and forth regularly (see Sights: Staten Island, p. 227). A walk along the Promenade affords a refreshing breath of sea air mixed with less invigorating carbon monoxide from the cars zipping by below. During the day, continue on to the Brooklyn Bridge for the mile-long walk into Manhattan. Many commuters prefer exercise, a view, and extra pocket change; they walk to work across the bridge.

To see the potpourri of 19th-century styles that developed in Brooklyn and that have come to represent U.S. architecture of that period, check out **Willow Street** between Clark and Pierrepont St. Numbers 155-159, in the Federal style, were the earliest houses here (c. 1825), with dormer windows punctuating the sloping roofs. The hand-hammered leadwork and small glass panes are part of the original doorways. Greek Revival fans should rally to the stone entrances of No. 101 and 103 (c. 1840) and the iron railings on No. 118-22. Numbers 108-12, built by William Halsey Wood in 1884, are Queen Anne-style houses where stone, stained glass, and slate have been pushed to their limits.

Continue along Willow and take a right on Orange St. to the **Plymouth Church of Pilgrims** (718-624-4743). The simple red-brick church is set with stained-glass windows by Lamb Studios, the oldest glass studio in America. The church was the center of New Yorker abolitionist sentiments before the Civil War under the leadership of its first minister, Henry Ward Beecher. His statue sits in the courtyard alongside a bas-relief of Abraham Lincoln, who visited the church. The Tiffany windows from an earlier church now reside in the modern church's Hillis Hall.

To get to Brooklyn Heights, follow Court St. from the Court St./Borough Hall station (or take the High St.-Brooklyn Bridge A,C subway and walk across Cadman Plaza).

NEIGHBORHOODS

■ Carroll Gardens and Red Hook

Just south of Atlantic Ave., centered around Court St., is a thriving Italian neighborhood. **Cobble Hill,** whose sidestreets are lined with gorgeous brownstones, stretches a few blocks down and segues into **Carroll Gardens.** The high Italian population here is evidenced by the numerous pasta and pastry shops lining Court St.**—old Italian guys** sit in lawn chairs and **chew the fat** in their native tongue—this was the location for much of *Moonstruck.* Many Manhattanites have recently made the move to Carroll Gardens, but with any luck such gentrification will not spell the end of Brooklyn's Little Italy. Stroll down Court St. to browse in the area's boutiques or to dine in its best restaurants. Carroll Park, a tiny postage stamp of a park, overflows with frolicking children on Court St. between President and Carroll St.

To the west, on the other side of the expressway, is the industrial waterfront area of **Red Hook.** Head west on Atlantic Ave. to the docks. On your right hovers one of the **Watchtower buildings,** which house the world headquarters of the Jehovah's Witness organization. Head south (left) on Columbia St. over trolley tracks and cobblestones. Follow the truck route signs one block west to Van Brunt St. From the end of this street, deep in Red Hook, you can take in a dazzling view of the harbor and the Statue of Liberty. If you turn around and take a right on Beard St., you will pass a number of lovely decaying industrial complexes. An ensuing left on Columbia St. followed by a right on Bay St. will bring you to a football field that draws young crowds for pick-up soccer games and white-clad Haitian immigrants for cricket. The Red Hook housing projects are just north of here. Avoid these sidestreets at night.

■ North Brooklyn

Nestled at the northern border with Queens, **Greenpoint** is the seat of an active Polish community (Subway: E or F to Queens Plaza, then G to Greenpoint Ave.). Manhattan Ave. intersects Greenpoint Ave. at the subway station and is at the heart of the neighborhood's bustling business district. Just west of Manhattan Ave.—bounded by Java St. to the north, Meserole St. to the south, and Franklin St. to the west—is the **Greenpoint Historic District.** The Italianate and Grecian houses were built in the 1850s, when Greenpoint was the home of a booming shipbuilding industry. The Union's iron-clad *Monitor,* which defeated the Confederacy's *Merrimac,* was built here. The historic district is hidden among the aluminum-sided post-war housing that predominates the area.

If you take Manhattan Ave. south to Driggs Ave., make a right, and go through McCarren Park, you'll meet up with the copper-covered domes and triple-slashed crosses of the **Russian Orthodox Cathedral of the Transfiguration of Our Lord,** at N. 12th St. Four blocks up is Kent Ave., which runs through a seedy industrial zone and under the Williamsburg Bridge to the monstrous Brooklyn Naval Yard.

Underground DaVincis and Urban Michelangelos

As the night shadows begin to lighten, the inspired artist puts the finishing touches on his canvas—he sprays some more paint on the rundown brick building—then sprints down an alley to avoid early morning police patrols. Graffiti is illegal and its practitioners must work invisibly. Using spray paint and urban resourcefulness, graffiti writers make art that reflects the city's vitality: colorful, intricate, fantastic, a mix of words and images painted on a wall, truck, or any available surface. Name 'tags' are common, and the more accomplished artists can transform a dingy wall into a virtuoso masterwork. Storefronts decorated by local talent abound in Brooklyn and the Bronx. Graffiti isn't meant to stay forever inside a museum, although New York artists Jean-Michel Basquiat and Keith Haring began their careers as graffiti writers and became famous for techniques learned on city walls.

South of Greenpoint is **Williamsburg** (Subway: J, M, or Z to Marcy Ave.), home to a large Hasidic Jewish population, mainly of the Satmar sect. In this part of town, which is bounded by Broadway, Bedford, and Union Ave., men wear long black coats and hats—dress which dates to early modern Eastern Europe. North of Broadway is a primarily Hispanic neighborhood. In recent years young artists have been drawn to Williamsburg for its affordable loft spaces which are reasonably close to Manhattan. A small but growing outcropping of hip restaurants, cafés, and bars has sprung up around them.

The L subway to Bedford Ave. will place you in the midst of Williamsburg's creative lofters. If you see an industrial warehouse-type building with lovely potted plants and flower beds in the window, then you've probably spotted a renovated loft. West on Berry St. and up N. 10th stands a fantastic **graffiti mural**—proving that spray painting city walls is a serious art form like any other. Going westward to the abandoned **East River piers** yields a relatively undiscovered view of the eastern edge of midtown Manhattan. Caution should be exercised—dangerous abandoned buildings and sketchy dead lots abound here. More *virtuoso* graffiti lurks northward at N. 10th and Union Ave.

Also located in Williamsburg is the **Brooklyn Brewery,** 118 N. 11th St., makers of New York's own Brooklyn Lager and Brooklyn Brown Ale. Call the brewery's main line (718-486-7422) for information about t-shirts and tours of the brewery.

Those venturing southeast into the neighborhoods of **Bushwick, Bedford-Stuyvesant,** and **Brownsville** should be cautious. Low public funding, high unemployment, and inadequate public works have created a high-crime ghetto. Major sights here are burnt-out buildings, patches of undeveloped land, and stagnant commercial zones. Still, social consciousness and political activism emerge from every pothole in these neglected streets. Wall murals portraying Malcolm X, slogans urging patronage of Black businesses, Puerto Rican flags, and leather Africa medallions all testify to a growing sense of racial and cultural empowerment. Spike Lee's explosive *Do the Right Thing* is set on the streets of Bed-Stuy.

Every year on the Fourth of July weekend, an African cultural celebration is held in Brownsville on the grounds of the **Boys and Girls School,** 1700 Fulton St. From noon to midnight for several days, you can hear rocking reggae bands and the slamming beats of local rap musicians. The Boys and Girls School is a community-controlled public school which grew out of the 1969 attempt to hand over control of the Ocean Hill-Brownsville School District to the community; the plan was derailed by a teachers' strike. The school's formation and subsequent problems were featured in the award-winning documentary film *Eyes on the Prize: America at the Racial Crossroads.*

At 770 Eastern Pkwy. in Crown Heights is the **world headquarters of Chabad,** (also known as the Lubavitchers), a Hasidic Jewish sect whose Grand Rebbe, Menachem Mendel Shneerson, died at the age of 92 in June of 1994. Prior to his death, many believed that the Rebbe was in fact the Messiah; even after his death some followers claim he will rise again. Shneerson was the last in a hereditary line of Grand Lubavitcher Rebbes; he did not have any children, nor did he name a successor. The future of this sect, which by most estimates commands the allegiance of hundreds of thousands of Jews worldwide, is presently uncertain. Friday night and Saturday are celebrated as the day of rest, *shabbat.* All of the many sects that coexist here strictly observe the Sabbath; if you intrude, you may feel unwelcome and conspicuous. You will likely feel unwelcome and conspicuous on days other than the Sabbath as well, unless you are dressed conservatively and, if you are male, wear a yarmulke or some other head covering.

■ Institute Park

Brooklyn's cultural focus, **Institute Park,** lies between Flatbush Ave., Eastern Parkway, and Washington Ave. (subway: #2 or 3 to Eastern Parkway-Brooklyn Museum). The area is unlike any other part of Brooklyn—large marble monuments and immense buildings sit quietly and virtually undiscovered and rise high above the surrounding area. The **Brooklyn Public Library** (718-780-7700) has its main branch here in a 1941 Art Deco building on the **Grand Army Plaza,** at the corner of Eastern Pkwy. and Flatbush Ave. The colossal library has a gold-plated magnificence that rivals the main branch at 42nd St. in Manhattan in its grandeur. It's more than a library; it's a monument to books. The library has spawned 53 branches and contains 1,600,000 volumes. There are changing exhibitions on the second floor (open Mon. 10am-6pm, Tues.-Thurs. 9am-8pm, Fri.-Sat. 10am-6pm, Sun. 1-5pm; closed Sun. June-Sept.). The **Brooklyn Museum** (718-638-5000), at the corner of Eastern Pkwy. and Washington Ave., has a large permanent collection and special exhibitions that regularly draw Manhattanites out of their borough. The building itself is a neoclassical wonder, with huge stone pillars and sculptures of 30 famous prophets and scholars (see Museums, p. 246).

The **Brooklyn Botanic Garden** (718-622-4433) blooms next to the museum, at 1000 Washington Ave. This 52-acre fairy-land was founded in 1910 on a reclaimed waste dump by the Brooklyn Institute of Art and Sciences. Throughout the garden are several stunning smaller gardens. The **Fragrance Garden for the Blind** is an olfactory carnival—in mint, lemon, violet, and more exotic flavors. All are welcome. The more formal **Cranford Rose Garden** crams in over 100 blooming varieties of roses. Every spring, visitors can take part in the Sakura Matsuri (Japanese cherry blossom festival) at the Cherry Walk and Cherry Esplanade. The woodsy **Japanese Garden** contains weeping willows and a viewing pavilion grouped around the turtle-stocked pond. Although artificial, the scenery here is realistic enough to fool the many water birds that flock to the site. The **Shakespeare Garden** displays 80 plants mentioned in the Bard's works. Toward the rear of the gardens are two cement pools of flowering lily-pads. The lilies create an intriguing combined effect: some come straight out of a Monet painting, while others are eerily reminiscent of the seed pods in *Invasion of the Body Snatchers.* (Open April-Sept. Tues.-Fri. 8am-6pm, Sat.-Sun. and holidays 10am-6pm; Oct.-March Tues.-Fri. 8am-4:30pm, Sat.-Sun. and holidays 10am-4:30pm. Admission $3, students and seniors $1.50, children 5-15 50¢. Free on Tuesdays.)

■ Park Slope and Prospect Park

The neighborhood called **Park Slope,** bounded by Flatbush Ave. to the north, 15th St. to the south, Fifth Ave. to the west, and Prospect Park to the east, combines a thriving business district with magnificent brownstone residences. Restaurants and stores line the north-south avenues, especially **Seventh Ave.,** and east-west streets like Carroll St. are lined with beautiful homes. The entire neighborhood is starting to bulge with yuppies and young artists. On the corner of Sixth Ave. and Sterling Pl., owls and angels adorn the graceful brownstone **St. Augustine Roman Catholic Church,** built in 1888. The attached academy has one entrance for boys, on Sterling Pl., and one entrance for girls, on Park Pl.

Just east of Park Slope, adjoining the southern border of Institute Park, is **Prospect Park** (718-965-8951). Take the #2 or 3 train to Grand Army Plaza, then head toward **Memorial Arch,** built in the 1890s to commemorate the North's victory over the South. The charioteer atop the arch is an emblem of Columbia, the Union. Visitors may climb up to the top of the arch for free on weekends from noon to 4pm.

Enter Prospect Park's northern corner through Grand Army Plaza. Frederick Law Olmsted and Calvert Vaux designed the park in the mid-1800s and supposedly liked it better than their Manhattan project, Central Park. This opinion of the 526-acre urban oasis is shared by many Brooklynites. The park's largest area is the sweeping 90-acre **Long Meadow,** the longest open urban parkland in North America. The **Friend's Cemetery,** a Quaker burial ground dating from 1846, remains intact in the western section of the park. Natural glacial pools and man-made Prospect Lake lie south of Long Meadow. **Lookout Hill** overlooks the lake and marks the site of a mass grave where the British buried American casualties during the Revolutionary War.

NEIGHBORHOODS

In the eastern part of the park, at Flatbush and Ocean Ave., you can see old Brooklyn preserved in **Leffert's Homestead** (718-965-6505), a Dutch farmhouse burned by George Washington's troops and rebuilt in 1777. The Homestead is available for free viewing Saturdays and Sundays; call for an appointment. The **Children's Historic House Museum** located inside the homestead is open weekends and holidays from noon to 4pm (free). Nearby, saddle a horse taken from Coney Island on the **1912 Carousel,** which plays an odd version of the Beatles' "Ob-La-Di, Ob-La-Da" (open Tues. and Fri. 10am-2pm, Sat.-Sun. noon-5pm; 50¢). The recently reopened **Prospect Park Wildlife Center** features live animal exhibits aimed mainly at children (open daily 10am-5:30pm; adults $2.50, seniors $1.25, children 3-12 50¢). In late summer, concerts are held at the bandshell in the northwestern corner of the park (events hotline 718-965-8999, park tours 718-287-3400).

Just southeast of Prospect Park is the neighborhood of **Flatbush,** home to significant Jamaican and other West Indian populations. Reggae music and exotic fruit stands fill major avenues such as Church Ave., Nostrand Ave., and Ave. J on summer days. At the corner of Flatbush Ave. and Clarkson St., down from Avi's Discount Center, you can spot the distinctive "tags" of graffiti artists Rock, Alan, Jew, and Picolo. At Flatbush and Church Ave. (subway: D to Church Ave.) stands the oldest church in Brooklyn, **Flatbush Dutch Reformed Church** (c. 1654). A few of the sanctuary windows are Tiffany stained glass, including one of Samson. The church has tolled the death of every U.S. president. Next door stands the second-oldest high school in North America, **Erasmus Hall Academy.** Not a single brick can be moved from the school's center building or the Dutch Reformed Church will repossess it. (Founding-fathers Aaron Burr, John Jay, and Alexander Hamilton all contributed to the school's building.) Although a strange concept today, the turn-of-the-century Manhattan aristocracy maintained summer homes in Victorian Flatbush (bounded by Coney Island and Ocean, Church, and Newkirk Ave.). You can wander around Argyle St. and Ditmas Ave. to see some of the old mansions. **Brooklyn College** (subway: #2 or 5 to Flatbush Ave./Brooklyn College), founded in 1930, includes the prestigious **Brooklyn Center for the Performing Arts** (718-951-4522). The Center often holds musical and dramatic performances for the community (see p. 270).

■ South Brooklyn and Coney Island

Greenwood Cemetery (718-469-5277), a vast, hilly kingdom of ornate mausoleums and tombstones, sits directly south of Park Slope and makes for a pleasant, if morbid, stroll (open daily 8am-4pm). Samuel Morse, Horace Greeley and Boss Tweed slumber here. This "Victorian Necropolis" is definitely worth a look—headstones here take the form of sinking ships, wrecked trains, empty beds and chairs, and fire hydrants in a morbid reminder of the means of death. The main entrance is at Fifth Ave. and 25th St. (subway: N or R to 25th St.; Tours ($5) Sun. at 1pm). South of the cemetery, on the southwest flank of Brooklyn, lies **Sunset Park,** a predominantly Latino neighborhood. Recently, Chinese immigrants have begun to establish a community on Eighth Ave. between 54th and 61st St., alongside a well established Arab population. The unique egg-shaped towers of **St. Michael's Roman Catholic Church** rise above the sidewalk on 42nd St. and Fourth Ave. Nearby, on the southwest corner of 44th St. and Fourth Ave., you can check out a famous graffiti piece by the infamous artist Dare. Between 41st and 44th St., up the hill from Fourth Ave. to Sixth Ave., is Sunset Park proper, the park for which the neighborhood is named. Here you'll find a sloping lawn with an extraordinary view of the Upper New York Bay, the Statue of Liberty, and lower Manhattan. Avid consumers flock to 5th Ave., which is lined with discount stores and odd hybrid restaurants. On the northwest corner of Fifth Ave. and 54th St. is a colorful mural (presumably painted by children) of happy people in front of the Manhattan and Brooklyn skyline. On 59th St. and Fifth Ave. stands an immense gray-stoned church, **Our Lady of Perpetual Help.** If you're in a car, you can head down to First Ave. and explore the trolley-scarred streets, the setting for Uli Wedel's *Last Exit to Brooklyn.*

NEIGHBORHOODS

Bay Ridge, south of Sunset, centers on Third Ave., also called "Restaurant Row." Nearby Shore Road is lined with mansions overlooking the Verrazano-Narrows Bridge and New York Harbor. Bay Ridge was the scene of John Travolta's strutting in the classic *Saturday Night Fever.* Sadly, the 2001 Odyssey disco is no longer operational. **Bensonhurst** became a household word and rallying cry in the fight against racism following the brutal murder of Yusef Hawkins in 1989. The predominantly Italian neighborhood centers around 86th St., and is chock full of Italian bakeries, pizza joints, rowdy youths, and discount stores, especially around 17th Ave.

North of Bensonhurst and east of Sunset Park, centered around 13th Ave. north of 65th St., is **Borough Park,** the largest Hasidic Jewish neighborhood in Brooklyn. In contrast to the more visible Crown Heights Lubavitchers, the Bobovers of Borough Park eschew, for the most part, the political and secular worlds, preferring to maintain an insular community. The main synagogue sits at 15th Ave. and 48th St. As in the other Hasidic neighborhoods of Brooklyn, visitors will feel more welcome if they are dressed conservatively. East of Ocean Parkway is the traditionally Jewish neighborhood of **Midwood** (subway: D or Q to Kings Hwy.). Once the home of the largest Sephardic Jewish community outside of Israel, the neighborhood has lately seen increasing numbers of Arabs, Italians, and non-Sephardic Jews. Nonetheless, kosher eateries still dot the major arteries such as Kings Hwy. and Ocean Avenue, along with halal markets and pizza joints.

The B, D, F, and N trains all plug into the Stillwell Ave. station in **Coney Island,** attesting to South Brooklyn's historic importance as a resort spot for the rest of the city. In the early 1900s, only the rich could afford the trip here. Mornings, they bet on horses at the racetracks in Sheepshead Bay and Gravesend; nights, they headed to the seaside for 50-dollar dinners. The introduction of nickel-fare subway rides to Coney Island made the resort accessible to the entire population. Millions jammed into the amusement parks, beaches, and restaurants on summer weekends. In the late 40s, the area became less attractive. Widespread car ownership allowed people to get even farther away from the city, and a few devastating fires in Coney Island soon cleared the way for urban housing projects throughout the area. However, Coney Island is still the place for an afternoon of amusement. During the summer months, the beach is usually crowded, and it's always fun to explore the boardwalk.

Some vestiges of the golden era linger. The **Cyclone** (718-266-3434), at 834 Surf Ave. and W. 10th St., built in 1927, is more than the most terrifying roller coaster ride in the world—couples have been married upon it and it's included on the National Register as an historic place (open daily mid-June to Labor Day noon-midnight; Easter weekend to mid-June Fri.-Sun. noon-midnight). Enter its 100-second-long screaming battle over nine hills of rickety wooden tracks—the ride's well worth $4. The 1920 **Wonder Wheel** ($2.50), in Astroland on Surf Ave., is the world's tallest at 150 feet and has a special twist that surprises everyone; make sure you get in a colored car. The **El Dorado** bumper car ($2.50), 1216 Surf Ave., still plays thumping 70s disco tunes and invites you to "bump, bump, bump your ass off!" The **Hellhole** ($2.50), on 12th St. between Bowery and the Boardwalk, is about as scary as a Munsters rerun, but has some fun, campy moments.

On the boardwalk at 12th St. is the **Coney Island Circus Sideshow** (open Fri. noon-sundown, Sat.-Sun. noon-10:30pm; admission $3, children $2). The Sideshow is run by a bunch of NYC hipsters who sponsor the annual **Coney Island Mermaid Parade** (usually the last Sat. in June), a huge costume-and-float parade with prizes at the end. Come watch, or even register from 10am to noon on the day of the parade at Steeplechase Park and join the festivities. The Sideshow also hosts numerous cultural events throughout the summer and fall, including great indie rock shows on most Friday nights (see Entertainment and Nightlife: Music, p. 273). Call 718-372-5159 for information on all Sideshow happenings.

The **New York Aquarium** (718-265-FISH/3474), on Surf and West Eighth St., offers a ride-free environment. The first beluga whale born in captivity was raised in these tanks. Watch a solitary scuba diver be immersed in a tank full of feeding sharks. There's also a new outdoor theater showcasing the aquarium's delightful dolphins (open daily 10am-5pm, holidays and summer weekends 10am-7pm; admission $7.75, children 2-12 and seniors $3.55).

You can head west on Surf Ave. or take the boardwalk to the corner of W. 16th St., where the majestically deceased **Thunderbolt** coaster stands in ruins—relentless greenery has grown over the lower half of the abandoned ride. The tall, rusted skeleton of the **Parachute Jump,** relocated to the edge of the boardwalk in 1941, once carried carts to the top and then dropped them for a few seconds of freefall before their parachutes opened. Once a year, on Puerto Rican National Day, a flag somehow gets tied to the top. The pier that juts out into the water from here makes a good place for fishing or taking a stroll.

East of Coney Island, Ocean Parkway runs on a north-south line through half of Brooklyn. An extension of Olmsted's Prospect Park, this avenue was constructed to channel traffic to the seaside. Beyond the parkway lies **Brighton Beach** (subway: D or Q to Brighton Beach), nicknamed "Little Odessa by the Sea" because of the steady stream of Russian immigrants who moved there in the early 80s. The 1995 film *Little Odessa,* about the Russian mafia, was set and filmed here. Take a stroll down Brighton Beach Ave. or the parallel boardwalk along the sea. In late June and early July, old Eastern Europeans complaining about their bodily ailments, Spandex-clad girls listening to Top-40 music on Walkmans, and middle-aged couples drowning sunburns in Noxzema are all wowed by the **Blue Angels air shows** that they watch from the boardwalk. On Fourth of July weekend, parachutists land near cheering seaside crowds. Through the summer, Brighton Beach residents sit in lawnchairs or on the benches, with the hot sun wrapped around them like a shroud of tranquility.

To the east lies **Sheepshead Bay** (subway: D or Q to Sheepshead Bay), named after the fish that has since abandoned its native waters for the cleaner Atlantic. Emmons Ave. runs along the bay and faces **Manhattan Beach,** a wealthy residential section of doctors and *mafioso* just east of Brighton Beach. In Sheepshead Bay, you can go after some blues (the fish, not the music) on any of the boats docked along Emmons Ave. (Boats depart 6am-8am; some also have evening trips leaving 5:30-6:30pm; $25-30.) Traditionally, a couple of dollars is collected from each passenger and the wad goes to the person who lands the biggest fish.

If you have a car, you can drive east along the Belt Parkway, which hugs Brooklyn's shores. Stop off at **Plumb Beach** for a more intimate sun-and-sand experience. At night, the parking lot here fills with big green Cadillacs and loving couples. Exit the Belt at Flatbush Ave., which leads south to the Rockaway beaches of Queens. Turn left just before the bridge and you can drive around the immense abandoned air strips of Floyd Bennett Field. Here, you will find information about **Gateway National Park** (718-338-3687; open daily dawn till dusk).

Continuing on the Belt will take you to **Starrett City,** based around Pennsylvania Ave. This development has its own schools, its own government, and its own source of electricity and heat. Originally, rent here was based on how much each resident's salary allowed. State legislators soon revoked this "un-American" policy. The complex was also famous for enacting a cap on the number of minority residents in an effort to achieve racial balance; this policy was overturned as well.

▓ Queens

With its endlessly shifting ethnic population, Queens is the true melting pot of the city. Immigrant populations nestle here in small pockets, bringing their customs, languages, and customs. With a foreign-born population of over 30%, the turn-over of cultures is constantly revitalizing Queens's demographic landscape. Formerly German and Irish areas are being reestablished by Indian and Caribbean influences. Queens has been the stomping ground of many a hopeful newcomer—it's a place where hard-working communities of every color and stripe can carve out a little bit of the Old Country in the New World.

Named in honor of Queen Catherine of Braganza, wife of England's Charles II, this rural colony was baptized in 1683. At the beginning of the 19th century, the small farms began to give way to industry, and, by the 1840s, the area along the East River in western Queens had become a busy production center. In 1898, Queens officially became a borough of the City of New York. The Long Island Railroad's construction of train tunnels under the East River in 1910 engendered much physical growth. Between 1910 and 1930, the population of the borough quadrupled to one million; in 1938, Queens accounted for almost three-quarters of all new construction in the city. The building boom of the 50s effectively completed the urbanization of Queens, establishing it as the new Lower East Side, home to a wave of late-20th-century immigrants. Today, in this medley of distinct neighborhoods, you can trace the history of ethnic settlement from block to block.

Although home to two of New York City's major airports, **LaGuardia** to the north and **JFK** to the south, much of Queens feels like a wholly separate city. It has even styled itself one. In response to ongoing concerns about taxes and city benefits (Queens maintains that it pays too much of the former and receives almost none of the latter), some uptight natives have lately called for secession. The city, meanwhile, has made noises about prioritizing outer-borough tourism. A Dinkins-inspired "New York: Yours to Discover" advertising blitz was supposed to divert flows of funds and people to Queens and other "neglected treasures," but a few fiscally lean years and cries for more crime-fighters on Manhattan's streets have shifted priorities. Until this program gets underway and Queens establishes its own tourism council, places like the **Queens Historical Society** (143-35 37th Ave., Flushing, NY 11354; 718-939-0647) pick up the slack. The society offers suggestions for self-guided tours of historical neighborhoods (such as the "Freedom Mile") and leads free guided tours. (Open daily 9:30am-4:30pm; visiting tours Tues., Sat., and Sun. 2:30pm-4:30pm; research library by appointment.)

ORIENTATION

Queens is geographically New York's largest borough, comprising over a third of the city's total area. Just across the East River from Manhattan lies the Astoria/Long Island City area, the northwest region of Queens. **Long Island City,** for many years Queens's industrial powerhouse, has a few residential pockets, but most people are here to work. In the 1930s, 80% of all industry in the borough was based here; Newtown Creek saw as much freight traffic as the Mississippi River. The area has lately acquired a reputation as a low-rent artists' community, though it remains to be seen whether the avant-garde will cross the river. **Astoria,** known as the Athens of New York, has by some estimates the second-largest Greek community in the world. The area is also home to a sizable Italian community.

Southeast of this section, in the communities of Woodside and Sunnyside, new Irish immigrants join their established countrymen. **Sunnyside,** a remarkable "garden community" built in the 1920s, gained notoriety during the Great Depression when over half the original owners were evicted because they weren't able to pay their mortgages. The neighborhood now commands international recognition as a model of middle-income housing. Southeast of Sunnyside lies **Ridgewood,** a neighborhood founded by Eastern European and German immigrants a century ago. More than 2000 of the distinctively European attached brick homes there receive protection as landmarks, securing Ridgewood a listing in the National Register of Historic Places, but the adjacent Brooklyn ghetto of Bushwick has frayed its edges.

East of Ridgewood, **Forest Hills** and **Kew Gardens** contain some of the most expensive residential property in the city. The Austin Street shopping district imports the luxury of Manhattan. Former Vice Presidential candidate Geraldine Ferraro has a house in Forest Hills. Originally called Whitepot, the land of Forest Hills was bought from the Indians for some white pots—a deal almost as unreal as Peter Minuit's Manhattan purchase. The Forest Hills/Kew Gardens region offers some of the most pleasant residential strolling areas in all the city. This pricey, upscale region nurses some Tudor-style residential architecture, as well as the **West Side Tennis Center,** whose courts have hosted some of tennis' elite. Just north of this area, **Flushing Meadows-Corona Park,** site of the World's Fair in both 1939 and 1964, still attracts crowds for

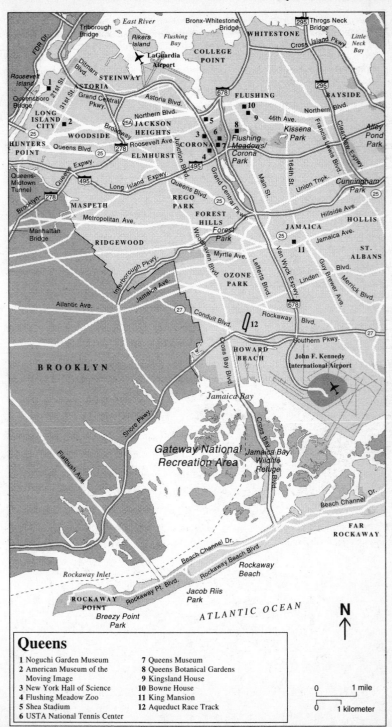

Queens

1 Noguchi Garden Museum
2 American Museum of the
   Moving Image
3 New York Hall of Science
4 Flushing Meadow Zoo
5 Shea Stadium
6 USTA National Tennis Center
7 Queens Museum
8 Queens Botanical Gardens
9 Kingsland House
10 Bowne House
11 King Mansion
12 Aqueduct Race Track

0   1 mile
0   1 kilometer

both its museums and its collection of open-air attractions. To the west, **Corona, Jackson Heights,** and **Elmhurst** have a large Hispanic population. To the east of the park, **Flushing** has become a "Little Asia" with a large Korean, Chinese, and Indian population, as well as a sizable number of Central and South American immigrants. Despite the dynamic demographic landscape, the area's elevated subway, some of the nation's oldest public transportation, retains the flavor of early 20th-century Queens. **Bayside,** east of Flushing, is a popular spot for bar-hopping in a relaxed, north shore atmosphere. **Jamaica,** located in the central part of the borough, and many of the neighborhoods to the southeast house prosperous West Indian and African-American communities. Along the south shore of Queens, the site of mammoth Kennedy Airport, you can find the **Jamaica Bay Wildlife Refuge.** Eastern Queens echoes the ethnic areas in a more diluted, upscale manner as the borough's borders give way to the true suburbia of Nassau.

Queens suffers from neither the monotonous grid of Upper Manhattan nor the slipshod angles of the streets in the Village. Most neighborhoods here developed independently, without regard for an overriding plan. Nevertheless, streets generally run north-south and are numbered from east to west, from First St. in Astoria to 271st St. in Glen Oaks. Avenues run perpendicular to streets and are numbered from north to south, from Second Ave. in the north to 165th Ave. in the south. The address of an establishment or residence usually tells you the closest cross-street; for example, 45-07 32nd Ave. is near the intersection with 45th St. But named streets sometimes intrude into the numerical system, and sometimes two different numbering systems collapse into one another. For added fun, Roads and Drives are frequently inserted between consecutive Avenues (as in these consecutive thoroughfares in Long Island City: 31st Road, 31st Drive, Broadway, 33rd Ave.), while Places are sometimes inserted between consecutive Streets.

■ Flushing

Flushing's melange of immigrant populations and historical landmarks (19 sites here comprise the "Flushing Freedom Mile") simultaneously typify and honor Queens unique culture. Moreover, getting here by subway couldn't be easier; the #7 Flushing line runs straight from Times Square.

Landmarks from before the American Revolution commingle with a downtown where the signs outside most stores are bilingual (and those signs which aren't are not likely to be in English). Up Main St. toward Northern Blvd., between 38th and 39th Ave., stands **St. George's Episcopal Church.** The present structure was built in 1853 to replace the original, where Francis Lewis, a signer of the Declaration of Independence, had once been a vestryman. Past the church about four blocks up and to the right, on Northern Blvd., sits a conspicuously shingled building at #137-16. This **Friends Meeting House** (718-358-9636), a national historic landmark, went up in 1694 and still serves as a place of worship for local Quakers. Meetings are held here at 11am every Sunday, and the main room, a severe and simple hall, is open on the first Sunday of every month. Across the street at 137-35 Northern Blvd., the **Flushing Town Hall** (718-463-7700), built in 1862, has recently been restored in the Romanesque tradition. Art and historical exhibitions await inside (suggested donation $2, students and seniors $1). Live jazz and classical concerts are offered here on Fridays, but call ahead to get a schedule ($15 each show, students and seniors $10).

For other points of historical interest, continue down Northern Blvd., past the Gothic monstrosity known as Flushing High School, to Bowne St., and make a right. About two blocks down, at #37-01, is **Bowne House** (718-359-0528). This low, unassuming structure, built in 1661, is the oldest remaining residence in New York City. Here, John Bowne defied Dutch governor Peter Stuyvesant's 1657 ban on Quaker meetings (around 1680, he held Quaker worship in his kitchen)—and was exiled for his efforts. Back in Holland, Bowne persuaded the Dutch East India Company to demand of the colony tolerance for all religious groups. This helped to establish the tradition of religious freedom enjoyed by Buddhist and Hindu newcomers in Flushing enjoy today. The house preserves such interesting antiques as a beehive oven, clay peace pipes, bone-handled utensils, and a walking stick Old Man Bowne used to kill wandering bears (open Tues. and Sat.-Sun. 2:30-4:30pm; admission $2, seniors and children under 14 $1).

Next to Bowne House lies a small park; head through it and past a playground on your left to the **Kingsland Homestead,** 143-35 37th Ave. (718-939-0647, visiting hours Tues., Sat., and Sun. 2:30-4:30pm). This large, decrepit house, built in 1775, is currently being restored and holds a permanent collection of antique china and memorabilia that belonged to the early trader Captain Joseph King. There is also a permanent collection of antique dolls and a fully furnished "Victorian Room." Don't be embarrassed to take a peek into "Aunt Marie's Secret Closet." As home of the **Queens Historical Society,** the Homestead displays three or four temporary exhibits each year concerning aspects of the borough's history. More academic adventurers can use the society's archival and genealogical research center by appointment. You can pick up a brochure here to guide you through the Flushing Freedom Mile Historic Tour. (Open Mon.-Sat. 9:30am-5pm; tours given Tues. and Sat.-Sun. 2:30-4:30pm; admission $2, seniors and students $1; admission to archives free with permission.)

Behind the house stands New York's only living landmark, a weeping beech tree planted in 1849 by nurseryman Samuel Parsons upon his return from Belgium. The first of its species in North America, it has a height of 65 feet and a circumference of 14 feet. The venerably twisted patriarch has spawned eight nearby trees, all "sons of beeches," and is the father of every other tree of its species on the continent.

Five blocks down Main St. toward Corona Park from the #7 subway station is the regal **Queens Botanical Garden** (718-886-3800; the Q44 bus toward Jamaica stops right in front of the Garden). Begun as a part of the 1939-40 World's Fair in nearby Flushing Meadows-Corona Park, the garden had to move when the park was being redesigned for the 1964-65 World's Fair. With the help of state-planning mastermind Robert Moses, the garden was relocated to its present site, where it now boasts a 5000-bush rose garden (the largest in the northeast), a 23-acre arboretum, and more than nine acres of "theme gardens" (open daily 8am-midnight; suggested donation $1, children 50¢). The beautiful, well kept Garden offers a pleasant excursion from the busy market area a few minutes' down on Main Street. On weekends, the Garden plays host to a cavalcade of wedding parties, each choosing its gazebos and fountains as a backdrop for commemorative photos.

Kissena Park, on Rose Ave. and Parsons Blvd., preserves nature on a more modest scale. The **Historic Grove** was planted here in the 19th century as part of Parson's Nursery and contains many exotic foreign tree species. As you enter from Rose Ave., pass tennis courts and a nature center; down the hill is beautiful Kissena Lake, circled by picnickers, cyclists, and even a few fisherfolk. Urban park rangers give walking tours (718-699-4204) and nature shows on Sundays at 2pm. Call the **Kissena Park Nature Center** for more information (718-353-2460; open Sat.-Sun. 10am-4pm). From the #7 subway stop at Main St., take the Q17 bus from in front of Model's to Rose Ave., and get out in front of Kissena Park.

To the east of Flushing, the 600-acre **Alley Pond Park/Environmental Center,** 228-06 Northern Blvd. (718-229-4000), just off the Cross-Island Pkwy., offers miles of nature trails through the park—a greenbelt of wetlands, woodlands, and marshes. A small exhibit in the back room of the center features live snakes, snapping turtles, frogs, and guinea pigs (open Tues.-Sat. 9:30am-4:30pm). To get there, take the #7 to Main St., Flushing. Then take the Q12 bus from Stern's department store on Roosevelt Ave., along Northern Blvd., to the center.

■ Flushing Meadows-Corona Park

Queens has hosted a pair of World's Fairs, both of them in Flushing Meadows-Corona Park, a 1255-acre former swamp sliced out of the middle of the borough. The park, developed during the 1939 Fair, was cultivated on the tip of a huge rubbish dump. Most of the park's present-day attractions were originally built for use at the 1964-65

Fair. Their somewhat shabby condition bears witness to better days. On weekends, local families come here to play frisbee and let off steam as cars and trucks race by on the nearby Van Wyck Expressway. The 380-ton steel globe (the **Unisphere**) that hovers nearby was constructed for the 1964 World's Fair and was intended as a symbol for the friendship of nations.

Like downtown Flushing, the park is on the #7 subway line from Times Square; get off at the 111th St. elevated station. (The next stop over, now known as the Willets Point/Shea Stadium station, was called the World's Fair Station in 1939.) Before leaving the platform, take a look at the huge, pale box of a building on stilts in the distance which reads "Terrace on the Park." Walk straight toward this along 111th St. for five blocks to a parking lot.

The building that houses the **New York Hall of Science** sits back across this parking lot, near the corner of 111th St. and 48th Ave. (718-699-0675 or 718-699-0005). Futuristic when it was constructed in 1964, it now stands on a neglected site, surrounded by rusty rockets. Its vision of the future may not have aged well on the outside, but the museum does a good job of making sure that its exhibitions inside are current and engaging. It even incorporates such neato technology as an electron microscope and powerful Macintosh computers. This "museum" certainly deserves a visit, especially if you bring children. Over 150 hands-on displays demonstrate a range of scientific concepts and encourage participation. Although the exhibits change with some frequency, recent hits have included "Giant Insects: Backyard Monsters," and "Seeing the Light," which demonstrated the principles behind lasers and prisms. If you time your visit just right, you may be lucky enough to witness one of the regularly scheduled **cow's-eye dissections** performed by a young and spirited staff "explainer" (open Wed.-Sun. 10am-5pm, June-Aug. Mon.-Tues. 10am-2pm; admission $4.50, seniors and children under 18 $3; free Wed.-Thurs. 2-5pm).

East of the building, following the walking path across the overpass and then turning right, you will come to the heart of the park and the **New York City Building.** The south wing houses winter ice skating (718-271-1996 for hours and prices; season runs Oct.-March), and the north wing is home to the **Queens Museum of Art** (718-592-5555). In the museum, you can see the "Panorama of the City of New York"—at 1800 square feet, the world's largest-scale model of an urban area. One hundred feet of New York correspond to one inch on the model, which re-creates over 865,000 buildings in miniature. The museum also displays casts of Classical and Renaissance architecture on loan from the Metropolitan Museum of Art (open Wed.-Fri. 10am-5pm, Sat.-Sun. noon-5pm).

The rest of the park's grounds are fun, too. Just south of the Hall of Science is a restored **Coney Island carousel** (718-592-6539) that pipes out mischievously off-key music at ear-splitting volume ($1 per ride; open Mon.-Fri. 10:30am-7:30pm, Sat.-Sun. 10:30am-8pm). The **Queens Wildlife Center and Zoo** (718-271-7761) next door features North American animals such as elk, bison, and bear, along with more exotic species such as sea lions, pumas, and sandhill cranes (oh my!). A petting zoo features sheep, goats, cows, and other standard petting zoo crew. (Open Mon.-Fri. 10am-5pm, Sat.-Sun. 10am-5:30pm; Nov.-March daily 10am-4:30pm. Tickets sold until ½-hr. before closing. Admission $2.50, seniors $1.25, children under 13 50¢.)

Also in the park, you can try your hand at a full (but short) course of pitch-'n'-putt golf (718-271-8182), which has 18 par-3 holes (open daily 8am-7pm; greens fee Sat.-Sun. $7, Mon.-Fri. $8; club rental $1 each), or cavort in a playground accessible to disabled children. In the southern part of the park, **Meadow Lake** offers paddle boating, rowboating, and duck-dunking, while **Willow Lake Nature Area** offers an occasional free tour; call the Urban Rangers at 718-699-4204 for more information.

Shea Stadium (718-507-8499 or 718-699-4220), to the north of the park, was built for the 1964 Fair, though the Mets now slug it out here (see Baseball, p. 282). Nearby, the **USTA National Tennis Center** (718-760-6200) holds the U.S. Open tennis championship each year (see Sports: Tennis, p. 283).

■ Astoria and Long Island City

In **Astoria,** Greek-, Italian-, and Spanish-speaking communities mingle amid lively shopping districts and top-flight cultural attractions. Astoria lies in the upper west corner of the borough, and **Long Island City** is just south of it, across the river from the Upper East Side. A trip on the N train from Broadway and 34th St. in Manhattan to Broadway and 31st St. at the (pseudo-) border between the two cities should take about 25 minutes. As you get off the train you will find yourself in the middle of the Broadway shopping district, a densely packed area where an average block includes three specialty delis, a Greek bakery, and an Italian grocery. Avid shoppers should go east eight blocks on Broadway to Steinway St., where the stores stretching block on block in both directions form a panoramic vista.

For those whose shopping appetites are satiated, two sculpture gardens provide a remarkable diversion from consumerism. From the Broadway station at 31st St., walk west along Broadway eight blocks toward the Manhattan skyline, leaving the commercial district for a more industrial area. At the end of Broadway, cross the intersection with Vernon Boulevard. The **Socrates Sculpture Garden** (718-956-1819) is located next to the steel warehouse. The N train to Broadway and an 8-block walk towards the East River will lead you to this intriguing land of 35 sculptures. The sight is stunning, if somewhat unnerving: modern day-glo and rusted metal abstractions *en masse* in the middle of nowhere, on the site of what was once an illegal dump. The sculptures on this five-acre waterfront plot challenge the viewer's interpretive skills, as does the "Sound Observatory" right on the edge of the East River. You could spend hours pitty-pat pattering on the tin drums and honking into the "vocal amplifier," which faces out onto the water (open daily 10am-sunset).

Two blocks south on Vernon Blvd., at 32-37, stands the **Isamu Noguchi Garden Museum** (718-204-7088 or 718-721-1932), established in 1985 next door to the world-renowned sculptor's studio. Noguchi (1904-88) designed and built this space, one of the few world-class museums that present a comprehensive survey of the work of a single sculptor. Inside, 12 galleries display Noguchi's breadth of vision. Head upstairs and take a look at the model of his proposed "Sculpture to Be Seen From Mars," a 2-mile-long face to be carved in the dirt next to Newark International Airport as a monument to man in the post-atomic age. His most inspired works, the smaller stone sculptures, are fantastically displayed in the indoor/outdoor galleries downstairs. Noguchi once said that he wanted "to look at nature through nature's eyes, and so ignore man as a special object of veneration." He worked with stones to "help them reveal their true souls, not to reshape them." In "The Well," which rests outside, Noguchi left large parts of the boulder uncut, but bored a large circular "belly button" into the top; water perpetually wells over and shimmers down the sides of the stone. The curators at the Metropolitan Museum liked this work so much that they commissioned one of their own. Films detailing Noguchi and his works are shown throughout the museum (open April-Nov. Wed., Fri. 10am-5pm and Sat.-Sun. 11am-6pm. Suggested contribution $4, students and seniors $2). A shuttle from Manhattan (718-721-1932; $5) leaves from the Asia Society on Park Ave. and 70th St. on Saturday and Sunday every hour on the half-hour from 11:30am to 3:30pm. It returns every hour on the hour until 5pm. A free long informative guided tour kicks off at 2pm.

Astoria is also home to the snazzy **Kaufman-Astoria Studio;** part of a 13-acre plant with eight sound stages, it's the largest studio in the U.S. outside of L.A. Paramount Pictures used these facilities to make such major motion pictures as *Ragtime, Arthur,* and *Secret of My Success.* The studios are closed to the public, but the complex contains the **American Museum of the Moving Image** (718-784-7777), at 35th Ave. and 36th St. The museum is accessible from the E, F, G, R, and N trains—from the elevated N-line stop on Broadway, walk five blocks on Broadway away from Manhattan to 36th St.; make a right and walk two blocks through the residential neighborhood. Galleries of wacky film and TV memorabilia and daily screenings serve up a hearty dose of pop culture (see Museums, p. 245).

Perhaps more than anything else in the borough, the **Steinway Piano Factory,** at 19th Rd. and 77th St. in northern Astoria (718-721-2600), puts Queens on the map. The Steinways moved their famous operation out to Astoria in the 1870s and had the place to themselves for quite some time. The area was named after pioneering William Steinway, who built affordable housing around the factory for his workers in the 19th century. The considerate Mr. Steinway threw in a library, a kindergarten, and athletic grounds. You can still see some of the rowhouse-style "piano houses" that he constructed on 20th Ave. between Steinway and 41st St. Free monthly walking tours, lasting from 9-11:30am, must be booked three months in advance.

The world-famous Steinway pianos continue to be manufactured in the same spot, in the same way. The 12,000 parts of the piano range from a 340-lb. plate of cast iron to tiny bits of the skin of a small Brazilian deer. Over 95% of public performances in the U.S. are played on Steinway grands. If you're in the area, you can also take a look at the **Steinway House,** 18-33 41st St., the spacious mid-19th-century mansion that belonged to William Steinway and is now protected by junkyard dogs.

Heading south of Astoria to Long Island City, you can gain some perspective on Manhattan from **Hunter's Point** on the East River. There, the brand-new **Citicorp Building,** the tallest building in New York outside of Manhattan and a harbinger of New York's 21st-century skyline, was completed in 1989. (From Astoria, the best option is to take the N line south to Queensboro Plaza and then walk 5 blocks southwest along Jackson Ave. to the Citicorp Bldg. From Manhattan, take the E or F train to 23rd St.-Ely Ave.; you'll come up right in front of the building on 44th Dr.) Its sleek glass exterior hulks over diminutive brick row houses, as if a butter-fingered planning official slipped somewhere, plopping a midtown monolith down on the wrong side of the river.

One block south of Citicorp to 45th Ave. and two blocks toward the Manhattan skyline lie the well kept brownstones of the **Hunter's Point Historic District.** Check out the facing of Westchester stone on the 10 Italianate row houses, rare examples of late 19th-century architecture.

If you make a left on 21st St. and go three blocks, you will come to a huge, red, stone Victorian building, at 46-01 21st St. This is the **Institute for Contemporary Art/PS1** (718-784-2084). The building housed the first public school in Queens; you can still see the word "Girls" cut into the stone lintel above the entrance (galleries open Wed.-Sat. 10am-6pm; suggested donation $2).

Long Island City commands an outstanding view of Manhattan and the East River. To get to the shorefront, walk toward the skyline along 45th Ave., go right on Vernon Blvd., and then take a left onto 44th Dr. Follow it to the public pier which juts into the river. To your right as you face the river lies the Queensboro Bridge, better known to Simon and Garfunkel fans as the **59th St. Bridge**. Directly in front of you, on the southern tip of Roosevelt Island, you can see the romantically turreted ruins of 19th-century hospital facilities. In addition to the highlights of the Manhattan skyline (the Art Deco Chrysler Building and the twin towers of the World Trade Center), there is a fine view of the United Nations complex—a wide gray tower facing out into the river, connected to a smaller domed annex with a satellite dish. The Citicorp Building boldly stands out directly behind you.

■ Central Queens: Jamaica, St. Albans, and Forest Park

Jamaica, named for the Jameco Indians, lies in the center of Queens and is the heart of the borough's African-American and West Indian community. To get here, take the E, J, or Z train to Jamaica Center. The main strip on Jamaica Ave., stretching between 150th and 168th St., is constantly bustling with activity. The **pedestrian mall** on 165th St. is lined with restaurants selling succulent Jamaican beef patties, stores peddling Malcolm X baseball caps and African clothing, and 30-foot-tall metal men waving with outstretched arms.

Like most other northeastern locales, Jamaica has its share of colonial history. The recently renovated **King Manor Museum,** Jamaica Ave. and 150th St. (718-206-0545), was the colonial residence of Rufus King, a signer of the Constitution, one of New York's first senators, and an early U.S. ambassador to Great Britain. His son was governor of New York. The house, set in 11-acre King Park, dates back to the early 1750s and combines examples of Georgian and Federal architecture (open Sat.-Sun. noon-4pm; Admission $2, students and seniors $1).

The **Jamaica Arts Center,** 161-04 Jamaica Ave. (718-658-7400) at 161st St., offers changing workshops, as well as frequent visual art exhibitions dealing with aspects of African-American or urban life. Recent exhibitions have included the photographic collection "African-Americans: A Self-Portrait," and "Songs of My People," a photo essay by aspiring artist Tyra Emerson (exhibition space open Mon.-Thurs. 9am-8:30pm, Fri.-Sat. 9am-5pm; free). Next door, the **Jamaica Savings Bank,** at 161-02 Jamaica Ave., is regarded by some as "the finest Beaux Arts building in Queens." Down a few blocks at Jamaica Ave. and 165th St. is the former **Valencia Theater,** now the "Tabernacle of Prayer." It was built in 1929 as one of several atmospheric "Wonder Theaters." While the elders of most religious institutions would probably treat the huge marquee in front with reserve, the Tabernacle's current occupants seem to feel quite lucky to have it. The building is open (for the most part) only on Sundays, but a peek into the front lobby will give you the idea.

While the area directly south of downtown Jamaica is fairly barren except for food-processing factories and crime, the middle- and upper-class African-American communities to its southeast are well kept residential areas with some interesting history. After WWII, **St. Albans,** the area centered on Linden Blvd. just east of Merrick Blvd., became the home of newly mobile African-Americans, many of whom were empowered by the GI Bill and the work of the NAACP. St. Albans in the 1950s recalled Harlem in the 1920s; jazz greats Count Basie, Fats Waller, and James P. Johnson as well as baseball stars like Jackie Robinson and Roy Campanella, all lived here—mostly in the Addisleigh Park area of western St. Albans. Today, wealthier African-Americans have moved southeast to communities like Laurelton, leaving behind St. Albans' homes and the West Indian bakeries and restaurants that now flourish in the lively shopping district along Linden Blvd. To get to St. Albans, take the E or J train to Jamaica Center, then the Q4 bus to Linden Blvd.

To the west of Jamaica, **Forest Park** (718-235-4100) is a densely wooded area with miles of park trails, a bandshell, a golf course (718-296-0999), a carousel ($1), baseball diamonds, tennis courts, and horseback riding (park open Mon.-Fri. 11am-6pm, Sat.-Sun. 11am-7pm). If you'd like to rent horses, both **Lynne's Riding School** (718-261-7679) and **Dixie Do Stables** (718-263-3500) will oblige you with a guided trail ride (both open 8am-7pm; $20 per hour). For information on upcoming park events, call the number above or 718-520-5941. Take the J or Z train to Woodhaven Blvd., or else take the L or M train to Myrtle/Wyckoff Ave., then the Q55 bus.

You can get a little taste of Old New York at the **Queens County Farm Museum** (718-347-3276), at 73-50 Little Neck Parkway, in Floral Park on the border of Nassau County. Built by Jacob Adriance in 1772 on 50 acres of land, this is the only working farm of its era that has been restored. Chicks and ducks and sheep better scurry when you take the E or F train to Kew Gardens/Union Turnpike, then the Q46 bus to Little Neck Pkwy. Walk three blocks north. (Farmhouse/museum open Sat.-Sun. noon-5pm. Grounds open Mon.-Fri. 9am-5pm, Sat.-Sun. 10am-5pm; tours given every hour on the half-hour. Donations requested.)

■ Southern Queens

The **Jamaica Bay Wildlife Refuge** (718-318-4340), near the town of Broad Channel in Jamaica Bay, is about the size of Manhattan and 10 times the size of Flushing Meadows-Corona Park. The refuge's western half dips into Brooklyn, and the entire place constitutes one of the most important urban wildlife refuges in the U.S., harboring more than 325 species of shore birds, water fowl, and small animals. Lined with benches and birdhouses, the miles of paths around the marshes and ponds resonate to the roar of planes leaving from nearby JFK. Beached wooden rowboats, a trout-mask replica, and the frequent egret or swan make this place a real oasis. Environmental slide shows and tours are available on weekends (Nature Center open Mon.-Fri. 8:30am-5pm, Sat.-Sun. 8:30am-6pm; free). To get to the refuge, take the A train to Broad Channel. Walk west along Noel Rd. (which is just in front of the station) to Crossbay Blvd., then turn right and walk about one mile to the center. Alternatively, take the E, F, G, or R line to 74th St.-Roosevelt Ave. in Jackson Heights, then the Q53 express bus to Broad Channel, and follow the directions above.

Just south of the refuge lies Rockaway Peninsula, named after a Native American word for "living waters." Here you'll find **Rockaway Beach,** immortalized by the Ramones in one of their pop-punk tributes. A public beach (718-318-4000) extends from Beach 3rd St. in Far Rockaway to Beach 149th St. in the west, lined by a boardwalk from Beach 3rd St. all the way to Beach 126th St. Between Beach 126th St. and Beach 149th St., the beach is divided between public and smaller, private waterfront areas; no street parking is allowed during the summer. To get to Rockaway Beach, take the A train to Broad Channel, then take a shuttle to 106th or 116th St.

Just west of Rockaway Beach (and separated from it by a huge chain-link fence) is **Jacob Riis Park,** part of the 26,000-acre **Gateway National Recreation Area** (718-318-4300), which extends into Brooklyn, Staten Island, and New Jersey. The park was named for Jacob Riis, a photographer and journalist, who in the early 1900s brought attention to the need for school playgrounds and neighborhood parks. He persuaded New York City to turn this overgrown beach into a public park. Today the park is lined with its own beauteous beach and boardwalk and contains basketball and handball courts, a golf course, and concession stands. Adjoining the park to the west is **Fort Tilden,** also a part of Gateway, where you can walk through the sand dunes past old Nike missile sites from the Cold War days, as well as the past sites of 16-inch shore guns from WWI and WWII, when this was a naval base. To get to Riis Park and Fort Tilden, take the #2 or 5 train to Flatbush Ave., then pick up the Q35 bus on Nostrand Ave. The Q22 bus connects Riis Park to the Beach 116th subway station in Rockaway Park.

■ The Bronx

The Bronx? No thonx.

—Ogden Nash

The Bronx has long exercised an unhealthy attraction on the American imagination, joined to Detroit, Watts, and Anacostia as a dark specter of urban decay, an apocalyptic city of doom. Much of the Bronx *is* characterized by deteriorating tenements, graffiti-covered homes, and chain-link fences topped with prison-style barbed wire. But while the Bronx is home to one of the poorest congressional districts in the country, several New York diamonds can be found in the rough here, including over 2000 acres of parkland, a great zoo, a classic baseball stadium, turn-of-the-century riverfront mansions, and thriving ethnic neighborhoods, including a Little Italy to shame its counterpart to the south. In addition, despite the rampant poverty, many Bronx residents have taken action to improve their neighborhoods by forming safety walks, clean-up patrols, and advocacy groups.

The only borough on the U.S. mainland, the Bronx took its name from the Bronx River, which in turn took its name from early Dutch settler Jonas Bronck, who claimed the area for his farm in 1636. Until the turn of the 19th century, the area consisted largely of cottages, farmlands, and wild marshes. Then, in the 1840s, the tide of immigration swelled, bringing scores of Italian and Irish settlers. Since then, the flow of immigrants (now mostly Hispanic and Russian) has never stopped.

ORIENTATION

If you're not heading for Yankee Stadium, for safety's sake stay out of the South Bronx unless you're in a car and with someone who knows the area. The northern and eastern parts of the borough are largely middle-class, with single-family houses and duplexes on (relatively) peaceful, tree-lined streets. Pelham Bay Park, in the northeastern part of the Bronx, is the city's largest park. In the center of the borough, on the banks of the Bronx river, Bronx Park contains the Bronx Zoo/Wildlife Conservation Park and its plant kingdom counterpart, the equally excellent New York Botanical Garden. At the western edge of Bronx Park's dynamic duo sits the campus of Fordham University. Van Cortlandt Park, in the northwest section of the borough, completes the trio of major open spaces. The subway will take you from Manhattan to the Bronx's attractions. The #1, 9, and 4 reach up to Van Cortlandt Park; the C and D lines serve Fordham Rd. and Bedford Park Blvd., near the Botanical Garden; the #2 and 5 skirt Bronx Park and the zoo; and the #6 stretches into Pelham Bay Park. The #4, C, and D trains whisk fans in and out of Yankee Stadium in the south of the borough. Scarce transfer stations make subway travel within the Bronx often time-consuming. If you're planning to travel around the Bronx, you're probably better off going by bus; ask for a bus map at a subway station.

■ Bronx Zoo/Wildlife Conservation Park

The most obvious reason to come to the Bronx is the **Bronx Zoo/Wildlife Conservation Park** (718-367-1010 or 718-220-5100), also known as the New York Zoological Society. The largest urban zoo in the United States, it provides a home for over 4000 animals. While the occasional building dots the zoo, this newly environmentally conscious park prefers to showcase its stars within the 265-acre expanse of natural habitats created for the animals' dwelling pleasure. While the timber rattlesnake and Samantha the python (the largest snake in the U.S.) have been sentenced to life in the Reptile House, more benign beasts have been loosed into the Park's "protected sanctuary," occasionally allowing for startlingly close interplay between inhabitant and visitor. Indian elephants frolic in a virtual Wild Asia while white-cheeked gibbons tree-hop in the JungleWorld.

Noteworthy natural habitats include the **Himalayan Highlands,** home to endangered snow leopards and fiery red pandas; **Wild Asia,** stalked by rhinoceroses, muntjacs, sambars, nilgais, and rare sika deer; **South America,** roamed by guanacos, babirusas, and pygmy hippos; and the **World of Darkness,** which swarms with scores of bats, bushbabies, and a not-to-be-missed display of naked mole rats. Kids imitate animals at the hands-on **Children's Zoo,** where they can climb a spider's web or try on a turtle shell. If you tire of the children, the crocodiles are fed Mondays and Thursdays at 2pm, sea lions at 3pm. *Let's Go* does not recommend feeding children to wild animals.

You can explore the zoo on foot or confuse the animals by traveling on the **Safari Train,** which runs between the elephant house and Wild Asia ($1). Soar into the air for a Tarzan's-eye view of the park from the **Skyfari** aerial tramway that runs between Wild Asia and the Children's Zoo ($2). Or hop aboard the **Bengali Express Monorail,** which glides around Wild Asia (20min.; $2). If you find the pace too hurried, saddle up a camel in the Wild Asia area ($3). **Walking tours** are given on weekends by the Friends of the Zoo; call 718-220-5142 three weeks in advance to reserve a place. Pamphlets containing self-guided tours are also available at the Zoo Center for 75¢. If you get hungry, several areas in the park feed humans daily, including the **Lakeside Cafe, African Market, Flamingo Pub,** and **Zoo Terrace.** Parts of the zoo close down during the winter (Nov.-April); call for more information. (Open Nov.-March daily 10am-4:30pm, April-Oct. Mon.-Fri. 10am-5pm, Sat.-Sun. and holidays 10am-5:30pm. Free on Wednesdays, otherwise admission $6.75, seniors and children $3. For disabled-access information, call 718-220-5188.)

To reach the zoo by car, take the Bronx River Pkwy. or (from I-95) the Pelham Pkwy. By subway take the #2 or 5 to E. Tremont Ave.-West Farms Sq. and walk four

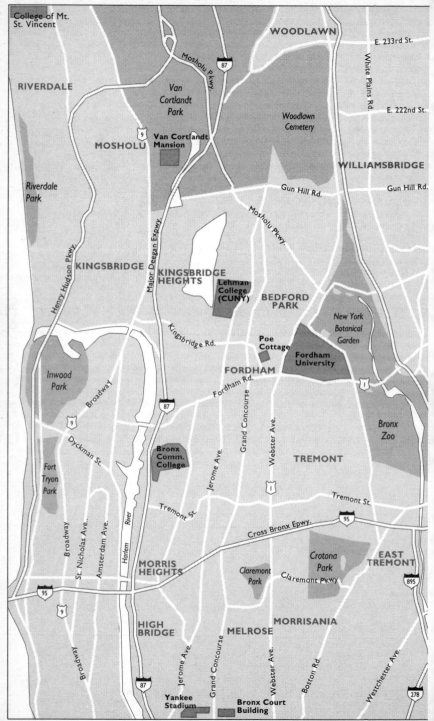

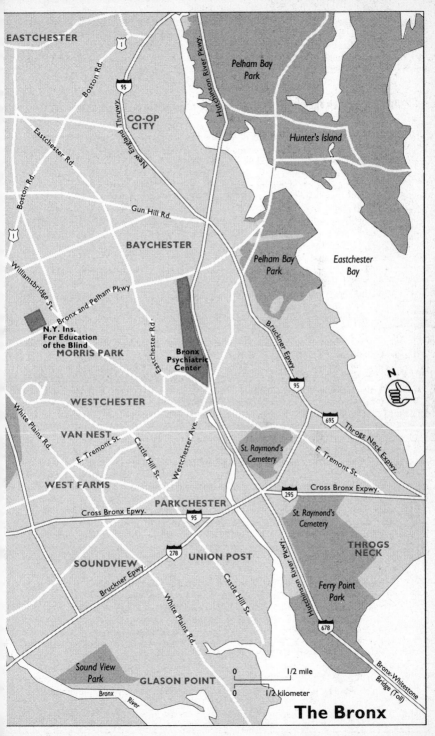

The Bronx

blocks north up Boston Rd. to the zoo entrance. Alternatively, take the D express to Fordham Rd., then the Bx12 bus to Southern Blvd. Walk east on Fordham Rd. to the Rainey Gate entrance. The express BxM11 bus leaves from Madison Ave. in Midtown for the Bronxdale entrance to the zoo ($3.75 each way) and runs back down the east side of Manhattan; call Liberty Lines at 718-652-8400 for details. Metro North also provides trains from Manhattan (call 212-532-4900).

■ Central Bronx: New York Botanical Garden, Etc.

North across East Fordham Rd. from the zoo sprawls the labyrinthine **New York Botanical Garden** (718-817-8705). Here, native New Yorkers cavort amid such oddities as trees, flowers, and the open sky. Snatches of forest and waterways attempt to recreate the area's original landscape. The 250-acre garden, one of the world's outstanding horticultural preserves, serves as both a research laboratory and a plant and tree museum. One can scope out the 40-acre hemlock forest kept in its natural state, the Peggy Rockefeller Rose Garden, the T.H. Everett Rock Garden and waterfall, the Native Plant Garden, the Snuff Mill restaurant (718-817-8687 to schedule a private meal), or a hands-on children's adventure garden. On weekends from April through October, tours available in 20 languages sweep the garden grounds at 1pm and 3pm, departing from the steps of the Visitor Information Center. If you go exploring by yourself, get a garden map; it's a jungle out there for the mapless. The 3-mile perimeter walk skirts most of the major sights. (Garden grounds open Tues.-Sun. 10am-6pm; $3, seniors, students, and children under 16 $1; children under 6 free. Free to all on Wed. and Sat. 10am-noon. Parking $4. Call 718-817-8705 for information.) If you're driving, the garden is easily reached via the Henry Hudson, Bronx River, or Pelham parkways. By subway, take the D or #4 to Bedford Park Blvd. Walk eight blocks east or take the Bx26, Bx12, Bx19, or Bx41 bus to the Garden. The Metro-North Harlem line goes from Grand Central Station to Botanical Garden Station, which lies right outside the main gate (call 718-532-4900 for details).

Fordham University (718-817-1000), begun in 1841 by John Hughes as St. John's College, has matured into one of the nation's foremost Jesuit schools. Robert S. Riley built the campus in classic collegiate Gothic style in 1936. It spans 80 fenced acres on Webster Ave. between E. Fordham Rd. and Dr. Theodore Kazimiroff Blvd. (subway: C or D to Fordham Rd.).

One of the more celebrated immigrant communities of the Bronx lies south of Fordham U. in **Belmont,** the uptown "Little Italy." In this neighborhood of two-story rowhouses and byzantine alleyways you'll find some of the best Italian food west of Naples. Outside the **Church of Our Lady of Mt. Carmel,** at 187th St. and Belmont Ave., stands a pair of ecclesiastical shops where you can buy a statuette of your favorite saint. The portable martyrs come in all sizes and in every color of the rainbow. The church holds high mass in Italian daily at 10:15am, 12:45pm, and 7:30pm. **Arthur Ave.** is home to some of the best homestyle southern Italian cooking (outside of Italy) in the world. At **Dominick's,** between 186th and 187th St., boisterous crowds at long communal tables put away pasta without recourse to ordering, prices, or menus. (Subway: C or D to Fordham Rd.) For the same dish on three different days you may pay three different prices, but you'll never leave kvetching (see Eating & Drinking: Bronx, p. 113).

The enthusiastic Bronx Historical Society maintains the **Edgar Allan Poe Cottage** (718-881-8900), built in 1812 and furnished in the 1840s. The morbid writer and his tubercular wife lived spartanly here at 2640 Grand Concourse off Kingsbridge Rd. (5 blocks west of Fordham U.) from 1846 until 1848. Here Poe wrote *Annabel Lee*, *Eureka*, and *The Bells*, a tale about the neighboring bells of Fordham. The museum displays a slew of Poe's manuscripts and other macabrabilia. (Open Wed.-Fri. 9am-5pm, Sat. 10am-4pm, Sun. 1-5pm. Call in advance for a tour. Admission $2. Subway: #4 or D to Kingsbridge Rd.)

The **Herbert H. Lehman College** (718-960-8000) rests at Jerome Ave. and E. 198th St., three blocks west and two long blocks north of the Poe House. Founded in 1931 as Hunter College, it is a fiefdom in the CUNY empire. The U.N. Security Council met in the gymnasium building in 1946. In 1980, the Lehmans endowed the first cultural center in the Bronx, the **Lehman Center for the Performing Arts,** on the Bedford Park Blvd. side of campus; the center is a 2300-seat concert hall, experimental theater, recital hall, library, dance studio, and art gallery in one. (Subway: #4 to Bedford Park Blvd.-Lehman College. Ticket office open Mon.-Fri. 10am-5pm; call 718-960-8000 for further info.) One block up through Harris Park, the **Bronx High School of Science** is a long-established center of academic excellence, as evidenced by the several Nobel Prize-winning scientists who matriculated here.

At Bronx Community College's **Hall of Fame for Great Americans,** at Martin Luther King Jr. Blvd. and W. 181st St. (718-289-5100), gape at the bronze busts of 102 great Americans set on beds of granite and weeds. Abe Lincoln, Booker T. Washington, and the Wright Brothers are just a few of the heads on display in this turn-of-the-century hall, owned by the City University of New York. (Open daily 9am-5pm. Free. Subway: #4 to Burnside Ave. See Museums, p. 248.)

■ Northern Bronx: Van Cortlandt Park

Van Cortlandt Park (718-430-1890), the city's third-largest, spreads across 1146 acres of ridges and valleys in the northwest Bronx. The slightly grungy park contains two golf courses, new tennis courts, baseball diamonds, soccer, football, and cricket fields, kiddie recreation areas, and a large swimming pool. In case you prefer food over recreation, the park also provides BBQ facilities. The park's **special-events office** (718-430-1848) offers information about the many concerts and sports activities that take place during the warmer months. While children of all ages swarm the various ball fields, nearby **Van Cortlandt Lake** teems with bemused fish. Hikers have plenty of clambering options—the **Cass Gallagher Nature Trail** in the park's northwestern section leads to rock outcroppings from the last ice age and to what is arguably the most untamed wilderness in the five boroughs. The **Old Putnam Railroad Track,** once the city's first rail link to Boston, now leads past the quarry that supplied the marble for Grand Central Station. The **Indian Field recreation area** was laid on top of the burial grounds of pro-rebel Stockbridge Indians who were ambushed and massacred by British troops during the Revolutionary War.

In the southwest of the park stands the **Van Cortlandt House** (718-543-3344), at 246th St., a national landmark built in 1748 by the prominent political clan of the same name. The house is the oldest building in the Bronx. George Washington made frequent visits here, including his 1781 meeting with Rochambeau to determine the final strategy of the Revolutionary War. George also began his triumphal march into New York City from here in 1783. Vague British nobility, aristocratic French, solitary Hessians, and continental Americans all showed up with their forces for the brief, historic sojourn. Musty masonry and peeling paint serve as reminders of this repeatedly restored mansion's distinguished history. Besides featuring the oldest dollhouse in the U.S., the house also sports a colonial-era garden and sundial. (Mansion open Tues.-Fri. 10am-3pm, Sat.-Sun. 11am-4pm. Admission $2, students and seniors $1.50. Kids under 12 free. The park and the mansion can both be reached by subway—#1 or 9 to 242nd St.)

Across from Van Cortlandt Park, atop a considerable hill, is **Manhattan College** (718-862-8000), a 100-year-old private liberal arts institution that began as a high school. Starting from the corner of Broadway and 242nd St. (Subway: #1 or 9 to 242nd St.), take 242nd up, up, *up*hill. As you scale the tortuous mound past Irish pubs and Chinese laundromats, watch for the college's pseudo-Federalist red-brick buildings and chapel. The campus sprawls over stairs, squares, and plateaus like a life-sized game of Chutes and Ladders. The second staircase on campus brings you to a sheer granite bluff crowned with a kitsch plaster Madonna, a likely kidnapping victim from a suburban garden. Hardy souls who attain the campus peaks can take in a cinemascopic view of the Bronx. In direct contrast to much of the poverty-stricken Bronx, this area features some extremely wealthy residences and a triumvirate of

N E I G H B O R H O O D S

esteemed private schools— **Fieldston School** (featured in Francis Ford Coppola's short film in *New York Stories*), **Horace Mann,** and **Riverdale.**

Wave Hill (718-549-3200), at 675 W. 252nd St., a pastoral estate in Riverdale, commands an astonishing view of the Hudson and the Palisades. Samuel Clemens (a.k.a. Mark Twain), Arturo Toscanini, and Teddy Roosevelt all resided in this impressive mansion. Donated to the city over 20 years ago, the estate currently offers concerts and dance amid its greenhouses and spectacular formal gardens. (Gardens open June to mid-Oct. Tues. and Thurs.-Sun. 9am-5:30pm, Wed. 9:30am-dusk; mid-Oct. through May Wed.-Sun. 10am-4:30pm. Tues.-Fri. free, Sat.-Sun. admission $4, seniors and students $2.) If you have a good sense of direction, Wave Hill is a hilly but pleasant half-hour walk from the 242nd St. subway. However, since the twists and turns of these streets can be confusing, a better bet would be the Metro North line to Riverdale Station.

The 1758 **Valentine-Varian House** (718-881-8900), the second-oldest building in the Bronx (Van Cortlandt got there first), also saw light action during the Revolution. It has since become the site of the **Museum of Bronx History,** which is run by the Bronx County Historical Society. The museum, at Bainbridge Ave. and E. 208th St., functions as the borough archive, profiling its heritage. The house has retained a few period furnishings but negligible Revolutionary ambience. (Open Sat. 10am-4pm, Sun. 1-5pm, otherwise by appointment. Admission $2. Subway: D to 205th St. or #4 to Mosholu Pkwy.)

■ Northeast Bronx: Pelham Bay Park

Pelham Bay Park has over 2100 acres of green saturated with playing fields, tennis courts, golf courses, picnic spaces, wildlife sanctuaries, a beach, and even training grounds for the city's mounted police force. The omniscient Park Rangers lead a variety of history- and nature-oriented walks for creatures great and small (call 718-430-1890 for a schedule). Inside the park, the Federalist **Bartow-Pell Mansion Museum** (718-885-1461), Shore Rd. opposite the golf courts, sits among prize-winning formal gardens landscaped in 1915. The interior decorator doted on the Empire/Greek-Revival style. (Open Wed., Sat.-Sun. noon-4pm. Closed three weeks in Aug. Admission $2.50, seniors and students $1.25. Children under 12 free, first Sun. of each month free to all. Subway: #6 to Pelham Bay Park.)

For a whiff of New England in New York, visit **City Island,** a community of century-old houses and sailboats complete with a shipyard. The **North Wind Undersea Museum** (718-885-0701) is a treat for sailors and landlubbers alike. Nautical treasures on display include a 100-year-old tugboat, antiquated diving gear, exotic sea shells, and enough whale bones to cause even Scandinavians to shiver their timbers. The Museum is also the home of "Physty the Whale," a life-size replica of the first beached whale ever to be saved by humankind (open Mon.-Fri. 10am-5pm, Sat.-Sun. noon-5pm; adults $3, children $2). Take the #6 subway to Pelham Bay Park and then board the #21 bus outside the station. Get off at the first stop on City Island; the museum is on your left.

■ South Bronx

This is most assuredly not the part of town you should be meandering through in search of bargains or out-of-the-way places—go directly to your destination and do not carry $200. That aside, sports fans and stair-master freaks will enjoy a visit to historic **Yankee Stadium,** on E. 161st St. at River Ave. Built in 1923, frequent remodeling has kept the aging stadium on a par with more recent constructions. The Yankees played the first night game here in 1946 and the first message scoreboard tallied points here in 1954. Inside the 11.6-acre park (the field measures only 3.5 acres), monuments honor such Yankee greats as Lou Gehrig, Joe DiMaggio, and the incomparable Babe Ruth. But besides conjuring thrills for baseball fans, Yankee Stadium provides much-needed income to area merchants struggling to keep the South Bronx's economy afloat. Controversial Yankees owner George Steinbrenner has announced a possible abandonment of The-House-That-Ruth-Built in the South Bronx for the more convenient and tourist-friendly confines of Midtown Manhattan. Needless to say, such a migration would hurt more than just a classic stadium and those who love it. (Subway: #4, C, or D to 161st St. See Sports: Baseball, p. 282.)

The **Bronx Museum of the Arts** (718-681-6000, ext. 141 for events), at 165th St. and Grand Concourse near Yankee Stadium, is another good reason to go south. Set in the rotunda of the Bronx Courthouse, the museum exhibits works by old masters as well as local talent, with a focus on contemporary Latino, African-American, and women artists. (Open Wed. 3pm-9pm, Thurs.-Fri. 10am-5pm, Sat.-Sun. 1-6pm. Suggested donation $3, students $2, seniors $1; Wed. free.)

■ Staten Island

In 1524, 32 years after Columbus patented the New World, a Florentine named Giovanni da Verrazano sailed into New York Harbor to get some fresh water. He refilled his casks on a sizable chunk of land and unwittingly stepped into history as the godfather of Staten Island. The name (originally Staaten Eylandt) comes courtesy of Henry Hudson, who plied his sail in the neighboring waters while on a 1609 voyage for the Dutch East India Company. In 1687, the sportive Duke of York sponsored a sailing contest, generously offering Staten Island as the prize. Manhattan's team won and has since called the island its own.

For the first 440 years after it was settled by Europeans, the only way to get from the island to New York proper was by boat. In 1713, a public ferry started running from Staten Island to the rest of the city. In spite of the new link, Staten Islanders still tended to look west to New Jersey, just a stone's throw away across the Arthur Kill, rather than north and east to the city. In 1964, builder Othmar "George Washington Bridge" Amman spanned the gap between Staten Island and Brooklyn with a 4260-foot-long suspension number, the **Verrazano-Narrows Bridge.** Visible from virtually everywhere on the island, the bridge has the distinction of being the world's second-longest suspension bridge, outspanned only by the Humber Bridge in England (it was also prominently featured in the John Travolta classic *Saturday Night Fever*). Amman's construction narrowly beats out San Francisco's Golden Gate Bridge for the honor by 60 feet.

Although traffic now flows more easily between Manhattan and Staten Island (via Brooklyn), the two boroughs exchange little save the barest cordiality. In recent years Staten Islanders have unsuccessfully lobbied borough, city, and state governments to have Staten Island declared an independent municipality. Many resent having to pay higher taxes to subsidize the poorer neighborhoods in New York's other boroughs. Manhattanites tend to lump Staten Island with New Jersey; most only go there in order to ride the ferry roundtrip (without getting off) or to take driving tests (the waiting list for appointments is shorter than in Manhattan and the driving substantially less frenetic). Moreover, many of the places worth visiting are scattered in locations that are only accessible by bus or car.

Yet, it only makes the few fine attractions seem even better for being undervalued and beyond the reach of the swarms of disinterested ferry riders. Snug Harbor is an idyllic oasis, the Tibetan Museum truly serene, and the Staten Island Mall belongs so solidly to the great American tradition of mall-dom that it's bound to make anyone visiting from the nation's heartland feel right at home.

To get to the **ferry terminal** in Manhattan (718-390-5253 for ferry info), take the #1 or 9 train to South Ferry (or take the N or R to Whitehall, then walk west about 3 blocks). Free to Staten Island and only 50¢ to ride back to Manhattan, the ferry is one of the best deals in the city. You can take in the splendid breeze and check out the lower Manhattan skyline, Ellis Island, the Statue of Liberty, and Governor's Island. The views are some of the best in the city, the frequent prey of postcard photographers and tourism bureaus. New York's scale is imprinted even on the boats and tankers, which are *huge,* and on the giant industrial structures lining the horizon. The

30-minute ride is particularly exhilarating at sunset or night; the ferry runs 24 hours. Sharing the trip with an automobile incurs a $3 charge

An **Information Center kiosk** by the Whitehall/South Ferry subway stop on Manhattan has plenty of tourist info, but, if you forget to arm yourself with brochures there, you can call the **Staten Island Chamber of Commerce,** 130 Bay St. (718-727-1900), for assistance (open Mon.-Fri. 8:30am-5pm). To get there, bear left from the ferry station onto Bay St. You can also call the Staten Island Institute of Arts and Sciences Arts Hotline (718-727-1135) to learn about regional art and exhibitions. Because of the hills and the distances (and some potentially dangerous neighborhoods in between), it's a bad idea to *walk* from one site to the next. Make sure to plan your excursion with the bus schedule in mind; it's available at the **New York Convention and Visitor's Bureau** (see Essentials: Tourist Information, p. 66), or at the South Ferry subway stop in Manhattan.

Just up the hill from the terminal, the second street on the right is Stuyvesant Place; follow it as it wraps up to the right, leading to the site of the imposing Federalist **Borough Hall** and its clocktower. The terraced garden nearby offers an eye-widening view of the harbor (as well as the chance to tweak the cheeks of Frank D. Paulo, depicted holding a pre-pubescent girl in a sculpture bearing the ambiguous inscription "A Public Man").

One block farther west at 75 Stuyvesant Pl., on the far corner of Wall St., are the galleries of the **Staten Island Institute of Arts and Sciences** (718-727-1135), which feature rotating displays pertaining to the art, science, and history of the region. The upstairs galleries feature temporary exhibits whose subjects vary widely, from the Staten Island Juried Art Exhibition to the "Fantastic World of Butterflies." (Open Mon.-Sat. 9am-5pm, Sun. 1-5pm. Suggested donation $2.50; seniors, students, and children under 12 $1.50).

At 1000 Richmond Terrace lies the **Snug Harbor Cultural Center** (718-448-2500), 83 sprawling, green, and amazingly well kept acres of the national Historic Landmark District. Founded in 1801, Sailors' Snug Harbor was the first maritime hospital and home for retired sailors in the U.S. (The iron fence barricading the grounds was meant to keep the old salts from quenching their thirst at nearby bars.) It was purchased by the City of New York in 1976 and now includes 28 historic buildings scattered over wonderfully placid and unpopulated parkland. The Center provides space for contemporary art, theater, recitals, outdoor sculpture, and concerts. You can get here by taking the S40 bus from the ferry terminal. The lovely uncrowded fields, gardens, and woodlands are a perfect antidote to Manhattanite cabin fever.

Once on the grounds, head toward the main cluster of buildings and follow the signs pointing you to the **Visitors' Center**, where you can pick up a map of the grounds and a schedule of the day's exhibitions and events (free tours of the grounds offered Sat.-Sun. 2pm). At the **Newhouse Center for Contemporary Art,** you'll be privy to the work of emerging and mid-career artists working in all media (open Wed.-Sun. noon-5pm; suggested donation $1). The **Staten Island Botanical Garden** (718-273-8200), also at the Center, tends a striking Butterfly Garden among the other beds of lilies, lilacs, sunflowers, and snapdragons on its 28 peaceful acres (open daily dawn to dusk; tours available by appointment). Another of the Center's tenants is the **Staten Island Children's Museum** (718-273-2060), which offers funky interactive exhibits. The recent "Water Wonder" exhibit was so encouraging of the hands-on ethic that it offered kids-sized rubber raincoats and rainpants for protection. The museum also features a "Walk-In Workshop" where kids can create their own art with a wide variety of media. "Science on Stage" performances by staff members run on weekends throughout the year (open June to mid-Sept. Tues.-Sun. 11am-5pm; mid-Sept. to May Tues.-Sun. noon-5pm; admission $4). Outdoor performances are often held in the Center's South Meadow; recent shows have included Buckwheat Zydeco and Arlo Guthrie (tickets $15 each show). Free family concerts are also held each Sunday at the Gazebo.

The **Staten Island Zoo** (718-442-3100), in Barrett Park at Broadway and Clove Rd., has moved all of its big animals permanently to Mexico (recent visitors have

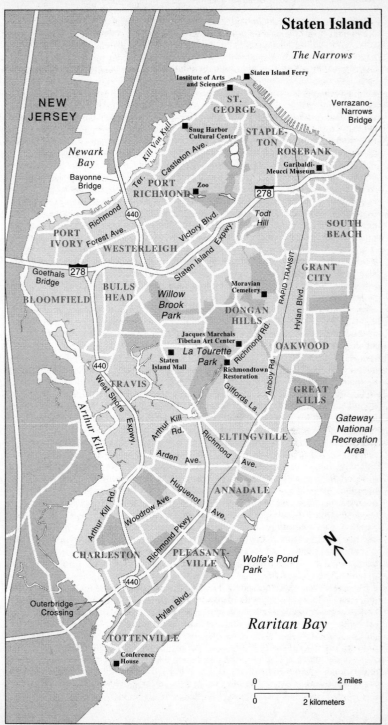

Staten Island

The Narrows

NEW JERSEY

Institute of Arts and Sciences

Staten Island Ferry

ST. GEORGE

STAPLE-TON

Verrazano-Narrows Bridge

Snug Harbor Cultural Center

ROSEBANK

Newark Bay

Kill Van Kull

Castleton Ave.

Garibaldi-Meucci Museum

Bayonne Bridge

Ter.

PORT RICHMOND

Zoo

278

Richmond

440

Victory Blvd.

Todt Hill

SOUTH BEACH

PORT IVORY

Forest Ave.

WESTERLEIGH

Staten Island Expwy.

RAPID TRANSIT

GRANT CITY

Goethals Bridge

278

BULLS HEAD

Willow Brook Park

Moravian Cemetery

Hylan Blvd.

BLOOMFIELD

DONGAN HILLS

OAKWOOD

Jacques Marchais Tibetan Art Center

Richmond Rd.

440

La Tourette Park

Staten Island Mall

Richmondtown Restoration

Amboy Rd.

GREAT KILLS

TRAVIS

West Shore Expwy.

Arthur Kill Rd.

Giffords La.

Gateway National Recreation Area

Arden Ave.

Richmond Ave.

ELTINGVILLE

Arthur Kill

Huguenot Ave.

ANNADALE

Woodrow Ave.

Richmond Pkwy.

CHARLESTON

PLEASANT-VILLE

Wolfe's Pond Park

440

Outerbridge Crossing

Hylan Blvd.

Raritan Bay

TOTTENVILLE

Conference House

N

| 0 | 2 miles |
| 0 | 2 kilometers |

remarked on a giant sucking sound). You can still toy with some of the world's finest reptiles for $3, $2 for children under 11, free admission Wednesday 2-4:45pm (open daily 10am-4:45pm). To reach the zoo, take the S48 bus from Ferry Terminal to Broadway, and then walk two and a half blocks south.

Designed like a small Tibetan mountain temple, the **Jacques Marchais Museum of Tibetan Art,** 338 Lighthouse Ave. (718-987-3500, 718-987-3478 for recorded schedule) displays one of the finest collections of Tibetan art in the Western hemisphere (see p. 249). To reach the Museum, take the S74 bus from the ferry to Lighthouse Ave., walk up Lighthouse Ave., and follow it as it bends to the right up the fairly steep hill; the Museum rests a few yards beyond the hill's crest.

Historic Richmond Town, 441 Clarke Ave., is a huge museum complex documenting three centuries of Staten Island's culture and history. Reconstructed 17th- to 19th-century dwellings are populated by "inhabitants," costumed master craftspeople and their apprentices. Thanks to budget cuts, only 10 of these buildings, spread over 100 acres, are permanently open to the public. Head for the **Voorlezer's House** (1695), the oldest surviving elementary school in the U.S. (also a church and home), the **General Store** (1840), and an 18th-century farmhouse. The buildings that are open to the public rotate, so call in advance to find out what's open, as well as to find out about the "living history" events, which take place on weekends throughout the summer. Tours of Richmond Town are sometimes available with advance notice. Call 718-351-1611 for tours or information on special events. (Open July-Aug. Wed.-Fri. 10am-5pm, Sat.-Sun. 1-5pm; Sept.-Dec. Wed.-Sun. 1-5pm. Admission $4; seniors, students, and children 6-16 $2.50.) To get here, take a 40-min. ride on the S74 bus from the ferry terminal.

The Vanderbilt saga comes to an end at the **Moravian Cemetery,** on Richmond Rd. at Todt Hill Rd. in Donegan Hills. Commodore Cornelius Vanderbilt and his clan lie in this ornate crypt, built in 1886 by Richard Morris Hunt. Central Park creator Frederick Law Olmsted contributed the landscaping. Alas, the crypt can be viewed only from the outside. Adjacent to the cemetery is the 72-acre **High Rock Park Conservation Center** (718-667-6042), with miles of well marked trails perfect for an afternoon stroll. The extremely friendly Urban Rangers lead tours of various parts of the park on Saturday and Sunday afternoons at 2pm (center open daily 9am-5pm; grounds open dawn to dusk). To get to the Center, take the S74 bus from the ferry terminal to the Rockland Ave. station, walk two blocks and go right onto Nevada; follow Nevada all the way to its end. The walk should take 20-25 minutes.

In the mid-1800s, Giuseppe Garibaldi, an Italian patriot and mastermind of Italy's reunification, took refuge on the island following his defeat at the hands of Napoleon III. He settled in an old farmhouse in Rosebank and proceeded to amass enough memorabilia to make the place into a museum: the **Garibaldi-Meucci Museum,** 420 Tompkins Ave. (718-442-1608). At one time the house belonged to Antonio Meucci, the less-than-celebrated inventor of the telephone (he had developed his first working model by 1851 and finally received a U.S. patent caveat in 1871, but died before being recognized as the inventor—luckily for Alexander Graham Bell). To get here, take the SIRTOA subway train from the ferry terminal station three stops to Clifton Station. Walk west three blocks on Vanderbilt Ave. to Tompkins Ave. and turn left; the museum is a few blocks ahead. The museum is open Tuesday through Sunday from 1 to 5pm and is free.

The only peace conference ever held between British forces and American rebels took place in Staten Island in the **Conference House** (718-984-2086). At the summit on Sept. 11, 1776, British commander Admiral Lord Howe met with three Continental Congress representatives—Benjamin Franklin, John Adams, and Edward Rutledge. Located at the foot of Hyland Blvd. in Tottenville, the house has become a National Historic Landmark. Inside, you can see period furnishings and refresh your knowledge of Revolutionary War minutiae (admission $2, seniors and children under 13 $1; guided tours by appointment Wed.-Sun. 1-4pm). To reach the Conference House, take the S78 bus to the last stop on Craig Ave. and walk west one block farther on

Hylan Blvd.; make a right on Satterlee St.; the Conference House is about 100 feet ahead on the left.

■ Hoboken, NJ

Right across the river from downtown Manhattan, Hoboken boasts not only a beautiful view of the New York skyline but also an increasingly legitimate cultural scene catering to the young and the hip. Sometimes considered a part of the Big Apple due to its proximity (10min. and $1 away via the PATH train) and spillover (Hoboken has become a haven for fun-loving twenty-somethings seeking lower rents), the city also boasts a bit of historical significance: Frank Sinatra and baseball were both born here. While honoring its heritage, Hoboken also remains thoroughly grounded in the 90s—it is famous for being the home and hangout of its own slacker culture as raucous (if not as varied) as that of its gargantuan neighbor. Following the cycles of urban cultural ecology, yuppies have started to crowd the young bohemians out of Hoboken, but this gentrification is still far from complete.

Today Hoboken is faced with unique problems, primarily centered around its Gen-X party town reputation. Many of the 33,000 residents move out once they de-slack, to counties with better schools and more suburban amenities (the average age here is 25). And the bar scene that emerged to serve the locals has attracted hordes of heavy-drinking frat-boy types, seen as a nuisance by many 'Bokenites. For now, though, Hoboken is still a great place to be when you're young and thirsty.

The mile-long city is laid out in a grid; the east-west streets are (from south to north) Newark St., First St., 2nd St.—all the way up to 14th St. The cross streets of note are River Rd. (a.k.a. Frank Sinatra Rd.), Hudson St., Washington St., Bloomfield St., and Willow St. Traipse up Washington St. for most of the action in Hoboken, but the streets around the PATH station and from First to 4th St. also bustle with activity. Be careful crossing the streets, though, as there are no crosswalks, and drivers here are even less friendly than those in the city.

To get to Hoboken, take the B, D, F, N, Q, or R train to 34th St., then the PATH train ($1) to the first stop in Hoboken. (The PATH train also leaves from the 23rd and 14th St. stations of the F train, as well as from its own stations at 9th St./Sixth Ave. and Christopher St./Greenwich St.)

Arising from the depths of the PATH station, turn to your right, and note the **Erie-Lackawanna Plaza.** This Beaux Arts station has been featured in a number of movies (no doubt because of the spectacular view), including *On the Waterfront* and Woody Allen's *Stardust Memories.* In the summer, the plaza features free movies on Thursday and Friday nights (starting at 9pm).

From here, walk the other direction along Hudson Pl. to Hudson St., take a right, then take a quick left onto Newark St. This area is littered with bars, probably due to its PATH proximity. Two blocks down Newark St., Hoboken's renowned **Pier Platters** wants you to album-browse. The local Bar/None label, original home of They Might Be Giants and Yo La Tengo, started nearby (see p. 292).

Washington Street, the main drag of the city, is just a little further down Newark St. Bars, restaurants, cafés, and realtors make up the bulk of the action here. At First and Washington St. sits the stately yet aging **Hoboken City Hall,** which often hosts

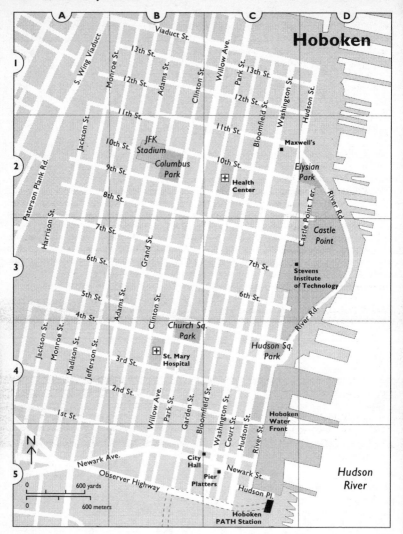

Hoboken

exhibitions by the Hoboken Historical Society. The 150th anniversary of baseball was proudly celebrated here in the summer of 1996. If you find Hoboken history intriguing, take a peek (201-656-2240; open Mon.-Fri. 8:30am-4:30pm).

Cruise on up Washington St. to 4th St. For those exhausted by punk rock and frat drinking antics ("Shotgun!"), take a left and walk two blocks to Garden St. and **Church Square Park.** Here swinging kids replace swinging singles, basketball hoops replace funnels, and summer concerts sound much more sedate than the screaming at Maxwell's or the grunting in the bars.

Back on Washington St., walk up to 8th St. and take a right up the very large hill which leads to the campus of the **Stevens Institute of Technology.** If you cut through the serene lawn and walk to the big cannons overlooking the edge of the hill, you'll be rewarded with quite a sight. This is **Castle Point,** where the view of Manhattan's west side, from Twin Towers to Empire State, is truly awe-inspiring.

From here, you'll probably want to descend the hill, with the frat-houses to your right, and keep on truckin' down Washington St. Brownstones in various shades line the street from 8th St. on up. On the right-hand side at 11th St., past the large sculpted elk, is the vaunted **Maxwell's** (see p. 275). On the left-hand side is an austere monument to the national pastime, which was supposedly first played in Hoboken, between the New Yorks and the Knickerbockers in 1846. Down 11th St. to the east, past Maxwell's, lies **Elysian Park,** the field where that legendary baseball game was played. Keep walking north and you'll end up in Weehawken—it's probably best to circle back at around 14th St.

■ Near Hoboken: Jersey City

Artists, further frustrated by the rising rent rates in Hoboken, have recently found refuge in the urban squalor of Jersey City, conveniently located on the PATH line from the World Trade Center. Jersey City's "scene" manages to stay off the streets; the city is in an economic depression, and most of the artistic settlement is near the Grove St. PATH station. The **Cathedral Art Gallery,** 39 Erie St. (201-451-1074), located in the Grace Church Van Voorst, can also be found a few blocks from the station; walk up Grove/Manila St. past Newark St. to 2nd St., go left one block to Erie St., then go left another block. Administered by the Cooper Art Gallery at 295 Grove St., the gallery features fine arts and crafts by local artists (open Tues.-Sat. noon-7pm). The **Jersey City Museum,** 472 Jersey Ave. (201-547-4514), two blocks up Newark St. from the Grove St. station, shows strong selections from the local scene (open Tues., Thurs., and Fri. 10:30am-5pm, Wed. 10:30am-8pm).

Liberty State Park (201-915-3411) is south of the Grove St. station. It contains a lot of state-run greenery, a science museum, and good views of Ellis Island and the Statue of Liberty. Take the #81 bus from the Hoboken Terminal (check for "Liberty State Park" on the LED board; $1).

NEIGHBORHOODS

Museums

New York has accumulated more stuff in more museums than any other city in the New World. Come witness a culture collecting itself. Swoon under a life-sized replica of a great blue whale at the American Museum of Natural History. Control a 900-ft. aircraft carrier at the Intrepid Sea-Air-Space Museum. Slip into the world of the 2000-year-old Egyptian Temple of Dendur or of Van Gogh's 100-year-old *Café at Arles* at the Metropolitan Museum of Art. Relax alongside Monet's *Water Lilies* at the Museum of Modern Art. Or analyze the question of engendered identity in the contemporary art at the Whitney.

Many New York museums request a donation instead of a fixed admission charge. No one will throw you out or even glare at you for giving less than the suggested donation; more likely, you'll feel slightly cheap and maybe guilty. Enjoy that sneaky feeling. Recently the Met has extended its hours so you can stay longer or take a break and come back for more (always keep your pin). Some museums have weekly "voluntary contribution" (read: free) times, typically in the evening.

During the annual **Museum Mile Festival** in June, Fifth Ave. museums keep their doors open until late at night, stage engaging exhibits, involve city kids in mural painting, and fill the streets with music and strolling dog-walkers. Many museums also sponsor film series and live concerts throughout the year (see Entertainment and Nightlife).

■ Metropolitan Museum of Art

In 1866, a group of eminent Americans in Paris enthusiastically received John Jay's proposal to create a "National Institution and Gallery of Art." Under Jay's leadership, the New York Union League Club rallied civic leaders, art collectors, and philanthropists, and launched the museum in 1870. At the time, the collection consisted of only 174 paintings—mostly Dutch and Flemish—and a handful of assorted antiquities. A decade later, the Metropolitan Museum settled at its present location in Central Park at Fifth Avenue and 82nd Street., despite the protests of park designer Frederick Law Olmstead. This once tiny project has since become an insatiable high-culture empire, spanning 1.4 million square feet. and housing 3.3 million works of art. The Met still constantly seeks, seduces, and seizes art objects from everyone and everywhere to display them for its enormous audience.

The museum's building, like the art it holds, is a sort of bridal composite, encompassing the old and the new, the borrowed and the blue (-blooded). The original, Gothic-style façade, which can now be seen only over the Lehman Wing on the western side, was later replaced with a more Neoclassical construction. This trend of expansion and rebuilding has continued for over a century as the ever-growing collection requires more and more space. Architects produce new walls designed in the style of the moment. Recent additions include the glass-enclosed Lila Acheson Wallace Wing and the Cantor Roof Garden, which contains changing sculpture exhibits in open air.

PRACTICAL INFORMATION AND ORIENTATION

The Met (879-5500) is located at Fifth Ave. and 82nd St. (Subway: #4, 5, or 6 to 86th St.) **Hours** are Sun. and Tues.-Thurs. 9:30am-5:15pm, Fri.-Sat. 9:30am-8:45pm. **Admission** is free to members and children under 12 (accompanied by an adult). Suggested donation is $7 for adults, $3.50 for seniors and students; if you can stomach the shame, disregard their suggestion and plunk down as little as you like. However, you must (and probably should) pay something.

Before subjecting yourself to the moral debate of pay-what-you-wish, you may want to stop by the **Visitors Center,** located at the information desk in the Great Hall, where you can stock up on brochures and grab a copy of the floor plan. In the Great

Hall, the **Foreign Visitors Desk** distributes maps and brochures and gives assistance in a number of languages. For information on **disabled access,** call Disabled Visitors Services (535-7710); for services for **hearing-impaired visitors,** call 879-0421. **Wheelchairs** are available upon request at coat-check areas.

If you feel you need special direction, you can rent **recorded tours** of the museum's exhibitions ($4, $3.50 for members or groups, free for high school students from New York, New Jersey, or Connecticut), or follow the multilingual tour guides. For tour info go to the Recorded Tour Desk in the Great Hall, or call 570-3821. Free **Gallery tours** in English roam daily. Inquire at the Visitors Center for schedules, topics, and meeting places. For recorded info on upcoming **concerts** and **lectures,** call 570-3949. Single tickets go on sale one hour before the event.

The museum's holdings sprawl over three floors. The **ground floor** houses the Costume Institute, European Sculpture and Decorative Arts, the Robert Lehman collection, and the Uris Center for Education, where public lectures, films, and gallery talks take place.

The **first floor** contains the extensive American Wing; the Arms and Armor exhibit; Egyptian Art; more European sculpture and decorative arts; Greek and Roman art; Medieval Art; Art of the Pacific Islands, Africa, and the Americas; the Lila Acheson Wallace Wing with its footloose collection of 20th-Century art; plus all the information facilities, shops, and restaurants.

The **second floor** brings you more of the American Wing; Ancient Near Eastern Art; Asian Art; a collection of drawings, prints, and photographs, yet another dose of European painting, sculpture, and decorative arts; a Greek and Roman Art encore; more Islamic art; musical instruments; the second installment of 20th-Century Art; and the R.W. Johnson Recent Acquisitions Gallery.

Don't rush the Metropolitan experience; you could camp out in here for a month. (In fact, two children lived here, in the children's book *From The Mixed-Up Files of Mrs. Basil E. Frankweiler.*) No one ever "finishes" the Met. If you only have a few hours, the Greeks and Egyptians should keep you occupied. Or dip into one of the funkier, smaller collections. If you plan to be in the city for a while, you may want to plan on several short trips to the Met. After a couple hours of nonstop aesthetic bombardment, the paintings begin to seem much more drab than they should.

COLLECTIONS

After receiving that M lapel pin, fasten it securely onto your clothing (or the guards won't let you in). One of the most heavily trafficked galleries on the first floor is the **Greek and Roman Gallery.** This expansive collection, spanning several millennia and the sweep of both empires, contains, among other notables, various Cypriot sculptures, Greek vases, Roman busts, and Augustine wall-paintings. Remarkable amid so many examples of Platonic idealism is the first century statue of an old, tired woman—it was vandalized by later generations for its "paganism" (i.e. its departure from classical notions of art).

For your wallet's sake, it's best to ignore the overpriced museum café and move into the **Michael C. Rockefeller Wing,** which contains the art of **Africa,** the **Pacific Islands,** and the **Americas.** This extensive wing features one of the largest collections of non-Western art in the West, and perhaps the most intriguing works in the museum. Totem poles, boats, ceremonial masks (many of which inspired the Cubist movement), musical instruments, and sculptures fill this spacious, light gallery. The African collection includes bronze sculpture from Nigeria and wooden sculpture by the Dogan, Bamana, and Senufo of Mali. From the Pacific come artifacts from Asmat, the Sepik provinces of New Guinea, and the island groups of Melanesia and Polynesia. Inuit and Native American artifacts, not to mention Aztec and Mayan art, are also represented.

Next is the **Lila Acheson Wallace Wing** of 20th-century art. The Met was at first reluctant to invest in controversial modern art—the Museum of Modern Art was built to house works that the Met would not accept (see Museum of Modern Art (MoMA), p. 238). But in 1967, the Met finally relented, establishing the **Department of 20th-**

Century Art, which has since welcomed, among others, Picasso, Bonnard, Pollock, Warhol, and Kandinsky. The Americans flex the most muscle here, with numerous paintings by the Eight, the Modernist Stieglitz Circle, Abstract Expressionists, and color field artists. You may or may not catch the big names, as the displays from the permanent collection change every six months or so, but if you're lucky you can catch such masterpieces as Picasso's *The Blind Minstrel,* typical of his blue period, and Grant Wood's *Ride of Paul Revere,* a canvas that proves that the *American Gothic* great was more than a one-hit wonder.

Just between the Wrightsman Galleries and the Henry Kravis Wing lies the **European Sculpture Garden.** This sunlit courtyard is a good place in which to take that moment's rest for which your feet are pleading. Marble people and animals, in various states of repose and anxiety, stand among children and parents in similar poses.

Through another door is the **European Sculpture and Decorative Arts** wing. Containing about 60,000 works, ranging from the early labors of the Renaissance to the early 20th century, the collection covers eight areas: sculpture, woodwork, furniture, ceramics, glass, metalwork, tapestries, and textiles. Note the impressive vases and tapestries created in honor of Napoleon, Catherine the Great, and other European dignitaries with money to burn.

Farther inside the department, the **Jack and Belle Linsky Galleries** emphasize precious and luxurious objects. Highlights of the collection include canvases by Lucas Cranach the Elder, Rubens, and Boucher; more than 200 Rococo porcelain figures from such renowned factories as Meissen and Chantilly; and exquisite 18th-century French furniture.

Nearby, the **Medieval Art** collection is housed in dark and mysteriously damp environs, featuring church paraphernalia, including paintings, stained glass, and a huge choir screen. The collection is not as large as it could be; the rest of the Met's Medieval collection is housed at **The Cloisters,** the Washington Heights branch of the Met (p. 247).

From the north end of the Medieval gallery, exit the old Met and enter a new gallery (the old brick exterior is now encased in an elaborate glass space), the **Robert Lehman Wing.** Opened to the public in 1975, it showcases an extraordinary collection assembled by the acquisitive Lehman clan. Italian paintings from the 14th and 15th centuries flank canvases by Rembrandt, El Greco, and Goya. French painters from the 19th and 20th centuries include Ingrès, Renoir, Chagall, and Matisse.

From here, head back through Medieval Art, swing over to the left, and start humming the "Star-Spangled Banner". The **American Wing** houses one of the nation's largest and finest collections of American paintings, sculptures, and decorative crafts. The paintings cover almost all phases of the history of American art from the early days of West and Trumbull to Sargent and Hopper. You can get some celebrated glimpses of early America in Gilbert Stuart's regal portraits of our country's founding father, Bingham's pensive *Fur Traders Descending the Mississippi,* and the heroic, if precariously perched, *George Washington Crossing the Delaware* by Emanuel Gottlieb Leutze. Of the 19th-century paintings, some of the more noteworthy include Sargent's *Madame X,* a stunning portrait of the notorious French beauty Mme Gautreau, and several breathtaking landscapes by the Hudson River School.

Twenty-five period rooms document the history of American interior design and decorative art since the Colonial period. Note the especially fun, sinuously curved Victorian *tête-à-tête*—an "S"-shaped love seat that looks like a pair of Siamese armchairs. Art Nouveau fans will gush at the ample selection of Louis Comfort Tiffany's glasswork, while admirers of American Modernism can pay their respects in the Frank Lloyd Wright Room. The room was ingeniously designed to be an integral and organic part of the natural world outside the windows, an example of Wright's concept of total design.

If your brain is feeling full, take a break and romp around in the **Arms and Armor** collection, nested just off the American collection. The armor collection contains a huge number of swords, rapiers, daggers, and other sharp pointy objects.

Around the corner, the **Department of Egyptian Art** occupies the entire northeast wing of the main hall, spanning thousands of years—from 3100 BCE to the Byzantine Period (CE 700)—and containing a galaxy of artifacts, from earrings to whole temples. One of the museum's true must-see's is the incredible **Temple of Dendur**. Preserved in its entirety, the temple was a gift from Egypt to the United States in 1965 in recognition of U.S. contributions to the Aswan dam and the preservation of Nubian monuments. Note the ubiquitous graffiti of long-dead hooligans, French soldiers during the Napoleonic occupation of Egypt. Elsewhere in the wing, mummies provide spooky fun for kids, young and old. Downstairs is the **Costume Institute.** The museum's rich costume holdings offer insightful commentary on the cultural evolution of our own time. Recent exhibitions have focused on Diana Vreeland (a fashion editor for *Vogue*) and the changing approach to waistlines.

Returning to the Great Hall, you can go up the huge flight of stairs, around the upstairs gift shop and past the statue of Perseus to examine the extensive collection of Chinese ceramics lining the Great Hall Balcony. To one side is more Greek and Roman art; on the other, the under-appreciated department of **Ancient Near Eastern and Islamic Art.** The collection of Ancient Near Eastern Art features artwork from ancient Mesopotamia, Iran, Syria, Anatolia, and a smattering of other lands, all produced during the period from 6000 BCE to the Arab conquest in CE 626. Behind is the Islamic Art room, where you can see an intact mid-14th-century Iranian *mihrab* (a niche in a house of worship that points in the direction of Mecca) covered entirely in blue glazed ceramic tiles. The tasteful exhibition space enhances the geometric intrigue of the tiles and panel designs.

Back on the Great Hall Balcony, on the right (facing Perseus—don't look at Medusa...or else!) lies the **Asian Art** department, with the best collection outside of Asia. Walk through to the new South Asian gallery, the **Florence and Herbert Irving Galleries for the Arts of South and Southeast Asia,** which features the rhythmic and contortionist sculptures of Buddhas and *bodhissatvas.* Encompassing the entire Southeast Asian peninsula from antiquity to the present, the gallery is arranged chronologically, with a Cambodian Khmer courtyard. Running parallel is the **Ancient Chinese** gallery, with Han-dynasty funeral statuary. Check out the little farmhouse with the pigs.

Down the hall, you have the choice of either going straight to examine one of the most extensive collections of Chinese painting in the world, taking a left for Japanese prints and paintings (the *ukiyo-e* prints shouldn't be missed), or shopping at yet another kiosk.

Finally, what remains of the second floor is the Met's "jewel in the crown," the astounding collection of **European Paintings.** The Italian, Flemish, Dutch, and French schools dominate the collection (as they do the pre-20th century art world), but British and Spanish works also make cameo appearances.

The Italian collection is particularly strong in early Renaissance paintings. Amid the plethora of Madonnas and beatific baby Jesuses, look for gems by Titian and Caravaggio. The Spaniards are less numerous, but El Greco and Goya are represented.

In the Flemish quarters, you'll find Van Eyck's *Crucifixion* and the macabre *Last Judgment*, in which an undernourished Christ presides over the heavens as reptiles munch on writhing sinners in Hell below. The enigmatic Hieronymus Bosch also makes a rare American appearance with his *Adoration of the Magi.*

The Dutch make a strong showing, led by Rembrandt, whose most emblematic canvases converge at the Met: *Flora, The Toilet of Bathsheba, Aristotle with a Bust of Homer,* and *Self Portrait* are all here. The Met is also one of the foremost repositories for the works of the Dutch master of light, Johannes Vermeer. Of fewer than 40 widely acknowledged Vermeer canvases, the Museum can claim five, including the celebrated *Young Woman with a Water Jug, The Allegory of Earth,* and the vaguely fetal *Portrait of a Young Woman.*

Also not to be missed are the many works of Impressionism and Post-Impressionism. The rich collection reads like an art history textbook: George Seurat's *Circus Sideshow* and Vincent Van Gogh's *Self-Portrait with a Straw Hat* are perhaps the

> ### Rest Dem Bones
>
> If you're aiming to see all there is to see in the Met, you're going to need a place to rest. There are many charming courts and gardens around the museum that allow you to take your ease while looking astute. Try the Charles Engelhardt court in the American Wing, or the European Sculpture Garden between the Wrightsman Galleries and the Kravis Wing. The Temple of Dendur also offers an area upon which you can sit like a Nubian bird on a wire—the enormous windows grant a splendid view of Central Park. And on cool, summer days, the Gerald and the Iris B. Cantor Roof Garden (6th floor) can't be beat for a little suntanning among the sculpture.

most immediately recognizable. Also featured are Degas' renowned ballet canvases and Monet's views of Rouen Cathedral.

The French contingent in the European collection may be the most comprehensive section of the museum, spanning the 16th through 19th centuries and reading like a Who's Who of the art world. Entire rooms are devoted to the works of Rodin, Cézanne, Gauguin, Monet, Manet, Degas, Renoir, and many others. The sheer volume of superior artwork in this section alone is staggering; make sure you've allotted yourself enough time to savor each one.

Exhibitions in the 1996-97 season are slated to include the works of Tiepolo (Jan. 20-April 27), the glory of Byzantium (March 11-July 6), and the jewelry creations of Cartier (April-Aug.).

■ Museum of Modern Art (MoMA)

Hipper than the Met but more traditional than the Whitney, MoMA commands one of the world's most impressive collections of post-Impressionist, late 19th- and 20th-century art. Founded in 1929 by scholar Alfred Barr in response to the Met's wariness of cutting-edge work, the museum's first exhibit, held in a Fifth Avenue office building, boasted such then-unknowns as Cézanne, Gauguin, Seurat, and van Gogh. But as the ground-breaking works of 1900 to 1950 have moved from cult to masterpiece status, MoMA, in turn, has shifted from revolution to institution, telling the more or less completed story of the Modernist revolt against Renaissance ways of seeing. Temporary exhibits keep the museum's energy level (and ability to attract viewers) at a high, but MoMA's true wealth lies in its permanent collection. Comparing works by Vuillard and Seurat or Mondrian and Kandinsky can be stimulating even for children. And the display of such tongue-in-cheek creations as the Oldenburg *Two Cheeseburgers with Everything* or the Duchamp *L.H.O.O.Q.* makes the MoMA a great place for lifting spirits, too.

PRACTICAL INFORMATION AND ORIENTATION

The Museum of Modern Art is located at 11 W. 53rd St., between Fifth and Sixth Avenue (708-9400, information and film schedules 708-9480. Subway: E or F to Fifth Avenue-53rd St. or B, D, Q to 50th St. Open Sat.-Tues. 11am-6pm, Thurs.-Fri. noon-8:30pm. Admission $8, seniors and students $5, children under 16 free. Pay what you wish Thurs. and Fri. 5:30-8:30pm. Films require tickets, which are free with the price of admission, and can obtained in advance from the information desk.)

Cesar Pelli's 1984 glass additions to the 1939 museum building doubled the gallery space and now flood the halls with natural light. The information desk, straight ahead as you enter, dispenses interesting free brochures as well as two printed guides ($2) that connect and contextualize the works in the permanent collection. Past the admission desk lies the Abby Aldrich Rockefeller Sculpture Garden, an expansive patio with a fountain, a drooping willow, and a world-class assemblage of modern sculpture, featuring works by Matisse, Picasso, and Henry Moore. Rodin's tormented Balzac overshadows its neighbors, although it stands in danger of being upstaged by Picasso's bloated, sickly she-goat. **Summergarden,** a museum tradition in which Juilliard School affiliates use the garden to present free avant-garde music, is presented here during July and August (see Classical Music, p. 267).

Near the entrance to the sculpture garden, a small space presents changing exhibitions by contemporary artists. To the left of the sculpture garden, the glass-walled **Education Center** shows films and posts a schedule of gallery talks. On the opposite side of the sculpture garden is the overpriced but crowded **Garden Café**. Take the escalator downstairs to temporary shows in the Theater Gallery and to foreign and domestic art films in the **Roy and Niuta Titus Theaters** (see Movies, p. 263).

COLLECTIONS

MoMA's impressive permanent display of paintings and sculptures begins on the **second floor**. The sequence of works in the numbered galleries follows the basic chronology of Western artistic production, from the origins of Modernism—as exemplified by the works of Paris Post-Impressionists and early Cubists—to the cold masterworks of 1970s minimalism, art history's *cul-de-sac*. The slide-show-quality comprehensiveness of MoMA's collection can provoke an open-mouthed *déjà vu;* these are the originals that inspire virtually all lectures on modern art and viewers will probably recognize at least one work in each room.

Gallery 1, beside Rodin's *John the Baptist* to the left of the escalator, is the beginning of your aesthetic journey. **Galleries 1-3** focus on Post-Impressionism, where the flourishing of the modern aesthetic is on full display in works by Cézanne, Seurat, van Gogh, and Rousseau. The big draw, aside from Henri Rousseau's symbolist *The Sleeping Gypsy,* is undeniably van Gogh's *The Starry Night,* covered by layers of paint so thick that patches near the bottom of the frame still seem wet.

Picasso and Braque, the fathers of Cubism (painting's answer to the challenge of photography), are featured in **Gallery 4.** Picasso's giant *Demoiselles d'Avignon,* the first Cubist masterpiece, highlights one wall. **Gallery 5** features lesser-known Cubists, while **Gallery 6** spotlights German Expressionism.

In **Gallery 7,** you can judge for yourself whether or not Kandinsky was successful in translating the euphoric effects of music into paint. Chagall's *I and the Village* is also displayed here. **Gallery 8** covers de Chirico, an Italian whose favorite topics include dreams, mannequins, dark green skies, classical architecture, and profound titles. **Gallery 9** is the first of many Picasso revisitations, along with works by Duchamp, while **Gallery 10** features the crisp lines, primary colors, and right angles of Piet Mondrian. Check out *Broadway Boogie-Woogie* (1944) to see how his conception of the city compares with your own. In the next few galleries, the famous paintings just keep on coming. **Gallery 12** showcases Henri Matisse's 1909 bacchanal *Dance (First Version)* while Gallery 13 is graced by Picasso's *Three Musicians.*

After a brief foray into the improvisational geometry of colorist Paul Klee in **Gallery 14, Gallery 13** offers a Picasso double-whammy—*Girl Before a Mirror* and *Seated Bather.* **Gallery 15** presents the works of elaborate, 1890s-inspired Max Ernst and high-concept prankster Marcel Duchamp, whose obsession with mathematics eventually led him out of painting and sculpture and into incessant games of chess. **Gallery 16** plumbs the Surrealist depths, with Dali's *Persistence of Memory* and Magritte's *False Mirror* vying for the attention of your subconscious.

To the left as you exit **Gallery 17** (where Jackson Pollock's work makes its first appearance) is the museum's display of **modern drawings**—some sketches for masterworks, some masterworks themselves. Seek out Kupka's colorful *Girl with Ball.* To the left of the exit in the drawing exhibit are MoMA's exhibits of **photography.** With hundreds of photos in under 10 rooms, the arrangement is rather daunting: temporary exhibits are in front, parts of the permanent photo collection in back.

Behind the escalator, across from the photography section, sits a room of Monet's *Water Lilies,* arranged in a diorama-like setting. Picture windows overlook the sculpture garden and douse both you and the screens that make up the painting in natural light; show up in the early afternoon and the screens seem washed-out. At other times, the effect can be magical.

The nine galleries on the **third** floor track American and European painting from the end of World War II to the late 60s. They feature works by Mark Rothko and Jackson Pollock (who created his gigantic "all-over" canvases by pouring and flinging industrial-quality paint); works by Robert Motherwell, Andrew Wyeth's *Christina's World,* Jasper Johns' studies of patriotic symbols, and pop-art demagogue Andy Warhol (whose gold Marilyn Monroe rests in **Gallery 26).**

MoMA owns much more 20th-century art than it will ever have space to display; an ever-changing assortment of works cavorts past **the third-floor stairwell.** Continue to find a chamber full of the museum's recent acquisitions. The selection here also changes rapidly, but there's always something of interest.

To the right of the exit from the **contemporary art** room is a small, dark room containing video compositions. On the third floor is MoMA's **prints** department; again, there are many works and they rotate frequently. A "reading room" lets you investigate old catalogs and defunct exhibitions.

Rise up once again to the **design exhibits** on the fourth floor. Scale models and blueprints for **Bauhaus** buildings accompany up-to-date displays of elegant **furniture,** Finnish tableware, political posters, and enough *chaise longues* to accommodate every psychoanalyst in New York.

The **bookstore** on the first floor (708-9702) sells MoMA merchandise such as art books, 50¢ postcards, and cool posters (open Sat.-Wed. 11am-5:45pm, Thurs.-Fri. 11am-8:45pm). The **MoMA Design Store,** across the street at 44 W. 53rd St., sells high-priced objects of contemporary design, along with interesting housewares including environmentally sound bowls, plates, and glasses stitched together from whole tropical leaves (open Sat. and Mon.-Wed. 10am-6pm, Thurs.-Fri. 10am-9pm, Sun. 11am-6pm).

■ American Museum of Natural History

The largest science museum (and home to the coolest dinosaurs) in the world broods in a suitably imposing structure. The four-block-long building holds 36 million items of varied appeal, ranging from exhibits on anthropology and biology to ecology and the natural sciences. The new **dinosaur halls,** which opened with much fanfare in the summer of 1995, are fascinating, as much for what they reveal about the evolution of popular and scientific perceptions of America's favorite extinct beasts as for what they reveal about the beasts themselves. Controversy surrounded the museum's decision to present the Apatosaurus with its tail high in the air, and shortly after the museum opened, *The New York Times* asserted that the Tyrannosaurus Rex's new image—turns out it never stood upright—had made it into "New York's newest media darling." While most museums display lightweight casts of fossils, which are much easier to mount and display, the Museum of Natural History insists on using real fossils in 85 percent of its displays (although, in fact, the difference is practically indiscernible). The museum contracted five artists, along with paleontological consultants, to mount the exhibit; it thus demonstrates an artistic sensibility unusual for a natural history display. In the first few weeks after it opened, the exhibit, which is on the museum's fourth floor, attracted 50 percent more visitors than in all of 1994. The crowds are not expected to disperse any time soon; take this into account when planning a visit.

The original museum building, constructed in 1877, has been almost entirely walled in by 21 additions. A statue of Theodore Roosevelt—in uniform and on horseback, flanked by a naked African man and a feather-clad Native American (both on foot)—stands near the newer Central Park West entrance. Efforts to ditch or alter this monument have been frustrated by its status as a national landmark. In the cavernous rotunda, the fossilized skeletons of **Barosaurus** and **Allosaurus** battle to the undeath. Maps are available at the **information desk** to the left of the entrance. The quotations and murals along the walls are all related to Teddy Roosevelt. His interests, background, and hunting hats are displayed on the first floor, in Hall 12.

Teddy's distant ancestors can be seen in the **Ocean Life and Biology of Fishes** display in Hall 10. A hulking two-story replica of a blue whale casts shadows on the black-lit fish in the surrounding tanks. Admire the largest unexploded Pop Rock on earth in Hall 6—the 34-ton Ahnghito, the biggest meteorite ever retrieved.

Also on the first floor, another new permanent exhibition, the **Hall of Human Biology and Evolution,** boasts skeletons that trace the last three million years. This and many other museum's halls feature computerized info-stops, allowing interactive appreciation of the fossils.

Stuffed stuff representing thousands of species can be discovered on floors one to three. A modest King Kong beats his breast in the **Hall of African Mammals** (Hall 13). A herd of Indian elephants runs riot through Hall 9, **Asiatic Mammals.** Toward the back of the second floor dwell huge and colorful anthropology exhibits; don't miss the costumed mannequins of "African Dance and Belief," and try not to wince at the more dated placards. **The Primates Wing,** on the third floor, demonstrates the evolutionary chain from a tree shrew to you. On the fourth floor, the "Mammals and Their Extinct Relatives" exhibit offers many large skeletons and fossils of extinct relations and the mammals who love them.

The **Alexander White Natural Science Center,** the museum's only room holding live animals, explains the ecology of New York City to kids, while the Discovery Room gives them artifacts they can touch. (Hours hover around Tues.-Fri. 2-4:30pm, Sat.-Sun. 1-4:30pm; closed September; call ahead to check.) **The People Center** hosts scholarly talks and demonstrations of traditional peoples' arts at scheduled times during the academic year.

The museum is located on Central Park West, at 79th to 81st St. (769-5100). (Subway: B or C to 81st St. Open Sun.-Thurs. 10am-5:45pm, Fri.-Sat. 10am-8:45pm. Suggested donation $6, seniors and students $4, children under 12 $3. Excellent wheelchair access.)

The museum also houses **Naturemax** (769-5650), a cinematic extravaganza on one of New York's largest movie screens, four stories high and 66 feet wide. (Admission $6, students and seniors $5, children under 12 $3; Fri.-Sat. double features $7.50, students and seniors $6.50, children under 12 $4.) **The Hayden Planetarium** (769-5100) offers outstanding multi-media presentations. This unique theater is an excellent movie alternative for a date and for young children (Open Mon.-Fri. 12:30-4:45pm, Sat. 10am-5:45pm, Sun. noon-5:45pm. Admission $5, seniors and students and adult groups of 10 or more $4, children under 12 $2.50.) Electrify your senses on Friday and Saturday nights with 3-D Laser Grunge or the perennial favorite, Laser Floyd (admission $8.50). Tickets available through Ticketron (307-7171).

▓ Guggenheim Museum

The Guggenheim's most famous exhibit is surely the building itself; the original, seven-story corkscrew of a museum dates to 1959 and is one of the only New York edifices that Frank Lloyd Wright deigned to design. The result is a curving, neofuturist construct that resembles the sort of alien organic citadel that would look right at home in a Tim Burton or Terry Gilliam film. But despite how cool it looks, Wright's design offered insufficient space as the museum's programmers tried for more and better exhibits; so from 1990 to 1992, the museum shut down for restoration and expansion. Offices moved out of the corkscrew, skylights and windows were replaced, and a new 10-story "tower gallery" sprouted behind the original structure, nearly doubling potential exhibit space. When the Guggenheim reopened in the summer of 1992, wags compared the new building to a Modernist toilet (Duchamp on the brain) while the *Village Voice* blasted the museum's fundraising methods. Gallery-goers, however, demonstrated enthusiastic support by mobbing the museum, the patio, the elevators, the restaurant, and the street outside.

The inside of the Guggenheim is no less intriguing. The curving white walls offer no distractions from the works on display. Light fills the museum from the numerous skylights and from the soft track lighting, amplifying the vacuum-seal approach to art appreciation. Every Manhattan-bred child has dreamt of skateboarding down the Guggenheim's spiraling hallway, which is capped by a huge skylight. Despite Wright's wish that visitors ride the elevator to the top of the spiral and "waft" down, exhibitions are usually arranged in ascending order instead. Each spin of the corkscrew holds one sequence or exhibit, while the newly constructed Tower Galleries, each accessible by the ramp or by elevator, may present a portion of the Thannhauser Collection of 20th-century works, including several by Picasso, Matisse, and Kandinsky. The rest of the permanent collection is especially strong in cerebral, geometric art, showcasing Mondrian and his Dutch *De Stijl* school, the Bauhaus experiments of German Josef Albers, and the Russian modernists. The collection also holds several Degas sculptures and works by German Expressionists Kirchner, Beckman, and Marc.

The museum is located at 1071 5th Ave. and 89th St. (recording 423-3500, human being 423-3662, TDD 423-3607; Subway: #4, 5, or 6 to 86th St.) There is also a new **Guggenheim Museum SoHo** (p. 247). (Fifth Avenue Guggenheim open Sun.-Wed. 10am-6pm, Fri.-Sat. 10am-8pm. Admission $7, students and seniors $4, children under 12 free; Fri. 6-8pm "pay what you wish." two-day pass to both Guggenheim museums $10, students and seniors $6; if you buy one in SoHo on Wed., it remains valid uptown for Fri.)

■ Whitney Museum

When the Metropolitan Museum of Art declined the donation of over 600 works from Gertrude Vanderbilt Whitney in 1929, Ms. Whitney, a wealthy patron and sculptor, decided to form her own museum. Opened on 8th Street in 1931, the Whitney has since moved twice, most recently in 1966 to an unusual and forbidding futuristic fortress designed by Bauhauser Marcel Breuer. The museum's collection is devoted solely to modern American art, including some 8500 sculptures, paintings, drawings, and prints.

As you enter, take note of the eerily timely mural of a bombing (complete with media omnipresence) by the stairs to the café. The first and second floors cover a wide range of changing exhibitions including theme shows, retrospectives, and contemporary work by avant-garde artists. The theater periodically shows films and videos from independent American artists. Check *This Week at the Whitney,* posted on a kiosk near the entrance, or call about special events, lectures, and guided tours.

The museum has assembled the largest collection of 20th-century American art in the world; if the varied (and often controversial) temporary exhibits don't float your boat, something in the permanent collection is bound to do so. Be warned, though; although the museum has dozens of American masterworks (including Ad Reinhardt's *Abstract Painting, Number 33,* Jasper John's *Three Flags,* Frank Stella's famous *Brooklyn Bridge,* Robert Rauschenberg's *Satellite,* Willem De Kooning's *Woman on Bicycle,* and Georgia O'Keefe's *Flower Collection*), don't expect to see them all. The Whitney's permanent collection is shown in bits and pieces; some selection of it is always on display, but specific works are called in and out of hibernation on a rotating basis. Contemporary works by Cindy Sherman, Barbara Krueger, Catherine Murphy, Frank Moore, Peter Saul, and many others will probably satisfy your aesthetic cravings, even if you can't see your favorites. Much of the Whitney's fame has come from its much-hyped **biennial exhibitions,** which showcase some of the most imaginative up-and-comers in the American art world. Although some of the older classics can't be found while the biennial exhibits are up, the remarkable creativity of many of the young artists on display provides ample compensation. Despite the occasional denunciation by the art critics of the NY press with ideological axes to grind, the Whitney features some of the most exciting and engaging contemporary art out there. Exhibits for 1996-97 are slated to include exhibits on artists Willem de Kooning and Paul Cadmus, as well as the New York Dada Movement.

There is expensive food downstairs and expensive museum souvenirs next door. Resist the temptation ($10 min. for lunch) and go to Third Ave. for food instead.

The museum is located at 945 Madison Ave. (570-3676), at 75th St. (Subway: #6 to 77th St. Open Wed. 11am-6pm, Thurs. 1-8pm, Fri.-Sun. 11am-6pm. Admission $7, students and seniors $5, children under 12 free; Thurs. 6-8pm $3.50.) Another branch of the Whitney is in the **Philip Morris** building, 120 Park Ave. at 42nd St., where a sculpture court features a changing array of installation pieces. Admission is free. Gallery talks, which occur frequently, are also free. Call 878-2453 for updates.

■ Cooper-Hewitt Museum

Since 1976 Andrew Carnegie's regal Georgian mansion has been the setting for the Smithsonian Institution's **National Museum of Design.** Pieces from the museum's vast permanent collection are culled for fascinating shows on aspects of contemporary or historical design.

The collection itself dates back to 1859, when Peter Cooper founded the Cooper Union for the Advancement of Science and Art. Cooper's granddaughters subsequently opened a museum in 1897, which was donated to the Smithsonian in 1963. In 1972, the collection found a new home in the Carnegie mansion. The largest group of holdings contains drawings and prints, primarily of architecture and design. Glass, furniture, porcelain, metalwork, stoneware, and textiles complete the catalogue, along with interesting knick-knacks such as a Russian chess set from the post-Revolution period that pits red communist pieces against pawn workers trapped in chains.

The museum itself is one of the more impressive design projects on the site. Cast-iron archways alternate with intricately carved ceilings and an operatic staircase, and everything basks in the pale, gilded glow of muted candelabras. You can pick out the Scottish bagpipes, an homage to Carnegie's heritage, in the moldings of the music room (now a gift shop). An unusually low doorway leads to what was once the 5'2" Carnegie's west library.

Exhibitions at the Cooper-Hewitt are often both sly and provocative. In the past, the museum has staged such playful offerings as a show of doghouses and a history of the pop-up book. Recent guest-curated shows have featured samples of 1950s wallpaper and studies of Dutch ceramics. With over two million volumes, the museum's library is one of the largest and most accessible scholarly resources in America for design (open by appt. until 5:30pm daily; call 860-6887 for details).

The extensive 1996 renovation of the Museum will connect the Carnegie Mansion with the townhouses on 90th St., allowing for more exhibition space. The 1996-97 exhibition schedule includes Italian Renaissance drawings, works of fashion designer Todd Oldham, and an outdoor exhibition on harnessing solar energy.

The museum is located at 2 E. 91st St. (860-6868), at Fifth Ave. (Subway: #4, 5, or 6 to 86th St. Open Tues. 10am-9pm, Wed.-Sat. 10am-5pm, Sun. noon-5pm. Admission $3, seniors and students $1.50, children under 12 free. Tues. 5-9pm free.)

■ Frick Collection

Upon his death, Pittsburgh steel magnate and 19th-century robber baron Henry Clay Frick secured his immortality by leaving his mansion and comprehensive art collection to the city. The collection showcases old masters and decorative arts in an intimate setting—a refreshing break from the warehouse ambience of New York's larger museums. However, this "mansion next door" ambience earns a price. As the works have not been organized and labelled, all but the most studious of art historians will be lost without a conveniently provided guidebook ($1).

On the other hand, since the collection remains much as it was when Mr. Frick originally arranged the works, the museum offers an intriguing look at Victorian conceptions of art. Some of the world's finest Old Masters are on display here, not to mention exquisite vases, sculptures, and bronzes—even furniture. Two of the 35 existing Vermeers hang in the **South Hall:** *Officer and Laughing Girl* and *Girl Interrupted at Her Music.* Also in the hall are a sassy and flirtatious portrait of Madame

MUSEUMS

Boucher by Monsieur Boucher and an early mother-and-child by Renoir. The nearby **Octagon Room** features a 15th-century altarpiece by Fra Filippo Lippi, while the anteroom showcases works by, among others, Van Eyck, El Greco, and Brueghel the Elder.

Moving through the numbered galleries, stop by Rococo foolishness and pink pink pink in the **Fragonard Room.** Here one can view Fragonard's *Progress of Love.* Although rejected by Mme Du Barry, these works are masterpieces of the Rococo style. In the **Living Hall,** El Greco's *St. Jerome* clasps his Latin translation of the Bible next to Titian's pensive *Portrait of a Man in a Red Cap,* Holbein's determined classic *Sir Thomas More,* and Giovanni Bellini's extraordinary 15th-century masterpiece *St. Francis in the Desert.* In the next room, the **Library** walls display Gainsborough and Reynolds portraits, a Constable landscape, a Turner seascape, a Gilbert Stuart likeness of George Washington, and a posthumously painted portrait of Henry Clay Frick surveying his domain. In the **North Hall,** on the way to the next room, the defiantly level-eyed Ingres portrait of the *Countesse d'Hausonville* will try to stare you down.

The largest room in the Frick, the **West Gallery,** has some stunning natural lighting from the skylight. Here, you can get more eye-candy with no less than three works of Rembrandt: the mysterious *Polish Rider; Nicholaes Ruts,* one of Rembrandt's earliest portrait commissions; and his sensitive 1658 *Self-Portrait,* a portrait of the artist as an aged man. Also note the works by Van Dyck (an elegant 1620 portrait of a close friend), Vermeer (an unfinished rendering of the opening of a letter), and Velázquez (a famous portrait of King Philip IV of Spain). Goya's depiction of blacksmiths at work in *The Forge* seems strangely out of place in this predominantly aristocratic collection, yet its harsh beauty transcends its relatively "proletarian" subject. The secret of the West Gallery is the interplay of light; for this reason in particular, the Dutch and Spanish works harmonize. Over at the head of the West Gallery, the **Enamel Room** contains a collection of Limoges enamels from the 16th and 17th centuries, as well as a penetrating evocation of Satan in Duccio di Buoninsegna's 1308 *The Temptation of Christ on the Mountain.*

The **Oval Room** features two Gainsborough women and two Van Dycks, all avoiding eye contact with each other (and you). Try to stand in a pose like theirs—these portraits are life-size. Also note the frisky and irreverent bronze *Diana* (also avoiding eye contact with the women), executed in 1776 by Jean-Antoine Houdon. The **East Gallery** holds several Whistlers with characteristically hue-orchestrated names: *Symphony in Flesh Color and Pink, Harmony in Pink and Grey,* and *Arrangement in Black and Brown.* They should be easy to tell apart. A fine Goya portrait of a young *Officer* also pouts here.

After walking through the least exhausting museum in New York, you can relax in the cool Garden Court and watch fountains of water burble up from the mouths of little stone frogs. The museum is located at 1 E. 70th St. (288-0700) at Fifth Avenue. (Subway: #6 to 68th St. Open Tues.-Sat. 10am-6pm, Sun. 1-6pm. Admission $5, students and seniors $3. Don't even try to broaden your child's mind: No children under 10 admitted; children under 16 must be accompanied by an adult. Group visits by appointment only.)

▓ Pierpont Morgan Library

The **Pierpont Morgan Library** contains a stunning collection of rare books, sculpture, and paintings gathered by the banker and his son, J.P. Morgan, Jr. This Low Renaissance-style *palazzo* was constructed with white marble bricks laid, in true Greek fashion, without mortar. Completed in 1907, the library remained private until 1924, when J.P. Morgan opened it to the public. Its permanent collection, not always on display, includes drawings and prints by Blake and Dürer, illuminated Renaissance manuscripts, a copy of the Louisiana Purchase, Napoleon's love letters to Josephine, a manuscript copy of Dickens's *A Christmas Carol,* and sheet music handwritten by Beethoven and Mozart.

Redefining the phrase,
"Budget Accommodations."

THE HERALD SQUARE AND THE PORTLAND SQUARE HOTELS

All the comfort and
important amenities of
New York's fine hotels,
for cost conscious
travellers who prefer
to spend their money
enjoying all of the
great and exciting
things that New York
has to offer.

Clean rooms,
courteous service,
color tv,
climate controlled,
charming atmosphere,
all ideally located
in the heart
of the city.

THE HERALD SQUARE HOTEL

31st St., between 5th & Broadway
(212) 279-4017   1 (800) 727-1888

Near Macy's and close to some
of the best shopping in the city!

THE PORTLAND SQUARE HOTEL

47th St., between 6th & Broadway
(212) 382-0600   1 (800) 388-8988

Within easy walking distance to
all the broadway shows, "restaurant
row" and the lights and dazzle
of Times Square!

A walk through the hall lined with medieval paraphernalia brings you to a circular room, which once served as the main entrance and which often features exhibitions. To the right, the **West Room,** Morgan Sr.'s opulent former office, has a carved ceiling made during the Italian Renaissance and stained glass taken from 15th and 17th century Switzerland. Two stately (if dour) Morgans stare down from the walls, daring you to touch the red velvet sofas.

To the left of the rotunda sits Morgan's library, a bibliophile's dream. Stacked with mahogany-colored bound volumes and encircled by two balconies, this room is often the site of additional exhibitions. Among the more notable items in the room: one of three existing likenesses of John "Lady of Christ" Milton, a fabulous 12th-century jewel-encrusted triptych believed to contain fragments from the Cross, and one of 11 surviving copies of the Gutenberg Bible, the first printed book. Exhibitions in 1996-97 will feature the works of Tiepolo and Charles Dickens

The museum is located at 29 E. 36th St. (685-0610), at Madison Avenue (Subway: #6 to 33rd St. Open Tues.-Sat. 10:30am-5pm, Sun. 1-6pm. $5, seniors and students $3. Free tours on various topics Tues.-Fri. 2:30pm.)

■ Other Major Collections

Alternative Museum, 594 Broadway (966-4444), 4th floor, near Houston and Prince St. in SoHo. Subway: B, D, F, or Q to Broadway-Lafayette St., or N or R to Prince St. Founded and operated by artists for non-established artists, the museum advertises itself as "ahead of the times and behind the issues." New visions and social critique are the name of the game, with an emphasis on the international, the unusual, and the socially conscious. For more info, try altmuseum@aol.com. Open Tues.-Sun. 11am-6pm. Suggested donation $3.

American Craft Museum, 40 W. 53rd St. (956-3535), across from the MoMA. Subway: E or F to Fifth Ave.-53rd St.; or B, D, or Q to 50th St. Not the old-fashioned quilts and Shaker furniture you might expect. This museum redefines the concept of crafts; don't expect wooden *tchotkes* here. Features modern pieces in wood, glass, metal, clay, plastic, paper, and fabric. Regular, ingenious exhibitions are shaped around particular subjects or materials. Past shows include "Made with Paper" and "Glass Installations," which evoked memories of Superman's home planet Krypton. Four floors of exhibits, changing every three months. Open Tues. 10am-8pm, Wed.-Sun. 10am-5pm. Admission $5, seniors and students $2.50, children under 12 free.

American Museum of the Moving Image, 35th Ave. at 36th St., Astoria, Queens (718-784-0077 for exhibition and screening information, 718-784-4777 for travel directions). Subway: N to 36th Ave. (Washington Ave.) at 31st St. Walk north along 31st St. one block to 35th Ave. and go right; walk five blocks east to 36th St. The museum promises a dedication to "the art, history, and technology of motion picture and television," but luckily it doesn't take itself quite that seriously. A gallery on the ground floor hosts somewhat bizarre changing exhibitions, such as a show on Hollywood hair and makeup design, and a let-you-play display of the newest in interactive CD-Rom video games. In the museum's permanent collection upstairs you can look in a Magic Mirror to see yourself as Marilyn Monroe, or gaze at a wall of Bill Cosby's sweaters (he never wears the same one twice). The upstairs memorabilia collection includes Mork and Mindy lunch boxes, Fonzie paper dolls, and the *Leave it to Beaver* "Ambush" game. Also upstairs is "King Tut's Fever Movie Palace," which shows flicks like *Batman and Robin* and *What Made Pistachio Nuts?*—the screening room downstairs regularly plays vintage films and rare collections of film shorts. New additions to the newly renovated building include "Behind the Screen," a demonstration of new visual media, and a closer view of David Letterman's original NBC set. Tours by appointment (718-784-4520). Open Tues.-Fri. noon-4pm, Sat.-Sun. noon-6pm. Admission $5, seniors $4, students and children under 12 $2.50.

The Asia Society, 725 Park Ave. (288-6400), at 70th St. Subway: #6 to 68th St. Exhibitions of Asian art are accompanied by symposia on related topics, musical performances, film screenings, and an acclaimed "Meet the Author" series. The art spans the Asian continent, from Iran to India to Southeast Asia to Japan to China to Korea, and even to Asian America. Particularly well-thought-out exhibitions on topics such as representations of primates in Asian art and "the object in context," a series which places one piece amidst others on loan and from the permanent collection to show the influences on and of that one piece. Open Tues.-Wed. and Fri.-Sat. 11am-6pm, Thurs. 11am-8pm, Sun. noon-5pm. Admission $3, seniors and students $1; Thurs. 6-8pm free. Tours Tues.-Sat. 12:30 pm, Thurs. also at 6:30pm, Sun. 2:30pm.

Audubon Terrace Museum Group, at Broadway and 155th St. in Harlem. Subway: #1 to 157th St. Once part of John James Audubon's estate and game preserve, the terrace now contains a number of museums and societies:

Hispanic Society of America, 613 W. 155th St. between Broadway and Riverside (926-2234). Devoted to Spanish and Portuguese arts and culture, including paintings, mosaics, and ceramics. Works by greats El Greco, Velázquez, and Goya. Spanish scholars will enjoy the 100,000-volume research library. Open Mon.-Sat. 10am-4:30pm, Sun. 1-4pm. Free.

American Numismatic Society (243-3130). Learn about the fascinating history of the penny! An extraordinary collection of coinage and paper money from prehistoric times to the present. Open Mon.-Sat. 9am- 5pm, Sun. 1-4pm. Free.

American Academy of Arts and Letters (368-5900). Honors American artists, writers, and composers; also offers occasional exhibits of manuscripts, paintings, sculptures, and first editions. Call for current exhibition details and times.

Black Fashion Museum, 157 W. 126th St. (666-1320), between Adam Clayton Powell Jr. Blvd. and Lenox/Malcolm X Blvd. Subway: #2 or 3 to 125th St. Founded in 1979, the B.F.M. maintains a permanent collection and mounts 2 yearly exhibits devoted to garments designed, sewn, or worn by black men and women from the 1860s to the present. Alongside the creations of contemporary black designers you'll find two slave dresses, a dress made by Rosa Parks, costumes from Broadway musicals like *The Wiz,* and a tribute to designer Ann Lowe, who designed the wedding dress for Jackie O's wedding to JFK. Open by appt Mon.-Fri. noon-6pm and the occasional Sat.; call 996-4470 or 666-1320 at least one day in advance. Suggested donation $3, students, seniors, and children under 12 $2.

Bronx Museum of the Arts, 165th St. and Grand Concourse (718-681-6000). Subway: C or D to 167th St. and south 3 blocks along Grand Concourse. Set in the rotunda of the Bronx Courthouse. The museum focuses on young talent, collecting works on paper by minority artists and sponsoring twice-yearly seminars for local artists, which culminate in group showings. Open Wed. 3pm-9pm, Thurs.-Fri. 10am-5pm, Sat.-Sun. 1-6pm. Suggested donation $3, students $2, seniors $1; Sun. free.

Brooklyn Museum, 200 Eastern Pkwy. (718-638-5000), at Washington Ave. Subway: #2 or 3 to Eastern Pkwy. The little sibling of the Metropolitan Museum—but not that little, and definitely worth the trip to Brooklyn. Check out the outstanding Ancient Greek, Roman, Middle Eastern, and Egyptian galleries on the 3rd floor; larger Egyptian collections are found only at London's British Museum and in Cairo. Crafts, textiles, and period rooms on the 4th floor provide respite from "higher" pursuits; the Moorish Room, a lush bit of exotica from John D. Rockefeller's Manhattan townhouse, is especially amusing. Gems from Sargent and the Hudson River School shine in the American Collection on the 5th floor. Nearby, the small, unusual contemporary gallery contains noteworthy work by Alfredo Jaar and Francis Bacon. On the same floor is European art from the early Renaissance to Post-Impressionism, including works by Rodin, Renoir, and Monet. Multi-media Asian art fills the 2nd floor. The enormous Oceanic and New World art collection takes up the central 2-story space on the 1st floor; the towering totem poles covered with human/animal hybrids could go nowhere else. The impressive African art collection here was the first of its kind in an American museum when it opened in 1923. Galleries downstairs put on temporary exhibits. Due to budget constraints, the museum is open only Wed.-Sun. 10am-5pm. Gift shop with jewelry and large art and travel-book collection open same hours. Gallery talks Wed.-Fri. at 2pm. Museum café open 10am-4pm. Suggested donation $4, students $2, seniors $1.50, children under 12 free.

China House Gallery, 125 E. 65th St. (744-8181), between Park and Lexington Ave. Subway: #6 to 68th St. This minute gallery within the China Institute showcases a broad spectrum of Chinese art, including calligraphy, ceramics, and bronzes, as well as occasional cultural-anthropological exhibits. Look for the lions guarding the red doors. Open Mon. and Wed.-Sat. 10am-5pm, Tues. 10am-8pm, Sun. 1-5pm. Suggested contribution $3.

The Cloisters, Fort Tryon Park (923-3700), in upper Manhattan. Subway: A to 190th St.; take the elevator up to the street, from the train station take a right onto Ft. Washington Ave. and head through Ft. Tryon Park. Or take the #4 bus from Fifth Ave. to the Cloisters' entrance (buses leave regularly from the Metropolitan Museum's main building on Fifth). In 1938, Charles Collen brought the High Middle Ages to the edge of Manhattan. Building a monastery from pieces of 12th- and 13th-century French and Spanish cloisters, he established this tranquil avatar of the Met. John D. Rockefeller, never short of a few bob, donated the entire site and many of the contents. Retreat to the air-conditioned Treasury to admire the Met's rich collection of medieval art. Examine countless books drawn by neurotic monks; when healthy people were off rampaging through the countryside looking for dragons, the monks were carving intricate 3-D biblical scenes in boxwood miniature. Follow the allegory told by the priceless Unicorn Tapestries, and wander through airy archways and manicured gardens bedecked with European treasures like the ghoulish marble fountain in the Cuxa Cloister. Open March-Oct. Tues.-Sun. 9:30am-5:15pm, Nov.-Feb. Tues.-Sun. 9:30am-4:45pm. Museum tours March-Oct. Tues.-Fri. at 3pm, Sun. at noon; Nov.-Feb. Wed. at 3pm. Suggested donation $6, students and seniors $3. Donation includes, and is included with, admission to the Metropolitan Museum's main building in Central Park.

Equitable Gallery, Equitable Center (554-4818), at Seventh Ave. and 51st St. Subway: N or R to 49th St. This small gallery presents 4 free exhibitions per year covering an eclectic array of subjects. An exhibition is always showing, save for the week or so of inter-exhibitional downtime; it's best to call ahead. Don't forget to check out the four-story Lichtenstein mural in the lobby of the building. Closed during summer. An exhibit on Cartier and Bresson is expected in 1997. Open Mon.-Fri. 11am-6pm, Sat. noon-5pm.

Forbes Magazine Galleries, 62 Fifth Ave. (206-5548), at 12th St. Subway: #4, 5, 6, L, N, or R to 14th St.-Union Sq. The holdings here, like those at the Frick Collection and the Morgan Library, were acquired by a multi-millionaire financier for his own pleasure and then turned over to the public. The late Malcolm Forbes's irrepressible penchant for the offbeat permeates this 20th-century collection. Eclectic exhibits occupy the ground floor of the late magnate's publishing outfit: 12,000 toy soldiers assuming various battle positions in the military-miniatures collection; a rotating exhibit of Presidential paraphernalia; the world's largest private collection of Fabergé eggs; and a completely random collection of 250 trophies known as "The Mortality of Immortality," including the prized trophy for the best White Leghorn chicken of the Northampton Egg Laying Trial. Rotating exhibits have recently included Victorian history paintings and World War II documents. Open Tues.-Sat. 10am-4pm. Free, but entry is limited to 900 persons per day; children under 16 must be accompanied by an adult. Thurs. is reserved for advance-notice group tours; call 206-5549.

Fraunces Tavern, 54 Pearl St. (425-1778) on 2nd and 3rd floors. Subway: #4 or 5 to Bowling Green, #1 or 9 to South Ferry, or N or R to Whitehall St. This museum primarily features two period rooms, along with the room where George Washington said goodbye to his troops after the Revolutionary War. The third floor features exhibits on the culture and history of early America, such as "The Changing Image of George Washington." Open Mon.-Fri. 10am-4:45pm, Sat. noon-4pm. Admission $2.50; seniors, students, and children $1.

Guggenheim Museum SoHo, 575 Broadway (423-3500) at Prince St. This branch of the Guggenheim occupies two spacious floors of an historic 19th-century building with selections from the museum's mammoth permanent collection of modern and contemporary works. The neighborhood and the breezy, stylish layout lends the place a gallery atmosphere (much unlike the corkscrew uptown). Special exhibitions, which change four times a year, are often exceptional: recently these have included a selection of watercolors by Kandinsky, and John Cage's "Rolywholyover: A Circus" which was a unique "composition for museum." They also host a children's "learning through art" exhibition each summer. Open Sun. and Wed.-Fri. 11am-6pm, Sat. 11am-8pm. Admission $6, students and seniors with ID $4, and children under 12 free. A seven-day pass is available for admission to both the Guggenheim Museum and the SoHo branch, $10, students and seniors with ID $6. The gallery store (423-3876), host to lots of artsy trinkets, is a nice place to meet a friend downtown.Wheelchair accessible.

Guinness World of Records, 350 Fifth Ave. (947-2335), located on the Concourse level of the Empire State Building at 34th St. Subway: N or R to 34th St.-Herald Sq., or #6 to 33rd St.-Park Ave. Synthesizer pop and enthusiastic recorded voices lure the unwary into the goofy world of Guinness. Primary colors exemplify the level of sophistication. See plastic replicas of the world's tallest man, heaviest man, longest neck, and the tattooed lady. Open 9am-10pm, adults $6.95, children $3.50, combination pass with **Empire State Building** observatory $9.95 adults, $5 children.

Hall of Fame for Great Americans, 181st St. and Martin Luther King Jr. Blvd. (718-289-5100). Subway: #4 to Burnside Ave. Walk 6 blocks west along Burnside Ave. as it becomes 179th St., then walk a block north. Located on the grounds of City University of New York in the Bronx, this poignant though decrepit hall features nearly 102 bronze busts of America's immortals, among them Alexander Graham Bell, George Washington Carver, Abraham Lincoln, Booker T. Washington, and the Wright brothers. Open daily 10am-5pm. Free.

International Center of Photography, 1130 Fifth Ave. (860-1777), at 94th St. Subway: #6 to 96th St. Housed in a landmark townhouse built in 1914 for *New Republic* founder Willard Straight. The foremost exhibitor of photography in the city and a gathering-place for its practitioners. Historical, thematic, and contemporary works, running from fine art to photo-journalism to celebrity portraits. The bookstore sells the bi-monthly booklet *Photography in New York*, a comprehensive guide to what is shown and where ($2.95). **Midtown branch** at 1133 Sixth Ave. (768-4680), at 43rd St. Both open Tues. 11am-8pm, Wed.-Sun. 11am-6pm. Admission $4, seniors and students $2.50, Tues. 6-8pm pay what you wish.

Intrepid Sea-Air-Space Museum, Pier 86 (245-0072), at 46th St. and Twelfth Ave. Bus: M42 or M50 to W. 46th St. One ticket admits you to the veteran World War II and Vietnam War aircraft carrier *Intrepid,* the Vietnam War destroyer *Edson,* the first and only publicly displayed guided-missile submarine *Growler,* and the lightship *Nantucket.* On the main carrier, Pioneer's Hall shows models, antiques, and film shorts of flying devices from the turn of the century to the 30s. You can also climb aboard the Intrepid's 900-ft. flight deck. Don't miss the Iraqi tanks parked near the gift shop; they were captured in the Gulf War. There are a number of guided tours of the museum and its different attractions which range from 10 min.-3hrs. in length. The museum offers a schedule of temporary and new exhibits and events; call for details. Open May 1-Sept. 30 daily 10am-5pm; Oct. 1-Apr. 30 Wed.-Sun. 10am-5pm, last admission one hour before closing. Admission $10, seniors and students and veterans $7.50, children 6-11 $5, children under 6 free.

The Jewish Museum, 1109 Fifth Ave. (423-3200, 423-3230 for exhibition and program information), at 92nd St. Subway: #6 to 96th St. The permanent collection of over 14,000 works details the Jewish experience throughout history, ranging from ancient Biblical artifacts and ceremonial objects to contemporary masterpieces by Marc Chagall, Frank Stella, and George Segal. Rotating exhibits fill the first two floors, while the permanent exhibition on the third and fourth floors, *Culture and Continuity: The Jewish Journey,* examines Jewish history and culture through art and artifacts. The other two floors host temporary exhibitions. Open Sun.-Mon. and Wed.-Thurs. 11am-5:45pm, Tues. 11am-9pm. Admission $7, seniors and students $5, children under 12 free; Tues. 5-8pm pay what you wish. Wheelchair accessible.

Lower East Side Tenement Museum, 97 and 90 Orchard St. (431-0233), near Broome St. Subway: B, D, or Q to Delancey St.; or J, M, or Z to Essex St. From Delancey St., walk 4 blocks east to Orchard St. and 1 block south. From Essex St., walk 2 blocks west to Orchard and 1 block south A preserved, early 20th-century Lower East Side tenement house, along with slideshows, documentaries, and displays about Lower East Side history. The museum gallery at 90 Orchard St. (open Tues.-Sun. 11am-5pm) offers free exhibits, and photographs documenting Jewish life on the Lower East Side. Guided historical walking tours depart from the corner at 90 Orchard St. on Sat. and Sun. Tours of the museum (the only way to view the exhibits) are conducted Tues.-Fri. at 1, 2, and 3pm, and Sat.-Sun. every 45 min. between 11am-4:15pm. Admission $7, seniors and students $6.

Jacques Marchais Museum of Tibetan Art, 338 Lighthouse Ave., Staten Island (718-987-3500). Take bus S74 from Staten Island Ferry to Lighthouse Ave., then turn right and walk up the fairly steep hill as it winds up to the right. Almost 2 hrs. from Manhattan but worth the trip for one of the largest private collections of Tibetan art in the West. Bronzes, paintings, and sculpture from Tibet and other Buddhist cultures. The museum, roosting atop a secluded hillside, is designed to resemble a small Tibetan mountain temple with terraced sculpture gardens and view of the distant Lower Bay. Sunday programs on Asian culture ($2 in addition to regular admission) are offered throughout the museum's season and cover topics ranging from photographs of Mongolia to origami "made easy" to Tibetan chanting. Call for current schedule. Open May-Oct. Wed.-Sun. 1-5pm, Nov.-April, call ahead to schedule a visiting time. Admission $3, seniors $2.50, children $1.

El Museo del Barrio, 1230 Fifth Ave. (831-7272), at 104th St. Subway: #6 to 103rd St. El Museo del Barrio is the only museum in the U.S. devoted exclusively to the art and culture of Puerto Rico and Latin America. Begun in an East Harlem classroom, the project has blossomed into a permanent museum that features video, painting, sculpture, photography, theater, and film. Permanent collection includes pre-Columbian art and *Santos de Palo,* hand-crafted wooden saint-figures from Latin America. Rotating exhibits often involve Latin American artists confronting the issues affecting the Hispanic-American community. Open Wed.-Sun. 11am-5pm, May-Sept. Wed., Fri.-Sun 9am-5pm, Thurs. noon-7pm. Suggested contribution $4, students and seniors $2.

The Museum for African Art, 593 Broadway (966-1313), between Houston St. and Prince St. in SoHo. Subway: N or R to Prince and Broadway. The museum has recently expanded to feature two major exhibits a year along with several smaller exhibitions of stunning and thoughtful African and African-American art, often with special themes. They also offer lecture series on Saturday afternoon (free with admission) and many hands-on family-oriented workshops on African culture (make your own gourd!); call for details. Open Tues.-Fri. 10am-5:30pm, Sat.-Sun. noon-6pm. Admission $4, students and seniors with ID $2.

Museum of American Folk Art, 2 Lincoln Center (595-9533, 977-7298 for recording), on Columbus Ave. between 65th and 66th St. Subway: #1 or 9 to 66th St. Three bright, white rooms devoted to crafts, from European-influenced quilts, needlepoint, and folk portraits to Navajo rugs and Mexican polychrome wooden animals. The museum provides special programs for children and crafts demonstrations for everyone, often enlivened by folk dancers and storytellers (call the administrative office at 977-7170 for information). Museum open Tues.-Sun. 11:30am-7:30pm. Wheelchair access. Suggested donation $2.

Museum of American Illustration, 128 E. 63rd St. (838-2560), between Park and Lexington Ave. Subway: #4, 5, or 6 to 59th St. or N or R to Lexington Ave. Changing exhibitions of illustrations from such diverse fields as Mad Magazine cartoons, children's books, and advertising. Open Tues. 10am-8pm, Wed. and Fri. 10am-5pm, Sat. noon-4pm. Free.

Museum of Bronx History (718-881-8900), at Bainbridge Ave. and 208th St. Subway: D to 205th St., or #4 to Mosholu Pkwy. Walk 4 blocks east on 210th St. and then south a block. Run by the Bronx Historical Society on the premises of the landmark Valentine-Varian House, this museum, as the name indicates, concerns itself with the history of the city's northernmost borough, from the pre-revolutionary era to the sometimes troubled present. Exhibits change regularly; call for schedule. Open Sat. 10am-4pm, Sun. 1-5pm, or by appointment. Admission $2.

Museum of the City of New York (534-1672), 103rd St. and Fifth Ave. in East Harlem next door to El Museo del Barrio. Subway: #6 to 103rd St. This fascinating museum details the history of the Big Apple. Permanent exhibits include a marine gallery, which contains figureheads of Andrew Jackson and Robert Fulton, models of various periods of New York sea life, and a gallery of dollhouses, whose minute and lavish detail tells much about the social history of the city. Open Wed.-Sat. 10am-5pm, Sun. 1-5pm. Contribution requested. Wheelchair accessible.

Museum of Television and Radio, 25 W. 52nd St. (621-6600, 621-6800 for daily activity schedule), between Fifth and Sixth Ave. Subway: B, D, F, Q to Rockefeller Center, or E, F to 53rd St. Formerly the Museum of Broadcasting, this museum has only one small gallery of exhibits and works primarily as a "viewing museum." With a collection of more than 60,000 TV and radio programs, the museum's library has a specially designed computerized cataloging system that allows you to find and select a program through the database, request it from a librarian, and privately watch or listen to it at one of the 96 TV and radio consoles. The museum also hosts a number of film series that focus on topics of social, historical, popular, or artistic interest; see the daily schedule at the front counter. Special screenings can be arranged for large groups. Open Tues.-Wed. and Fri.-Sun. noon-6pm, Thurs. noon-8pm. Hours extended until 9pm on Fri. for theaters only. Suggested donation $6, students $4, seniors and children under 13 $3.

National Academy Museum, 1083 Fifth Ave. (369-4880), between 89th and 90th St. Subway: #4, 5, or 6 to 86th St. Founded in 1825 to advance the "arts of design" in America: painting, sculpture, architecture, and engraving. Currently the academy hosts exhibits, trains young artists, and serves as a fraternal organization for distinguished American artists. Such notables as Winslow Homer, Frederic Edwin Church, John Singer Sargent, and Thomas Eakins represent the 19th century in the permanent collection, while the roster of contemporary artists and architects includes Isabel Bishop, Robert Rauschenberg, Robert Venturi, and Philip Johnson. Regular exhibitions explore the history of American design and its European influences. Open Wed.-Thurs. and Sat.-Sun. noon-5pm, Fri. noon-8pm. Admission $5; seniors, students, and children under 16 $3.50. Free Fri. 5-8pm.

National Museum of the American Indian, 1 Bowling Green (668-6624), in the US Customs House. Subway: #4 and 5 to Bowling Green. This newly re-opened museum exhibits the best of the Smithsonian's vast collection of Native American artifacts, in galleries and exhibitions designed by Native American artists and craftsmen as well as historians. The galleries are organized thematically, as opposed to by tribe or geographical area. The museum also shows works by contemporary artists, as a means of bringing American Indian culture into the present and the future. Open daily 10am-5pm. Free.

New Museum of Contemporary Art, 583 Broadway (219-1222), between Prince and Houston St. Subway: N or R to Prince; or B, D, F, or Q to Broadway-Lafayette. Dedicated to the roles "art" plays in "society", the New Museum supports the hottest, the newest, and the most controversial. Interactive exhibits and video tricks aplenty. Many works deal with politics of identity—sexual, racial, and ethnic. Most major exhibitions are complemented by "Gallery Talks" in which the artist holds court at the museum to discuss the work and answer questions. Open Wed.-Fri. and Sun. noon-6pm, Sat. noon-8pm. Admission $4, artists, seniors, and students $3, children under 12 free. Sat. 6-8pm free.

New York City Fire Museum, 278 Spring St. between Varick and Hudson St. (691-1303). Housed in a renovated 1904 firehouse, this museum is for all those kids who wanted to be firemen when they grew up or for all those people who saw *Backdraft* a dozen times and still couldn't get enough. They have everything from the history of the sliding pole to snapshots of local firemen and full-size horse-drawn fire engines. Many of the staff are actual NYC firemen. The museum's café, which serves up live music along with refreshments, is open on Thurs. 4pm-9pm. Admission is $4 for adults, $2 for students and seniors, and $1 for children under 12. Open Tues.-Sat. 10am-4pm, Thurs. until 9pm.

Old Merchants House, 29 E. 4th St. (777-1089), between Lafayette St. and the Bowery. Subway: #4, 5, or 6 to Bleecker St. Walk 3 blocks north up Lafayette St. and a block east. New York City's only preserved 19th-century family home. Built in 1832, the house was owned by Seabury Tredwell, a prosperous merchant, and preserves his family's furniture, clothing, and memorabilia. Open Sun.-Thurs. 1-4pm or by appointment. Admission $3, seniors and students $2.

Parsons Exhibition Center, at Parsons School of Design, 2 W. 13th St. (229-8987), at Fifth Ave. Subway: #4, 5, 6 or L, N, R to 14th St. A variety of exhibitions, many of student and faculty work, including photography, computer art, painting, and sculpture. Open Mon.-Sat. 9am-6pm. Free.

Police Academy Museum, 235 E. 20th St. (477-9753), near Second Ave. Subway: #6 to 23rd St. On the second floor of the city's police academy. An esoteric and somewhat perplexing collection of crime-related artifacts. Intriguing displays of counterfeit money and firearms, including Al Capone's personal machine gun. Interspersed throughout are intimidatingly posed mannequins in uniform, as well as old trophies that the police squad's various sports leagues have won. Open Mon.-Fri. 9am-3pm. Free.

Nicholas Roerich Museum, 319 W. 107th St. (864-7752; fax 864-7704), between Broadway and Riverside Dr. Subway: #1 or 9 to 110th St. A friend and close collaborator of Stravinsky on Diaghilev's *Ballets Russes,* Nicholas Roerich painted, philosophized, archaeologized, studied things Slavic, and founded an educational institution to promote world peace through the arts. Located in a stately old townhouse, the museum brims with Roerich's landscape paintings, books, and pamphlets on art, culture, and philosophy. The museum also hosts a music series on Sundays at 5pm, October-May. Open Tues.-Sun. 2-5pm. Free.

Schomburg Center for Research in Black Culture, 515 Lenox/Malcolm X Ave. (491-2200), at 135th St. Subway: #2 or 3 to 135th St. This branch of the New York Public Library has one of the world's largest collections of documentation on black history and culture, including taped oral histories, photographs, and personal papers. Shows by African and African-American artists, and regular exhibitions concerning African-American issues. Call for hours of special collections and upcoming events. Tickets are sold in the gift shop. Open Mon.-Wed 12pm-8pm, Thurs.-Sun. 10am-6pm. Free.

Abigail Adams Smith Museum, 421 E. 61st St. (838-6878), between York and First Ave. Subway: #4, 5, 6, N, or R to 59th St.-Lexington Ave. Although the house bears her name, Abigail never actually lived (or even slept) here; in fact, this building was once her stable. Now refurbished with nine rooms of 18th-century articles, including a letter from George Washington. Open Tues.-Sun. 11am-4pm, Admission $3, students and seniors $2. Children under 12, free.

Studio Museum in Harlem, 144 W. 125th St. (864-4500), between Adam Clayton Powell Jr. Blvd. and Lenox/Malcolm X Ave. Subway: #2 or 3 to 125th St. Founded in 1967 at the height of the Civil Rights movement and dedicated to the collection and exhibition of works by black artists. Photographs, paintings, and sculptures in three broad categories: African-American art, Afro-Caribbean paintings, and African art and sculpture. Open Wed.-Fri. 10am-5pm, Sat.-Sun. 1-6pm. Admission $5, seniors and students $3, children $1; seniors free on Wed.

Ukrainian Museum, 203 Second Ave. (228-0110), between 12th and 13th St. Subway: L to Third Ave. This tiny upstairs museum exhibits late 19th- and early 20th-century Ukrainian folk art, including pottery, hand-carved candelabra, and traditional embroidered ceremonial clothing. Also hosts special shows, such as the recent exhibition of art by New Yorkers of Ukrainian descent. Seasonal exhibits on Christmas and Easter crafts as well as numerous courses in Ukrainian embroidery, baking, and Christmas ornament-making. Open Wed.-Sun. 1-5pm. Admission $1, seniors and students 50¢, children under 12 free.

Yeshiva University Museum, 185th St. (960-5390) at Amsterdam Ave. Subway:#1 or 9 to 181st or 190th St. Features exhibitions concerning the Jewish community. Open Tues.-Thurs. 10:30am-5pm, Sun. noon-6pm, or call for an appointment. Closed Aug. Admission $3, seniors and children under 17 $1.50.

Galleries

New York's museums may be the vanguard of art history, maintaining priceless collections and orchestrating blockbuster exhibitions, but New York galleries are where art *happens*. Contemporary art, such as it is, lives, breathes, trades hands, and all too often goes belly-up in these spaces. Think of the city's galleries as high culture's pet stores—you're not supposed to touch anything and half the fun is in seeing what's on display, looking cute, eager, and ready for purchase. Don't worry about how expensive it all is—the owners don't really expect you, budget traveler, to buy anything. It's best to ignore any snootiness you might encounter and have a blast. Galleries are *free* culture—go, and go often.

To get started, pick up a free copy of *The Gallery Guide* at any major museum or gallery; it lists the addresses, phone numbers, and hours of virtually every showplace in the city and comes equipped with several handy maps to orient you on your art odyssey. Extensive gallery information can also be found in the "Art" section of *New York* magazine as well as in the omniscient "Goings On About Town" in *The New Yorker*.

SoHo is a wonderland of galleries, with a particularly dense concentration of more than 40 different establishments lining Broadway between Houston and Spring St. **Madison Avenue** between 70th and 84th has a generous sampling of ritzy showplaces, and another group of galleries festoons **57th St.** between Fifth and Sixth Ave. Most galleries are open from Tuesday to Saturday, from 10am or 11am to 5pm or 6pm. In the summer, galleries often close on Saturdays and many are open by appointment only (and, for the most part, only to those serious about buying) from late July through early September.

Nearly all galleries host "openings" for their exhibitions; these are sometimes open to the public, offering the chance to drink wine, eat cheese, and pose, pose, pose (check *The Village Voice*, *The New Yorker*, and *The New York Press*). Stumbling upon an installation-in-progress can also be interesting, as walls are painted, bulky structures are erected, and artsy types sweat from physical exertion.

▉ SoHo

Hard economic times have sent the galleries in SoHo into a state of flux. Not only do they open and close with amazing rapidity, but many of them have had to cut their losses and sell what they call "bread and butter" art—a landscape that goes well with a sofa or a soothing sunset to remind the investment banker of his upcoming Club Med holiday. The avant-garde is having trouble getting its foot into the door of the ground-level, more commercial galleries that line West Broadway. So take a look on the second or third floors of gallery-packed buildings if you want to see the more experimental art that SoHo has to offer. The following is a sampling of the different types of galleries to be found in the neighborhood.

Holly Solomon Gallery, 172 Mercer (941-5777), at Houston St. This SoHo matriarch is an excellent place to start a tour of downtown galleries. Three or four artists are always showing in this multi-floored space, providing newcomers with an accessible array of avant-garde art. Strengths include upper-tier video, illustration, photography, and installation art; unlike other galleries, Solomon's has a sense of humor. William Wegman and Nam tune Paik are represented here. Open Sept.-June Tues.-Sat. 10am-6pm; July-Aug. Tues.-Fri. 10am-5pm.

Mary Boone, 417 W. Broadway (752-2929). Hot, hot, hot contemporary art. Names like Barbara Krueger and Richard Artschwager sell here—this is the big time. Perhaps the epitome of a SoHo gallery. Open Tues.-Sat. 10am-6pm.

Pace Gallery, 142 Greene St. (431-9224), between Prince and Houston. This famous gallery has two locations in the city. Its SoHo branch consists of one massive room displaying the works of biggies like Julian Schnabel and Claes Oldenburg. Exhibitions rotate every four weeks in this hot spot of the art world. Open Tues.-Sat. 10am-6pm; June-Aug. Mon.-Fri. 10am-6pm.

Sonnabend, 420 W. Broadway (966-6160). This prominent gallery shows contemporary paintings by well known American and European artists. Jeff Koons, John Baldessari, and Robert Rauschenburg top the bill. Open Tues.-Sat. 10am-6pm. By appointment only July -Aug.

Gagosian, 36 Wooster St. (228-2828). Big, bad art in the best possible way. Home to the notorious Damien Hirst show *cum* media blitz, where overhyped British art met overhyped British pop amid beachballs and vivisected livestock. If you're here to see galleries, you should probably see what's up here—more than likely, it'll be fun. Open Tues.-Sat. 10am-6pm. Closed in August.

David Zweirner, 43 Greene St. (966-9074), at Grand St. A small gallery that pulls together excellent, elegant one-person shows with a strong conceptual punch, frequently graceful in its curation. Some of the smartest contemporary art around ends up on Zweirner's walls. Open Tues.-Sat. 10am-6pm, closed Sat. in July.

Feature, 76 Greene St. (941-7077), second floor. Good and risky. Daring, straightforward selections of contemporary art. Don't miss their out-of-the-way back showroom when you visit. Open July-Aug. Tues.-Fri. 10am-5pm, Sept.-May Tues.-Fri. 10am-6pm.

Gavin Brown's Enterprise, 558 Broome St. (431-1512), just west of 6th Ave. Literally and figuratively as far left as you'd want to get without a map, this tiny gallery specializes in fun, interesting contemporary work. Japanese art, Steve Pippen (the bathroom artist), and other *uber*contemporary stuff. Not much artwork, but the artwork-to-crap ratio is much higher than in most galleries. Open Wed.-Sat. noon-6pm. Call first in the summer.

Exit Art, 548 Broadway (466-7745), between Prince and Spring St., on the second floor. A fun and happening "transcultural" and "transmedia" non-profit space, featuring successful and not-so-successful experiments in presentation and curation of visual art, theater, film, and video. The Café Cultura, open Fri. and Sat. from noon-8pm, lets you hang out and grab a beer ($3) while absorbing the culture. About as friendly and young as it gets in the NYC art scene. Open Tues.-Thurs. 10am-6pm, Fri. 10am-8pm, Sat. 11am-8pm. Closed in August.

American Primitive, 594 Broadway (966-1530), second floor. This small space shows only works by folk or self-taught American artists of the 19th and 20th centuries, focusing on contemporary works. The sculptures and paintings range from very colorful depictions of urban settings to more faded, craft-style works. Proudly and aggressively out of the art scene—so uncool they're cool. Open Mon.-Sat. 11am-6pm; closed Sat. during July-Aug.

Drawing Center, 35 Wooster St. (219-2166). Specializing exclusively in unique works on paper, this non-profit space manages to set up reliably high-quality exhibits. Shows range from historical to contemporary—the drawings are a terrific visual respite from the frequently garish and extravagant SoHo streets. Open Tues., Thurs.-Fri. 10am-6pm, Wed. 10am-8pm, Sat. 11am-6pm.

Artists Space, 38 Greene St. (226-3970), at Grand St., third floor. Another non-profit and non-stuffy gallery. Performance is stressed here, with experimental theater, video art, and sculpture featured year-round. A slide file of unaffiliated artists gives those without backing a chance to shine. Open Tues.-Sat. 10am-6pm; slide file open Wed.-Fri. 1-6pm. Frequent evening performances—call for schedule.

Stuart Levy Gallery, 588 Broadway (941-0009), third floor. Presenting five to six one-person shows and several group shows each year, this large gallery specializes in works in various media which incorporate photography. Open Tues.-Sat. 10am-6pm and by appointment Sept.-June.

Printed Matter, Inc., 77 Wooster St. (925-0325). Here, they hope to shake up your definition of "books." Featuring the best artist books and magazines in the biz, this non-profit bookshop/gallery makes a fascinating reading list any day of the year. Artists like John Baldessari, Barbara Krueger, Cindy Sherman, and Kiki Smith are all associated with this place, but it is their commitment to displaying books by unknowns which make them such a valuable resource in SoHo. Perpetual exhibitions and installations—always free, always fascinating. Open Tues.-Fri. 10am-6pm, Sat. 11am-7pm.

GALLERIES

■ Upper East Side

M. Knoedler & Co., Inc., 19 E. 70th St. (794-0550). One of the oldest and most respected galleries in the city, it shows Abstract Expressionists like Olitski and Motherwell. Recently, contemporary trends have infiltrated the time-honored institution, which now mounts shows like "Robert Rauschenberg: Bicyclords, Urban Bourbons & Eco-Echo." Open Mon.-Fri. 9:30am-5pm.

Hirschl and Adler Galleries, 21 E. 70th St. (535-8810), between Fifth and Madison Ave. A wide variety of 18th- to 20th-century European and American art. Open Mon.-Fri. 9:30am-4:45pm. Also **Hirschl and Adler Modern** upstairs.

Jane Kahan Gallery, 922 Madison Ave. (744-1950), between 73rd and 74th St. Specializes in 19th- and 20th- century greats such as Chagall, Arp, Calder, Matisse, and Renoir. Emphasis on Picasso ceramics. Open Tues.-Sat. 10am-6pm.

Thomson Studio Gallery, 19 E. 75th St. (249-0242), between Fifth and Madison Ave. This establishment's particular strength is late 19th- and early 20th-century American painting and sculpture, including some from the Salmagundi school. Open Mon.-Fri. 9:30am-5pm.

■ 57th Street

Fuller Building, 41 E. 57th St., between Madison and Park Ave. Stylish Art Deco building harbors 12 floors of galleries. Contemporary notables such as Robert Miller, André Emmerich, and Susan Sheehan; collectors of ancient works like Frederick Schultz; and several galleries handling modern works. The **André Emmerich Gallery** (752-0124) features important contemporary work by Hockney et al. Most galleries in the building keep hours of Mon.-Sat. 10am-6pm, but there is extreme variation and, from Oct.-May, most will be closed Mon.

Marlborough Gallery, 40 W. 57th St. (541-4900), between Fifth and Sixth Ave. A great diversity of forms, including painting, mixed media, and sculpture, featuring artists from throughout the world. Artists of note include Red Grooms, John Davies, and Marisol. Open Mon.-Sat. 10am-5:30pm.

Pace Gallery, 32 E. 57th St. (421-3292). Four floors dedicated to the promotion of widely disparate forms of art. **Pace Gallery** specializes in painting, sculpture, and drawing; **Pace Editions** in prints both old and new; **Pace MacGill** in photography; and the unfortunately named **Pace Primitive** in African works. Open Tues.-Fri. 9:30am-5:30pm, Sat. 10am-6pm.

Sidney Janis Gallery, 110 W. 57th St. (586-0110), between Sixth and Seventh Ave., sixth floor. Spanning artistic epochs from Cubism to Minimalism, this gallery has hosted shows by de Kooning, Gorky, Gottlieb, Pollock, and Rothko. It has also examined the links between its favored artists in large-scale conceptual shows, like the recent American Homage to Matisse, which included works by Avery, Kelly, Lichtenstein, and others. Open Tues.-Sat. 10am-5:30pm. Closed July-Aug.

Entertainment & Nightlife

Although always an exhilarating, incomparable city, New York only becomes *New York* when the sun goes down. From the blindingly bright lights of Times Square to the dark, impenetrably smoky atmosphere of a Greenwich Village or SoHo bar, the Big Apple pulls you in a million directions at once. Find some performance art, hear some jazz, go to an all-night diner, twist the night away—heck, even get a tattoo. A cab ride home at 4:30am through empty streets with the windows down is always sure to make your spirits soar. This city never sleeps, and, at least for a few nights, neither should you.

Choosing a show or club from among the city's dizzyingly broad array of entertainment and cultural activity is a common problem. The theaters, halls, clubs, and hundreds of other independent venues that are together responsible for New York's cultural hegemony over the rest of the country all compete fiercely for popular attention and critical credibility. *Let's Go* lists New York's more essential venues and hot spots, but be sure to check local sources to find out about other places and to get the scoop on present offerings. A number of publications print daily, weekly, and monthly entertainment and nightlife calendars; try *New York* magazine, the *Village Voice,* and *The New York Times* (particularly the Sunday edition). The most comprehensive survey of the theater and movie scene can be found in *The New Yorker.* The monthly *Free Time* calendar ($1.25) lists free cultural events throughout Manhattan. Try the NYC Parks Department's **entertainment hotline** (360-3456; 24hr.) for the lowdown on special events in parks throughout the city. Call the **NYC/ON STAGE hotline** (768-1818) for a comprehensive listing of all the theater, dance, and music events taking place each week. Also try **765-ARTS** (765-2787), which lists music, theater, art, and other events at more than 500 venues.

▓ Theater

Broadway is currently undergoing a revival—ticket sales are booming, and mainstream musicals are receiving more than their fair share of attention. Old-fashioned productions such as *Showboat* and *Grease* are very popular, and tickets can be hard to come by. The many Off-Broadway and Off-Off-Broadway shows throughout the city offer a cheaper and less mainstream alternative for theatergoers.

Consult *The New Yorker* for superior short descriptions of current shows, or try *The New York Times.* For listings of Broadway, Off-Broadway, and Off-Off-Broadway shows, see *Listings,* a weekly guide to entertainment in Manhattan ($1). **The Broadway Line** (563-2929) is an interactive phone service that gives show descriptions, performance schedules, and ticket prices for all types of shows, and even forwards your call to a ticket agent if you're ready to make a purchase. For information on shows and ticket availability, you can also call the **NYC/ON STAGE hotline** at 768-1818. The NYC Department of Cultural Affairs **Arts Hotline** (956-2787) offers an actual person to advise you (open Mon.-Fri. 9am-5pm).

Though Broadway tickets usually run upwards of $50, there are many ways to save money. Some theaters have recently introduced $15 seats in the farthest reaches of the balcony, though these seats are predictably hard to come by. **TKTS** (768-1818 for recorded info) sells half-price tickets to many Broadway and some of the larger Off-Broadway shows on the same day of the performance, from a booth in the middle of Duffy Square (the northern part of Times Square, at 47th and Broadway). The board near the front of the line posts the names of the shows with available tickets. There is a $2.50 service charge per ticket, and only cash or traveler's checks are accepted. (Tickets sold Mon.-Sat. 3-8pm for evening performances; Wed. and Sat. 10am-2pm for matinees; and Sun. noon-8pm for matinees and evening performances.) The lines can be long, snaking around the traffic island a few times, but they move fairly quickly. To beat the lines, arrive before selling time. The lines are often shorter downtown, where TKTS has an indoor branch in the mezzanine of 2 World Trade Center (booth operates Mon.-Fri. 11am-5:30pm, Sat. 11am-3:30pm; Sunday matinee tickets sold on Sat.).

You can get a similar discount with **"twofers"** (i.e., two fer the price of one), ticket coupons that float around the city at bookstores, libraries, and the New York Visitors and Convention Bureau. They are usually for old Broadway warhorses—shows that have been running strong for a very long time.

Full-price tickets may be reserved over the phone and paid for by credit card through: **Tele-Charge** (239-6200; 24hr.) for Broadway shows, **Ticket Central** (279-4200, open 1-8pm daily) for Off-Broadway shows, and **Ticketmaster** (307-7171, 24hr.) for all types of shows. All three services assess a per-ticket service charge; make sure you ask before purchasing. These fees can be evaded by purchasing tickets directly from the box offices.

The renowned **Shakespeare in the Park** series, founded by the same Joseph Papp who founded the Joseph Papp Public Theater (see below), is a New York summer tradition that practically everyone in the city has attended (or attempted to attend). From late June through August, two Shakespeare plays are presented at the Delacorte Theater in Central Park, near the 81st St. entrance on the Upper West Side, just north of the 79th St. Transverse (861-7277 or 598-7100). The glorious outdoor amphitheater overlooks Turtle Pond and its mini-Dunsinane. Top-notch productions—plus the opportunity to perform Shakespeare in the great outdoors—attract the most important actors around. Recent performances have included *Richard III* with Denzel Washington, *Othello* with Raoul Julia and Christopher Walken, and *The Tempest* with Patrick Stewart. Kevin Kline serves as the festival's artistic director. For free tickets, wait in line at the Delacorte Theater. (Tickets available from 1pm; try to get there by 11:30am. Also available from 1-3pm at the Public Theater at 425 Lafayette St. downtown. Limit of two tickets per person. Doors open Tues.-Sun. at 7:30pm, shows start at 8pm.)

For years, the **Joseph Papp Public Theater,** 425 Lafayette St. (598-7150), was inextricably linked with its namesake founder, one of the city's leading producers and favorite sons (he died in 1991). The six theaters here present a wide variety of shows; recently, an exhaustive and exhausting Shakespeare Marathon included every single one of the Bard's plays down to *Timon of Athens* (Ticket prices $15-35). The Public Theater saves about one quarter of the seats for every production, to be sold for about $10 on the day of performance (starting at 6pm for evening performances and 1pm for matinees).

The city also boasts the widest variety of ethnic theater in the country. The **Repertorio Español,** currently housed in the Gramercy Arts Theater at 138 E. 27th St. (889-2850), presents many Spanish productions (tickets $15-20). The **Negro Ensemble Company** (575-5860) rents out space to perform works by and about African-Americans (tickets $15-20). The **Pan Asian Repertory Theater** (245-2660), in the Church of St. Clements at Playhouse 46, 423 W. 46th St., is the largest Asian-American theater in the U.S. The **Irish Arts Center,** at 553 W. 51st St. (757-3318), presents contemporary and classic Irish and Irish-American plays (tickets $20-25).

New York is the birthplace of the elusive amalgam called **performance art,** a combination of stand-up comedy, political commentary, theatrical monologue, and video art (or just some guy standing onstage slapping meat on his head). The Brooklyn Academy of Music's famous **Next Wave festival** specializes in performance art, as do these Manhattan venues: **The Kitchen,** at 512 W. 19th St. (255-5793), **Franklin Furnace,** at 112 Franklin St. (925-4671), **Performance Space 122 (P.S. 122),** at 150 First Ave. (477-5288), and the **Theater for the New City,** at 155 First Ave. (254-1109). **La Mama,** at 74a E. 4th St. (254-6468), the most venerable of the lot, helped Sam Shepard get started.

BROADWAY

Most Broadway theaters are located north of Times Square, between Eighth Avenue and Broadway and the streets that connect them. Broadway theaters are open only when a play is in production, and most don't have phones. Call **Ticketmaster** (307-4100) or one of the other lines listed above for information, or check the papers.

Ambassador Theater, 219 W. 49th St., between Broadway and Eighth Ave. Built on a slant. Spencer Tracy played here in *The Last Mile* in 1930. In *The Straw Hat Revue* (1939), Danny Kaye, Jerome Robbins, and Imogene Coca parodied Broadway shows, anticipating *Forbidden Broadways* to come. The Ambassador is currently showing the 4-Tony-winning rap/tap blockbuster *Bring in da Noise, Bring in da Funk* (see So What's On?, p. 263). Tickets $20-67.50.

Belasco Theater, 111 W. 44th St., between Sixth and Seventh Ave. Built in 1907 by David Belasco, a producer extraordinaire who acted, designed, directed, and believed fervently in spectacle. He equipped the place with an elevated stage that could be lowered for set changes as well as a backstage elevator that would ascend to his private apartments. In 1935, the legendary Group Theater brought Clifford Odets' *Awake and Sing* to the Belasco. The Group Theater proved the most politically explicit act on Broadway, and 4 decades later the very nude revue *Oh! Calcutta!* exploded here as the most sexually explicit.

Booth Theater, 222 W. 45th St., between Broadway and Eighth Ave. Designer Herts dressed it up in early Italian Renaissance in 1913 and Melanie Kahane modernized it in 1979. Kaufman and Hart's *You Can't Take It With You* opened here, as did Noel Coward's *Blithe Spirit.* Ntozake Shange's poetic *For Colored Girls Who Have Considered Suicide When the Rainbow is Enuf* lasted 742 performances. Recent productions include *Having Our Say,* the autobiography of two century-old African-American women. Tickets $15-49.50.

Broadhurst Theater, 235 W. 44th St., between Broadway and Eighth Ave. Designed in 1917 by Herbert J. Krapp, the man who churned out theaters at the top of the century. Helen Hayes crowned the place with her legendary performance in *Victoria Regina* back in 1935. *Grease* first rocked here, as did *Godspell.* Ian McKellan played Saliere to Tim Curry's Mozart and Jane Seymour's Constanze in the American premier of *Amadeus.* Patrick Stewart has shed his Star Trek uniform the past two holiday seasons for an energetic one-man performance of Dickens's classic *A Christmas Carol.* The theater's most successful recent production was *Kiss of the Spider Woman,* starring Vanessa Williams, which won 7 Tony Awards in 1993, including Best Musical.

Broadway Theater, 1681 Broadway, between 52nd and 53rd St. Built as a movie house in 1924 with a whopping capacity of 1765. Its first theatrical venture, *The New Yorkers* by Cole Porter and Herbert Fields, closed in 20 weeks—it was hard to sell tickets for $5.50 during the Depression. Benefits, including Irving Berlin's *This Is the Army* with a cameo by Irv himself, raised money for the Emergency Relief fund during World War II. Soon Oscar Hammerstein did a jazzed-up all-black *Carmen.* A few operas and dance troupes later, the stage saw another musical: *Mr. Wonderful,* starring Sammy Davis, Jr. and Sr. *The Most Happy Fella* dropped in, *The Body Beautiful* dropped out, and Les Ballets de Paris, the Beryozka Russian Dance Company, and the Old Vic flew in to do Shakespeare. Then Ethel Merman brought musical comedy belting back with *Gypsy.* In 1972, *Fiddler on the Roof* ended its run here, breaking previous records with its tally of 3242 performances. Harold Prince revived Leonard Bernstein's *Candide* with labyrinthine staging and multi-level seating; he then staged *Evita* here. Here, Anthony Quinn starred in the *Zorba* revival, and most recently, the theater has hosted *Miss Saigon,* which in 1996 was in its sixth year and running strong (tickets $15-70).

Brooks Atkinson Theatre, 256 W. 47th St. (719-4099), between Broadway and Eighth Ave. Designed in 1926 as the Mansfield by very busy architect Herbert J. Krapp. In 1930 *The Green Pastures* opened here, setting Southern blacks amid Old Testament events; it enjoyed a run of 640 performances and won the Pulitzer Prize. Marc Blitzstein's revolutionary *The Cradle Will Rock* opened here during the memorable snowstorm of December 26, 1947. In the 50s, the struggling theater served as a TV playhouse. Then, in 1960, it was named for the much-loved *New York Times* theater critic and Harvard grad who had retired from reviewing plays that spring. John Steinbeck's *Of Mice and Men* was revived here with James Earl Jones as Lenny. Ellen Burstyn and Charles Grodin conducted their annual fling here in *Same Time, Next Year* for 1453 performances. *She Loves Me* played here recently.

Circle in the Square Theatre, on W. 50th St., between Broadway and Eighth Ave. Delightfully in the round, a charming hotbed of things Shavian and Shepardian. Modeled after—but half the size of—the downtown theater by the same name, it opened with *Mourning Becomes Elektra* in 1972. The circular stage has brimmed with sand for Tina Howe's *Coastal Disturbances* and was once strung up with laundry for a production of *Sweeney Todd*. Much Molière here, too.

Cort Theater, 138 W. 48 St., between Sixth and Seventh Ave. Built in the style of Louis XVI, with a lobby of Pavanozza marble and 999 seats. Katherine Hepburn made her debut here in 1928 in *These Days;* it closed in a week, but she returned in the 50s to star in a blockbuster run of *As You Like It*. Grace Kelly made her first Broadway appearance here. In summer 1995, the production was *The Heiress,* a Tony Award-winning play based on James' *Washington Square*.

Ethel Barrymore Theater, 243 W. 47th St., between Broadway and Eighth Ave. In 1927, the celebrated Ethel was blithely appearing in a Maugham play at another theater when playwright Zoe Atkins approached her and promised that the Shuberts would build her a theater if she would agree to do a play called *The Kingdom of God*. Ethel Barrymore read and liked it and soon found herself starring in this play as well as a series of others. Alfred Lunt, Lynn Fontanne, and Noel Coward appeared here in Coward's *Design for Living*. Described as "a kettle of venom" by Brooks Atkinson, Claire Booth Luce's scathing play *The Women,* with a cast of 40 females, ran for 657 performances. *A Streetcar Named Desire* opened here in 1947, starring Jessica Tandy and Marlon Brando, as did Lorraine Hansbery's acclaimed *Raisin in the Sun,* starring Sidney Poitier. Oscar Wilde's *An Ideal Husband* was running in 1996. Tickets $30-55.

Eugene O'Neill Theater, 230 W. 49th St., between Broadway and Eighth Ave. Using the Georgian style, Krapp designed this one, too, born as the Forrest Theater back in 1925. In 1959, it was renamed in honor of playwright Eugene O'Neill, who had died in 1953. Arthur Miller's *All My Sons* opened here, as did his *A View From the Bridge*. A slew of musicals have come and gone here, followed by a host of Neil Simon plays and some sterner stuff. Recently, Trumpette Marla Maples starred here in *The Will Rogers Follies*. In 1994 the O'Neill began an ongoing revival of *Grease;* to promote the musical, the outside of the theater was painted fluorescent pink and covered with black graffiti. Tickets $30-67.50.

Gershwin Theater, on W. 50th St. (586-6510), between Broadway and Eighth Ave. Neo-Art Nouveau. It started up in 1972 as the Uris, hosting *Porgy and Bess, Sweeney Todd,* and *The Pirates of Penzance,* which spent the summer in Central Park. Both *The King and I* and *Mame* were revived here. The mammoth revival of *Showboat* should still be rolling along.

Golden Theater, 252 W. 45th St., between Broadway and Eighth Ave. Built by Krapp and commissioned by the Chanin brothers, the production whiz-kids who wanted the 800-seat space to accommodate intimate artistic work. When *Angel Street,* a strange piece of Victoriana, opened here, skeptical producers ordered only 3 days' worth of playbills—but the show ran for 1293 (3 x 431) performances. Some revues swept through—starring Mike Nichols and Elaine May, Yves Montand, and finally the likes of Peter Cook and Dudley Moore in *Beyond the Fringe*. Tickets $35-75.

Helen Hayes Theater, 240 W. 44th St. (944-9450), between Broadway and Eighth. It opened in 1912 with only 299 seats and was soon appropriately christened the Little Theatre. Originally designed to stage intimate and non-commercial works, it fared poorly commercially and closed. It served as New York Times Hall from 1942-1959 and as the ABC TV Studio from 1959-1963, but then hosted the long-running comedy *Gemini* and Tony-winning *Torch Song Trilogy*.

Imperial Theater, 249 W. 45th St., between Broadway and Eighth Ave. Built in 1923, it entered the big leagues with *Oh, Kay!* by the Gershwins (story by P.G. Wodehouse and Guy Bolton). Rodgers and Hart, with George Abbot, conflated

American musicals and Russian ballet in their 1935 hit *On Your Toes*. Cole Porter's *Leave It To Me* introduced Mary Martin and a chorus blue-boy named Gene Kelly to the Broadway stage. Martin returned in *One Touch of Venus*, a show by unlikely collaborators Kurt Weill, S. J. Perelman, and Ogden Nash. Ethel Merman proved there's no business like show business in *Annie Get Your Gun*. *Fiddler on the Roof* opened here on September 22, 1964. *Cabaret* had a brief stint, followed by *Zorba* and *Minnie's Boys*, a musical about the Marx Brothers. *Les Misérables* has jerked tears here since October 1990, and almost certainly will continue through 1997 (tickets $15-70).

Lunt-Fontanne Theater, 205 W. 46th St. (575-9200), between Broadway and Eighth Ave. Built in 1910 as the Globe. Carrière and Hastings planned the seating and equipped the place with an oval ceiling-panel that could be removed in fair weather. Fanny Brice dazzled here in the *Ziegfeld Follies of 1921*. *No, No, Nanette*, featuring the song "Tea for Two," was a hit here in the 20s. The Globe went dark during the Depression, and then became a movie house. In 1957, the City Investing Company fixed it up and named it after dashing drama couple Alfred Lunt and Lynn Fontanne. The restored house hosted new musicals *The Sound of Music* and *The Rothschilds* as well as revivals *A Funny Thing Happened on the Way to the Forum* and *Hello, Dolly!* Sandy Duncan flew here as *Peter Pan*.

Lyceum Theater, 149 W. 45th St., between Sixth and Seventh Ave. The oldest of the lot, designed by Herts and Tallant back in 1903, topped by a 10-story tower with scene shops, carpentry studios, and extra dressing rooms galore. It faced demolition in 1939; playwrights George S. Kaufman and Moss Hart chipped in with some friends, bought it in 1940, and sold it to the Shubert Organization in 1945. *Born Yesterday*, with Judy Holliday, opened here in 1946. *Look Back in Anger* stormed over from England in 1957. In 1980, the 1939 flop *Morning's at Seven* was revived here—and won a Tony Award.

Majestic Theater, 247 W. 44th St., between Broadway and Eighth Ave. The largest legit theater in the district and the last of the former Chanin chain. Rodgers and Hammerstein's *Carousel* opened here, as did their short-lived *Allegro* and their hot ticket *South Pacific,* which ran for 1925 performances. *Camelot,* with Julie Andrews and Richard Burton, charmed Broadway for 873 performances. Nowadays, Andrew Lloyd Webber's *Phantom of the Opera* skulks on after nine lucrative years. Tickets $15-70.

Marquis Theater, 211 W. 45th St., at Broadway. Opened with Robert Lindsay's star turn in *Me and My Girl*. Other shows include Tyne Daly's shot at *Gypsy* and Jerry Lewis' Broadway debut in *Damn Yankees*. Currently running is a stage version of *Victor/Victoria,* starring Julie Andrews. Tickets $20-75.

Martin Beck Theatre, 302 W. 45th St., between Eighth and Ninth Ave. When built in 1924, it was the only Byzantine-style American theater. The Abbey Irish Theater Players performed here in 1932 in classics like *Juno and the Paycock* and *Playboy of the Western World.* Katharine Cornell played Juliet here to Basil "Sherlock" Rathbone's Romeo and Orson Welles's Tybalt. Tennessee Williams found his way here with *The Rose Tattoo,* starring Maureen Stapleton and Eli Wallach, and *Sweet Bird of Youth,* starring Geraldine Page and Paul Newman. Liz Taylor made her Broadway debut here in *The Little Foxes*. A revival of the classic musical *Guys and Dolls* recently played here.

Minskoff Theatre, 200 W. 45th St., at Broadway. Less streamlined than its neighbor, the Gershwin, but equally high-tech. Its 1621 seats are 35ft. in the air. It opened on March 13, 1973, with Debbie Reynolds in a revival of *Irene*. Rudolf Nureyev pirouetted through here with the Murray Lewis Dance Company in 1978, followed by a series of short-lived musicals: *The King of Hearts,* a *West Side Story* revival, and *Can-Can,* a fast-stomping extravaganza that closed after 5 days. *Sunset Boulevard* premiered here in November 1994 and should still be running in 1996 with new star Betty Buckley. Tickets $25-70.

Music Box Theater, 239 W. 45th St., between Broadway and Eighth Ave. Cute, charming, built in 1921 by Sam Harris and Irving Berlin to house Berlin's *Music Box Revues*. This stage braved the Depression with French comedy *Topaze* by Marcel Pagnol and Noel Coward's "Mad Dogs and Englishmen" ditty (not to be confused with Joe Cocker's flailing album of the same name), sung by Beatrice Lillie in

The Third Little Show. The Music Box production *Of Thee I Sing* became the first musical comedy to win the Pulitzer Prize. When romantic comedies upstaged revues, the Music Box churned out the tuneless *I Remember Mama,* introducing a young Marlon Brando to the stage; Tennessee Williams's *Summer and Smoke;* and William Inge's *Bus Stop. Sleuth* mysteriously endured for 1222 performances, *Deathtrap* for a prime 1609. Irving Berlin maintained a lively financial and emotional interest in the theater until his death.

Nederlander Theater, 208 W. 41st St., between Seventh and Eighth Ave. It opened as the National Theater in 1921. Noel Coward and Gertrude Lawrence trod the stage in a group of plays called *Tonight at 8:30.* Orson Welles and John Houseman transported their Shakespearean productions from the smaller Mercury Theater. Here Sir John Gielgud and Lillian Gish starred in a failed production of *Crime and Punishment,* and Edward Albee premiered his successful *Who's Afraid of Virginia Woolf?* and his more obscure *Tiny Alice.* The Royal Shakespeare Company's *A Midsummer Night's Dream* directed by Peter Brook, came to visit, as did Tom Stoppard's *Jumpers* and Harold Pinter's *Betrayal.* In 1980 the National-turned-Billy Rose-turned-Trafalgar was dubbed "The Nederlander" in honor of late theater owner David Tobias Nederlander. The East Village rock-tragedy *Rent* currently plays here (see So What's On?, p. 263). Tickets $30-67.50.

Neil Simon Theater, 250 W. 52nd St., between Broadway and Eighth Ave. Tireless designer Herbert J. Krapp built this in 1927 as the Alvin Theater with a capacity of 1400. The Lunts' *The Taming of the Shrew,* staged for the Finnish Relief Fund, was followed by Robert E. Sherwood's Pulitzer Prize-winning *There Shall Be No Night,* about Russia's invasion of Finland. The Alvin found lighter fare with long-running *A Funny Thing Happened on the Way to The Forum* and Tom Stoppard's landmark farce *Rosencrantz and Guildenstern Are Dead.* The theater is now running *The King and I.* Tickets $25-75.

Palace Theatre, 1564 Broadway, at 47th St. Sarah Bernhardt, Ethel Barrymore—you name them, they played the Palace. Once a vaudeville haunt for Houdini, W.C. Fields, and the Marx Brothers, the Palace became a movie house with few spells of musical theater from the 30s to the 50s. Then in 1965, James Nederlander restored it. Lauren Bacall stopped by to be *The Woman of the Year,* later followed by the more outrageous men of the year in *La Cage aux Folles.* The Palace debuted Disney's blockbuster musical adaptation *Beauty and the Beast* in 1994; it should continue through 1997. Tickets $22.50-70.

Plymouth Theater, 236 W. 45th St., between Broadway and Eighth Ave. Designed by Krapp to seat 1000, the Plymouth was built in 1917. Thornton Wilder's *The Skin of Our Teeth* played here in 1942. A British invasion began with *Equus, Piaf,* and *The Real Thing;* English visitors completely reconstructed the house for the Royal Shakespeare Company's 8-hr. Dickensian marathon, *Nicholas Nickleby,* which won Tonys for actor Roger Rees and directors Trevor Nunn and John Caird. Tickets $25-45.

Richard Rodgers Theatre, 226 W. 46th St., between Broadway and Eighth Ave. Krapp sloped the seats L-Z upward for short people in the back. Here *Finian's Rainbow* charmed Broadway with an Irish lilt—725 performances' worth. *Guys and Dolls* opened here in 1950, won 8 Tony Awards, and lasted 1194 performances. Audrey Hepburn was transmogrified into Jean Giraudoux's lyrical sprite in *Ondine* in 1954. In 1975, Sir John Gielgud directed Maggie Smith in a revival of *Private Lives,* and Bob Fosse staged the hit *Chicago.* The 80s brought the sizzling musical *Nine,* based on Fellini's *8½. How to Succeed in Business Without Really Trying,* starring Matthew Broderick, opened here in 1995.

Roundabout Theatre, 1530 Broadway (869-8400). This tiny, 500-seat theater is just large enough to be considered Broadway. It produces classics and revivals of plays and musicals. Tickets $45-60.

Royale Theater, 242 W. 45th St., between Broadway and Eighth Ave. Designed by Krapp, this house seats over 1000 and caters mostly to musicals. Tennessee Williams's first Broadway play, *The Glass Menagerie,* starring Laurette Taylor, moved here from the Off-Broadway Playhouse. Julie Andrews made her debut in *The Boy Friend,* a 1954 takeoff on 1920s musicals. Thornton Wilder's *The Matchmaker* previously flopped as *The Merchant of Yonkers* and later got musicalized as *Hello,*

Dolly! here in 1955. Mary Tyler Moore took the man's role in *Whose Life Is It Anyway?*, continuing the tradition of profuse gender confusion initiated by Jagger, Bowie, and the rest of the "glam" movement of the 70s.

St. James Theater, 246 W. 44th St., between Broadway and Eighth Ave. Built in 1927. Seats 1600 in Georgian splendor. Here, John Houseman and Orson Welles collaborated on Richard Wright's chilling *Native Son. Oklahoma!* whirled in 1943, dazzling New York, running for 2248 performances, and launching Rodgers and Hammerstein. Yul Brynner first took the Broadway stage here in *The King and I* in 1951. Laurence Olivier and Anthony Quinn even traded roles at whim in their remarkable production of Anouilh's *Becket.* Joseph Papp brought his musical version of *Two Gentlemen of Verona.* Tickets $25-70.

Shubert Theatre, 225 W. 44th St., between Broadway and Eighth Ave. Built in 1913 by Lee and J.J. Shubert in memory of their deceased brother Sam. 1932 brought *Americana,* with its Depression song "Brother, Can You Spare a Dime?" In 1943, Paul Robeson played Othello, co-starring with Uta Hagen and José Ferrer. Katherine Hepburn thrilled audiences with *The Philadelphia Story* for 417 sold-out performances. *A Chorus Line* opened and closed here after its record-breaking run. The musical *Crazy for You* will be into its sixth year as of February 1996.

Virginia Theater, 245 W. 52nd St., between Broadway and Eighth Ave. On April 13, 1925, President Coolidge pushed a button in Washington, D.C., that set the floodlights flowing over Shaw's *Caesar and Cleopatra,* starring Helen Hayes and Lionel Atwill. Next, Lunt and Fontanne came here with Shaw's *Arms and the Man.* Edward G. Robinson graced the stage in 1927 in Pirandello's *Right You Are (It is So if You Think it is So).* A series of flops forced the Theater Guild to lease out the place as a radio playhouse from 1943-50. The American National Theater and Academy (ANTA) then took over and started sponsoring experimental productions and straight plays such as *J.B., A Man For All Seasons,* and a revival of *Our Town* with Henry Fonda. Currently *Smokey Joe's Café: the Songs of Leiber and Stoller* is playing here. Tickets $49.50-70

Walter Kerr Theater, 225 W. 48th St. Built in a record 66 days in 1921 as The Ritz and only recently christened the Walter Kerr in honor of the gentle critic. When it was the WPA Theater, the Federal Theater Project staged *Pinocchio* and T.S. Eliot's *Murder in the Cathedral* here. Renovated in 20s-style by Karen Rosen, the Kerr reopened in 1983 with the juggling, entertaining *Flying Karamazov Brothers.* Tony Kushner's extraordinary *Angels in America,* a two-part epic on gay life comprising of *Millennium Approaches* and *Perestroika,* played here recently, as did August Wilson's *Seven Guitars.*

Winter Garden Theater, 1634 Broadway, between 50th and 51st St. It opened in 1911 as a hall "devoted to novel, international, spectacular, and musical entertainment." Al Jolson first appeared in blackface here. The Winter Garden has always been graced by new musical successes, from *Wonderful Town* to *West Side Story* to *Funny Girl.* Here Zero Mostel revived *Fiddler on the Roof,* Angela Lansbury revived *Gypsy,* and the multi-media blitz *Beatlemania* revived Beatles worship. Most recently, designer John Napier clawed the place apart to create his fantasy set for *Cats,* which will likely continue to play through 1997. Tickets $37.50-65.

OFF-BROADWAY AND OFF-OFF-BROADWAY

Off-Broadway theaters are a group of smaller theaters, mostly located downtown. Officially, these theaters have between 100 and 499 seats; only Broadway houses have over 500. Off-Broadway houses frequently offer more offbeat or quirky shows, with shorter runs, but occasionally these shows have long runs or jump to Broadway houses. Many of the best of the Off-Broadway houses huddle in the Sheridan Square area of the West Village. Eugene O'Neill got his break at the **Provincetown Playhouse,** and Elisa Loti made her American debut at the **Actors Playhouse.** Tickets cost $15-45; TKTS sells tickets to the larger Off-Broadway houses. It is often possible to see shows for free by arranging to usher; this usually entails dressing neatly and showing up at the theater around 45 minutes ahead of curtain, helping to seat ticket-holders, and then staying for 10 minutes after the performance to help clean up. Call the the-

ENTERTAINMENT

ater after 5pm and speak with the House manager far in advance to set this up (your goal: free seats; your opponents, the savvy theater crowd).

Off-Off-Broadway is not a joke but an actual category of cheaper, younger, and smaller theaters. Some Off- and Off-Off Broadway theaters have easily definable missions and aesthetics. **Playwrights Horizons** and **Manhattan Theater Club,** for instance, are among the nation's most prestigious launching pads for new American plays. Other theaters, such as **The Ontological Hysteric Theater at St. Mark's Church** (533-4650), are less easy to define—and more adventurous. Check out the Hysterics *Blueprint Series* in July for a respected taste of new and emerging talent.

Many of the theaters listed below have varied and eclectic offerings, and many of them host several different companies. Your best bet is to check the listings and reviews in the *Village Voice*.

Actors Playhouse, 100 Seventh Ave. S. (691-6226). Recent shows include *Making Porn*, featuring unclothed former gay porn star Rex Chandler. Tickets $25-30.

Alice's Fourth Floor, 432 W. 42nd St. (967-0400), between Dyer and 10th Ave. Home to theater workshops as well as performances.

American Place Theater, 111 W. 46th St. (840-2960 for a schedule, 840-3074 for the box office). Contemporary drama such as Barnaby Spring's *The Mayor of Boys Town*, which ran in 1994.

Astor Place Theater, 434 Lafayette St. (254-4370). Currently showing *The Blue Man Group*. Tickets $35-45.

Cherry Lane, 38 Commerce St. (989-2020), at Grove St. Started in the 1920s by theater mavens unhappy with what they perceived as the commercial drift of the Provincetown Playhouse, Cherry Lane has hosted such avant-garde productions as Beckett's *Waiting for Godot* and plays by Ionesco and Albee.

Circle in the Square Downtown, 159 Bleecker St. (254-6330), at Thompson St. The original Circle in the Square company of the 1950s got their name from their round theater within Sheridan Square. At their new, non-round space on Bleecker St., Eugene O'Neill's *The Iceman Cometh* was put on. Jason Robards and Geraldine Page got their starts with this company.

Douglas Fairbanks Theatre, 432 W. 42nd St. (239-4321). Currently showing the musical comedy *Party*. Tickets around $40.

Ensemble Studio, 549 W. 52nd St. (247-4982), at Eleventh Ave. A bit off the beaten path. Produces non-musicals and compilations of short plays by both established and lesser-known playwrights. Tickets free to $25.

Harold Clurman Theater, 412 W. 42nd St. (279-4200).

Here, 145 Ave. of the Americas (647-0202). Experimental musical, poetic, and dramatic performances. Tickets $10-25.

John Houseman Theater, 450 W. 42nd St. (967-9077). Home to Studio Theater, Studio Too, The New Group, Houseman Theater Co., and Gotham City Improv.

Joseph Papp Public Theater, 425 Lafayette St. (598-7150) See above.

Lamb's, 130 W. 44th St. (997-1780). Two spaces (one with 349 seats, the other with 29) host family-oriented plays and musicals such as *Johnny Pie* and *Smoke on the Mountain*. Tickets $25-35.

Lucille Lortel, 121 Christopher St. (924-8782). Primarily known for its 1950s production of the *Threepenny Opera* by Brecht, with a cast that included Bea Arthur, Ed Asner, and John Astin.

Manhattan Theater Club, 131 W. 55th St. (581-1212). This extremely successful theater company's recent productions have included *Lips Together, Teeth Apart* and *Love! Valour! Compassion!*

Orpheum, 126 Second Ave. (477-2477). This theater recently scored a success with Mamet's *Oleanna*. Currently playing *Stomp*.

Pan Asian Repertory, 423 W. 46th St. (245-2660). Works by and about Asian life. (see above)

Playhouse 91, 316 E. 91st St. (831-2000). Currently houses the Jewish Repertory Theater. Under the artistic direction of Ran Avni, the JRT puts on plays inspired by the Jewish experience.

Playwrights Horizons, 416 W. 42nd St. (279-4200), between 9th and 10th Ave. Dedicated to the support of new American playwrights, lyricists, composers, and

---

So What's On?

Here are a few of Broadway and Off-Broadway's most popular offerings:

Blue Man Group/Tubes, Astor Place Theater. Somewhere between stand-up, performance art, and a one-ring circus. Three guys painted blue do some weird stuff.

The Fantasticks, Sullivan St. Playhouse, The longest running show in Broadway history—a love story involving a boy, a girl, two dads, and a fence.

Rent, Nederlander Theater. Winner of the 1996 Pulitzer Prize for drama, *Rent* translated Puccini's *La Bohème* into a rock tragedy set in Alphabet City, where youths suck the marrow out of life against a backdrop of AIDS, struggling artists, homelessness, and other hard realities of bohemian living.

Bring In 'Da Noise, Bring in 'Da Funk, Ambassador Theater. A rap/tap epic about the history of Black America from slave ships to modern New York City. It won 4 Tony awards in 1996, and tickets still start at $20.

---

productions of their work. They have developed and produced more than 300 new plays and musicals, including three Pulitzer Prize winners. Tickets $10-30.

Promenade Theatre, 2162 Broadway (580-1313). Recently performed the eclectic *All Wicked Songs.* Tickets $40-42.50.

Provincetown Playhouse, 133 MacDougal St. (674-8043). Some of the most noteworthy Villagers are associated with this playhouse, including Eugene O'Neill and Edna St. Vincent Millay. Starting out in 1915 as plays produced on a porch in Cape Cod, the Provincetown put on many controversial, avant-garde acts in the 1920s, such as Dada drama and the puzzling works of e.e. cummings. An historical luminary in Village theater, its prominence has dimmed in the wake of the confrontational theater of the 90s.

Ridiculous Theatrical Company, 1 Sheridan Sq. (691-2271). Alternative theater at its height. The company starts its 32nd year of productions in 1997.

Samuel Beckett Theater, 410 W. 42nd. St. (522-2858), between Ninth and Tenth Ave. Artsy productions of contemporary drama, sometimes including post-performance discussions with members of the cast. Tickets $8-12.

SoHo Repertory Theatre, 46 Walker St. (977-5955), between Broadway and Church St. This 100-seat theater stages contemporary avant-garde works by American playwrights. Tickets $10-15.

Sullivan Street Playhouse, 181 Sullivan St. (674-3838). Home to *The Fantasticks* since May 1960, making it the longest running show in U.S. history. Grab a twofer pass. All seats $35; shows Tues.-Fri. 8pm, Sat. 3 and 7pm, Sun. 3 and 7:30pm.

Theater at Saint Peter's Church, 619 Lexington Ave. (935-2200). Recently performed the religiously themed *Act of Providence.* Tickets $25.

Vineyard Theater, 309 E. 26th St. (683-9772). Recently performed *The Peculiar Works Project.*

Westside Theater, 407 W. 43rd St. (315-2244). Rental theater hosting a variety of plays, comedies, and musicals, including the likes of Penn and Teller. Recently featured Sherry Glaser's one-woman comedy *Family Secrets.* Tickets $30-40.

■ Movies

If Hollywood is *the* place to make films, New York City is *the* place to see them. Most movies open in New York weeks before they're distributed across the country, and the response of Manhattan audiences and critics can shape a film's success or failure nationwide. Dozens of revival houses show motion picture classics year-round, and independent filmmakers from around the reel world come to New York to flaunt their work.

First-run movies show all over the city. Big-screen fanatics should check out the cavernous **Ziegfeld,** 141 W. 54th St. (765-7600), between Sixth and Seventh Ave., one of the largest screens left in America, showing first-run films. Consult local newspapers for complete listings. Tickets run $8 for adults and $4.25 for children under

12. **MoviePhone** (777-FILM) allows you to reserve tickets for most major movie-houses and pick them up at showtime from the theater's automated ticket dispenser; you charge the ticket price plus a $1.50 fee over the phone. For more extensive listings of revival houses and independent films check *The Village Voice* or *The New Yorker*.

MUSEUMS AND OTHER VENUES

Adam Clayton Powell, Jr., State Office Building, 163 W. 125th St. (873-5040 or 749-5298), at Adam Clayton Powell Blvd. 2nd-floor gallery highlights contemporary and classic cinema created by and about African-Americans, as well as work done by black filmmakers from South America, Africa, and the Caribbean. Spike Lee has screened films here. Admission $5, seniors and students with ID $3. Lectures by contemporary filmmakers $3, but prices and schedules vary; call ahead.

American Museum of the Moving Image, 35th Ave. at 36th St., Astoria, Queens (718-784-0077). Has three full theaters showing everything from silent classics to retrospectives of great directors. Recent programs have ranged from 1950s *Father of the Bride* to *Fast Cars and Women*. Free with admission to museum: $5, seniors $4, students and children under 12 $2.50.

The Asia Society, 725 Park Ave. (288-6400), at 70th St. Subway: #6 to 68th St. Films from or about Asia. Ticket prices vary. Call 517-ASIA for tickets.

China Institute, 125 E. 65th St. (744-8181, at Lexington Ave. Sponsors Chinese and Chinese-American film series. Call for a schedule. Tickets $5.

Cineplex Odeon Worldwide, 340 W. 50th St. (246-1583), between Eighth and Ninth Ave. Offers second-run, big Hollywood movies on 7 screens for $3. Box office opens at 12:30pm. All films in super Dolby sound.

French Institute/Alliance Française, in Florence Gould Hall, 55 E. 59th St. (355-6100). Francophiles can satisfy their craving for Godard by inquiring about current film offerings. Films are screened Tues. at Tinker Auditorium, 22 E. 60th St. Tickets $7, students $5.50.

Goethe Institute, 1014 Fifth Ave. (439-8706), between 82nd and 83rd St. Shows German films (usually with English subtitles) each week at locations around the city. Ticket prices vary.

Japan Society, 333 E. 47th St. (752-0824). Mounts yearly retrospectives of the greatest Japanese achievements in film. Schedule can be obtained by visiting the society or by calling. Tickets $7, students, seniors, and members $5.

Metropolitan Museum of Art, Fifth Ave. at 82nd St. (570-3930). The Met shows art-related movies throughout the week, as well as artsy classic and foreign films on Saturdays, at 4pm and 6:30pm. They are free with museum admission. Box office at the Uris Center Information Desk opens at 5pm on the day of the performance; limit 4 tickets per person.

Museum of Modern Art: Roy and Niuta Titus Theaters, 11 W. 53rd St. (708-9480). The MoMA serves up an unbeatable diet of great films daily in its two lower-level theaters. The film department holds what it claims to be "the strongest international collection of film in the United States," and it's hard to doubt them. Film tickets are included in the price of admission and are available upon request. Also ask about screenings in the video gallery on the third floor.

New York Public Libraries: For a real deal, check out a library, any library. All show free films: documentaries, classics, and last year's blockbusters. Screening times may be a bit erratic, but you can't beat the price. (For complete information on New York libraries, see Essentials: Libraries, p. 15.)

Symphony Space, 2537 Broadway (box office 864-5400; open daily noon-7pm), at 95th St. Subway: #1, 2, 3, or 9 to 96th St. Primarily a live performance space, but every July the Foreign Film Festival showcases the expanding canon of quality foreign films. Tickets $7.

Walter Reade Theater, at Lincoln Center (875-5600). Subway: #1 or 9 to 66th St. New York's performing arts octopus flexes yet another cultural tentacle with this two-year-old theater in the Rose Building next to the Juilliard School. Foreign, famous, and critically-acclaimed American independent films dominate. General admission $7.50. Call the box office at 875-5601; it opens daily at 1:30pm.

REVIVAL AND INDEPENDENT FILM HOUSES

Angelika Film Center, 18 W. Houston St. (995-2000), at Mercer St. Subway: #6 to Bleecker St. or B, D, F, Q to Broadway-Lafayette. Eight screens of alternative (not-quite-underground) cinema. Come here to see the movies that hipper-than-thou people at cocktail parties mention—the films that everyone has seen reviews of but never got around to seeing. Come early on weekends. The pricey café upstairs has excellent espresso, as well as pastries and sandwiches. Tickets $8, seniors and children under 12 $4.

Anthology Film Archives, 32 Second Ave. (505-5181), at E. 2nd St. Subway: F to Second Ave. A forum for independent filmmaking, focusing on the contemporary, off-beat, and avant-garde chosen from U.S. and foreign production. The resident cinema guru has created the Archives' most enduring series—"The American Narrative"—featuring 300 great American films. Tickets $7, students with ID $6.

Bryant Park Film Festival, Bryant Park (512-5700), at 42nd St. and 6th Ave. Subway: B, D, F, Q, N, R, S, 1, 2, 3, 7, or 9 to 42nd St. Running from late June to August, this free outdoor series features classic revivals such as *Mr. Smith Goes to Washington, Citizen Kane,* and *The Sound of Music.* Movies begin at sunset, and the rain date is Tuesday nights.

Cinema Village, 22 E. 12th St. (924-3363), at University Pl. Subway: N, R, L, 4, 5, or 6 to Union Sq. Features independent documentaries and foreign films. Great seats that lean back. Tickets $8, seniors $4 on weekdays.

Film Forum, 209 W. Houston St. (727-8110), near Sixth Ave. and Varick St. Subway: C or E to Spring St., or 1 or 9 to Houston St. Three theaters showing the best in independent filmmaking, classics, and foreign films. Tickets $8, seniors $4.50.

Joseph Papp Public Theater, 425 Lafayette St. (260-2400). Subway: #6 to Astor Pl. Quirky selection of old movies, particularly "art" classics and film history milestones. There is also a theater auditorium featuring live "experimental" performance pieces. No screenings on Mon. Tickets $5-8.

The Kitchen, 512 W. 19th St. (255-5793), between Tenth and Eleventh Ave. Subway: C or E to 23rd St. World-renowned showcase for off-beat happenings. Features experimental and avant-garde film and video, as well as concerts, dance performances, and poetry readings. Most shows are from New York-based struggling artists. Season runs Oct.-June. Call for information or check advertisements in *The Village Voice.* Ticket prices vary by event.

Lighthouse Cinema, 116 Suffolk St. (979-7571), between Delancey and Rivington St. Subway F, M, J, or Z to Delancey St. Reliably bizarre selection shines with vintage educational and documentary films (such as CBS' Special Report on Homosexuality) enjoyed for their clinical absurdity. The appropriately titled *Give Me Liberty Psychedelic Summer Anything Goes Filmfest* recently ran archival Dada documentary footage one evening with Scalpel Fetish Night (a few people always pass out watching open-heart surgery) the next. The oddities will cost you $7.

Millennium Film Workshop, 66 E. 4th St. (673-0090). Subway: F to Second Ave. More than just a theater, this group presents an extensive program of experimental films from October to June and offers classes and workshops. Tickets $6.

■ Television: Live in the Studio

In New York you can bring your TV fantasies to life. Here, you can ask Montel's guest that tough question, get harassed by Dave in person, snicker at Rush's Hillary-bashing with other well-to-dos, or decide for yourself what happened to the humor on SNL. Plan ahead, though. It's best to order your tickets two to three months in advance, although standby tickets are often available. Here's a little sampler of what the Big Four are offering and how to get on the ticket.

CBS (975-3247) scored big by bringing David Letterman into its fold—his contract was recently extended until 2002. Order tickets for his *Late Show* well in advance by writing: Dave Letterman Tickets, 1697 Broadway, NY, NY 10019. Day-of-show standby tickets are given out at 9am at the Ed Sullivan Theater, 1697 Broadway, at 53rd St., but lines can be long; it's best to call CBS to find when you should get in line.

Daytime talker Geraldo Rivera also tapes through CBS. Call 265-1283 for more information.

NBC currently opens two shows to guests: *Saturday Night Live* and *Late Night with Conan O'Brien.* Call 664-3055 for general information. Only *Late Night* is active during the summer; tapings are scheduled Monday through Friday 5:30-6:30pm, and tickets are given out on the day of the show only, beginning at 9am, from the page desk in the main lobby of NBC at Rockefeller Center (call 664-3056 or 664-3057 to make phone reservations). *SNL* goes on hiatus June-August; order tickets for these shows well in advance by sending one postcard per show to NBC Tickets, 30 Rockefeller Plaza, New York, NY 10012. Be warned, though: not only are you not given the option to choose specific dates, but because requests are lotteried, you might not find out you've been rejected until four months after you send off your request. SNL accepts ticket orders during the month of August only. You just might want to get in line on the mezzanine level of Rockefeller Center (50th St. side) at 8am the morning of the show for a chance at standby tickets. You must be at least 16 to attend these tapings.

For general information on **ABC's** offerings, call 456-7777. *Regis and Kathie Lee* and *Rolonda* (650-2020) are the only shows to which ABC admits guests (456-3537). Send a postcard with name, address, phone number, and your request for up to four tickets to Live Tickets, Ansonia Station, P.O. Box 777, 10023. Expect an eight month wait. For standby tickets, line up at the corner of 67th St. and Columbus Ave. at 8am, or even earlier. No one under 18 admitted to these ones, unless you've been working in a Honduran sweatshop.

Fox (452-3600) currently opens several shows to audiences: *Rush Limbaugh* (397-7367), *Gordon Elliot* (975-8540), *Mark Walberg* (527-6400), and *Montel Williams* (840-1700). Call for further information.

■ Opera

Lincoln Center (875-5000) is New York's one-stop shopping mall for high-culture consumers; there's usually opera or dance at one of its many venues. Write Lincoln Center Plaza, New York, NY 10023, or drop by its Performing Arts Library (870-1930) for a full schedule and a press kit as long as the *Ring* cycle. The **Metropolitan Opera Company** (362-6000), opera's premier outfit, plays on a Lincoln Center stage as big as a football field. Regular tickets run as high as $160—go for the upper balcony (around $22; the cheapest seats have an obstructed view) unless you're prone to vertigo. You can stand in the orchestra ($14) along with the opera freakazoids who've brought along the score, or all the way back in the Family Circle ($15). (Regular season runs Sept.-April Mon.-Sat.; box office open Mon.-Sat. 10am-8pm, Sun. noon-6pm.) In June, watch for free concerts in city parks (call the Met ticket line at 362-6000). The 1996-97 season will include such new productions as *A Midsummer Night's Dream* and *Eugene Onegin.*

At right angles to the Met, the **New York City Opera** (870-5570) has come into its own under the direction of Christopher Keene, who has been general director since 1989. "City" now has a split season (Sept.-Nov. and March-April) and keeps its ticket prices low year-round ($15-73). Call on the night before the performance you want to attend to check the availability of $10 rush tickets, then wait in line the next morning.

In July, look for free performances by the **New York Grand Opera** at Central Park Summerstage (360-2777) every Wednesday night. Check the papers for performances of the old warhorses by the **Amato Opera Company,** 319 Bowery (228-8200; Sept.-May). Music schools often stage opera as well; (see Classical Music, p. 267).

■ Dance

The New York State Theater (870-5570), another Lincoln Center fixture, is home to the late, great George Balanchine's **New York City Ballet,** the country's oldest dance company. Though Balanchine is best-known for modern, abstract master-pieces such as *Apollo* and *Jewels,* his versions of the classics are still the repertoire's biggest sellers. Decent tickets for the *Nutcracker* in December sell out almost imme-diately. (Performances Nov.-Feb. and April-June. Tickets $12-57, standing room $8.) The *New Yorker,* among other critics, has recently lambasted the NYC ballet as too much of an old girl's network. For a more energetic and vivacious bunch, the **Amer-ican Ballet Theater** (477-3030) dances at the Metropolitan Opera House at Lincoln Center from late April to mid-June. Under the guidance first of Baryshnikov and now Kevin McKinsey, A.B.T.'s eclectic repertoire has ranged from grand Kirov-style Rus-sian, for which it is best known, to experimental American (tickets $16-95). Unlike its more stuffy rival, the A.B.T. is well respected for its commitment to fostering and pro-moting younger dancers—look here for the talent of tomorrow.

The **Alvin Ailey American Dance Theater** (767-0940) bases its repertoire of modern dance on jazz, spirituals, and contemporary music. It often takes its moves on the road, but always performs at the **City Center** in December. Tickets ($15-40) can be difficult to obtain. Call the City Center box office (581-7907) weeks in advance if possible. Look for half-price tickets at the Bryant Park ticket booth (A few day-of-show tickets are available to students with ID for $8; call the box office for information.

The **Martha Graham Dance Co.,** 316 E. 63rd St. (832-9166), performs original Graham pieces during its October New York season. The founder of modern dance and of perhaps the most famous experimental company, Graham revolutionized 20th-century movement with her psychological, rather than narrative, approach to choreography (tickets $15-40).

Keep an eye out for performances of the **Merce Cunningham Dance Company** (255-8240), of John Cage fame, and the **Paul Taylor Dance Company** (431-5562). Both companies stage a one- to two-week season of performances at the City Center (581-1212) each year, along with other performances throughout New York and the rest of the country. The **Dance Theater Workshop** (691-6500) also stages works in Manhattan throughout the year, and the Joyce Theater, 175 Eighth Avenue (242-0800), between 18th and 19th St., offers a year-round schedule of experimental dance troupes (tickets $15-40).

In Queens, the **Ballet Folklorica de Dominican Republic,** 104-11 37th Ave. (718-651-8427), in Corona, specializes in traditional ethnic folk dance. Meanwhile, **Cen-tral Park Summerstage** (320-2777) hosts dance companies from around the world. Ballet connoisseurs should call the Brooklyn Center for Performing Arts at Brooklyn College (see Classical Music, below), which introduces a major foreign ballet com-pany to New York every year.

Half-price tickets for many music and dance events can be purchased on the day of performance at the **Bryant Park** ticket booth, on W. 42nd St. (382-2323) between Fifth and Sixth Avenue (open Tues.-Sun. noon-2pm and 3-7pm; tickets for Mon. shows available Sun.; cash and traveler's checks only). Call for daily listings. Full-price tickets are also available here for all TicketMaster events.

■ Classical Music

Musicians advertise themselves vigorously; you should have no trouble finding the notes. Begin with the ample listings in *The New York Times, The New Yorker,* or *New York* magazine. The *Free Time* calendar ($2) can clue you in on the city's free classical events throughout the city. Remember that many events, such as outdoor music, are seasonal.

LINCOLN CENTER

The Lincoln Center Halls have a wide, year-round selection of concerts. The **Great Performers Series** (875-5020), featuring musicians famous and foreign, packs the

Avery Fisher and Alice Tully Halls and the Walter Reade Theater, from October until May (call 721-6500; tickets from $11).

Avery Fisher Hall (875-5030) paints the town ecstatic with its annual **Mostly Mozart Festival,** featuring performers like Itzhak Perlman, Alicia de Larrocha, Jean-Pierre Rampal, and Emanuel Ax. Show up early; major artists and rising stars usually give half-hour pre-concert recitals, beginning one hour before the main concert and free to ticketholders. The festival runs from July to August, with tickets to individual events running from $12 to $30. The **New York Philharmonic** (875-5656) begins its regular season at Fisher Hall in mid-September. Tickets range from $10 to $60. (Call CenterCharge for tickets at 721-6500; open Mon.-Sat. 10am-8pm, Sun. noon-8pm.) During the Philharmonic's regular season, students and seniors can sometimes get **$5 tickets;** call ahead to check availability, then show up 30 minutes before the concert (Tues.-Thurs. only). Ten-dollar tickets are sometimes sold for the odd morning rehearsal; again, call ahead (anyone is eligible for these). In August for a couple of weeks, the Philharmonic heads for the hills and lawns of New York's parks. Kurt Masur and friends lead the posse at **free concerts** on the Great Lawn in Central Park, in Prospect Park in Brooklyn, in Van Cortland Park in the Bronx, and around the city. Select nights are enlivened by fireworks after the program. For information on these outdoor events call the summer hotline at 875-5709.

Alice Tully Hall, in the Juilliard School at Lincoln Center, features an eclectic mix of music, dance, theater, video, and performance art. Composer Philip Glass is a regular here. Founded six years ago, the **Serious Fun!** Series brings big-name avant-garde, mixed-media, and performance artists into the realm of corporate sponsorship. Recent performers have included the Mark Morris Dance Company and Toni Morrison, and Max Roach and Bill T. Jones in a multimedia performance. The series lasts three weeks in July; tickets go from $22 to $30 per event (875-5050; box office open Mon.-Sat. 11am-6pm, Sun. noon-6pm, or call CenterCharge at 721-6500). The **Chamber Music Society** offers students and seniors heavily discounted seats for its performances in Alice Tully Hall (call 875-5788; students from $9, seniors from $14, others from $20).

The **Juilliard School of Music** itself is one of the world's leading factories of classical musicians. Juilliard's **Paul Recital Hall** hosts free student recitals almost daily during the school year from September until May; Alice Tully Hall holds larger student recitals, also free, most Wednesdays from September to May at 1pm. Orchestral recitals, faculty performances, chamber music, and dance and theater events take place regularly at Juilliard and never cost more than $10—you can see the next generation's Yo-Yo Ma for a third of the cost of seeing this one's. Call 769-7406 for a complete Juilliard schedule.

Free outdoor events at Lincoln Center boggle the mind every summer, with everything from modern dance premieres to country-music festivals; call 875-5400 for the daily boggle.

OTHER HALLS AND VENUES

Carnegie Hall (247-7800), Seventh Ave. at 57th St. Subway: N or R to 57th St., or B, D, or E to Seventh Ave. The New York Philharmonic's original home was saved from demolition in the 1960s by Isaac Stern and is still the favorite coming-out locale of musical debutantes. Top soloists and chamber groups are booked regularly. Box office open Mon.-Sat. 11am-6pm, Sun. noon-6pm; tickets $10-60. See Sights: Sightseeing Tours, p. 123, for more about the hall.

92nd Street Y, 1395 Lexington Ave. (996-1100). Subway: #6 to 96th St. Cultural life on the Upper East Side revolves around the 92nd Street Y. The Y's Kaufmann Concert Hall seats only 916 people and offers an intimate setting unmatched by New York's larger halls, with flawless acoustics and the oaken ambience of a Viennese salon. The Y is the home of the **New York Chamber Symphony** under the fiery direction of Gerard Schwartz. The Chamber Symphony's repertoire covers everything from Telemann and Rameau to the works of contemporary masters like Pijton, Diamond, and Stravinsky. In addition, the Y plays host to a panoply of world-class visiting musicians. The Distinguished Artists Series, dating back to the late 30s, has featured all the big names from Segovia and Schnabel to Yo-Yo Ma, Alfred Brendel, and Schlomo Mintz. Other notable series include Chamber Music at the Y, Lyrics and Lyricists, Keyboard Conversation, and Young Concert Artists. Non-musical events include an ongoing series of literary readings at the Poetry Center and some of most engaging lectures in New York. Readings $8-12, lectures $15, concerts $15-40.

Town Hall, 123 W. 43rd St. (840-2824), between Sixth Ave. and Broadway. Subway: #1, 2, 3, 9, N, or R to 42nd St. This landmark is an elegant pavilion with excellent acoustics. Tenacious trio McKim, Mead & White designed the place in 1921; it has since hosted a wide variety of cultural events, including lectures by such luminaries as Sandra Bernhard, jazz festivals, and concerts of all kinds. Joan Sutherland made her debut here. The building has a seating capacity of 1495. Box office open Mon.-Sat. noon-6pm, open until showtime on day of show.

Merkin Concert Hall, 129 W. 67th St. (362-8719), between Broadway and Amsterdam Ave. Subway: #1 or 9 to 66th St. Quartered in Abraham Goodman House, the Merkin Concert Hall offers eclectic, ethnic, and contemporary music alongside more conventional selections. A typical week at the Merkin might include love songs and dirges spanning 400 years, classical and modern Chinese music, and the choral, folk-inspired works of Bartok and Shostakovich. Traditional Jewish and 20th-century classical music seem to be Merkin's specialties. One of New York's best spaces for chamber music, the intimate theater seats 457. Season Sept.-June; tickets $10-15.

Symphony Space (864-5400), at Broadway and 95th. Subway: #1 or 9 to 96th St. The misleadingly named Symphony Space is a former skating rink and cinema that now hosts all kinds of cultural events. The performance season (Sept.-June) corrals classical and traditional ethnic musical performances along with plays, dance companies, and the "Selected Shorts" program of fiction readings by famous actors. An annual Gilbert and Sullivan operetta packs the space, and during the summer it sponsors an ambitious program of old and new foreign films. Pick up a Symphony Space program guide at the Space itself. Box office open daily noon-7pm. Most movies $6, other events free or up to $35.

Metropolitan Museum of Art (535-7710; see Museums, p. 234). The Met posts a schedule of performances covering the sound spectrum from traditional Japanese music and Russian balalaika to all-star classical music recitals. Chamber music in the bar and piano music in the cafeteria on Fri. and Sat. evenings, free with museum admission; some of the other concerts charge $15 and up for tickets. For ticket information or brochure, call Concerts and Lectures at 535-7710.

Museum of Modern Art (708-9491; see Museums, p. 238). On most weekends in July and Aug., the Museum of Modern Art's "Summergarden" program presents free concerts of "avant-garde" contemporary classical music by Juilliard students in the museum's Sculpture Garden; concerts are on Fri. and Sat. at 8:30pm. Enter the Sculpture Garden through the (normally locked) back gate at 14 W. 54th St. between 6pm and 10pm.

Frick Collection (288-0700; see Museums, p. 243). From Oct. through May, the Frick Collection hosts free classical music concerts Sundays at 5pm (occasional summer concerts Tues. at 5:45pm). Tickets are limited to 2 per applicant; written requests must be received by the third Mon. before the concert. If you're not in the mood to fill out forms, show up 5 minutes before the show and try to steal the seats of no-shows.

Cooper-Hewitt Museum (860-6868; see Museums p. 243). Free concerts—ranging from classical to soul to hip-hop—come to the garden of the Cooper-Hewitt Museum from late June through Aug.

Cathedral of St. John the Divine, 1047 Amsterdam Ave. (662-2133), at 112th St. Subway: #1 or 9 to 110th St. Presents an impressive array of classical concerts, art exhibitions, lectures, plays, movies, and dance events. Ticket prices vary, so call.

Theater at Riverside Church (864-2929), on Riverside Dr. between 120th and 122nd St. Subway: #1 or 9 to 125th St. Hosts theater, music, dance, and video performances for up to 275 people. Prices vary.

ENTERTAINMENT

St. Paul's Chapel (602-0747, 602-0873), on Broadway between Church and Fulton St. Subway: A or C to Broadway-Nassau St. Built in 1766, St. Paul's is Manhattan's only surviving pre-Revolutionary War church. George Washington came here to pray after his inauguration. The exquisite interior, lit by Waterford crystal chandeliers, provides the perfect setting for concerts of well-loved classical standards by Mozart, Haydn, Shostakovich, Bach, et al., as well as occasional lesser-knowns. Noon concerts (Sept.-June) Mon. and Thurs.; additional concerts throughout the season. Suggested donation $2.

Trinity Church, 74 Trinity Pl. (602-0873), at Wall St. Subway: #4 or 5 to Wall St. With St. Paul's Chapel, Trinity Church presents the **Sundays at Four** classical concert series Sept.-June, in addition to other concerts throughout the year. Tickets $15-20, students and seniors can reserve standard seating for $10.

World Financial Center (945-0505), Battery Park City. Subway: C or E to World Trade Ctr. Free concerts at the Winter Garden, the Center's main atrium, feature fascinating world music concerts such as Finnish roots music, Brazilian *souk,* and according-driven zydeco.

Brooklyn Academy of Music, 30 Lafayette St. (718-636-4100), between Felix and Ashland Pl. Subway: #2, 3, 4, 5, D, or Q to Atlantic Ave. Founded in 1859, the Brooklyn Academy of Music (B.A.M.) has compiled a colorful history of magnificent performances: here Pavlova danced, Caruso sang, and Sarah Bernhardt played Camille. The oldest performing arts center in the country, it focuses on new, nontraditional, multicultural programs (though it sometimes features classical music as well). Jazz, blues, performance art, opera, and dance can be enjoyed here. Every May brings Dance Africa, which features West African dancing as well as crafts. Call for the constantly changing schedule. B.A.M.'s annual Next Wave Festival, Oct.-Dec., features contemporary music, dance, theater, and performance art; it broke artists like Mark Morris and Laurie Anderson. B.A.M. is home to the **Brooklyn Philharmonic Orchestra,** which performs from Sept.-March and hosts a brief opera season March-June. Orchestra and opera tickets $10-40. Manhattan Express Bus makes the round trip to B.A.M. from 51st St. and Lexington Ave. for each performance ($4); subway: #2, 3, 4, 5, D, Q to Atlantic Ave., or B, M, N, R to Pacific St.

Brooklyn Center for Performing Arts (718-951-4500 or 951-4522), 1 block west of the junction of Flatbush and Nostrand Ave. on the campus of Brooklyn College. Subway: #2 or 5 to Flatbush Ave. The Brooklyn Center for Performing Arts at Brooklyn College (B.C.B.C.) prides itself on presenting many exclusive events each year. In recent years it has showcased Leontyne Price, André Watts, the Garth Fagan Dance Company with Wynton Marsalis, Joan Rivers, and Jerry Lewis. Season Oct.-May; tickets $20-40.

Colden Center for the Performing Arts (718-793-8080), at Queens College in Flushing, Queens. Subway: #7 to Main St., Flushing, then Q17 or Q25-34 bus to the corner of Kissena Blvd. and the Long Island Expressway. The Colden Center has a beautiful, 2143-seat theater, which houses the **Queens Symphony Orchestra** and hosts an excellent program of jazz and dance concerts. Special effort is made to present work by emerging artists whose works reflect the borough's cultural diversity. Season Sept.-May; tickets $12-25.

Ukrainian Bandura Ensemble of New York, 84-82 164th St. (718-658-7449) in Jamaica, Queens. This ensemble keeps the 56-stringed bandura alive, playing at parades, festivals, and various other events around the city as the occasion arises.

MUSIC SCHOOLS

One of the best ways for the budget traveler to absorb New York musical culture is to visit a music school. Except for opera and ballet productions ($5-12), concerts at the following schools are free and frequent (especially September to May): the **Juilliard School of Music,** Lincoln Center (see above); the **Mannes School of Music,** 150 W. 85th (580-0210), between Columbus and Amsterdam Ave.; the **Manhattan School of Music,** 122 Broadway (749-2802); the **Bloomingdale House of Music,** 323 W. 108th St. (663-6021), near Broadway.

■ Jazz

Since its beginnings in the early part of the century, jazz has been an important part of the New York music scene. From Big Band orchestras and traditional stylists to free, fusion, and avant-garde artists, jazz can be found in all its various forms in venues across the city. You can check out one of the many hazy dens that bred lingo like "cat" and "hip" (a "hippie" was originally someone on the fringes of jazz culture who talked the talk but was never really in the know), or more highbrow shows at Lincoln Center. Summer spawns humid sets in parks and plazas. Throughout the year, many museums offer free jazz in their gardens and cafés. To find a current listing of jazz venues around the city, whether seasonal or mainstays, check the *Village Voice*, the *New Yorker*, the *New York Free Press*, or *New York* magazine.

Central Park Summerstage, at 72nd St. (360-2777) in Central Park, divides its attention between many performing arts, including jazz, opera, rock, and folk. Call or pick up Central Park's calendar of events, which is available at the Dairy in Central Park (see Sights: Central Park, p. 183). The season runs from mid-June to early Aug., and concerts are free.

Head to the **Lincoln Center Plazas** and Damrosch Park's **Guggenheim Bandshell** to hear free jazz, salsa, and Big Band delights. The Lincoln Center's new **Midsummer Night Swing Dancextravaganza**, held from late June until late July every night from Wednesday to Saturday, invites couples and singles to tango, swing, shimmy, or fox-trot. The center provides a dance floor, a café, and bands fronted by such musicians as Illinois Jacquet (dancing Wed.-Sat. 8:15pm, lessons Wed.-Thurs. 6:30pm). **Alice Tully Hall,** also at Lincoln Center, presents a summer jazz series (875-5299). Guest soloist Wynton Marsalis trumpeted the inaugural season.

The **JVC Jazz Festival** blows into the city in June. All-star performances of past series have included Julius Hemphill, Ray Charles, Billy Taylor, and Mel Torme. Tickets go on sale in early May, but many events take place outdoors in the parks and are free. **Bryant Park** hosts a large number of these concerts, as does **Damrosch Park** at Lincoln Center. Call 501-1390 in the spring for information, or write to: JVC Jazz Festival New York, P.O. Box 1169, Ansonia Station, New York, NY 10023.

The **Guggenheim Museum** (423-5000; see Museums, p. 241) has live jazz, Brazilian, and world beat music in its rotunda on Fridays and Saturdays from 5 to 8pm. Museum admission is required, but Fridays 5 to 8pm is pay-what-you-wish. The **Museum of Modern Art** (708-9480; see Museums, p. 238) also has jazz in its Garden Café on Fridays from 5:30-7:45pm. Museum admission is required, but Fri. 5:30-8:30pm is pay-what-you-wish. The **World Financial Center Plaza** (945-0505) hosts free concerts (infrequently) from June to September, featuring jazz styles ranging from Little Jimmy Scott to the Kit McClure Big Band, an all-female jazz orchestra. The **World Trade Center,** on Church St. at Dey St. (435-4170), hosts free lunchtime jazz concerts in its plaza each Wednesday during July and August. Two performers are featured each week, one performing at noon and the other at 1pm. The **South Street Museum** (732-7678) sponsors a series of outdoor concerts from July to early September at Pier 17, Ambrose Stage, and the Atrium.

In the heart of Rockefeller Center, entertainment palace **Radio City Music Hall** (247-4777) boasts a bill of great performers that reads like an invitation list to the Music Hall of Fame; Ella Fitzgerald, Frank Sinatra, Ringo Starr, Linda Ronstadt, and Sting, among others, have all performed at the legendary venue. The Rockettes still kick out the lights here every year at Christmas and Easter (box office at 50th St. and Sixth Ave; open Mon.-Sat. 10am-8pm, Sun. 11am-8pm). Tickets range from $20 to $1000 for the "Night of 100 Stars."

New York's churches wed the pristine to the upbeat in their capacity as music halls. Though the true godfathers of gospel keep the faith farther uptown, the midtown sacred-jazz scene belongs to **Saint Peter's,** 619 Lexington Ave. (935-2200) at 52nd St. On the first Sunday of every month, St. Peter's hosts a gala jazz mass. On other Sundays, jazz vespers are intoned at 5pm, followed at 7pm or 8pm by a full-fledged jazz concert ($5-10 donation for the concert). Informal jazz concerts are also held Wednesdays at 12:30pm ($4 donation), and classical concerts are given on Sunday afternoons (except in summer). In addition, the hippest ministry in town brings you art openings and exhibits, theater, lectures, and more (see Sights: East Midtown, p. 169). Call ahead for a current schedule of St. Peter's offerings; John Garcia Geyel, Pastor to the Jazz Community, oversees all tuneful good deeds.

Most of the music schools and halls listed under Classical Music have jazz offerings. And the **Coca Cola Concert Series,** though primarily a rock festival, also brings jazz and reggae concerts to **Jones Beach** (516-221-1000; June-early Sept.; tickets $20-27.50).

JAZZ CLUBS

Expect high covers and drink minimums at the legendary jazz venues. Most of them crowd tables together and charge $5 per drink. While hearing the jazz gods costs an arm and a leg, there are a few bars, like Indigo Blues, which supply a reliable selection of no-names free of charge.

Apollo Theatre, 253 W. 125th St. (749-5838, box office 864-0372), between Frederick Douglass Blvd. and Adam Clayton Powell Blvd. Subway: #1, 2, 3, or 9 to 125th St. Historic Harlem landmark has heard Duke Ellington, Count Basie, Ella Fitzgerald, Lionel Hampton, Billie Holliday, and Sarah Vaughan. A young Malcolm X shined shoes here. Now undergoing a resurgence in popularity. Ticket prices vary. A big draw is the legendary Amateur Night ($5), where acts are either gonged (ouch!) or rated "regular," "show-off," "top dog," or "super top dog." Tickets $9-30 for Amateur Night.

Birdland, 2745 Broadway (749-2228), at 105th St. Subway: #1 or 9 to 103rd St. A supper club serving reasonably good cajun food and top jazz. The place feels Upper West-nouveau but the music is smoked-out-and-splendid 52nd St. Blue Note Records makes recordings here. Appetizers $5-7, entrees $11-16, sandwiches $8-11. Sun. jazz brunch. Fri.-Sat $10 cover (includes free drink), $10 cover and $10 min. per person at tables. Sun.-Thurs. $5 cover plus $5 min. per set at tables; no cover at bar. No cover for brunch Sun. noon-4pm. Open Mon.-Sat. 5pm-2am, Sun. noon-4pm and 5pm-2am. First set nightly at 9pm.

Blue Note, 131 W. 3rd St. (475-8592), near MacDougal St. Subway: A, B, C, D, E, F, or Q to Washington Sq. The legendary jazz club is now a commercialized concert space with crowded tables and a tame audience. Often books big name performers. Cover $20 and up, $5 drink min. More reasonable Sun. jazz brunch includes food, drinks, and jazz for $14.50 (noon-6pm, shows at 1 and 3:30pm; reservations recommended). Other sets daily 9 and 11:30pm.

Bradley's, 70 University Pl. (473-9700), at 11th St. Subway: #4, 5, 6, L, N, or R to Union Sq. Nightly piano and bass duos (and other small ensembles) cut through the smoke. Usually crowded. $8 drink min. with cover charge approx. $15. Sets at 10pm, midnight, 2am. Music daily 9:45pm-4am.

Cotton Club, 666 W. 125th St. (663-7980), between Broadway and Riverside Dr. More tourists than regulars at this jazz hall of the greats. Most shows are expensive, but some are affordable. Cover $8-27.50. Shows at 8 and 10pm.

Dan Lynch, 221 Second Ave. (677-0911), between 13th and 14th St. Subway: #4, 5, 6, L, N, or R to Union Sq. Dark smoky room with Casablanca fan, long bar, and "all blues, all the time." Swinging, beautifully friendly deadhead crowd envelops the dance floor. Pool table in back. Blues and jazz start at 10pm. Jam session Sat.-Sun. 4-9pm. Cover Fri.-Sat. $5.

Indigo Blues, 221 W. 46th St. (221-0033), between Broadway and Eighth Ave. Subway: #1, 2, 3, 9, N, or R to 42nd St., or C or E to 50th St. Located in the basement of the Hotel Edison; look for a little gray door squeezed between the hotel and an Italian restaurant. Jazz and blues served up nightly in a high-modernist glass and brick den. Heavyweight guests have included Milt Jackson, Freddie Hubbard, Frank Bruno, Betty Carter, and Stanley Jordan. Music starts after 9pm. Cover $10-20 depending on the attraction, plus a variable min. if you sit at a table (no ingestive min. at the bar). Occasional nights of comedy; call ahead.

Michael's Pub, 211 E. 55th St. (758-2272), at Third Ave. Subway: #4, 5, or 6 to 59th St. New Orleans traditional jazz. Woody Allen occasionally plays clarinet here on Mon. nights, more frequently since the brouhaha over his domestic troubles. ("He needs the adulation," said one commentator.) Mel Torme and other jazz stars also come in sometimes; call ahead for a schedule. Sets Mon. 9 and 11pm, Tues.-Sat. 9pm, 10:45pm and midnight "if people are still here." Cover Tues.-Thurs. $15, Fri.--Sat. $20, Mon. $25. Open Mon.-Sat. 6pm-2am.

Red Blazer Too, 349 W. 46th St. (262-3112), between Eighth and Ninth Ave. Subway: C or E to 50th St. Dance cheek to cheek in the stardust of fab golden oldies. Fri.-Sat. is blistery Dixieland, and on the other nights you can catch swing, ragtime, and related musical romps from yesteryear. Jazz Age crowd. Sun. jazz brunch 1-5pm. Music nightly; Sun. brunch noon-5pm, closes at midnight. Mon. 8pm-midnight, Tues.-Thurs. 8:30pm-12:30am, Fri.-Sat. 9pm-1:30am. Cover $5 and 2-drink min. except Mon.

Sweet Basil, 88 Seventh Ave. (242-1785), between Bleecker and Grove St. Subway: #1 or 9 to Christopher St./Sheridan Sq. Serves mostly traditional jazz with dinner. Lots of tourists, some regulars. Occasional star sets—check ahead. Cover $17.50, plus $10 min. No cover for jazz brunch (Sat.-Sun. 2-6pm). Shows Mon.-Fri. 9 and 11pm, Sat.-Sun. 9, 11pm, and 12:30am. Open daily noon-2am.

Village Vanguard, 178 Seventh Ave. (255-4037), south of 11th St. Subway: #1, 2, 3, or 9 to 14th St. A windowless, wedge-shaped cavern, as old and hip as jazz itself. The walls are thick with memories of Lenny Bruce, Leadbelly, Miles Davis, and Sonny Rollins. Every Mon. the Vanguard Orchestra unleashes its torrential Big Band sound on sentimental journeymen at 10pm and midnight. Cover $15 plus $10 min., Fri.-Sat. $15 plus $8 min. Sets Sun.-Thurs. 9:30 and 11:30pm, Fri.-Sat. 9:30, 11:30pm, and 1am.

■ Rock, Pop, Punk, Funk, and Folk

New York City has a long history of producing bands on the vanguard of popular music and performance, from the New York Dolls to the Velvet Underground, from Dee-Lite to the Beastie Boys. If New York's home-grown bands fail to satisfy the craving for live music, keep in mind that virtually every band that tours the U.S. comes to the city. Call the **Concert Hotline** (249-8870), or check out the exhaustive and indispensable club listings in the *Village Voice* to find out who's in town.

Music festivals are also hot tickets and provide the opportunity to see tons of bands at a (relatively) low price. The mother of all such showcases, the New Music Seminar, recently folded under the weight of its own enormitude; prices had been rising steadily and the crowds had begun to look more and more like industry cronies. The **CMJ Music Marathon** runs for four nights in September and includes over 400 bands, ranging from bigger names like David Byrne, G. Love and Special Sauce, and the Pizzicato Five to up-and-comers. A recent addition to the music scene, the **Macintosh New York Music Festival** presents over 350 bands over a week-long period.

At 12th St. in Coney Island, Brooklyn, is the **Coney Island Circus Sideshow,** which features great indie rock shows as part of its "Sideshows by the Seashore" program on most Friday nights during the summer (admission $6; first band at 10pm). The adjacent snack bar is a great place to sip Rolling Rock ($2) and chat with NYC underground rock luminaries. Call 718-372-5159 for information on all Sideshow happenings.

If arena rock is more your style, check out **Madison Square Garden (MSG),** Seventh Avenue and W. 33rd St. (465-6000), perhaps America's premier entertainment facility, hosting over 600 events and nearly 6,000,000 spectators every year. Apart from rock concerts, regular offerings include exhibitions; trade shows; boxing matches; rodeos; monster trucks; dog, cat, and horse shows; circuses; tennis games; and the odd presidential convention (tickets $20-50). **Radio City Music Hall** (247-4777) and New Jersey's **Meadowlands** (201-935-3900) also occasionally stage equally high-priced performances.

ENTERTAINMENT

ABC No Rio, 156 Rivington St. (254-3697), near Clinton St. Subway: B, D, or Q to Essex St. Walk a block north and then 3 blocks east. A non-profit, community-run space featuring lots of hardcore and punk-related genres, as well as occasional poetry readings, art exhibitions, etc. No alcohol served. All ages. Cover $2-5.

A.K.A., 77 W. Houston St. (673-7325), between W. Broadway and Wooster St. Subway: #1 or 9 to Houston St., or N or R to Prince St./Broadway. Dark, gothic and hard to find (look for the small green awning and head upstairs), A.K.A. draws all sorts of bands, from heavy metal to acid jazz, into its excellent room. Mainly a chic crowd of in-the-know locals. Live acts Wed.-Sat. Cover $5-10.

Beacon Theatre, 2124 Broadway (496-7070), between 74th and 75th St. Subway: #1, 2, 3, or 9 to 72nd St. Mid-sized concert hall featuring mid-sized alternative rock names, as well as special events such as world beat concerts and multi-media performance events. Call or check the *Village Voice* for schedule; there's nearly something every weekend. Tickets $15-40.

The Bitter End, 147 Bleecker St. (673-7030), at Thompson St. Subway: A, B, C, D, E, F, or Q to W. 4th St., or #6 to Bleecker St. Small space hosts sweet-sounding folk and country music; they claim artists like Billy Joel, Stevie Wonder, Woody Allen, and Rita Rudner all got their start here. Look for their likenesses in the gaudy mural behind the bar. Call for show times. Cover $5-15. Open Sun.-Thurs. 7:30pm-3am, Fri.-Sat. 7:30pm-4am.

Bottom Line, 15 W. 4th St. (228-7880 or 228-6300), at Mercer St. Subway: #1 or 9 to Christopher St., or A, B, C, D, E, F, or Q to W. 4th St. A somber, loft-like space where rainbows weave on the walls against a black background. If you can't find a seat, you can sit at the comfy bar (even without ordering a drink) surrounded by old show photos. A mixed bag of music and entertainment—from jazz to kitsch to country to theater to good old-time rock-and-roll by over-the-hill singer/songwriters. Recent shows include Marianne Faithfull, Harvey Fierstein, and a tribute to Frank Zappa. Double proof of age (21+) required, but some all-ages performances. Shows nightly 7:30 and 10:30pm. Cover $20.

CBGB/OMFUG (CBGB's), 315 Bowery (982-4052), at Bleecker St. Subway: #6 to Bleecker St. The initials have stood for "country, bluegrass, blues, and other music for uplifting gourmandizers," since 1976, but everyone knows this club has been all about punk rock. Blondie and the Talking Heads got their starts here, and the club continues to be *the* place to see great alternative rock. CB's has adjusted to the post-punk 90s with more diverse offerings, including a website (http://www.cbgb.com), but the punk spirit lives on in the grotty, famously narrow interior, the multi-colored layers of graffiti on the bathroom walls, and the wistful eyes of some of the clientele. Shows nightly at around 8pm. Cover $5-10. **CB's Gallery** next door also offers live music.

Coney Island High, 15 St. Mark's Place (475-9726). Subway: N or R to 8th St. or #6 to Astor Place. High energy venue offering several different themes—it may not be Coney Island but it is a ride. If you miss the scum and glam of the 80s, you'll want to check out **Greendoor** every other Sat. night, a self-described trash rock party. Wed. is **Fraggle Rock,** a queer nite with Iggy Pop-style live music. Cover ranges from free to $10, depending on the night.

Continental Divide, 25 Third Ave. (529-6924), at St. Mark's Pl. Subway: #6 to Astor Pl. An East Village fixture booking lots and lots of local bands—some good, some bad, most ugly. No cover Sun.-Thurs.; Fri.-Sat. $5.

The Cooler, 416 W.14th St. (229-0785), at Greenwich St. Subway: 1, 2, 3, A, C, or E, to 14th St. In the heart of the meat-packing district, The Cooler showcases funk, alternative, acid-jazz, and some of the smartest DJs in town in a huge vault of a room. With meat hooks and scales on gory display, all they need is a Damian Hirst sculpture. Cover varies. Doors open Sun.-Thurs. 8pm, Fri.-Sat. 9pm.

Fez, 380 Lafayette St. (533-2680) behind the Time Café. Subway: #6 to Astor Pl. This lushly appointed, Moroccan-decorated club draws an extremely photogenic crowd, especially on Thurs. nights, when the Mingus Big Band holds court (sets at 9 and 11pm, reservations suggested). Other nights vary: music ranges from jazz to alt-pop, with the occasional *chanteuse* thrown in for good measure. Kitchen open 8:30pm-midnight. Call for dates, prices, and reservations.

Irving Plaza, 17 Irving Pl. (777-6800 or 777-1224 for concert info), at 15th St., between Third Ave. and Union Sq. Subway: #4, 5, 6, L, N, or R to 14th St.-Union Sq. A mid-sized venue decorated in a puzzling *chinoiserie* style. Features rock, comedy, feminist performance art, and other entertainment in its barn-like perfomance space. Sat. night becomes **Grey Gardens** dance club. Cover varies. Doors open at 8pm, unless otherwise noted. Box office open Mon.-Fri. 11am-6pm.

Knitting Factory, 74 Leonard St. (219-3055), between Broadway and Church St. Subway: #1, 2, 3, 6, 9, A, C, or E to Canal. Walk up Broadway to Leonard St. Free-thinking musicians anticipate the Apocalypse with a wide range of edge-piercing performances complemented by great acoustics. Several shows nightly. Sonic Youth played here every Thurs. night for years (alas, no more). The last Sun. of each month features **Cobra,** a musical genre invented by avant-garde jazz composer John Zorn. The Factory recently hosted the **"What is Jazz"** festival, an exploration of the musical form that promises to become a regular on the summer festival circuit. Cover (usually $10) for entrance to the back room/performance space only; entry to the cozy bar up front is always free. $3 pints of Brooklyn Brown Ale and Brooklyn Lager are yummy.

Maxwell's, 1039 Washington St. (201-798-4064), at 11th St. in Hoboken, NJ. Subway: B, D, F, N, Q, or R to 34th St., then PATH train ($1) to the first stop in Hoboken. Once there, walk along Hudson Pl. to Hudson St., up one block to Newark St., left two blocks to Washington St., and right 10 blocks to 11th St. Strong underground acts from America and abroad have plied their trade in the back room of this Hoboken restaurant for about 15 years (see Hoboken, NJ, p. 231). New Order played its first U.S. show here. Recent visitors include Superchunk, Stereolab, and G. Love and Special Sauce. Cover $5-10; shows occasionally sell out, so get tix in advance from Maxwell's, Pier Platters in Hoboken (see Shopping: Record Stores, p. 292), See Hear in the East Village, or TicketMaster.

McGovern's, 305 Spring St. (627-5037), between Greenwich and Hudson St. Subway: #1, 9, A, L, or E to Canal St. Tiny, worn, and a little bit seedy, in comparison to the glitz and glamour of the rest of SoHo. Out of the way, with a mostly young, local crowd; live rock nightly. Cover Fri.-Sat. after 10pm $5.

Mercury Lounge, 217 E. Houston St. (260-4700), at Ave. A. Subway: F to 2nd Ave.-E. Houston St. Once a gravestone parlor, the Mercury has attracted an amazing number of big-name acts to its fairly small-time room, running the gamut from folk to pop to noise. Past standouts have included Lenny Kravitz, Morphine, and They Might Be Giants. Music nightly; cover usually $5-15.

New Music Café, 380 Canal St. (941-1019), at W. Broadway. Subway: #1, 6, 9, J, N, or R to Canal St. Tends to be more upscale and mainstream than avant-garde; music ranges from acid jazz to noise pop. Music nightly; cover about $10.

Rock-n-Roll Café, 149 Bleecker St. (677-7630), two blocks west of Broadway. Subway: B, D, or F to Broadway/Lafayette, or #6 to Bleecker St. All covers, all the time. This club books tribute bands only. Recent doppelgangers include facsimiles of the Beatles, Jimi Hendrix, the Doors, Van Halen, and Ozzy Ozbourne. Shows Sun.-Thurs. 8 and 9:30pm, Fri.-Sat. 8:30 and 10:30pm. Cover varies.

Roseland, 239 W. 52nd St. (247-0200), at Eighth Ave. and Broadway. Subway: C or E to 50th St. Decently priced concert club featuring mostly They-Might-Be-Giants-esque, major-label college rock, with forays into large-scale rave events and Mötley Crüe-type territory. Also the occasional night of ballroom dancing, harkening back to the club's origins. Tickets $15-25.

Tramps, 45 W. 21st St. (727-7788), between Fifth and Sixth Ave. Subway: F, N, or R to 23rd St. Screaming violins and clattering washboards pack the sweaty dance floor. Louisiana zydeco rocks nightly with help from blues, reggae, and indie rock bands. Surprisingly agile crowd. Sets usually around 8:30 and 11pm. Doors open at 7pm. There's a new **Tramps Café** next door with moderately priced "new Southern" cuisine. Cover $5-15.

Wetlands Preserve, 161 Hudson St. (966-5244), near Laight St. in TriBeCa. Subway: #1, 9, A, C, or E to Canal St. A giant Summer of Love mural in the back room sets the tone, a Volkswagen bus curio shop swims in tie-dyes, and mood memorabilia hearken to the Woodstock years in this 2-story whole-earth spectacular. The back-to-nature theme is backed up by regular Tues. night "Ecosaloon" lectures on environmental concerns (7pm, free). Nightly live music includes Grateful Dead tributes (which have become more crowded since Jerry's death) each Tues., "Psychedelic Psaturdays," and rock-underground-alternative-whatever Wed.-Fri. Sunday caters to the 16-and-over crowd, otherwise 18+. Cover $7-10; shows usually kick off at either 9 or 10pm.

OTHER MUSIC CLUBS

Louisiana Community Bar & Grill, 622 Broadway (460-9633), between Bleecker and Houston St. Subway: B, D, F, or Q to Broadway-Lafayette St., or N or R to Prince St. Large and youthful NYU crowd. Interior is an attempt to create a pure Cajun atmosphere, with open beams across the ceiling, "unfinished walls," and massive alligators made of papier-mâché. Soul, blues, folk, and zydeco nightly; never a cover. They really stick you with the beer prices (up to $4 a bottle), so do your drinking before you arrive. Set times vary, usually starting around 8 or 9pm, though some shows start as late as 1am.

Sounds of Brazil (SOB's), 204 Varick St. (243-4940), at the corner of Seventh and Houston in the Village. Subway: #1 or 9 to Houston. Celebrating 14 years of making the world beat, this luncheonette-turned-dance-club presents bopping musicians playing the sounds of Brazil, Africa, Latin America, and the Caribbean in a setting overrun with tropicana. Look for the occasional R&B, Latin jazz, or acid- jazz set. Open for dining Tues.-Thurs. 7pm-2:30am, Fri.-Sat. 7pm-4am. Most shows Sun.-Thurs. 8 and 10pm; Fri.-Sat. 10:30pm and 1am; or, alternately, 10pm, midnight, and 2am. Sat. sees live samba with free admission before 9pm. Cover $10-16, depending on the act. Fri. no cover.

■ Dance Clubs

A wilderness of human flesh / Crazed with avarice, lust and rum / New York, thy name's Delirium.
—Byron R. Newton, Ode to New York, 1906

The New York club scene is an unrivaled institution. The crowd is aggressively uninhibited, the music unparalleled, and the fun can be virtually unlimited—as long as you uncover the right place. Honing in on the hippest club in New York isn't easy without connections. Clubs rise, war, and fall and even those "in the know" don't always know where to find the hot spot. The best parties are often raves, advertised only by word of mouth, the Internet, and psychedelic flyers and convening late at night in abandoned warehouses, closed bars, or unknown clubs. Many clubs move from space to space each week, although true clubbers still manage to find them. Make friends with someone on the inside, or check out the cooler record stores for directional flyers.

The rules are relatively simple. You have to have "the look" to be let in. Doorpeople are the clubs' fashion police and nothing drab or conventional will squeeze by. Wear black clothes or rave gear and drape your most attractive friends on your arms. Don't look worried; act like you belong. Most clubs open their doors around 9pm, but come after 11pm unless you crave solitude; things don't really get going until 1 or 2am. Most clubs stay open until 4am; a few non-alcoholic after-hours clubs keep getting busy until 5 or 6am, or even later.

Even the best clubs are only good on one or two nights a week. The right club on the wrong night can be a big mistake, particularly if you've already paid the $5-15 cover charge. The cover can rise to $20 on weekend nights when the B&T crowd (who reach Manhattan from New Jersey and Long Island by bridge and tunnel) attempts to get past the bouncers *en masse.*

Let's Go has ranked the following dance clubs according to fun and value. The suggestions could well have changed by the summer of '97, as hip is by its nature an elusive commodity. Call ahead to make sure that you know what (and whom) you'll find when you arrive.

Welcome to the Jungle

Early in the 90s, black Londoners spawned **jungle,** a frantic urban music style that has adapted well to New York City, the original urban jungle, although here the crowd is comprised mostly of white post-ravers. Jungle incorporates the slow, dubby basslines of reggae with sped-up hip-hop breakbeats and recombinant sampling strategies, stewed thick and fast with inflections of techno. The result is edgy, experimental, and futuristic. New York now offers about four jungle club nights a week. **Konkrete Jungle** (604-7959) is the most established while **Jungle Nation** (802-7495) throbs with a more serious crowd. DJs to look for include Dara, Delmar, Soulslinger, DB, Cassien, and Peshy.

Bar Room, 432 W. 14th St. (366-5680), at Washington St. Subway: A, C, or E to 14th St. Although this hidden club reaches its zenith with the **Clit Club** or **Jackie 60**, the Bar Room gets serious on Saturdays with **Jungle Nation.** The dedicated crowd is refreshingly low on attitude. Cover $5 before midnight, $7 with flyer, and $10 without. Doors open at 10:30pm (see Gay and Lesbian Clubs, p. 278).

Tunnel, 220 Twelfth Ave. (695-7292 or 695-4682), at 27th St. Subway: C or E to 23rd St. The name may refer to the cavernous space or to the mostly Jersey crowd, but this is the party that everyone's invited to. An immense club—3 floors and a mezzanine packed with 2 dance floors, lounges, glass-walled live shows, and a skateboarding cage. Enough room for a multitude of diverse parties in this labyrinthine place. The one and only Junior Vasquez spins here on Sat. Open Fri.-Sat.; Sat. nights are queer. Cover $20.

Webster Hall, 125 E. 11th St. (353-1600), between Third and Fourth Ave. Subway: #4, 5, 6, N, or R to Union Sq.-14th St. Walk 3 blocks south and a block east. New and very popular club offers a rock/reggae room and a coffeeshop in addition to the main, house-dominated dance floor. **Psychedelic Thursdays** often feature live bands and $2.50 beers. Fri.-Sat. see the motto of "4 floors, 5 eras, 4 DJs...and 40,000 sq. ft. of fun" put into effect. Open Wed.-Sat. 10pm-4am. Cover $15-20.

Robots, 25 Ave. B (995-0968), at 3rd Ave. Subway: F to Second Ave. For 14 years, Robot has been the place to go when other clubs have closed but your energy has yet to wear off. Open bar before midnight; most guests arrive around 4am and stay until 10am. Thursday's **Killer** offers a strong dose of acid trance and progressive house. Open Wed.-Thurs. 10pm-7am, Fri.-Sat. 10pm-noon. Cover $6-15.

Twilo, 530 W. 27th St. (268-1600). Subway: #1 or 9 to 28th St. or C or E to 23rd St. Located in the former Sound Factory. A crowded scene earlier in the night, with meaty shirtless glam boys and a healthy bridge and tunnel crowd mixing with the occasional 8-ft.-tall drag queen. Later, the music gets deeper and the crowd more serious. If you stay past the 4am clearout, expect to stay until breakfast time. Cover $15-20. Doors open around midnight.

Limelight, 660 Sixth Ave. (807-7850). Subway: F or R to 23rd St. One of NYC's landmark dance clubs—other clubs across the country have been named after it. Once a church, despite what you may have heard about its recently arrested owner. The real attraction is Wed. night's Disco 2000 party, where funky things happen. Queer on Fri. and Sat. nights. Sun. night is live heavy metal. Cover usually $15. Open until 4am.

Nell's, 246 W. 14th St. (675-1567), between Seventh and Eighth Ave. Subway: #1, 2, 3, or 9 to 14th St. A legendary hotspot in slight decline; faithful admirers hang on for reliable jazzy, soulful music upstairs and phat beats below. On Monday nights the popular **Funky Buddha** hip-hop fest rages on. Racially diverse crowd. Cover Mon.-Wed. $7; Thurs., Sun. $10; Fri.-Sat. $15. Open daily 10pm-4am.

Palladium, 126 E. 14th St. (473-7171), at Third Ave. Subway: #4, 5, 6, L, N, or R to 14th St. Started by megaclub moguls Steve Rubell and Ian Schrager. Once Madonna and her friends set the pace; now the club lags under its own hype, although it remains packed with enthusiastic clubbers. Club MTV used to be filmed here. Funky. Mainstream, but funky. **Bump!** on Sundays is a muscle-bound gay night. Open Fri.-Sat. 10pm-4am. Cover $20.

Analog, 416 W. 14th St. (229-0785), between 9th and 10th Ave. Deep within the Cooler on Tuesdays, Analog spins all kinds of electronic music, including hard-house, trip-hop, and illbient. Live electronic musicians often share the floor with DJs. Cover $10. Doors open at 8pm.

The Bank, 225 E. Houston St. (505-5033 or 334-7474) at Ave. A. Subway: F to Delancey St. A stately bank converted into a gritty club, with a heavy Goth-boy and chain concentration. Clear sight-lines make it great for live music. Reliable, if journeyman, music. Underground vault a great spot for the wee hours. Call for information on the erratic schedule. Cover usually around $8.

China Club, 2130 Broadway (877-1166), at 75th St. Subway: #1, 2, 3, or 9 to 72nd St. Rock-and-roll hot spot where Bowie and Jagger come on their off nights. Models and long-haired men make it a great people-watching spot. Pudgy, rich men trying to get by the doorman make it a great people-mocking spot. Mon. night is one of New York's hottest club nights for the "beautiful people" crowd. Be well-dressed or you won't get in. Go elsewhere for great dancing. Cover around $20. Opens daily at 10pm.

■ Gay and Lesbian Clubs

The New York gay scene extends visibly throughout the city. The West Village, especially around Christopher St., has long been the hub of the city's alternative life. Chelsea, just north of Village, has emerged as the new hangout for gay men fed up with the Guppie lifestyle. A hard-core gay crowd also occupies the East Village on First and Second Avenue south of E. 12th St. Wealthier types cruise the Upper West Side in the upper 70s. Gay communities are not restricted to Manhattan; Park Slope in Brooklyn has long been home to a large and important lesbian community.

Each week the *Village Voice* and *New York Native* publish full listings of gay events. The *New York Free Press* is also a good resource. The Gay and Lesbian Student Organization of Columbia University sponsors a huge dance on the first Friday and the third Saturday of each month in Earl Hall at 116th St. and Broadway (subway: #1 to 116th St.; cover $7, students with ID $5). The *Pink Pages* is a phone book for the queer community with all sorts of listings, including bars and clubs. You can pick one up in some of the gay/lesbian bars.

Following is a list of clubs (some of them dance-oriented, others geared more towards conversation and drinking) at the center of gay and lesbian nightlife. Remember to bring two forms of ID to prove you're over 18 or 21, as needed. Also remember that some of these clubs are geared exclusively towards lesbians or gay men and may frown on letting in hopefuls of the opposite sex. Finally, if you and a friend of the opposite sex want to go to any of these clubs together, you should certainly avoid behaving like a heterosexual couple in front of the bouncer. *Let's Go* has ranked the clubs, taking fun and value into account.

Clit Club, 432 W. 14th St. (529-3300), at Washington St. Subway: A, C, or E to 14th St. Fri. nights in the Bar Room. The grandmother of NY dyke clubs, the Clit still draws one of the younger and more diverse crowds around. This is *the* place to be for young, beautiful, queer grrls. Host Julie throws the hottest party around every Fri. night, with go-go girls, house music, and babes galore. Hit on the femme of your dreams at the pool table, or just chill out in the video room. Women only. Cover $3 before 11pm, $5 after 11pm. Doors open at 9:30pm.

Bar D'o, 29 Bedford St. (627-1580). The coziest lounge with the most sultry lighting in the city. Superb performances by drag divas Joey Arias and Raven O Tues. and Sat.-Sun. nights ($3). Even without the fine chanteuses, this is a damn fine place for a drink. Women's night on Mon. packs a glam night of drag kings. Go early for the atmosphere, around midnight for the performances, and 2am to people-watch/gender-guess (Is that a boy or a girl?). Don't try to leave in the middle of a show, or you'll be in for a nasty tongue-lashing. Doors open around 10am.

Meow Mix, 269 E. Houston St. (254-1434), at Suffolk St. A major party scene Tues.-Sun. nights for East Village lesbians. Especially hot on Sat. Lots of events, including comedy, readings, performances, and the occasional *Xena: Warrior Princess* swordfight. Friendly staff. Call for schedule. Cover usually $2-5.

Fraggle Rock, 15 St. Mark's Place (334-7474), at Coney Island High (see p. 274). Bimonthly gatherings of the queercore tribes. Rockin' proof that gay nightlife isn't just dance clubs. There's a house band and queer/gay positive rock groups. Alternate Wed. Open 9pm-4am. Cover $8.

Cake, 99 Ave. B. (505-2226 or 674-7957), at 6th St. A laid back early-evening lounge for village lesbians looking for a drink. Fab theme nights, like Cream (Wed.) and Hustler (Thurs.), get it moving later in the evenings. Sun. night offers a drag king show. Most nights boy- and girl-friendly. Doors open around 8pm.

Jackie 60, 432 W. 14th St. (366-5680), at Washington St. Tues. nights at the Bar Room. Drag queens work it while the (sometimes) celebrity crowd eggs them on to even more fabulous feats of glamour. Tues. is David Bowie night. Cover $10. Doors open at 10pm.

Wonder Bar, 505 E. 6th St. (777-9105). On a strip crowded with bars, Wonder Bar stands out. Decorated in zebra chic and laid back neutrals, Wonder Bar is frequented by fun young males and lipstick lesbians. Open Wed.-Sat. 10pm-4am.

W.O.W!, 248 W. 14th St. (631-1102), at 7th Ave. This Wednesday party at **Zi's** attracts a happy-hour crowd of professional women. If you're tired of the grrls at Clit Club and the East Village hangouts, then you're ready for this crowd. Occasional erotic readings by lesbian writers. Happy hour 6:30-10pm offers $2 margaritas. Cover $3 before 9pm, $5 thereafter.

Boiler Room, 86 E. 4th St. (254-7536), between First and Second Ave. Hip East Village hangout that sees a mixed crowd with a strong dyke contingency. Drag kings nightly. Open daily 4pm-4am.

Uncle Charlie's, 56 Greenwich Ave. (255-8787), at Perry St. Subway: #1 or 9 to Christopher St. Biggest and best-known gay club in the city. Mainstream and preppy, with guppies galore. It's still fun, if a bit crowded on the weekends. Women are welcome, but few come. Open daily 3pm-4am. No cover.

Duplex, 61 Christopher St. (255-5438), at Seventh Ave. Bright lights, drag queens, cabarets... it's not a Madonna show, it's the Duplex, the oldest cabaret in the city. The place hosts singers, comedians, theatrical presentations (such as "nuns against filth," where porn meets the Pope), and celebrity impersonators, including transvestite versions of Meryl Streep, Liz Taylor, and Julie Andrews. Cover varies: $3-12. 2-drink min. Concerts start at 8 or 10pm. Open daily 4pm-4am.

Flamingo East, 219 2nd Ave. (533-2860), between 13th and 14th St. Subway: L to 3rd Ave. or 4,5, or 6 to Union Square. So swank, so kinky, so hip. This place transcends lounge kitsch and takes you to the next level. Try Sunday nights for splendid Hawaiian lounge at *The 999999's.* A good place for your fabb-est duds—nothing is too vintage, too outrageous, or too much. Doors open around 10pm.

The Cubbyhole, 281 W. 12th St. (243-9041), at 4th St. Subway: A, C, E, or L to 14th St. Yes, these two streets do intersect in the non-Euclidean West Village near Eighth Ave. Piano bar provides a relaxed scene for lesbians. Very low-key, but definitely queer. No cover. Happy hour 4-7pm daily. Open daily 9am-4am.

The Spike, 120 11th Ave. (243-9688), at W. 20th St. Subway: C or E to 23rd St. Caters to an adventurous crowd of leather-clad men (and some women) who know how to create a spectacle. Open daily 9pm-4am.

The Monster, 80 Grove St. (924-3558), at 4th St. and Sheridan Sq. Subway: #1 or 9 to Christopher St. Look for the snarl of Christmas lights above the door. Cabaret-style piano bar with downstairs disco; heats up on Fri. and Sat. nights. Crazy singles scene amid decadently lush vegetation. Bring a pen. Cover Fri.-Sat. $5. Open daily 4pm-4am.

The Pyramid, 101 Ave. A (420-1590), at 6th St. Subway: #6 to Astor Pl. Look for the lavender pyramid. Also known by its street address, this dance club mixes gay, lesbian, and straight folks. Vibrant drag scene. Pushes the limits of exotic with their fresh remixes. Fri. is straight night. Cover $5-10. Open daily 9pm-4am.

Crazy Nanny's, 21 Seventh Ave. South (366-6312, 929-8356), near LeRoy St. Subway: #1 or 9 to Houston St. Glamour dykes and the women who love them come here to shoot some pool and just hang out. Happy hour Mon.-Sat. 4-7pm, 2-for-1 drinks. Dancing nightly. Open daily 4pm-4am.

Henrietta Hudson, 438 Hudson St. (924-3347), between Morton and Barrow St. Young, clean-cut lesbian crowd. Mellow in the afternoon, packed at night and on the weekends. Try the Henrietta Girlbanger or the Girl Scout ($6.50). Happy hour (2 for 1) Mon.-Fri. 5-7pm. No cover. Open daily 3pm-4am.

■ Miscellaneous Hipster Hangouts

A New York night is filled with attractions and events that defy categorization, from performance art to free-floating parties and shows to poetry slams. Many hot spots don't have defined locations: mobile parties like **Giant Step**, **SoundLab** and **Soul Kitchen** move from club to club with an ardent crowd of followers, drawn in by the innovative amalgamations of jazz, funk, and techno beats. The cover varies from show to show. Check the *Village Voice* for upcoming locations.

The Anyway Café, 34 E. 2nd St. (473-5021), at 2nd Ave. This off-the-beaten track hangout serves up a full menu of creative outlets: Mon. (8pm-1am) open mike music and poetry, Tues. (8pm-1am) open mike jazz jam, Thurs. "open wall" art show (bring your own art), Fri.-Sat. live jazz from 9pm on, and Sun. at 7pm is Russian Karaoke (believe it or not...). This joint is friendly and free of the smoky pretention which all-too-often plagues such venues. Also a great place to kick back with homemade sangria and sample some gourmet Russian specialties (all under $10). Open Sun.-Thurs. noon-1am, Fri.-Sat. 11am-2am.

Collective Unconscious, 145 Ludlow St. (254-5277), south of Houston St. A performance space collectively (and unconsciously) run by eight local artists who put up their own shows and provide a venue/studio/rehearsal space/you-name-it for the Village artistic community at large. Frequent open-mike events, including, but not limited to, Wed. nights, as well as an ongoing serial play on Sat. at 8pm ($5). Lots of men sporting the bald/potbelly/goatee look. Friendly people and usually something interesting to see. No frills—you might have to sit on the floor. No alcohol or other refreshments served either, but you're welcome to bring your own. Cover $3-10. Call for a schedule of events.

Mission Café, 82 2nd Ave. (505-6616), between 4th and 5th St. This theater hotspot hosts astrologers giving cheap readings on Wed. nights, and professional tarot readings on Thurs. They also feature a different artist on the wall every month. In the morning, try their steamed eggs, made on the espresso machine with Jack Cheese, scallions, and tomato on a bagel ($3.50). Come in and read a magazine, or have the astrologer read you. Coffee and juices (including specialty drinks) 75¢-$3.25. Open Mon.-Fri. 8am-11pm, Sat. 9am-11pm, Sun. 9am-8pm.

Nuyorican Poets Café, 236 E. 3rd St. (505-8183), between Ave. B and Ave. C. Subway: F to Second Ave. Walk 3 blocks north and 3 blocks east. New York's leading venue for the currently-in-vogue "poetry slams" and spoken word performances. Several regulars have been featured on MTV's Spoken Word series. A mixed bag of unintentioned doggerel with occasional gems. If you don't like the performers, don't worry—the bartender will heckle them like you wouldn't believe. Other types of performances too, as well as workshops for your inner poet, DJ-enhanced parties, and occasional risque acts like "Erotic words en Español." Cover $5-10.

■ Baths

Tenth Street (Russian and Turkish) Baths, 268 E. 10th St. (674-9250), between First Ave. and Ave A. Expert masseur Boris runs this co-ed bathhouse that offers all conceivable (and legal) bodily services—oak-leaf massages, salt scrubs, oil massages, and black mud treatments. More conventional services are also provided, such as saunas, steam rooms, and an ice-cold pool. Admission $19. Open daily 9am-10pm; Thurs. and Sun. are men-only, Wed. is women-only.

■ Comedy Clubs

The Next Big Thing only a few years ago, comedy clubs are now on the wane. While venues vary tremendously in size and atmosphere, nearly all impose a hefty cover and a drink minimum that's more like a maximum on Fridays and Saturdays. Invariably, there'll be an annoying emcee who'll jab at the Kansans in the front row between acts; if you dare to sit up close, be prepared.

Comic Strip Live, 1568 Second Ave. (861-9386), between 81st and 82nd St. Subway: #6 to 77th St. Sunday comics' characters Dagwood and Dick Tracy line the four-color walls of this well established pub-style club. Former denizens include just about everyone in the post-SNL pantheon. Mon. is audition night, when lucky wanna-bes who signed up the previous Fri. are chosen by lot for their moment in the spotlight, to be humiliated en masse. Shows Sun.-Thurs. 8:30pm, Fri. 8:30 and 10:30pm, Sat. 8pm, 10:15pm and 12:30am. On Sun. and Tues.-Thurs. $8 cover and $9 drink min., Fri.-Sat. $12 cover and 2-drink min. Make reservations.

Dangerfield's, 1118 First Ave. (593-1650), between 61st and 62nd St. Subway: #4, 5, or 6 to 59th St., or N or R to Lexington Ave. Rodney's respectable comic launching pad. Rising stars from throughout the country perform here, and HBO specials featuring the likes of Roseanne Barr, the late Sam Kinison, and Jerry Seinfeld have all been taped at the club. Be prepared for a surprise (the line-up is only available the day of the show, and unannounced guest comedians occasionally appear). Popular with the post-prom crowd. Shows Sun.-Thurs. 9pm; Fri. 9 and 11:15pm; Sat. 8, 10:30pm, and 12:30am. Cover Sun.-Thurs. $12.50, Fri.-Sat. $15.

The Original Improvisation, 433 W. 34th St. (279-3446), between Ninth and Tenth Ave. Subway: A, C, or E to 34th St. A quarter-century of comedy—acts from Saturday Night Live, Johnny Carson, and David Letterman. Richard Pryor and Robin Williams got started here. Off the beaten path but well worth the trip for comedy diehards. Shows Thurs.-Sat. 9pm, Fri.-Sat. at 8:30 and 10:30pm. Cover $12, $9 drink or food min.

■ Radio

In New York City, the radio spectrum serves up everything from soulless elevator instrumentals (WLTW 106.7 FM) to pirate radio broadcasts of underground sounds and community activism (see p. 159). As with most American radio, the lower on the dial, the less-commercial (and more innovative) the sounds will be. WFMU 91.1 is a college radio station without a college—Upsala College collapsed in 1994 and the acclaimed high quality eclecticism of FMU enabled it to continue as the college's only surviving department. FMU broadcasts genre-defying freeform music to a devoted listenership and is strongest in obscure guitar-based music from the 20s to the present day. Another college radio gem is Columbia's WKCR 89.9 FM—playing everything but rock. KCR's "Out to Lunch" weekdays from noon to 3pm airs a spectrum of jazz and is knowledgeable about the current scene. For hardcore hip-hop and underground rap, check out Stretch Armstrong's Thurs. 1-5am show on KCR. WQHT 97.1 FM sends out more commercial styles, beginning each weekday with Dr. Dre and Ed Lover's morning show of phat beats, dope rhymes, and fast-paced talk. In the evenings QHT becomes more daring, offering ground-breaking cutting scratching, and record recombination.

Classical: WNYC 93.9, WQXR 96.3
Jazz: WBGO 88.3, WCWP 88.1, WQCD 101.9
College/Indie/Alternative: WNYU 89.1, WKCR 89.9, WSOU 89.5, WFMU 91.1, WDRE 92.7, WHTZ 100.3, WAXQ 104.3, WNEW 102.7
Classic Rock: WXRK 92.3
Top 40: WPSC 88.7, WRKS 98.7, WPLJ 95.5, WRCN 103.9, WMXV 105.1
Hip Hop/R&B/Soul: WQHT 97.1, WBLS 107.5, WWRL 1600AM
Oldies: WRTN 93.5, WCBS 101.1
Foreign-language Programming: WADO 1280AM, WWRV 1330AM, WKDM 1380AM, WZRC 1480AM, WNWK 105.9
News: WABC 770AM, WCBS 880AM, WINS 1010AM, WBBR 1130AM
Public Radio: WNYC 93.9, WNYC 820AM, WBAI 99.5
Sports: WFAN 660AM

ENTERTAINMENT

Sports

While most cities would be content to field a major-league team in each big-time sport, New York opts for the Noah's Ark approach: two baseball teams, two NHL hockey teams, two NFL football teams (although the Giants and Jets are now quartered across the river in New Jersey), an NBA basketball team and an MLS soccer squad. In addition to local teams' regularly scheduled season games, New York hosts a number of celebrated world-class events such as the New York Marathon and the United States Tennis Association Open (a.k.a. the U.S. Open). The city papers overflow with information on upcoming events.

■ Spectator Sports

BASEBALL

The once-proud national pastime thrives in New York from late March to early October, when two high-exposure teams make their exploits off the field almost as melodramatic as those on it. The legendary **New York Yankees** play ball at **Yankee Stadium** in the Bronx (718-293-6000), though short-tempered boss George Steinbrenner is threatening to move the Yanks elsewhere. Relations with the Bronx turned particularly sour in 1994, when a member of the Yankees front management allegedly likened the neighborhood youths to "monkeys." On the playing field, Paul O'Neill, Wade Boggs, and Jimmy Key have joined long-time Yank Don Mattingly in propelling the club to the upper tier of the division, after some dismal seasons in the late 80s. The team has also greatly benefitted from the substance-abusing superstar duo of Dwight Gooden and Darryl Strawberry. But given the 1995 baseball strike, the Yankees and the sport itself have been waning in popularity of late. Plenty of tickets are usually available, from $6.50 for bleacher seats to $17 for lower box seats. On Family Day every Monday, the deserving brood can get half-price seats.

In 1986, the **New York Mets** won the World Series for the second time in franchise history and the city went wild. But over the past few years, the Mets have lost virtually all their superstars, including Howard Johnson, Doc Gooden, and Darryl Strawberry. Nowadays, the line-up features such up-and-comers as Todd Hundley and Jose Vizcaino. If baseball can withstand the soccer onslaught, there's always 1997 for the pennant. Watch them go to bat at **Shea Stadium** in Queens (718-507-8499). Tickets range from $6.50 for bleacher seats to $15 for lower box seats, the best of which are often difficult to obtain. On promotion dates, sponsors give away baseball cards, action figures, wallets, helmets, banners, and other memorabilia. Avoid family days unless you really adore screaming kids.

BASKETBALL

Once universally considered mediocre, the **New York Knickerbockers** (usually referred to as the Knicks) are finally a force in the NBA, winning the Eastern Conference in 1994 under the towering leadership of center Patrick Ewing but losing in the NBA Finals to Houston in seven games. The Knicks repeated the Eastern Conference victory in 1995, but failed to make it to the playoffs, despite stellar performances by Ewing, John Starks, and Charles Oakley. In a bid to beat the 1996 championship Bulls, the Knicks recently spent the off-season refitting their team for 1997, trading Anthony Mason for Charlotte Hornets star Larry Johnson and taking on promising new talent like John Wallace and Dantae Jones. The Knicks do their dribbling at **Madison Square Garden** (MSG) (465-6741) from late fall to late spring. Tickets, which start at $13, are fairly hard to come by and nearly impossible to find during the playoffs. On the college level, the second-tier N.I.T. and Big East collegiate tournaments take place at MSG in March.

FOOTBALL

Though both New York teams once battled in the trenches at Shea Stadium, nowadays they play across the river at **Giants Stadium** (201-935-3900) in East Rutherford, New Jersey. The mighty **New York Giants** are looking for their third Super Bowl ring. Meanwhile, the **Jets,** playing at the Meadowlands in NJ, long seeking to return to the glory of the Namath years, have played well recently but have yet to return to their former prominence. Jets tickets are hard to come by; Giants tickets nigh impossible—season ticket holders have booked them all for the next **40 years.** See *Let's Go: New York City 2037* for details. Try any local sports bar for the best view of the action you're likely to get. Tickets for the Jets start at $25 (cash only at the Meadowlands box office).

HOCKEY

In a town known for its speed and turbulence, it's not hard to understand why New Yorkers attend hockey games with such fervor. The **New York Rangers** play at **Madison Square Garden** (MSG, 465-6741 or 308-6977) from late fall to late spring. Long-suffering fans, after enduring 54 dry years, were finally rewarded with a huge, gleaming piece of silverware when their Rangers captured the Stanley Cup in June 1994. Indoor fireworks exploded as the final buzzer sounded, and one ecstatic fan spoke for many when he held up a sign saying, "Now I can die in peace!" The Rangers recently signed the Great One, Wayne Gretzky, for the 1997 season. Tickets start at $12; reserve well in advance. Meanwhile, the lowly **New York Islanders** are now mired near the bottom of the league, after winning four consecutive Stanley Cups in the early 80s. They hang their skates at the **Nassau Coliseum** (516-794-9300) in Uniondale, Long Island. Tickets range between $19-60.

SOCCER

Buoyed by swelling youth interest and the recent 1994 World Cup, soccer has undergone a meteoric rise in popularity in the past few years, culminating in the start of a new American league, **Major League Soccer (MLS).** Since the league's inception in 1996, New Yorkers have wasted no time learning what the rest of the world has known for decades—no other sport can compare to *futbol*. With foreign powerhouses like Italy's Roberto Donadoni and local talents like star midfielder Tab Ramos and former U.S. national team goalie Tony Meola, the **New York/New Jersey Metrostars** have had a promising first season, selling out record crowds if not yet captivating television audiences. The Metrostars play at **Giants Stadium** (201-935-3900) in the football off-season. At this rate, they'll rename it Metrostars Stadium soon enough.

TENNIS

Tennis enthusiasts who get their tickets three months in advance can attend the prestigious **U.S. Open,** held in late August and early September at the United States Tennis Association's (USTA) Tennis Center in Flushing Meadows Park, Queens (718-760-6200). Tickets are $20-210 for day matches and $25-225 for evening matches. The **Virginia Slims Championship,** featuring the world's top women players, comes to MSG (465-6741) in mid-November. Tickets for the opening rounds start at $25.

HORSERACING

Forsake the rat race for some equine excitement. Thoroughbred fans can watch the stallions go at **Belmont Park** (718-641-4700) every day except Monday from May through July and from September to mid-October, and may even catch a grand slam event. The **Belmont Stakes,** run in early summer, is one leg in the Triple Crown. The "Belmont Special" train leaves from Penn Station every 20 minutes from 9:45am to noon ($7 roundtrip, including $1 off admission). Meanwhile, **Aqueduct Racetrack** (718-641-4700), next to JFK Airport, has races from late October to early May, every day except Monday and Tuesday. (Subway: A or C to Aqueduct.) Grandstand seating at both tracks costs $2. Racing in New York is suspended during the month of August, when the action goes upstate to Saratoga.

PEOPLERACING

On the first Sunday in November, two million spectators line rooftops, sidewalks, and promenades to cheer 22,000 runners in the **New York City Marathon** (16,000 racers actually finish). The race begins on the Verrazano Bridge and ends at Central Park's Tavern on the Green.

■ Participatory Sports

Amateur and recreational athletes also twist and flex in New York, and you can too! Although space in much of the city is at a premium, the **City of New York Parks and Recreation Department** (360-8111; 360-3456 for a recording of park events) manages to maintain numerous playgrounds and parks in all boroughs, for everything from baseball and basketball to croquet and shuffleboard.

SWIMMING

Beaches

Coney Island Beach and Boardwalk (2½ mi.), on the Atlantic Ocean, from W. 37th St. to Corbin Pl., in Brooklyn (718-946-1350). Subway: B, D, F, or N to Coney Island.

Manhattan Beach (¼ mi.), on the Atlantic Ocean, from Ocean Ave. to Mackenzie St. in Brooklyn (718-946-1373).

Orchard Beach and Promenade (1¼ mi.), on Long Island Sound in Pelham Bay Park, Bronx (718-885-2275). Subway: #6 to Pelham Bay Park.

Rockaway Beach and Boardwalk (7½ mi.), on the Atlantic Ocean. From Beach 1st St., Far Rockaway, to Beach 149th St., Neponsit, Queens (718-318-4000). Lifeguards on duty daily 10am-6pm through the summer. Subway: A or C.

Staten Island: South Beach, Midland Beach, and **Franklin D. Roosevelt Boardwalk** (2½ mi.), on Lower New York Bay. From Fort Wadsworth to Miller Field, New Dorp. Take bus #51 from the ferry terminal.

Jones Beach State Park, on Long Island Sound in Nassau County (516-785-1600). Take LIRR to Freeport or Wantaugh, and catch a shuttle to the beach.

Pools

Public pools are scattered throughout all the boroughs of New York, but they can be dangerous, since several incidents of sexual assault have occurred in the past couple years. Often this takes the form of girls or women being surrounded by a circle of boys or men, who close in and molest the victim in what is called "whirlpooling." The NYC Parks Department has added security and is considering segregating some pools by sex. If you can find the few pools that aren't in troubled neighborhoods, though, public pools can be a cheap way to escape from the sweltering summer heat. Some of the nicer pools include **John Jay Pool,** east of York Ave. at 77th St., and **Asser Levy Pool,** at 23rd and Asser Levy Place (next to the East River). All outdoor pools are open from early July through Labor Day from 11am to 7 or 8pm, depending on the weather. Both are free, although the latter's heated indoor pool is open only to members. Call the Parks Aquatic Information Line at 718-699-4219.

Indoor pools can be somewhat safer than outdoor pools and tend to be open year-round, but most require some sort of annual membership fee of $10 and up.

BASKETBALL

Basketball is one of New York's favorite pastimes. Courts can be found in parks and playgrounds all over the city, and most are frequently occupied. **Pickup basketball** games can also be found in various parts of the city, each with its own rituals, rulers, and degree of intensity. **The Cage,** at W 4th and Sixth Avenue, is home to some of the City's best amateur players: rumor has it that scouts for college and pro teams occasionally drop by incognito to ferret out some new talent. Other pickup spots worth checking out (if you're any good) include courts at **Central Park, 96th and Lexington Ave.,** and **76th and Columbus Ave.**

BICYCLING

From spring to fall, daily at dawn and dusk and throughout the weekend, packs of dedicated (and fashion-conscious) cyclists dressed in biking shorts navigate the trails and wide roads of **Central Park.** (The circular drive is car-free Mon.-Thurs. 10am-3pm and 7-10pm, and Fri. 10am-3pm and 7pm until Mon. 6am; see Jogging below for tips on where to ride in Central Park.) On the West Side, along the Hudson bank, **Riverside Park** between 72nd and 110th St. draws more laid-back riders. Other excellent places to cycle weekends include the deserted **Wall Street** area or the unadorned roads of Brooklyn's **Prospect Park.** For quick same-day excursions, plenty of bike shops around Central Park rent out two-wheelers by the hour. (For more info on biking in New York City, see Essentials: Getting Around, p. 65.)

JOGGING

In New York, joggers and cyclists go hand in hand—not exactly a harmonious combination. When running in **Central Park** during no-traffic hours (see Bicycling, above), stay in the right-hand runners' lane to avoid being mowed down by some reckless pedal-pusher. *Stay in populated areas and stay out of the park after dark.* Avoid venturing up beyond 96th St. unless you have a companion or are familiar with the route. Recommended courses include the 1.58-mile jaunt around the Reservoir and a picturesque 1.72-mile route starting at Tavern on the Green along the West Drive, heading south to East Drive, and then circling back west up 72nd St. to where you started. Another beautiful place to run is **Riverside Park,** which stretches along the Hudson River bank from 72nd to 116th St.; for safety's sake, don't stray too far north. (For more information on jogging in New York, see Essentials: Getting Around, p. 66).

Hell On Wheels

The Rollerblading craze has hit New York hard. Messengers career through crowded streets on their skates, oblivious to the flow of traffic around them, and park paths are often clogged with talented (and not-so-talented) bladers. The type of skating varies from space to space; some areas have slalom courses and half-pipes set up similar to skateboarding courses. The following open stretches feature good views and a skate-happy crowd:

Battery Park: try skating from the tip of Manhattan through Battery Park City on the west side of the island. Great view of the harbor and skyline, extremely flat skating surface.
West Street: the city has blocked off about ten blocks stretching from Christopher to Horatio St. Big crowd of heavy-duty skaters. View of the Hudson (but you're looking at New Jersey).
Chelsea Piers: brand new roller rink in an equally new sports and entertainment complex, at 23rd St. and 12th Ave. Very popular with in-line hockey players. Juts out into the Hudson for a great view.
East River Promenade: Slightly narrow strip of boardwalk running from 81st to 60th St. The path is very low and close to the river, with great views of Roosevelt Island.
Central Park: The park maintains several roller-zones, including the Outer Loop, which circles the park, and a slalom course near Tavern on the Green (67th St.).

BOWLING

There are only a few places left for strikes and spares in Manhattan. Try the 44-lane **Bowlmor,** 110 University Pl. (255-8188), near 13th St., on the third and fourth floors. With such limited alley space, call ahead to check lane-availability. ($3.25 per game each person, shoe rental $1. Open Sun.-Wed. 10am-1am, Thurs. 10am-2am, Fri.-Sat. 10am-4am.) **Tennis** courts are on the higher floors; call 989-2300 to reserve space and check admission.

GOLF

Although New York golf courses don't measure up to those at Pebble Beach, New Yorkers nonetheless remain avid golfers, jamming all of the 13 well manicured city courses during the weekends. Most are found in the Bronx or Queens, including **Pelham Bay Park** (718-885-1258), **Van Cortlandt Park** (718-543-4595), and **Forest Park** (718-296-0999). Greens fees are $19 during the week and $21 Saturdays and Sundays for non-NYC residents. Reservations for summer weekends are suggested seven to ten days in advance.

ICE SKATING

The first gust of cold winter air brings out droves of aspiring Paul Wylies and Oksana Baiuls. While each of the rinks in the city has its own character, nearly all have lockers, skate rentals, and a snack bar. The most popular and expensive is the famous sunken plaza in **Rockefeller Center,** Fifth Avenue and 50th St. (757-5730), which doubles as the chic American Festival Café during the spring and summer months. The Rockefeller rink is always crowded during the winter months, and throngs of spectators stand around the outside edges, just observing the skating below. You can do your Bolero thing at the Donald Trump-owned **Wollman Memorial Rink** (517-4800), located in a particularly scenic section of Central Park near 64th St. (For more information on hours and rates, see Sights: Central Park, p. 152)..**Sky Rink** (336-6100), at W. 21st St. and the Hudson River, boasts two full-sized Olympic rinks. Call for hours, prices, and skate rental fees for recreational skating.

HORSEBACK RIDING

Horseback riding in Central Park, for those experienced in English saddle, operates out of **Claremont Stables,** at 175 W. 89th St. (724-5100; open Mon.-Fri. 6am-10pm, Sat.-Sun. 6:30am-5pm; $33 per hour; make reservations). In Queens, **Lynne's Riding School** (718-261-7679) and **Dixie Do Stables** (718-263-3500) give guided trail rides through Forest Park (open 8am-7pm; $20 per hour). Lynne's requires some riding experience.

CRICKET AND CROQUET

The two bastions of British civilization, cricket and croquet, are both played in this most un-English of cities. You won't see Ian Botham swinging his chunk of willow, but you can turn your arm over for a few overs of off-spin at **cricket fields** throughout the boroughs. Fields include **Flushing Meadows-Corona Park** in Queens (call 718-520-5932 for the $10 permit); **Canarsie Beach Park** in Brooklyn (718-965-8919); and **Van Cortlandt Park** in the Bronx (718-430-1890 for the $25 permit). During the summer months, weekend permits at any of the three parks are nearly impossible to come by. All welcome spectators, though, and Flushing Meadows-Corona Park has just added three new fields.

For a quick dose of mallet and wicket, head to the croquet lawn in Central Park, north of Sheep Meadow (call 696-2512 for permits; open May-Nov.).

Shopping

If something exists, it can be purchased somewhere in New York City. The shopping experience runs the gamut from the glitzy departments stores and boutiques on Fifth and Madison Ave. to the hole-in-the-wall record stores of St. Mark's Place to the throb of techno tunes emanating from the arbiters of cool in SoHo. It's easy to get wrapped up in New York's conspicuous consumption. One of the less official shopping zones is the streets themselves. Vendors hawk everything from tapes to socks to fruit to jewelry. Just be aware that that Rolex watch and that Gucci bag are either extremely hot or extremely fake—the bargain is a bargain for a reason.

■ Department Stores and Shopping Malls

New York has more ritzy department stores than Beverly Hills. Start with **Macy's,** the world's "finest" department store; it used to bill itself as the world's "largest" until recently, when a store in Germany was built one square foot larger. You can eat breakfast, lunch, and dinner at Macy's, get a facial and a haircut, mail a letter, have your jewelry appraised, exchange currency, purchase theater tickets, and get lost. Of course, you can also shop. The chaotic colossus sits at 151 W. 34th St. (695-4400), between Broadway and Seventh Ave.

Grab a store directory at the entrance to help you navigate Macy's mazes. Macy's has its own Visitors Center, located on the first-floor balcony, where a concierge (560-3827) will assist anyone looking for anything. They will also arrange dining or theater reservations, provide information on upcoming city-wide events, and arrange for interpreters to assist non-English speakers in the store. Those too busy making money to spend any of it themselves can hire others to spend it for them, using the "Macy's by Appointment" service on the third floor. A staff of fashion consultants, home-accessories experts, and corporate specialists act as consumer therapists, walking clients through the store, if necessary, to help them discover what they really want (for an appointment, call 494-4181). All of these services are free. (Open Mon.-Sat. 10am-8:30pm, Sun. 11am-7pm. Subway: #1, 2, 3, or 9 to Penn Station, or B, D, F, N, Q, or R to 34th St.)

Courtly **Lord and Taylor,** 424 Fifth Ave. (391-3344), between 38th and 39th St., features ten floors of fashion frenzy. Scores of New Yorkers come to be shod at the acclaimed shoe department and treated in Lord's manner—caring service and free early morning coffee. Lord and Taylor also offers legendary Christmas displays. The first in history to use the picture window as a stage for anything other than merchandise, the store began this custom in 1905 during an unusually balmy December that failed to summon the appropriate meteorological garnish; Lord and Taylor filled its windows with mock blizzards, reviving the Christmas spirit for gloomy city-dwellers. (Open Mon.-Tues. 10am-7pm, Wed.-Fri. 10am-8:30pm, Sat. 9am-7pm, Sun. 11am-6pm. Subway: B, D, or F to 42nd St., or N or R to 34th St.)

Also renowned for its window displays is **Barney's New York** (945-1600). The mother store, a 10,000-sq.-ft. coliseum, overlooks the Hudson River at Two World Financial Center. Barney's features stunning (and painfully pricey) collections of sportswear, formalwear, shoes, and housewares (open Mon.-Fri. 10am-7pm, Sat. 10am-6pm, Sun. noon-5pm). Another, equally large outfit does business at Madison and 66th St., featuring the **mad66** Café, a great place to spot celebrity shoppers sipping lattè as they rest their weary legs and bag-laden arms. (Open Mon.-Thurs. 10am-9pm, Fri. 10am-8pm, Sat. 10am-7pm; Sept.-June also Sun. noon-6pm.)

Saks Fifth Avenue, 611 Fifth Ave. (753-4000), between 49th and 50th St., is subdued and chic. This institution has aged well and continues to combine good taste with smooth courtesy. The perfume-sprayers are more restrained, although no less adept, than those at Bloomingdale's (open Mon.-Wed. and Fri.-Sat. 10am-6:30pm, Thurs. 10am-8pm, Sun. noon-6pm).

Bloomingdale's, 1000 Third Ave. (705-2000), at E. 59th St., affectionately known as Bloomie's, is "an extraordinary shopping experience." More to the point, Bloomie's is nine floors dedicated to decadence—the totally consuming need to shop. Sidestep the eternal tango between casual shoppers and perfume spritzers on the first floor, and dodge the throngs of foreign tourists buying up the Clinique counter. There's something for everyone here, but most of it is far too hopelessly chic for the average budget peasant. Just remember: bathrooms are on floors 2, 7, and 8, the chairs are soft and cushy for when your friend takes longer in the fur salon than you'd anticipated, and there's 8.25% sales tax on all purchases in NYC. (Open Mon. and Fri.-Sat. 10am-7pm, Tues.-Wed. 10am-10pm, Thurs. 10am-9pm, Sun. 11am-7pm.)

Sit in luxury's lap at the legendary, extortionate **Bergdorf-Goodman** clothing mansion, on both sides of the street at 745 and 754 Fifth Ave. (753-7300), between 57th and 58th St., where conspicuous consumers buy pricey jewelry and swank outfits by the crystal light of chandeliers. Try not to swallow your tongue (open Mon.-Wed. and Fri.-Sat. 10am-6pm, Thurs. 10am-8pm).

If the name doesn't set you rolling, the smorgasbord of bizarre merchandise will; **Hammacher Schlemmer,** 157 E. 57th St. (421-9000), between Third and Lexington Ave., is a gadget-fancier's fantasyland. Marvel at such essential items as a self-stirring French saucepan, an air-conditioned doghouse, a computerized fortune teller, and the Whiz Bang Popcorn Wagon. More redeemingly, Hammacher's zeal for automated convenience has also provided the world with the steam iron, the electric razor, and the pressure cooker. Masquerade as a serious consumer while test-driving the floor models of various massage machines (open Mon.-Sat. 10am-6pm).

Stern's Department Store and many other smaller chain stores ascend to commodity heaven on eight levels of fashion, toys, electronics, and hard-to-find items.in the **Manhattan Mall** (465-0500) at Sixth Ave. and 33rd St. The mall's colored lights and fantasy-land exterior appear to herald an amusement park, and all is movement inside, with the silver escalators and the constant parade of humanity. Four glass elevators haloed in lightbulbs slide up and down the walls, eliciting the same sinking feeling as an advanced-technology ferris wheel. The building is twisted into a doughnut shape to focus shoppers' attention inward and away from real life on the streets outside. The top level, called "Taste of the Town," is an international food court, an entire floor of noshing and funk (open Mon.-Sat. 10am-8pm, Sun. 11am-6pm).

Trump Tower (832-2000), at 57th St. and Fifth Ave., gleams with marble and gold. Inside, a fountain of plenty climbs the walls of a six-story atrium jampacked with upmarket boutiques and restaurants. The 1980s have gone into hiding here, waiting for the nostalgia gap to catch up and send them back out into the world at large. (Boutiques open Mon.-Sat. 10am-6pm. Atrium open daily 8am-6pm.)

Mall-shopping on a global scale transpires at the 60 shops and restaurants in the concourse of the **World Trade Center** (435-4170), at West and Liberty St. (shops open Mon.-Fri. 7:30am-6:30pm, Sat. 10am-5pm).

Anyone from the American hinterland who's feeling a little homesick won't want to miss the **Staten Island Mall,** off Richmond Rd., near the center of the island. With a huge, sprawling, one-floor selection, it's so similar to malls all over the country that it's easy to imagine yourself anywhere but Staten Island, New York. Roam from Sears to Macy's to the Gap to B. Dalton—all the big names of Mall-dom are here (Mall open Mon.-Sat. 10am-9:30pm, Sun. noon-6pm). To get here, take the S44 bus from the ferry terminal and ride for about 45 minutes.

▓ Clothes

In SoHo, enormous **Canal Jean Co.,** 504 Broadway (226-1130), between Prince and Broome St., the original home of the surplus clinic, brims with neon ties, baggy pants, and silk smoking jackets. Artsy hipsters can buy their black slim-fitting jeans here. Poke around in the bargain bins out front (open Sun.-Thurs. 10:30am-8pm, Fri.-Sat. 10:30am-9pm). On weekends, check out the **flea market** at the western end of Canal St. for honest-to-goodness antiques along with the usual funk junk.

In the NYU area, the **Antique Boutique,** 712 Broadway (460-8830) near Astor Pl., blares better techno than many clubs, and sells both stunning vintage clothing and interesting (but expensive) new designs. As with most outfitters of club gear, expect a lot of shiny plastics and outrageous attitudes (10% discount for students with ID; open Mon.-Sat. 10am-11pm, Sun. noon-9pm). **Reminiscence,** 74 Fifth Ave. (243-2292), near 14th St., is happily stuck in a 70s groove. But now it's even cheaper—a few items cost under $10 (another store at 109 Ave. B (353-0626), near 14th St.; both stores open Mon.-Sat. 11am-8pm, Sun. noon-7pm). At 16 W. 8th St., between Fifth and Sixth Ave., the clothes at **Andy's Chee-pee's** (460-8488) aren't really all that chee-pee, but are definitely worth a peek (if only for that distinctive vintage clothing aroma; open Mon.-Sat. 9am-8pm, Sun. noon-7pm). Another location exists at 691 W. Broadway near W. 4th St. (420-5980; open Mon.-Sat. 9am-11pm, Sun. noon-8pm). **Cheap Jack's,** 841 Broadway (777-9564), between 13th and 14th St., has racks and racks of worn jeans, old flannels, leather jackets, and other vintage treats in its cavern of a store (open Tues.-Sun. 11:30am-7pm). **Patricia Field,** 10 E. 8th St. (254-1699), near Fifth Ave., offers a fabulous array of costly hipster gear; the colors of choice are neon and the fabric vinyl. The wig selection is extensive as well (open Mon.-Sat. noon-8pm, Sun. 1-7pm).

In SoHo, cutting-edge boutiques abound. For women's clothing, **Betsey Johnson,** 130 Thompson St. (420-0169), between Prince and Houston St. (open daily 11am-7pm) and **Anna Sui,** 113 Greene St. (941-8406), between Spring and Prince St. (open Mon.-Sat. noon-7pm, Sun. noon-6pm) offer new (if pricey) duds.

If you're looking to blend into the hip SoHo scene, you might want to get yourself a pair of oh-so-cool glasses. A primo shopping stop is **Selina Optique,** 99 Wooster (343-9490), at Broome St., where an almost infinite array of hand-crafted and self-consciously clunky glasses and sunglasses await your perusal. Don't be daunted by the boutique atmosphere—the impeccably dressed French and Japanese staff is extremely helpful and friendly. One caveat: Genuine SoHo attitude carries a hefty price—some pairs can run upwards of $500.

The shopping experience on the Upper West Side along Columbus Ave. is designed primarily for those with Roman numerals after their names. Hit the boutiques during the January and July sales. A few havens for the not-so-rich-or-famous do exist. Still a favorite of the young and hip is **Alice Underground,** 380 Columbus Ave. (724-6682) at 78th St. (also at 481 Broadway; 431-9067). Alice Underground offers wonderful cummerbunds, bow ties, and silk dinner jackets to give men that "Bond, James Bond sheen." Women have choices galore, from chic to funk to Victorian (open on Columbus Sun.-Fri. 11am-7pm, Sat. 11am-8pm; on Broadway daily 11am-7:30pm). Daryl Hannah, Diane Keaton, and Annie Lennox stop at **Allan and Suzi,** 416 Amsterdam Ave. (724-7445), at 80th St. From new Gaultier Madonna-wear at 70% off to $40 original Pucci dresses, this store is cheap, chic chaos. A large assortment of platform shoes surrounds the melee. Sorry guys—no men's clothes for sale (open daily noon-8pm).

Across town, highfalutin' second-hand designer clothes await you at **Encore,** 1132 Madison Ave., second floor (879-2850), at 84th St. (open Mon.-Wed. and Fri. 10:30am-6:30pm, Thurs. 10:30am-7:30pm, Sat. 10:30am-6pm, Sun. noon-6pm; closed Sun. July through mid-Aug.), or at **Michael's,** 1041 Madison Ave., second floor (737-7273), between 79th and 80th (open Mon.-Wed. and Fri.-Sat. 9:30am-6pm, Thurs. 9:30am-8pm). **Daffy's,** 335 Madison Ave. (557-4422), at 44th St., or 111 Fifth Ave. (529-4477), at 18th St, is the place for new mid-range designer clothes. Be prepared to go through piles of unsorted items to find those 70%-off gems you thought you'd never have (Madison branch open Mon.-Fri. 8am-8pm, Sat. 10am-6pm, Sun. noon-6pm; Fifth Ave. branch open Mon.-Sat. 10am-9pm, Sun. 11am-6pm). Great bargains on normally expensive designer clothes can be had at **Dollar Bills,** 99 E. 42nd St. (867-0212), at Vanderbilt Ave., right outside Grand Central Station. It's hit or miss, but when you hit, you hit big. Armani, Fendi, and other chic European designers can all be found here with careful sifting and a little luck (open Mon.-Fri. 8am-7pm, Sat. 10am-6pm, Sun. noon-5pm).

Striped oxfords, tasteful ties, Father's Day every day—why, it's **Brooks Brothers!** At 346 Madison Ave. (682-8800) at E. 44th St., stock up on male-related accoutrements and finger the ties admiringly (open Mon-Wed. 8:30am-6:30pm, Thurs. 8:30am-7:30pm, Fri. 8:30am-6pm, Sat. 9am-6pm).

Underpaid artists and well-to-do Manhattan hipsters head southward to **Domsey's** (718-384-6000), the best vintage clothing store in the city. The sprawling warehouse rests at 431 Kent Ave. in Brooklyn. Astounding bargains await the diligent shopper— such as fine corduroys for $5. The selection is vast in one of the few stores in the city where used clothing is actually cheap. (Subway: J, M, or Z to Marcy; open Mon.-Fri. 8am-5:30pm, Sat. 8am-6:30pm, Sun. 11am-5:30pm.)

■ Computers and Electronics

Amps, CD players, cameras, tape decks, VCRs—you name it, New York sells it for less. Every other block has a combo camera/electronics/luggage store. With few exceptions, be wary of these tourist traps; the salespeople may try to sell you something you'll regret buying. When dealing with equipment costing several hundred dollars or more, try to stick to new goods with the original manufacturer's warranties.

To eliminate most hassles, shop at the bigger and more reputable electronics stores in New York. Recently, **The Wiz** has been publicizing their long-held but formerly obscure policy of matching advertised competitors' prices. They proudly proclaim that "Nobody Beats The Wiz" and then dare you to find a lower-priced ad for anything sold in their stores. If you find a valid ad, they'll beat it and return 10% of the price difference. If you want to take them up on their little challenge, get hold of the Sunday *New York Times* or the latest copy of the *Village Voice*, in which you'll find ads from **6th Ave. Electronics** and **Uncle Steve,** two stores that consistently beat The Wiz's prices. In Manhattan, The Wiz's locations include 337 Fifth Ave. (684-7600), at 33rd St. opposite the Empire State Building; 871 Sixth Ave. (594-2300), at 31st St.; 12 W. 45th St. (302-2000), between Fifth and Sixth Ave.; and 17 Union Sq. West (741-9500), at 15th St. (All open Mon.-Sat. 10am-7pm, Sun. 1-7pm.) **J & R Music World,** at 23 Park Row (732-8600), near City Hall, will also meet most of your electronics needs with competitive prices. (Open Mon.-Sat. 9am-6:30pm, Sun. 11am-6pm. Subway: #4, 5, or 6 to City Hall.) Mega-store **47th Street Photo,** 67 W. 47th St. (921-1287), deals in cameras, dark room equipment, computers, and electronics at great prices. Get your *Empire Strikes Back* mouse pad here (open Mon.-Wed. 9:30am-7pm, Thurs. 9:30am-8pm, Fri. 9:30am-3pm, Sun. 10am-5pm).

■ Record Stores

They're not just for records anymore, as CDs, cassettes, and even music videos tend to dominate many so-called "record stores." But whatever the format (unless you're looking for the new Tori Amos 8-track), in New York you can get your eardrums buzzing with music from almost every era and genre.

If you're not the scrounge-and-search type, go straight to **Tower Records,** 692 Broadway (505-1500), at E. 4th St. This one-stop music emporium, nearly a block long with four full floors of merchandise, is one of the largest on the East Coast. Gadgets like the music-video computer let you preview select songs before purchasing them, while a touch-screen store directory makes tracking down that elusive album by your favorite mainstream artist a cinch. There are other branches uptown at 1535 3rd Ave., at 86th St., and at 2107 Broadway, at 74th St. (Open daily 9am-midnight; subway: #6 to Bleecker St.)

HMV, at 86th St. and Lexington Ave., is another "music superstore," looking like dad's study filled with CDs and large posters of the newest Big Thing. His Master's Voice provides a wide range of classical, jazz, new age, show tunes, and rock pop schlock for you and your little disc-spinnin' dog. There's also a branch at Broadway and 72nd St. (both open Sun.-Thurs. 9am-10pm, Fri.-Sat. 9am-11pm).

For those music enthusiasts on the lookout for more obscure titles or labels, at least a dozen smaller stores can be found east of Tower Records in the East Village and round about Bleecker St. in the West Village. Though they may lack the stock and organization of larger stores, many of these places specialize in hard-to-find alternative rock imports, dance remixes, rare oldies, and the insurgent 7-inch single. Several of these smaller stores also sell used records, cassettes, and CDs at bargain prices. Perseverance pays off in this city; if you can't find what you want here, you're probably not looking hard enough.

Bleecker St. Golden Disc, 239 Bleecker St. (255-7899). Subway: A, B, C, D, E, F, or Q to W. 4th St. This vintage shop specializes in vinyl platters from eras past. The basement holds a heavy jazz LP concentration, and the street level stocks old rock, blues, country, and soul. Open Mon.-Tues. 11am-8pm, Wed.-Sat. 11am-9pm, Sun. 1pm-7pm.

Colony Records, 1619 Broadway (265-2050), at 49th St. Subway: #1 or 9 to 50th St., or N, R to 49th St. You really can't miss the big neon sign, not even in its Times Square locale. Extensive selection of all forms of new and used music on CD, tape, and vinyl—from rock to Cajun to folk. Check out the vintage sheet music and the selection of autographs, memorabilia, and movie scripts. Open Mon.-Sat. 9:30am-1am, Sun. 10am-midnight.

Disc-O-Rama, 186 W. 4th St. (206-8417), between Sixth and Seventh Ave. Subway: #1 or 9 to Christopher St.; or A, B, C, D, E, F, or Q to W. 4th St. Cheap popular albums. All CDs (all!!) $10 or below; grab a coupon from the *Voice* and knock off a buck more. Strong alternative section in addition to the more standard Mariah Carey-type Top 40. The CDs aren't alphabetized, so be prepared for a search (the top 200 are nicely organized). Open Mon.-Thurs. 11am-10:30pm, Fri.- Sat. 11am-1am, Sun. noon-8pm.

Downtown Music Gallery, 211 E. 5th St. (473-0043). Subway: #6 to Astor Place or N,R to 8th St. Dense and diverse, the selection of CDs and vinyl should please most non-mainstream music enthusiasts. The gallery's "downtown, prog, avant, and japanoise" section is very strong—virtually all of John Zorn's many musical projects are available. The staff knows the music well and is ready to dispense advice. Open Sun.-Wed. noon-9pm, Thurs. noon-10pm, Fri.-Sat. noon-11pm.

Generation Records, 210 Thompson St. (254-1100), between Bleecker and 3rd St. Subway; A, B, C, D, E, F, or Q to W. 4th St. All kinds of alternative and underground rock on CD and vinyl—the hardcore and roots industrial selection is especially strong. Fairly low prices (CDs $11-13) and the best assortment of hard-to-find imports in the Village. Some good deals on used merchandise can be found downstairs. Open Mon.-Thurs. 11am-10pm, Fri.-Sat. 11am-1am, Sun. noon-10pm.

Gryphon Record Shop, 251 W. 72nd St., #2F (874-1588), near West End Ave. Subway: #1, 2, 3, or 9 to 72nd St. A 2nd-floor apartment with walls, tables, and crates of classical LPs, many rare or out of print. Real collector atmosphere; proprietor has the knowledge to match. Open Mon.-Sat. 11am-7pm, Sun. noon-6pm.

Jammyland, 60 E. 3rd St. (614-0185), between First and Second Ave. Subway #6 to Bleecker St. Head to Jammy's for a generous selection of reggae, roots, dub, dance-hall, ska, and other Jamaican innovations. Open Tues.-Sun. noon-midnight.

Kim's Video and Audio, 6 St. Mark's Place (598-9985). Subway: N or R to 8th St., or #6 to Astor Place. This is the mothership of Kim's outposts. Upstairs is a tremendous video showcase specializing in independent and foreign films, and downstairs holds a startlingly strong selection of independent and import CDs and records for reasonable prices. The supply of experimental beats—from 70s Jamaican dub to avant-jazz to futuristic jungle—is exhaustive. The other Kim's locations (144 and 350 Bleecker St. or 85 Ave. A., 260-1010, 675-8996, and 529-3410 respectively) offer smaller music departments with the same high quality. Open daily 10am-midnight.

Liquid Sky Temple, 241 Lafayette St. (431-6472). Subway: #6 to Spring St. or N, R to Prince St. A sheet of cascading water behind the storefront window announces the presence of this post-rave record and clothing shop. Since this is a store for techno DJs (and DJ-wannabees), most of the music is on vinyl, but there is a decent selection of pricey CDs and mixtapes. Good location to find discount flyers for underground clubs and rave events. Open Mon.-Sat. 1-8pm, Sun. 2-7pm.

Midnight Records, 263 W. 23rd St. (675-2768), between Seventh and Eighth Ave. Subway: #1, 9, C, or E to 23rd St. A mail-order and retail store specializing in hard-to-find rock records. Posters plaster the walls; every last mildewy nook is crammed with records—over 10,000 in stock. Prices aren't cheap, but if you're looking for the Prats' album *Disco Pope,* this may be the only place to find it. Lots of 60s and 70s LPs. Most LPs $9-20. Open Tues.-Sat. noon-6pm.

Other Music, 15 E. 4th St. (477-8150) across from Tower. Subway: #6 to Bleecker. Specializing in the alternative and avant-garde, from Stereolab to recordings of static and feedback. Obscure stuff abounds, but you can avoid steep import prices with the sizeable used CD section. Posters and flyers keep the clientele updated on where to see performers who push the boundaries of "music." Open Mon.-Wed. 11am-10pm, Thurs.-Sat. 11am-11pm, Sun. noon-8pm.

Pier Platters, 56 Newark St. (201-795-4785 and -9015), in Hoboken. Subway: B, D, F, N, Q, or R to 34th St., then PATH train ($1) to the first stop in Hoboken. Walk along Hudson Pl. to Hudson St., up one block to Newark St., then left. In 1982, a homesick Irishman started this independent record store, now Maxwell's companion in leading the Hoboken alternative. Celebrated members of the musical underground (particularly those playing at Maxwell's) shop here regularly, perusing the incredibly extensive, high-quality collection of rare singles and full-length records, with an emphasis on independent releases from the U.S. and New Zealand. Open Mon.-Sat. 11am-9pm, Sun. noon-8pm.

Second Coming Records, 235 Sullivan St. (228-1313), near W. 3rd St. Subway: A, B, C, D, E, F, or Q to W. 4th St. Vinyl, and lots of it. An especially strong selection of underground 7"s. Thanks to a recent expansion, the CD stock now accommodates a wide range of alternative and popular releases, both new and used. Very into the local scene—come here to see who's playing where. Also good for alternative imports and bootlegs. Open Sun.-Thurs. 11am-8pm, Fri.-Sat. 11am-10pm.

Smash Compact Discs, 33 St. Mark's Pl. (473-2200), between Second and Third Ave. Subway: #6 to Astor Pl. Come here if you can't find that classic-rock album at Sounds. Used CDs $3-10. Open Mon.-Thurs. 11am- 10pm, Fri.-Sun. 11am-11pm.

Sounds, 20 St. Mark's Pl. (677-3444), between Second and Third Ave. Subway: #6 to Astor Pl. Good, fair-priced selection of alternative and dance music. Used CD folders offer the best values, but be prepared to search. Racks of used LPs. New CDs $9-13, used ones $5-9. For used CDs, they'll pay (in cash) up to 50% of their resale value. **CD & Cassette Annex** at 16 St. Mark's Pl. (677-2727). Open Mon.-Thurs. noon-10:30pm, Fri.-Sat. noon-11:30pm, Sun. noon-9pm.

Vinylmania, 60 Carmine St. (924-7223), at Bedford St. Subway: A, B, C, D, E, F, or Q to W. 4th St. The dance center—they carry house, hip-hop, rap, R&B, and some jazz as well. Vinyl in the front (better for DJ manipulation) and CDs in the back. A good place for club flyers. Open Mon.-Fri. 11am-9pm, Sat.-Sun. 11am-7pm.

■ Toys and Games

Children of Paradise, 154 Bleecker St. (473-7146), at Thompson St. Subway: A, B, C, D, E, F, or Q to W. 4th St. Tiny store absolutely crammed with toys new and old, from the fanciest Kung-Fu Grip Mighty Morphin' Power Ranger to some of the earliest Barbies. Check out the wide array of old-school *Star Wars* Kenner toys. Open Mon.-Sat. 11am-7pm, Sun. noon-7pm.

Dollhouse Antics, 1343 Madison Ave. (876-2288), at 94th St. Subway: #6 to 96th St. Furniture that'll fit your tiny NYC hovel of a room! First-class doll real estate plus most miniaturized mundanities: coffee sets, Scrabble boards, toilets, napkins, and tables covered by artfully stitched baby-tablecloths. Immortalize your own family pet in a hand-painted 2- by 3" portrait to hang above a Lilliputian mantle ($75, clear photo required). Open Mon.-Fri. 11am-5:30pm, Sat. 11am-5pm; hours may vary in the summer, so call ahead.

Game Show, 1240 Lexington Ave. (472-8011), at 83rd St. Subway: #4, 5, or 6 to 86th St. Sick of painting the town red? Why not stay inside and play board games? Everything from *Monopoly* and *Pictionary* to the ever-lovin' *Kosherland,* the original *Hüsker Dü* (Bob Mould not included), and a discreet section of "adult" games like *Talk Dirty to Me.* Lots of puzzles too. Open Mon.-Wed., Fri.-Sun. 11am-6pm, Thurs. 11am-7pm.

The Leather Man, 111 Christopher St. (243-5339), between Bleecker and Hudson St. Subway: #1 or 9 to Christopher St. Check out that window display! Not for the timid—chains, leather, and, in the basement, all manner of sex toys (and supplements). Plenty of gifts for the folks. Staff is friendly and helpful towards all genders and orientations. Open daily noon-midnight.

Soccer Sport Supply, 1745 First Ave., (800-223-1010), between 89th and 90th St. Subway: #4, 5, or 6 to 86th St. New York's soccer outlet since 1933. Carries goalie jerseys, shinguards, and everything else you need to play the world's most popular sport. Open Mon.-Fri. 10am-6pm, Sat. 10am-5pm.

Star Magic, 1256 Lexington Ave. (988-0300), at 85th St. Subway: #4, 5, or 6 to 86th St. Specializing in "space age gifts," this store carries everything from telescopes to dried astronaut ice cream to tarot decks. Get some crystal or holographic jewelry to impress your New Age friends. Ravers can pick up glow-sticks and other glowing apparel. Other branches at 745 Broadway (228-7770), at 8th St., and at 275 Amsterdam Ave. (769-2020), at 73rd St. Open Mon.-Sat. 10am-8:30pm, Sun. 11am-7:30pm.

Tenzig & Pena, 916 Madison Ave. (288-8780), between 75th and 76th St. Subway: #4, 5, or 6 to 77th St. An educational toy- and bookstore with plenty of jigsaw puzzles, learning games, and the like. Perfect place to pick up tons of stocking stuffers and gifts for your niece's/nephew's birthday for under $12, including shark puppets, fighting nuns, and picture books. Open Mon.-Sat. 10am-6pm, Sun. noon-6pm.

Village Chess Shop, 230 Thompson St. (475-9580), between Bleecker and 3rd St. Subway: A, B, C, D, E, F, or Q to W. 4th. St. The Village's keenest intellects square off in rigorous strategic combat while sipping coffee ($1) and juice ($1.50). Play is $1 or $1.60 for clocked play per hour per person. Don't ₁%$# swear or you'll be penalized 25¢. Novices can get their game analyzed for $3. The shop also showcases several breathtaking antique chess sets, as well as more recent models based on Tolkien's *Lord of the Rings,* the Simpsons, Shakespearean characters, and the Civil War. Check it out. Open daily noon-midnight.

■ Specialty Stores

All of New York is a specialty store. From the highbrow chic boutiques to the funky avant-garde, if it's been made, you'll find it in this city. Here's a partial list of interesting places to browse:

The Ballet Shop, 1887 Broadway (581-7990), at 62nd St. Subway: #1 or 9 to 66th St. LPs, CDs, photographs, books, posters, and memorabilia related to ballet. Open Mon.-Sat. 11am-6pm, Sun. noon-5pm; Sept.-March Mon.-Sat. 11am-6pm.

Books and Binding, 33 W. 17th St. (229-0004), between Fifth and Sixth Ave. Subway: L or F to Sixth Ave.-14th St. A budget bookstore with a bookbinding department on the 2nd floor ($30-125). Open Mon.-Fri. 9:30am-8pm, Sat. 10am-7pm.

Condomania, 351 Bleecker St. (691-9442), near W. 10th St. Subway: #1 or 9 to Christopher St. "America's first condom store," it's basically just condoms, dental dams, and lube. Be sure to pick up some XXX-rated fortune cookies or a box of "Penis Pasta" with your order. Friendly staff answers all questions and gives safer-sex tips. Open Sun.-Thurs. 11:30am-10:45pm, Fri.-Sat. 11:30am-midnight.

The Counter Spy Shop, 499 Madison Ave. (688-8500), between 49th and 50th St. Subway: #6 to 51st St. James Bond fans and clinical paranoids will love this small store, devoted to the technology of subterfuge and deception. Expensive bulletproof vests, hidden cameras, and domestic lie detectors share the racks with false-bottom cans ($20) and junior spy t-shirts ($10). Open Mon.-Fri. 9am-6pm, Sat. 10am-4pm.

The How-To Video Source, 953 Third Ave. (486-8155), at 57th St. Subway: #4, 5, or 6 to 59th St., or N or R to Lexington Ave. As the name implies, a store that specializes in how-to videos. Learn how to meet the mate of your dreams while picking up Cajun cooking, martial arts, and sign language. While you're at it, let John

Cleese teach you how to irritate people ($19.95). Only in New York. Open Mon.-Fri. 10am-8pm, Sat.-Sun. 11am-7pm.

Little Rickie, 49½ First Ave. (505-6467), at 3rd St. Subway: F to Second Ave. Collectible offbeat cultural icons, like Pee Wee Herman decals, Madonna tapestries, and Elvis lamps, as well as marionettes of the Pope and Indonesian penis dolls. Open Mon.-Sat. 11am-8pm, Sun. noon-7pm.

Maxilla & Mandible, 451-5 Columbus Ave. (724-6173), between 81st and 82nd St. Subway: #1 or 9 to 79th St. Shelves and boxes of well-displayed shells, fossils, eggs, preserved insects, and—most of all—bones from every imaginable vertebrate (including *Homo sapiens*). A giant walking-stick insect under glass and an 11-ft. alligator skeleton stand out prominently among the merchandise. Malachite-colored jewel beetles "for the kids" $9. Caters to international collectors. Macabre but neato. Open Mon.-Sat. 11am-7pm, Sun. 1-5pm.

The Pop Shop, 292 Lafayette St. (219-2784), at Houston St. Subway: B, D, F, or Q to Broadway-Lafayette St. The late 80s Pop artist Keith Haring's cartoonish, socially-conscious artwork can be found on posters and postcards all over the city, but where else could you find Haring-decorated dominoes, backpacks, pull toys, or stocking caps? Opened in 1985, the shop was handpainted by the late artist in his distinctive style, and all proceeds benefit the Keith Haring Foundation, which supports a wide range of social causes. Open Tues.-Sat. noon-7pm, Sun. noon-7pm.

Rita Ford Music Boxes, 19 E. 65th St. (535-6717), between Madison and Fifth Ave. Subway: #6 to 68th St. Tinkle, tinkle, tinkle. Not just a plastic pop-up ballerina in a box here; all kinds of music boxes, from 19th-century antiques to Disney-endorsed *Beauty and the Beast* models. Expensive, yes (no budget buys here), but well worth a peek. Open Mon.-Sat. 9am-5pm.

Schoepfer Studios, 138 W. 31st St. (736-6939), between Sixth and Seventh Ave. Subway: N or R to 34th St. A gallery-store of great breadth in the realm of stuffed and mounted dead animals. Buy a genuine rattlesnake (from $100), or get just the rattles in the form of a pair of earrings ($18). Steer skulls start at $75, and the mounted barnyard chicken goes for $175. Snake-head keychains also available. Open Mon.-Thurs. 10am-4:30pm, Fri. 10am-4pm.

Spike's Joint, 1 S. Elliot Pl. (718-802-1000), in Brooklyn. Subway: G to Fulton. Head down Lafayette, take a left past the quiet brownstones of South Elliot. A small boutique filled with clothing, merchandise, and memorabilia from Spike Lee's film company, *Forty Acres and a Mule Filmworks.* Located in Spike's neighborhood of Fort Greene. Open Mon.-Sat. 10am-7pm, Sun. noon-6pm.

Tender Buttons, 143 E. 62nd St. (758-7004), between Third and Lexington Ave. Subway: #4, 5, or 6 to 59th St., or N, R to Lexington Ave. A treasure-trove of billions of buttons. If you carelessly lost the button on your favorite Renaissance doublet, you will find a replacement here. Also has cuff links and buckles to match buttons, or vice versa. Fork out $1000 for a button off one of George Washington's coats. Beware bloodthirsty button addicts. Open Mon.-Fri. 11am-6pm, Sat. 11am-5pm.

Television City, 64 W. 50th St. (246-4234), at Fifth Ave. Subway: #6 to 51st St. Paraphernalia from just about any television show that ever was. From *Mork and Mindy* lunchboxes to *Seinfeld* CD-ROMS to Kermit the Frog bags. Don't forget your *Melrose Place* t-shirt. Worth a visit if only to hear the TV theme songs played on the sound system. What ever happened to Nell Carter, anyway? Open Mon.-Fri. 10am-7pm, Sat.-Sun. 11am-6pm.

Warner Bros. Studio Store, 1 E. 57th St. (754-0300), at Fifth Ave. Subway: B or Q to 57th St.-Sixth Ave., or N or R to 57th St.-Seventh Ave. A three-story shrine to Warner Bros. most profitable icons, from the Looney Tunes gang to the Batman movies. Find Bugs Bunny, the Tasmanian Devil, Elmer Fudd, and Yosemite Sam emblazoned and embroidered on every conceivable type of item, from hats to housewares. No, you can't get any of those Acme products that Wile E. Coyote relied upon, but you can get Acme-label clothing. That's all, folks. Open Mon.-Sat. 10am-8pm, Sun. 11am-6pm.

■ Bookstores

Whether your taste runs to esoteric cosmology or Third World revolution, whether you seek the newest *Let's Go* guide or a first-edition copy of Joyce's *Dubliners,* Manhattan is the island for you. Chains like **Barnes and Noble** (807-0099), **B. Dalton** (674-8780), **Doubleday** (397-0550), and **Waldenbooks** (269-1139) discount current best-sellers, but patronizing smaller bookshops can be a much more interesting experience. If the books you want are hard to find, you should try one of the larger shops like the **Strand** (nearly 2 million tomes) or a specialized shop like **Murder Ink.**

GENERAL INTEREST

Barnes and Noble, 105 Fifth Ave. (807-0099), at W. 18th St. Subway: L or F to Sixth Ave.-14th St. Although part of a chain, this store began it all. The "biggest bookstore in the world" with tons of titles, many at heavy discounts. Buys college textbooks for up to ½-price. Open Mon.-Fri. 9:30am-7:45pm, Sat. 9:30am-6:15pm, Sun. 11am-5:45pm. Check out the **Barnes and Noble Bargain Annex,** 128 Fifth Ave. (633-3500) too. The B&N information line is 675-5500.

Barnes and Noble, 2289 Broadway (362-8835), at 82nd St. Subway: #1 or 9 to 79th St. Bigger than the Chelsea branch, this vast store offers comfortable chairs and couches to read in, a café, a well-stocked magazine section, and just about any book you want (don't forget though, that by patronizing this behemoth you are helping to squeeze out smaller local stores). Reportedly, this is one of the hot new pick-up scenes for literary-minded New Yorkers. Open Sun.-Thurs. 9am-11pm, Fri.-Sat. 9am-midnight.

Books and Company, 939 Madison Ave. (737-1450), between 74th and 75th St. Subway: #6 to 77th St. A helpful and gracious staff make this two-story bookstore and excellent place to shop or browse. The reading series takes place in the Fall and Spring. Isabelle Allende, Gary Snyder, and Jamaica Kincaid have all read in this small store. Excellent section of literature, criticism, and literary periodicals. Call for information on free (but often extremely crowded) readings. Open Mon.-Fri. 10am-7pm, Sat. 10am-6pm, Sun. noon-6pm.

Coliseum Books, 1771 Broadway (757-8381), at 57th St. Subway: #1, 9, A, B, C, or D to 59th St. Mainly stocks new releases, but also has a fine selection of drama and music (the store is just a stone's throw from Lincoln Center and Carnegie Hall), as well as poetry. Open Mon-Tues. 8am-10pm, Wed.-Thurs. 8am-11pm, Fri. 8am-11:30pm, Sat. 10am-11:30pm, Sun. noon-8pm.

Crawford Doyle Booksellers, 1082 Madison Ave. (288-6300), at 81st St. Subway: #6 to 77th St. This newly-renovated bookshop synthesizes computer technology and old-fashioned customer care to serve all your bookstore needs. Open Mon.-Sat. 10am-6pm, Sun. noon-5pm.

Gotham Book Mart, 41 W. 47th St. (719-4448). Subway: B, D, F, or Q to 47-50th St. This bookstore smuggled to America censored copies of works by Joyce, Lawrence, and Miller—the same shop where then-unknown LeRoi James and Allen Ginsberg worked as clerks. Legendary and venerable, Gotham's renowned selection of new and used volumes of 20th century writing has made it a favorite among the New York literati. The cozy, cluttered aisles also contain a wealth of rare and contemporary poetry, prose, philosophy, and journals. An upstairs gallery features changing exhibits. Open Mon.-Fri. 9:30am-6:30pm, Sat. 9:30am-6pm.

Gryphon, 2246 Broadway (362-0706), between 80th and 81st St. Subway: #1 or 9 to 79th St. Small and homey, with lots and lots of used books. Varied selection. Open daily 10am-midnight.

Shakespeare and Company, 2259 Broadway,(580-7800), between 81st and 82nd St. A local institution, this relatively large bookstore used to be the pick-up spot for the Upper West Side set before that other store moved in next door. Still a scene unto itself., although the store is undergoing lease troubles. Great selection of literature, art, and theater books in addition to general interest, plus a huge periodical section. Open daily 10am-10:30pm.

St. Mark's Bookshop, 31 Third Ave. (260-7853), at 9th St. Subway: #6 to Astor Pl. The ultimate East Village bookstore. Excellent selection, with an emphasis on current literary theory, fiction, and poetry. Helpful staff. Open daily 10am-midnight.

Strand, 828 Broadway (473-1452), at 12th St. Subway: #4, 5, 6, L, N, or R to 14th St. The world's largest and New York's most-loved used-book store. A must-see. 8 mi. of shelf space holding nearly 2 million books. Staffers will search out obscure titles at your bidding. Ask to see a catalog, or better yet, get lost in the shelves on your own. The best of the best. Open Mon.-Sat. 9:30am- 9:30pm, Sun. 11am-9:30pm.

SPECIALTY BOOKS

A Different Light, 151 West 19th St. (989-4950), at 7th Ave. Subway: #1 or 9 to 18th St. This fabulous bookstore offers an amazing selection of lesbian and gay readings—everything from the latest queer sci-fi thriller to anthologies of transgender theory. The store really shines with its near-daily readings by prominent names in lesbigay literary circles. In the café section, you can sip the "Gertrude Stein" (a lattè is a lattè is a lattè, $2.25), "James Baldwin" (americano, $1.25), or any of several similarly named beverages. Stop by for a schedule of the free Sunday movie series, featuring such films as the Marilyn Monroe drag classic *Some Like It Hot.* Open daily 10am-midnight.

Applause Theater and Cinema Books, 211 W. 71st St. (496-7511), at Broadway. Subway: #1, 2, 3, or 9 to 72nd St. Great selection of scripts, screenplays, and books on everything from John Wayne to tap dancing. Over 4000 titles. Knowledgable staff. Open Mon.-Sat. 10am-8pm, Sun. noon-6pm.

Argosy Bookstore, 116 E. 59th St. (753-4455). Subway: #4, 5, or 6 to 59th St.; or N or R to Lexington Ave. Buys and sells rare and used books, along with as autographed editions, Americana, and some truly swell maps. Extremely helpful staff and a friendly clientele to boot. Many racks of $1 books. Open Mon.-Fri. 9am-6pm; Oct.-May also Sat. 10am-6pm.

Asahiya Bookstore, 52 Vanderbilt Ave. (883-0011), at E. 45th St. Subway: #4, 5, 6, 7, or S to 42nd St. Japanese books and periodicals. Origami, some stationery, and a few English-language books on Japan for the *kanji/hiragana*-illiterate. Open daily 10am-8pm.

Biography Bookstore, 400 Bleecker St. (807-8692), at W. 11th St. Subway: #1 or 9 to Christopher St. Let us sit upon the ground and tell sad tales of the deaths of kings, presidents, rock idols, and other personalities. Biography-browsing at its best. Very strong gay/lesbian section as well as bestsellers. Open Mon.-Thurs. noon-8pm, Fri. noon-10pm, Sat. 11am-11pm, Sun. 11am-7pm.

Books of Wonder, 132 Seventh Ave. (989-3270), at 18th St. Subway: #1 or 9 to 14th St. Small bookstore stocked with children's literature. The selective used-book section is worth exploring. Open Mon.-Sat. 11am-7pm, Sun. noon-6pm.

The Complete Traveller Bookstore, 199 Madison Ave. (685-9007), at 35th St. Subway: #6 to 32nd St. Possibly the widest selection of guidebooks on the Eastern Seaboard. New addition of antiquarian travel guides. Most importantly, the store carries a full assortment of *Let's Go* guidebooks. Open Mon.-Fri. 9am-7pm, Sat. 10am-6pm, Sun. 11am-5pm.

Hacker Art Books, 45 W. 57th St. (688-7600), between Fifth and Sixth Ave. Subway: B or Q to 57th St. Perched on rows upon rows of unmarked shelves five flights up from the rumble of the street, Hacker's volumes comprise one of the best art book selections anywhere. From catalogues of Picasso's ceramics to an obscure text examining food, New York City's urban structure, and modern art, the selection here should satisfy art historians, do-it-yourself birdhouse builders, fans of prehistoric stoneware, and, of course, the art-minded Let's Go traveler. Open. Mon-fri. 9:30am-6pm.

Harris' Books, 81 Second Ave. (353-1119), between 4th and 5th St., second floor. Subway: #6 to Bleecker St. Harris won the "Best of the *New York Free Press"* two years in a row. Only in New York could someone open up their apartment and call it a bookstore. This little shop specializes in alternative/underground books. Harris knows all 6,000 of them and sells them cheaper than most. Open Mon.-Thurs. 2pm-10pm, Fri.-Sat. 2pm-midnight.

Kitchen Arts and Letters, 1435 Lexington Ave. (876-5550), at 93rd St. Subway: #6 to 96th St. The wide range of cookbooks here will help you break away from the monotony of bland Chinese and cheap burger joints. Also books on wine and culinary history and scholarship, as well as antique culinary tomes. Open Mon. 1-6pm, Tues.-Fri. 10am-6:30pm, Sat. 11am-6pm. Closed Sat. late-July-Aug.

Liberation Bookstore, 421 Lenox Ave. (281-4615), at 131st St. Subway: #2 or 3 to 135th St. This small store houses a great selection of African and African-American history, art, poetry, and fiction. Open Mon.-Fri. 11am-7pm, Sat. 11:30am-6pm.

Murder Ink, 2486 Broadway (362-8905), between 92nd and 93rd St. Subway: #1, 2, 3, or 9 to 96th St. New and used, happily cluttered. Decorated in the official colors of murder (red and black), this store is loaded with enough whodunits to have you looking over your shoulder for a lifetime. Also at 1465b Second Ave. (517-3222), bet. 76th and 77th St. Open Mon.-Sat. 10am-7:30pm, Sun. 11am-7pm.

A Photographer's Place, 133 Mercer St. (431-9358), between Prince and Spring St. Subway: R to Prince St. This small, quiet store contains photography books, both new and rare, even out of print ones, as well as a wide selection of neat postcards. The staff is friendly and knowledgeable about photo matters in general. Open Mon.-Sat. 11am-8pm, Sun. noon-6pm.

Revolution Books, 9 W. 19th St. (691-3345), at Fifth Ave. Subway: #4, 5, 6, L, N, or R to 14th St. Ironically one of the most successful chains of independent booksellers, a real entrepreneur in books on Marx, Mao, and Martin Luther King, Jr. Recently moved to a new location. Open Mon.-Sat. 10am-7pm, Sun. noon-5pm.

See Hear, 33 St. Mark's Place (505-9781), between Second and Third Ave. Subway: #6 to Astor Pl. A small store exclusively (well, almost exclusively) dedicated to books, 'zines, and magazines about rock music, mostly of the underground variety. Excellent selection of Chick religious tracts (fundamentalist religious comic books) as well. Open daily 11am-11pm.

Sportsworld, Ltd., 1475 Third Ave. (772-8729), between 83rd and 84th St. Subway: #4, 5, or 6 to 86th St. New York's all-sports bookstore. Besides covering the big four, Sportsworld offers a wide selection in topics ranging from jai alai to crew. Open Mon.-Wed. 11am-6pm, Thurs.-Fri. 11am-7pm, Sat. 10:30am-5pm, Sun. noon-5pm.

Zakka, 510 Broome St. (431-3961). If Japanese pop/punk teen culture is what you crave, you won't want to miss this boutique/bookstore/toy store/video palace, which stocks all the latest paraphernalia pertaining to androgynous Asian pop-eyed anime. all kinds of hip Tokyo magazines, and a decent collection of cutting-edge design and photography books. Zakka features such mags as *Cutie*, billed for "independent girls", in which pink-haired Japanese teenagers profess their affection for Shonen Knife and Courtney Love. Sassy wishes they were this cool. Open daily noon-8pm, closed 1st and 3rd Tues. of every month.

■ Posters and Comics

Anime Crash, 13 E. 4th St. (254-4670), between Lafayette and Broadway. Japanese pop culture, from Akira to Zandor. Import comics, model sets, huge posters, and assorted cool miscellany. CDs, videos, and laserdiscs also on sale. Open Mon.-Thurs. 11am-9pm, Fri.-Sat. 11am-11pm, Sun. noon-7pm.

Forbidden Planet, 821 Broadway (473-1576), at 12th St. Subway: N, R, L, 4, 5, or 6 to Union Sq.-14th St. New and used comic books, D&D figurines, a whole section of V.C. Andrews books, piercing books, and a shelf of serial killers at this large sci-fi/fantasy warehouse. Unhealthily thin boys and the death-goth girls who love them congregate here. Here's where you can get all those missing back issues of *Cerebus the Aardvark.* Open daily 10am-8:30pm.

The Postermat, 37 W. 8th St. (982-2946 or 228-4027), between Fifth and Sixth Ave. Located in anarchy grand central, this store proclaims itself to be the original and largest poster shop in the city, serving Village hipsters for over thirty years. Besides the vast collection of t-shirts and posters commemorating musicians, movies, lifestyles, and alternative living in general, the Postermat also sells some toys and candy, including Sea Monkeys and hard-to-find Pez dispensers. Open Mon.-Sat. 10am-9pm, Sun. 11am-9pm.

Daytripping from NYC

This city drives me crazy, or, if you prefer, crazier; and I have no peace of mind or rest of body till I get out of it.
—Lafcadio Hearn, 1889 (he later fled to Tokyo)

■ Atlantic City

For over 50 years, coffee-table high-rollers have been struggling for control of the likes of St. James Place and Ventnor Avenue. When these thoroughfares were immortalized in *Monopoly*, Atlantic City was *the* beachside hotspot among resort towns, frequented by wealthy families like the Vanderbilts and the Girards. The opulence has since faded; with the rise of competition from Florida resorts, the community chest closed, and Atlantic City suffered decades of decline, unemployment, and virtual abandonment. Even today, 15% of the city's 38,000 residents don't have jobs.

But the decline was not completely irreversible. With the legalization of gambling in 1976, casinos soon rose from the rubble of Boardwalk. Today, velvet-lined temples of tackiness (each with a dozen restaurants and big-name entertainment) blight the beach and draw all kinds of tourists from international jet-setters to seniors clutching plastic coin cups. One can even take a casino-sponsored bus from Manhattan—pay $20 for the trip and get it all back in quarters upon arrival. But only a few blocks from this indulgence lies an impoverished and crime-ridden community. Glitz and glamour no longer thrive on Baltic Avenue and the only people vying for control of Atlantic Avenue are peep-show owners and pickpockets.

And yet, a boom of sorts has recently hit the Boardwalk. With the announced opening of five new casino hotels in the past 18 months, and big players like Donald Trump and Arnold Schwarzenegger investing heavily, Atlantic City may once again be the bastion of glam it once was.

PRACTICAL INFORMATION AND ORIENTATION

Visitor Information: Atlantic City Convention Center and Visitors Bureau, 2314 Pacific Ave. (449-7130, 800-262-7395 ext. 5087; "Under the Boardwalk" plays while you're on hold). Home of the Miss America Pageant. Main entrance on the Boardwalk between Mississippi and Florida Ave. Another booth on the Boardwalk at Mississippi Ave. Personal assistance daily 9am-5pm; leaflets available 24hr.

Atlantic City International Airport: (645-7895 or 800-451-2564). Located just west of Atlantic City in Pamona with service to Washington, D.C., Philadelphia, and New York (around $50 one way). Served by Spirit, USAir, and Continental.

Train: Amtrak: (800-872-7245), at Kirkman Blvd. near Michigan Ave. Follow Kirkman to its end, bear right, and follow the signs. To New York (1 per day, 2½hr., $28). Open Sun.-Fri. 9:30am-7:40pm, Sat. 9:30am-10pm.

Buses: Greyhound (345-6617). Buses every hr. to New York (2½hr., $20). **New Jersey Transit** (800-582-5946). Runs 6am-10pm. Hourly service to New York ($21). Also runs along Atlantic Ave. (base fare $1). Both lines operate from **Atlantic City Municipal Bus Terminal,** Arkansas and Arctic Ave. Both offer casino-sponsored roundtrip discounts, including cash back on arrival in Atlantic City. Many casinos will give the bearer of a bus ticket receipt $10-15 in quarters and sometimes a free meal. **Gray Line Tours** (397-2600) offers several roundtrip excursions daily to Atlantic City ($26 on weekends, 3hr.). Your ticket receipt is redeemable for up to $15 in cash, chips, or food from a casino when you arrive. Caesar's, the Taj Mahal, and TropWorld have the best offers ($15 in cold, flexible cash). The bus drops you at the casino and picks you up three hours later. Overnight package $88—call 212-397-3807 for info. Terminal open 24hr.

Bookstore: Atlantic City News and Book Store (344-9444), at the intersection of Pacific and Illinois Ave. Most comprehensive collection of strategic gambling literature east of Las Vegas. Buy with your head, not over it. Open 24hr.

Pharmacy: Parkway, 2838 Atlantic Ave. (345-5105), one block from TropWorld. Delivers locally and to the casinos. Open Mon.-Fri. 9am-7pm, Sat. 9am-6pm.

Hospital: Atlantic City Medical Center (344-4081), at the intersection of Michigan and Pacific Ave.

Help Lines: Rape and Abuse Hotline (646-6767). 24-hr. counseling, referrals, and accompaniment. **Gambling Abuse** (800-GAMBLER/426-2537). 24-hr. help for gambling problems. **AIDS Hotline** (800-281-2437). Open Mon.-Fri. 9am-5pm.

Emergency: 911.

Post Office: (345-4212), at Martin Luther King and Pacific Ave. Open Mon.-Fri. 8:30am-6pm, Sat. 8:30am-noon. **ZIP code:** 08401.

Area Code: 609.

Atlantic City lies about halfway down New Jersey's coast, is accessible via the **Garden State Parkway** and the **Atlantic City Expressway,** and is easily reached by train from Philadelphia and New York.

Atlantic City's attractions cluster on and around the Boardwalk, which runs east-west along the Atlantic Ocean. All but two of the casinos (the Trump Castle and Harrah's) overlook this paradise of soft-serve ice cream and fast food. Running parallel to the Boardwalk, Pacific and Atlantic Avenues offer cheap restaurants, hotels, convenience stores, and 99¢ emporiums. But Atlantic Avenue can be dangerous after dark, and any street farther out can be dangerous even by day.

Getting around Atlantic City is easy on foot. When your winnings become too heavy to carry, you can hail a **Rolling Chair,** quite common along the Boardwalk ($5 for 5 blocks, $15 for ½hr.). Sometimes-entertaining Atlantic City locals or erudite foreign students might chat with you while they push. The less exotic and less expensive **yellow tram** runs continuously for $2 one way or $5 for an all-day pass. On the streets, catch a **jitney** ($1.25), which runs 24 hours up and down Pacific Avenue (call 344-8642 for frequent rider and senior citizen passes), or a NJ Transit Bus ($1) covering Atlantic Avenue. **Parking** at the Sands Hotel is free, but "for patrons only," so go spend a few dollars at the slots after partaking of this little-known convenience. If you want to park in a **lot,** park as close to the Boardwalk as possible. It'll run about $5-7 per hour, but the $3 lots several blocks away offer dubious security.

ACCOMMODATIONS AND CAMPING

Large, red-carpeted beachfront hotels have bumped smaller operators a few streets back. Smaller hotels along **Pacific Avenue,** a block from the Boardwalk, have rooms that run about $60-95 in the summer. Rooms in the city's guest houses are reasonably priced, though facilities there can be dismal. Reserve ahead, especially on weekends, as rooms go very quickly. Many hotels lower their rates mid-week. Winter is also slow in Atlantic City, as water temperature, gambling fervor, and hotel rates all drop significantly. Campsites closest to the action cost the most; the majority close September through April. Reserve a site if you plan to visit in July or August.

Inn of the Irish Pub, 164 St. James Pl. (344-9063), near the Ramada Tower, just off the Boardwalk. Big, clean, pretty rooms, decorated with antiques. No TVs, phone, or A/C, but in the summer the breeze from the beach keeps things cool. Some rooms have a view of the sea. Plush lobby with TV and pay phone. Porch sitting area complete with rocking chairs and seniors. Coin-op laundry in hotel next door. Single with shared bath $29, with private bath $51.40. Double with shared bath $45.80, with private bath $80. Prices include tax. Key deposit $5. Breakfast and dinner $10, children $8.

Hotel Cassino, 28 Georgia Ave. (344-0747), at Pacific Ave. behind Trump Plaza. Slightly run-down, but clean and cheap. 50 rooms with shared baths. Family-run business. Rates negotiable. Singles $25-35. Doubles $30-45. Key deposit $10. Open May 15-Oct. 29.

Birch Grove Park Campground (641-3778), Mill Rd. in Northfield. About 6 mi. from Atlantic City, off Rte. 9. 50 sites. Attractive and secluded. Sites $18 for 4 people, with hookup $24. Sites available April-Oct.

Since budget bargains get booked quickly in the summer, if you have a car it pays to stay in Absecon, about 8 miles from Atlantic City. Exit 40 from the Garden State Parkway will take you to Rte. 30, which is lined with great deals. The **American Lodge,** 232 E. White Horse Pike (800-452-4050), ½mile east from the parkway at exit 40, offers large rooms with king-size beds, cable, and A/C (rooms $35, $45 with a jacuzzi; 4-person max. with no charge; $5 per additional person thereafter).

FOOD

The food in Atlantic City may not be particularly good, but it *is* cheap. 75¢ hotdogs and $1.50 pizza slices crowd the Boardwalk. After cashing in your chips, you can visit a **casino buffet** (about $10 for dinner, $6-7 for lunch). The cheapest casino buffet in town is on the sixth floor of the **Claridge.** All-you-can-eat breakfast is $3.77, lunch and dinner $4.72. However, the town provides higher-quality meals in a less noxious atmosphere. For a complete rundown of local dining, pick up a copy of *TV Atlantic Magazine, At the Shore,* or *Whoot* (all free) from a hotel lobby, restaurant, or local store, or hang around casino gambling dens and score free pretzels, coffee, cookies, juice, and even yogurt provided to high rollers.

Your best bet for cheap dining in Atlantic City is the **Inn of the Irish Pub,** at 164 St. James Pl. (345-9613), which serves hearty, modestly priced dishes like deep-fried crab cakes ($4.50), honey-dipped chicken ($4.50), and Dublin beef stew ($5). The lunch special (Mon.-Fri. 11am-2pm) includes a pre-selected sandwich and cup of soup for $2. This oaky, inviting pub has a century's worth of Joycean élan and Irish memorabilia draped on the walls. Draft mugs of domestic cost $1. (Open 24hr.)

Pacific Avenue is cramped with steak, sub, and pizza shops. Celebrity supporters of the **White House Sub Shop,** 2301 Arctic Ave. (345-1564, 345-8599), include Bill Cosby, Johnny Mathis, and Frank Sinatra, who is rumored to have these immense subs flown to him while he's on tour ($4.50-9; open Mon.-Sat. 10am-1am, Sun. 11am-1am). For renowned Italian food, including the best pizza in town, hit **Tony's Baltimore Grille,** 2800 Atlantic Ave. at Iowa Ave. (345-5766). Sit in one of the large booths and twiddle the knobs on your own personal jukebox (pasta around $5.50, pizza $5-8; open daily 11am-3am; bar open 24hr.). Though the crowds may put you off, you can get great slices of pizza ($1.75) from one of the many **Three Brothers from Italy** joints on the Boardwalk. For a traditional and toothsome oceanside dessert, try custard ice cream or saltwater taffy, both available at vendors along the Boardwalk. **Custard and Snackcups,** between South Carolina and Ocean Ave. (345-5151), makes 37 flavors of soft-serve ice cream and yogurt, ranging from peach to tutti-frutti. (Cones $2.25; open Sun.-Thurs. 10am-midnight, Fri.-Sat. 10am-3am.)

CASINOS

You don't have to spend a penny to enjoy yourself in Atlantic City's casinos, but it helps; their vast, plush interiors and spotless marble bathrooms could feasibly entertain a resourceful and voyeuristic budget traveler for hours. You can watch the blue-haired old ladies with vacant, zombie-like stares shove quarter after quarter in the slot machines. You can gaze in admiration at the fat, 70-something men dressed in polyester, trying to act like Bond at the blackjack tables. As a matter of fact, you're not the only one watching—discreet cameras monitor the heavy bid tables and suited men politely observe all aspects of the games, from dealers to players.

Thousands of square feet of flashing lights and plush carpet stupefy the gaping crowds; everyone pretends not to notice the one-way ceiling mirrors concealing big-brother gambling monitors. The alluring rattle of chips, clicking of slot machines, and clacking of coins never stops. Outside the gambling matrix, coffee shops teem with con-men and early-bird-special-chomping seniors. Meanwhile, glittery crooners crow away.

The casinos on the Boardwalk all fall within a dice toss of one another. The farthest south is **The Grand** (347-7111), between Providence and Boston Ave., and the farthest north is **Showboat** (343-4000), at Delaware Ave. and Boardwalk. If you liked

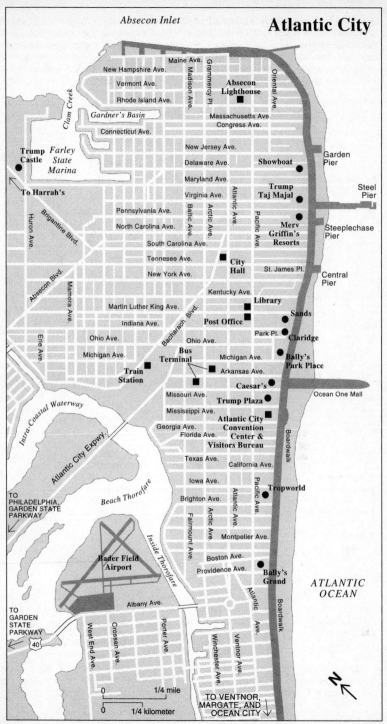

Atlantic City

Absecon Inlet

Maine Ave.
New Hampshire Ave.
Vermont Ave.
Rhode Island Ave.
Gardner's Basin
Connecticut Ave.
Massachusetts Ave.
Congress Ave.
Clam Creek
Farley State Marina
New Jersey Ave.
Delaware Ave.
Maryland Ave.
Virginia Ave.
Pennsylvania Ave.
North Carolina Ave.
South Carolina Ave.
Tennessee Ave.
New York Ave.
Kentucky Ave.
Martin Luther King Ave.
Indiana Ave.
Ohio Ave.
Michigan Ave.
Ohio Ave.
Michigan Ave.
Arkansas Ave.
Missouri Ave.
Mississippi Ave.
Georgia Ave.
Florida Ave.
Texas Ave.
California Ave.
Iowa Ave.
Brighton Ave.
Montpelier Ave.
Boston Ave.
Providence Ave.
Albany Ave.

Madison Ave.
Grammercy Pl.
Oriental Ave.
Atlantic Ave.
Baltic Ave.
Arctic Ave.
Pacific Ave.
Bacharach Blvd.
St. James Pl.
Park Pl.
Boardwalk
Pacific Ave.
Atlantic Ave.
Arctic Ave.
Fairmount Ave.
Atlantic Ave.
Ventnor Ave.
Winchester Ave.
Porter Ave.
Crossan Ave.
West End Ave.

Absecon Lighthouse
Showboat
Trump Taj Majal
Merv Griffin's Resorts
City Hall
Library
Sands
Post Office
Claridge
Bus Terminal
Bally's Park Place
Train Station
Caesar's
Trump Plaza
Atlantic City Convention Center & Visitors Bureau
Tropworld
Bally's Grand

Trump Castle
To Harrah's
Huron Ave.
Brigantine Blvd.
Absecon Blvd.
Mamora Ave.
Erie Ave.
Intra-Coastal Waterway
Atlantic City Expwy.
Beach Thorofare
Inside Thorofare
Bader Field Airport
TO PHILADELPHIA, GARDEN STATE PARKWAY
TO GARDEN STATE PARKWAY
40

Garden Pier
Steel Pier
Steeplechase Pier
Central Pier
Ocean One Mall

ATLANTIC OCEAN

0   1/4 mile
0   1/4 kilometer

N

TO VENTNOR, MARGATE, AND OCEAN CITY

Aladdin, you'll love the **Taj Mahal** (449-1000), at 1000 Boardwalk, Donald Trump's meditation on how to exploit sacred Indian art and architecture. Here, you can eat at the "Gobi Dessert" or "The Delhi Deli." It was missed payments on this tasteless tallboy that cast the financier into his billion-dollar tailspin. It will feel like *Monopoly* when you realize Trump owns three other hotel casinos in the city: **Trump Plaza** (441-6100) and **Trump Regency** (344-400) on the Boardwalk, and **Trump Castle** (441-2000) at the Marina.

The outdoor Caesar at **Caesar's Boardwalk Resort and Casino** (348-4411) at Arkansas Ave. has moved indoors, replaced by a kneeling Roman gladiator heralding the entrance to **Planet Hollywood.** Come, see, and conquer at the only casino with 25¢ video blackjack. Play slots at the feet of a huge **Statue of David** as well. The parking lot behind Caesar's is also worth a look. Made to resemble a Roman temple, this colossal structure has classical Ionic pillars and seven statues of Caesar in various states of grace. The **Sands** (441-4000) at Indiana Ave. is big and ostentatious with its pink-and-green seashell motif.

The other casinos are also worth exploring: **Bally's Park Place** (340-2000), **Harrah's Marina Hotel** (441-5000), the **Claridge** (340-3400) at Indiana Ave., **Showboat** (343-4000) at States Ave., **TropWorld Casino** (340-4000) at Iowa Ave., and **Bally's Grand** (347-7111) at Georgia Ave. Be sure to check out the celebrity handprints at the main entrance to Merv Griffin's **Resorts International** (344-6000) at North Carolina Ave. and Boardwalk. Merv's is also a great place to park your car—$3 self-park to stay as long as you want.

Open nearly all the time, casinos lack windows and clocks, denying you the time cues that signal the hours slipping away. Free drinks (coffee and juice) and bathrooms at every turn keep you peppy and satisfied. To curb inevitable losses, stick to the cheaper games: blackjack, slot machines, and the low bets in roulette and craps. Minimum bets go up in the evenings and on weekends. Stay away from the cash machines. A book like John Scarne's *New Complete Guide to Gambling* will help you plan an intelligent strategy, but keep your eyes on your watch or you'll have spent five hours and five digits before you know what hit you. If you're on a tight budget, play the **5¢ slots** available only at Trump Plaza, TropWorld, Bally's Grand, and Taj Mahal. You can gamble for hours on less than $10. If you don't know the finer points of multiple action blackjack, baccarat, chemin de fer, or pai gow poker, pick up a free *Gaming Guide* at any of the casinos—a security guard can point you toward this complete listing of rules and odds.

The minimum gambling age of 21 is strictly enforced. Even if you sneak by the bouncers posted at the doors, you cannot collect winnings if you are underage. When an underage gambler hit a $200,000 jackpot, claiming his father had won, the casino reviewed videos to discover the kid had pulled the lever. It was the casino's lucky day, not his.

BEACHES AND BOARDWALK

There's something for everyone at Atlantic City, thanks to the Boardwalk. For those under 21 (or those tired of the endless cycle of losing and winning money at big casinos), **gamble for prizes** at one of the many arcades that line the Boardwalk. It feels like real gambling, but that cute teddy bear in the window is easier to get than the $2 million grand prize at a resort.

The **Steel Pier,** an extension in front of the Taj Mahal, is an amusement park with the usual standbys: roller coaster, ferris wheel, tilt-a-whirl, carousel, kiddie rides, and lots of games of "skill." Rides cost $1.50 to 3 each (open daily noon-midnight in the summer; call the Taj Mahal for winter hours). Ride the **Go-Carts** at Schiff's Central Pier (off of St. James Place); $6 includes one adult and one child.

There are places to eat cheap food, ice cream, fried dough, and anything else you could want from end to end of the Boardwalk. There are also 99¢ novelty shops and dozens of stores at which to purchase tacky and tasteless souvenirs.

Your winnings can be rapidly blown at the **Shops On Ocean One** (347-8086) on the Boardwalk opposite Caesar's. This complex features 120 stores of typical mall variety. (Open daily 10am-10pm; restaurants open earlier and stay open later.)

Those tired of spending money can take a swim at the **beach.** The sand and water are clean, there's a nice breeze and a beautiful view of the ocean, though the beach is inevitably crowded with older couples, families, and others bored of gambling. Or walk or bike west to adjacent **Ventnor City's** sands, which are quieter.

If the Guinness book museum in the Empire State Building wasn't enough to satisfy your kitsch quota, Atlantic City offers skeptical consumers the **Ripley's Believe It or Not Museum** (347-2001) at New York Ave. and Boardwalk. Here you can see silly wonders like a roulette table made of jelly beans (open Sun.-Thurs. 10am-10pm, Fri.-Sat. 10am-11pm; admission $8, children $6).

▧ Long Island

While in theory "Long Island" includes the entire 120-mile-long fish-shaped landmass, in practice the term excludes the westernmost sections of Brooklyn and Queens. There is no typical Island dweller; many different types of folk (displaced Brooklynite, small-town fisherman, vacationing investment banker) make their abode here. One thing binds them together—an effort to escape "The City." East of the Queens-Nassau line, people read *Newsday* rather than the *Times* or the *Daily News;* they back the Islanders rather than the Rangers; and they enjoy their role as neighbor to, rather than part of, the great metropolis.

Until the 20th century, Long Island was a sparsely populated, typically Northeastern jumble of potato farms and villages; its docks and ports sustained a strong maritime industry. Parts of Suffolk County still preserve the small-town tradition (although for the most part they preserve it in order to capitalize on its value as a tourist draw). Many of the island's major roads and highways are flanked by vegetable stands and "pick your own" strawberry, pea, and potato farms.

In the early part of the 20th century, Long Island became the playground for Manhattan's rich and famous. New York millionaires built their country houses on the rocky north shore, creating the exclusive "Gold Coast" captured in its 1920s heyday by F. Scott Fitzgerald in *The Great Gatsby.* Later emigrés pushed farther east to Montauk and the Hamptons. The 1950s were a turning point for the Island; New York City expanded, cars became more affordable, and young couples enjoying postwar prosperity sought dream houses for their baby-boom families. Most importantly, new Long Island neighborhoods such as Levittown provided an escape from the city as well as a safe, wholesome environment in which to raise children. This suburban ideal later turned sour for some; the decay of the postwar dream in Long Island communities has been portrayed in such films as Oliver Stone's *Born on the Fourth of July.* Yet, although drugs and crime have seeped into a few of Long Island's myriad communities, by and large a drive through the area reveals miles and miles of minivans, white picket fences, and obsessively mowed lawns.

The 1950s also saw the expansion of Long Island's highway system, the essential link to New York City for hordes of commuters. For years, the Long Island Railroad (LIRR) provided the only major connection from Long Island across the Nassau-Queens border and into the city. During the 50s, the Island's main artery, the Long Island Expressway (LIE, officially called State Highway 495), grew to include 73 exits on the 85-mile stretch from Manhattan to Riverhead. Despite the continued expansion, the Island's population has outgrown all its forms of transportation and traffic jams are seemingly incessant on the expressway during rush hour (which basically extends from 7am to midnight). Because of this traffic, many natives commute to the city by train, but Long Island's sights are most easily accessible by car.

PRACTICAL INFORMATION AND ORIENTATION

Visitor Information: Long Island Convention and Visitors Bureau (516-951-2423). This number offers an interactive recorded schedule of events with available operators. The Bureau also operates two visitors centers. The first is located on the LIE, eastbound between exits 51 and 52 (open May-Sept. daily 9:30am-4:30pm). The second is on the Southern State Pkwy., eastbound between exits 13 and 14, opposite the State Police Barracks (open May-Sept. Wed.-Sun. 9:30am-4:30pm). There are also a number of regional or village-specific tourist centers along the LIE and other main roads.

Trains: Long Island Railroad (LIRR) (train information 516-822-5477, tour information 718-990-7498, lost and found 718-643-5228, open 7am-7pm). The Island's main public-transportation facility has 5 central lines, all but one of which meet at the main station in Jamaica, Queens. In Manhattan, you can connect from the subway to the LIRR at Penn Station (34th St. at 7th Ave.), which is served by the #1, 2, 3, 9, A, C, and E subway lines. In Brooklyn, you can transfer from the subway to the LIRR at the Flatbush Ave. station, which is served by the #2, 3, 4, 5, B, D, M, N, Q, and R subway lines. In Queens, the #7 subway line connects with the LIRR at stations in Long Island City, Hunters Point Ave., Woodside, and Main St., Flushing. The E, J, and Z subway lines connect with the LIRR at Jamaica Station. Fares vary according to destination and time of day ("peak" or "off-peak"). Peak fares (charged on trains scheduled to arrive at western terminals between 6 and 10am, and on trains departing those terminals between 4 and 7pm) range from $4.75-15.25. Off-peak fares (usually about 30% less) range from $3.25-10.25. Tickets may be purchased aboard trains, but you will be surcharged on board if the station ticket office is open. The LIRR offers educational and recreational tours, as well as escorted sightseeing tours May-Nov.

Buses:

Long Island Bus: Daytime bus service in Queens, Nassau, and western Suffolk (718-766-6722). Service runs along major highways, but the routes are complex and irregular—make sure you confirm your destination with the driver. Some buses run every 15min., others every hr. In Nassau, the roundtrip fare is $2, but crossing over into Queens from Nassau Cty. costs an additional 50¢; transfers are 25¢. Disabled travelers and senior citizens pay half fare. The MSBA has daily service to and from Jones Beach during the summer months, connecting with the LIRR in Freeport, Nassau ($1.50 each way). Buses also run in summer from the LIRR station in Babylon, Nassau to Robert Moses State Park on Fire Island ($1.75 each way). Call for current schedule.

Suffolk Transit: (516-852-5200). Open Mon.-Fri. 8am-4:30pm. Fare policy same as Nassau. The S-92 bus loops-the-loop back and forth between the tips of the North and South Forks, with 9 runs daily, most of them between East Hampton and Orient Point. Call to confirm stops and schedules. The route also connects with the LIRR at Riverhead, where the Forks meet. No service Sun. Fare $1.50, seniors and the disabled 50¢. Transfers 25¢. Children under 5 ride free.

Greyhound: 24-hr. reservation number 800-231-2222. Terminal locations in Hempstead (516-483-3230), Melville (516-427-6897), and Islip (516-234-2445). Manhattan to Hempstead $7 each way. Manhattan to Huntington $8 each way. Manhattan to Islip $10 each way. More expensive and less comfortable than the LIRR.

Hampton Express: (516-286-4600). Buses depart 10-11 times on Fri., 6-7 times per day Sat.-Thurs. Buses to destinations on the South Fork depart Manhattan from 86th and Columbus, 81st and Third, 42nd and Third, 72nd and Madison, and 72nd and Lexington. Fare $15 to all destinations, children 4-11 $10. Reservations recommended, but tickets may be purchased aboard bus. Call for schedule information and exact locations of stops.

Sunrise Express: (800-527-7709, in Suffolk 516-477-1200). Their "NY Express" runs 4 times per day Fri.-Sat. and 3 times per day Sun.-Thurs. from Manhattan to the North Fork ($15, $29 roundtrip). Catch buses on the southwest corner of 44th St. and Third Ave. or in Queens (LIE exit 24 to Kissena Blvd., in front of Queens College's Colden Ctr. at the Q88 bus stop). They go directly to River-

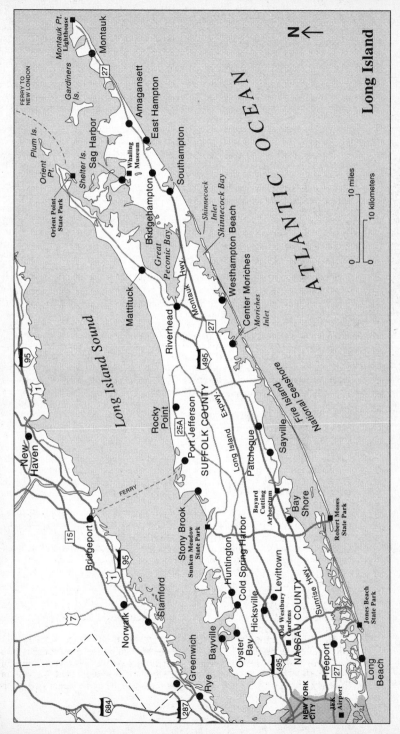

head, then stop at almost all villages on the North Fork to Greenport. The Greenport stop is right near the Shelter Island Ferry terminal. Disabled travelers pay $22 roundtrip and kids on laps ride free. Reservations recommended. Bicycles ($10) and pets ($5) allowed. Call for schedule information.

Taxis and Car Services: See the phone book for local cab companies; the following are useful for longer distances:

Ollie's Airport Service (516-829-8647) in Nassau. Vans, limousines, and cars. Ollie's runs on fixed routes from the major airports in Queens out to Nassau. They're cheaper than taxis, but more costly than public transportation. Open 24hr.

Long Island Airports Limousine Service (516-234-8400; Queens 718-656-7000). Similar to Ollie's; focuses on van lines from the Queens airports out onto the island at less-than-taxi rates. The farthest this "line-service" extends is Riverhead in Suffolk City. Also standard taxi service. Buses, cabs, and vans 9am-midnight.

Car Rental:

Avis Rent-a-Car (nationwide reservations 800-331-1212). In Nassau, 900 Old Country Rd. (516-222-3255), in Garden City (open Mon. and Fri. 7am-8pm, Tues.-Thurs. 7am-7pm, Sat.-Sun. 9am-5pm). In Suffolk, 135 West Jericho Turnpike (271-9300), Huntington Station (open Mon.-Fri. 7am-8pm, Sat.-Sun. 9am-5pm). Any rental will run upwards of $50 per day, even on multi-day packages (but free unlimited miles!). Renting from a smaller outfit in Manhattan is definitely advised, though car quality may be less consistent (see Car Rental, p. 64). Must have a major credit card. Additional charge of $32 for those under 25.

Hertz Rent-a-Car (worldwide reservations 800-654-3131). In Islip, Suffolk Cty., at the MacArthur Airport (516-737-9200; open Mon.-Fri. 6am-midnight, Sat.-Sun. 7am-midnight). Also at the East Hampton Airport in Suffolk Cty. (516-537-3987; open Sun.-Thurs. 9am-5pm, Fri.-Sat. 9am-7pm). Upwards of $50 per day during the week, reaching $100 per day on weekends. Rent in Manhattan and save a lot of dough (see Car Rental, p. 64). Must be at least 25 with a major credit card.

Bicycle Rental:

Country Time Cycles, 11500 Main Rd. (516-298-8700), in Mattituck. All bikes $15 per day or $50 for 5 days. Open Mon.-Sat. 10am-6pm, Sun. 10am-3pm. Credit card required.

Piccozzi's Service Station, Rte. 114 (516-749-0045), at the Mobil in Shelter Island Heights. A 10-min. walk from the north ferry up Rte. 114 (Bridge St.). 3-speeds $13 per 4hr., $17 per 8hr.; 12-speeds $14 per 4hr., $19 per 8hr.; 21-speeds and mountain bikes $17 per 4hr., $21 per 8hr. Open daily 7:30am-7:30pm. Cash deposit or credit card required.

Help Line: Rape Hotline 222-2293.

Area Code: 516.

■ Nassau County

Nassau is the eerie suburbia that bridges the chaotic urbanity of New York City with the rural splendor of nearby Suffolk. Here prosperous folk from the outer boroughs of the city get their first taste of luxury amid sprawling mansions, towering trees, and forbidding iron gates. Despite the prolific strip malls and cookie-cutter residential architecture, Nassau offers numerous peaceful spots to unwind.

ACCOMMODATIONS

Finding a place to stay in Nassau County can be a daunting prospect for the budget traveler. Daytrippers would probably be better off heading back to the city to crash for the night. Most of the decent larger hotels in Nassau exact indecent rates ($100-150 per night) and cater to a Big-Mac-eating, mini-van driving, family-of-four set, while the few smaller hotels which rent for less are often seedy enough to make you want to keep driving (some advertise rates for "short stays"). Yet there are a few good motels and inns that are cheap enough to make an overnight stay affordable.

Freeport Motor Inn and Boatel, 445 South Main St. (516-623-9100), in Freeport, LIE Exit 38. Head south on the Meadowbrook State Pkwy. to exit M9. Turn right off the exit and bear left onto Mill Rd. Turn left onto South Main and it's a few minutes ahead on the left. Only minutes from Jones Beach, next to a marina and a nice strip of water. Aqua-green doors and a welcoming plastic fisherman enhance the water-side effect. Clean and comfortable, with cable TVs, private baths, and phones in all rooms. Sun.-Thurs. singles $63, doubles $70. Fri.-Sat. singles and doubles $75. Continental breakfast. Reservations urged for summer weekends.

Days Inn, 828 S. Oyster Bay Rd. (516-433-1900; fax 516-433-0218), in Syosset. LIE Exit 435, then right (south) on S. Oyster Bay Rd. The Inn is about 2¼mi. ahead on your right (a little south of Old Country Rd.). Your standard "budget" motel room—clean, spacious, and comfortable. Singles $80. Doubles $86. Specials as low as $59 run throughout the year. Reservations recommended for summer weekends. Continental breakfast Mon.-Fri. 7am-10am, Sat.-Sun. 8am-10:30am. All have baths and cable TV; kitchenette units available ($86 single occupancy).

CAMPING

Camping makes by far the most financial sense if you plan to spend any amount of time on the Island without spending too much money. On the down side, there are only a few months when the weather blows fair enough for comfort and, even then the humidity can be oppressive. You may also find the island's campsites tangled in a mystifying web of local, state, and federal regulations. State parks are generally the most welcoming to visitors and a few private campgrounds open their arms as well. There are few enough campgrounds and high enough demand that reservations are recommended, if not required, at most sites.

Battle Row (516-572-8690), in Old Bethpage, Nassau. Take LIE Exit 48 and go south on Old Swamp Rd. At the fourth traffic light, turn left onto Bethpage-Sweethollow Rd., then make the first right onto Claremont St. Adjacent to the Village Restoration. 12 tent sites and 52 trailer sites (39 have electricity and water) available on a first-come, first-served basis. Electricity, restrooms, showers, grills, and a playground. Tent sites $6.25 for Nassau residents, $8.75 for visitors. Trailer sites $15 for visitors. 21 and over—unless you're a family. Nowhere near the beach. Reservations strongly recommended.

Heckscher Park (800-456-2267 or 516-581-4433) in East Islip, Suffolk. Take LIE Exit 53 and go south on the Sagtikos State Pkwy. Follow signs onto the Southern State Pkwy. east and follow it as it turns south and becomes the Heckscher Spur Pkwy. The Park is at the end of the Pkwy. A state-run facility with access to a beautiful beach. Make reservations by calling the toll-free state number. 69 tent and trailer sites (none have electricity and water). Restrooms, showers, food, grills, a pool, and a beach. $15 for the first night, $14 per additional night. Limit of two tents and six people per site. Reservations recommended and must be made at least 3 days in advance. Open May-Sept. Someone should be 21 years or older.

FOOD

Nobody has ever confused Long Island with a hungry budget traveler's paradise. Restaurants catering to islanders, on the other hand, do very well for themselves. Many of these island favorites specialize in such ethnic fare as Chinese, Italian, and Greek. You might have to overcome your hangups about style and locale, though; if you refuse to eat in a strip mall, you're seriously limiting your options.

An amazing variety of reasonably priced restaurants, from Turkish to Viennese, helps to diversify Nassau, pleasing those whose wallets have been depleted in New York. You can count on a good meal at one of the island's Chinese eateries, which are found at virtually every shopping center in Nassau. Some good moo-shi vegetables or beef and broccoli can fill even the emptiest of stomachs for less than $10.

No trip to Long Island is complete without a stop at one of its **diners.** Originally, these were decommissioned dining cars parked on street-sides to provide short-order cooking; the diner on Long Island has since become a fieldstone-modernist extravaganza, with potted palms, hosts, mints at the exit, and two-foot glossy menus. These diners, which line the highways, are probably the closest thing to an indigenous Long Island dining experience.

To Fu, 8025 Jericho Tpke. (516-921-7981 or 516-921-7983), in Woodbury. Take LIE Exit 43N and turn left (north) at the light onto S. Oyster Bay Rd. Hang a right (go east) on Jericho Tpke. and it's on the left after the third light. A huge menu of Chinese and Japanese food to rave about. Huge family groups sit alongside smiling couples in this huge restaurant, located in the mall at Jericho Plaza in Woodbury. Mint grey décor with bright pagoda-like canopies over the sushi bar. Sauteed shrimp/scallop with string bean, $6 for lunch. Seafood specials change nightly. Open Mon.-Thurs. 11:30am-10pm, Fri. 11:30am-11pm, Sat. noon-11pm, Sun. 1-10pm.

Christiano's, 19 Ira Rd. (516-921-9892), in Syosset. LIE to Exit 41N (S. Oyster Bay Rd.), go north, cross the Jericho Tpke., continue on Jackson Ave. for 1mi., and hang a right onto Ira Rd. Who can argue with Billy Joel? The red tablecloths and lively bar charmed the superstar to immortalize this homey eatery with "Scenes from an Italian Restaurant." The locals have been dining here since 1958—every spring the magnanimous owner offers favorite dishes at 1958 prices. Italian casseroles like baked ravioli ($7-9) as well as "Americanos"—dishes like roast chicken $7.50. Open Mon.-Thurs. 11am-1am, Fri.-Sat. 11am-2am, Sun. noon-1am.

Stango's, 19 Grove St. (516-671-2389), in Glen Cove. LIE Exit 39N onto Glen Cove Rd. heading north. Bear right at the fork onto Cedar Swamp Rd. (and away from Rte. 107). At the fourth traffic light make a left onto Grove St. On a side street in a less polished area of Glen Cove, Stango's serves up southern Italian cuisine at budget-friendly prices. Established in 1919, the building resembles a little house that has opened its doors to serve delicious food. Sausage pepper mushroom *frittata* $7.25, baked dishes $8-12. Open Tues.-Sun. 4-11:30pm.

SIGHTS

Nassau's distinctive regional museums, sprawling garden estates, and historical preserves offer a relaxed alternative to the hectic Manhattan scene, although negotiating through the traffic you may meet in reaching these places can often leave you feeling anything but relaxed. Many of the following sights can be reached by public transport from Manhattan via the Long Island Railroad and the public bus lines. Directions are almost always complicated, though, especially when trying to get from one sight to another. The best idea is to call ahead and speak to a staff member directly. An even better idea is to take a car.

Now obscured by car dealerships and chain restaurants, the ghost of a luxury lifestyle is preserved at the **Old Westbury Gardens.** Once the home of a Gold Coast millionaire, the huge, elegant manor house roosts comfortably amid acres of formal, flower-filled gardens. The grounds-only admission here is a true budget treasure.

The two nearby lakes are ornamented by sculptures, gazebos, and water lilies. A vast rose garden adjoins a number of theme gardens (such as the Grey Garden, which contains only plants in shades of silver and deep purple). Sunday afternoon classical concerts are performed by Juilliard students on occasion in May, June, September, and October (free with regular admission). (Open Wed.-Mon. 10am-5pm. Last ticket sold at 4pm. Garden admission $6, seniors $4, children 6-12 $3. House and garden admission $10, seniors $7, children 6-12 $6. To reach the gardens, take LIE to Exit 39S. Follow the service road parallel to the expressway eastbound for 1.2mi. and turn right onto Old Westbury Rd.)

Nestled among the sportscar-filled grounds of contemporary Oyster Bay affluence is the **Planting Fields Arboretum.** Insurance magnate William Robertson Coe once counted his coins at his mansion here at nearby **Coe Hall** (516-922-0479 or -9206). Constructed in 1921 in the Tudor Revival style, the residence has rows upon rows of mind-boggling windows. Unfortunately, only eight decorated rooms are open to the public; the inside is better left to the interiors enthusiast. (House open daily 12:30-3:30pm; admission $3.50, seniors $2, children 7-12 $1.) The massive arboretum consists of 409 acres of some of the most valuable real estate in the New York area. Two huge greenhouses, covering 1½ acres, contain the largest camellia collection in the Northeast. The flowers burst into bloom during the unlikely months of January, February, and March, when most city-dwellers have begun to forget what flora looks like. Other quirky highlights include a "synoptic garden" of plants obsessively alphabetized according to their Latin names; every letter is represented except J and W. The **Fall Flower Show,** held for two weeks in early October, attracts huge crowds every year. The arboretum hosts a summer concert series; past seasons have seen Joan Baez, the Indigo Girls, and Spyro Gyra (call for concert schedule and times). (Grounds open daily 9am-5pm; admission $3 per vehicle. To reach the arboretum, take LIE to 41N, go north on U.S. 106 to Rte. 25A, take a left, and follow the signs.)

Those tired of manicured gardens and pruned trees can find wilder nature at one of the preserves scattered throughout the county. The **Garvies Point Museum and Preserve,** Barry Dr. (516-571-8010), in Glen Cove, includes a museum devoted to regional geology and Native American archaeology and 62 acres of woods, thickets, fields, and ponds. The preserve is right on the shore and offers access to many secluded beaches and spectacular overlooks—pick up a trail map at the museum. The museum hosts a popular annual **Indian Feast** the weekend before Thanksgiving. (Museum open Wed.-Sun. 10am-4pm, Sun. 1-4pm. Admission $1, children 5-12 50¢. Take LIE to Exit 39N and follow Glen Cove Rd. north. Continue on the Glen Cove bypass (Rte. 107)—keep left at the fork—to its end, and follow the signs.)

Perhaps the most precious jewel in the Oyster Bay crown is **Sagamore Hill** (516-922-4447), off Sagamore Hill Rd., northeast of Oyster Bay. Once the summer presidential residence of Theodore Roosevelt, this National Historic Site reflects the importance of nature and wildlife in the philosophy of the conservationist President. In the summer of 1905, Roosevelt met here with envoys from Japan and Russia to set in motion negotiations that would lead to the Treaty of Portsmouth, which ended the Russo-Japanese War. The house is jam-packed with "Teddy" memorabilia and its Victorian clutter convincingly evokes Roosevelt's era; the collection of antlers, for instance, reflects his sporting interests. (Open Wed.-Sun. 9:30am-5pm. Tours ($2) leave every ½hr.; you must have a tour ticket to enter. To get there, take LIE Exit 41N to Rte. 106 north, turn right (east) at the junction with Rte. 25A and follow the signs.)

Since the days of Herman Melville, American culture has given a suitably prominent place to that largest of mammals, the whale. When it comes to indulging cetacean obsessions, nothing compares to the **Cold Spring Harbor Whaling Museum** (516-367-3418) on Main St. in Cold Spring Harbor. Built in honor of the small whaling fleet that sailed from Cold Spring Harbor in the mid-19th century, the museum features a 30-foot-long, fully rigged vessel, one of only six remaining whaleboats of its kind in the world. The collection of scrimshaw—detailed whalebone carvings done to pass the long hours at sea—testifies to the joys and ennui of the seafaring tradition. (Open daily 11am-5pm; closed Mon. in fall and winter. Admission $2, seniors and children 6-12 $1.50. To get here, take LIE Exit 41 N to Rte. 106 north, and turn right (east) at the junction with Rte. 25A. Follow this all the way into Cold Spring Harbor, where it becomes Main St. The museum is past the commercial center a short distance on the left.)

The **United States Merchant Marine Museum,** on Steamboat Rd. in King's Point (516-773-5000 for recording, 516-773-5515 for a staff member), is located on the grounds of the U.S. Merchant Marine Academy. The museum houses exhibits on the history and past glories of the Merchant Marines. (Open Aug.-June Tues.-Wed. 11am-3pm, Sat.-Sun. 1-4:30pm. Donation requested. Take LIE to Exit 33 and go north on Community Dr. Continue to the road's end and then go right on W. Shore Rd. Take a right on King's Point Rd. and then a left on Steamboat Rd.)

The **Old Bethpage Village Restoration** (516-572-8401) on Round Swamp Rd. in Old Bethpage, is a "history preserve," in which fragments of Long Island's 19th-century heritage have been gathered and reassembled in the form of a typical pre-Civil War village. The recreation features a general store, a blacksmith's shop, and sheep shearing. This is a particularly charming site to visit with children. Columbus Day weekend brings the **Long Island Fair,** a popular old-fashioned festival. (Village open

Wed.-Sun. 10am-5pm. Admission $5, seniors and children 5-12 $3. Take LIE to Exit 48, then hang a right onto Round Swamp Rd. and a left onto the driveway.)

BEACHES AND PARKS

Jones Beach State Park (785-1600) is convenient and crowded, overflowing with daytrippers from the city. There are nearly 2500 acres of beachfront here and the parking area accommodates 23,000 cars. Only 40 minutes from the City, Jones Beach packs in the crowds during the summer months; the beach becomes a sea of umbrellas and blankets with barely a patch of sand showing. Along the 1½-mile boardwalk you can find deck games, roller-skating, miniature golf, basketball, and nightly dancing. The **Marine Theater** inside the park often hosts rock concerts. There are eight different public beaches on the rough Atlantic Ocean and the calmer Zachs Bay, plus a number of beaches restricted to residents of certain towns in Nassau County. In the summer you can take the LIRR to Freeport or Wantaugh, where you can take a bus to the beach. **Recreation Lines** (718-788-8000) provides bus service straight from mid-Manhattan from Memorial Day to Labor Day on Saturday and Sunday. Buses leave Manhattan from 56th St. at Second Ave. at 8:30 and 9am, and return from the beach at 4 and 4:30pm; the roundtrip fare is $18. By car, take the LIE east to the Northern State Pkwy., go east to the Meadowbrook (or Wantaugh) Pkwy., and then south to Jones Beach. The park closes at midnight, except to those with special fishing permits.

Sunken Meadow State Park (516-269-4333) is one of the less frequented beaches in Nassau. With smaller waves than those found at its South Shore counterparts, Sunken Meadow serves as a more family-oriented, island resident beach. This is the place to be if you're sick of trying to enjoy the beach with a couple thousand of your closest friends. There's plenty of parking, picnic tables, a boardwalk, concession stand, basketball courts, and playgrounds. The bathhouse is clean and the lifeguards friendly. Beach and park open 8am-8pm; parking costs $4 before 4pm. Take LIE Exit 51N to the Sunken Meadow State Pkwy., which runs straight into the park.

Bethpage State Park (516-249-0700) is one of the only state parks in the county not located on the beach, but that doesn't keep a mostly residential crowd from partaking of its bridle paths, picnic tables, and driving ranges. Bethpage is a great place to stop and stroll through well-kept fields and lawns—just watch out for flying golf balls (golf open Mon.-Fri. 5am-7pm, Sat.-Sun. 4am-7pm). The park is open 8am-8pm. Take LIE Exit 44S to Central Avenue and follow the signs from there.

ENTERTAINMENT AND NIGHTLIFE

The best nightlife for most Long Islanders exists in Manhattan. However, that's no reason to sit at home reading a book after the sun sets over Long Island Sound. Huge multi-screen theaters pepper the island and tickets are cheaper than in the city. See *Newsday* for full listings.

Post-movie options are limited, but some of the metropolitan, city-that-never-sleeps nightlife of Manhattan has spread to Nassau. You can relax to some live jazz at **Sonny's Place,** 3603 Merrick Rd. (516-826-0973), in Seaford. Sonny extracts an $8 cover charge on Friday and Saturday nights and enforces a two-drink minimum. During the week the music plays on without the cover or minimum if you sit or stand at the bar but, for those sitting at tables, a $2 cover and 2-drink minimum applies. Music plays Sunday through Thursday 9pm-1am, Friday and Saturday 9:30pm-2am. From the LIE, take Exit 44S to the Seaford-Oyster Bay Expressway and head south; take Exit 1W onto Merrick Rd. and go west one block.

For dancing, try **Gatsby's,** a fashionable spot on a stretch past the green light at 1067 Old Country Rd. in Westbury (516-997-3685). The DJ starts spinning at 9pm from Tuesday to Saturday and there are occasional live shows on Thursday, Friday, and Saturday nights. Cover for live shows is usually about $5; women sometimes drink free—call for details.

Nassau also bows to the more refined. The **Long Island Philharmonic** (516-293-2222) performs at the **Tilles Center for the Performing Arts** (516-299-2752, box office 516-299-3100) and offers free evening concerts at area parks during the summer (call for info). Located on the C.W. Post Campus of Long Island University, on Northern Blvd. in Greenvale, the Tilles Center sponsors a wide variety of performances throughout the academic year. The **Arena Players Repertory Theater,** 296 Rte. 109 in East Farmingdale (516-731-1100), and the **Broadhollow Theater** at 229 Rte. 110, Farmingdale (516-752-1400), have full calendars of productions. Performance quality can be inconsistent, especially by New York standards, and shows are often overly commercial. Still, the theaters have matured and are worth a look when a favorite goes up. The Arena Players recently featured *The Owl and the Pussycat* while the Broadhollow presented *Company.* Ticket prices vary but are rarely expensive. Local universities also have active theaters—notably the **John Cranford Adams Playhouse** at Hofstra University, on Fulton Ave. in Hempstead (463-6644), which offers several plays a year. (Call for schedule; tickets $15.)

National rock concert tours stop during the summer at the **Jones Beach Marine Theater,** Jones Beach State Park, Wantaugh (516-221-1000, recorded concert hotline 516-422-9222). Joining the bandmembers for some slam-dancing is impossible here unless you have a rowboat; the stage is separated from the bleachers by a wide stretch of water. In a production of *Showboat,* the actors made their entrances and exits by motorboat. Now the theater hosts concerts exclusively. The **Westbury Music Fair,** on Brush Hollow Rd. in Westbury (516-334-0800), has a theater in the round and hosts big names on tour.

■ Suffolk County

The eastern half of the island, with its two long forks and small offshore islands, makes up Suffolk County. For the most part, Suffolk is filled with small, relatively quaint towns (so small and quaint that they are self-proclaimed villages or hamlets). Many residents proudly hang American flags from the porches of paint-chipped white farmhouses and weekend activity is characterized by antique-shopping and barn sales galore. In this rural, small-town America atmosphere, the bowling alley and the Shelter Island Ferry are about as fast-paced as it gets.

The cluster of communities along the South Fork, collectively known as **the Hamptons,** is home to wealthy summering Manhattanites, modern-day Gatsbys, and displaced West Coast stars. The area jams in July, as traffic backs up for miles on Highway 27. Each Hampton has its own style and stereotype. Look in Southampton for old money, Westhampton for new money, and East Hampton for artists. Bridgehampton, appropriately enough, lies between Southampton and East Hampton

---

Stargazing?

Some famous faces you might see in the Hamptons: Billy Joel (singer/songwriter), Kim Basinger and Alec Baldwin (acting duo), Tom Wolfe (*Bonfire of the Vanities* author), Jann Wenner (*Rolling Stone* publisher), Steven Spielberg (auteur), Donna Karan (fashion designer), and Barbra Streisand (Barbra).

ACCOMMODATIONS

Suffolk County provides a wider variety of housing and, with its open spaces, more opportunities for camping. However, places generally close during the off-season and fill up quickly during the summer.

Montauket, Tuthill Rd. (516-668-5992), in Montauk. Follow the Montauk Hwy. to Montauk. At the traffic circle take Edgemere, which becomes Flamingo, and make a left onto Fleming and then another left. The island's best bargain, though difficult to find. This little gem tucked in a cove at the end of winding roads is a homestyle alternative to the more commercialized hotels along Rte. 27. The simple rooms are adorned only with watercolor scenes of the ocean: perfect for vacationing students or budget-conscious lovers who hunger for a view of the rocky shores but can't stomach the precipitous prices in town. No TV, no A/C; most rooms have two single beds. From March-May and Oct.-Nov. 15, only 4 rooms are open; the whole hotel opens for the summer season. Make reservations in March for summer weekends—it fills up quickly. Almost always full on weekends. Doubles $35, with private bath $40. Lively bar/restaurant is one of Montauk's best-kept secrets.

Sands Motel, Montauk Highway (516-668-5100), right in Montauk. Take the Montauk Highway to Montauk; the motel is on the right just before you reach the main shopping area. Just a 5-min. walk from the beach, this motel has the standard amenities (telephones, refrigerators, cable TV). Beach view and proximity to town restaurants are a plus. Efficiencies and deluxe suites as well as single and double bedrooms. Off-season rates $50-110; summer rates $96-175.

Easterner Resort, 639 Montauk Hwy. (516-283-9292), in Southampton. Sunrise Hwy. Exit 66 to the Montauk Hwy. Make a left onto Country Rd. #39. Travel ¼mi., then go east 1½ miles on Montauk Hwy. Fully renovated in spring of 1994. Very nice 1- and 2-bedroom cottages with kitchenettes, TV, and A/C. Swimming pool. Sun.-Thurs. $65, summer weekend packages from $135 per night (and generally a 2-night min. stay required). Open June-Sept. Call ahead for weekend reservations.

Pines Motor Lodge, corner of Rte. 109 and 3rd St. (516-957-3330), in North Lindenhurst. LIE to Southern State Pkwy. E., Exit 33. Go southeast on Babylon Farmingdale Rd. (which is Rte. 109); it's just beyond the intersection of Straight Path. Affordable roadside motel. Rooms clean, with all the standard amenities (TV, private bath, phone). Fri.-Sat. singles $70, doubles $80. Sun.-Thurs. singles $59. Lower off-season rates; call ahead.

Blue Dolphin Motel, Main Road (516-477-0907), in East Marion. Take LIE Exit 71 to Riverhead; go around traffic circle to Hwy. 25 E (otherwise known as Main Rd.); motel is on the right in East Marion. Just outside of Greenport and only 15min. from the loveliest beach on the North Shore, this motel in blue is an excellent choice for an inexpensive, quiet getaway. The Blue Dolphin has a small café, outdoor dining area, and a swingset. Singles and doubles $60-65. Triples $70. Quads $70-80. Rooms also available by the week. Open May-Oct.

132 North Main Guest House (516-324-2246 or 516-324-9771), in East Hampton, 1mi. from the beach. LIE Exit 70 to Sunrise Hwy., which becomes Montauk Hwy., which in turn becomes Main Rd.; veer left onto N. Main at the fork in front of the windmill green. Century-old guest house with meticulously maintained farmhouse and cottage. Twelve rooms decorated in different colors; all have A/C. Breakfast included. Sun.-Thurs. Singles or doubles $80-150, Fri.-Sat. $130-220.

Referral Services

A Reasonable Alternative, Inc., 117 Spring St., Port Jefferson, NY 11777 (516-928-4034). Rooms in private homes all along the shores of Nassau and Suffolk. Prices increase the farther east you go. Singles or doubles $50-100.

CAMPING

Suffolk County's campgrounds are for nature lovers. Commercial, RV-friendly grounds are few and far between. But if the grime of the city has gotten to you, Suffolk's woodsy landscape and beachy terrain will cure the grimmest cabin fever. Be Young. Have Fun. Go Camping.

Hither Hills State Park (516-668-2554 or 800-668-7600) on the Old Montauk Hwy. near Montauk. This park offers lovely views, swimming, and picnicking spots. Reservations are required and you must stay for at least one week (fee $119 per week). Reservations are taken up to 90 days in advance and, seriously, should be made as close to 90 days in advance as possible. Camp office open 8am-9pm.

Cedar Point County Park (516-852-7620). Take LIE Exit 68S to Hwy. 27; go east until East Hampton. Take Hwy. 40 and follow signs from there. This family-oriented public park offers campsites for $20 per night and also provides bathrooms, showers, picnic area, nature trails, beaches, and rowboats. Ranger booth open daily until 10pm.

Wildwood Park (800-456-2267 or 516-668-7600) at Wading River. LIE Exit 68 and go north onto Rte. 46 (Wm. Floyd Pkwy.); follow it to its end and go right (east) on Rte. 25A. Follow the signs from there. Former estate of Charles and John Arbuckle, multi-millionaire coffee dealers who, brilliantly, packaged coffee instead of selling it in bulk. 300 tent sites and 80 trailer sites with full hook-ups, restrooms, showers, food, and a beach. Tent sites $13 first night and $10 per additional night; sites with a concrete platform $14 first night and $11 thereafter. Reservations urged for summer weekends and must be made at least a week in advance. $6.75 non-refundable service charge for reservations.

FOOD

In Suffolk, budget bargains are difficult to find—the ample tourist culture has sprouted a host of high-priced (and sometimes low-value) eateries. Farm stands and seafood restaurants are your best bet for inexpensive eats in Suffolk. In general, inland cities that cater to Long Island residents are good bets for bargain dining.

On the North and South Forks, upscale seafood eateries abound. Trust decor as an indicator of price, but not necessarily of the food quality; sometimes the best meal can come from the most inconspicuous of places.

For a truly wholesome food experience, stop at any roadside produce stand that looks appealing; or, if you're feeling particularly participatory, visit one of **Lewin Farms'** two separate picking patches. At the one on Sound Avenue in Wading River (516-929-4327), you can pick your own apples, nectarines, and peaches. (Open May-Dec. Mon.-Tues. 9am-4pm, Wed.-Sun. 8am-5:30pm. LIE to Exit 68, go north to Rte. 25A and east to Sound Avenue—it's the first farm on Sound Ave.) At the other, 123 Sound Ave. in Calverton (516-727-3346), you can pick strawberries, raspberries, plums, pears, peaches, nectarines, beans, onions, peas, squash, and tomatoes. Pumpkins, too! (Open late May-late Nov. daily 9am-4pm. LIE to Exit 71N; drive on Edwards Ave. to Sound Ave.; the farm is ¼mi. down on the left.) Crops are (obviously) seasonal, so call ahead to confirm that some crop is ripe for the picking.

La Superica (516-725-3388), Long Island Ave. and Main St., in Sag Harbor, at the foot of the bridge. This colorful Mexican restaurant serves up fresh fare with California-style influences and specializes in seafood dishes. Although the menu is a bit expensive, the portions are hefty enough to make you skip your next meal. The nachos loaded with beans, cheese, sour cream, guacamole, and jalapenos ($8) are exquisite. Frequent happy hour bargains on tasty margaritas. Open Mon.-Fri. 5:30-11pm, Sat.-Sun. 5:30-midnight.

Peter's Pasta Specialties, 132 W. Main St. (516-422-9233), in Babylon. Take the Southern State Parkway East to Exit 33. Go south on Rte. 109 all the way to Rte. 27A (Main St.) in Babylon Village and turn left. Local flavor hits the jackpot in this cozy little Italian restaurant. A veritable cornucopia of pasta and sauce selection—you can custom-design your own pasta fantasy. Open Mon.-Thurs. noon-9:30pm, Fri.-Sat. noon-3pm and 5-10:30pm, Sun. 3:30-9pm.

Cappucino Cottage, 209 Front St. (516-477-8455), in Greenport. Take the Main Road (Hwy. 25) east to Greenport. A friendly, unpretentious juice-and-coffee establishment. Drinks $1-3. Open Mon.-Thurs. 9am-9:30pm, Fri.-Sun. 9am-11:30pm

Pizza Village, 700 Montauk Highway (516-668-2232), in Montauk. Take the Montauk Highway east to Montauk; the restaurant is on the right. This popular pizza joint serves up delicious heros, pizzas, and pastas. You can eat in or take out—they'll even deliver. Pizzas come in 4-slice ($5), 6-slice ($7.75), and 8-slice ($9) pies. Open daily 11am-10pm.

Fish Net, 122 Montauk Hwy. (516-728-0115), Hampton Bays, ¼mi. west of the Shinnecock Canal Bridge. Some of the best local fish on the South Fork, served in a worn, homey atmosphere and eaten with sleeves rolled up. Shoes required, but all else is optional. Still, though, the prices are strictly South Fork: dinners $11-26. Open Sun.-Thurs. 11:30am-10pm, Fri.-Sat. 11:30am-10:30pm.

Driver's Seat, 62 Jobs Lane (516-283-6606), in Southampton; Jobs Ln. begins just across from Hill St. (Rte. 27E) in the town center. A well known meeting place in the posh Hamptons. Eat indoors, outdoors, or at the bar. Entrees like jumbo burgers, quiche, and local seafood run $6-18. On Wed. entrees are 2-for-1. Open daily 11:30am-11pm. On weekends burgers and bar food served until midnight.

Candy Kitchen, 1925 Main St. (516-537-9885), in Bridgehampton. Take Rte. 27E to Main St. in Bridgehampton. Well-dressed vacationers and savvy locals congregate in this long-standing luncheonette for traditional American sweets and sandwiches. Pancakes ($3.25), sandwiches ($1.75-7). Open daily 7am-9:30pm.

Amagansett Sweets, 135 Main St. (516-267-3099), in Amagansett. Take Rte. 27 to Main St. in Amagansett. Strolling couples and neighborhood kids in the know all stop in here for a delicious scoop of ice cream ($2.35) or brownie. Open Sun.-Thurs. 11am-10pm, Fri.-Sat. 11am-11pm.

SIGHTS

Far from the frenzied hubbub of Manhattan, the peaceful villages of Suffolk County, only a few hours' drive from Manhattan, are New York's version of the tradition-steeped towns of New England. Many of Suffolk's roots have been successfully preserved and the county offers some fine colonial house-museums. Salty old towns full of shady streets—refreshing retreats from New York's din—line the lazy coast.

A summer visit to Suffolk requires the strategic timing of a wartime general. Hotel rates skyrocket and traffic likens itself to a parade in freeze-frame. When visiting for the weekend, leaving before 2pm or late (11pm) on Friday will decelerate your pace to a scene-savoring crawl. Or visit mid-week, when lodging is cheaper (rates can often double on weekends) and beaches are nearly empty.

After shopping at the Walt Whitman Mall, the nearby **Walt Whitman's Birthplace** (516-427-5240) will seem a more appropriate memorial to the great American poet whose 1855 *Leaves of Grass* introduced a democratic free-verse style that revolutionized poetry. The small, weathered farmhouse at 246 Old Walt Whitman Rd., Huntington Station, was built in 1816 by Walt Whitman, Sr., a carpenter and the father of the Bard of Long Island. The family moved to Brooklyn when the poet was only four years old, but the house still offers an interesting commentary on his life. Especially worthwhile is the short still-frame movie consisting of pictures of the poet's life and loves, accompanied by passages from *Leaves of Grass.* (Open Wed.-Fri. 1-4pm, Sat.-Sun. 10am-4pm. Free. Take LIE to Exit 49N, drive 1¾ mi. on Rte. 110, and turn left onto Old Walt Whitman Rd.; signs will guide you.)

Sagtikos Manor (516-665-0093), on Rte. 27A in Bay Shore on the South Bay, was originally 1210 acres but has now downsized to 10. Built in 1697, it remains the finest example of Colonial architecture on the Island. The hub of Long Island's pre-Revolutionary aristocracy, the 42-room manor has housed the commander of the British forces during the Revolution and then perfidiously hosted George Washington during a tour of Long Island. Built by the Van Cortlandt family, it soon passed into the hands of the Thompsons, who lived here until the 20th century. Its current owner, Robert Gardiner, is related to the original owners through an uncle. The entire original colonial structure (as opposed to the several later additions) is open to the public. Highlights include the fine period rooms—one containing an ancient desk with a set of cubby-holes used for James Madison and Thomas Jefferson's mail when they were on the island—like the parlor, which still displays the house's original paint made of lime, buttermilk, and blueberries. (Open July-Aug. Wed.-Thurs. and Sun. 1-4pm; June and Sept. Sun. 1-4pm. Admission $3, children under 12 $1.25. Take the Southern State Pkwy. to Exit 40 and go south on the Robert Moses Causeway. Turn left (east) on the Montauk Hwy. (Rte. 27A) and go 1½ mi. The Manor is on the left just past Manor Ln.)

Historians and sadists alike should check out the **Southampton Historical Museum** (516-283-2494), located near the center of town at the corner of Meeting House Lane and Main St.—it brings substance to another era's concept of "family values." Thieves and adulterers tasted their peers' wrath in the **pillory:** here they were relieved of several layers of skin when publicly flayed. Before modern psychotherapy, alcoholics and sassy children were "corrected" via the humiliating **stocks,** a rigor mortis dress rehearsal. The museum also boasts an excellent collection of old children's toys, which includes a merry-go-round and several rocking horses, as well as some fascinating dolls and dollhouses. Downstairs displays the whaling logs which 18th-century captains kept while at sea. (Open in summer Tues.-Sun. 11am-5pm. Admission $3, children 6-11 50¢. Take Rte. 27E to Southampton Center.)

The **Guild Hall Museum,** 158 Main St. (516-324-0806), in East Hampton, ensures that sophisticated New Yorkers escaping to the Hamptons won't have to suffer from complete art withdrawal. The collection specializes in well known artists of the eastern Island region, from the late 19th century to the present. Guild Hall hosts changing exhibitions, films, lectures, concerts, plays, art classes, and special events. A recent major exhibition displayed a number of important works by Willem de Kooning (open daily June-Aug. 11am-5pm; Sept.-May Wed.-Sun. 11am-5pm; admission $5).

For animal lovers, the **Long Island Game Farm and Zoo** (516-878-6644) in Manorville (2mi. south of LIE, Exit 70) is the perfect place to go for a hands-on good time. Check out the petting zoo, where many of the zoo's countless farm animals make their home. (Open April-July Mon.-Fri. 10am-5pm, Sat.-Sun. 10am-6pm; Sept.-April Mon.-Fri. 10am-4pm. Admission to park, shows, and all rides except the Sky Slide $12, seniors $7, children 2-11 $10.)

Wine Country

Long Island does not readily conjure up images of plump wine-grapes just waiting to be plucked by epicurean islanders, but a visit to one of the East End's more than 40 vineyards can be a pleasant surprise. The wineries and vineyards here produce the best Chardonnay, Cabernet Sauvignon, Merlot, Pinot Noir, and Riesling in New York State. Local climate and soil conditions rival those of Napa Valley. Many of the island wineries offer free tours and tastings; call ahead to make an appointment (all tastings for those 21 and over).

To get to the wine district, take the LIE to its end (Exit 73), then Rte. 58, which becomes Rte. 25 (Main Rd.). North of and parallel to Rte. 25 is Rte. 48 (North Rd. or Middle Rd.), which claims a number of wineries. Many wineries ferment on the South Fork as well.

Palmer Vineyards, 108 Sound Ave. (516-722-9463), in Riverhead. Embark on a guided or self-guided tour of the most advanced equipment on the Island and enjoy a tasting room with an interior assembled from two 18th-century English pubs. On Oct. weekends you can take a hayride to the vineyards. Open daily 11am-6pm. Self-guided tours 50¢-$1. Always 3 free tastings; other tastings available for a fee. Hours and tours shorter in off-season; call ahead. Open Nov.-May daily 11am-5pm.

Bridgehampton Winery (516-537-3155), Sag Harbor Tpke., Bridgehampton. Holds special summer events, including the effervescent Chardonnay Festival in mid-Aug. Open June-Sept. daily 11am-5pm. Free tastings.

Mattituck Hills Winery (516-298-9150), Bergen and Sound Ave., Mattituck. Hosts both a Strawberry Festival (in which you can sample chocolate-covered strawberries with house wines) and a Pre-Harvest Festival (which includes a grape stomp). Free daily tastings and tours on summer weekends. Open Mon.-Fri. 11am-5:15pm, Sat.-Sun. 11am-6pm.

Sag Harbor

Out on the South Fork's north shore droops **Sag Harbor,** one of the best-kept secrets of Long Island. Founded in 1707, this port used to be more important than New York Harbor, since its deep shore made for easy navigation. In 1789 Washington signed the document creating ports of entry to the United States and, of the two named, "Sagg Harbour" appeared before New York City. At its peak, this winsome village was the fourth-largest of the world's whaling ports. James Fenimore Cooper began his first novel, *Precaution,* in a Sag Harbor hotel in 1824. During the Prohibition years, the harbor served as a major meeting-place for smugglers and rum-runners from the Caribbean.

In the past few years, an increasing number of tourists have returned to the quiet, tree-lined streets of salt-box cottages and Greek Revival mansions. This is a different crowd than that of years past, but the legacy of Sag Harbor's former grandeur survives in the second-largest collection of Colonial buildings in the U.S. and in the cemeteries lined with the gravestones of Revolutionary soldiers and sailors. In town, check out the **Sag Harbor Whaling Museum** (516-725-0770), in the former home of Benjamin Hunting, a 19th-century whale-ship owner. A huge whale rib towers in an arch over the front door. Note the antique washing-machine, made locally in 1864, and the excellent scrimshaw collection. (Open May-Sept. Mon.-Sat. 10am-5pm, Sun. 1-5pm; admission $4, children 6-13 $1; tours by appointment.)

Montauk

As the easternmost point of the South Fork, Montauk offers an unobstructed view of the Atlantic Ocean. Despite the slightly commercialized tourist/hotel areas and the three hour drive, the peaceful salty air is well worth the drive. Take the LIE to Exit 70 (Manorville), then go south to Sunrise Hwy. (Rte. 27), which becomes Montauk Hwy., and drive east. It's impossible to go too far—at least without turning the inside of your car into an aquarium.

At the island's edge stands the **Montauk Point Lighthouse and Museum** (516-668-2544). The 86-foot structure went up in 1796 by special order of President George Washington, but back then it was 297 feet off the shoreline. Thanks to the wonders of geology, it's now fully attached, surrounded by the Montauk Pt. State Park. If your lungs are willing, you should definitely climb the 138 spiraling steps to the top to look out over the seascape, across the Long Island Sound to Connecticut and Rhode Island. Try to spot the *Will o' the Wisp,* a ghostly clipper ship sometimes sighted on hazy days under full sail with a lantern hanging from its mast. Experts claim that the ship is a mirage resulting from the presence of phosphorus in the atmosphere, but what do they know? (Open Sun.-Fri. 10:30am-6pm, Sat. 10:30am-8pm. Admission $2.50, children 6-11 $1. Parking $3 until 4pm, free after 4pm.)

Try **Viking** (516-668-5700) or **Lazybones'** (516-668-5671) for half-day fishing cruises ($24; equipment and bait included). Cruises sail at 8am and 1pm. During the summer, most trips go after fluke, but these two companies also offer seasonal outings for bluefish, cod, and tuna. **Okeanos Whale Watch Cruise** (516-728-4522) offers excellent six-hour trips for spotting fin, minke, and humpback whales ($30, children under 13 $15).

BEACHES AND PARKS

Orient Beach State Park (323-2440). From the LIE take Hwy. 25E on the North Fork to the end and follow the signs into the park. Beautiful, secluded beach with lots of shaded picnic tables. Perhaps the nicest, most well kept beach on the north shore. Parking is $4 until 4pm, $5 thereafter. Open 8am-8pm.

Montauk Point State Park and Montauk Downs (668-2554). Take Montauk Hwy. east along the South Fork past Montauk and follow signs for the park. Montauk Downs has driving ranges for golfers and a great beach. The state park is basically for fisherfolk. Park closes at 8pm, unless you have a night-fishing permit.

NIGHTLIFE AND ENTERTAINMENT

The most exciting nighttime entertainment in Suffolk (besides breathing the night air and listening to the crickets) can be found on the grounds of the parks and museums, which host harpsichord and piano recitals. This outdoor musical life, as with most things in Suffolk, becomes much more active in the summer. Performance dates and times vary; ask at community museums or pick up a copy of one of the free papers or magazines such as *Dan's Papers* (see below), which are ubiquitous around the entrances of most establishments. Some of these parks restrict admission to local residents or charge exorbitant fees to exclude tourists like yourself—get the straight dope before setting out. The **Guild Hall Museum** in East Hampton hosts a number of impressive films, lectures, concerts, plays, and special events. The Guild Hall's **John Drew Theater** hosts most of these performances, including a series of readings by such prominent writers as Robert Bly and Robert Lipsyte. The Hall's Jazz Concert series takes place in the latter half of July (call 516-324-0806 for information). Past performers include Robert Cray and Dave Brubeck. *Dan's Papers,* published in Bridgehampton, provide info on concerts and other nighttime happenings.

CPI (the Canoe Place Inn), located on the East Montauk Hwy. east of Hampton Bays (516-728-4126 or 516-728-4130), is by far the South Fork's biggest draw for the college and twentysomething crowd. It's not uncommon for CPI to feature three DJs and two live bands in a single night (for a cover of about $10). Live shows can sometimes be great bargains—the Violent Femmes, Joan Jett, and 38 Special played recent shows here which were free before 11pm and $5 thereafter (open Fri.-Sat. 10pm-4am, with occasional special shows on Wed. nights).

Another big draw for the post-college crowd is **Co-Co's Water Café,** at 117 New York Ave., Huntington (516-271-5700), but beware: the minimum age for men is always 23 and rises to 28 on singles night (Tues.). Women need only be 21—we're not sure why (open nightly until 4am).

On the South Fork, **East Hampton Bowl,** 71 Montauk Hwy. (516-324-1950), just west of East Hampton, offers a great escape from the big-money scene. And yes—it is a spot for nightlife; the bowling alley and attached bar stay open until at least midnight every night and Sat. nights feature "Rock-'n'-Bowl," a big draw in which the lights fade and a disco ball descends, a live DJ starts to play and, of course, people keep on bowling (bowling $4.25 per game before 6pm, $5 after; shoe rental $2.75).

The **New Community Cinema,** 423 Park Ave., Huntington (516-423-7653), just over the Nassau border, is a local secret and one of the only places on Long Island where you can safely call your movie a "film." The cinema screens offbeat documentaries and foreign art-flicks. Shows are often preceded by introductions or concluded with question-and-answer sessions with the filmmakers themselves, or simply those in the know. Eat brownies and siphon herbal tea while you wait for the lights to go down—they won't start the film until everyone is seated. (Tickets cost $6.50, students with ID $4.50, children under 12 $3. Shows on Fri. and Sat. after 6pm are $1 more. To get here take LIE Exit 49N to Rte. 110 and continue north into the village of Huntington; take a right onto Park Ave.)

■ Long Island's Islands: Fire and Shelter

Fire Island, one of the more extraordinary natural sites off Long Island's shores, is a 32-mile-long barrier island buffering the South Shore from the roaring waters of the Atlantic. The state has designated most areas of Fire Island either a state park or a federal "wilderness area"—both of which are legally protected from development—but 17 summer communities have designated the rest of it their resort area and forged their own niche here. Fire Island's unique landscape will make you forget there ever was such a city as New York. Cars are allowed only on the easternmost and westernmost tips of the island; there are no streets, only "walks." Fire Island, a hip counterculture spot during the 60s and home to the burgeoning disco scene of the early-to-mid 70s, still maintains a laid-back atmosphere. Two of Fire Island's many resorts, Cherry Grove and The Pines, are home to predominantly gay communities. (For ferry info see Getting There, below.)

The **Fire Island National Seashore** (516-289-4810 for the headquarters in Patchogue) is the main draw and, in summer, it offers fishing, clamming, and guided nature walks. The facilities at **Sailor's Haven** (just west of the Cherry Grove community) include a marina, a nature trail, and a famous beach. Similar facilities at **Watch Hill** (516-597-6455) include a 20-unit campground, where reservations are required. **Smith Point West,** on the eastern tip of the island, has a small visitor-information center and a nature trail with disabled access (516-281-3010; center open daily 9am-5pm). Here you can spot horseshoe crabs, white-tailed deer, and monarch butterflies, which flit across the country every year to winter in Baja California.

The **Sunken Forest,** so called because of its location down behind the dunes, is another of the Island's natural wonders. Located directly west of Sailor's Haven, its soils support an unusual and attractive combination of gnarled holly, sassafras, and poison ivy. From the summit of the dunes, you can see the forest's trees laced together in a hulky, uninterrupted mesh.

Shelter Island bobs in the protected body of water between the North and South Forks. Accessible by ferry or by private boat, this island of about 12 square miles offers wonderful beaches (locals tend to favor beaches Wade and Hay) and a serene sense of removal from the intrusions of the city. But you don't have to rough it; the island has virtually everything that you could need, including a coalyard, four insurance agencies, and a real estate attorney. A detailed map of the island is available from most inns and other places of business. If you don't have, or choose not to bring, a car, you might want to rent a bike—the island has no public transport.

GETTING THERE

Ferries: Listed below are several of the ferry services from Long Island to the various islands. Call for schedules, which vary with day and destination.

To Fire Island: From **Bay Shore** (516-665-3600), ferries sail to Fair Harbor, Ocean Beach, Ocean Bay Park, Saltaire, and Kismet. Roundtrip fare $11, children under 12 $5. From **Sayville** (516-589-8980), ferries leave for Sailor's Haven (roundtrip fare $8, children under 12 $4.50) and Cherry Grove and Fire Island Pines (roundtrip fare for either one $10, children under 12 $5). Ferries leave about every hour. From **Patchogue** (516-475-1665), ferries go to Davis Park and Watch Hill (roundtrip to either $10, children under 12 $5.50). LIRR stations lie within a short distance of the 3 ferry terminals, making access from New York City relatively simple. All ferries run May-Nov.

To Shelter Island: from the North and South Forks. **North Fork: Greenport Ferry** (516-749-0139), North Ferry Rd., on the dock. Passenger and driver $6.50, roundtrip $7, each additional passenger $1, walk-on (without a car) $1. Ferries run daily every 10min., with the first ferry leaving Greenport at 6am and the last ferry departing the island at midnight. **South Fork: North Haven Ferry** (749-1200), 3mi. north of Sag Harbor on Rte. 114, on the dock. Car and driver $6 one way, $6.50 roundtrip, additional passengers $1 each, walk-ons $1 round-trip. Ferries run daily at approximately 10min. intervals 6am-1:45am.

ACCOMMODATIONS AND CAMPING

The Belle Crest Inn, 163 North Ferry Rd. (749-2041), in Shelter Island Heights. Just up the hill from the north ferry. Beautiful old country home feels like you're house-esitting for country relatives. Large rooms furnished with an eye toward antique detail—most beds have canopies. Great spot for a romantic getaway. From May 1 to Oct. 31: Mon.-Thurs. doubles with shared bath $65-70, with private bath $95; Fri.-Sun. $80 and $165. Two-night min. for weekends in summer. Off-season rates dip as low as $45 for a shared bath; call for details. Full country breakfast included. Reservations strongly recommended, but off-season rooms are somewhat easier to come by.

Smith Point West on Fire Island. Camping is free but requires a hike of about 1mi. to get into the camping area. You must pick up a permit from the Smith Point Visitors Center (281-3010; open daily 9am-5pm) on the day you go down. To get to Smith Point, take LIE Exit 68, head south, and follow the signs.

FOOD

Shelter Island Pizza and Eatery (749-0400), Rte. 114 at Jaspa Rd., Shelter Island, near the Shelter Island Center. Scrumptious array of finger foods—great for a snack or a budget-conscious dinner out. Calzones $4, deep-dish pizza $12. Open daily 11am-9pm.

UPSTATE NEW YORK

■ Catskills

The Catskills are widely known as the site of the century-long repose of Rip Van Winkle, but these sleepy bucolic parts aren't just for napping—these mountains are home to quiet villages, sparkling streams, and miles of hiking and skiing trails, all of which can be found in the state-managed Catskill Preserve. Amid the Catskill's purple haze lies Woodstock, site of the famous 1969 rock festival (and of the 1994 marketing rehash). Music history aside, Woodstock is a small, peaceful city that offers a welcoming contrast to the metropolis to the South.

Practical Information Adirondack Pine Hill Trailways provides excellent service through the Catskills. The main stop is in **Kingston,** at 400 Washington Ave. on the corner of Front St. (914-331-0744 or 800-858-8555). Buses run to New York City (11 per day, 2hr., $18.50; same-day round trip $25 or $35, depending on the day). Other stops in the area include Woodstock, Pine Hill, Saugerties, and Hunter; each connects with New York City, Albany, and Utica. (Ticket office open daily 6am-11:30pm.) The **Ulster County Public Information Office,** 244 Fair St., 5th Floor (914-340-3566 or 800-342-5826), six blocks from Kingston bus station, has a helpful travel guide and a list of Catskill hiking trails (open Mon.-Fri. 9am-5pm). Four stationary **tourist cabooses** dispense info at the traffic circle in Kingston, on Rte. 28 in Shandaken, on Rte. 209 in Ellenville, and on Rte. 9W in Milton (open in summer Fri.-Sun.; hours vary depending on volunteer availability). Rest stop **visitors centers** along I-87 can advise you on area sights.

■ Catskill Forest Preserve

The 250,000-acre **Catskill Forest Preserve** contains many small towns which host travelers looking for outdoor adventure. The required permits for **fishing** (non-NY residents, $20 per 5 days) are available in any sporting goods store. Ranger stations distribute free permits for **back-country camping** necessary for stays of more than three days. Though trails are maintained year-round, lean-to's are sometimes dilapidated and crowded. Always boil or treat water with chemicals, and remember to pack out your garbage. For more information on fishing, hunting, or environmental issues, call the **Department of Environmental Conservation** (914-256-3000). **Adirondack Trailways'** buses from Kingston service most trail heads—drivers will let you out anywhere along secondary bus routes.

Accessible by bus from Kingston, **Phoenicia** is a fine place to anchor a trip to the Catskills. The **Esopus River,** to the west, has great trout fishing, and **The Town Tinker,** 10 Bridge St. (688-5553), rents inner-tubes for summertime river-riding. (Inner-tubes $7 per day, with a seat $15. Driver's license or $15 required as a deposit. Transportation $4. Life jackets provided. Open May-Sept. daily 9am-6pm; last rental 4:30pm.) Artifacts from the late-19th-century glory days of the steam engine fill the **Empire State Railway Museum** (688-7501), on High St. off Rte. 28. It features train rides on the Catskill Mountain Railroad (open weekends and holidays 10am-6pm). At the 65-foot-high **Sundance Rappel Tower,** Rte. 214 (688-5640), visitors climb up and return to earth the hard way. (4 levels of lessons; beginner, 3-4hr., $20. Lessons only held when a group of 4 is present. Reservations required.)

If your karma is running out of gasma, you can stop at **Woodstock,** between Phoenicia and Kingston. Though a haven for artists and writers since the turn of the century, Woodstock is best known for the concert which bore its name, an event which actually took place in nearby Saugerties. Since then, the tie-dyed legacy has faded, and Woodstock has become an expensive, touristed town. You can soothe your soul and chant your mantra at the **Zen Mountain Monastery,** S. Plank Rd., P.O. Box 197, Mt.

Tremper 12457 (688-2228), a few miles from Woodstock off Rte. 28N from Mt. Tremper. The 8:45am Sunday services include an OM-azing demonstration of zazen meditation (weekend and week-long retreats from $175).

What is now **Historic Kingston** was once a defensive stockade built by Peter Stuyvesant. Stroll down Wall St., Fair St., or North Front St. and defend yourself against the cutesy shops that have taken its place. Live out your childhood firefighting fantasies at the **Volunteer Fireman's Hall and Museum,** 265 Fair St. (331-0866; open Wed.-Fri. 11am-3pm, Sat. 10am-4pm). Head to the **Woodstock Brewing Company,** 20 James St. (331-2810), for a taste of beer brewed right in the Hudson Valley. Nat Collins, the owner and brewmaster, will give you a free tour and tasting in his (and one of the state's only) complete microbrewery (tours Sat. 1pm on the first and third Sat. of each month).

Camping and Accommodations Huddle around the fire and shiver to ghost stories at any of the **state campgrounds.** Reservations (800-456-2267) are vital during the summer, especially Thursdays through Sundays. (Sites $9-12; $1.50 registration fee; phone reservation fee $7; $2 more for partial hook-up. Open May-Sept.) The **Office of Parks** (518-474-0456) distributes brochures on the campgrounds. **North Lake/South Lake** (518-589-5058), Rte. 23A three miles northeast of Haines Falls, rents canoes ($15 per day) and features two lakes, a waterfall, hiking, and 219 campsites ($15, reserve 7 days in advance; day use $5). **Kenneth L. Wilson** (914-679-7020), an 8-mile hike from the Bearsville bus stop, has well-wooded campsites ($12), showers, a pond-front beach, and a family atmosphere. A bit more primitive, **Woodland Valley** (914-688-7647), 5 miles southeast of Phoenicia, does have flush toilets and showers, and sits on a good 16-mile hiking trail (sites $9).

If the thought of sleeping outside in the land of the headless horseman makes your blood run cold, you can take refuge in a giant room with cable TV at the **Super 8 Motel,** 487 Washington Ave. (338-3078), in Kingston two blocks from the bus station. (Weekdays singles from $55; doubles from $57; weekends singles from $60; doubles from $62; senior discounts available. Reserve for summer weekends.) In Phoenicia, the **Cobblestone Motel** (688-7871), on Rte. 214, has an outdoor pool and well worn but very clean rooms (singles $40; doubles $44; rooms with kitchenette $55). Countless other motels, motor inns, economy cabins, and the like line Rte. 28 between Kingston and Phoenicia. For a true bargain, follow Rte. 28 off the beaten path to the **Belleayre Hostel** (254-4200). Bunks and private rooms, in a rustic setting not far from Phoenicia, all have sinks, radios, kitchen access, a picnic area, and sporting equipment. Call for directions. (Bunks in summer $9, in winter $12. Private rooms $20-25. Efficiency cabins for up to four $35-45.)

■ Tarrytown

A convenient day trip from New York City, Tarrytown is a sleepy suburban hollow near the Tappan Zee bridge on the Hudson River. This area provided the inspiration for Washington Irving's tales of Rip Van Winkle and *The Legend of Sleepy Hollow.* Irving's home, **Sunnyside,** Sunnyside Lane (914-591-8763) is where the irreverent writer re-created a Dutch country cottage and hosted nine nieces and a brother. You won't blame Irving for leaving his Wall St. birthplace when you see this expansive estate which he maintained on a writer's salary—he's believed to be the first American to have made a living so. August events include annual storytelling and jazz festivals (open March-Dec. Wed.-Mon. 10am-5pm; Admission $7, seniors $6, ages 6-17 $4, grounds only $4). Near Sunnyside is **Lyndhurst,** 635 South Broadway (914-631-4481), the sumptuous summer palace of various New York tycoons. This stately manor has wonderful grounds, including a rose garden, a horseman-less carriage house, and the remains of what was once the largest greenhouse in America. The manor itself is nice, but if you're looking to save a few bucks, skip it and just enjoy the magnificent grounds. (Open May-Oct. Tues.-Sun. 10am-5pm; Nov.-April Sat.-Sun. 10am-3:30pm. $7, seniors $6, children $3, grounds only $3; joint tickets for Sunnyside and

Lyndhurst $12, seniors $10.) Head over to neighboring **North Tarrytown** (just down Rte. 9) to **Philipsburg Manor** (914-631-3992), a neat living history venue (a la Colonial Williamsburg) that features a working waterwheel on a replicated, but functioning, colonial farm. (Open March-Dec. Wed.-Mon. 10am-5pm; Jan-Feb. Sat-Sun. 10am-5pm; Admission $7, seniors $6, ages 6-14 $4, students $4.)

For a nature break, roll out to Rockefeller State Park Reserve, Rte.117, one mile off Rte. 9 (914-631-1470), where you can bike, fish, or ride a horse (permit required; open daily 8am-sunset; free). The real must-see of the entire region, however, is the stupendous **Rockwood,** Rte. 117 (914-631-1470, 914-631-8200 for tour). Here you can climb over the fountains of a former Rockefeller estate and enjoy views of the Hudson River Valley that are head and shoulders above any other around. Tours must be arranged in advance—the estate features sculpture by Brancusi, Calder, Moore, and Picasso. Or you can picnic in the hillside meadows and fall asleep under a tree. The park is open 7am-sunset. All the fixin's for a picnic in one of the spots in Tarry-town are available at the **Grand Union,** 1 Courtland Avenue and Wilton St. (open Mon.-Sat. 7am-11pm, Sun. 8am-9pm).

Tarrytown is accessible from New York by a scenic 50-60 minute ride on the **Metro-North Commuter Rail** (800-METRO-INFO/63876-4636) which runs from Grand Central Station. (Train runs 6:20am-1:20am, $5 off-peak, $6.75 rush hour.)

■ Bear Mountain

If the noises of the city and other urban blights have frayed your nerves, **Bear Mountain State Park** is a wonderful place to recommune with nature and soothe your inner child. The site, which includes over 80 square miles of near wilderness and 140 miles of marked trails, also boasts some of the taller Catskill mountains, several lakes (including the large, sparkling **Hessian Lake**) and a section of the **Hudson River.** The main attraction, other than the land and the lakes themselves, is the **Trailside Museum and Zoo,** the oldest of its kind in the U.S. The zoo allows visitors to safely view the region's more ferocious wildlife, while the museum focuses on other aspects of the park, such as history (Fort Clinton, a Revolutionary War battle site, is nearby) and archaeology, including some mastodon skeletons unearthed in 1902 (museum/zoo open daily 9am-4:30pm). Also scattered throughout the park are various intriguing statues, including an inquisitive **Walt Whitman,** standing atop a promontory in mid-stride, and a huge antelope head overlooking the Hudson. Hikers may be interested to know that the earliest segment of the **Appalachian Trail** is located in the park, along with several other meandering wilderness paths.

The park also offers many huge playing fields and picnic benches, so don't forget the frisbee and the briquets. For slightly cooler weather, Bear Mountain has cross-country skiing trails, an ice rink (which doubles as a roller rink) and a ski jump.

Guarded by two big-stick-wielding bear sculptures, the **Bear Mountain Inn,** designed in Swiss Chalet style, is located at the hub of the park. Romantics looking for a more secluded spot should check out the **Stone Lodges** by Hessian Lake, while Stephen King fans may prefer to stay at the **Overlook Lodge** (the park requests that you leave all telepathic children at home), also near Hessian Lake. Call 914-786-2701 to make reservations at any of the hotels. (A room is $59 weeknights and $84 on weekends. One night's deposit due 7 days after reservation). The **restaurant** and **cafeteria** within the Inn are on a bit on the pricey side—picnic fixings might accord better with budget travel (restaurant/cafeteria open Mon.-Thurs. 8am-3pm and 5pm-9pm; Fri.-Sat. 8am-3pm and 5pm-10pm, Sun. 8am-3pm and 4-9pm).

Bear Mountain is located on Rte. 9 and can be reached via **Short Line Buses,** which run from Port Authority and take about an hour (round trip ticket $20). For further information, call the **Park Visitor Center** at 914-786-5003 (open Apr.-Oct. 8am-6pm, Nov.-March 8am-5pm).

■ West Point

Those who love straight men (and women) in uniform and those curious to know about the people who protect New Yorker's rights to be crazy will definitely want to spend a few hours at **West Point,** a Revolutionary War site and America's premier service academy. Since the nation's inception, West Point has dominated the American military—55 of the 60 major battles of the Civil War were commanded by West Point grads on both sides. Indeed, virtually every U.S. military leader of note (George Marshall and Stonewall Jackson being exceptions) served their time at the Point.

A visit to West Point should probably begin at the **Visitor's Center,** just outside of **Thayer Gate** (just off Rte. 9). There you can pick up the appropriate brochures, see a replica of a cadet's room, and pick up some army memorabilia (open daily 9am-4:30pm). While there, be sure to visit the **West Point Museum,** containing a plethora of uniforms, weapons, and trophies dating as far back as the 16th century (open daily 10:30am-4:15pm).

After reviewing all the army facts you'll probably ever need, you're ready to enter the Academy. Unlike his more stuffy counterparts at Buckingham Palace, the cadet at the gate will not only speak to you, he'll tell you where to go first. (You probably shouldn't salute him unless you're related to the military in some fashion.)

Aside from a few restricted areas, visitors pretty much have the run of the place. Two Revolutionary War sites are situated here—**Fort Clinton** and **Fort Putnam,** the latter originally under the command of George Washington. Also note the assortment of war monuments around the campus, particularly **Trophy Point,** the storehouse for many intriguing U.S. war relics, and the **Battle Monument,** the largest single piece of granite in the Western hemisphere (and you wondered where the defense budget went). Also not to be missed are the **Cadet Chapel,** an exercise in military Gothic with the world's largest pipe organ, and **"The Plain,"** the fabled West Point parade ground.

West Point is located on Rte. 9 and can also be reached via **Short Line Bus** from the New York Port Authority (roundtrip about $20). For more information call the Visitor's Center at 914-938-2638.

Appendices

▨ When to Go

CLIMATE

New York's weather is the worst of both worlds: summers are hot and sticky, and yet winters can still compete with neighboring New England for cold and snow. Winter snowfalls are common, but the city usually clears streets within a day for traffic. In the spring and fall, frequent impromptu showers make umbrellas a good idea.

MONTH	HIGH	LOW
January	38°	26°
February	40°	27°
March	49°	34°
April	61°	44°
May	72°	53°
June	80°	63°
July	95°	68°
August	90°	67°
September	76°	60°
October	66°	50°
November	54°	41°
December	42°	30°

U.S. HOLIDAYS

Martin Luther King, Jr.'s Birthday is celebrated on the third Monday in January (Jan. 20 in 1997), **Presidents' Day** (honoring Presidents Washington and Lincoln) on the third Monday in February (Feb. 17). **Memorial Day,** falling on the last Monday of May (May 26), honors U.S. veterans who died in combat and signals the unofficial start of summer. Halfway through summer, **Independence Day** explodes on July 4. Americans usually celebrate their independence from England with barbecues, parades, and fireworks. Summer unofficially ends with another long weekend, **Labor Day,** on the first Monday of September (Sept. 1). The increasingly controversial **Columbus Day** comes on the second Monday in October (Oct. 13), while **Thanksgiving,** the fourth Thursday of November (Nov. 27), celebrates the more appreciated arrival of the Pilgrims at Plymouth, MA in 1620. The holiday and shopping seasons peak at **Christmas** (Dec. 25) and run through **New Year's Day** (Jan. 1). All public agencies and offices and many businesses close on these holidays.

▨ Nuts and Bolts

TIME

U.S. residents tell time on the 12-hour, not 24-hour, clock. Hours after noon are *post meridiem* or pm (e.g. 2pm); hours before noon are *ante meridiem* or am (e.g. 2am). Noon is sometimes referred to as 12pm and midnight as 12am; *Let's Go* uses "noon" and "midnight." The continental U.S. is divided into four **time zones:** Eastern, Central, Mountain, and Pacific. Hawaii and Alaska claim their own time zones as well. When it's noon Eastern time, it's 11am Central, 10am Mountain, 9am Pacific, 8am Alaskan, and 7am Hawaiian-Aleutian. New York City follows Eastern Standard Time (EST) and, like most states, advances its clocks by one hour for **daylight saving time.** In 1997, daylight saving time will begin on Sunday, April 5, at 2am. It will end on Sunday, October 25, at 2am; set your clocks back one hour to 1am then. Or, in the words of the old adage, spring ahead, fall back.

MEASUREMENTS

Although the metric system has made considerable inroads into American business and science, the British system of weights and measures continues to prevail in the U.S. The following is a list of U.S. units and their metric equivalents:

1 inch (in.) =	25.4 millimeters (mm)
1 foot (ft.) =	0.30 meter (m)
1 yard (yd.) =	0.91 meter (m)
1 mile (mi.) =	1.61 kilometers (km)
1 ounce (oz.; mass) =	28.35 grams (g)
1 fluid ounce (fl. oz.; volume) =	29.59 milliliters (mL)
1 pound (lb.) =	0.45 kilogram (kg)
1 liquid quart (qt.) =	0.95 liter (L)
1 gallon (gal.) =	3.78 liter (L)

ELECTRICAL OUTLETS, TEMPERATURE, AND OTHER AMERICAN DEVIATIONS

Outlets throughout the U.S., Canada, and Mexico provide current at 117 volts, 60 cycles (Hertz), and American plugs usually have two rectangular prongs; plugs for larger appliances often have a third prong for the purpose of grounding. Appliances designed for the European electrical system (220 volts) will not operate without a transformer and a plug adapter. Transformers are sold to convert specific wattages (e.g., 0-50 watt transformers for razors and radios, larger watt transformers for hair dryers and other appliances).

Moreover, the U.S. uses the Fahrenheit **temperature scale** rather than the Centigrade (Celsius) scale. To convert Fahrenheit to Centigrade temperatures, subtract 32, then multiply by 5 and divide the result by 9. 32°F is the freezing point of water, 212° its boiling point, and room temperature usually hovers around 70°.

▓ Free New York

The city may cost an arm and a leg to live in, but you can still visit without having to pawn any of your precious limbs. Free entertainment abounds; you just need to know where to look. Both the *New York Times* (especially good on Fridays) and *the Village Voice* (each Wednesday) print extensive lists of free events throughout the city, as does the *Free Time* monthly ($1.25).

Some museums—such as the **Cooper-Hewitt** on Tuesdays—have weekly free times. Others have voluntary-donation policies; if you're on a budget, you can choose to pay less at the **Alternative Museum,** the **American Museum of Natural History,** the **Black Fashion Museum,** the **Brooklyn Museum,** the **China House Gallery,** the **Cloisters,** the **Metropolitan Museum,** the **Museum of American Folk Art,** and the **Museum of Television and Radio.** On Friday from 6 to 8pm, the **Guggenheim** invites visitors to "pay what you wish." The Museum of Modern Art offers the same policy Thursday and Friday 5:30-8:30pm, as does the New Museum of Contemporary Art Saturday 6-8pm. Smaller galleries and some museums never charge admission; without spending a penny, you can visit the **American Numismatic Society,** the **Forbes Magazine Galleries,** the **Garibaldi-Meucci Museum** on Staten Island, the **Hall of Fame for Great Americans,** the **Hispanic Society of America,** the **Museum of American Illustration,** the **Nicholas Roerich Museum,** the **Police Academy Museum,** the **Schomburg Center for Research in Black Culture,** and countless art galleries clustered throughout SoHo and the rest of the city. For those who prefer more animate entertainment, the **Bronx Zoo** is free Wednesday.

For free, you can tour **Grand Central Station,** the **Lincoln Center Library,** the **New York Stock Exchange,** and the **Commodities Exchange Center** at the World Trade Center. Paying your respects at **Grant's Tomb** and the **U.N. General Assembly** (Sept.-Dec.) costs nothing. And colonial dwellings like the **Dyckman House** and **Hamilton Grange** welcome their modern-day visitors free of charge.

Shakespeare shows for free in Central Park, but to obtain a ticket, you have to wake up early. Central Park's **Summerstage** brings amazing music and writers for free performances from late June through early August; check the *Village Voice* or call 360-2777. Past performers include Buddy Guy, Juliana Hatfield, Elvis Costello, Patti Smith, Joan Baez, and more. Music schools don't charge for their concerts: try **Juilliard,** the **Greenwich Music School,** and the **Bloomingdale House of Music.** You can listen to a prestigious free lecture series at the **Cooper Union** or to free poetry at the **92nd Street Y.**

Come summertime, troopers willing to brave the heat can enjoy concerts, dances, comedy, theater, and film at absolutely no charge. The *Summer in New York* brochure, available free at the Visitors Bureau and other information booths (see Essentials: Tourist Information, p. 66), presents a full catalog of gratis summertime events.

The **JVC Jazz Festival** (787-2020) and the **Serious Fun!** comedy series offer several free events throughout the city's parks in June and July. Try the 24-hour information line of the **City of New York Parks and Recreation Department** (360-3456) for a schedule of concerts and events. **Bryant Park,** at Sixth Ave. between 40th and 42nd St., offers many lunchtime jazz recitals during the summer, as well as free screenings of classic movies on Monday nights June-August.

Assorted corporate magnates mount their own musical agendas. From June through August, **Rockefeller Center** (632-3975) holds concerts on Tuesdays and Thursdays at 12:30pm at the Garden at 1251 Sixth Ave. On Wednesdays in July and August, the Rockefeller series moves to the McGraw Hill Minipark at 48th St. and Sixth Ave. (also at 12:30pm). The **World Financial Center** (945-0505) hosts its own summer bash from June to September, mostly free: a fittingly global parade of art, chamber music, contemporary dance, and jazz by greats like Dave Brubeck. The Duke Ellington Orchestra, the Artie Shaw Orchestra, and Buster Poindexter have all played here in the past. Serious classical music wafts alongside strains of classic rock and roll; the Shostakovich String Quartet once shared the bill with Flash Cadillac and the beat boys from *American Graffiti.*

The **World Trade Center** (435-4170) also maintains a full summer entertainment schedule in July and August at its Austin J. Tobin Plaza. Each day has a different theme, such as oldies, opera, or jazz. Most concerts start at 12:15pm and are then repeated at 1:15pm. In August, **Lincoln Center** (875-5400) holds a series of music and dance concerts six days a week, during the day and evening, on the plazas. Offerings include folk, blues, and classical music. **Damrosch Park,** at Lincoln Center, sponsors shows several nights a week in the summer.

The **South Street Seaport Museum** (732-7678) presents a wide variety of free outdoor entertainment, ranging from rock concerts to classical recitals to celebrations of street hockey. The **Museum of Modern Art** (708-9480) holds its free **Summergarden Series** of classical music in its delightful sculpture garden at 14 W. 54th St. (July-Aug. Fri.-Sat. 7:30pm).

The Central Park **Dairy** (794-6564) provides information on free New York parks activities, like the Dairy's calcium-enriched Sunday afternoon recitals. The **Lower Manhattan Cultural Council** (432-0900) stages music and dance performances and public readings at various downtown sites; it also organizes and provides information on the free concerts held at the World Trade and Financial Centers. **American Landmark Festivals** (866-2086) include a series of free concerts year-round at various locales.

The **Brooklyn Summer Series** fills the bill with concerts in Brooklyn parks, playgrounds, and even shopping malls. **Celebrate Brooklyn** (718-788-0055), a multimedia extravaganza, swarms Brooklyn's Prospect Park Bandshell with jazz, rock, world beat, blues, and big brass, as well as dance, ballet, and theater. The **Brooklyn Botanical Garden** (718-622-4433) hosts summer Shakespeare and outdoor chamber music.

The **Queens Council on the Arts** (718-647-3377) organizes its own **Arts in the Park Festival** at the Forest Park Seufert Bandshell, at Forest Park Dr. and Woodhaven Blvd. Concerts take place July through August in the late afternoon and evenings and feature a variety of musical styles, ranging from gospel to classical to country; concerts for children are held on Thursday mornings. Check the council's bimonthly calendar of events, the *Queens Leisure Guide,* or call the above number.

■ Major Annual Events

January	Winter Festival	Central Park
	National Boat Show, Jan. 5-14	Jacob Javits Convention Center
February	Jazz Festival	Snug Harbor Cultural Center, Staten Island
	Black History Month	Events throughout the city
	Chinese New Year	Chinatown
March	Ringling Bros. and Barnum & Bailey Circus	Madison Square Garden
	St. Patrick's Day Parade	Fifth Avenue
April	Easter Show	Radio City Music Hall
	International Auto Show	Jacob Javits Convention Center
	Spring Flower Show	Brooklyn Botanical Garden
	Cherry Blossom Festival	Brooklyn Botanical Garden
	Earth Day Parade	TBA
May	Fleet Week '96	Intrepid Museum
	Ninth Ave. International Food Festival	Ninth Ave. between 37th and 57th St.
	Memorial Day Celebration	South Street Seaport
	Seafest '96	South Street Seaport
June	Tony Awards	TBA
	Bang on a Can Festival	Lincoln Center
	Summer Stage	Central Park
	Bronx Week	events throughout the borough
	Buskers Fare Festival	street performances in lower Manhattan
	Puerto Rican Day Parade, Jun. 12	Fifth Ave.
	Museum Mile Festival	Fifth Ave. museums open free, 6pm-9pm
	Midsummer Night Swing Dances	outdoors under the stars at Lincoln Center
	Mermaid Parade	Coney Island
July	Macy's Firework Display (July 4)	lower Hudson River
	Mostly Mozart Music Festival	Lincoln Center
	Serious Fun Festival	avant garde performing arts at Lincoln Center
	Salute to New York City	New York Philharmonic in Central Park, with fireworks
	free Shakespeare performances	Delacorte Theater, Central Park
	Macy's "Tap A Mania"	34th St. and Broadway
August	U.S. Open	National Tennis Stadium, Flushing, Queens
	Harlem Week	Harlem
	Summer Stage	Central Park
September	New York Film Festival	Lincoln Center

	Chile Pepper Fiesta	Brooklyn Botanic Gardens
	ice skating begins	Rockefeller Center and Wollman Rink, Central Park
	New York Book Fair	events TBA
October	Halloween Parade	Sixth Ave. from Spring St. to 23rd St.
	Washington Heights Week	Throughout Washington Heights
November	New York City Marathon	Fifth Avenue
	Macy's Thanksgiving Day Parade	Broadway (Huge balloon floats assembled the previous evening at 79th and Central Park West)
December	Christmas Tree lighting, Dec. 2	Rockefeller Center
	Lighting of Giant Menorah	Fifth Ave. and 59th St.
	New Year's Eve	Times Square—at midnight, ball drops from Times Tower
	New Year's Eve Fireworks	South Street Seaport and Prospect Park, Brooklyn

Index

INDEX

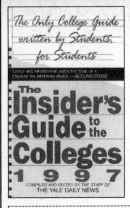

★Let's Go 1997 Reader Questionnaire ★

Name: _____ **What book did you use?**_____

Address: _____

City: _____ **State:** _____ **Zip Code:** _____

How old are you? under 19   19-24   25-34   35-44   45-54   55 or over

Are you (circle one)   in high school   in college   in grad school
employed   retired   between jobs

Have you used Let's Go before?   yes   no

Would you use Let's Go again?   yes   no

How did you first hear about Let's Go?   friend   store clerk   CNN
bookstore display   advertisement/promotion   review   other

Why did you choose Let's Go (circle up to two)?   annual updating
reputation   budget focus   price   writing style
other: _____

Which other guides have you used, if any?   Frommer's $-a-day   Fodor's
Rough Guides   Lonely Planet   Berkeley   Rick Steves
other: _____

Is Let's Go the best guidebook?   yes   no

If not, which do you prefer? _____

**Which part of Let's Go do you feel needs most to be improved, if any
(circle up to two)?**   packaging/cover   practical information
accommodations   food   cultural introduction   sights
practical introduction ("Essentials")   directions   entertainment
gay/lesbian information   maps   other: _____

How would you like to see these things improved?

_____

_____

How long was your trip?   one week   two weeks   three weeks
one month   two months or more

Have you traveled extensively before?   yes   no

Do you buy a separate map when you visit a foreign city?   yes   no

Have you seen the Let's Go Map Guides?   yes   no

Have you used a Let's Go Map Guide?   yes   no

If you have, would you recommend them to others?   yes   no

Did you use the internet to plan your trip?   yes   no

Would you buy a Let's Go   phrasebook   adventure/trekking guide
gay/lesbian guide

**Which of the following destinations do you hope to visit in the next three
to five years (circle one)?**   Australia   China   South America   Russia
other: _____

Where did you buy your guidebook?   internet   chain bookstore
independent bookstore   college bookstore   travel store
other: _____